The Twin Earth Chronicles

The Twin Earth Chronicles

Twenty Years of Reflection on
Hilary Putnam's
"The Meaning of 'Meaning' "

Edited by

Andrew Pessin

and

Sanford Goldberg

M.E. Sharpe
Armonk, New York
London, England

Library of Congress Cataloging-in-Publication Data

The twin earth chronicles : twenty years of reflection on
Hilary Putnam's "The meaning of 'meaning'" / edited by
Andrew Pessin and Sanford Goldberg.
p.   cm.
Includes the text of Hilary Putnam's The meaning of "meaning."
Collection of twenty-one previously published articles, 1975–1992.
Includes bibliographical references and index.
ISBN 1-56324-873-5. — ISBN 1-56324-874-3 (pbk.)
1. Putnam, Hilary. Meaning of "meaning." 2. Language
and languages—Philosophy. 3. Meaning (Psychology)
I. Pessin, Andrew. II. Goldberg, Sanford. III. Putnam, Hilary.
Meaning of "meaning."
P106.P883T88   1995
149'.94—dc20   95-10001
CIP
Printed in the United States of America

The paper used in this publication meets the minimum requirements of
American National Standard for Information Sciences—
Permanence of Paper for Printed Library Materials,
ANSI Z 39.48-1984.

EB (c)   10   9   8   7   6   5   4   3   2   1
EB (p)   10   9   8   7   6   5   4   3   2   1

*This volume is dedicated,
with love and thanks, to our wives,
Sarah and Judy.*

Contents

IV. *Self-Knowledge*

Introduction   319

Acknowledgments

Every ATTEMPT HAS BEEN MADE to trace the ownership of all copyrighted material included in this book and to make proper acknowledgement thereof. If an error has inadvertently occurred, the editors will make the necessary correction in subsequent editions provided notification is received.

1. "The Meaning of 'Meaning' " by Hilary Putnam originally appeared in *Language, Mind, and Knowledge*, Minnesota Studies in the Philosophy of Science, vol. VII, 131–93. Ed. K. Gunderson. © 1975 by the University of Minnesota. Published by University of Minnesota Press. Reprinted by permission of the author and University of Minnesota Press.

2. "Putnam's Theory on the Reference of Substance Terms" by Eddy Zemach originally appeared in *The Journal of Philosophy* LXXIII, 5 (March 11, 1976) 116–27. Reprinted by permission of the author and *The Journal of Philosophy*.

3. "Natural Kinds" by D. H. Mellor originally appeared in *British Journal for the Philosophy of Science* 28 (1977) 299–312. Reprinted by permission of *British Journal for the Philosophy of Science*.

4. "Putnam on Artifacts" by Stephen Schwartz originally appeared in *The Philosophical Review* LXXXVII, 4 (October 1978) 566–74. Reprinted by permission of the author and *The Philosophical Review*.

5. The selection by John Searle is excerpted from his book *Intentionality* (Cambridge: Cambridge University Press, 1983) 197–208. © 1983 by Cambridge University Press. Reprinted by permission of the author and Cambridge University Press.

6. "Natural Kind Terms" by Kim Sterelny originally appeared in *Pacific Philosophical Quarterly* 64 (1983) 110–25. Reprinted by permission of *Pacific Philosophical Quarterly*.

7. "Individualism and the Mental" by Tyler Burge originally appeared in *Midwest Studies in Philosophy Vol. IV*, 73–122; the excerpt here is from 73–87. Eds. P. French, T. Uehling, and W. Wettstein. © 1979 by the University of Minnesota. Published by University of Minnesota Press. Reprinted by permission of the author and University of Minnesota Press.

8. "Other Bodies" by Tyler Burge originally appeared in *Thought and Object: Essays on Intentionality*, ed. A. Woodfield (Oxford: Clarendon Press, 1982), 97–120. © 1982 by Tyler Burge. Reprinted by permission of the author and Oxford University Press.

9. "Beyond Belief" by Daniel Dennett originally appeared in *Thought and Object: Essays on Intentionality*, ed. A. Woodfield (Oxford: Clarendon Press,

1982), 1–96; the excerpt here is from 36–60. © 1982 by Daniel Dennett. Reprinted by permission of the author and Oxford University Press.

10. "Social Content and Psychological Content" by Brian Loar was read at the Oberlin Colloquium in 1985 and originally appeared in *Contents of Thought: Proceedings of the 1985 Oberlin Colloquium in Philosophy* (Tucson: University of Arizona Press 1988), pp. 99–110. Eds. R. Grimm and D. Merrill. Reprinted by permission of University of Arizona Press.

11. This selection by Jerry Fodor is chapter 2 from his book *Psychosemantics* (Cambridge: MIT Press, 1987), pp. 27–53. © 1987 by the Massachusetts Institute of Technology. Reprinted by permission of the author and MIT Press.

12. "Functionalism and Broad Content" by Frank Jackson and Philip Pettit originally appeared in *Mind* XCVII, 387 (July 1988) 382–400. Reprinted by permission of the authors and Oxford University Press.

13. "On What's in the Head" by Robert Stalnaker originally appeared in *Philosophical Perspectives 3: Philosophy of Mind and Action Theory*, ed. J. Tomberlin (Atascadero, CA: Ridgeview Publishing Company, 1989), 287–316. Reprinted by permission of Ridgeview Publishing Company.

14. The selection by Colin McGinn is excerpted from his book *Mental Content* (Oxford, England: Blackwell Publishers, 1989), 157–59. Reprinted by permission of Blackwell Publishers.

15. "A Modal Argument for Narrow Content" by Jerry Fodor originally appeared in *The Journal of Philosophy* LXXXVIII, 1 (January 1991) 5–26. Reprinted by permission of the author and *The Journal of Philosophy*.

16. "All the Difference in the World" by Tim Crane originally appeared in *The Philosophical Quarterly* 41, 162 (1991), 1–26. Reprinted by permission of Blackwell Publishers.

17. "Putnam on Mind and Meaning" by John McDowell originally appeared in *Philosophical Topics* 20, 1 (Spring 1992), 35–48. Reprinted by permission of the author and *Philosophical Topics*.

18. "Knowing One's Own Mind" by Donald Davidson originally appeared in *Proceedings and Addresses of the American Philosophical Association* 61 (1987), 441–58. Reprinted by permission of the author and the American Philosophical Association.

19. "Individualism and Self-Knowledge" by Tyler Burge originally appeared in *The Journal of Philosophy* LXXXV, 11 (November 1988), 649–63. Reprinted by permission of the author and *The Journal of Philosophy*.

20. "Anti-Individualism and Privileged Access" by Michael McKinsey originally appeared in *Analysis* 51, 1 (1991), 9–16. Reprinted by permission of the author.

21. "Can Externalism Be Reconciled With Self-Knowledge?" by Akeel Bilgrami originally appeared in *Philosophical Topics* 20, 1 (Spring 1992), 233–67. Reprinted by permission of the author and *Philosophical Topics*.

Preface

Andrew Pessin and Sanford Goldberg

"THAT PSYCHOLOGICAL STATE DOES NOT determine extension will now be shown with the aid of a little science-fiction." With that humble sentence in 1975 Hilary Putnam changed the face of philosophy forever. Twin Earth burst on the scene like the legendary meteor that did in the dinosaurs; it has been reverberating through philosophy ever since. With implications stretching far beyond its original domain in the philosophy of language and philosophy of psychology, it has left almost no area of contemporary analytic philosophy untouched. Indeed Twin Earth and "The Meaning of 'Meaning'," the article in which it became famous, comprise perhaps the most influential single philosophical episode in the past half century. Here in 1995, therefore, in celebration of its twentieth anniversary, we have collected in this volume some of the best writings, by some of the best philosophers, on Twin Earth and its implications.

Twin Earth, of course, is very much like Earth. In fact it is *exactly* like Earth, molecule for molecule if you like; the reader may even suppose that he himself has a *Doppelgänger*, an identical copy, on Twin Earth. In the original version of the tale there is only one small difference between Earth and Twin Earth: the liquid called "water" there is not H_2O, but a different liquid with a long and complicated chemical formula abbreviated XYZ. This XYZ, however, is indistinguishable from water under normal conditions. It tastes like water, and quenches thirst like water, and fills the oceans and lakes and rivers of Twin Earth, etc.—but it isn't water. Otherwise everything else on the two planets is the same.

This simple-sounding scenario (along with its variations), however, conceals many complex problems and issues, and so has given rise to many extended debates. Some of these problems were explicitly treated by Putnam, while others were first addressed by his commentators and disputants, but all have proved important and difficult. For example, does the word "water" differ in meaning as it is used on the Twin planets? Does it even differ in denotation? How are answers to these questions affected if we change the scenario by rolling the time back to about 1750, before the chemistry of water was understood, such that nobody, not even "experts," could distinguish between H_2O and XYZ? How, further, do views on the meanings of terms for natural kinds like "water" transfer to other sorts of terms, such as artifact terms, color adjectives, social-role terms, legal terms, etc.? And how are views about term meanings (in particular for natural kinds) related to views about what natural kinds in fact *are*? (Must they, for example, have essences?)

Similar problems and debates arose as the focus turned from words to the corresponding concepts. What is the relationship between knowing a meaning and being in a psychological state? Are two Twins, each thinking on his respective planet, "I sure could go for some water," thinking the same thought? What are the implications of attributing to them *different* thoughts for other views on the relationship between minds and brains, and the nature of scientific psychology? What are the implications for the possibility of "self-knowledge," our apparent ability to know what we are thinking, and, indeed, to do so authoritatively? These and many related questions will be debated vigorously throughout this volume.

Putnam himself in "The Meaning of 'Meaning'" focuses on challenging two very important assumptions made about the nature of meaning and its relation to psychology: (1) that knowing the meaning of a term is just a matter of being in a certain psychological state; and (2) that the meaning of a term (its "intension") determines its extension (i.e., denotation). More precisely, what he challenges is the cotenability of these assumptions. He argues, that is, "that these two assumptions are not jointly satisfied by *any* notion, let alone any theory of meaning." Twin Earth was introduced as part of this argument to show, as noted above, that psychological state does not determine extension—and so ultimately to show, in the famous phrase, that " 'meanings' just ain't in the head!"

Along the way, however, Putnam introduces various concepts that were to spawn, in effect, whole industries. Among others we find:

(1) "Methodological solipsism"—a methodological assumption that no psychological state presupposes the existence of any individual other than the subject to whom that state is ascribed.

(2) The "division of linguistic labor"—the phenomenon, roughly, that while most people can quite correctly use and understand most of the terms of ordinary language, few of them know or need to know very much about the nature of what those terms refer to. For example, it isn't necessary for me to know very much about gold, or about how to distinguish gold from other similar looking things, in order to use the word "gold" correctly; I can leave tasks such as those to experts and rely, in effect, on their word (or on the word of those who rely directly on the experts).

(3) The "indexicality of natural kind terms"—the fact that terms for natural kinds, such as "water," have a hidden "indexical" component allowing their extension to be dependent in a certain way upon contexts. Thus, as Putnam puts it, " 'water' is stuff that bears a certain similarity relation to the water *around here*," where the emphasized phrase picks out the extension-determining context. This in turn connects to Kripke's doctrine that natural kind terms are rigid designators; that is, they refer to the same substance in every possible world in which they refer to anything at all. Together these two notions worked to define a realism which, amongst other consequences, helped overturn the reigning description theory of meaning.

(4) "Stereotypes"—conventional ideas, which may be wildly inaccurate, of what some object or substance looks like or acts like or is. While the concept itself wasn't new, its application in the theory of meaning was.

These, plus detailed discussion of the relevant writings of Quine, Davidson, and Carnap, amongst others, plus more still constitute this remarkable—and enduring—essay. It is now twenty years old, but its importance and relevance continue to grow. This volume aims to reflect that.

We have had quite a bit of help in assembling and preparing this volume. For contributions of various sorts we would like to thank David Chalmers, Judy Levey, Sarah Pessin, our editor Nick Street, all the contributing authors, Kenyon College, and Columbia University.

Introduction

Hilary Putnam

THE PAPERS IN THIS COLLECTION represent a range of responses to my essay "The Meaning of 'Meaning.' " The editors have made an excellent selection, and a reader who works through this collection of essays will certainly be abreast of the debate about my "semantic externalism." To comment on each of the individual papers would require a whole series of essays rather than an "introduction," and I shall not attempt it. Instead, I shall offer a few general remarks, and comment on just two of the reactions to my "Twin Earth" thought experiment and to semantic externalism in general.

"The Meaning of 'Meaning' " was itself a reaction to an assumption about concepts that is literally millennia-old, and I have never ceased to be surprised and gratified by the speed with which and the extent to which the view I proposed in that essay became widespread. When I speak of a millennia-old assumption about concepts, I am not overlooking the fact that there has been disagreement about concepts and about conceptual thought ever since Aristotle disagreed with Plato about the nature of "ideas" in the Greek sense of that word (often translated as "forms"). For example, according to Plato, ideas are extra-mental entities, but knowledge of them is supposed to be innate in the mind, and capable of being brought to consciousness by an act of "recollection." For Aristotle, they are both mental and extra–mental. The very same "idea" or "form" is supposed to be capable of existing in things, but also, minus its matter, in the mind. In the middle ages, Conceptualist and Nominalist views were added to the Platonic and Aristotelian alternatives. For the Conceptualists ideas are explicitly mental entities; for the Nominalists they are, of course, "names," but the understanding of "names" is supposed to lie in each individual mind. In the modern period, for an empiricist like Hume, ideas are hardly distinguished from mental images, and are certainly in the mind. Thus, in spite of the variety of metaphysical theories about the nature of concepts, this much was not doubted: concepts were uniformly thought of as capable of being completely contained in or recollected by "the mind" (which was itself conceived of as a private theater, isolated from other individuals and from the "external world").

It was also taken for granted by almost all the philosophers in the tradition that the idea in the mind, or the possession or recollection of the idea by the mind, determines the extension of the "name" associated with the idea or concept: a name, say, "dog," is *true of* a particular thing inasmuch as that particular thing falls under the concept in the mind, or the concept recollected by the mind. In short, it is a feature of all these views that *one individual in isolation* can, in principle, grasp any concept whatsoever, and that the individual's grasp of his or her concepts totally determines[1] the extension of all the individual's terms. *Knowledge of meanings is private mental property.*

It was against this conception of meanings and of knowledge of meanings as private mental property that I wrote "The Meaning of 'Meaning,' " and the Twin Earth thought experiment was only one of a number of arguments that I used to argue that, contrary to these traditional views, knowledge of meanings is not something that is possible for a thinker in isolation, and that it presupposes both interactions with the world and interactions with other language users. The interaction with other language users is something that I illustrated with the aid of words which we are all competent to use, but the members of whose extension most of us are not able to recognize. For me at that time the word "elm" was such a word. I possessed what normally counts as "knowledge of the meaning" of the word "elm." For example, I knew that elms are deciduous trees, that they are common in North America and in Europe, I knew the approximate height of a typical elm (I knew that it was not a miniature tree or a bush). True, I was quite unable to distinguish an elm from a beech; yet, to say that I *did not know the meaning of the word "elm"* could, *pace* John Searle, have been to confuse lack of botanical knowledge with lack of linguistic competence. Or (another example I used), take the word "gold." I suppose that no one who is not a chemist or a metallurgist or a miner or a jeweller can distinguish true gold from fake gold with genuine reliability; the rest of us have to rely on these experts when we purchase gold jewelry in order to avoid being fooled. Yet this does not mean that we lack knowledge of the meaning of the word "gold." My suggestion was that knowing the meaning of the word "gold" or of the word "elm" is not a matter of *knowing that* at all, but a matter of *knowing how*; and what you have to *know how* is to play your part in an intricate system of social cooperation. Language, I said, is not a tool like a hammer, that anyone can use by him- or herself. It is a tool like a large ship, which it takes many people working together to operate. I can refer to gold, talk about gold, purchase gold, etc., perfectly well without being able reliably to distinguish gold from non-gold because there are others in the community— experts—upon whom I can rely. In short, there is a *linguistic division of labor.*

There are, however, words whose extension we are all competent at determining (at least in normal circumstances). All of us, for example, are extremely reliable at identifying water, at least under normal circumstances (although under doubtful circumstances even here we might have to consult an expert). But even the understanding of a word like "water" is not, I argued, simply a matter of having an item tucked away in a private mental theater.

In arguing that meaning depends not only on other speakers, but also on the environment, I used several examples (in "The Meaning of Meaning' " and its predecessor, "Is Semantics Possible?").[2] For instance, I imagined at one point that the words "aluminum" and "molybdenum" had their meanings unintentionally *switched* by English-speaking colonists on another planet. (Something like this happened when English colonists came to the United States and ignorantly applied words like "sparrow" to species of birds which are not called "sparrows" in

England.) What I associate with the word "aluminum" is not very different from what I associate with the word "molybdenum" (if we prescind from the knowledge that pots and pans are often made of aluminum and not of molybdenum— but we can also imagine that on the colony, pots and pans are normally made of molybdenum). Thus, we can imagine that an English-speaker on Terra and an English-speaker on one of Terra's colonies might be in the same brain state, at least in all relevant respects, on a particular occasion of the use of the sentence, "This pot is made of aluminum," and yet one of them might be *saying* that the pot is made of aluminum and the other might be saying that it is made of molybdenum. To mean *aluminum* when one uses the word "aluminum," I argued, it is not enough to have certain associations, certain mental images, etc.; it is necessary that the metal referred to in the linguistic community by that name *actually be aluminum*, and whether that is the case depends on whether one has certain direct or indirect interactions with aluminum itself, including interactions that go through experts in one's community.

The example that became the most famous, however, and the one that gives this anthology its title, was the one involving Twin Earth. I wrote,

> One of the peculiarities of Twin Earth is that the liquid called "water" is not H_2O but a different liquid whose chemical formula is very long and complicated. I shall abbreviate this chemical formula simply as XYZ. I shall suppose that XYZ is indistinguishable from water at normal temperatures and pressures. In particular, it tastes like water and it quenches thirst like water. Also, I shall suppose that the oceans and lakes and seas of Twin Earth contain XYZ and not water, that it rains XYZ on Twin Earth and not water, etc.
>
> If a spaceship from Earth ever visits Twin Earth, then the supposition at first will be that "water" has the same meaning on Earth and on Twin Earth. This supposition will be corrected when it is discovered that "water" on Twin Earth is XYZ, and the Earthian spaceship will report somewhat as follows: "On Twin Earth, the word 'water' means XYZ."[3]

I went on to claim that the difference in the meaning of the word "water" existed even *before* chemistry was developed on either Earth or on Twin Earth (say, in 1750); it is just that in 1750 neither community knew the chemical nature of the substance each called "water." *The meaning was different because the stuff was different.* And I pointed out that an Earth speaker and his Twin Earth *Doppelgänger* might be in the same brain state *neuron for neuron*, and it would still be the case that what the Earthian meant by his word "water" was not what his Twin Earthian *Doppelgänger* meant by the word. It was at this point that I wrote, "Cut the pie any way you like, 'meanings' just ain't in the *head*."

Of course, denying that meanings are in the head must have consequences for the philosophy of mind, but at the time I wrote those words I was unsure as to just what those consequences were. After all, such accomplishments as *knowing the meaning of words* and *using words meaningfully* are paradigmatic "mental abilities";

yet, I was not sure, when I wrote "The Meaning of 'Meaning,' " whether the moral of that essay should be that we shouldn't think of the meanings of words as lying in the mind at all, or whether (like John Dewey and William James) we should stop thinking of the mind as something "in the head" and think of it rather as a system of environment-involving capacities and interactions. In the end, I equivocated between these views. I said, on the one hand, that "meanings just ain't in the head," and, on the other hand, that the notion of the mind is ambiguous, and that, in one sense of "mental state" (I called mental states, in this supposed sense, 'narrow mental states'), our mental states *are* entirely in our heads, and in another sense (I called mental states in this supposed second sense "broad mental states"), a sense which includes such states as *knowing the meaning of a word*, our mental states are individuated by our relations to our environment and to other speakers and not simply by what goes on in our brains. Subsequently, under the influence of Tyler Burge and more recently of John McDowell as well, I have come to think that this conceded too much to the idea that the mind *can* be thought of as a private theater (situated inside the head).

SEARLE'S REACTION

John Searle's view[4] is that meanings are literally in the head. He replies to the arguments in "The Meaning of 'Meaning' " by claiming that English speakers who are not able to tell elms from beeches "don't know the meaning or know it imperfectly." At the same time, he holds that even such speakers have a different *concept* of an elm and of a beech; for, he argues, they have "enough conceptual knowledge to know the two are distinct species." Here, I can reply that if, indeed, they "don't know the meaning" *at all*, then it follows at once that this "conceptual knowledge," whatever it is, is not *meaning*. So let us assume that Searle's assertion that they "know it imperfectly" or "don't know it at all" was a slip.

The only "conceptual knowledge" about elms and not about beeches that such a speaker typically possesses is that elms are trees that experts upon whom he or she relies refer to by the name "elm." Does the existence of such conceptual knowledge show that meanings *are* in the head as Searle believes? (Searle regards all mental states as "features of the brain."[5])

Well, if it does, then "the tree that experts upon whom I rely call an 'elm' " must be part of what such a speaker *means* by "elm," for otherwise *nothing* in the the part of the meaning known to the speaker (in the "Intentional content" of "elm," to employ Searle's notion) distinguishes elms from beeches. (I mean, of course, that this is a consequence of *Searle's* view; in my view, knowing the meaning of "elm" isn't, for the most part, a matter of *knowing that* at all, but of participating successfully in the linguistic division of labor. And, in my view, the *sound and spelling* of the word, although of course known to speakers, are not part of its meaning.)

The whole notion of "Intentional content" on which Searle relies seems to me intensely problematic for reasons which I shall explain shortly. But, in any case, even if there were Searlian "Intentional contents," they could not be identical with the meanings of words in a public language. I don't mean to say that some *other* objects are the meanings of words in a public language; in my view, meanings aren't objects at all. I agree with Wittgenstein and with Quine that the idea of its meaning as some kind of "entity" with which a word is "associated" and which determines how the word is to be used in every context, is as untenable today as belief in Homeric gods.[6] The real questions are (as many philosophers have pointed out) not what meanings *are*, but (1) what it is *to know the meaning* of a word; and (2) when should we say that two words have the *same* meaning, i.e., how to understand the relation of *synonymy*. When I say that "Intentional contents" in Searle's sense (if there are such things) are not the same as meanings in a public language at all, I mean that sameness of "Intentional contents" in Searle's sense does not have the *properties* that synonymy has, or even that *similarity* of meaning has, in a public language. Wittgenstein famously remarked that for many purposes (though not for all) we may say that the meaning of a word is its use in the language. Thus, to say of words in a public language, or in two different public languages, that they have "the same meaning" is to say that in certain respects they have the same use. But to know what *that* comes to (and it comes to different things in different cases[7]), we have to know in each case which features to discount and which features are relevant. For example, when we say that in English the word "elm" has the same meaning as the word "Ulme" in German, we discount the differences in the sound and spelling of the words themselves. But on Searle's theory (as I just argued) what an English speaker means by the word "elm" would be *the kind of tree that experts upon whom I rely refer to by the name "elm"* and what the German speaker means by the word "Ulme" is *the kind of tree that experts upon whom I rely refer to by the name "Ulme."* These are two entirely different "Intentional contents." Thus, if we suppose that Searle's theory of "Intentional contents" is a theory of *meaning in a public language*, we would have to say that a word and its translation do not have the same meaning at all. Indeed, they don't even have similar meanings—for let us suppose that, by some accident, some group of English speakers have switched the words "elm" and "beech." Let us suppose that in Nova Scotia, as it might be, beeches are called "elms" and elms are called "beeches." On Searle's theory, the word "elm" would, in this case, have the *same* meaning in Massachusetts and in Nova Scotia, notwithstanding the fact that (speaking as we ordinarily speak) in Nova Scotia "elm" means "beech," while "elm" in English and "Ulme" in German would have totally different meanings. Our actual practices of individuating the meanings of words would, in fact, be totally ignored by such a theory.

More importantly (since this is an anthology of papers on Twin Earth), Searle denies that the Twin Earth thought experiment shows that meanings aren't just features of the brain. According to Searle, "most people do not go around baptizing natural kinds; they just intend to use words to mean and refer to whatever the community at large, including the experts, use the words to mean and refer to." What this seems to mean is that, for most people, "water" *means* "stuff that the community at large, including the experts, call 'water.' " This account has the same defects as the account of the meaning of "elm" I just considered.

Searle also argues that even if the meaning of water did have an indexical (ostensive) element of the kind I suggested in "The Meaning of 'Meaning,' " that would not mean that it was not a private mental content. What a typical Earthian English speaker might mean by the word "water" is, he suggests, "whatever is identical in structure to this stuff," and a typical Twin Earth English speaker might associate the very same "Intentional content" with the word. Thus, on this alternative proposal, the word would have exactly the same meaning on Earth and Twin Earth; however, it would have a different extension because the Earth speakers are referring to what comes out of Earth faucets and the Twin Earth speakers are referring to what comes out of Twin Earth faucets. Such a view, it seems to me, fails to conform to our actual practice of deciding on sameness/similarity of meaning in a public language by denying that *what we are in fact referring to* plays any role at all.

In addition, it is uncertain whether Searlian "Intentional contents" really exist at all. How is the Searlian speaker in isolation* supposed to *have* the notion of an "expert"? What is the "Intentional content" of "expert"? Perhaps Searle would say that the "Intentional content" of "expert" is: *speaker whom other speakers call an "expert."* But then how is the "intension" of "speaker" supposed to be fixed? Perhaps Searle would say that the "Intentional content" of "speaker" is: *person with whom I engage in a certain kind of communication.* But then how is the "Intentional content" of "communication" fixed?

It is clear that Searle is making the assumption that at least some very significant concepts (concepts like "speaking," "communicating," and "calling something a so-and-so") are concepts that a speaker *could* master and possess without relying on the actual nature of any of the objects with which he or she interacts, and without the benefit of a linguistic division of labor. This is a sort of "private language" assumption. I myself do not believe that mysterious "Intentional contents," totally inside the head but with the power of fixing reference to external realities all by themselves, exist at all.[8] But I do not need to argue against Searle's metaphysics here—for, in any case, as I have just shown, even if there *were* Searlian "Intentional contents," sameness and difference of Searlian "Intentional contents" could not be the same thing as sameness and difference of meaning or concept as meanings and concepts are actually individuated.

---

* Remember, "Intentional contents" are supposed to be *features of the brain*, and thus presumably do not depend on relations to the environment or to other speakers at all!

TYLER BURGE'S CRITICISM AND A CONCLUDING REMARK

Tyler Burge's criticism comes, so to speak, from the opposite direction. Burge agrees with my semantic externalism, but argues that I did not carry it far enough. In Burge's view, my attempt in "The Meaning of 'Meaning' " to hold a place open for a notion of "narrow content" and for "narrow mental states" represented a confusion on my part, and I have come to believe that he right. But, since I agree with his paper, I will only refer the reader to it rather than attempt to summarize his arguments.

In this Introduction, I have focused on the two doctrines in "The Meaning of 'Meaning' " that have aroused the most controversy: semantic externalism and the division of linguistic labor. Unfortunately, more than one author has misread the essay by overlooking the fact that it asserted that there are additional factors involved in meaning. "The Meaning of 'Meaning' " also contains the beginning of a theory of the semantics of natural–kind words, and that theory does *not* claim that their meaning is entirely determined by the nature of the objects in their extension (whatever that nature is discovered to be by scientific investigation), although I did and do still claim that it is *partly* so determined. Another factor that partly determines the meaning of a natural–kind term is the stereotype that speakers have of a typical member of the kind. If there is an area in which there is further work to be done (linguistically and historically as well as philosophically), it is the study of the ways in which these two components—the stereotype and the objective nature of the objects in question—interact with one another. I assume that the reader of this anthology will read (or re–read) "The Meaning of 'Meaning' " itself. I urge him or her not to neglect the less thematized but nevertheless (I believe) important discussions sprinkled through it of such matters as stereotypes, the various senses that natural–kind words can have, the problems with what I called "California semantics," etc.

HILARY PUTNAM
Cambridge, Massachusetts
Spring 1995

ENDNOTES

1. There are only two exceptions to this generalization. One, which I knew of when I wrote, and which partly inspired, "The Meaning of 'Meaning,' " is a remark somewhere in Mill's *Logic* to the effect that while the concept in the mind does most of the work in fixing the extension of a natural-kind term (I believe that Mill was here thinking primarily of terms for species, e.g., "cow" or "wolf"), it does not do so completely; the fixing of the extension is completed *by the species itself*, or words to that effect. The other, which was only called to my attention recently by Dan Warren, is a passage in Kant's

first Critique (A728) according to which the extension of the term "water" is not precisely fixed by the concept, but rather by *experiments*.

2. Both of these papers are collected in my *Mind, Language and Reality; Philosophical Papers*, vol. 2 (Cambridge: Cambridge University Press, 1975). "The Meaning of 'Meaning' " is, of course, reprinted in the present collection.

3. "The Meaning of 'Meaning'," p. 3–52 (in the present volume). I go on to explain that I am *not* saying that on Twin Earth "water" and "XYZ" are synonyms, but rather that the extension—the substance referred to, not its chemical description—is one *component* of the meaning of the word "water," both on Earth and on Twin Earth.

4. See the selection from Searle's *Intentionality* (New York: Cambridge University Press, 1983) reprinted in the present volume. I believe that this was also Russell's view when he wrote *Problems of Philosophy*.

5. Searle's *Minds, Brains and Science* (Cambridge, MA: Harvard University Press, 1984), p. 19.

6. Cf. Wittgenstein's reference to "a *mythological* description of the use of a rule" (*Philosophical Investigations*, §221, emphasis added).

7. This is something emphasized by Charles Travis in his important book on Wittgenstein's philosophy of language, *The Uses of Sense* (Oxford: Oxford University Press, 1989).

8. For a view of the mind totally opposed to Searle's mentalism, see my "Sense, Nonsense, and the Senses: An Inquiry into the Powers of the Human Mind," "The Dewey Lectures, 1994," in *The Journal of Philosophy*, vol. XCI, no. 9, September 1994.

Part I
Where It All Began

1

The Meaning of "Meaning"[1]

Hilary Putnam

LANGUAGE IS THE FIRST BROAD area of human cognitive capacity for which we are beginning to obtain a description which is not exaggeratedly oversimplified. Thanks to the work of contemporary transformational linguists,[2] a very subtle description of at least some human languages is in the process of being constructed. Some features of these languages appear to be *universal*. Where such features turn out to be "species-specific"—"not explicable on some general grounds of functional utility or simplicity that would apply to arbitrary systems that serve the functions of language"—they may shed some light on the structure of mind. While it is extremely difficult to say to what extent the structure so illuminated will turn out to be a universal structure of *language*, as opposed to a universal structure of innate general learning strategies,[3] the very fact that this discussion can take place is testimony to the richness and generality of the descriptive material that linguists are beginning to provide, and also testimony to the depth of the analysis, insofar as the features that appear to be candidates for "species-specific" features of language are in no sense surface or phenomenological features of language, but lie at the level of deep structure.

The most serious drawback to all of this analysis, as far as a philosopher is concerned, is that it does not concern the meaning of words. Analysis of the deep structure of linguistic forms gives us an incomparably more powerful description of the *syntax* of natural languages than we have ever had before. But the dimension of language associated with the word "meaning" is, in spite of the usual spate of heroic if misguided attempts, as much in the dark as it ever was.

In this essay, I want to explore why this should be so. In my opinion, the reason that so-called semantics is in so much worse condition than syntactic theory is that the *prescientific* concept on which semantics is based—the prescientific concept of *meaning*—is itself in much worse shape than the prescientific concept of syntax. As usual in philosophy, skeptical doubts about the concept do not at all help one in clarifying or improving the situation any more than dogmatic assertions by conservative philosophers that all's really well in this best of all possible worlds. The reason that the prescientific concept of meaning is in bad shape is not clarified by some general skeptical or nominalistic argument to the effect that meanings don't exist. Indeed, the upshot of our discussion will be that meanings don't exist in quite the way we tend to think they do. But electrons don't exist in quite the way Bohr thought they did, either. There is all the distance in the world between this assertion and the assertion that meanings (or electrons) "don't exist."

3

I am going to talk almost entirely about the meaning of words rather than about the meaning of sentences because I feel that our concept of word-meaning is more defective than our concept of sentence-meaning. But I will comment briefly on the arguments of philosophers such as Donald Davidson who insist that the concept of word-meaning *must* be secondary and that study of sentence-meaning must be primary. Since I regard the traditional theories about meaning as myth-eaten (notice that the topic of "meaning" is the one topic discussed in philosophy in which there is literally nothing but "theory"—literally nothing that can be labelled or even ridiculed as the "commonsense view"), it will be necessary for me to discuss and try to disentangle a number of topics concerning which the received view is, in my opinion, wrong. The reader will give me the greatest aid in the task of trying to make these matters clear if he will kindly assume that *nothing* is clear in advance.

MEANING AND EXTENSION

Since the Middle Ages at least, writers on the theory of meaning have purported to discover an ambiguity in the ordinary concept of meaning, and have introduced a pair of terms—*extension* and *intension*, or *Sinn* and *Bedeutung*, or whatever—to disambiguate the notion. The *extension* of a term, in customary logical parlance, is simply the set of things the term is true of. Thus, "rabbit," in its most common English sense, is true of all and only rabbits, so the extension of "rabbit" is precisely the set of rabbits. Even this notion—and it is the *least* problematical notion in this cloudy subject—has its problems, however. Apart from problems it inherits from its parent notion of *truth*, the foregoing example of "rabbit" *in its most common English sense* illustrates one such problem: strictly speaking, it is not a term, but an ordered pair consisting of a term and a "sense" (or an occasion of use, or something else that distinguishes a term in one sense from the same term used in a different sense) that has an extension. Another problem is this: a "set," in the mathematical sense, is a "yes-no" object; any given object either definitely belongs to S or definitely does not belong to S, if S is a set. But words in a natural language are not generally "yes–no": there are things of which the description "tree" is clearly true and things of which the description "tree" is clearly false, to be sure, but there are a host of borderline cases. Worse, the line between the clear cases and the borderline cases is itself fuzzy. Thus the idealization involved in the notion of *extension*—the idealization involved in supposing that there is such a thing as the set of things of which the term "tree" is true—is actually very severe.

Recently some mathematicians have investigated the notion of a *fuzzy set*— that is, of an object to which other things belong or do not belong with a given probability or to a given degree, rather than belong "yes–no." If one really wanted to formalize the notion of extension as applied to terms in a natural language, it would be necessary to employ "fuzzy sets" or something similar rather than sets in the classical sense.

The problem of a word's having more than one sense is standardly handled by treating each of the senses as a different word (or rather, by treating the word as if it carried invisible subscripts, thus: "rabbit$_1$" animal of a certain kind; "rabbit$_2$"— coward; and as if "rabbit$_1$" and "rabbit$_2$" or whatever were different words entirely). This again involves two very severe idealizations (at least two, that is): supposing that words have discretely many senses, and supposing that the entire repertoire of senses is fixed once and for all. Paul Ziff has recently investigated the extent to which both of these suppositions distort the actual situation in natural language;[4] nevertheless, we will continue to make these idealizations here.

Now consider the compound terms "creature with a heart" and "creature with a kidney." Assuming that every creature with a heart possesses a kidney and vice versa, the extension of these two terms is exactly the same. But they obviously differ in meaning. Supposing that there is a sense of "meaning" in which meaning = extension, there must be another sense of "meaning" in which the meaning of a term is not its extension but something else, say the "concept" associated with the term. Let us call this "something else" the *intension* of the term. The concept of a creature with a heart is clearly a different concept from the concept of a creature with a kidney. Thus the two terms have different intension. When we say they have different "meaning," meaning = intension.

INTENSION AND EXTENSION

Something like the preceding paragraph appears in every standard exposition of the notions "intension" and "extension." But it is not at all satisfactory. Why it is not satisfactory is, in a sense, the burden of this entire essay. But some points can be made at the very outset: first of all, what evidence is there that "extension" is a sense of the word "meaning?" The canonical explanation of the notions "intension" and "extension" is very much like "in one sense 'meaning' means *extension* and in the other sense 'meaning' means *meaning*." The fact is that while the notion of "extension" is made quite precise, relative to the fundamental logical notion of *truth* (and under the severe idealizations remarked above), the notion of intension is made no more precise than the vague (and, as we shall see, misleading) notion "concept." It is as if someone explained the notion "probability" by saying: "in one sense 'probability' means frequency, and in the other sense it means *propensity*." "Probability" *never* means "frequency," and "propensity" is at least as unclear as "probability."

Unclear as it is, the traditional doctrine that the notion "meaning" possesses the extension/intension ambiguity has certain typical consequences. Most traditional philosophers thought of concepts as something *mental*. Thus the doctrine that the meaning of a term (the meaning "in the sense of intension," that is) is a concept carried the implication that meanings are mental entities. Frege and more recently Carnap and his followers, however, rebelled against this "psychologism," as they termed it. Feeling that meanings are *public* property—that the *same* meaning can be "grasped" by more than one person and by persons at different times—they identified concepts (and hence "intensions" or meanings) with abstract entities rather than mental entities. However, "grasping" these abstract entities was still an individual psychological act. None of these philosophers doubted that understanding a word (knowing its intension) was just a matter of being in a certain psychological state (somewhat in the way in which knowing how to factor numbers in one's head is just a matter of being in a certain very complex psychological state).

Second, the timeworn example of the two terms "creature with a kidney" and "creature with a heart" does show that two terms can have the same extension and yet differ in intension. But it was taken to be obvious that the reverse is impossible: two terms cannot differ in extension and have the same intension. Interestingly, no argument for this impossibility was ever offered. Probably it reflects the tradition of the ancient and medieval philosophers who assumed that the concept corresponding to a term was just a conjunction of predicates, and hence that the concept corresponding to a term must *always* provide a necessary and sufficient condition for falling into the extension of the term.[5] For philosophers like Carnap, who accepted the verifiability theory of meaning, the concept corresponding to a term provided (in the ideal case, where the term had "complete meaning") a *criterion* for belonging to the extension (not just in the sense of "necessary and sufficient condition," but in the strong sense of *way of recognizing* if a given thing falls into the extension or not). Thus these positivistic philosophers were perfectly happy to retain the traditional view on this point. So, theory of meaning came to rest on two unchallenged assumptions:

(I) That knowing the meaning of a term is just a matter of being in a certain psychological state (in the sense of "psychological state," in which states of memory and psychological dispositions are "psychological states"; no one thought that knowing the meaning of a word was a continuous state of consciousness, of course).

(II) That the meaning of a term (in the sense of "intension") determines its extension (in the sense that sameness of intension entails sameness of extension).

I shall argue that these two assumptions are not jointly satisfied by *any* notion, let alone any notion of meaning. The traditional concept of meaning is a concept which rests on a false theory.

"PSYCHOLOGICAL STATE" AND METHODOLOGICAL SOLIPSISM

In order to show this, we need first to clarify the traditional notion of a psychological state. In one sense a state is simply a two-place predicate whose arguments are an individual and a time. In this sense, *being 5 feet tall, being in pain, knowing the alphabet*, and even *being a thousand miles from Paris* are all states. (Note that the *time* is usually left implicit or "contextual"; the full form of an atomic sentence of these predicates would be "x *is five feet tall at time* t," "x *is in pain at time* t," etc.) In science, however, it is customary to restrict the term state to properties which are defined in terms of the parameters of the individual which are fundamental from the point of view of the given science. Thus, being five feet tall is a state (from the point of view of physics); being in pain is a state (from the point of view of mentalistic psychology, at least); knowing the alphabet might be a state (from the point of view of cognitive psychology), although it is hard to say; but being a thousand miles from Paris would *not* naturally be called a *state*. In one sense, a psychological state is simply a state which is studied or described by psychology. In this sense it may be trivially true that, say *knowing the meaning of the word "water"* is a "psychological state" (viewed from the standpoint of cognitive psychology). But this is not the sense of psychological state that is at issue in the above assumption (I).

When traditional philosophers talked about psychological states (or "mental" states), they made an assumption which we may call the assumption of methodological solipsism. This assumption is the assumption that no psychological state, properly so called, presupposes the existence of any individual other than the subject to whom that state is ascribed. (In fact, the assumption was that no psychological state presupposes the existence of the subject's *body* even: if P is a psychological state, properly so called, then it must be logically possible for a "disembodied mind" to be in P.) This assumption is pretty explicit in Descartes, but it is implicit in just about the whole of traditional philosophical psychology. Making this assumption is, of course, adopting a *restrictive program*—a program which deliberately limits the scope and nature of psychology to fit certain mentalistic preconceptions or, in some cases, to fit an idealistic reconstruction of knowledge and the world. Just *how* restrictive the program is, however, often goes unnoticed. Such common or garden variety psychological states as *being jealous* have to be reconstructed, for example, if the assumption of methodological solipsism is retained. For, in its ordinary use, x *is jealous of* y entails that y exists, and x *is jealous of* y's *regard for* z entails that both y and z exist (as well as x, of course). Thus *being jealous* and *being jealous of someone's regard for someone else* are not psychological states permitted by the assumption of methodological solipsism. (We shall call them "psychological states in the wide sense" and refer to the states which are permitted by methodological solipsism as "psychological states in the narrow sense.") The reconstruction required by methodological solipsism would be to reconstrue *jealousy* so that I can be jealous of my own hallucinations, or of figments of my imagination, etc. Only if we assume that psychological states in the narrow sense have a significant degree of causal closure (so that restricting ourselves to psychological states in the narrow sense will facilitate the statement of psychological *laws*) is there any point in engaging in this reconstruction, or in making the assumption of methodological solipsism. But the three centuries of failure of mentalistic psychology is tremendous evidence against this procedure, in my opinion.

Be that as it may, we can now state more precisely what we claimed at the end of the preceding section. Let A and B be any two terms which differ in extension. By assumption (II) they must differ in meaning (in the sense of "intension"). By assumption (I), *knowing the meaning of* A and *knowing the meaning of* B are psychological states *in the narrow sense*—for this is how we shall construe assumption (I). *But these psychological states must determine the extension of the terms A and B just as much as the meanings ("intensions") do.*

To see this, let us try assuming the opposite. Of course, there cannot be two terms A and B such that *knowing the meaning of* A is the same state as *knowing the meaning of* B even though A and B have different extensions. For *knowing the meaning of* A isn't just "grasping the intension" of A, whatever that may come to; it is also knowing that the "intension" that one has "grasped" *is* the intension of A. Thus, someone who knows the meaning of "wheel" presumably "grasps the intension" of its German synonym *Rad*; but if he doesn't know that the "intension" in question is the intension of Rad he isn't said to "know the meaning of Rad." If A and B are different terms, then *knowing the meaning of* A is a different state from *knowing the meaning of* B whether the meanings of A and B be themselves the same or different. But by the same argument, if I_1 and I_2 are different *intensions* and A is a term, then *knowing that* I_1 *is the meaning of* A is a different psychological state from *knowing that* I_2 *is the meaning of* A. Thus, there cannot be two different logically possible worlds L_1 and L_2 such that, say, Oscar is in the *same* psychological state (in the narrow sense) in L_1 and in L_2 (in all respects), but in L_1 Oscar understands A as having the meaning I_1 and in L_2 Oscar understands A as having the meaning I_2. (For, if there were, then in L_1 Oscar would be in the psychological state *knowing that* I_1 *is the meaning of* A and in L_2 Oscar would be in the psychological state *knowing that* I_2 *is the meaning of* A, and these are different and even—assuming that A has just *one* meaning for Oscar in each world—incompatible psychological states in the narrow sense.)

In short, if S is the sort of psychological state we have been discussing—a psychological state of the form *knowing that* I *is the meaning of* A, where I is an "intension" and A is a term—then the *same* necessary and sufficient condition for falling into the extension of A "works" in *every* logically possible world in which the speaker is in the psychological state S. For the state S *determines* the intension I, and by assumption (II) the intension amounts to a necessary and sufficient condition for membership in the *extension*.

If our interpretation of the traditional doctrine of intension and extension is fair to Frege and Carnap, then the whole psychologism/Platonism issue appears somewhat a tempest in a teapot, as far as meaning-theory is concerned. (Of course, it is a very important issue as far as general philosophy of mathematics is concerned.) For even if meanings are "Platonic" entities rather than "mental" entities on the Frege–Carnap view, "grasping" those entities is presumably a psychological state (in the narrow sense). Moreover, the psychological state uniquely determines the "Platonic" entity. So whether one takes the "Platonic" entity or the psychological state as the "meaning" would appear to be somewhat a matter of convention. And taking the psychological state to be the meaning would hardly have the consequence that Frege feared, that meanings would cease to be public. For psychological states are "public" in the sense that different people (and even people in different epochs) can be in the *same* psychological state. Indeed, Frege's argument against psychologism is only an argument against identifying concepts with mental particulars, not with mental entities in general.

The "public" character of psychological states entails, in particular, that if Oscar and Elmer understand a word A differently, then they must be in different psychological states. For the state of *knowing the intension of* A *to be, say, I* is the *same* state whether Oscar or Elmer be in it. Thus two speakers cannot be in the same psychological state in all respects and understand the term A differently; the psychological state of the speaker determines the intension (and hence, by assumption (II), the extension) of A.

It is this last consequence of the joint assumptions (I), (II) that we claim to be false. We claim that it is possible for two speakers to be in exactly the *same* psychological state (in the narrow sense), even though the extension of the term A in the idiolect of the one is different from the extension of the term A in the idiolect of the other. Extension is not determined by psychological state.

This will be shown in detail in later sections. If this is right, then there are two courses open to one who wants to rescue at least one of the traditional assumptions; to give up the idea that psychological state (in the narrow sense) determines *intension*, or to give up the idea that intension determines extension. We shall consider these alternatives later.

ARE MEANINGS IN THE HEAD?

That psychological state does not determine extension will now be shown with the aid of a little science-fiction. For the purpose of the following science-fiction examples, we shall suppose that somewhere in the galaxy there is a planet we shall call Twin Earth. Twin Earth is very much like Earth; in fact, people on Twin Earth even speak *English*. In fact, apart from the differences we shall specify in our science-fiction examples, the reader may suppose that Twin Earth is *exactly* like Earth. He may even suppose that he has a *Doppelgänger*—an identical copy—on Twin Earth, if he wishes, although my stories will not depend on this.

Although some of the people on Twin Earth (say, the ones who call themselves "Americans" and the ones who call themselves "Canadians" and the ones who call themselves "Englishmen," etc.) speak English, there are, not surprisingly, a few tiny differences which we will now describe between the dialects of English spoken on Twin Earth and Standard English. These differences themselves depend on some of the peculiarities of Twin Earth.

One of the peculiarities of Twin Earth is that the liquid called "water" is not H_2O but a different liquid whose chemical formula is very long and complicated. I shall abbreviate this chemical formula simply as XYZ. I shall suppose that XYZ is indistinguishable from water at normal temperatures and pressures. In particular, it tastes like water and it quenches thirst like water. Also, I shall suppose that the oceans and lakes and seas of Twin Earth contain XYZ and not water, that it rains XYZ on Twin Earth and not water, etc.

If a spaceship from Earth ever visits Twin Earth, then the supposition at first will be that "water" has the same meaning on Earth and on Twin Earth. This supposition will be corrected when it is discovered that "water" on Twin Earth is XYZ, and the Earthian spaceship will report somewhat as follows:

"On Twin Earth the word 'water' means XYZ."

(It is this sort of use of the word "means" which accounts for the doctrine that extension is one sense of "meaning," by the way. But note that although "means" does mean something like *has as extension* in this example, one would *not* say

"On Twin Earth the meaning of the word 'water' is XYZ."

unless, possibly, the fact that "water is XYZ" was known to every adult speaker of English on Twin Earth. We can account for this in terms of the theory of meaning we develop below; for the moment we just remark that although the verb "means" sometimes means "has as extension," the nominalization "meaning" *never* means "extension.")

Symmetrically, if a spaceship from Twin Earth ever visits Earth, then the supposition at first will be that the word "water" has the same meaning on Twin Earth and on Earth. This supposition will be corrected when it is discovered that "water" on Earth is H_2O, and the Twin Earthian spaceship will report

"On Earth[6] the word 'water' means H_2O."

Note that there is no problem about the extension of the term "water." The word simply has two different meanings (as we say) in the sense in which it is used on Twin Earth, the sense of water$_{TE}$, what *we* call "water" simply isn't water; while in the sense in which it is used on Earth, the sense of water$_E$, what the Twin Earthians call "water" simply isn't water. The extension of "water" in the sense of water$_E$ is the set of all wholes consisting of H_2O molecules, or something like that; the extension of water in the sense of water$_{TE}$ is the set of all wholes consisting of XYZ molecules, or something like that.

Now let us roll the time back to about 1750. At that time chemistry was not developed on either Earth or Twin Earth. The typical Earthian speaker of English did not know water consisted of hydrogen and oxygen, and the typical Twin Earthian speaker of English did not know "water" consisted of XYZ. Let Oscar$_1$ be such a typical Earthian English speaker, and let Oscar$_2$ be his counterpart on Twin Earth. You may suppose that there is no belief that Oscar$_1$ had about water that Oscar$_2$ did not have about "water." If you like, you may even suppose that Oscar$_1$ and Oscar$_2$ were exact duplicates in appearance, feelings, thoughts, interior monologue, etc. Yet the extension of the term "water" was just as much H_2O on Earth in 1750 as in 1950; and the extension of the term "water" was just as much

XYZ on Twin Earth in 1750 as in 1950. $Oscar_1$ and $Oscar_2$ understood the term "water" differently in 1750 *although they were in the same psychological state,* and although, given the state of science at the time, it would have taken their scientific communities about fifty years to discover that they understood the term "water" differently. Thus the extension of the term "water" (and, in fact, its "meaning" in the intuitive preanalytical usage of that term) is *not* a function of the psychological state of the speaker by itself.

But, it might be objected, why should we accept it that the term "water" has the same extension in 1750 and in 1950 (on both Earths)? The logic of natural-kind terms like "water" is a complicated matter, but the following is a sketch of an answer. Suppose I point to a glass of water and say "this liquid is called water" (or "this is called water," if the marker "liquid" is clear from the context). My "ostensive definition" of water has the following empirical presupposition that the body of liquid I am pointing to bears a certain sameness relation (say, *x is the same liquid as* y, or *x is the same$_L$ as* y) to most of the stuff I and other speakers in my linguistic community have on other occasions called "water." If this presupposition is false because, say, I am without knowing it pointing to a glass of gin and not a glass of water, then I do not intend my ostensive definition to be accepted. Thus the ostensive definition conveys what might be called a defeasible necessary and sufficient condition: the necessary and sufficient condition for being water is bearing the relation same$_L$ to the stuff in the glass; but this is the necessary and sufficient condition only if the empirical presupposition is satisfied. If it is not satisfied, then one of a series of, so to speak, "fallback" conditions becomes activated.

The key point is that the relation same$_L$ is a *theoretical* relation whether something is or is not the same liquid as *this* may take an indeterminate amount of scientific investigation to determine. Moreover, even if a "definite" answer has been obtained either through scientific investigation or through the application of some "common sense" test, the answer is *defeasible*: future investigation might reverse even the most "certain" example. Thus, the fact that an English speaker in 1750 might have called XYZ "water," while he or his successors would not have called XYZ water in 1800 or 1850 does not mean that the "meaning" of "water" changed for the average speaker in the interval. In 1750 or in 1850 or in 1950 one might have pointed to, say, the liquid in Lake Michigan as an example of "water." What changed was that in 1750 we would have mistakenly thought that XYZ bore the relation same$_L$ to the liquid in Lake Michigan, while in 1800 or 1850 we would have known that it did not (I am ignoring the fact that the liquid in Lake Michigan was only dubiously water in 1950, of course).

Let us now modify our science-fiction story. I do not know whether one can make pots and pans out of molybdenum; and if one can make them out of molybdenum, I don't know whether they could be distinguished easily from aluminum pots and pans (I don't know any of this even though I have acquired the word "molybdenum.") So I shall suppose that molybdenum pots and pans *can't* be distinguished from aluminum pots and pans save by an expert. (To emphasize the point, I repeat that this could be true for all I know, and *a fortiori* it could be true for all I know by virtue of "knowing the meaning" of the words *aluminum* and *molybdenum*.) We will now suppose that molybdenum is as common on Twin Earth as aluminum is on Earth, and that aluminum is a rare on Twin Earth as molybdenum is on Earth. In particular, we shall assume that "aluminum" pots and pans are made of molybdenum on Twin Earth. Finally, we shall assume that the words "aluminum" and "molybdenum" are *switched* on Twin Earth: "aluminum" is the name of *molybdenum* and "molybdenum" is the name of *aluminum*.

This example shares some features with the previous one. If a spaceship from Earth visited Twin Earth, the visitors from Earth probably would not suspect that the "aluminum" pots and pans on Twin Earth were not made of aluminum, especially when the Twin Earthians *said* they were. But there is one important difference between the two cases. An Earthian metallurgist could tell very easily that "aluminum" was molybdenum, and a Twin Earthian metallurgist could tell equally easily that aluminum was "molybdenum." (The shudder quotes in the preceding sentence indicate Twin Earthian usages.) Whereas in 1750 no one on either Earth or Twin Earth could have distinguished water from "water," the confusion of aluminum with "aluminum" involves only a part of the linguistic communities involved.

The example makes the same point as the preceding one. If Oscar$_1$ and Oscar$_2$ are standard speakers of Earthian English and Twin Earthian English respectively, and neither is chemically or metallurgically sophisticated, then there may be no difference at all in their psychological state when they use the word "aluminum"; nevertheless we have to say that "aluminum" has the extension *aluminum* in the idiolect of Oscar$_1$ and the extension *molybdenum* in the idiolect of Oscar$_2$. (Also we have to say that Oscar$_1$ and Oscar$_2$ mean different things by "aluminum," that "aluminum" has a different meaning on Earth than it does on Twin Earth, etc.) Again we see that the psychological state of the speaker does *not* determine the extension (*or* the "meaning," speaking preanalytically) of the word.

Before discussing this example further, let me introduce a *non*-science-fiction example. Suppose you are like me and cannot tell an elm from a beech tree. We still say that the extension of "elm" in my idiolect is the same as the extension of "elm" in anyone else's, viz., the set of all elm trees, and that the set of all beech trees is the extension of "beech" in *both* of our idiolects. Thus "elm" in my idiolect has a different extension from "beech" in your idiolect (as it should). Is it really credible that this difference in extension is brought about by some difference in our *concepts*? My concept of an elm tree is exactly the same as my concept of a beech tree (I blush to confess). (This shows that the identification of meaning "in the sense of intension" with *concept* cannot be correct, by the way.) If someone heroically attempts to maintain that the difference between the extension of "elm" and the extension of "beech" in *my* idiolect is explained by a difference in my psychological state, then we can always refute him by constructing a "Twin Earth" example—just let the words "elm" and "beech" be switched on Twin

Earth (the way "aluminum" and "molybdenum" were in the previous example). Moreover, I suppose I have a *Doppelgänger* on Twin Earth who is molecule for molecule "identical" with me (in the sense in which two neckties can be "identical"). If you are a dualist, then also suppose my *Doppelgänger* thinks the same verbalized thoughts I do, has the same sense data, the same dispositions, etc. It is absurd to think *his* psychological state is one bit different from mine: yet he "means" *beech* when he says "elm" and *I* "mean" *elm* when I say elm. Cut the pie any way you like, "meanings" just ain't in the *head!*

A SOCIOLINGUISTIC HYPOTHESIS

The last two examples depend upon a fact about language that seems, surprisingly, never to have been pointed out: that there is *division of linguistic labor*. We could hardly use such words as "elm" and "aluminum" if no one possessed a way of recognizing elm trees and aluminum metal; but not everyone to whom the distinction is important has to be able to make the distinction. Let us shift the example: consider *gold*. Gold is important for many reasons: it is a precious metal, it is a monetary metal, it has symbolic value (it is important to most people that the "gold" wedding ring they wear *really* consist of gold and not just *look* gold), etc. Consider our community as a "factory": in this "factory" some people have the "job" of *wearing gold wedding rings*, other people have the "job" of *selling gold wedding rings*, still other people have the "job" of *telling whether or not something is really gold*. It is not at all necessary or efficient that everyone who wears a gold ring (or a gold cufflink, etc.), or discusses the "gold standard," etc., engage in buying and selling gold. Nor is it necessary or efficient that everyone who buys and sells gold be able to tell whether or not something is really gold in a society where this form of dishonesty is uncommon (selling fake gold) and in which one can easily consult an expert in case of doubt. And it is *certainly* not necessary or efficient that everyone who has occasion to buy or wear gold be able to tell with any reliability whether or not something is really gold.

The foregoing facts are just examples of mundane division of labor (in a wide sense). But they engender a division of linguistic labor: everyone to whom gold is important for any reason has to *acquire* the word "gold"; but he does not have to acquire the *method of recognizing* if something is or is not gold. He can rely on a special subclass of speakers. The features that are generally thought to be present in connection with a general name—necessary and sufficient conditions for membership in the extension, ways of recognizing if something is in the extension ("criteria"), etc.—are all present in the linguistic community *considered as a collective body*; but that collective body divides the "labor" of knowing and employing these various parts of the "meaning" of "gold."

This division of linguistic labor rests upon and presupposes the division of *non*linguistic labor, of course. If only the people who know how to tell if some metal is really gold or not have any reason to have the word "gold" in their vocabulary, then the word "gold" will be as the word "water" was in 1750 with respect to that subclass of speakers, and the other speakers just won't acquire it at all. And some words do not exhibit any division of linguistic labor: "chair," for example. But with the increase of division of labor in the society and the rise of science, more and more words begin to exhibit this kind of division of labor. "Water," for example, did not exhibit it at all prior to the rise of chemistry. Today it is obviously necessary for every speaker to be able to recognize water (reliably under normal conditions), and probably every adult speaker even knows the necessary and sufficient condition "water is H_2O," but only a few adult speakers could distinguish water from liquids which superficially resembled water. In case of doubt, other speakers would rely on the judgement of these "expert" speakers. Thus the way of recognizing possessed by these "expert" speakers is also, through them, possessed by the collective linguistic body, even though it is not possessed by each individual member of the body, and in this way the most recherche fact about water may become part of the *social* meaning of the word while being unknown to almost all speakers who acquire the word.

It seems to me that this phenomenon of division of linguistic labor is one which it will be very important for sociolinguistics to investigate. In connection with it, I should like to propose the following hypothesis:

HYPOTHESIS OF THE UNIVERSALITY OF THE DIVISION OF LIN-GUISTIC LABOR: Every linguistic community exemplifies the sort of division of linguistic labor just described: that is, possesses at least some terms whose associated "criteria" are known only to a subset of the speakers who acquire the terms, and whose use by the other speakers depends upon a structured cooperation between them and the speakers in the relevant subsets.

It would be of interest, in particular, to discover if extremely primitive peoples were sometimes exceptions to this hypothesis (which would indicate that the division of linguistic labor is a product of social evolution), or if even they exhibit it. In the latter case, one might conjecture that division of labor, including linguistic labor, is a fundamental trait of our species.

It is easy to see how this phenomenon accounts for some of the examples given above of the failure of the assumptions (I), (II). Whenever a term is subject to the division of linguistic labor, the "average" speaker who acquires it does not acquire anything that fixes its extension. In particular, his individual psychological state *certainly* does not fix its extension; it is only the sociolinguistic state of the collective linguistic body to which the speaker belongs that fixes the extension.

We may summarize this discussion by pointing out that there are two sorts of tools in the world: there are tools like a hammer or a screwdriver which can be used by one person; and there are tools like a steamship which require the cooperative activity of a number of persons to use. Words have been thought of too much on the model of the first sort of tool.

INDEXICALITY AND RIGIDITY[7]

The first of our science-fiction examples—"water" on Earth and on Twin Earth in 1750—does not involve division of linguistic labor, or at least does not involve it in the same way the examples of "aluminum" and "elm" do. There were not (in our story, anyway) any "experts" on water on Earth in 1750, nor any experts on "water" on Twin Earth. (The example *can* be construed as involving division of labor *across time*, however. I shall not develop this method of treating the example here.) The example *does* involve things which are of fundamental importance to the theory of reference and also to the theory of necessary truth, which we shall now discuss.

There are two obvious ways of telling someone what one means by a natural-kind term such as "water" or "tiger" or "lemon." One can give him a so-called ostensive definition—"this (liquid) is water"; "this (animal) is a tiger"; "this (fruit) is a lemon"; where the parentheses are meant to indicate that the "markers" *liquid, animal, fruit,* may be either explicit or implicit. Or one can give him a *description*. In the latter case the description one gives typically consists of one or more markers together with a *stereotype* [see chapter 8 in Putnam (1975a)]—a standardized description of features of the kind that are typical, or "normal," or at any rate stereotypical. The central features of the stereotype generally are *criteria*—features which in normal situations constitute ways of recognizing if a thing belongs to the kind or, at least, necessary conditions (or probabilistic necessary conditions) for membership in the kind. Not all criteria used by the linguistic community as a collective body are included in the stereotype, and in some cases the stereotypes may be quite weak. Thus (unless I am a very atypical speaker), the stereotype of an elm is just that of a common deciduous tree. These features are indeed necessary conditions for membership in the kind (I mean "necessary" in a loose sense; I don't think "elm trees are deciduous" is *analytic*), but they fall far short of constituting a way of recognizing elms. On the other hand, the stereotype of a tiger does enable one to recognize tigers (unless they are albino, or some other atypical circumstance is present), and the stereotype of a lemon generally enables one to recognize lemons. In the extreme case, the stereotype may be *just* the marker: the stereotype of molybdenum might be *just* that molybdenum is a *metal*. Let us consider both of these ways of introducing a term into someone's vocabulary.

Suppose I point to a glass of liquid and say "*this* is water," in order to teach someone the word "water." We have already described some of the empirical presuppositions of this act, and the way in which this kind of meaning-explanation is defeasible. Let us now try to clarify further how it is supposed to be taken.

In what follows, we shall take the notion of "possible world" as primitive. We do this because we feel that in several senses the notion makes sense and is scientifically important even if it needs to be made more precise. We shall assume further that in at least some cases it is possible to speak of the same individual as existing in more than one possible world.[8] Our discussion leans heavily on the work of Saul Kripke, although the conclusions were obtained independently.

Let W_1 and W_2 be two possible worlds in which I exist and in which this glass exists and in which I am giving a meaning explanation by pointing to this glass and saying "this is water." (We do *not* assume that the *liquid* in the glass is the same in both worlds.) Let us suppose that in W_1 the glass is full of H_2O and in W_2 the glass is full of XYZ. We shall also suppose that W_1 is the actual world and that XYZ is the stuff typically called "water" in the world W_2 (so that the relation between English speakers in W_1 and English speakers in W_2 is exactly the same as the relation between English speakers on Earth and English speakers on Twin Earth). Then there are two theories one might have concerning the meaning of "water":

(1) One might hold that "water" was *world-relative* but *constant* in meaning (i.e., the word has a *constant relative meaning*). In this theory, "water" *means the same* in W_1 and W_2; it's just that water is H_2O in W_1 and water is XYZ in W_2.

(2) One might hold that water is H_2O in all worlds (the stuff called "water" in W_2 isn't water), but "water" doesn't have the same meaning in W_1 and W_2.

If what was said before about the Twin Earth case was correct, then (2) is clearly the correct theory. When I say "*this* (liquid) is water," the "this" is, so to speak, a *de re* "this"—i.e., the force of my explanation is that "water" is whatever bears a certain equivalence relation (the relation we called "same$_L$" above) to the piece of liquid referred to as "this" *in the actual world*.

We might symbolize the difference between the two theories as a "scope" difference in the following way. In theory (1), the following is true:

(1') (For every world W) (For every x in W) (x is water $\equiv x$ bears same$_L$ to the entity referred to as "this" in W_1)

while on theory (2):

(2') (For every world W) (For every x in W) (x is water $\equiv x$ bears same$_L$ to the entity referred to as "this" *in the actual world W_1*).

(I call this a "scope" difference because in (1') "the entity referred to as 'this' " is within the scope of "For every world W"—as the qualifying phrase "in W" makes explicit, whereas in (2') "the entity referred to as 'this' " means "the entity referred to as 'this' *in the actual world*," and has thus a reference *independent* of the bound variable "W.")

Kripke calls a designator "rigid" (in a given sentence) if (in that sentence) it refers to the same individual in every possible world in which the designator designates. If we extend the notion of rigidity to substance names, then we may express Kripke's theory and mine by saying that the term "water" is *rigid*.

The rigidity of the term "water" follows from the fact that when I give the ostensive definition "*this* (liquid) is water" I intend (2') and not (1').

We may also say, following Kripke, that when I give the ostensive definition "this (liquid) is water," the demonstrative "this" is *rigid*.

What Kripke was the first to observe is that this theory of the meaning (or "use," or whatever) of the word "water" (and other natural-kind terms as well) has startling consequences for the theory of necessary truth.

To explain this, let me introduce the notion of a *cross-world relation*. A two-term relation R will be called *cross-world* when it is understood in such a way that its extension is a set of ordered pairs of individuals *not all in the same possible world*. For example, it is easy to understand the relation *same height as* as a cross-world relation: just understand it so that, e.g., if x is an individual in a world W_1 who is five feet tall (in W_1) and y is an individual in W_2 who is five feet tall (in W_2), then the ordered pair x, y belongs to the extension of *same height as*. (Since an individual may have different heights in different possible worlds in which that same individual exists, strictly speaking it is not the ordered pair x, y that constitutes an element of the extension of *same height as*, but rather the ordered pair x-*in-world*-W_1, y-*in-world*-W_2.)

Similarly, we can understand the relation $same_L$ (same liquid as) as a cross-world relation by understanding it so that a liquid in world W_1 which has the same important physical properties (in W_1) that a liquid in W_2 possesses (in W_2) bears $same_L$ to the latter liquid.

Then the theory we have been presenting may be summarized by saying that an entity x, in an arbitrary possible world, is *water* if and only if it bears the relation $same_L$ (construed as a cross-world relation) to the stuff *we* call "water" in the *actual* world.

Suppose, now, that I have not yet discovered what the important physical properties of water are (in the actual world)—i.e., I don't yet know that water is H_2O. I may have ways of *recognizing* water that are successful (of course, I may make a small number of mistakes that I won't be able to detect until a later stage in our scientific development) but not know the microstructure of water. If I agree that a liquid with the superficial properties of "water" but a different microstructure *isn't really* water, then my ways of recognizing water (my "operational definition," so to speak) cannot be regarded as an analytical specification of *what it is to be* water. Rather, the operational definition, like the ostensive one, is simply a way of pointing out a standard—pointing out the stuff *in the actual world* such that for x to be water, in *any* world, is for x to bear the relation $same_L$ to the *normal* members of the class of *local* entities that satisfy the operational definition. "Water" on Twin Earth is not water, even if it satisfies the operational definition, because it doesn't bear $same_L$ to the *local* stuff that satisfies the operational definition, and local stuff that satisfies the operational definition but has a microstructure different from the rest of the local stuff that satisfies the operational definition isn't water either, because it doesn't bear $same_L$ to the *normal* examples of the local "water."

Suppose, now, that I discover the microstructure of water—that water is H_2O. At this point I will be able to say that the stuff on Twin Earth that I earlier *mistook* for water isn't really water. In the same way if you describe not another planet in the actual universe, but another possible universe in which there is stuff with the chemical formula XYZ which passes the "operational test" for *water*, we shall have to say that that stuff isn't water but merely XYZ. You will not have described a possible world in which "water is XYZ," but merely a possible world in which there are lakes of XYZ, people drink XYZ (and not water), or whatever. In fact, once we have discovered the nature of water, nothing counts as a possible world in which water doesn't have that nature. Once we have discovered that water (in the actual world) is H_2O, *nothing counts as a possible world in which water isn't H_2O.* In particular, if a "logically possible" statement is one that holds in some "logically possible world," *it isn't logically possible that water isn't H_2O.*

On the other hand, we can perfectly well imagine having experiences that would convince us (and that would make it rational to believe that) water *isn't* H_2O. In that sense, it is conceivable that water isn't H_2O. It is conceivable but it isn't logically possible! Conceivability is no proof of logical possibility.

Kripke refers to statements which are rationally unrevisable (assuming there are such) as *epistemically necessary*. Statements which are true in all possible worlds he refers to simply as necessary (or sometimes as "metaphysically necessary"). In this terminology, the point just made can be restated as: a statement can be (metaphysically) necessary and epistemically contingent. Human intuition has no privileged access to metaphysical necessity.

Since Kant there has been a big split between philosophers who thought that all necessary truths were analytic and philosophers who thought that some necessary truths were synthetic *a priori*. But none of these philosophers thought that a (metaphysically) necessary truth could fail to be *a priori*: the Kantian tradition was as guilty as the empiricist tradition of equating metaphysical and epistemic necessity. In this sense Kripke's challenge to received doctrine goes far beyond the usual empiricism/Kantianism oscillation.

In this paper our interest is in theory of meaning, however, and not in theory of necessary truth. Points closely related to Kripke's have been made in terms of the notion of *indexicality*.[9] Words like "now," "this," "here," have long been recognized to be *indexical*, or *token-reflexive*—i.e., to have an extension which varied from context to context or token to token. For these words no one has ever suggested the traditional theory that "intension determines extension." To take our Twin Earth example: if I have a *Doppelgänger* on Twin Earth, then when I think "I have a headache," *he* thinks "I have a headache." But the extension of the particular token of "I" in his verbalized thought is himself (or his unit class, to be precise), while the extension of the token of "I" in *my* verbalized thought is *me* (or my unit class, to be precise). So the same word, "I," has two different extensions in two different idiolects; but it does not follow that the concept I have of myself is in any way different from the concept my *Doppelgänger* has of himself.

Now then, we have maintained that indexicality extends beyond the *obviously* indexical words and morphemes (e.g., the tenses of verbs). Our theory can be summarized as saying that words like "water" have an unnoticed indexical component: "water" is stuff that bears a certain similarity relation to the water *around here*. Water at another time or in another place or even in another possible world has to bear the relation same$_L$ to *our* "water" *in order to be water*. Thus the theory that (1) words have "intensions," which are something like concepts associated with the words by speakers; and that (2) intension determines extension— cannot be true of natural-kind words like "water" for the same reason the theory cannot be true of obviously indexical words like "I."

The theory that natural-kind words like "water" are indexical leaves it open, however, whether to say that "water" in the Twin Earth dialect of English has the same *meaning* as "water" in the Earth dialect and a different extension (which is what we normally say about "I" in different idiolects), thereby giving up the doctrine that "meaning (intension) determines extension"; or to say, as we have chosen to do, that difference in extension is *ipso facto* a difference in meaning for natural-kind words, thereby giving up the doctrine that meanings are concepts, or, indeed, mental entities of *any* kind.

It should be clear, however, that Kripke's doctrine that natural-kind words are rigid designators and our doctrine that they are indexical are but two ways of making the same point. We heartily endorse what Kripke says when he writes:

> Let us suppose that we do fix the reference of a name by a description. Even if we do so, we do not then make the name synonymous with the description, but instead we use the name rigidly to refer to the object so named, even in talking about counterfactual situations where the thing named would not satisfy the description in question. Now, this is what I think is in fact true for those cases of naming where the reference is fixed by description. But, in fact, I also think, contrary to most recent theorists, that the reference of names is rarely or almost never fixed by means of description. And by this I do not just mean what Searle says: "It's not a single description, but rather a cluster, a family of properties that fixes the reference." I mean that properties in this sense are not used at all. [Kripke (1971), p. 157]

LET'S BE REALISTIC

I wish now to contrast my view with one which is popular, at least among students (it appears to arise spontaneously). For this discussion, let us take as our example of a natural-kind word the word *gold*. We will not distinguish between "gold" and the cognate words in Greek, Latin, etc. And we will focus on "gold" in the sense of gold in the solid state. With this understood, we maintain: "gold" has not changed its *extension* (or not changed it significantly) in two thousand years. Our methods of *identifying* gold have grown incredibly sophisticated. But the extension of χρυσὸς in Archimedes's dialect of Greek is the same as the extension of *gold* in my dialect of English.

It is possible (and let us suppose it to be the case) that just as there were pieces of metal which could not have been determined *not* to be gold prior to Archimedes, so there were or are pieces of metal which could not have been determined not to be gold in Archimedes's day, but which we can distinguish from gold quite easily with modern techniques. Let X be such a piece of metal. Clearly X does not lie in the extension of "gold" in standard English; my view is that it did not lie in the extension of χρυσὸς in Attic Greek, either, although an ancient Greek would have *mistaken* X for gold (or, rather, χρυσὸς).

The alternative view is that "gold" *means* whatever satisfies the *contemporary* operational definition of gold. "Gold" a hundred years ago meant whatever satisfied the "operational definition" of *gold* in use a hundred years ago; "gold" now means whatever satisfies the operational definition of *gold* in use in 1973; and χρυσὸς meant whatever satisfied the operational definition of χρυσὸς in use *then*.

One common motive for adopting this point of view is a certain skepticism about *truth*. In the view I am advocating, when Archimedes asserted that something was gold (χρυσὸς) he was not just saying that it had the superficial characteristics of gold (in exceptional cases, something may belong to a natural kind and *not* have the superficial characteristics of a member of that natural kind, in fact); he was saying that it had the same general *hidden structure* (the same "essence," so to speak) as any normal piece of local gold. Archimedes would have said that our hypothetical piece of metal X was gold, but he would have been wrong. But who's to say he would have been wrong?

The obvious answer is: *we are* (using the best theory available today). For most people either the question (*who's to say?*) has bite, and our answer has no bite, or our answer has bite and the question has no bite. Why is this?

The reason, I believe, is that people tend either to be strongly antirealistic or strongly realistic in their intuitions. To a strongly antirealistic intuition it makes little sense to say that what is in the extension of Archimedes's term χρυσὸς is to be determined using *our* theory. For the antirealist does not see our theory and Archimedes's theory as two approximately correct descriptions of some fixed realm of theory-independent entities, and he tends to be skeptical about the idea of "convergence" in science—he does not think our theory is a *better* description of the *same* entities that Archimedes was describing. But if our theory is *just* our theory, then to use *it* in deciding whether or not X lies in the extension of χρυσὸς is just as arbitrary as using Neanderthal theory to decide whether or not X lies in the extension of χρυσὸς. The only theory that it is *not* arbitrary to use is the one the speaker himself subscribes to.

The trouble is that for a strong antirealist *truth* makes no sense except as an intra-theoretic notion [see Putnam (1975a) chapter 11 for a discussion of this point]. The antirealist can use truth intra-theoretically in the sense of a "redundancy theory"; but he does not have the notions of truth and reference available *extra-theoretically*. But *extension is tied to the notion of truth*. The extension of a term is just what the term is true of. Rather than try to retain the notion of extension via an awkward operationalism, the antirealist should reject the notion of extension as he does the notion of truth (in any extra-theoretic sense). Like Dewey, for example, he can fall back on a notion of "warranted assertibility" instead of truth (relativized to the scientific method, if he thinks there is a *fixed* scientific method, or to the best methods available at the time, if he agrees with Dewey that the scientific method itself evolves). Then he can say that "X is gold (χρυσὸς)" was warrantedly assertible in Archimedes's time and is not warrantedly assertible today (indeed, this is a *minimal* claim, in the sense that it represents the minimum that the realist and the antirealist can agree on); but the assertion that X was in the extension of χρυσὸς will be rejected as meaningless, like the assertion that "X is gold (χρυσὸς)" was *true*.

It is well known that narrow operationalism cannot successfully account for the actual use of scientific or common-sense terms. Loosened versions of operationalism, like Carnap's version of Ramsey's theory, agree with, if they do not account for, actual scientific use (mainly because the loosened versions agree with any possible use!), but at the expense of making the communicability of scientific results a *miracle*. It is beyond question that scientists use terms as if the associated criteria were not *necessary and sufficient conditions*, but rather *approximately* correct characterizations of some world of theory-independent entities, and that they talk as if later theories in a mature science were, in general, *better* descriptions of the *same* entities that earlier theories referred to. In my opinion the hypothesis that this is *right* is the only hypothesis that can account for the communicability of scientific results, the closure of acceptable scientific theories under first-order logic, and many other features of the scientific method.[10] But it is not my task to argue this here. My point is that if we are to use the notions of truth and extension in an extra-theoretic way (i.e., to regard those notions as defined for statements couched in the languages of theories other than our own), then we should accept the realist perspective to which those notions belong. The doubt about whether *we* can say that X does not lie in the extension of "gold" as *Jones* used it is the *same* doubt as the doubt whether it makes sense to think of Jones's statement that "X is gold" as *true or false* (and not just "warrantedly assertible for Jones and not warrantedly assertible for us"). To square the notion of truth, which is essentially a realist notion, with one's antirealist prejudices by adopting an untenable theory of meaning is no progress.

A second motive for adopting an extreme operationalist account is a dislike of unverifiable hypotheses. At first blush it may seem as if we are saying that "X is gold (χρυσὸς)" was false in Archimedes's time although Archimedes could not *in principle* have known that it was false. But this is not exactly the situation. The fact is that there are a host of situations that *we* can describe (using the very theory that tells us that X isn't gold) in which X would have behaved quite unlike the rest of the stuff Archimedes classified as gold. Perhaps X would have separated into two different metals when melted, or would have had different conductivity properties, or would have vaporized at a different temperature, or whatever. If we had performed the experiments with Archimedes watching, he might not have known the theory, but he would have been able to check the empirical regularity that "X behaves differently from the rest of the stuff I classify as χρυσὸς in several respects." Eventually he would have concluded that "X may not be gold."

The point is that even if something satisfies the criteria used at a given time to identify gold (i.e., to recognize if something is gold), it may behave differently in one or more situations from the rest of the stuff that satisfies the criteria. This may not *prove* that it isn't gold, but it puts the hypothesis that it may not be gold in the running, even in the absence of theory. If, now, we had gone on to inform Archimedes that gold had such and such a molecular structure (except for X), and that X behaved differently because it had a different molecular structure, is there any doubt that he would have agreed with us that X isn't gold? In any case, to worry because things may be *true* (at a given time) that can't be *verified* (at that time) seems to me ridiculous. In any reasonable view there are surely things that are true and can't be verified at *any* time. For example, suppose there are infinitely many binary stars. *Must* we be able to verify this, even in principle? [See chapter 22 in Putnam (1975a); chapters 17 and 18 in Putnam (1970), vol. 1.]

So far we have dealt with *metaphysical* reasons for rejecting our account. But someone might disagree with us about the empirical facts concerning the intentions of speakers. This would be the case if, for instance, someone thought that Archimedes (in the *Gedankenexperiment* described above) would have said: "it doesn't matter if X *does* act differently from other pieces of gold; X is a piece of gold, because X has such-and-such properties and that's all it takes to be gold." While, indeed, we cannot be certain that natural-kind words in ancient Greek had the properties of the corresponding words in present-day English, there cannot be any serious doubt concerning the properties of the latter. If we put philosophical prejudices aside, then I believe that we know perfectly well that no operational definition does provide a necessary and sufficient condition for the application of any such word. We may give an "operational definition," or a cluster of properties, or whatever, but the intention is never to "make the name *synonymous* with the description." Rather "we use the name *rigidly*" to refer to whatever things share the *nature* that things satisfying the description normally possess.

OTHER SENSES

What we have analyzed so far is the predominant sense of natural-kind words (or, rather, the predominant *extension*). But natural-kind words typically possess a number of senses. (Ziff has even suggested that they possess a *continuum* of senses.)

Part of this can be explained on the basis of our theory. To be water, for example, is to bear the relation same$_L$ to certain things. But what is the relation same$_L$?

X bears the relation same$_L$ to y just in case (1) x and y are both liquids, and (2) x and y agree in important physical properties. The term "liquid " is itself a natural-kind term that I shall not try to analyze here. The term "property" is a broad-spectrum term that we have analyzed in previous papers. What I want to focus on now is the notion of *importance*. Importance is an interest-relative notion. Normally the "important" properties of a liquid or solid, etc., are the ones that are *structurally* important: the ones that specify what the liquid or solid, etc., is ultimately made out of—elementary particles, or hydrogen and oxygen, or earth, air, fire, water, or whatever—and how they are arranged or combined to produce the superficial characteristics. From this point of view the characteristic of a typical bit of water is consisting of H_2O. But it may or may not be important that there are impurities; thus, in one context "water" may mean *chemically pure water*, while in another it may mean the stuff in Lake Michigan. And a speaker may sometimes refer to XYZ as water if one is *using* it as water. Again, normally it is important that water is in the liquid state; but sometimes it is unimportant, and one may refer to a single H_2O molecule as water, or to water vapor as water ("water in the air").

Even senses that are so far out that they have to be regarded as a bit "deviant" may bear a definite relation to the core sense. For example, I might say "did you see the lemon," meaning the *plastic* lemon. A less deviant case is this: we discover "tigers" on Mars. That is, they look just like tigers, but they have a silicon-based chemistry instead of a carbon-based chemistry. (A remarkable example of parallel evolution!) Are Martian "tigers" tigers? It depends on the context.

In the case of this theory, as in the case of any theory that is orthogonal to the way people have thought about something previously, misunderstandings are certain to arise. One which has already arisen is the following: a critic has maintained that the *predominant* sense of, say, "lemon" is the one in which anything with (a sufficient number of) the superficial characteristics of a lemon is a lemon. The same critic has suggested that having the hidden structure—the genetic code—of a lemon is necessary to being a lemon only when "lemon" is used as a term of *science*. Both of these contentions seem to me to rest on a misunderstanding, or, perhaps, a pair of complementary misunderstandings.

The sense in which literally *anything* with the superficial characteristics of a lemon is necessarily a lemon, far from being the dominant one, is extremely deviant. In that sense something would be a lemon if it looked and tasted like a lemon, even if it had a silicon-based chemistry, for example, or even if an electron-microscope revealed it to be a *machine*. (Even if we include growing "like a lemon" in the superficial characteristics, this does not exclude the silicon lemon, if there are "lemon" trees on Mars. It doesn't even exclude the machine-lemon; maybe the tree is a machine too!)

At the same time the sense in which to be a lemon something has to have the genetic code of a lemon is *not* the same as the technical sense (if there is one, which I doubt). The technical sense, I take it, would be one in which "lemon" was *synonymous* with a description which *specified* the genetic code. But when we said (to change the example) that to be *water* something has to be H_2O we did not mean, as we made clear, that the *speaker* has to *know* this. It is only by confusing *metaphysical* necessity with *epistemological* necessity that one can conclude that, if the (metaphysically necessary) truth-condition for being water is being H_2O, then "water" must be synonymous with H_2O—in which case it is certainly a term of science. And similarly, even though the predominant sense of "lemon" is one in which to be a lemon something has to have the genetic code of a lemon (I believe), it does not follow that "lemon" is synonymous with a description which specifies the genetic code explicitly or otherwise.

The mistake of thinking that there is an important sense of "lemon" (perhaps the predominant one) in which to have the superficial characteristics of a lemon is at least *sufficient* for being a lemon is more plausible if among the superficial characteristics one includes *being cross-fertile with lemons*. But the characteristic of being cross-fertile with lemons presupposes the notion of being a lemon. Thus, even if one can obtain a sufficient condition in *this* way, to take this as inconsistent with the characterization offered here is question-begging. Moreover the characterization in terms of *lemon*-presupposing "superficial characteristics" (like being cross-fertile with *lemons*) gives no truth-condition which would enable us to decide which objects in other possible worlds (or which objects a million years ago, or which objects a million light years from here) are lemons. (In addition, I don't think this characterization, question-begging as it is, is *correct*, even as a sufficient condition. I think one could invent cases in which something which was not a lemon was cross-fertile with lemons and looked like a lemon, etc.)

Again, one might try to rule out the case of the machine-lemon (lemon-machine?) which "grows" on a machine-tree (tree-machine?) by saying that "growing" is not really *growing*. That is right; but it's right because *grow* is a natural-kind *verb*, and precisely the sort of account we have been presenting applies to *it*.

Another misunderstanding that should be avoided is the following: to take the account we have developed as implying that the members of the extension of a natural-kind word necessarily *have* a common hidden structure. It could have turned out that the bits of liquid we call "water" had *no* important common physical characteristics *except* the superficial ones. In that case the necessary and sufficient condition for being "water" would have been possession of sufficiently many of the superficial characteristics.

Incidentally, the last statement does not imply that water could have failed to have a hidden structure (or that water could have been anything but H_2O). When we say that it could have *turned out* that water had no hidden structure what we mean is that a liquid with no hidden structure (i.e., many bits of different liquids, with nothing in common *except* superficial characteristics) could have looked like water, tasted like water, and have filled the lakes, etc., that are actually full of water. In short, we could have been in the same epistemological situation with respect to a liquid with no hidden structure as we were actually with respect to water at one time. Compare Kripke on the "lectern made of ice" [Kripke (1971)].

There are, in fact, almost continuously many cases. Some diseases, for example, have turned out to have no hidden structure (the only thing the paradigm cases have in common is a cluster of symptoms), while others have turned out to have a common hidden structure in the sense of an etiology (e.g., tuberculosis). Sometimes we still don't know; there is a controversy still raging about the case of multiple sclerosis.

An interesting case is the case of *jade*. Although the Chinese do not recognize a difference, the term "jade" applies to two minerals: jadeite and nephrite. Chemically, there is a marked difference. Jadeite is a combination of sodium and aluminum. Nephrite is made of calcium, magnesium, and iron. These two quite different microstructures produce the same unique textural qualities!

Coming back to the Twin Earth example, for a moment; if H_2O and XYZ had both been plentiful on Earth, then we would have had a case similar to the jade/nephrite case: it would have been correct to say that there were *two kinds of "water."* And instead of saying that "the stuff on Twin Earth turned out not to really be water," we would have to say "it turned out to be the XYZ *kind of water.*"

To sum up: if there is a hidden structure, then generally it determines what it is to be a member of the natural kind, not only in the actual world, but in all possible worlds. Put another way, it determines what we can and cannot counterfactually suppose about the natural-kind ("water could have all been vapor?" yes/"water could have been XYZ" no). But the local water, or whatever, may have two or more hidden structures—or so many that "hidden structure" becomes irrelevant, and superficial characteristics become the decisive ones.

OTHER WORDS

So far we have only used natural-kind words as examples, but the points we have made apply to many other kinds of words as well. They apply to the great majority of all nouns, and to other parts of speech as well.

Let us consider for a moment the names of artifacts—words like "pencil," "chair," "bottle," etc. The traditional view is that these words are certainly defined by conjunctions, or possibly clusters, of properties. Anything with all of the properties in the conjunction (or sufficiently many of the properties in the cluster, on the cluster model) is necessarily a *pencil, chair, bottle,* or whatever. In addition, some of the properties in the cluster (on the cluster model) are usually held to be *necessary* (on the conjunction-of-properties model, *all* of the properties in the conjunction are necessary). Being an artifact is supposedly necessary, and belonging to a kind with a certain standard purpose—e.g., "pencils are artifacts," and "pencils are standardly intended to be written with" are supposed to be necessary. Finally, this sort of necessity is held to be *epistemic* necessity—in fact, analyticity.

Let us once again engage in science fiction. This time we use an example devised by Rogers Albritton. Imagine that we someday discover that *pencils are organisms.* We cut them open and examine them under the electron microscope, and we see the almost invisible tracery of nerves and other organs. We spy upon them, and we see them spawn, and we see the offspring grow into full-grown pencils. We discover that these organisms are not imitating other (artifactual) pencils—there are not and never were any pencils except these organisms. It is strange, to be sure, that there is *lettering* on many of these organisms—e.g., BONDED *Grants* DELUXE made in U.S.A. No. 2.—perhaps they are intelligent organisms, and this is their form of camouflage. (We also have to explain why no one ever attempted to manufacture pencils, etc., but this is clearly a possible world, in some sense.)

If this is conceivable, and I agree with Albritton that it is, then it is epistemically possible that *pencils could turn out to be organisms.* It follows that *pencils are artifacts* is not epistemically necessary in the strongest sense and, *a fortiori,* not analytic.

Let us be careful, however. Have we shown that there is a possible world in which pencils are organisms? I think not. What we have shown is that there is a possible world in which certain organisms are the *epistemic counterparts* of pencils (the phrase is Kripke's). To return to the device of Twin Earth: imagine this time that pencils on Earth are just what we think they are, artifacts manufactured to be written with, while "pencils" on Twin Earth are organisms à la Albritton. Imagine, further, that this is totally unsuspected by the Twin Earthians—they have exactly the beliefs about "pencils" that we have about pencils. When we discovered this, we would not say: "some pencils are organisms." We would be far more likely to say: "the things on Twin Earth that pass for pencils aren't really pencils. They're really a species of organism."

Suppose now the situation to be as in Albritton's example both on Earth and on Twin Earth. Then we would say "pencils are organisms." Thus, whether the "pencil-organisms" on Twin Earth (or in another possible universe) are really *pencils* or not is a function of whether or not the *local* pencils are organisms or not. If the local pencils are just what we think they are, then a possible world in which there are pencil-organisms is *not* a possible world in which *pencils are organisms;* there are *no* possible worlds in which pencils are organisms in this case (which is, of course, the actual one). That pencils are artifacts *is* necessary in the sense of true in all possible worlds—metaphysically necessary. But it doesn't follow that it's epistemically necessary.

It follows that "pencil" is not *synonymous* with any description—not even loosely synonymous with a *loose* description. When we use the word "pencil," we intend to refer to whatever has the same *nature* as the normal examples of the local pencils in the actual world. "Pencil" is just as *indexical* as "water" or "gold."

In a way, the case of pencils turning out to be organisms is complementary to the case we discussed some years ago [see my (1970), vol. 1, chapter 15] of cats turning out to be robots (remotely controlled from Mars). In Katz (forthcoming), Katz argues that we misdescribed this case: that the case should rather be described as its *turning out that there are no cats in this world.* Katz admits that we might *say* "Cats have turned out not to be animals, but robots"; but he argues that this is a semantically deviant sentence which is glossed as "the things I am referring to as 'cats' have turned out not to be animals, but robots." Katz's theory is bad linguistics, however. First of all, the explanation of how it is we can *say* "Cats are robots" is simply an all-purpose explanation of how we can say *anything*. More important, Katz's theory predicts that "Cats are robots" is *deviant*, while "There are no cats in the world" is nondeviant, in fact standard, in the case described. Now then, I don't deny that there *is* a case in which "There are not (and never were) any cats in the world" would be standard: we might (speaking epistemically) discover that we have been suffering from a collective hallucination. ("Cats" are like pink elephants.) But in the case I described, "Cats have turned out to be robots remotely controlled from Mars" is surely nondeviant, and "There are no cats in the world" is highly deviant.

Incidentally, Katz's account is not only bad linguistics; it is also bad as a rational reconstruction. The reason we *don't* use "cat" as synonymous with a description is surely that we know enough about cats to know that they do have a hidden structure, and it is good scientific methodology to use the name to refer rigidly to the things that possess that hidden structure, and not to whatever happens to satisfy some description. Of course, if we *knew* the hidden structure we could frame a description in terms of *it*; but we don't at this point. In this sense the use of natural-kind words reflects an important fact about our relation to the world: we know that there are kinds of things with common hidden structure, but we don't yet have the knowledge to describe all those hidden structures.

Katz's view has more plausibility in the "pencil" case than in the "cat" case, however. We think we *know* a necessary and sufficient condition for being a *pencil*, albeit a vague one. So it is possible to make "pencil" synonymous with a loose description. We *might* say, in the case that "pencils turned out to be organisms" *either* "Pencils have turned out to be organisms" *or* "There are no pencils in the world"—i.e., we might use "pencil" either as a natural-kind word or as a "one-criterion" word.[11]

On the other hand, we might doubt that there *are* any true one-criterion words in natural language, apart from stipulative contexts. Couldn't it turn out that pediatricians aren't doctors but Martian spies? Answer "yes," and you have abandoned the synonymy of "pediatrician" and "doctor specializing in the care of children." It seems that there is a strong tendency for words which are introduced as "one-criterion" words to develop a "natural-kind" sense, with all the concomitant rigidity and indexicality. In the case of artifact-names, this natural-kind sense seems to be the predominant one.

(There is a joke about a patient who is on the verge of being discharged from an insane asylum. The doctors have been questioning him for some time, and he has been giving perfectly sane responses. They decide to let him leave, and at the end of the interview one of the doctors inquires casually, "What do you want to be when you get out?" "A teakettle." The joke would not be intelligible if it were literally inconceivable that a person could be a teakettle.)

There are, however, words which retain an almost pure one-criterion character. These are words whose meaning derives from a transformation: *hunter = one who hunts.*

Not only does the account given here apply to most nouns, but it also applies to other parts of speech. Verbs like "grow," adjectives like "red," etc., all have indexical features. On the other hand, some syncategorematic words seem to have more of a one-criterion character. "Whole," for example, can be explained thus: *The army surrounded the town* could be true even if the A division did not take part. *The whole army surrounded the town* means every part of the army (of the relevant kind, e.g., the A Division) took part in the action signified by the verb.[12]

MEANING

Let us now see where we are with respect to the notion of meaning. We have now seen that the extension of a term is not fixed by a concept that the individual speaker has in his head, and this is true both because extension is, in general, determined *socially*—there is division of linguistic labor as much as of "real" labor—and because extension is, in part, determined *indexically*. The extension of our terms depends upon the actual nature of the particular things that serve as paradigms,[13] and this actual nature is not, in general, fully known to the speaker. Traditional semantic theory leaves out only two contributions to the determination of extension—the contribution of society and the contribution of the real world!

We saw at the outset that meaning cannot be identified with extension. Yet it cannot be identified with "intension" either, if intension is something like an individual speaker's *concept*. What are we to do?

There are two plausible routes that we might take. One route would be to retain the identification of meaning with concept and pay the price of giving up the idea that meaning determines extension. If we followed this route, we might say that "water" has the same *meaning* on Earth and on Twin Earth, but a different *extension*. (Not just a different *local* extension but a different *global* extension. The XYZ on Twin Earth isn't in the extension of the tokens of "water" that I utter, but it is in the extension of the tokens of "water" that my *Doppelgänger* utters, and this isn't just because Twin Earth is far away from me, since molecules of H_2O are in the extension of the tokens of "water" that I utter no matter how far away from me they are in space and time. Also, what I can counterfactually suppose water to be is different from what my *Doppelgänger* can counterfactually suppose "water" to be.) While this is the correct route to take for an *absolutely* indexical word like "I," it seems incorrect for the words we have been discussing. Consider "elm" and "beech," for example. If these are "switched" on Twin Earth, then surely we would *not* say that "elm" has the same meaning on Earth and Twin Earth, even if my *Doppelgänger*'s stereotype of a beech (or an "elm," as he calls it) is identical with my stereotype of an elm. Rather, we would say that "elm" in my *Doppelgänger*'s idiolect means *beech*. For this reason, it seems preferable to take a different route and identify "meaning" with an ordered pair (or possibly an ordered *n-tuple*) of entities, *one of which is the extension*. (The other components of the, so to speak, "meaning vector" will be specified later). Doing this makes it trivially true that *meaning determines extension* (i.e., difference in extension is *ipso facto* difference in meaning), but totally abandons the idea that if there is a difference in the meaning my *Doppelgänger* and I assign to a word, then there *must* be some difference in our concepts (or in our psychological state). Following this route, we can say that my *Doppelgänger* and *I mean something different* when we say "elm," but this will not be an assertion about our psychological states. All this means is that the tokens of the word he utters have a different extension than the tokens of the word I utter; but this difference in extension is not a reflection of any difference in our individual linguistic competence considered in isolation.

If this is correct, and I think it is, then the traditional problem of meaning splits into two problems. The first problem is to account for the *determination of extension*. Since, in many cases, extension is determined socially and not individually, owing to the division of linguistic labor, I believe that this problem is properly a problem for sociolinguistics. Solving it would involve spelling out in detail exactly how the division of linguistic labor works. The so-called "causal theory of reference," introduced by Kripke for proper names and extended by us to natural-kind words and physical-magnitude terms, falls into this province. For the fact that, in many contexts, we assign to the tokens of a name that I utter whatever referent we assign to the tokens of the same name uttered by the person from whom I acquired the name (so that the reference is transmitted from speaker to speaker, starting from the speakers who were present at the "naming ceremony," even though no fixed *description* is transmitted) is simply a special case of social cooperation in the determination of reference.

The other problem is to describe *individual competence*. Extension may be determined socially, in many cases, but we don't assign the standard extension to the tokens of a word *W* uttered by Jones *no matter how* Jones uses *W*. Jones has to have some particular ideas and skills in connection with *W* in order to play his part in the linguistic division of labor. Once we give up the idea that individual competence has to be so strong as to actually determine extension, we can begin to study it in a fresh frame of mind.

In this connection it is instructive to observe that nouns like "tiger" or "water" are very different from proper names. One can use the proper name "Sanders" correctly without knowing anything about the referent except that he is called "Sanders"—and even that may not be correct. ("Once upon a time, a very long time ago now, about last Friday, Winnie-the-Pooh lived in a forest all by himself under the name of Sanders.") But one cannot use the word tiger correctly, save *per accidens*, without knowing a good deal about tigers, or at least about a certain conception of tigers. In this sense concepts *do* have a lot to do with meaning.

Just as the study of the first problem is properly a topic in sociolinguistics, so the study of the second problem is properly a topic in psycholinguistics. To this topic we now turn.

STEREOTYPES AND COMMUNICATION

Suppose a speaker knows that "tiger" has a set of physical objects as its extension, but no more. If he possesses normal linguistic competence in other respects, then he could use "tiger" in *some* sentences: for example, "tigers have mass," "tigers take up space," "give me a tiger," "is that a tiger?", etc. Moreover, the *socially determined* extension of "tiger" in these sentences would be the standard one, i.e., the set of tigers. Yet we would not count such a speaker as "knowing the meaning" of the word *tiger*. Why not?

Before attempting to answer this question, let us reformulate it a bit. We shall speak of someone as having *acquired* the word "tiger" if he is able to use it in such a way that (1) his use passes muster (i.e., people don't say of him such things as "he doesn't know what a tiger *is*," "he doesn't know the meaning of the word 'tiger'," etc.); and (2) his total way of being situated in the world and in his linguistic community is such that the socially determined extension of the word "tiger" in his idiolect is the set of tigers. Clause (1) means, roughly, that speakers like the one hypothesized in the preceding paragraph don't count as having acquired the word "tiger" (or whichever). We might speak of them, in some cases, as having *partially acquired* the word; but let us defer this for the moment. Clause (2) means that speakers on Twin Earth who have the same linguistic habits as we do, count as having acquired the word "tiger" only if the extension of "tiger" in their idiolect is the set of tigers. The burden of the preceding sections of this paper is that it does *not* follow that the extension of "tiger" in Twin Earth dialect (or idiolects) is the set of tigers merely because their linguistic habits are the same as ours: the nature of Twin Earth "tigers" is also relevant. (If Twin Earth organisms have a silicon chemistry, for example, then their "tigers" aren't really tigers, even if they look like tigers, although the linguistic habits of the lay Twin Earth speaker exactly correspond to those of Earth speakers.) Thus clause (2) means that in this case we have decided to say that Twin Earth speakers have not acquired our word "tiger" (although they have acquired another word with the same spelling and pronunciation).

Our reason for introducing this way of speaking is that the question "does he know the meaning of the word 'tiger'?" is biased in favor of the theory that acquiring a word is coming to possess a thing called its "meaning." Identify this thing with a concept, and we are back at the theory that a sufficient condition for acquiring a word is associating it with the right concept (or, more generally, being in the right psychological state with respect to it)—the very theory we have spent all this time refuting. So, henceforth, we will "acquire" words, rather than "learn their meaning."

We can now reformulate the question with which this section began. The use of the speaker we described does not pass muster, although it is not such as to cause us to assign a nonstandard extension to the word "tiger" in his idiolect. Why doesn't it pass muster?

Suppose our hypothetical speaker points to a snowball and asks, "is that a tiger?" Clearly there isn't much point in talking tigers with *him*. Significant communication requires that people know something of what they are talking about. To be sure, we hear people "communicating" every day who clearly know nothing of what they are talking about; but the sense in which the man who points to a snowball and asks "is that a tiger?" doesn't know anything about tigers is so far beyond the sense in which the man who thinks that Vancouver is going to win the Stanley Cup, or that the Vietnam War was fought to help the South Vietnamese, doesn't know what he is talking about as to boggle the mind. The problem of people who think that Vancouver is going to win the Stanley Cup, or that the Vietnam War was fought to help the South Vietnamese, is one that obviously cannot be remedied by the adoption of linguistic conventions; but not knowing what one is talking about in the second, mind-boggling sense can be and is prevented, near enough, by our conventions of language. What I contend is that speakers are *required* to know something about (stereotypical) tigers in order to count as having acquired the word "tiger"; something about elm trees (or anyway, about the stereotype thereof) to count as having acquired the word "elm"; etc.

This idea should not seem too surprising. After all, we do not permit people to drive on the highways without first passing some tests to determine that they have a *minimum* level of competence; and we do not dine with people who have not learned to use a knife and fork. The linguistic community too has its minimum standards, with respect both to syntax and to "semantics."

The nature of the required minimum level of competence depends heavily upon both the culture and the topic, however. In our culture speakers are required to know what tigers look like (if they acquire the word "tiger," and this is virtually obligatory); they are not required to know the fine details (such as leaf shape) of what an elm tree looks like. English speakers are *required by their linguistic community* to be able to tell tigers from leopards; they are not required to be able to tell elm trees from beech trees.

This could easily have been different. Imagine an Indian tribe, call it the Cheroquoi, who have words, say *uhaba'* and *wa'arabi* for elm trees and beech trees, respectively, and who make it *obligatory* to know the difference. A Cheroquoi who could not recognize an elm would be said not to know what an *uhaba'* is, not to know the meaning of the word *uhaba'* (perhaps, not to know the word, or not to *have* the word); just as an English speaker who had no idea that tigers are striped would be said not to know what a tiger is, not to know the meaning of the word "tiger" (of course, if he at least knows that tigers are large felines we might say he knows part of the meaning, or partially knows the meaning), etc. Then the translation of *uhaba'* as "elm" and *wa'arabi* as "beech" would, in our view, be only *approximately* correct. In this sense there is a real difficulty with radical translation,[14] but this is not the abstract difficulty that Quine is talking about.[15]

WHAT STEREOTYPES ARE

I introduced the notion of a "stereotype" in my lectures at the University of Washington and at the Minnesota Center for the Philosophy of Science in 1968. The subsequently published "Is semantics possible?" [see chapter 8 in Putnam (1975a)] follows up the argumentation, and in the present essay I want to introduce the notion again and to answer some questions that have been asked about it.

In ordinary parlance a "stereotype" is a conventional (frequently malicious) idea (which may be wildly inaccurate) of what an X looks like or acts like or is. Obviously, I am trading on some features of the ordinary parlance. I am not concerned with malicious stereotypes (save where the language itself is malicious); but I am concerned with conventional ideas, which may be inaccurate. I am suggesting that just such a conventional idea is associated with "tiger," with "gold," etc., and, moreover, that this is the sole element of truth in the "concept" theory.

In this view someone who knows what "tiger" means (or, as we have decided to say instead, has acquired the word "tiger") is *required* to know that *stereotypical* tigers are striped. More precisely, there is *one* stereotype of tigers (he may have others) which is required by the linguistic community as such; he is required to have this stereotype, and to know (implicitly) that it is obligatory. This stereotype must include the feature of stripes if his acquisition is to count as successful.

The fact that a feature (e.g., stripes) is included in the stereotype associated with a word X does not mean that it is an analytic truth that all X's have that feature, nor that most X's have that feature, nor that all normal X's have that feature, nor that some X's have that feature.[16] Three-legged tigers and albino tigers are not logically contradictory entities. Discovering that our stereotype has been based on nonnormal or unrepresentative members of a natural kind is not discovering a logical contradiction. If tigers lost their stripes they would not thereby cease to be tigers, nor would butterflies necessarily cease to be butterflies if they lost their wings.

(Strictly speaking, the situation is more complicated than this. It is possible to give a word like "butterfly" a sense in which butterflies would cease to be butterflies if they lost their wings—through mutation, say. Thus one can find *a* sense of "butterfly" in which it is analytic that "butterflies have wings." But the most important sense of the term, I believe, is the one in which the wingless butterflies would still be butterflies.)

At this point the reader may wonder what the value to the linguistic community of having stereotypes is, if the "information" contained in the stereotype is not necessarily correct. But this is not really such a mystery. Most stereotypes do in fact capture features possessed by paradigmatic members of the class in question. Even where stereotypes go wrong, the way in which they go wrong sheds light on the contribution normally made by stereotypes to communication. The stereotype of gold, for example, contains the feature *yellow* even though chemically pure gold is nearly white. But the gold we see in jewelry is typically yellow (due to the presence of copper), so the presence of this feature in the stereotype is even useful in lay contexts. The stereotype associated with *witch* is more seriously wrong, at least if taken with existential import. Believing (with existential import) that witches enter into pacts with Satan, that they cause sickness and death, etc., facilitates communication only in the sense of facilitating communication internal to witch-theory. It does not facilitate communication in any situation in which what is needed is more agreement with the world than agreement with the theory of other speakers. (Strictly speaking, I am speaking of the stereotype as it existed in New England 300 years ago; today that witches aren't *real* is itself part of the stereotype, and the baneful effects of witch-theory are thereby neutralized.) But the fact that our language has *some* stereotypes which impede rather than facilitate our dealings with the world and each other only points to the fact that we aren't infallible beings, and how could we be? The fact is that we could hardly communicate successfully if most of our stereotypes weren't pretty accurate as far as they go.

THE "OPERATIONAL MEANING" OF STEREOTYPES

A trickier question is this: how far is the notion of stereotype "operationally definable." Here it is necessary to be extremely careful. Attempts in the physical sciences to *literally* specify operational definitions for terms have notoriously failed; and there is no reason the attempt should succeed in linguistics when it failed in physics. Sometimes Quine's arguments against the possibility of a theory of meaning seem to reduce to the demand for operational definitions in linguistics; when this is the case the arguments should be ignored. But it frequently happens that terms do have operational definitions not in the actual world but in idealized circumstances. Giving these "operational definitions" has heuristic value, as idealization frequently does. It is only when we mistake operational definition for more than convenient idealization that it becomes harmful. Thus we may ask: what is the "operational meaning" of the statement that a word has such and such a stereotype, without supposing that the answer to this question counts as a theoretical account of what it is to be a stereotype.

The theoretical account of what it is to be a stereotype proceeds in terms of the notion of *linguistic obligation*; a notion which we believe to be fundamental to linguistics and which we shall not attempt to explicate here. What it means to say that being striped is part of the (linguistic) stereotype of "tiger" is that it is *obligatory* to acquire the information that stereotypical tigers are striped if one acquires "tiger," in the same sense of "obligatory" in which it is obligatory to indicate whether one is speaking of lions in the singular or lions in the plural when one speaks of lions in English. To describe an idealized experimental test of this hypothesis is not difficult. Let us introduce a person whom we may call the linguist's *confederate*. The confederate will be (or pretend to be) an adult whose command of English is generally excellent, but who for some reason (raised in an alien culture? brought up in a monastery?) has totally failed to acquire the word "tiger." The confederate will say the word "tiger" or, better yet, point to it (as if he wasn't sure how to pronounce it), and ask "What does this word mean?" or "What is this?" or some such question. Ignoring all the things that go wrong with experiments in practice, what our hypothesis implies is that informants should typically tell the confederate that tigers are, *inter alia*, striped.

Instead of relying on confederates, one might expect the linguist to study children learning English. But children learning their native language aren't taught it nearly as much as philosophers suppose; they learn it but they aren't taught it, as Chomsky has emphasized. Still, children do sometimes ask such questions as "What is a tiger?" and our hypothesis implies that in these cases too informants should tell them, *inter alia*, that tigers are striped. But one problem is that the informants are likely to be parents, and there are the vagaries of parental time, temper, and attention to be allowed for.

It would be easy to specify a large number of additional "operational" implications of our hypothesis, but to do so would have no particular value. The fact is that we are fully competent speakers of English ourselves, with a devil of a good sense of what our linguistic obligations are. Pretending that we are in the position of Martians with respect to English is not the route to methodological clarity; it was, after all, only when the operational approach was abandoned that transformational linguistics blossomed into a handsome science.

Thus if anyone were to ask me for the meaning of "tiger," I know perfectly well what I would tell him. I would tell him that tigers were feline, something about their size, that they are yellow with black stripes, that they (sometimes) live in the jungle, and are fierce. Other things I might tell him too, depending on the context and his reason for asking; but the above items, save possibly for the bit about the jungle, I would regard it *obligatory* to convey. I don't have to experiment to know that this is what I regard it as obligatory to convey, and I am sure that approximately this is what other speakers regard it as obligatory to convey too. Of course, there is some variation from idiolect to idiolect; the feature of having stripes (apart from figure-ground relations, e.g., are they black stripes on a yellow ground, which is the way I see them, or yellow stripes on a black ground?) would be found in all normal idiolects, but some speakers might regard the information that tigers (stereotypically) inhabit jungles as obligatory, while others might not. Alternatively, some features of the stereotype (big-cat-hood, stripes) might be regarded as obligatory, and others as *optional*, on the model of certain syntactical features. But we shall not pursue this possibility here.

QUINE'S "TWO DOGMAS" REVISITED

In "Two dogmas of empiricism" Quine launched a powerful and salutory attack on the currently fashionable analytic-synthetic distinction. The distinction had grown to be a veritable philosophical man-eater: analytic *equalling* necessary *equalling* unrevisable in principle *equalling* whatever truth the individual philosopher wished to explain away. But Quine's attack itself went too far in certain respects; some limited class of analytic sentences can be saved, we feel [see chapter 2 in Putnam (1975a)]. More important, the attack was later construed, both by Quine himself and by others, as implicating the whole notion of meaning in the downfall of the analytic-synthetic distinction. While we have made it clear that we agree that the traditional notion of meaning has serious troubles, our project in this paper is constructive, not destructive. We come to revise the notion of meaning, not to bury it. So it will be useful to see how Quine's arguments fare against our revision.

Quine's arguments against the notion of analyticity can basically be reduced to the following: that no behavioral significance can be attached to the notion. His argument (again simplifying somewhat) was that there were, basically, only two candidates for a behavioral index of analyticity, and both are totally unsatisfactory, although for different reasons. The first behavioral index is *centrality*: many contemporary philosophers call a sentence analytic if, in effect some community (say, Oxford dons) holds it immune from revision. But, Quine persuasively argues, maximum immunity from revision is no exclusive prerogative of analytic sentences. Sentences expressing fundamental laws of physics (e.g., the conservation of energy) may well enjoy maximum behavioral immunity from revision, although it would hardly be customary or plausible to classify them as analytic. Quine does not, however, rely on the mere implausibility of classifying all statements that we are highly reluctant to give up as analytic; he points out that "immunity from revision" is, in the actual history of science, a *matter of degree*. There is no such thing, in the actual practice of rational science, as *absolute* immunity from revision. Thus to identify analyticity with immunity from revision would alter the notion in two fundamental ways: analyticity would become a matter of degree, and there would be no such thing as an absolutely analytic sentence. This would be such a departure from the classical Carnap-Ayer-*et al.* notion of analyticity that Quine feels that if *this* is what we mean to talk about, then it would be less misleading to introduce a different term altogether, say, *centrality*.

The second behavioral index is *being called "analytic."* In effect, some philosophers take the hallmark of analyticity to be that trained informants (say, Oxford dons) *call* the sentence analytic. Variants of this index are: that the sentence be deducible from the sentences in a finite list at the top of which someone who bears the ancestral of the graduate-student relation to Carnap has printed the words "Meaning Postulate"; that the sentence be obtainable from a theorem of logic by substituting synonyms for synonyms. The last of these variants looks promising, but Quine launches against it the question, "what is the criterion of synonymy?" One possible criterion might be that words W_1 and W_2 are synonymous if and only if the biconditional (x) (x is in the extension of W_1 $<==>$ x is in the extension of W_2) is *analytic*; but this leads us right back in a circle. Another might be that words W_1 and W_2 are synonymous if and only if trained informants *call* them synonymous; but this is just our second index in a slightly revised form. A promising line is that words W_1 and W_2 are synonymous if and only if W_1 and W_2 are interchangeable (i.e., the words can be switched) *salva veritate* in all contexts of a suitable class. But Quine convincingly shows that this proposal too leads us around in a circle. Thus the second index reduces to this: a sentence is analytic if either it or some expression, or sequence of ordered pairs of expressions, or set of expressions, related to the sentence in certain specified ways, lies in a class to all the members of which trained informants apply a certain *noise*: either the *noise* ANALYTIC, or the *noise* MEANING POSTULATE, or the *noise* SYNONYMOUS. Ultimately, this proposal leaves "analytic," etc., *unexplicated noises*.

Although Quine does not discuss this explicitly, it is clear that taking the intersection of the two unsatisfactory behavioral indexes would be no more satisfactory; explicating the analyticity of a sentence as consisting in centrality *plus* being called ANALYTIC is just saying that the analytic sentences are a subclass of the central sentences without in any way telling us wherein the exceptionality of the subclass consists. In effect, Quine's conclusion is that analyticity is either centrality misconceived or it is nothing.

In spite of Quine's forceful argument, many philosophers have gone on abusing the notion of analyticity, often confusing it with a supposed highest degree of centrality. Confronted with Quine's alternatives, they have elected to identify analyticity with centrality, and to pay the price of classifying such obviously synthetic-looking sentences as "space has three dimensions" as analytic, and the price of undertaking to maintain the view that there is, after all, such a thing as absolute unrevisability in science in spite of the impressive evidence to the contrary. But this line can be blasted by coupling Quine's argument with an important argument of Reichenbach's.

Reichenbach [(1965) p. 31] showed that there exists a *set* of principles each of which Kant would have regarded as synthetic *a priori*, but whose conjunction is incompatible with the principles of special relativity and general covariance. (These include normal induction, the continuity of space, and the Euclidean character of space.) A Kantian can consistently hold on to Euclidean geometry come what may; but then experience may force him to give up normal induction or the continuity of space. Or he may hold on to normal induction and the continuity of space come what may; but then experience may force him to give up Euclidean geometry (this happens in the case that physical space is not even homeomorphic to any Euclidean space). In his article in Schilpp (1951), Reichenbach gives essentially the same argument in a slightly different form.

Applied to our present context, what this shows is that there are principles such that philosophers fond of the overblown notion of analyticity, and in particular philosophers who identify analyticity with (maximum) unrevisability, would classify then as analytic, but whose conjunction has testable empirical consequences. Thus either the identification of analyticity with centrality must be given up once and for all, or one must give up the idea that analyticity is closed under conjunction, or one must swallow the unhappy consequence that an analytic sentence can have testable empirical consequences (and hence that an *analytic* sentence might turn out to be *empirically false*).

It is no accident, by the way, that the sentences that Kant would have classified as synthetic *a priori* would be classified by these latter-day empiricists as analytic; their purpose in bloating the notion of analyticity was precisely to dissolve Kant's problem by identifying *apriority* with analyticity and then identifying analyticity in turn with truth by convention. (This last step has also been devastatingly criticized by Quine, but discussion of it would take us away from our topic.)

Other philosophers have tried to answer Quine by distinguishing between *sentences* and *statements*: all *sentences* are revisable, they agree, but some *statements* are not. Revising a sentence is not changing our mind about the statement formerly expressed by that sentence just in case the sentence (meaning the syntactical object together with its meaning) after the revision is, in fact, not synonymous with the sentence prior to the revision, i.e., just in case the revision is a case of meaning change and not change of theory. But (1) this reduces at once to the proposal to explicate analyticity in terms of synonymy; and (2) if there is one thing that Quine has decisively contributed to philosophy, it is the realization that meaning change and theory change cannot be sharply separated. We do not agree with Quine that meaning change cannot be defined at all, but it does not follow that the dichotomy "meaning change or theory change" is tenable. Discovering that we live in a non-Euclidean world *might* change the meaning of "straight line" (this would happen in the—somewhat unlikely—event that something like the parallels postulate was part of the stereotype of straightness); but it would not be a *mere* change of meaning. In particular it would not be a change of *extension*: thus it would not be right to say that the parallels postulate was "true in the former sense of the words." From the fact that giving up a sentence S would involve meaning change, it does not follow that S is *true*. Meanings may not fit the world; and meaning change can be forced by empirical discoveries.

Although we are not, in this paper, trying to explicate a notion of analyticity, we are trying to explicate a notion that might seem closely related, the notion of meaning. Thus it might seem that Quine's arguments would also go against our attempt. Let us check this out.

In our view there is a perfectly good sense in which being striped is part of the meaning of "tiger." But it does not follow, in our view, that "tigers are striped" is analytic. If a mutation occurred, all tigers might be albinos. Communication presupposes that I have a stereotype of tigers which includes stripes, and that you have a stereotype of tigers which includes stripes, and that I know that your stereotype includes stripes, and that you know that my stereotype includes stripes, and that you know that I know . . . (and so on, à la Grice, forever). But it does not presuppose that any particular stereotype be *correct*, or that the majority of our stereotypes remain correct forever. Linguistic obligatoriness is not supposed to be an index of unrevisability or even of truth; thus we can hold that "tigers are striped" is part of the meaning of "tiger" without being trapped in the problems of analyticity.

Thus Quine's arguments against identifying analyticity with centrality are not arguments against identifying a feature's being "part of the meaning" of X with its being obligatorily included in the stereotype of X. What of Quine's "noise" argument?

Of course, evidence concerning what people *say*, including explicit meta-linguistic remarks, is important in "semantics" as it is in syntax. Thus, if a speaker points to a *clam* and asks "is that a tiger?" people are likely to guffaw. (When they stop laughing) they might say "he doesn't know the meaning of 'tiger'," or "he doesn't know what tigers are." Such comments can be helpful to the linguist. But we are not *defining* the stereotype in terms of such comments. To say that being "big-cat-like" is part of the meaning of tiger is not merely to say that application of "tiger" to something which is not big-cat-like (and also not a tiger) would provoke certain *noises*. It is to say that speakers acquire the information that "tigers are (stereotypically) big-cat-like" as they acquire the word "tiger" and that they feel an obligation to guarantee that those to whom they teach the use of the word do likewise. Information about the minimum skills required for entry into the linguistic community is significant information; no circularity of the kind Quine criticized appears here.

RADICAL TRANSLATION

What our theory does not do, by itself at any rate, is solve Quine's problem of "radical translation" (i.e., translation from an alien language/culture). We cannot translate our hypothetical Cheroquoi into English by matching stereotypes, just because finding out what the stereotype of say, *wa'arabi* is involves translating Cheroquoi utterances. On the other hand, the constraint that each word in Cheroquoi should match its image in English under the translation-function as far as stereotype is concerned (or approximately match, since in many cases exact matching may not be attainable), places a severe *constraint* on the translation function. Once we have succeeded in translating the basic vocabulary of Cheroquoi, we can start to elicit stereotypes, and these will serve both to constrain future translations and to check the internal correctness of the piece of the translation-function already constructed.

Even where we can determine stereotypes (relative, say, to a tentative translation of "basic vocabulary"), these do not suffice, in general, to determine a unique translation. Thus the German words *Ulme* and *Buche* have the same stereotype as elm; but *Ulme* means "elm" while *Buche* means "beech." In the case of German, the fact that *Ulme* and "elm" are cognates could point to the correct translation (although this is far from foolproof—in general, cognate words are not synonymous); but in the case of Greek we have no such clue as to which of the two words ὀξύα, πτελέα means *elm* and which *beech*; we would just have to find a Greek who could tell elms from beeches (or *oxya* from *ptelea*). What this illustrates is that it may not be the *typical* speakers' dispositions to assent and dissent that the linguist must seek to discover; because of the division of linguistic labor, it is frequently necessary for the linguist to assess who are the experts with respect to *oxya*, or *wa'arabi*, or *gavagai*, or whatever, before he can make a guess at the socially determined extension of a word. Then this socially determined extension *and* the stereotype of the *typical* speaker, inexpert though he is, *will* both function as constraints upon the translation-function. Discovery that the stereotype of *oxya* is wildly different from the stereotype of "elm" would disqualify the translation of *oxya* by "elm" in all save the most extensional contexts; but the discovery that the *extension* of *oxya* is not even approximately the class of elms would wipe out the translation altogether, in all contexts.

It will be noted that we have already enlarged the totality of facts counted as evidence for a translation-function beyond the ascetic base that Quine allows in *Word and Object*. For example, the fact that speakers say such and such when the linguist's "confederate" points to the word *oxya* and asks "what does this mean?" or "what is this?" or whatever is not allowed by Quine (as something the linguist can "know") on the ground that this sort of "knowledge" presupposes already having translated the query "what does this word mean?" However, if Quine is willing to assume that one can *somehow* guess at the words which signify *assent* and *dissent* in the alien language, it does not seem at all unreasonable to suppose that one can somehow convey to a native speaker that one does not understand a word. It is not necessary that one discover a locution in the alien language which literally means "what does this word mean?" (as opposed to: "I don't understand this word," or "this word is unfamiliar to me" or "I am puzzled by this word," etc.). Perhaps just saying the word *oxya*, or whatever, with a tone of puzzlement would suffice. Why should *puzzlement* be less accessible to the linguist than *assent*?

Also, we are taking advantage of the fact that segmentation into *words* has turned out to be linguistically universal (and there even exist tests for word and morpheme segmentation which are independent of meaning). Clearly, there is no motivated reason for allowing the linguist to utter whole sentences and look for assent and dissent, while refusing to allow him to utter words and morphemes in a tone of puzzlement.

I repeat, the claim is not being advanced that enlarging the evidence base in this way solves the problem of radical translation. What it does is add further constraints on the class of admissible candidates for a correct translation. What I believe is that enlarging the class of constraints can determine a unique translation, or as unique a translation as we are able to get in practice. But constraints that go beyond linguistic theory proper will have to be used, in my opinion; there will also have to be constraints on what sorts of beliefs (and connections between beliefs, and connections of beliefs to the culture and the world) we can reasonably impute to people. Discussion of these matters will be deferred to another paper.

A CRITIQUE OF DAVIDSONIAN SEMANTIC THEORY

In a series of publications, Donald Davidson has put forward the interesting suggestion that a semantic theory of a natural language might be modeled on what mathematical logicians call a *truth definition* for a formalized language. Stripped of technicalities, what this suggestion comes down to is that one might have a set of rules specifying (1) for each word, under what conditions that word is true of something (for words for which the concept of an extension makes sense; all other words are to be treated as syncategorematic); (2) for sentences longer than a single word, a rule is given specifying the conditions under which the sentence is true as a function of the way it is built up out of shorter sentences (counting words as if they were one-word sentences, e.g., "snow" as "that's snow"). The choice of one-word sentences as the starting point is my interpretation of what Davidson intends; in any case, he means one to start with a *finite* stock of *short* sentences for which truth conditions are to be laid down *directly*. The intention of (2) is not that there should be a rule for each sentence not handled under (1), since this would require an infinite number of rules, but that there should be a rule for each sentence *type*. For example, in a formalized language one of the rules of kind (2) might be: if S is (S_1 & S_2) for some sentences S_1, S_2, then S is true if and only if S_1, S_2, are both true.

It will be noticed that, in the example just given, the truth condition specified for sentences of the sentence type (S_1 & S_2) performs the job of specifying the meaning of "&." More precisely, it specifies the meaning of the structure (——— & ———). This is the sense in which a truth definition can be a theory of meaning. Davidson's contention is that the *entire* theory of meaning for a natural language can be given in this form.

There is no doubt that rules of the type illustrated can give the meaning of some words and structures. The question is, what reason is there to think that the meaning of most words can be given in this way, let alone all?

The obvious difficulty is this: for many words, an extensionally correct truth definition can be given which is in no sense a theory of the meaning of the word. For example, consider *"Water" is true of x if and only if x is* H_2O. This is an extensionally correct truth definition for "water" (strictly speaking, it is not a truth definition but a "truth of" definition—i.e., a *satisfaction*-in-the-sense-of-Tarski definition, but we will not bother with such niceties here). At least it is extensionally correct if we ignore the problem that water with impurities is also called "water," etc. Now, suppose most speakers don't *know* that water is H_2O. Then this formula in no way tells us anything about the *meaning* of "water." It might be of interest to a chemist, but it doesn't count as a theory of the meaning of the term "water." Or, it counts as a theory of the *extension* of the term "water," but Davidson is promising us more than just that.

Davidson is quite well aware of this difficulty. His answer (in conversation, anyway) is that we need to develop a theory of *translation*. This he, like Quine, considers to be the real problem. Relativized to such a theory (relativized to what we admittedly don't yet have), the theory comes down to this: we want a system of truth definitions which is simultaneously a system of translations (or approximate translations, if perfect translation is unobtainable). If we had a theory which specified what it is to be a good translation, then we could rule out the above truth definition for "water" as uninteresting on the grounds that *x is* H_2O is not an acceptable translation or even near-translation of *x is water* (in a prescientific community), even if water = H_2O happens to be true.

This comes perilously close to saying that a theory of meaning is a truth definition plus a theory of meaning. (If we had ham and eggs we'd have ham and eggs—*if* we had ham and *if* we had eggs.) But this story suffers from worse than promissoriness, as we shall see.

A second contention of Davidson's is that the theory of translation that we don't yet have is necessarily a theory whose basic units are *sentences* and not *words* on the grounds that our *evidence* in linguistics necessarily consists of assent and dissent from sentences. Words can be handled, Davidson contends, by treating them as sentences ("water" as "that's water," etc.).

How does this ambitious project of constructing a theory of meaning in the form of a truth definition constrained by a theory of translation tested by "the only evidence we have," speakers' dispositions to use sentences, fare according to the view we are putting forward here?

Our answer is that the theory cannot succeed in principle. In special cases, such as the word "and" in its truth-functional sense, a truth definition (strictly speaking, a clause in what logicians call a "truth definition"—the sum total of all the clauses is the inductive definition of "truth " for the particular language) can give the meaning of the word or structure because the stereotype associated with the word (if one wants to speak of a stereotype in the case of a word like "and") is so strong as to actually constitute a necessary and sufficient condition. If all words were like "and" and "bachelor" the program could succeed. And Davidson certainly made an important contribution in pointing out that linguistics has to deal with inductively specified truth conditions. But in the great majority of words, the requirements of a theory of truth and the requirements of a theory of meaning are mutually incompatible, at least in the English–English case. But the English–English case—the case in which we try to provide a significant theory of the meaning of English words which is itself couched in English—is surely the basic one.

The problem is that in general the only expressions which are both coextensive with X and have roughly the same stereotype as X are expressions containing X itself. If we rule out such truth definitions (strictly speaking, clauses, but I shall continue using "truth definition" both for individual clauses and for the whole system of clauses, for simplicity) as

"X is water" is true if and only if X is water

on the grounds that they don't say anything about the meaning of the word "water," and we rule out such truth definitions as

"X is water" is true if and only if X is H₂O

on the grounds that what they say is wrong as a description of the *meaning* of the word "water," then we shall be left with nothing.

The problem is that we want

W is true of x if and only if ———

to satisfy the conditions that (1) the clause be extensionally correct (where ——— is to be thought of as a condition containing "x," e.g., "x is H_2O"); (2) that ——— be a *translation* of W—on our theory, this would mean that the stereotype associated with W is approximately the same as the stereotype associated with; (3) that ——— not contain W itself, or syntactic variants of W. If we take W to be, for example, the word "elm," then there is absolutely no way to fulfill all three conditions simultaneously. Any condition of the above form that does not contain "elm" and that is extensionally correct will contain a ——— that is absolutely terrible as a *translation* of "elm."

Even where the language contains two exact synonyms, the situation is little better. Thus,

"Heather" is true of x if and only if x is gorse

is true, and so is

"Gorse" is true of x if and only if x is heather

—*this* is a *theory* of the *meaning* of "gorse" and "heather"?

Notice that the condition (3) is precisely what logicians do *not* impose on *their* truth definitions.

"Snow is white" is true if and only if snow is white

is the paradigm of a truth definition in the logician's sense. But logicians are trying to give the extension of "true" with respect to a particular language, not the meaning of "snow is white." Tarski would have gone so far as to claim he was giving the *meaning* (and not just the extension) of "true"; but he would never have claimed he was saying *anything* about the meaning of "snow is white."

It may be that what Davidson really thinks is that a theory of meaning, in any serious sense of the term, is impossible, and that all that is possible is to construct translation-functions. If so, he might well think that the only "theory of meaning" possible for English is one that says "'elm' is true of x if and only if x is an elm," "'water' is true of x if and only if x is water," etc., and only rarely something enlightening like "S_1 & S_2 is true if and only if S_1, S_2 are both true." But if Davidson's "theory" is just Quinine skepticism under the disguise of a positive contribution to the study of meaning, then it is a bitter pill to swallow.

The contention that the only evidence available to the linguist is speakers' dispositions with respect to whole sentences is, furthermore, vacuous on one interpretation, and plainly false on the interpretation on which it is not vacuous. If dispositions to say certain things *when queried about individual words or morphemes or syntactic structures* are included in the notion of dispositions to use sentences, then the restriction to dispositions to use sentences seems to rule out nothing whatsoever. On the nonvacuous interpretation, what Davidson is saying is that the linguist cannot have access to such data as what informants (including the linguist himself) say when asked the meaning of a word or morpheme or syntactic structure. No reason has ever been given why the linguist cannot have access to such data, and it is plain that actual linguists place heavy reliance on informants' testimony about such matters, in the case of an alien language, and upon their own intuitions as native speakers, when they are studying their native languages. In particular, when we are trying to translate a whole sentence, there is no reason why we should not be guided by our knowledge of the syntactic and semantic properties of the constituents of that sentence, including the deep structure. As we have seen, there are procedures for gaining information about individual constituents. It is noteworthy that the procedure that Quine and Davidson claim is the only *possible* one—going from whole sentences to individual words—is the *opposite* of the procedure upon which every success ever attained in the study of natural language has been based.

CRITIQUE OF CALIFORNIA SEMANTICS

I wish now to consider an approach to semantic theory pioneered by the late Rudolf Carnap. Since I do not wish to be embroiled in textual questions, I will not attribute the particular form of the view I am going to describe to any particular philosopher but will simply refer to it as "California semantics."

We assume the notion of a *possible world*. Let f be a function defined on the "space" of all possible worlds whose value $f(x)$ at any possible world x is always a subset of the set of entities in x. Then f is called an intension. A term T has meaning for a speaker X if X associates T with an intension f_T. The term T is *true of* an entity e in a possible world x if and only if e belongs to the set $f(x)$. Instead of using the term "associated," Carnap himself tended to speak of "grasping" intensions; but, clearly, what was intended was not just that X "grasp" the intension f, but that he grasp *that f* is the intension *of T*—i.e., that he *associate f* with T in some way.

Clearly this picture of what it is to understand a term disagrees with the story we tell in this paper. The reply of a California semanticist would be that California semantics is a description of an *ideal* language; that actual language is *vague*. In other words, a term T in actual language does not have a single precise intension; it has a set—possibly a fuzzy set—of intensions. Nevertheless, the first step in the direction of describing natural language is surely to study the idealization in which each term T has exactly one intension.

(In his book *Meaning and Necessity*, Carnap employs a superficially different formulation: an intension is simply a *property*. An entity e belongs to the extension of a term T just in case e has whichever property is the intension of T. The later formulation in terms of functions f as described above avoids taking the notion of *property* as primitive.)

The first difficulty with this position is the use of the totally unexplained notion of *grasping* an intension (or, in our reformulation of the position, *associating* an intension with a term). Identifying intensions with set-theoretic entities f provides a "concrete" realization of the notion of intension in the current mathematical style (relative to the notions of possible world and set), but at the cost of making it very difficult to see how anyone could have an intension in his mind, or what it is to think about one or "grasp" one or "associate" one with anything. It will not do to say that thinking of an intension is using a word or functional substitute for a word (e.g., the analogue of a word in "brain code," if, as seems likely, the brain "computes" in a "code" that has analogies to and possibly borrowings from language; or a thought form such as a picture or a private symbol, in cases where such are employed in thinking) which *refers* to the intension in question, since *reference* (i.e., being in the extension of a term) has just been defined in terms of *intension*. Although the characterization of what it is to think of an abstract entity such as a function or a property is certainly correct, in the present context it is patently circular. But no noncircular characterization of this fundamental notion of the theory has ever been provided.

This difficulty is related to a general difficulty in the philosophy of mathematics pointed out by Paul Benacerraf [Benacerraf (1973)]. Benacerraf has remarked that philosophies of mathematics tend to fall between two stools: either they account for what mathematical objects are and for the necessity of mathematical truth and fail to account for the fact that people can *learn* mathematics, can *refer to* mathematical objects, etc., or else they account for the latter facts and fail to account for the former. California semantics accounts for what intensions *are*, but provides no account that is not completely circular of how it is that we can "grasp" them, associate them with terms, think about them, *refer to* them, etc.

Carnap may not have noticed this difficulty because of his Verificationism. In his early years Carnap thought of understanding a term as possessing the *ability to verify* whether or not any given entity falls in the extension of the term. In terms of intensions: "grasping" an intension would amount, then, to possessing the ability to verify if an entity e in any possible world x belongs to $f(x)$ or not. Later Carnap modified this view, recognizing that, as Quine puts it, sentences face the tribunal of experience collectively and not individually. There is no such thing as the way of verifying that a term T is true of an entity, in general, independent of the context of a particular set of theories, auxiliary hypotheses, etc. Perhaps Carnap would have maintained that something like the earlier theory was correct for a limited class of terms, the so-called "observation terms." Our own view is that the verifiability theory of meaning is false both in its central idea and for observation terms, but we shall not try to discuss this here. At any rate, if one is *not* a verificationist, then it is hard to see California semantics as a theory at all, since the notion of *grasping* an intension has been left totally unexplained.

Second, if we assume that "grasping an intension" (associating an intension with a term T) is supposed to be a *psychological state* (in the narrow sense), then California semantics is committed to both principles (1) and (2) that we criticized in the first part of this paper. It must hold that the psychological state of the speaker determines the intension of his terms which in turn determines the extension of his terms. It would follow that if two human beings are in the same total psychological state, then they necessarily assign the same extension to every term they employ. As we have seen, this is totally wrong for natural language. The reason this is wrong, as we saw above, is in part that extension is determined socially, not by individual competence alone. Thus California semantics is committed to treating language as something private—to totally ignoring the linguistic division of labor. The extension of each term is viewed by this school as totally determined by something in the head of the individual speaker all by himself. A second reason this is wrong, as we also saw, is that most terms are *rigid*. In California semantics every term is treated as, in effect, a *description*. The *indexical* component in meaning—the fact that our terms refer to things which are similar, in certain ways, to things that we designate *rigidly*, to *these* things, to the stuff we call "water," or whatever, *here*—is ignored.

But what of the defense that it is not actual language that the California semanticist is concerned with, but an idealization in which we "ignore vagueness," and that terms in natural language may be thought of as associated with a set of intensions rather than with a single well-defined intension?

The answer is that an *indexical* word cannot be represented as a vague family of non-indexical words. The word "I," to take the extreme case, is *indexical* but not *vague*. T is not synonymous with a *description*; neither is it synonymous with a fuzzy set of descriptions. Similarly, if we are right, "water" is synonymous neither with a description nor with a fuzzy set of descriptions (intensions).

Similarly, a word whose extension is fixed socially and not individually is not the same thing as a word whose extension is *vaguely* fixed individually. The reason my individual "grasp" of "elm tree" does not fix the extension of elm is not that the word is vague—if the problem were simple vagueness, then the fact that my concepts do not distinguish elms from beeches would imply that elms are beeches, as I use the term, or, anyway, borderline cases of beeches, and that beeches are elms, or borderline cases of elms. The reason is rather that the extension of "elm tree" in my dialect is not fixed by what the average speaker "grasps" or doesn't "grasp" at all; it is fixed by the community, including the experts, through a complex cooperative process. A language which exemplifies the division of linguistic labor cannot be approximated successfully by a language which has vague terms and no linguistic division of labor. Cooperation isn't vagueness.

But, one might reply, couldn't one replace our actual language by a language in which (1) terms were replaced by coextensive terms which were *not* indexical (e.g., "water" by "H_2O," assuming "H_2O" is not indexical); and (2) we eliminated the division of linguistic labor by making every speaker an expert on every topic?

We shall answer this question in the negative; but suppose, for a moment, the answer were "yes." What significance would this have? The "ideal" language would in no sense be similar to our actual language; nor would the difference be a matter of "the vagueness of natural language."

In fact, however, one can't carry out the replacement, for the very good reason that *all* natural-kind words and physical-magnitude words are indexical in the way we have described, "hydrogen," and hence "H_2O," just as much as "water." Perhaps "sense data" terms are not indexical (apart from terms for the self), if such there be; but "yellow" as a *thing* predicate is indexical for the same reason as "tiger"; even if something *looks* yellow it may not *be* yellow. And it doesn't help to say that things that look yellow in normal circumstances (to normal perceivers) are yellow; "normal" here has precisely the feature we called indexicality. There is simply no reason to believe that the project of reducing our language to non-indexical language could be carried out in principle.

The elimination of the division of linguistic labor might, I suppose, be carried out "in principle." But, if the division of linguistic labor is, as I conjectured, a linguistic universal, what interest is there in the possible existence of a language which lacks a constitutive feature of *human* language? A world in which every one is an expert on every topic is a world in which social laws are almost unimaginably different from what they now are. What is the *motivation* for taking such a world and such a language as the model for the analysis of *human* language?

Incidentally, philosophers who work in the tradition of California semantics have recently begun to modify the scheme to overcome just these defects. Thus it has been suggested that an intension might be a function whose arguments are not just possible worlds but, perhaps, a possible world, a speaker, and a nonlinguistic context of utterance. This would permit the representation of some kinds of indexicality and some kinds of division of linguistic labor in the model. As David Lewis develops these ideas, "water," for example, would have the same *intension* (same function) on Earth and on Twin Earth, but a different extension. [In effect, Lewis retains assumption (1) from the discussion in the first part of this paper and gives up; (2) we chose to give up (1) and retain (2).] There is no reason why the formal models developed by Carnap and his followers should not prove valuable when so modified. Our interest here has been not in the utility of the mathematical formalism but in the philosophy of language underlying the earlier versions of the view.

SEMANTIC MARKERS

If the approach suggested here is correct, then there is a great deal of scientific work to be done in (1) finding out what sorts of items can appear in stereotypes; (2) working out a convenient system for representing stereotypes, etc. This work is not work that can be done by philosophical discussion, however. It is rather the province of linguistics and psycholinguistics. One idea that can, I believe, be of value is the idea of a *semantic marker*. The idea comes from the work of J. Katz and J. A. Fodor; we shall modify it somewhat here.

Consider the stereotype of "tiger" for a moment. This includes such features as being an animal; being big-cat-like; having black stripes on a yellow ground (yellow stripes on a black ground?); etc. Now, there is something very special about the feature *animal*. In terms of Quine's notion of *centrality* or *unrevisability*, it is qualitatively different from the others listed. It is not impossible to imagine that tigers might not be animals (they might be robots). But spelling this out, they must always have been robots; we don't want to tell a story about the tigers being *replaced* by robots, because then the robots wouldn't be tigers. Or, if they weren't always robots, they must have *become* robots, which is even harder to imagine. If tigers are and always were robots, these robots mustn't be too "intelligent," or else we may not have a case in which tigers aren't animals—we may, rather, have described a case in which some robots are animals. Best make them "other directed" robots—say, have an operator on Mars controlling each motion remotely. Spelling this out, I repeat, is difficult, and it is curiously hard to think of the case to begin with, which is why it is easy to make the mistake of thinking that it is "logically impossible" for a tiger *not* to be an animal. On the other hand, there is no difficulty in imagining an individual tiger that is not striped; it might be an albino. Nor is it difficult to imagine an individual tiger that doesn't look like a big cat: it might be horribly deformed. We can even imagine the whole species losing its stripes or becoming horribly deformed. But tigers ceasing to be animals? Great difficulty again!

Notice that we are not making the mistake that Quine rightly criticized, of attributing an absolute unrevisability to such statements as "tigers are animals," "tigers couldn't change from animals into something else and still be tigers." Indeed, we can describe farfetched cases in which these statements would be given up. But we maintain that it is *qualitatively* harder to revise "all tigers are animals" than "all tigers have stripes"—indeed, the latter statement is not even true.

Not only do such features as "animal," "living thing," "artifact," "day of the week," "period of time," attach with enormous centrality to the words "tiger," "clam," "chair," "Tuesday," "hour"; but they also form part of a widely used and important *system of classification*. The centrality guarantees that items classified under these headings virtually never have to be reclassified; thus these headings are the natural ones to use as category-indicators in a host of contexts. It seems to me reasonable that, just as in syntax we use such markers as "noun," "adjective," and, more narrowly, "concrete noun," "verb taking a person as subject and an abstract object," etc., to classify words, so in semantics these category-indicators should be used as markers.

It is interesting that when Katz and Fodor originally introduced the idea of a semantic marker, they did not propose to exhaust the meaning—what we call the stereotype—by a list of such markers. Rather, the markers were restricted to just the category-indicators of high centrality, which is what we propose. The remaining features were simply listed as a "distinguisher." Their scheme is not easily comparable with ours, because they wanted the semantic markers *plus* the distinguisher to always give a necessary and sufficient condition for membership in the extension of the term. Since the whole thing—markers and distinguisher—were supposed to represent what every speaker implicitly knows, they were committed to the idea that every speaker implicitly knows of a necessary and sufficient condition for membership in the extension of "gold," "aluminum," "elm"—which, as we have pointed out, is not the case. Later Katz went further and demanded that *all* the features constitute an *analytically* necessary and sufficient condition for membership in the extension. At this point he dropped the distinction between markers and distinguishers; if all the features have, so to speak, the infinite degree of centrality, why call some "markers" and some "distinguishers"? From our point of view, their original distinction between "markers" and "distinguisher" was sound—provided one drop the idea that the distinguisher provides (together with the markers) a necessary and sufficient condition, and the idea that any of this is a theory of *analyticity*. We suggest that the idea of a semantic marker is an important contribution, when taken as suggested here.

THE MEANING OF "MEANING"

We may now summarize what has been said in the form of a proposal concerning how one might reconstruct the notion of "meaning." Our proposal is not the only one that might be advanced on the basis of these ideas, but it may serve to encapsulate some of the major points. In addition, I feel that it recovers as much of ordinary usage in common sense talk and in linguistics as one is likely to be able to conveniently preserve. Since, in my view something like the assumptions (I) and (II) listed in the first part of this paper are deeply embedded in ordinary meaning talk, and these assumptions are jointly inconsistent with the facts, no reconstruction is going to be without some counterintuitive consequences.

Briefly, my proposal is to define "meaning" not by picking out an object which will be identified with the meaning (although that might be done in the usual set-theoretic style if one insists), but by specifying a normal form (or, rather, a *type* of normal form) for the description of meaning. If we know what a "normal form description" of the meaning of a word should be, then, as far as I am concerned, we know what meaning is in any scientifically interesting sense.

My proposal is that the normal form description of the meaning of a word should be a finite sequence, or "vector," whose components should certainly include the following (it might be desirable to have other types of components as well): (1) the syntactic markers that apply to the word, e.g., "noun"; (2) the semantic markers that apply to the word, e.g., "animal," "period of time"; (3) a description of the additional features of the stereotype, if any; (4) a description of the extension.

The following convention is a part of this proposal: the components of the vector all represent a hypothesis about the individual speaker's competence, *except the extension*. Thus the normal form description for "water" might be, in part:

Syntactic Markers	Semantic Markers	Stereotype	Extension
mass noun; concrete;	natural-kind; liquid;	colorless; transparent; tasteless; thirst-quenching; etc.	H_2O(give or take impurities)

—this does not mean that knowledge of the fact that water is H_2O is being imputed to the individual speaker or even to the society. It means that (*we* say) the extension of the term "water" as *they* (the speakers in question) use it is *in fact* H_2O. The objection "who are *we* to say what the extension of *their* term is in fact" has been discussed above. Note that this is fundamentally an objection to the notion of *truth*, and that extension is a relative of truth and inherits the family problems.

Let us call two descriptions *equivalent* if they are the same except for the description of the extension, and the two descriptions are coextensive. Then, if the set variously described in the two descriptions is, *in fact*, the extension of the word in question, and the other components in the description are correct characterizations of the various aspects of competence they represent, *both* descriptions count as correct. Equivalent descriptions are both correct or both incorrect. This is another way of making the point that, although we have to use a *description* of the extension to *give* the extension, we think of the component in question as being the *extension* (the *set*), not the description of the extension.

In particular the representation of the words "water" in Earth dialect and "water" in Twin Earth dialect would be the same except that in the last column the normal form description of the Twin Earth word "water" would have XYZ and not H_2O. This means, in view of what has just been said, that we are ascribing the *same* linguistic competence to the typical Earthling/Twin Earthian speaker, but a different extension to the word, nonetheless.

This proposal means that we keep assumption (II) of our early discussion. Meaning determines extension—by construction, so to speak. But (I) is given up;

the psychological state of the individual speaker does not determine "what he means."

In most contexts this will agree with the way we speak, I believe. But one paradox: suppose Oscar is a German–English bilingual. In our view, in his total collection of dialects, the words "beech" and *Buche* are *exact synonyms*. The normal form descriptions of their meanings would be identical. But he might very well not know that they are synonyms! A speaker can have two synonyms in his vocabulary and not know that they are synonyms!

It is instructive to see how the failure of the apparently obvious "if S_1 and S_2 are synonyms and Oscar understands both S_1 and S_2 then Oscar knows that S_1 and S_2 are synonyms" is related to the falsity of (I), in our analysis. Notice that if we had chosen to omit the extension as a component of the "meaning-vector," which is David Lewis's proposal as I understand it, then we would have the paradox that "elm" and "beech" have the *same meaning* but different extensions!

On just about any materialist theory, believing a proposition is likely to involve processing some *representation* of that proposition, be it a sentence in a language, a piece of "brain code," a thought form, or whatever. Materialists, and not only materialists, are reluctant to think that one can believe propositions *neat*. But even materialists tend to believe that, if one believes a proposition, *which* representation one employs is (pardon the pun) immaterial. If S_1 and S_2 are both representations that are *available* to me, then if I believe the proposition expressed by S_1 under the representation S_1, I must also believe it under the representation S_2—at least, I must do this if I have any claim to rationality. But, as we have just seen, this isn't right. Oscar may well believe that *this* is a "beech" (it has a sign on it that says "beech"), but not believe or disbelieve that this is a "*Buche*." It is not just that belief is a process involving representations; he believes the proposition (if one wants to introduce "propositions" at all) under one representation and not under another.

The amazing thing about the theory of meaning is how long the subject has been in the grip of philosophical misconceptions, and how strong these misconceptions are. Meaning has been identified with a necessary and sufficient condition by philosopher after philosopher. In the empiricist tradition, it has been identified with a method of verification, again by philosopher after philosopher. Nor have these misconceptions had the virtue of exclusiveness; not a few philosophers have held that meaning = method of verification = necessary and sufficient condition.

On the other side, it is amazing how weak the grip of the facts has been. After all, what have been pointed out in this essay are little more than home truths about the way we use words and how much (or rather, how little) we actually know when we use them. My own reflection on these matters began after I published a paper in which I confidently maintained that the meaning of a word was "a battery of semantical rules," [see chapter 6 in Putnam (1975a)] and then began to wonder how the meaning of the common word "gold" could be accounted for in this way. And it is not that philosophers had never considered such examples: Locke, for example, uses this word as an example and is not troubled by the idea that its meaning is a necessary and sufficient condition!

If there is a reason for both learned and lay opinion having gone so far astray with respect to a topic which deals, after all, with matters which are in everyone's experience, matters concerning which we all have more data than we know what to do with, matters concerning which we have, if we shed preconceptions, pretty clear intuitions, it must be connected to the fact that the grotesquely mistaken views of language which are and always have been current reflect two specific and very central philosophical tendencies: the tendency to treat cognition as a purely *individual* matter and the tendency to ignore the *world*, insofar as it consists of more than the individual's "observations." Ignoring the division of linguistic labor is ignoring the social dimension of cognition; ignoring what we have called the *indexicality* of most words is ignoring the contribution of the environment. Traditional philosophy of language, like much traditional philosophy, leaves out other people and the world; a better philosophy and a better science of language must encompass both.

ENDNOTES

1. First published in K. Gunderson, ed., (1975).
2. The contributors to this area are now too numerous to be listed; the pioneers were, of course, Zellig Harris and Noam Chomsky.
3. For a discussion of this question, see Putnam (1967) and Noam Chomsky (1971), especially chapter 1.
4. This is discussed by Ziff (1972), especially chapter VIII.
5. This tradition grew up because *the* term whose analysis provoked all the discussion in medieval philosophy was the term "God," and the term "God" was thought to be defined through the conjunction of the terms "Good," "Powerful," "Omniscient," etc.—the so-called "Perfections." There was a problem, however, because God was supposed to be a Unity, and Unity was thought to exclude His essence being complex in *any* way—i.e., "God" was defined through a conjunction of terms, but God (without quotes) could not be the logical product of properties, nor could He be the unique thing exemplifying the logical product of two or more *distinct* properties, because even this highly abstract kind of "complexity" was held to be incompatible with His perfection of Unity. This is a theological paradox with which Jewish, Arabic, and Christian theologians wrestled for centuries (e.g., the doctrine of the Negation of Privation in Maimonides and Aquinas). It is amusing that theories of contemporary interest, such as conceptualism and nominalism, were first proposed as solutions to the problem of predication in the case of God. It is also amusing that the favorite model of definition in all of this theology—the conjunction-of-properties model—should survive, at least through its consequences, in philosophy of language until the present day.
6. Rather, they will report: "On Twin Earth (*the Twin Earthian name for Terra*—H. P.), the word 'water' means H_2O."
7. The substance of this section was presented at a series of lectures I gave at the

University of Washington (Summer Institute in Philosophy) in 1968, and at a lecture at the University of Minnesota.

8. This assumption is not actually needed in what follows. What *is* needed is that the same *natural kind* can exist in more than one possible world.

9. These points were made in my 1968 lectures at the University of Washington and the University of Minnesota.

10. For an illuminating discussion of just these points, see R. Boyd's *Realism and Scientific Epistemology* (unpublished: Xerox draft circulated by the author, Cornell Department of Philosophy).

11. The idea of a "one-criterion" word, and a theory of analyticity based on this notion, appears in Putnam [(1975a), chapter 2].

12. This example comes from an analysis by Anthony Kroch (in his M.I.T. doctoral dissertation, 1974, Department of Linguistics).

13. I *don't* have in mind the Flewish notion of "paradigm" in which any paradigm of a *K* is *necessarily* a *K* (in reality).

14. The term is due to Quine (in *Word and Object*): it signifies translation without clues either from shared culture or cognates.

15. For a discussion of the supposed impossibility of uniquely correct radical translation see Putnam (1975a), chapter 9.

16. This is argued in Putnam (1975a), chapter 8.

Part II
Natural Kinds and Philosophy of Language

Introduction

ONE OF THE CENTRAL LINES of argument in Putnam's "The Meaning of 'Meaning' " concerns a bundle of doctrines in the philosophy of language; the most important of these have to do with the meaning and reference of a certain class of referring terms. (Just how large this class is, is a matter of debate; see below.) Putnam's explicit target is the Fregean account of these terms. But as the result of his critique of the Fregean view, Putnam's article has also contributed to contemporary discussions about necessary truth: if his anti-Fregean account is correct, there are necessary truths (in particular about natural kinds) that are not analytic truths. Putnamiam issues in the philosophy of natural kinds and the philosophy of language, then, are the main focus of Part II.

We should begin with the Fregean account itself, the target of Putnam's Twin Earth reflections. There are two components of this view: one, a thesis about the meaning of these referring expressions; the other, a thesis about the relation between the meaning and the reference (or extension class) of these expressions. The first Fregean thesis is that the meaning of any term or expression consists of the *concepts*, or beliefs, that the relevant speaker(s) associate with it.[1] The second Fregean thesis is that the meaning of a referring expression *determines* or *fixes* its reference (extension class). Together these two claims imply that a referring expression refers to all and only those objects that fall under the concepts which the relevant speaker(s) associate(s) with the expression. It is for this reason that Frege's theory is often called a *description theory of reference*: the associated concepts constitute a description, and all and only the objects that satisfy this description make up the extension class of the expression.

Putnam's Twin Earth example is supposed to show that both claims in Frege's description theory of reference are false. Putnam actually gives two independent examples that are supposed to make this point. In each, Putnam holds the speakers'

53

beliefs (concepts) constant, while a relevant difference in their environments makes for a difference in the extension of their referring expression. One involves a difference in the chemical microstructure of what are macroscopically indistinguishable substances; the other involves a difference in the community's usage of terms. In both cases the upshot is supposed to be that the reference of the expressions cannot be a function of the speakers' concepts or beliefs; and, on the basis of pretheoretical intuitions about meaning, Putnam suggests that this should convince us to abandon the identification of meaning with associated concepts (beliefs).

In the former case we have the familiar Twin Earth scenario. The point of the story is to contrast the extension of the term "water" on each planet, even though *Doppelgängers* share identical associated beliefs. That is, when the Earthling says, "That's water," pointing at the wet stuff on Earth, the extension of her term "water" is H_2O; when the Twin Earthling says, "That's water," pointing at the wet stuff on Twin Earth, the extension of *her* term "water" is XYZ. And if we imagine this story taking place before it was known that (Earthly) water is H_2O, then there would be no *concepts* possessed by anyone that would pick out Earth water but not Twin Earth water. Hence, there is a difference in extension despite identical associated beliefs (or concepts).

In Putnam's second case against the Fregean account we are to imagine two worlds different only in: (i) the frequency of two particular metals, aluminum and molybdenum; and (ii) the usage of two (technical) terms "aluminum" and "molybdenum." On Earth "aluminum" is used to refer to aluminum, a metal that is relatively common here; on Twin Earth "aluminum" is used to refer to a metal that is relatively common *there*, but that happens to be molybdenum. Again, it is assumed that laypersons cannot tell the difference between the two metals. As a result of this, people on Earth have the same attitudes towards aluminum as people on Twin Earth have towards molybdenum.

Next, Putnam introduces his division-of-linguistic-labor hypothesis: the term "aluminum" as used by the Earthly layperson refers to aluminum, and as used by the Twin Earthly layperson refers to molybdenum, although neither speaker has concepts that enable her to distinguish between the two metals, because each defers to—and so inherits the reference from—the experts, who *can* so distinguish them. Once again, we have a term ("aluminum") whose extension differs on Earth and Twin Earth, despite identical associated concepts (in the mind of the layperson).

One final feature of Putnam's examples is worth underlining with regard to the selections below. This is his positive account of the reference of these natural-kind terms. In his view, these terms involve a hidden indexical element: "water" refers to whatever stuff has the same chemical microstructure—whatever it happens to be—as *this wet stuff* here on Earth. So the reference of a natural kind term is fixed by an *ostensive indication* of a paradigm instance (as in, "That stuff there is water"). An implication of this account is that there is a class of truths that are necessary without being analytic.[2] This is the class of sentences that express the relevant identifications: "water is H_2O," etc. Their necessity derives from *the way in which the terms get their reference*—so long as the chemical microstructure of the stuff ostensively indicated as water is H_2O, water *could not be anything but* H_2O. At the same time, this necessity does not depend on the meaning, understood here as the speaker's associated beliefs, of the term itself; water would be H_2O no matter what beliefs the lay speaker may have.

The articles that follow, like the responses that Putnam's article has elicited in philosophy of language discussions, can be separated into two main groups, according to the focus of the discussion. In one group are those that, provisionally accepting Putnam's account, attempt to discern the class of referring terms for which his account is adequate. In the other are those that try to decide the question whether Putnam has indeed succeeded in showing that the Fregean and other accounts of reference fail.

The only example from the first group included in this section is Stephen Schwartz's "Putnam on Artifacts" (1978).[3] Schwartz argues that while the indexical account of referring expressions serves for natural-kind terms, it will not do for artifact terms, such as "pencil." The problem, he thinks, is that artifact terms are a subclass of what he calls "nominal-kind terms." Such terms are unlike natural kind terms in one crucial respect. Natural-kind terms have an extension class the nature of whose members invites talk of underlying essences that we might fail to know at present; these essences, according to Putnam's theory, are what fix the reference of the terms. In contrast, nominal-kind terms refer, and nominal kinds themselves are identified, strictly on the basis of certain observable properties. In the case of artifacts, they are properties of form and function. But if this is correct, then in such cases the indexical account is unmotivated: nominal kinds do not possess an *underlying* nature at all, and so no underlying nature with which to fix the reference of the terms. Worse yet, the indexical account implies that pencils, for example, could not grow on trees since "pencil" refers to what on Earth are artifacts, and only things like these can be pencils; yet (Schwartz argues) this implication is counterintuitive. He concludes that the indexical account will not do for artifact terms.

All of the other articles included below offer arguments evaluating the success that Putnam's reflections have against the Fregean and other accounts of reference.

Eddy Zemach, in his "Putnam's Theory on the Reference of Substance Terms" (1976), begins the assault on Putnam's view of reference. Zemach's thesis is that as a theory of the reference of substance terms, Putnam's account "is, first of all, unreasonable or incoherent, and, secondly, . . . in any case it presupposes some traditional theory it deems false and attempts to replace." To show this Zemach goes over three ways in which Putnam might try to establish his view of reference and criticizes each.

Zemach begins by quoting Putnam to the effect that the reference of a substance term is determined by the nature of the stuff that speakers from a linguistic community have called by that term. If this is taken to be the central thesis, then

Putnam's claim, that the term "water" has a different extension on Earth and Twin Earth, is in trouble. Presumably some speakers of English would call the Twin Earth liquid "water" even after they found out about its different chemical microstructure. One way to undercut this possibility, Zemach writes, would be for Putnam to say that in such a use "water" would no longer be a natural-kind term. This move is objectionable, Zemach says, because it would transform Putnam's thesis into an *a priori* claim about what it is for a term to be a natural-kind term. On such a reading the only question that remains is whether we actually do, and whether we ought to, use these terms in this way. Zemach responds to both in the negative.

A second argument is directed against an alternative reading of Putnam's thesis. In this reading, the reference of a substance term is fixed by the original ostensive indication, so that "water" refers to whatever has the same nature as the original sample indicated when "water" was first introduced. This reading avoids the earlier problem, but it runs up against the objection that no one knows what the objects were like at this original baptism. Indeed, Zemach writes, with this reading it is possible that what we call "water" is not water at all—a most unpalatable conclusion.

Zemach also challenges the inference from the division-of-linguistic-labor hypothesis to Putnam's view of reference. Zemach argues that the hypothesis itself does not entail, nor does it give us a compelling reason to accept, this theory of reference. On the contrary, this hypothesis can be accepted by people who oppose Putnam's views about reference: theorists who hold (for example) that the reference of a term depends on the concepts that the speaker associates with it, or on the use that the speaker makes of it, etc. But if this is the case, Zemach concludes, then there can be no straightforward inference from the division-of-linguistic-labor hypothesis to Putnam's view of reference.

In "Natural Kinds" (1977), D. H. Mellor continues the Fregean response to Putnam. In the first instance Mellor is interested in showing that, contrary to what Putnam holds, the Twin Earth reflections offer no convincing argument for the doctrine of essentialism about natural kinds.[4] But one of Mellor's counter-arguments to the alleged case for essentialism is to show that the Fregean account of natural-kind terms is better than Putnam's rival account. Here the issue, whether there are necessary truths about natural kinds that do not derive from analyticities, is made to turn on the question which account of natural-kind terms is superior. Mellor's claim is that the Fregean account is superior, so the Twin Earth examples provide us with no reason to think that there are such truths.

Mellor's counterargument has two stages. In the first Mellor defends the Fregean account of natural-kind terms against Putnam's arguments in a way that is similar to Zemach's case against Putnam. What is new is the second stage of Mellor's argument, in which he tries to establish the superiority of the newly resuscitated Fregean account of natural-kind terms. The problem with Putnam's account, he argues, is that it requires that there be a paradigm example that, when indicated ostensively, fixes the reference of the natural-kind term. To Mellor this is objectionable, first, because our use of kind terms does not depend on making such ostensive indication; and second, because even where ostensive indication is used, objects are designated to exemplify certain types in virtue of the fact that the objects satisfy certain theoretical beliefs about such objects. Thus, Mellor concludes, the Fregean account predicts our actual use of these terms better than Putnam's account does.

The most hard core of the neo-Fregeans, however, is John Searle, as represented in the selection from his book *Intentionality* (1983). This selection is part of his larger project to develop and defend a neo-Fregean account of meaning and reference. In the chapter from which a part is reprinted here, Searle seeks to repudiate Putnam's slogan that "'meanings' just ain't in the head!"

Searle's strategy is to reinterpret the Twin Earth examples in such a way that one need neither abandon the Fregean account of meaning nor accept the view that meanings are not in the head. The novelty of his position—Searle responds to the division-of-labor example as both Zemach and Mellor do—lies in his claim that *even if* we accept Putnam's claim that the extension of a natural-kind term is determined indexically, neither Putnam's theory of reference nor his conclusion that meanings are not in the head follows. All that follows is that the meaning of these terms will itself contain the indexical element. However, this implies both that meanings "ain't in the head" *only if* indexical beliefs are not in the head, and that meaning does not determine extension *only if* indexical contents do not determine extension. To resist both of these implications, Searle offers his own (Fregean) account of how indexical contents determine extension; they do so, in this view, self-referentially. (For a more detailed account of this self-referentiality, see chapter 2 of Searle's book.) Searle concludes that all Putnam has done is "to offer us an alternative Intentionalistic account, based on indexical presentations, of the meanings of a certain class of general terms."

A response to Zemach and Mellor, and a defense of a view that is developed out of Putnam's account of natural-kind terms, is found in Kim Sterelny's "Natural Kind Terms" (1983). He begins by challenging the claim that "water" refers to both H_2O and XYZ; in Sterelny's view, this claim is too costly to accept. Sterelny also criticizes their response to the division of labor case as relying on a notion of reference-borrowing from the expert, a notion for which (he writes) there is no Fregean account.

Next, Sterelny develops his own version of a "causal theory" of natural-kind terms. He focuses his attention on the task of characterizing the *grounding* of natural-kind terms, i.e., of giving an account of the direct link between the terms themselves and examples of the natural kind they denote. Following Putnam's lead regarding the nature of this grounding, Sterelny writes that natural-kind terms themselves are introduced into the language by "ostensive contact with samples of the kind," and that the extension of the term is then "the class of all objects that bear the relation 'same kind as' to the ostensively given samples." He then modifies this account to meet the various criticisms that have been made against Putnam's original formulation.

Foremost among these criticisms is Mellor's objection that some kind terms are introduced in the absence of samples. Sterelny responds by conceding that descriptions have a role to play in the grounding of some natural-kind terms. However, this is not an outright concession to the Fregean because the role they play is fundamentally referential rather than attributive (in Donnellan's sense). At bottom, the description-object link is itself grounded in the perceptual link between the description's user and the object to which the user is perceptually linked; this link holds regardless of whether the description is true of the object at the end of the link. In cases not involving any samples, Sterelny allows that the descriptions are initially attributive; however, once the term is introduced, and the effects and interactions of the kind it names are traced, causal grounding of the term proceeds as above. This is crucial, according to Sterelny, since "it is in virtue of such causal groundings that we are able to regard superseded theories as partly true, and their special vocabulary non-empty."

A second criticism to which Sterelny responds is "the qua problem." A given sample s is of indefinitely many kinds: a particular cat is a sample of the kind *cat*, but also of *mammal, animal, pet, physical object*, etc. So when it is said that a natural-kind term is grounded by ostensively indicating an object, in virtue of what is the extension of the term fixed? (How is this range of exemplified kinds restricted to the right one?) Sterelny's response is to say that the kind that an ostensively indicated object is meant to exemplify is determined by the speaker's knowledge of the object's causal powers; hence, the concession that the grounding of a term "will typically involve a cluster of beliefs."

One final criticism Sterelny treats is the objection that causal theories cannot allow for referential failure or reference change. Sterelny responds to the charge of not allowing for reference failure by appealing to his concession that grounding involves clusters of beliefs about an item's causal powers. If a natural-kind term is associated with a host of false causal beliefs—"witch" is a good example of such a term—then even though it is introduced ostensively it will fail to refer. And to the charge of not allowing for reference change, he suggests the causal theorist need only acknowledge that names are multiply grounded.

So modified, Sterelny's causal theory of natural-kind terms is (he claims) superior to previous causal theories. Its main strengths include those of traditional causal theories—their account of the semantics of simple expressions, their account of theory change and meaning change, their allowing people to refer to a kind without knowing necessary and sufficient conditions for being of that kind—yet avoids some of the drawbacks of the traditional accounts. He ends the article by wondering whether the account can be extended to the special sciences; Sterelny concludes that while it cannot it is no worse off in this respect than its rivals.

ENDNOTES

1. There is room for Fregeans to differ over who the relevant speaker(s) is (are): there is debate whether the relevant person is the speaker using the term, the experts, or some suitably high percentage of all competent native speakers, etc. In their respective contributions to this volume, Zemach and Mellor, both critical of Putnam's theory of reference, appear to exploit expert beliefs. But they leave unchallenged the idea that such an appeal implies that the individual's concepts alone don't fix the reference of the term. Searle, in his contribution, follows them in appealing to expert beliefs but challenges the idea that this appeal implies that the speaker's concepts don't suffice. Sterelny criticizes the very idea that an appeal to expert beliefs can be part of a Fregean theory of reference. (See below.)
2. Kripke (1972) offers an account of the reference of proper names that have the same implication.
3. See, however, the Burge selections from the next section: Burge *extends* Twin Earth-style considerations to cover not only natural-kind terms, but also artifact terms, color adjectives, social-role terms, abstract nouns, action verbs, legal terms, etc.
4. Essentialism is the thesis that what makes something a natural kind x is that it has a certain underlying essence, or set of properties that science discovers. Possession of these properties is thus said to be a necessary and sufficient condition for being of kind x.

2

Putnam's Theory on the Reference of Substance Terms

Eddy Zemach

THE THEORY THAT I SHALL here call "the historico-scientific theory of reference" was originally suggested by Saul Kripke as an account of the reference of rigid designators [which include, according to Kripke (1972), both proper names and names of substances]. Recently there have been several attempts to further develop this theory: Keith Donellan (1974) has done so with respect to proper names, and Hilary Putnam did it with respect to names of substances [Putnam (1973); all parenthetical page references in this paper are to that article]. In the present article I shall try to examine Putnam's theory. I shall try to prove that it is, first of all, unreasonable or incoherent, and, secondly, that in any case it presupposes some traditional theory it deems false and attempts to replace.

I

Putnam's thesis is basically this. Traditionally, he says, the "theory of meaning came to rest on two unchallenged assumptions: (1) That knowing the meaning of a term is just a matter of being in a certain psychological state . . . (2) That the meaning of a term determines its extension" (700). Putnam claims that these two assumptions cannot be jointly satisfied and that in order to have an adequate theory of reference one must give up either assumption (1) or assumption (2). [Putnam's own preference is to renounce (1) and retain (2).] On the alternative theory of reference he offers, something is, e.g., water, if it has the same *nature* as the entity called "water" by members of the linguistic community that uses the term "water," *regardless* of whether they know *what* the nature of water is, and *regardless* of *what* concepts they associate with the term "water." Thus, reference is determined by: (1) identifying the substance referred to by users of the substance-term in question; and then by (2) discovering the nature of said substance. For example, if the term "N" is used in a linguistic community S to refer to N's and if (because N's are believed by members of S to be essentially similar to O's, and not to P's, although the reverse is actually the case) "N" is later applied to O's and not to P's, then, regardless of the concepts members of S associate with "N" and regardless of what they wish to mean by "N," they are wrong: P's and N, and O's are not N.

Putnam presents several test cases which are intended to show the plausibility of his view and the untenability of rival accounts. All these cases involve, more or less, the same kind of story (in the following I have condensed the story somewhat, but the relevant details are unchanged). Suppose that, on the planet Twin Earth, which is almost exactly similar to Earth, the colorless, tasteless, liquid that fills the lakes and oceans, comes down in rain, etc., is not composed of H_2O molecules but of XYZ molecules. Suppose, further, that Twin Earthians use the term "water" to refer to the said substance [let us call it "water (TE)"]. Now suppose that the Twin Earthians do not know that the chemical structure of water (TE) is XYZ, and Earthmen do not know that the structure of water is H_2O. Say, the time is 1750 and chemistry yet undeveloped. Thus an Earthman and his identical twin on Twin Earth can be in the same psychological state (have the same concepts, beliefs, etc.) with respect to the word "water" and its extension. Yet, Putnam says, the extension of "water" as used by Earthmen is water, i.e., H_2O, and the extension of "water" as used by Twin Earthians is water (TE), i.e., XYZ. Thus, we have a dilemma. We can say that since the Earthman and his Twin Earthian counterpart are in the same psychological state, the word "water" they use has the same meaning for both, but two different extensions: "water" on Earth denotes H_2O, and "water" on Twin Earth denotes XYZ; hence, reference is independent of meaning. The other possibility is to maintain that difference in extension lies difference in meaning, and hence "water" on Earth and "water" on Twin Earth do not have the same meaning, although their users are in exactly the same psychological state. Rather, on this option, what a term means is determined by the nature of the substance in question, and that nature, known to the scientists, need not be known to all or even to most of the users of the term "water." To conclude: either meaning is independent of reference or else knowing a meaning is not being in a certain psychological state. Q.E.D.

To begin the examination of Putnam's view, let us ask, first of all, whether he is right in assuming that "water" on Earth and "water" on Twin Earth have different extensions. Putnam says that

> . . . in the sense in which it is used on Twin Earth . . . what *we* call "water" simply isn't water, while in the sense in which it is used on Earth . . . what the Twin Earthians call "water" simply isn't water (701).

But is this true? We remember that, according to Putnam, in order to determine whether something is water or not, we should find out whether it has the same nature as "most of the stuff I and other speakers in my linguistic community have, on other occasions, called 'water'" (702). But who are the members of this linguistic community? Whom does it include? Does it include all speakers of English? If so, it includes the Twin Earthians who, by hypothesis, are speakers of English. Since (again, by hypothesis) water (TE) is no less abundant than water, it follows that most of the stuff I and other speakers of English call "water" is neither

H_2O nor XYZ but (H_2O v XYZ). Therefore, the extension of "water" as used on Earth and on Twin Earth is identical.

To undercut this argument, Putnam would obviously like to exclude Twin Earthians from the community the linguistic habits of which single out *which* stuff is to be examined by the scientist in order to determine what water is. For the argument's sake, I shall assume that Putnam can find a way of doing this without begging the question (which he would do if he were to say, "The Twin Earthians do not speak my language because they call 'water' something which isn't water.") In fact I do not see how Putnam can exclude the Twin Earthians from his linguistic community without also excluding Australians, South Africans, and, in the final account, everyone except Hilary Putnam himself. But let this pass. Let us assume that Putnam does succeed and the Twin Earthians are somehow excluded from the linguistic community in question. Still the problem is not solved since Earthmen, too, may call the substance in the seas, lakes, etc., of Twin Earth by the name "water." They will certainly do so before they become chemically sophisticated and discover that Earth water has a different molecular structure from that of Twin Earth water, and they might continue to do so even after having made this discovery. That is, they may say that what has been discovered is that some water is made out of H_2O molecules and some water is made out of XYZ molecules, but both are equally water. After all, this is exactly what we say of so many other materials: paper may have widely different chemical structures, and so may sand, and cloth, and stone, and hair, and glue, and . . . Chemical constitution is not always decisive in determining our usage of substance names.

A defender of Putnam may protest and say, "Yes, *ordinary* speakers of English may go on to call the stuff on Twin Earth by the name 'water,' but Putnam's point is precisely that they would be *wrong*; it is experts, i.e., scientists, and not standard speakers who determine the reference of a substance-term." But this argument is, obviously, based on a gross misunderstanding of Putnam's position. At the stage we are dealing with one *cannot*, as yet, invoke the scientist's verdict, because, in Putnam's view, we must first of all single out the stuff that is to be examined by the scientist; and *which* stuff it is, is determined not by the scientist but by what "I and other speakers in my linguistic community have, on other occasions, called" by that substance-word. If, however, the way we actually use substance-words is not determined by chemical considerations, then the stuff called by a given English substance-word can be said either not to have any common nature, or else to have a "disjunctive" nature. Thus, the nature of the stuff called "water" may turn out to be precisely H_2O v XYZ.

As a matter of fact, "water" *is* used in this way. Consider the case of heavy water. Nothing that is composed of D_2O molecules is composed of H_2O molecules, yet (Saul Kripke to the contrary) heavy water is commonly regarded as a kind of water. The same holds for aggregates of T_2O, HDO, HTO, and DTO molecules (the number of varieties is eighteen, since in each case the oxygen can be either O^{16}, or O^{17}, or O^{18}). All these, we say, are different kinds of water. Moreover, there is no chemical constitution common to all bodies of ordinary water; different samples differ chemically. Ordinary water normally contains some D_2O, some H_2O_2, some H_2O_3, a large amount of sodium chloride, and various minerals. Hard water, soft water, mineral water, salt water and distilled water are all different chemicals. To which of these has this glass of liquid to bear the relation *Same Liquid* in order to qualify as a glass of water? But if English speakers have the right to call all these liquids "water," they may also add aggregates of XYZ molecules to this list, and Putnam will have to accept this classification as an uncontestable datum.

One may wish to answer that D_2O, for example, is said to be chemically similar to H_2O, whereas Putnam has stipulated that XYZ is essentially dissimilar to H_2O. This, indeed, is true. One must remember, however, that (if linguistic usage is what singles out the reference of "water") it is a historical fact that "water" was regularly used to refer to a great variety of chemically dissimilar liquids, among which are tears, urine, sweat, saliva, solutions of ammonia and camphor, etc. There is hardly any single "nature" that is common to all of these.

How would Putnam respond to these charges? He would not, I think, deny that people may wish to apply the term "water" both to aggregates of H_2O and to aggregates of XYZ molecules. He may even admit that, as used by some people, "water" refers not only to collections of H_2O molecules but to other substances as well. What he would, perhaps, say is that, in the dialect of people who use "water" in this way, the term "water" is not a name of a natural kind. It is like "air" (very different combinations of gases can be called "air"), "oil," "dust," "dirt," "glass," "plastic" or even "red stuff." If this is the way "water" is used, then there simply *is* no substance called "water." If, however, "water" is meant to be a substance-name, we must stipulate that it refers to a natural kind, e.g., to collections of H_2O molecules only (including, perhaps, some other *essentially similar* liquids).

Yet, if this ploy is adopted, Putnam's thesis must undergo a very serious meta-morphosis. It will no longer be a claim about the reference of some ordinary English terms, such as "elm," "water," "gold" or "aluminum." Instead, it will become an *a priori* claim about what is it for x to be a natural-kind term, whether or not there are any such terms in English. The claim is clearly *a priori* since no fact about the use of any term can falsify it. Any counterevidence about the actual use of a certain substance-term will prove only that the term in question is not really a substance-term. The question is no longer whether English substance-terms refer in the way Putnam alleges they do, since it is now stipulated that nothing is a substance-term unless it refers in this way. The only serious questions that remain are, whether we do, and whether it is desirable that we should, employ in our language substance-terms whose reference is stipulated in the way suggested above.

The answer, I believe, is negative, on both questions: we neither do nor is it desirable that we should use such substance-terms. Science is characterized by radical changes in what is considered to be the essence of objects and, hence, in the ways of classifying them. Stuffs and objects that looked alike on the molar level have turned out to differ widely on the molecular (or the atomic, or the subatomic) level. Putnam's story itself can serve as an example. In the course of scientific progress, Putnam tells us, we have discovered that, molar properties notwithstanding, water (TE) is essentially different from Earth water. Is it so unreasonable to expect, then, that with further developments in science we may discover that on a more fundamental level some H_2O molecules are essentially different from other H_2O molecules? It may even be the case that, in the new classification, one kind of H_2O molecule will turn out to be essentially closer to the XYZ molecule than to some other kind of the H_2O molecule. What, then, will the reference of "water" be? If Putnam's recommendations on the reference of substance-terms are adopted we may have to reach the conclusion that there are no substance-terms in English at all.

This argument is not overdramatized. Consider all the substance-terms taken by the science of some period or other to be names of natural kinds. Of the four natural kinds of Greek science—Fire, Air, Earth, and Water—only the last perhaps is still considered to be a natural kind. It would certainly be too rash to guarantee it or any other currently fashionable candidate (or any of Putnam's other candidates for natural kindness: aluminum, molybdenum, birch, elm, gold) eternal life as natural kind. Coal and diamond, on the other hand, were discovered to be chemically similar (members of the same natural kind?), yet no new substance-term was coined in English to refer to these and their kin.

To prevent a misunderstanding let me hasten add that the above argument is perfectly compatible with Kripke's thesis that a statement may be necessary *de re* and epistemically *a posteriori*. I agree that it is logically possible that contemporary physics is, after all, ultimate and thus determines cosmic taxonomy. I therefore admit that, if this is so, any bit of matter composed of H_2O molecules is so composed in all possible worlds in which it exists. But this admission helps Putnam not at all, since it is also possible that, in the final account, "water" is not a rigid designator and "red" is. Thus, if there are any substance-terms, we do not know which are they. To summarize: (a) the reference of extant English substance-terms does not correspond to the substance taxonomy of contemporary physics, and (b) even if we redefine some English substance-terms so as to create such correspondence by stipulation, the chance that the current taxonomy is identical with the ultimate one is probably nil. Thus Putnam cannot escape the conclusion that, in all probability, there are no substance-terms in English. As a thesis about the semantics of natural language, this is patently absurd.

II

So far, I have considered Putnam's thesis under one interpretation, the interpretation that seemed to me most faithful to his actual words. There is, however, another interpretation of the same thesis which, if adopted, can avoid all the objections I have previously raised against it. In the beginning of this paper I have called Putnam's theory a "historico-scientific theory of reference," but hitherto I have said very little about the *historical* element in it. This omission was not accidental: it is difficult to know what weight Putnam does place on this, the more

Kripkean, element of his theory. At any rate, it is clear that if he *were* to stress the historical element and use it, e.g., in the way that Kripke uses the historical chain in determining the reference of proper names, all my previous objections would dissipate. I have argued that *if* the substance whose nature is to determine the reference of the substance-term is to be singled out through the linguistic practices of a community of speakers, it is almost certain that no such common nature can be discovered, and what is discovered is something Putnam does not want. But one need not say that the substance to be examined by the scientist is singled out in this way. Instead, one may say that water is everything that has the same nature as the substance that was originally called "water." Under this interpretation, Putnam's theory is this: at some historical point in the development of English some *x* was indexically ostended, or otherwise identified, and referred to as "water." That *x*, and every *y* that has the same nature as that *x*, is water— regardless of what the original, or any subsequent, speaker believed about that nature, regardless of what *y*'s are believed to share this nature with *x*, and hence regardless of the way standard speakers apply the term "water." It is possible that most speakers misapply the term if they have mistaken beliefs about the nature of *x*, or about the nature of some *y*s.

It is clear that all my previous objections are powerless against this "historical" version of Putnam's theory of reference. But the obvious difficulty of this version— indeed, its complete futility—lies in the fact that no one knows, nor can even hope to know, on what occasions and with respect to what objects our ordinary English substance-terms were first uttered. We do not even know whether the substance that was originally referred to as "water" *was* indeed water (i.e., was the substance we call "water"). According to this version of Putnam's theory, it is possible that we, all of us, are utterly mistaken, and what we call "water" is simply not water. It is possible that only, say, spittle, or milk, is water, and nothing else is. I have heard some followers of Putnam answer that this objection is irrelevant because it is based upon epistemological considerations that need not concern a semanticist. But it seems to me that this answer is totally unacceptable. Any theory which has as a result that we do not and cannot know what is the correct reference of the word "water," or any other English substance-term, cannot be right.

An adherent of this version of the historico-scientific theory of reference may retort again that it is *possible* that the historical chain (leading back from our use of "water" to the first referential use of this word) terminates in a token referring to a body of water. Since it is also possible for us to believe that this is the case, we may have a *true belief* that the substance in our lakes and seas is water. But this is not nearly enough, as a simple *Gedankenexperiment* can prove. Suppose we discover that "water" was originally used by the Saxons to refer to urine only. Later on, because of their mistaken beliefs about chemistry, they have extended the use of this term until it reached its present employment. Would we then recant and say that there is no water in the sea? I am sure we would not. It is not only logically possible, but conceptually necessary, that our prime example of water is water. Any theory that contests this fact must be false.

The same argument can be developed from another angle. Suppose that we have fortunately preserved this original body of liquid termed "water." Let us suppose ourselves even more fortunate and assume that, upon investigation, our scientists declare that ordinary water does bear the relation $same_L$ to it. Could we, under these conditions, adopt Putnam's view on reference? I believe we could not. As Putnam himself correctly notes, "the relation $same_L$ is a *theoretical* relation: whether something is or is not the same liquid as *this* may take an indeterminate amount of scientific investigation to determine" (702). Scientific investigation is fallible, and gives us good approximations rather than absolute truths. Therefore, it is *logically possible* that at some future time we shall reverse our verdict and declare the original sample not to bear $same_L$ to any of our prime examples of water. But then, I believe, no amount of scientific investigation can *possibly* have the result that the stuff we call "water" is not water. What we would say, under these circumstances, is rather that the liquid originally called "water" has just been discovered not to be water at all.

III

Let me turn now to another component of Putnam's theory, i.e., to his views about the Division of Linguistic Labor (henceforth, DLL). Putnam argues, very plausibly, that it is not the case that everyone who uses some substance-term, e.g., "gold," should "be able to tell with any reliability whether or not something is gold" (705). Only few, the experts, need have the skill to tell gold from other substances that superficially resemble gold. Furthermore, the use of the term "gold" "by other speakers depends upon a structured cooperation between them and the experts" (706). This thesis, as interpreted by Putnam, seems to challenge both the Wittgensteinian view on reference (because now it seems that if x is not an expert on gold then the extension of "gold" in his idiolect is not determined by *his use* of the term "gold") and the mentalistic view on reference (because it now seems that if x is not an expert on gold then the extension of "gold" in his idiolect is not determined by *his concept*, or his grasp of the meaning, of the term "gold"). Putnam, therefore, appears to have another powerful argument for his view that either (a) what x refers to by a certain substance-word is independent of what he means by this word; *or else* (b) what x means by a certain word is independent of his psychological states.

Now what I would like to question is not the Hypothesis of the Division of Linguistic Labor (HDLL) itself—I believe it is a very plausible hypothesis indeed—but the conclusion that its truth lends support to Putnam's view on reference. That is, I claim not that the premise is false, but that the argument in which it is used is invalid. I shall argue that both the Wittgensteinians and the mentalists can adopt HDLL in their theories of reference. It does not support either theory.

Let us assume that HDLL is true. Putnam does not claim, however, that HDLL is true with respect to every term. On the contrary, he insists that "some words do not exhibit any division of linguistic labor: "chair," for example" (705). Again, some words that at one time "did not exhibit it [DLL] at all" may, later on, "begin to exhibit this kind of division of labor" (705). Let me, then, take one of Putnam's own examples: the story of Oscar who is no expert on chemistry and cannot distinguish between aluminum and molybdenum. There are two possibilities now: (1) DLL is applied to "aluminum" in Oscar's idiolect; (2) DLL is not applied to "aluminum" in Oscar's idiolect. How can we find out which is the case? Finding out what the experts refer to by "aluminum" will not help us in this task since here we investigate *Oscar's* idiolect. For all we know, Oscar might be using "aluminum" to refer to a geranium! Now the mentalist would say that in order to know what "aluminum" refers to in Oscar's idiolect, we must inspect Oscar's *concept* of aluminum and see, e.g., whether he *intends* "aluminum" to mean whatever the experts mean by this term. Only by examining Oscar's intentions (the mentalist would say) can we know whether he wishes to defer to any experts in applying "aluminum" and, if so, to which experts (chemists? botanists?) he intends to defer. The Wittgensteinian would say the same thing about Oscar's behavior: in order to find out what "aluminum" refers to in Oscar's idiolect we must inspect his *use* of "aluminum"; only thus can we know whether he wishes to use this term in the way the experts use it, whether he intends to defer to any experts in applying "aluminum," and to which experts he intends to defer. So far, then, HDLL does not seem to challenge the traditional views on reference in any way: on the contrary, it seems to presuppose one or the other of them.

Let us go, then, to the second stage. Suppose that, by using one of the above methods, we have found out whether "aluminum" in Oscar's idiolect does or does not exemplify DLL. Assume, first of all, that the answer is negative: DLL is not applied to "aluminum" in Oscar's idiolect. Since, by hypothesis, Oscar cannot distinguish between aluminum and molybdenum, it follows that the extension of "aluminum" in his idiolect is: aluminum *or* molybdenum. Putnam asked us to imagine another Oscar, $Oscar_2$, who lives on Twin Earth, where molybdenum is found in exactly those places where, on Earth, aluminum is found, and vice versa. This $Oscar_2$, being $Oscar_1$'s counterpart, is as ignorant is our Oscar, and so, like him, he does not apply DLL to "aluminum" in his idiolect. But then Putnam is just wrong when he claims, "we have to say that 'aluminum' has the extension *aluminum* in the idiolect of $Oscar_1$, and the extension *molybdenum* in the idiolect of $Oscar_2$. . . . Also we have to say that $Oscar_1$ and $Oscar_2$ mean different things by 'aluminum'" (703). Surely we have to say no such thing. We have to say so only if both $Oscar_1$ and $Oscar_2$ apply DLL to "aluminum" in their respective idiolects. If they do not (as Putnam must admit to be possible) then "aluminum" has the *same* extension in both idiolects, i.e., the class of everything that is either aluminum or molybdenum.

Let us then make a third step and assume that the Oscars do apply DLL to "aluminum." That is, although they cannot tell aluminum from molybdenum, they are willing to apply the term "aluminum" to all substances that the experts call "aluminum" and to these only. Can we now say that, at least in this case, the psychological states of the Oscars with respect to "aluminum" do not fix the extension of this term? Certainly not. The mentalist would say that it is precisely the psychological state that determines the meaning of "aluminum"; it is the *belief* of each Oscar that what "aluminum" means is what the scientists take it to mean. Thus, HDLL again fails to challenge the mentalist's contention that "meanings are in the head." The Wittgensteinian will, of course, make an exactly parallel move with respect to the *use* of the term "aluminum" by the two Oscars.

Finally, let us grant Putnam's last assumption, too, and accept, without further ado, his test case exactly as he presents it. Again, Oscar$_1$ is the Earthman, Oscar$_2$ is his Twin Earthian counterpart. "Aluminum" in Earth languages denotes aluminum; "aluminum" in Twin Earth languages denotes molybdenum. Oscar$_1$'s conception of the meaning of the Earthian word "aluminum" is the same as Oscar$_2$'s conception of the Twin Earthian word "aluminum" (that is, neither can distinguish between aluminum and molybdenum). Now add the final premise, and assume that both Oscars apply DLL to "aluminum." Can Putnam *now* draw the coveted conclusion, namely that, although both Oscars are in the same psychological state with respect to "aluminum," the term "aluminum" in their respective idiolects has different extensions? The answer is, No. The logical howler is buried in the glib expression, "both Oscars apply DLL to 'aluminum'." This gives the impression that both Oscars do the same thing with respect to "aluminum"; but this is a mistake. Oscar$_1$ applies DLL because he believes that aluminum is the stuff that *Earth* scientists call "aluminum," but Oscar$_2$ applies DLL because he believes that aluminum is the stuff that *Twin Earth* scientists call "aluminum." Thus, the two Oscars have widely different beliefs about "aluminum." We would not say, e.g., that two persons have the same beliefs about "democracy" if one of them believes that the reference of this term is determined by the Communist Party while the other believes that Senator Goldwater is the expert on its reference. The Oscars, therefore, are *not* in the same psychological state with respect to "aluminum." Nor do they behave in the same way with respect to it. Although both defer to scientists in applying "aluminum," it is to different scientists that they defer; and while Earth scientists apply "aluminum" to aluminum, Twin Earth scientists apply "aluminum" to molybdenum. Thus, the extensions of "aluminum" in the idiolects of the two Oscars are indeed distinct, but so are their psychological states and their behavior. Putnam has failed to show that any two people can mean two different things by a certain term although they are in the same psychological state or exhibit the same behavior, with respect to it. He has also failed to show that "the traditional concept of meaning is a concept which rests on a false theory" (700). On the contrary, I have tried to show that the very intelligibility of HDLL rests on some traditional concept of meaning and would have been altogether inconceivable on the historico-scientific theory of reference only.

3

Natural Kinds

D. H. Mellor

1. Some notable philosophers have recently used new arguments to revive essentialism, and have prescribed their essences for a variety of metaphysical fears and ailments. The essence of a self has been said to guarantee its ancestry; mental essence has been promoted as a sure defense against materialism; and diamonds have been warranted in all possible worlds against being paste. I mistrust these prescriptions, especially the claims made for their active ingredients: possible worlds and necessary identity. However, I don't mean here to resist all applications of these notions, nor to dispute all forms of essentialism. I mean only to supply an antidote to the natural-kind essences widely advertised by Professors Kripke (1972, 1972a) and Putnam (1975).

Kripke and Putnam claim that natural kinds have essential properties; that is, properties which nothing can lack and still be of the kind. The kinds involved include the traditional natural kinds: elements and compounds like gold and water, and biological and botanical species like tigers and elm trees. Modern essences, however, come in a wider range. Essential properties are claimed also, for example, for temperatures and lengths.[1] These do not traditionally form natural kinds, but it will be convenient here to stretch the term to match the doctrine.

Properties alleged to be essential typically involve the microstructure of things. Having atomic number 79 is said to be the essential property of gold [Kripke (1972), p. 327]; being H_2O the essential property of water [Putnam (1975), p. 233]. Genetic makeup similarly provides essential properties for animals and plants,[2] and mean molecular kinetic energy for temperature. These essential properties of natural kinds are supplied by the natural sciences: "In general, science attempts, by investigating basic structural traits, to find the nature, and thus the essence (in the philosophical sense), of the kind" [Kripke (1972), p. 330].

The necessity of essential properties is metaphysical, not epistemic. The claim is that things of a kind have its essential properties in all possible worlds, not that its essential properties are knowable *a priori*.[3] In particular it is not supposed to be analytic to ascribe its essential properties to things of a kind. Kinetic theory gives the essence of temperature, not the meaning of "temperature." Essentialism needn't therefore dispute Quinean critiques of the analytic-synthetic distinction on the one hand, nor on the other need it plague theoretical conflict with the problems of incommensurability [Feyerabend (1962); Kuhn (1962)] or indeterminacy of translation [Quine (1960)]:

69

Note that on the present view, scientific discoveries of species' essence do not constitute a "change of meaning" . . . We need not ever assume that the biologist's denial that whales are fish shows his "concept of fishhood" to be different from that of the layman; he simply corrects the layman, discovering that "whales are mammals, not fish" is a necessary truth. Neither "whales are mammals" nor "whales are fish" was supposed to be *a priori* or analytic in any case. [Kripke (1972), p. 330]

So proponents of rival theories are not doomed by essentialism to Kuhn's (1970) and Feyerabend's (1970) dialogue of the deaf. We need not, therefore, continue that prolonged dialogue here.

2. Essentialism about kinds has various sources. It derives partly from the plausibility of examples such as those given above. Some among the properties common to things of a kind undoubtedly matter more than others. In particular, some will be more central than others to a theory which explains the properties and relations of things of that kind. I consider in 7 whether properties being important in that sense is in fact best explained by, and thereby lends support to, the claim that they are essential properties of the kind; and I conclude that it is not.

Individual essences are a classic source of essentialism about kinds. Some kinds may provide criteria for the reidentification of things of that kind, such that no thing of the kind could survive change in the specified respect. It is arguable, for example, that a man could not survive the loss or drastic transformation of the body whose spatio-temporal continuity settles questions of human reidentification. I don't think that is true, but even if it were, it would follow neither that any men, nor that all men, must have bodies of the kind specified. In the first place, John's inability as a man to *become* a beetle is compatible with the possibility of his always having been one; in the second, there *could* still have been *men* (other than the men there actually are) who lacked these bodily features and would be reidentified over time by different criteria. Anyway, arguments from individual essence, if they worked at all, would not work for kinds, such as water and gold, that provide no criteria for the reidentification of things. Perhaps there are characteristics a gold cup cannot come to have, but that will not show that other gold objects cannot have them.

There are, I believe, no sound inferences from individual essences to kind essences; but that point is not new, and I need not argue it further here. My concern here is with two other, newly fashionable, arguments for essentialism about kinds. One, due to Putnam (1975), derives essentialism directly from a theory about how the extension of kind terms is fixed. The other, due to Kripke [(1972), (1972a)], derives it indirectly via a theory of the singular reference of natural kinds and other seemingly general terms, from whose necessary self-identity essentialism is taken to follow:

When we have discovered that heat is molecular motion we've discovered an identification which gives us an essential property of this phenomenon.

We have discovered a phenomenon which in all possible worlds will be molecular motion—which could not have failed to be molecular motion, because that's what the phenomenon is. [Kripke (1972), p. 326]

Putnam's theory of the extension of kind terms, and Kripke's theory of their reference, are alike in denying traditional accounts that make the reference (or extension) of terms a function *inter alia* of something like their Fregean sense.[4] As applied to kinds in particular, the new theories deny that the extension of kind terms is any function of descriptions believed by their users to be true of things of the kind [Putnam (1975), p. 221]. Fregeans, who believe the contrary, need not, of course, deny that there are nonanalytic essences of kinds [Dummett (1973), p. 117], but Fregean theories of how kind terms get their extension give no especial reason to think there are any. Fregean theories in general and description theories of kind terms in particular, yield necessity only as a by-product of analyticity. (Had our Fregean sense of "water" made us apply it only to what we believe "H_2O" applies to, then—at least for us in this world—water would in all possible worlds have been H_2O. But that, as we have seen, is not why essentialists think being H_2O is of the essence of water.)

To provide essence without analyticity, an alternative is needed to the Fregean sense of what water is. Putnam to that end tells two tales designed to bury Frege, as a prelude to recommending his own essentialist account of natural kinds. In fact, Putnam buries Frege alive and well; and that fact must be shown first, before we can profitably turn to the deficiencies of Putnam's and Kripke's rival theories.[5]

3. Putnam's tales are aimed at the idea of a kind term's extension being *any* Fregean function of its users' beliefs. The tales therefore present cases where such an extension differs for two groups of users with relevantly identical beliefs. First, we suppose a Twin Earth somewhere, which is just like Earth except for a different microstructure, XYZ, of what they, too, call "water." Macroscopically XYZ is indistinguishable from H_2O, and it plays just the same part in Twin Earth life that H_2O does here. By 1950, however, it has become common knowledge on each planet that the other lives off different stuff. But back in 1750 no one knew about the microstructure of water, and each planet had identical beliefs about the stuff they so called. Yet "the extension of the term 'water' was just as much H_2O on Earth in 1750 as in 1950; and the extension of the term 'water' was just as much XYZ on Twin Earth in 1750 as in 1950" [Putnam (1975), p. 224]. Now the local stuff was no doubt in the extension of "water" as used on each planet in 1750. If the stuff on the other planet was different in kind, it was presumably not in fact in the term's extension, even though the users then would have mistakenly thought it was. Hence, the anti-Fregean conclusion: "water" can have different extensions in the same world for different users who give it the same Fregean sense.

I agree that "water" had (tenselessly) the same extension in 1750 as it had in 1950; what I deny is that at either time that extension was different on Earth and on Twin Earth. The fact that Twin Earth's 1950 beliefs about local water differed from ours doesn't begin to show that the extension of their term "water" differed from that of ours. It doesn't even follow that the senses of the term differed; and if they did, the whole point of the sense/reference distinction is to allow sameness of reference (or extension) to accompany difference of sense. It is indeed quite plain to my Fregean eye that in 1950, as in 1750, "water" had the same extension on Twin Earth as it had here. There was water on both planets alike, and there still is. We simply discovered that not all water has the same microstructure; why should it? Because its microstructure is an essential property of water? Well, that is what's in question.

Fregeans need not resort to science fiction to recommend their reading of this tale. There is a perfect precedent in the discovery of isotopes. If Zemach's [(1976), p. 120 (reprinted here—ed.)] heavy waters are too rare and exotic to convince, try the two common isotopes of chlorine. Note that in these real cases the various isotopes occur together in natural samples; they aren't segregated onto separate planets. It is therefore undeniable that the extension of "chlorine" included both isotopes before their discovery, and so presumably includes both isotopes now.[6] What Putnam must say is that chlorine and water have been found not to be natural kinds after all, but rather mixtures of natural kinds. But in that case, as Zemach [(1976), p. 122] observes, it will very likely turn out that we have no natural-kind terms. Anyway, the pertinent point is that the first Twin Earth tale doesn't compel that conclusion, which it would have to do to dispose of Frege. The Fregean reading that Putnam overlooks is *prima facie* at least as plausible as his own.

Putnam, however, has another Twin Earth tale that won't admit this Fregean reading. This time we suppose that aluminum and molybdenum are practically indistinguishable, that molybdenum is as common on Twin Earth as aluminum is here, and consequently that on Twin Earth all our Earthly uses of the two metals are interchanged. Moreover, like Americans, Twin Earthians don't call aluminum "aluminum"; they (unlike Americans) call it "molybdenum." The term "aluminum" they reserve for molybdenum. Now most people, both here and there, can't tell the metals apart; call these people "laymen." Laymen here are therefore in the same psychological state about aluminum that laymen there are about what they also call "aluminum." Yet the extension of "aluminum" as laymen use the term there is indubitably molybdenum and, thus, quite different from the extension of "aluminum" as laymen use the term here.

My Fregean waterworks, chlorinated or not, will not wash with this tale. Our laymen know that aluminum isn't molybdenum, even if they can't tell what the difference is. So we can't make our term "aluminum" apply also to Twin Earth molybdenum as we made "water" apply also to XYZ. The reason of course is that there are high priests as well as laymen, experts who *can* tell the difference. Our experts fix the extensions of "aluminum" and "molybdenum" for laymen here; experts on Twin Earth fix them the other way round for laymen there. There is, as Putnam [1975) p. 227] puts it, a "division of linguistic labor."

Very well. It need not be *my* beliefs that fix the reference or extension of terms which I can use quite well in my limited way. So I defer to experts, whose job it is to say what such a term really applies to. The reference or extension in any possible world of the term as we use it may nevertheless still be some Fregean function of our *experts'* beliefs. In Australia, for example, to be "back of Bourke" is to be way out in the outback. That Bourke is at an edge of Australian civilization is all I know about that place, certainly not enough to enable me to tell Bourke from several other places. Yet I can still refer to Bourke, as I have just done, by taking it to be whatever place would best fit more expert geographers' beliefs about it. Our knowledge of most things and places must be like this; certainly most of our knowledge of natural kinds. So no doubt the labor of reference is divided, as Putnam says, but it may be a Fregean labor for all that [Dummett (1973), pp. 138–139; (1974), pp. 530–51].

4. Fregeans can cope with Putnam's Twin Earth tales. Frege is still in the ring; so how does Putnam fare on points? His rival theory gives the extension of natural-kind terms in two stages. First, archetypes in this world, paradigm specimens of the kind. Then anything, in any possible world, that has a suitable "same-kind" relation to the archetypes. It is for science to tell us what the same-kind relation is for any category of kinds (for H_2O, Putnam proposes, implausibly enough, a same-*liquid* relation!). Generally, Putnam assumes that the relation will specify a shared microstructure. But whatever shared properties Putnam's same-kind relation picks out will be essential properties of the kind, since the relation is assumed to be an equivalence relation that holds across all possible worlds [Putnam (1975), p. 232], not just in this one. So not just actual specimens of the kind share the specified properties: nothing could be of the kind and not share them with the kind's archetypes.

Putnam's necessity is metaphysical, not epistemic. A natural kind may be known long before its essential microstructure is known. Putnam's theory is radically anti-Fregean: given archetypes, a kind term's extension is fixed by its same-kind relation, regardless of what anyone believes.

Putnam's argument for kind essences credits kinds both with archetypes and with cross-world equivalence relations holding between all things of the kind. Real natural kinds need have neither. Take archetypes. Their role is to fix the kind term's extension without recourse to its Fregean sense. Putnam takes it that they must therefore be in this world, so that they can be picked out ostensively. Thus, pointing out Lake Michigan as an archetypal sample of water (Putnam's example) fixes the extension of "water" regardless of its sense (just as naming the lake "Lake Michigan" is supposed to fix the reference of that expression regardless of *its* sense). Then the rest of the extension of "water," in any possible world, is just what stands in the relevant same-kind relation to *this* archetype. That is why Putnam [(1975) p. 234] says that kind terms are "indexical," like "I," "now," "here," and "this."

Ostensive reference, to just *this* archetype in *this* world, is thus essential to the mechanism of Putnam's essentialist theory. He must show, therefore, that our use of kind terms actually incorporates it. An extension of Kripke's causal theory of naming offers to show this. The theory has some irrelevantly contentious aspects, about how users of names pass them on;[7] all we need here is that, roughly, some archetype must be causally "upwind" of any use of a natural-kind term. Thus, our uses of "water" and "aluminum" are supposed to derive causally from our (or our experts') causal acquaintance with archetypal specimens of H_2O and aluminum respectively; and that is supposed to be why H_2O and aluminum are what we refer to by those terms. The corresponding Twin Earth uses derived causally from archetypes of XYZ and molybdenum, which is why those are the kinds they refer to by the same terms.

That is the theory. Unfortunately, archetypes do not constrain our use of natural-kind terms in that way. True, botanists designate type specimens of plant species, and geneticists designate cultures to exemplify gene types. But these specimens are causally downwind of the usage they are supposed to constrain. They are chosen to fit botanical and genetic knowledge, not the other way round. They are certainly not the specimens whose classification caused the corresponding kind terms to be used in the first place; they may well indeed not even be of the same kind as those specimens. Hence, as Nicholas Jardine (in a Cambridge University Moral Sciences Club paper) and Zemach [(1976) pp. 123–24] have observed, our most authoritative specimens of a kind might on Putnam's account not even *be* of that kind.

So some archetypal natural kinds have the wrong archetypes; others have none at all. Consider elements high in the periodic table, that do not occur in nature and have never been made. We have names for them, but there may never be archetypes to constrain our use of the names. Even if specimens eventually appear, the discovery, creation or synthesis of previously unknown fundamental particles, elements and compounds can surely be *predicted*. The term "neutrino" applied to just the same particles when it was used to predict their existence as it has applied to since their discovery. Ostensive reference (say to a bubble-chamber photograph) could not have fixed its extension then; why suppose exactly the same extension is fixed that way now?

Even if we were to grant Putnam his archetypes, however, his essentialism would still fail to follow. No reason is given why particular properties must be common to all things in all possible worlds that are of the same kind as the archetypes. Suppose that all samples of water in fact share ten "important" properties, but that water could lack any one of them, so that only the disjunction of all conjunctions of nine of them is essential. In this case of course, sameness of kind is not the equivalence relation Putnam [(1975), p. 231] says it is, since it is not transitive: two merely possible samples of water could differ in two of the ten properties. But Putnam's account doesn't in fact provide transitivity, since what makes things water in other possible worlds is their likeness to archetypes in *this* world, not their likeness to each other. To claim that the relation is an equivalence relation, so that archetypes have to share the *same* properties with all possible samples of the kind, is just gratuitously to assume the essentialist conclusion.

5. Putnam's account of the extension of kind terms both fails to be true and fails to entail essentialism. I turn now to Kripke's derivation of essentialism from the necessary self-identity of natural kinds. In evaluating his argument it is essential to keep the reference of a kind term clearly distinguished from its extension. To which end I hereafter distinguish the supposedly singular term "water" from the corresponding predicate ". . . is water," and likewise for other kind terms. Now Kripke [(1972), p. 349] admits that a causal mechanism is not needed to secure the reference of natural-kind terms. "Neutrino" could be introduced, as it was, by theoretical description and still be applied rigidly in Kripke's sense. That is, we can still consider the consequences of just *that* kind of particle failing in this or that respect to satisfy the theoretical descriptions which in fact served to identify it. "Neutrino," so understood, is for Kripke a non-Fregean rigid designator since its reference in other possible worlds is not constrained to satisfy these theoretical descriptions, which must be supposed to provide its Fregean sense. For this to work, of course, there must actually be neutrinos, near enough as specified. They needn't be in the observed past, to serve as archetypes; but they do need to be somewhere in this world—past, present, or future. Otherwise the requisite uniqueness of reference would not be secured. Many different kinds of particles will satisfy our theoretical descriptions of neutrinos in various possible worlds; and nothing but the reality of one of these will single it out as the unique referent of the term "neutrino." Were there in fact no neutrinos, the term could for Kripke no more designate a natural kind than "unicorn" can [Kripke (1972), p. 763].

However, there are neutrinos, just as there is H_2O. Let us therefore grant for the moment that "H_2O," like "neutrino," can be made a non-Fregean rigid designator by theoretical description and Kripkean fiat. Grant also that "water" is such a designator, in this case perhaps even because our use of the term derives causally from Putnamesque archetypes like Lake Michigan. What more is needed for "water" and "H_2O" to designate the *same* kind? And how is sameness of kind related to coextensiveness in the corresponding predicates ". . . is water" and ". . . is H_2O," which is what matters for essentialism?

We must in fact tackle the latter question first in order to answer the former. As referents of singular terms, kinds are obscure entities, not notably clearer than properties or attributes in their criteria of identity. If the necessary self-identity of kinds is to have any implications for essentialism, these criteria will have to be spelled out in terms of predicate extensions. One such criterion presents itself at once. For water to be the same natural kind as H_2O, it seems at least to be necessary for ". . . is water" and ". . . is H_2O" to be coextensive in all possible worlds; otherwise some possible world would contain something whose membership of the kind depended on what the kind was called, which seems implausible.

But then it looks as if "Water is H_2O," construed as an identity statement containing rigid designators, already and trivially entails that all samples of water in all possible worlds are also samples of H_2O. Far from the *necessity* of this identity establishing that being H_2O is an essential property of water, that is just what must be the case for the identity claim to be true at all. It is indeed not clear what more the metaphysical necessity of "Water is H_2O" could consist in, since we have already used up our possible worlds in saying what makes it true. So no doubt it is necessary if true; but only because if in this world ". . . is water" and ". . . is H_2O" are coextensive-in-all-worlds, then so they are in all other worlds.[8] In short, because the identity criteria of kinds have thus to be given in terms of their extensions, there is no useful inference to essentialism from the necessity of identity, even if the kind terms involved are admitted to be rigid designators; if anything, the inference will be the other way.

One might try arguing, however, that the requirements of natural-kind identity have been pitched too high. Perhaps what is needed is coextensiveness, not in all possible worlds, but in this world and in those nearest to it. After all, science is supposed to give us essences; yet the most scientists can show us in fact is lawful coextensiveness between ". . . is water" and ". . . is H_2O." That is, we suppose they can show that not only *are* all samples of water samples of H_2O, but that if anything *were* a sample of water it would be a sample of H_2O. Now that need not be a claim about all possible worlds, since the consequent of a true subjunctive conditional need not be true in all possible worlds in which the antecedent is true: it need only be true in those worlds which are sufficiently like ours [Lewis (1973)]. Waiving the difficulties of characterizing lawfulness in terms of truth in nearby worlds without begging the question, suppose for the sake of argument that the lawfulness of "All and only samples of water are samples of H_2O" so characterized, suffices for the identity of water and H_2O. Will the rigidity of "water" and "H_2O" now secure necessity for this identity and thus coextensiveness in all worlds, however remote, for ". . . is water" and ". . . is H_2O"?

To see that it will not do the latter, we must appreciate how loose the connection is between the reference of "water" (say) and the extension of ". . . is water" in various possible worlds. Obviously there could be much more water than there is, or much less. That is to say, there are possible worlds with samples of water that don't exist in this world, and others in which some real watery individuals (like Lake Michigan) don't exist at all. Consequently, in yet other possible worlds, there is water all right, although no individual sample of it is identical with any of the real samples that we have. In each of these worlds the singular term "water" has the same reference (namely, of course, water—whatever that is), while the extension of the predicate ". . . is water" may differ totally from what it is here or in other possible worlds.

Now we are at present supposing, for the sake of Kripke's argument, that coextensiveness between ". . . is water" and ". . . is H_2O" in all worlds is not required for the identity of water and H_2O, only coextensiveness in this and some suitable class of nearby worlds. We now see that in other worlds the extension of ". . . is water" may be quite different from its extensions hereabouts; and so may that of ". . . is H_2O." And whatever the necessity of identity may do to secure that "water" and "H_2O" have the same reference in these other worlds, it will do nothing to secure that ". . . is water" and ". . . is H_2O" have the same extensions, which is what essentialism needs.

6. Even if "water," "H_2O," and similar kind terms were rigid designators, therefore, essentialism would get no help from the supposed necessity of identities like "Water is H_2O," however the reference of the singular terms involved is related to the extension of the corresponding predicates. But there is anyway no good reason to admit that these terms are non-Fregean rigid designators. Kripke [(1971) pp. 146–48] implies that without rigid designators we would need Lewis's (1973) "counterparts" in order to state counterfactuals about things (and kinds). I share Kripke's distaste for counterparts, but this is a false dichotomy. Fregean names may designate the same things or kinds in many possible worlds, namely in all those that can be specified by Fregeanly intelligible counterfactuals about them. On a "cluster" version of the description theory [e.g., Searle (1958)], taking account of Putnam's division of linguistic labor, such counterfactuals can suppose the lack of almost any property of the thing, or of things of the kind, and of all such properties attributed by any one nonexpert speaker. That is quite enough to give a specious appearance of non-Fregean rigidity to what may in fact be Fregean names. Of course it is trivially true that "water" applies to water whatever intelligible counterfactual supposition we make about it. The question is whether something like a Fregean sense of "water" limits the range of such suppositions. I see no reason to deny that it does, and equally none to assert that anything about water itself makes the antecedents of any such counterfactuals necessarily false.

7. We have seen that essentialism can be extracted neither from Putnam's archetypes, nor from a merely stipulated rigidity of reference via modish truisms about identity. The existence of essences in Kripke's and Putnam's theories is no more than a gratuitous assumption on their part. Its appeal lies solely in that of the stock exemplars of essential properties; and that appeal, I shall argue in conclusion, is specious.

In biological species, for example, there is a distinct dearth of suitable properties shared even in this world. Capacity to interbreed with fertile offspring is the obvious candidate, but even that is well known to lack the transitivity Putnam's same-kind relation would need in order to yield essentialism. It usually doesn't hold between all and only members of the same species here, never mind in other possible worlds. Nor [*pace* Dummett (1973), pp. 143–45] can coming of a common stock be essential to a species,[9] which could easily have been cross-bred from independent mutations.

Elements and chemical compounds offer more scope for essentialism, since all their specimens at least share some properties in this world. Of properties supposed to be shared in all possible worlds, we have seen that microstructure provides the stock exemplars; it is worth asking why. Scientists commonly employ a principle of "microreduction" [Schlesinger (1963), chapter 2], i.e. roughly the principle that properties of things should be explained in terms of the properties and relations of their spatial parts. Many properties can indeed be so explained; and the assumption that they can underlies standard techniques for studying things in convenient (e.g. laboratory) isolation from their normal surroundings.

Microreductive theories are thus relatively easily testable, which is a well-known Popperian virtue in science. It is therefore both good method to look for microreductive explanation of kinds of things and an importantly pervasive fact that they can be found. Where, moreover, such explanation is both comprehensive and deductive, we may be able to replace reference to things of a kind with reference to their parts. So it is, roughly, that reference to gas samples was made eliminable, by the classical kinetic theory, in favor of reference to gas particles.

Suppose we now adopt a Quinean view of ontology, and admit only kinds of things that *need* to be referred to in stating what we know. Since kinetic theory makes reference to gas samples redundant, they disappear from our ontology. Similarly, let us suppose, with water and gold. Microreductive theories make reference to anything more than H_2O molecules and gold atoms redundant. There is, we might say, nothing to water and gold but the particles of which they are composed. And this, I reckon, is the source of the idea that water would have to be H_2O in any possible world, because H_2O is all there is to water.

The inference is specious. This way of removing items from our ontology requires deducibility. Unless all the macroscopic properties of a kind are deducible from its microstructure, reference to things of the kind is still required. And if they are deducible, then they occur in any possible world the microstructure occurs in. So if the microstructure is essential for this reason, so are all the macroscopic properties it explains.

So-called "essential" properties are thus really no more essential than any other shared properties of a kind. They are just properties ascribed by the primitive predicates in a comprehensive deductive theory of the kind. That is presumably what makes them what Putnam [1975], p. 232] calls "the important physical properties" of the kind; and the principle of microreduction will no doubt ensure that such properties will most commonly concern the kind's microstructure.

Our anti-Fregean essentialists must now suppose a property's "importance," so construed, to be a feature of the world independent of our beliefs and theories. If we knew everything, perhaps that would be so, as Ramsey (1928) thought in 1928. But as Ramsey (1929) observed in 1929, we don't know everything. Even microreductive theories cannot be construed as claiming completeness merely by virtue of claiming truth. For there may always be more smaller-scale detail to the world than any such theory describes. Its presently primitive predicates may, therefore, cease to be primitive at any time, when it is itself explained by yet another such theory, without at all impugning either its truth or its explanatory value. Water may still be H_2O, however much we subsequently learn of the nuclear structure of hydrogen and oxygen atoms.

8. I have tried in this paper to dispose of some of modern essentialism's newer and more seductive arguments. Putnam's Twin Earth tales do not, as he supposes, dispose of Fregean alternatives to essentialist theory. His own account of the extension of natural-kind terms is false of nearly all natural kinds and would not yield essentialism even if it were true. Kripke's theory of the reference of kind terms likewise fails to yield essentialism as a product of the necessary self-identity of natural kinds. The stock candidates for essential properties, moreover, are either not even shared in this world by all things of the kind, or their status is evidently more a feature of our theories than of the world itself.

In short, our essentialists' premises are false, their arguments invalid, and the plausibility of their conclusions specious. Their essences can go back in their Aristotelian bottles, where they belong.

ENDNOTES

1. "It is going to be *necessary* that heat is the motion of molecules" [Kripke (1971), p. 160]. The proposition "The standard meter rod (S) is 1 meter long" [Kripke (1972), p. 275] takes to be a contingent *a priori* truth—*a priori* because S sets the standard, contingent because S might have been shorter, longer, or nonexistent. But if S in fact fixed the extension of "1 meter" as Putnam prescribes (see below), then whatever shared properties in fact make distant objects the same length as S would be essential properties of being 1 meter long.
2. ". . . animals with the appearance of cats but reptilic internal structure . . . would not be cats; but 'fools' cats'" [Kripke (1972, p.321].
3. Kripke [(1971), pp. 150–51; (1972), pp. 260–63). I have used Dummett's term for the latter notion since I incline to accept his account, on which "epistemic necessity is a stronger notion . . . a statement may be [metaphysically] but not epistemically necessary, but the converse could not occur. Kripke, however, claims the properties of being *a priori* and being necessary to be quite independent" [Dummett (1973), p. 121].
4. I say *"inter alia"* because Fregean reference or extension is obviously a function also of context (e.g., in indirect speech, according to Frege, a name refers to what is normally its sense) and of what the world contains (e.g., whether "gold" applies to my tiepin depends on whether my tiepin is gold) [cf. Dummett (1973) chapters 5 and 9].
5. My arguments against Putnam's interpretation of his two tales overlap with those of Zemach (1976), but my further purposes make it desirable to restate them here in my own way.
6. The sense of "chlorine" *might* of course have changed in the wake of this discovery, to make the term apply only to the more common isotope; just as the sense of "water" might have changed to exclude XYZ or D_2O. But that is not what happened and anyway not what Putnam needs. If changes of belief about the microstructure of kinds do produce changes of extension in kind terms, that rather recommends a Fregean view.
7. "When the name is 'passed from link to link', the receiver of the name must, I think, intend when he learns it to use it with the same reference as the man from whom he heard it" [Kripke (1972), p. 302]. Intention isn't enough, however: "I am asked to name a capital city and I say "Kingston is the capital of Jamaica"; . . . [I] said something strictly

and literally true even though it turns out that the man from whom I picked up this scrap of information was actually referring to Kingston-upon-Mames and making a racist observation" [Evans (1973), p. 194]. "We are left with this: that a name refers to an object if there exists a chain of communication, stretching back to the introduction of the name as standing for that object, at each stage of which there was a *successful* intention to preserve its reference. This proposition is indisputably true; but hardly illuminating" [Dummett (1973), p. 151]. See also Altham (1973).

8. I ignore as incredible accounts of metaphysical (as opposed to epistemic) necessity in which this does not follow—i.e., in which the accessibility relation between possible worlds is not transitive [Hughes and Cresswell (1968)]; but see below.

9. I fear this idea derives partly from Kripke's [(1972), pp. 312–14] claim that an offspring's parents are essential to it—a claim of which it may suffice to remark that "If John hadn't been a Kennedy he wouldn't have been shot" is a plainly intelligible contingent statement [cf. Dummett (1973), p. 132].

4

Putnam on Artifacts

Stephen P. Schwartz

IN A RECENT SERIES OF papers, Hilary Putnam has presented us with a very compelling view of the functioning of natural-kind terms.[1] Putnam holds that natural-kind terms like "gold," "tiger," and "water" are indexical or rigid. This means that contrary to traditional theories, the meaning of such a term is not given by a conjunction or cluster of properties semantically associated with the term. At best the features associated with such a term serve as good indicators of the presence of a real essence or nature that determines what it is to be a member of that natural kind. The extension of the term is part of the meaning, but criteria specifiable in terms of superficial properties are not. This means that, except for trivial analytic statements such as "Gold is gold," there are no analytic statements with an indexical term as subject.

I have no disagreement with Putnam so long as he restricts his analysis to natural-kind terms, but in several places he claims that his indexical approach can be extended to all of the referring terms of language.[2] In this paper I shall focus on the terms for kinds of artifacts, such as "chair," "pencil," "bottle," and argue that the indexical account does not fit them well. I will show that Putnam's arguments fail to demonstrate that artifact terms are indexical. Furthermore, artifact terms are a subclass of what I call "nominal-kind terms," none of which can be treated as indexical. Indeed, some version of the traditional theory rejected by Putnam is likely to be substantially correct about them.

Putnam holds that we use natural-kind terms to refer to whatever has a common hidden structure. Thus, we use "water" to refer to all bodies of H_2O. The use of a natural-kind term carries with it the presumption of a shared common nature, even if we do not yet know what this nature is:

> A natural kind term . . . is a term that plays a special kind of role. If I describe something as a lemon, or as an acid, I indicate that it is likely to have certain characteristics (yellow peel, or sour taste in dilute water solution, as the case may be); but I also indicate that the presence of these characteristics, if they are present, is likely to be accounted for by some "essential nature" which the thing shares with other members of the natural kind. What the essential nature is is not a matter of language analysis but of scientific theory construction; today we would say that it is chromosome structure, in the case of lemons, and being a proton-donor, in the case of acids.[3]

Since Putnam believes that terms for kinds of artifacts are indexical, he believes that kinds of artifacts share a nature, or that at least we presume that they do, and that we intend our artifact terms to refer to whatever shares this nature:

> It follows that "pencil" is not synonymous with any description—not even loosely synonymous with a loose description. When we use a word "pencil," we intend to refer to whatever has the same nature as the normal examples of the local pencils in the actual world. "Pencil" is just as indexical as "water" or "gold."[4]

"Pencil" here is being used by Putnam as a standard example of an artifact term, so he means his point to apply to all or most terms for kinds of artifacts.

Putnam, of course, does not hold that pencils, chairs, tables, and so on, have a biological or chemical nature. Instead he holds that they have, or at least we believe they have, an artifactual nature. That they have an artifactual nature is, according to Putnam, a matter of fact not language, and thus, contrary to what he claims the traditional theory would suggest, we can imagine discovering that pencils are organisms. It is important to examine this claim in detail, before we go on to consider the plausibility of holding that pencils have an artifactual nature.

Putnam has us imagine the following about those things we call pencils:

> We cut them open and examine them under the electron microscope, and we see the almost invisible tracery of nerves and other organs. We spy upon them, and we see them spawn, and we see the offspring grow into full-grown pencils.[5]

Putnam claims that this is all epistemically possible. In spite of all we currently believe to the contrary it could turn out that pencils are organisms.

What is the point of imagining that pencils are discovered to be organisms? It is impossible to determine by the actual behavior of speakers under ordinary circumstances whether they are using the term "pencil" as indexical or not.[6] In a sense, this is like a case of Quinean indeterminacy. Here we have two people one of whom uses the term "pencil" indexically and another who has decided to apply the term to all and only those objects that satisfy a certain superficial specification having to do with form and function. If we start questioning our informants about objects we should get the same answers from each of them; "pencil" or "not pencil" in the same cases. The one believes that it is just a fact about pencils that they are the way they are, whereas the other would refuse to call anything that was not like them a pencil, but they nevertheless call the same things pencils. The only way we can distinguish the indexical user from the nonindexical user is by determining how they would behave in certain counterfactual situations. The point of imagining that we discover that pencils are organisms is that the indexical user of "pencil" will supposedly withhold the term from these organisms since he now knows that they do not satisfy the specification associated with "pencil" by him. On the other hand the indexical user will be surprised by such a discovery but will nevertheless apply "pencil" to these organisms just as he did when he believed that they were artifacts. What he will say is that he now knows what the nature of pencils is. Namely, they are a certain kind of organism. He will now refuse to extend "pencil" to candidates that are not of this kind. In other words, according to Putnam, the nonindexical user could not discover that *pencils* were organisms since then they just would not be pencils, whereas the indexical user could imagine discovering that pencils are organisms. Since *we* can imagine discovering that pencils are organisms we must be using the term indexically.

Note, however, that this thought experiment will distinguish between the indexical user and the nonindexical user only if "pencils are not organisms" follows from the specification that the nonindexical user associates with "pencil." In other words the reason that the nonindexical user cannot discover that pencils are organisms is that it is analytic that "pencils are not organisms" because being an artifact is part of the specification of "pencil." If, on the other hand, the specification associated with "pencil" by the nonindexical user only includes features having to do with form and function and does not include anything about origin, the nonindexical user could discover that pencils are organisms just as readily as the indexical user. So even if we agree with Putnam that we could discover that pencils are organisms this does not imply that "pencil" is indexical. All that has been shown is that either "pencil" is indexical or that if it is not indexical "being an artifact" is not part of its meaning. I argue below that in fact it does not seem plausible that "being an artifact" is part of the analytic specification of what pencil, chair, lamp, and so forth is. Thus, I agree with Putnam that it is a matter of fact that all of our pencils are artifacts. However, I do not agree that its being a matter of fact shows that "pencil" is indexical.[7]

Let us see how Putnam's example of the organism pencils must be extended if it is genuinely to distinguish the indexical from the nonindexical users of "pencil." In order to distinguish the indexical from the nonindexical users of "pencil" we must see how they would each react to counterexamples to claims about the nature of pencils. This is because statements that describe the nature of the things that fall under an indexical general term are not subject to disproof by counterexample. If we discover a lone robot in the form of a cat, we do not reject the claim that cats are animals. Rather we say that this robot is not a cat. Analogously, if we discovered of a bit of metal that everyone took to be gold that it was not an element but some elaborate compound we would not say that we have discovered some gold that is not an element. Rather we would say that this bit of metal is not gold. Such claims as "water is H_2O," "lead is an element," "tigers are animals" are not subject to disproof by single counterexample. We just never would count anything as a counterexample to the claim that all tigers are animals. This, of course, does not mean that such statements are analytic or incorrigible in any sense. If we discovered that all cats were robots then we would reject the claim that cats are animals.

Suppose now that we discover that the local pencils are all organisms, as Putnam imagines. The nonindexical user is able to abide this discovery, since being an artifact is not part of the specification semantically associated with "pencil" by him. But then we make a further discovery. In some distant place we discover something that meets all the specifications that the nonindexical user imposes on "pencil" but is *not* an organism. It is not important what it is, just that it does not share the same biological nature as the local pencil organisms. I am imagining that it is something that we would all call a pencil on the basis of superficial observation and inspection, it even fools the indexical users at first. If this were to happen the indexical user would withdraw "pencil" when he discovers that the object is not an organism because he will not allow "pencils are organisms" to be falsified by counterexample. The nonindexical user, for whom "pencils are organisms" had the status of a truth, but otherwise no special status, will say "See, we have a counterexample to the claim that all pencils are organisms." This imagined circumstance is one that does distinguish the indexical user from the nonindexical user. My intuition is that we would react as the nonindexical user does, indicating that "pencil" is nonindexical for us. The example is, however, too elaborate and implausible to give clear answers. But then at least this much is clear; Putnam cannot use this thought experiment to prove that "pencil" is indexical for us.

On the other hand, what about "pencils are artifacts"? Since in the actual word pencils are artifacts, according to Putnam it is necessary that pencils are artifacts, and this will be a claim that is not subject to disproof by counterexample, if "pencil" is indexical. He says that pencils are "artifacts manufactured to be written with. . . ." From this it follows "That pencils are artifacts is necessary in the sense of true in all possible worlds—metaphysically necessary."[8] Just as, if the local water is H_2O, anything that is not H_2O is not water, so if "pencil" and "chair" are indexical and we correctly believe that the local chairs and pencils that serve to determine the reference of these terms are artifacts, then anything that was not an artifact could not be a chair or pencil. Putnam's position is that the nature of pencils is that they are artifacts made for writing, just as the nature of water is H_2O. (Of course, these statements of nature are not incorrigible.)

If "pencils are artifacts" is corrigible but not subject to disproof by counterexample, then this is a strong indication that "pencil" is indexical. I have already agreed that it is corrigible, but I do not see how Putnam can be so sure that there cannot be counterexamples to the claim that "pencils are artifacts." Can't we imagine that somewhere they grow pencils? Their pencil bushes have regular hexagonal branches, graphite cores, and so on. The people in harvesting the pencils break them off about eight inches below the end on which nature has fixed an eraser, sharpen them up, and there you have it, a new pencil. These pencils are not organisms, of course, but they are not artifacts either. Putnam argues that "pencils are artifacts" is not subject to disproof by counterexample by having us imagine that we discover that what passes for pencils on Twin Earth are organisms. Perhaps Putnam is correct in holding that these pencil mimics are not really pencils. However, something can fail to be an artifact and yet not be an organism. The reason that these Twin Earth organisms are not pencils may be that "organism" is itself indexical. The difficulty may come from that side. In any case in order to show that "pencils are artifacts" is not subject to disproof by counter-example it is not sufficient to show that there could not be organism counter-examples. One must show that given that the local pencils are artifacts there could not be any nonartifactual pencils.

I have already suggested that nonartifactual pencils could be discovered grow-ing on trees. There might also be other ways that a pencil could be produced naturally, as it were. For example, I do not see the metaphysical impossibility of a pencil springing forth *ex nihilo*. Such a pencil, produced say by a lightning bolt, would be a very special pencil indeed. It would be amazing given the probabilities against such a thing happening that it did happen, but this is not to say that it is impossible. But it would be impossible if "pencil" were indexical. It would be just as impossible for a lightning bolt to produce a pencil as it would be for it to produce some water that is not H_2O or some gold that is not an element.

If "pencil" were indexical then it would also be the case that the term could be extended to things that did not superficially resemble the paradigm pencils, so long as they had the same nature or underlying trait. If water is H_2O then any stuff that is H_2O is water, regardless of whether or not it superficially resembles the paradigm water.[9] In this sense of "nature" we do not have the remotest idea of what the nature of pencils is. If "pencil" were indexical and pencils were organ-isms, then we could say that what makes something a pencil is whatever makes something to be this kind of organism, that is, a genetic code or something like that. This serves to show the contrast between what Putnam supposes and what is actually the case. As it is, Putnam does not even give a hint as to what such an underlying nature might be in the case of pencils.

I believe, of course, that there is no such underlying nature of pencils, nor is there a presumption of such a nature. What makes something a pencil are superficial characteristics, such as a certain form and function. There is nothing underlying about these features. They are analytically associated with the term "pencil," not disclosed by scientific investigation. (Being an artifact is not, however, one of these features, since as I have already argued it is not necessary that pencils be artifacts, *a fortiori*, it is not analytic that pencils are artifacts.)

We stated earlier that the use of a natural kind term carries with it the presumption of a shared common nature. This presumption of a common nature need not, however, be true. It could have turned out that the bodies commonly called "water" shared no common hidden structure. "The local water, or what-ever, may have two or more hidden structures—or so many that 'hidden structure' becomes irrelevant. . . ."[10] Thus, Putnam does not want to assert that the exten-sion of a natural-kind word necessarily has a common hidden structure. He says, "It could have turned out that the bits of liquid we call 'water' had no important common physical characteristics except the superficial ones."[10] Such a state of affairs has an important effect on whether or not a natural-kind term is indexical. "In that case [where there are no important shared physical characteristics except the superficial ones] the necessary and sufficient condition for being 'water' would have been possession of sufficiently many of the superficial characteristics."[10] If the necessary and sufficient condition for being water would have been possession of sufficiently many of the superficial characteristics, then we could give an analytic specification of the meaning of "water" along the lines suggested in traditional theories. As we have seen there seems to be no candidate for the nature of artifact kinds, so artifact kinds like pencils, chairs, lamps, are just like water would be if we discovered that there was no chemical nature common to all bodies of water. The superficial characteristics take over and serve to provide necessary and sufficient conditions for being a member of the kind. The big difference between artifact kinds and water is that we do not presuppose that there is any underlying nature that makes something to be the kind of artifact that it is. Terms for kinds of artifacts do not even start out as indexical. When I say that there is no common nature that all pencils have, I mean that there is nothing apart from some set of superficial characteristics that all pencils have in common. If something is a pencil because it has all or enough of some set of superficial characteristics, then "pencil" is not indexical. It is not having the same nature as some local pencils that makes something a pencil, but rather it is satisfying the description of the characteristics that make it a pencil.

Since terms like "chair," "pencil," "lamp" are not indexical, and it is not analytic that chairs, pencils, and lamps are artifacts, I call them nominal kinds[11] to distinguish them from natural kinds. Members of a nominal kind do not share a common hidden nature, and we can give an analytic specification in terms of form and function of what it is to be a member of the nominal kind.[12]

One reason for distinguishing nominal kinds is that they do not support inductions in the following sense. The fact that several examined chairs are upholstered, say, does not support the claim that all chairs are chairs are upholstered. The fact that the examined chairs are wooden does not support the contention that all chairs are wooden and so on. In fact if a scientist were interested in chairs as a subject of scientific study and got a good specimen, and started to examine it closely in order to discover the nature of chairs, we would think that he was crazy. Compare this with the zoologist interested in snakes and so obtains a fine specimen and begins to dissect it.

It seems to me that the following statement of Putnam's applies to all nominal kinds: "Bachelors are a kind of synthetic 'class'. They are not a natural kind in Mill's sense. They are rather grouped together by ignoring all aspects except a single legal one."[13] I am not sure if terms for kinds of artifacts like "pencil," "chair," or "lamp" are one-criterion terms, but they are like "bachelor" in that they name synthetic classes. In order to see what is meant by synthetic class, consider the difference between "dog" and "cat" on the one hand, and "pet" on the other. "Dog" and "cat" are natural-kind terms, but "pet" is a nominal-kind term. Something is a pet if it satisfies certain descriptions. We do not presume that pets share a common underlying nature, other than being animals, perhaps. Something is a pet not because of its nature but because of its relationship to other things, its function or role, and so on. "Pet" is not the name of a natural kind, rather, pets form a synthetic class.

Putnam has been willing to allow that there are some nonindexical terms in our language, but he seems to think that there are very few and that they are quite unimportant philosophically. In the "Meaning of 'Meaning'" Putnam asserts that the indexical account applies to most nouns and even to other parts of speech.

> So far we have only used natural-kind words as examples, but the points we have made apply to many other kinds of words as well. They apply to the great majority of all nouns, and to other parts of speech as well.[14]

I am not sure how we decide how many terms are indexical and how many are nominal, but it seems clear to me that large segments of the natural language include terms that are names of nominal kinds. We have already mentioned "pencil," "lamp," and "chair" as examples of nominal-kind terms. In general the names of kinds of furniture, household articles, implements, tools, ornaments, and so on will be nominal-kind terms.

If the above list of nominal kinds is correct, then it is simply wrong to assert that most terms of natural language are indexical. The list is far from complete, and yet would contain thousands of words. The correct approach to ordinary language, it seems to me, is to combine both Putnam's insights and the traditional approach. It is clear that Putnam is correct about natural-kind terms, his error is in extending his analysis to nominal-kind terms. On the other hand, followers of the traditional approach are correct about nominal-kind terms, and their error has been in attempting to extend their analysis to natural-kind terms. The correct theory of natural language will recognize that natural-kind terms are indexical, while at the same time recognizing that nominal-kind are not. Putnam suggests both in "The Analytic and the Synthetic" and in "Meaning and Reference" that there is nothing for philosophers to do in the study of language. There is plenty of work for psycholinguists and sociologists but none for philosophers:

> It is the belief that there are synonymies and analyticities of a deeper nature—synonymies and analyticities that cannot be discovered by the lexicographer or the linguist but only by the philosopher—that is incorrect.[15]

If I am right that many of the ordinary terms of our language are not indexical, but are nominal-kind terms, there are deep synonymies and analyticities of the kind Putnam denies. Of course, it would not be the case that these could not be discovered by the lexicographer or linguist since they could be discovered by anyone with ability and an interest in looking closely at the use of language. The question is who is going to be most interested in these deep synonymies and analyticities. If it turns out that the terms around which the traditional questions in philosophy revolve are nominal-kind terms, then they will be in need of philosophical analysis. And this philosophical analysis will be an important tool in approaching these questions.

ENDNOTES

1. See in particular: "Is Semantics Possible?" and "Meaning and Reference," both in Schwartz (1977); "Explanation and Reference," in Pearce and Maynard (1973); Putnam (1975b).
2. See Putnam [(1975b), p. 160]; "Is Semantics Possible?", pp. 104–5.
3. "Is Semantics Possible?", p. 104.
4. Putnam [(1975b), p. 162].
5. Putnam [(1975b), p. 161]. The example is attributed to Albritton.
6. For an argument supporting a similar claim about proper names see Donellan [(1977), pp. 13–16]. Donnellan says, "I believe the conclusion from this is that in the absence of stipulation that the name shall be one or the other, it would be indeterminate whether a name introduced by means of a description is a rigid designator or an abbreviation, so long as the name continues to be pegged to the description" (p. 16).
7. I would like to thank Carol Kates for helping me to formulate this point.
8. Putnam [(1975b), p. 162].
9. See Kripke's discussion of Polywater in Kripke (1972).
10. Putnam [(1975b), pp. 159–60].
11. I mean to suggest by this term Locke's notion of nominal essence, which, unlike real essences, are the workmanship of the understanding rather than nature.
12. I do not want to be taken as holding to the idea that an analytic specification in terms of a strict conjunction of characteristics can always be given for a nominal kind. It is quite possible that some version of the cluster theory is correct for many nominal-kind terms.
13. Hilary Putnam, "The Analytic and the Synthetic," in Rosenberg and Travis [(1971), p. 115].
14. Putnam [(1975b), p. 160].
15. "The Analytic and the Synthetic," p. 98.

5

From *Intentionality*: Are Meanings in the Head?

John Searle

THE FUNDAMENTAL QUESTION OF THE philosophy of language has always been: How does language relate to reality? The answer I proposed to that question in *Speech Acts* was that language relates to reality in virtue of the fact that speakers so relate it in the performance of linguistic acts. The original question then reduces to one of analyzing the nature and conditions of the possibility of these acts. In *Intentionality* I have tried to ground that analysis further in the Intentionality of the mind: the question, "How does language relate to reality?", is only a special case of the question, "How does the mind relate to reality?", and just as the question about language is reduced to one about various sorts of speech acts, so the question about the mind reduces to one about the various forms of Intentionality, the representational capacities of speech acts being simply a special case of derived Intentionality.

On one interpretation of Frege, my general approach to Intentionality is a matter of revising and extending Frege's conception of "*Sinn*" to Intentionality in general, including perception and other forms of self-reference; and my approach to the special problem of reference is in some respects Fregean in spirit, though, of course, not in detail. Specifically, it is possible to distinguish at least two independent strands in Frege's account of the relations between expressions and objects. First, in his account of the *Sinn* and *Bedeutung* of *Eigennamen*, an expression refers to an object because the object fits or satisfies the *Sinn* associated with the expression. Second, in his fight against psychologism Frege felt it necessary to postulate the existence of a "third realm" or abstract entities: senses, propositions, etc. Communication in the utterance of an expression is possible only because both the speaker and the hearer can grasp a common abstract sense associated with the expression. My own account is Fregean in accepting the first of these strands, but I reject the second. Linguistic reference is a special case of Intentional reference, and Intentional reference is always by way of the relation of fitting or satisfaction. But it is not necessary to postulate any special metaphysical realms in order to account for communication and shared Intentionality. If you think about the Evening Star under the mode of presentation "Evening Star," and I think about the same planet under the same mode of presentation, the sense in which we have an abstract entity in common is the utterly trivial sense in which, if I go for a walk in the Berkeley hills and you go for exactly the same walk, we share an abstract entity, the same walk, in common. The possibility of shared Intentional contents does not require a heavy metaphysical apparatus any more than the possibility of shared walks.

Both the Fregean and the present account of meaning are internalist in the sense that it is in virtue of some mental state in the head of a speaker and hearer—the mental state of grasping an abstract entity or simply having a certain intentional content—that speaker and hearer can understand linguistic references. At the time of this writing, the most influential theories of reference and meaning reject a Fregean or internalist analysis. There is a variety of reasons for which the anti-internalist position has become fashionable, and there is considerable disagreement among the anti-internalists as to what the correct analysis of reference and meaning is. In this chapter [of *Intentionality*] and the next I will consider and answer at least some of the more influential attacks on the internalist, Fregean, or Intentionalistic tradition. These chapters, therefore, are more argumentative than those which preceded them: my aim is not only to present an Intentionalistic account of reference but to do so by way of answering what I believe is a family of mistaken doctrines in contemporary philosophy. Here, in no special order, are some of the most influential theses urged against the internalist picture.

1. There is supposed to be a fundamental distinction between *de re* and *de dicto* beliefs and other sorts of propositional attitudes. *De re* beliefs are relations between agents and objects, they cannot be individuated solely in terms of their mental contents (*de dicto*) because the object itself (*res*) has to be part of the principle of individuation of the belief.

2. There is supposed to be a fundamental distinction between the "referential" and the "attributive" use of definite descriptions. Only in the case of attributive uses of definite descriptions does a speaker "refer" to an object in virtue of the fact that his Intentional content sets conditions which the object satisfies, but these are not genuine cases referring at all; in the referential use of definite descriptions the speaker need not use an expression that the object referred to satisfies.[1]

3. Indexical expression, e.g., "I," "you," "this," "that," "here," and "now," are supposed to be impossible for an internalist theory to account for, since their utterance lacks a "completing Fregean sense."

4. Exponents of the so-called causal theory of names and the causal theory of reference are supposed to have refuted something called the "descriptivist theory" of names and of reference and, thereby to have refuted any internalist or Fregean account, and to have shown that reference is achieved in virtue of some *external* causal relations.

5. The causal theory of reference is supposed to be applicable to a large class of general terms, the natural-kind terms and perhaps others; and for these terms there are supposed to be decisive arguments showing that knowing their meanings cannot consist in being in psychological states of any sorts,

but must involve some more direct causal relations with the world. It is supposed to have been shown that "meanings are not in the head."

I believe that all these views are false. Furthermore, they share a family resemblance; they suggest a picture of reference and meaning in which the speaker's internal Intentional content is insufficient to determine what he is referring to, either in his thoughts or in his utterances. They share the view that in order to account for the relations between words and the world we need to introduce (for some? for all? cases) external contextual, nonconceptual, causal relations between the utterance of expressions and the features of the world that the utterance is about. If these views are correct then the account I have given of Intentionality must be mistaken. At this point then I see no alternative to mounting a series of set-piece philosophical arguments. The justification for making such a fuss over views I believe are false anyway has to do with the size of the issues involved. If we are unable to account for the relation of reference in terms of internal Intentional contents, either the contents of the individual speaker or the linguistic community of which he is a part, then the entire philosophical tradition since Frege, both the analytic and the phenomenological strands, is mistaken and we need to start over with some external causal account of reference in particular, and the relation of words to the world in general.

I. MEANINGS IN THE HEAD

I shall begin by considering Hilary Putnam's argument that "meanings are not in the head."[2] I think in the relevant sense that meanings are precisely in the head—there is nowhere else for them to be—and that Putnam's arguments fail to show anything to the contrary.

Putnam considers two views:

(1) Knowing the meaning of a word or expression consists in being in a certain psychological state.
(2) Meaning (intension) determines extension.

Appropriately construed these two entail a third:

(3) Psychological states determine extension.

Putnam tries to show that we cannot hold both (1) and (2) together and that (3) is false. He proposes to reject (1) and (3) while accepting a revised version of (2). In the discussion which follows it is important to point out that nothing hangs on accepting the traditional analytic-synthetic distinction; for the purposes of this discussion both Putnam and I accept holism, and nothing in our dispute turns on that issue.

Putnam's strategy is to try to construct intuitively plausible cases where the same psychological state will determine different extensions. If type-identical psychological states can determine different extensions, then there must be more to the determination of extension than psychological states, and the traditional view is, therefore, false. Putnam offers two independent arguments to show how the same psychological state can determine different extensions. He sometimes talks as if they were part of the same argument but, in fact, they are quite independent and, I believe, only the second is really serious. I will, therefore, deal rather briefly with the first.

The first argument concerns what he calls the principle of "the linguistic division of labor," i.e., the principle that in any linguistic community some people have more expertise in applying certain terms than others do. For example, in our community some people know more about trees than others and so can tell which trees are, for example, beeches and which are elms. Others, such as myself, don't know much about the difference between beech trees and elm trees, insofar as there is any *concept* attaching to the words "beech" and "elm" for me; they are pretty much the same concept. In both cases I have the concept of a big, deciduous tree growing in the eastern part of the United States. Therefore, according to Putnam, in my idiolect the concept or "intension" is the same, but the extension is clearly different. "Beech" denotes beech trees and "elm" denotes elm trees: same psychological state, different extensions.

I really don't believe any defender of the traditional view would be worried by this argument. The thesis that meaning determines reference can hardly be refuted by considering cases of speakers who don't even know the meaning or know it only imperfectly. Or to put the same point another way, the notions of intension and extension are not defined relative to idiolects. As traditionally conceived, an intension or Fregean *Sinn* is an abstract entity which may be more or less imperfectly grasped by individual speakers. But it does not show that intension does not determine extension to show that some speaker might not have grasped the intension, or grasped it only imperfectly; for such a speaker hasn't got a relevant extension either. The notion of the "extension in my idiolect" has no application for cases where one does not know the meaning of the word.

To make out the case, Putnam would have to argue that the collectivity of speakers' Intentional states, including those of all the ideal experts, does not determine the correct extensions. But if the argument is to be based on linguistic and factual ignorance, the very doctrine of the linguistic division of labor would seem to refute the argument from the start, because the doctrine is that where one speaker is ignorant he can appeal to the experts: what is and what is not an elm is for the experts to decide. That is, where *his* intension is inadequate he lets *their* intension determine extension. Furthermore, if we assume that Putnam *knows* this argument to be valid, we get something very much like an inconsistency as follows:

1. My (Putnam's) concept of "elm" = my concept of "beech" but
2. The extension of "elm" in my idiolect ≠ the extension of "beech" in my idiolect.

How do I know 2 to be true? Obviously because:

3. I know that beeches are not elms, and elms are not beeches.

And how do I know that? I know that because I know that elms and beeches are two *different* species of trees. Imperfect as my grasp of the relevant concepts is, at least I have enough conceptual knowledge to know that the two are distinct species. But for this very reason,

4. Number 3 states conceptual knowledge.

If such knowledge is not conceptual knowledge, nothing is. Therefore,

5. Contrary to 1, my concept of "elm" ≠ my concept of "beech."

In his more important and influential second argument Putnam tries to show that even the collectivity of speakers' Intentional states might be insufficient to determine extension, for there might be two communities with the same set of collective intensions but with different extensions. Imagine that in a distant galaxy there was a planet very similar to ours with people like ourselves speaking a language indistinguishable from English. Imagine, however, that on this Twin Earth the stuff they call "water" is perceptually indistinguishable from what we call "water," but in fact it has a different chemical composition. What is called "water" on Twin Earth is a very complicated chemical compound, the formula for which we will abbreviate as "XYZ." According to Putnam's intuitions, the expression "water" on Earth in 1750, before anything was known about the chemical composition of water referred to H_2O; and "water" on Twin Earth in 1750 referred to XYZ. Thus, even though the people on both Earth and Twin Earth were all in the same psychological state relative to the word "water," they had different extensions and, therefore, Putnam concludes that psychological states do not determine extension.

Most people who have criticized Putnam's argument have challenged his intuitions about what we would say concerning the Twin Earth example. My own strategy will be to accept his intuitions entirely for the purpose of this discussion, and then argue that they fail to show that meanings are not in the head. But I want to digress for a moment and consider what the traditional theorists would say about the example as presented so far. I think it would go something like this. Up to 1750, "water" meant the same on both Earth and Twin Earth and had the same extension. After it had been discovered that there were two different chemical compositions, one for Earth and one for Twin Earth, we would have a choice. We could *define* "water" as H_2O, which is what we have, in fact, done; or we could just say that there are two kinds of water, and that water on Twin Earth is constructed differently from water on Earth. There is, indeed, some support for these intuitions. Suppose, for example, there had been a great deal of going and coming between Earth and Twin Earth, so that speakers were likely to have encountered both. Then it seems likely that we would construe water as we now construe jade. Just as there are two kinds of jade, nephrite and jadeite (Putnam's example), so there would be two kinds of water, H_2O and XYZ. Furthermore, it looks like we pay a high price for accepting his intuitions. A very large number of things have water as one of their essential components, so if the stuff on Twin Earth is not water then presumably their mud is not mud, their beer is not beer, their snow is not snow, their ice cream is not ice cream, etc. If we take it really seriously, indeed, it looks as if their chemistry is going to be radically different. On our Earth if we drive cars we get H_2O, CO, and CO_2 as products of the combustion of hydrocarbons. What is supposed to come out of the cars on Twin Earth? I think that a defender of the traditional view might also point out that it is odd that Putnam assumes that "H_2O" is fixed and that "water" is problematic. We could equally well imagine cases where H_2O is slightly different on Twin Earth from what it is on Earth. However, I don't want to pursue these alternative intuitions to Putnam's; rather, I want to accept his intuitions for the purpose of the argument and continue with his positive account of how extension is determined.

On Putnam's theory the extension of a general term like "water," and indeed on his theory just about any general term, is determined *indexically* as follows. We identify a kind of substance, such as water, by certain surface features. These are such things as that water is a clear, tasteless, colorless liquid, etc. The crucial point is that the extension of the word "water" is then determined as whatever is identical in structure with this stuff, whatever that structure is. Thus, on his account the reason that "water" on Twin Earth has a different extension from "water" on Earth is that the stuff identified indexically has a different structure on Twin Earth from the structure that it has on Earth, and "water" is simply defined as whatever bears the relation "same L" to this stuff.

Now from the point of view of a traditional theorist, what exactly does this argument achieve? Even supposing Putnam is right about his intuitions, all he has done is substitute one Intentional content for another. For the traditional cluster-of-concepts Intentional content, Putnam has substituted an indexical Intentional content. In each case it is a meaning in the head that determines extension. In fact, Putnam's suggestion is a rather traditional approach to natural-kind terms: a word is defined ostensively as whatever bears the right relation to the denotation of the original ostension. "Water" has simply been defined as whatever is identical in structure to this stuff whatever that structure is. And this is simply one case among others in which intensions, which are in the head, determine extensions.

On the traditional Lockean view, water is defined (nominal essence) by a checklist of concepts: liquid, colorless, tasteless, etc. On the Putnam proposal, water is defined (real essence) indexically by identifying something that satisfies the nominal essence and then declaring that water is to be defined as whatever has the same real essence as the stuff so identified. This may be an improvement on Locke but it certainly does not show that meanings are not in the head.

I believe Putnam would not regard this as an adequate response, since the whole tone of his writings on this topic is to suggests that he takes himself not to be proposing a variation of the traditional view that meanings are in the head but to be rejects the tradition altogether. The interest of this discussion for the present work only becomes clear when we examine the underlying assumptions about Intentionality that lead him to suppose that the alternative account of meaning that he proposes is somehow fundamentally inconsistent with the view that meanings are in the head. Let us try to state his position a little more precisely. We can distinguish three theses:

(1) The associated cluster of concepts does not determine extension,
(2) The indexical definition does determine extension, and
(3) What is in the head does not determine extension.

Now (3) does not follow from (1) and (2). To suppose that it does one must assume that the indexical definition is not in the head. Putnam uses (1) and (2) to argue for (3) and thereby assumes that the indexical definition is not in the head. Now, why does he think that? Why does he think that in the case of these indexical definitions what is in the head does not determine extension? I believe that there are two reasons why he makes this fallacious move. First, he supposes that since we don't know the microstructure, and since it is the microstructure that determines extension, then what is in the head is insufficient to determine extension.

But that, I believe, is simply a mistake; and we can illustrate the way it is a mistake by considering the following example. The expression, "The murderer of Brown," has an intension which determines as its extension the murderer of Brown.[3] The intension, "The murderer of Brown," fixes the extension even though it is a fact about the world who murdered Brown. For someone who does not know who murdered Brown the extension of the expression, "The murderer of Brown," is still the murderer of Brown even though he does not know who it is. Now analogously, the Intentional content "identical in structure with this (indexically identified) stuff" is an Intentional content that would determine an extension, even if we don't know what that structure is. The theory that intension determines extension is the theory that intensions set certain conditions which anything has to meet in order to be part of the extension of the relevant intension. But that condition is satisfied by Putnam's example: the indexical definition of water has as Intentional content, that is, it sets certain conditions which any potential sample has to meet if it is to be part of the extension of "water," in exactly the same sense that the expression "The murderer of Brown" sets certain conditions which any potential candidate has to meet if he or she is to be the extension of "The murderer of Brown." But in both cases it is a matter of fact about the world, whether or not some existing entities satisfy the Intentional content. It is, therefore, just a mistake to suppose that because we define "water" in terms of an unknown microstructure, that intension does not determine extension.

But there is a second and deeper reason why Putnam supposes that his analysis shows that meanings are not in the head. He makes certain assumptions about the nature of Intentional contents and the nature of indexical expressions, and especially about the way Intentional contents, relate to indexical expressions, which we must now explore. The assumptions emerge when he says:

> For these (indexical) words no one has ever suggested the traditional theory that "intension determines extension." To take our Twin Earth example: if I have a *Doppelgänger* on Twin Earth, then when I think, "I have a headache," *he* thinks "I have a headache." But the extension of the particular token of "I" in his verbalized thought is himself (or his unit class, to be precise), while the extension of the token of "I" in *my* verbalized thought is *me* (or my unit class, to be precise). So the same word, "I," has two different extensions in two different idiolects; but it does not follow that the concept I have of myself is in any way different from the concept my *Doppelgänger* has of himself.[4]

This passage makes it clear that Putnam supposes both that the traditional view that what is in the head determines extension cannot be applied to indexicals and that if two speakers, I and my "*Doppelgänger*," have type-identical mental states our states must have the same condition of satisfaction. I believe both these assumptions are false. I want to argue, first, that if by "intension" we mean Intentional content, then the intension of an utterance of an indexical expression precisely does determine extension; and, second, that in perceptual cases two people can be in type-identical mental states, indeed we can even suppose that a man and his *Doppelgänger* can be type-identical down to the last microparticle, and their Intentional contents can still be different; they can have different conditions of satisfaction. Both perceptual Intentionality and indexicality are cases of self-referentiality of Intentional or semantic content. We will explore the self-referentiality of indexical propositions later in this chapter. For present purposes it is sufficient to remind ourselves of the causal self-referentiality of perceptual experience that we explored in Searle [(1983); see chapters 2 and 4], and to show how it is relevant to the Twin Earth argument.

Let us suppose that Jones on the Earth in 1750 indexically identifies and baptizes something as "water," and Twin Jones on Twin Earth also indexically identifies and baptizes something as "water." Let us also suppose that they have type-identical mental contents and type-identical visual and other sorts of experiences when they make the indexical identification. Now, since they give the same type-identical definitions—namely, "water" is defined as whatever is identical in structure with this stuff—and since they are having type-identical experiences, Putnam supposes that we cannot account for how "water" has a different extension on Earth from the extension on Twin Earth in terms of their mental contents. If their experiences are the same, how can their mental contents be different? On the account of Intentionality presented in this book [Searle (1983)] the answer to that problem is simple. Though they have type-identical visual experiences in the situation where "water" is for each indexically identified, they do not have type-identical Intentional contents. On the contrary, their Intentional contents can be different because each Intentional content is causally self-referential in the sense that I explained earlier. The indexical definitions given by Jones on Earth of "water" can be analyzed as follows: "water" is defined indexically as whatever is identical in structure with the stuff causing *this* visual experience, whatever the structure is. And the analysis for Twin Jones on Twin Earth is: "water" is defined indexically as whatever is identical in structure with the stuff causing *this* visual experience, whatever the structure is. Thus, in each case we have type-identical experiences, type-identical utterance, but in fact in each case something different is meant. That is, in each case the conditions of satisfaction established by the mental content (in the head) is different because of the causal self-referentiality of perceptual experiences.

This account does not have the consequence that different speakers on Earth must mean something different by "water." Most people do not go around baptizing natural kinds; they just intend to use words to mean and refer to whatever the community at large, including the experts, uses the words to mean and refer to. And even when there are such public baptisms they would normally involve on the part of the participants shared visual and other experiences of the sort that we discussed in chapter 2 [of *Intentionality*]. But the account does have the consequence that, in making indexical definitions, directly speakers *can* mean something different because their Intentional contents are self-referential to the token Intentional experiences. I conclude, then, that even if we accept all of his intuitions—which many of us will not—Putnam's arguments do no show that meanings are not in the head. Quite the contrary, what he has done is to offer us an alternative Intentionalistic account, based on indexical presentations, of the meanings of a certain class of general terms.

ENDNOTES

1. I will not discuss this view further in the book since I have attempted to refute it elsewhere; see "Referential and Attributive" in Searle [(1979), pp. 137–61].
2. Putnam, "The Meaning of 'Meaning' ", in Putnam [(1975a), pp. 215–71].
3. Strictly speaking it determines the unit class whose sole member is the murderer of Brown, but for the purposes of this argument we can ignore this distinction.
4. *Op. cit.*, p. 234.

6

Natural-Kind Terms

Kim Sterelny

I. INTRODUCTION

In this paper I present a causal theory of natural-kind terms (hereafter, NKTs) resembling those already given for names. The theory is a development of Putnam's sketch in his (1975). I proceed as follows. In section II I motivate causal theories of kind terms. In sections III and IV the theory defended in this paper is developed and shown to be superior to cruder causal theories. In the final section I consider whether causal theories can be extended to cover the kind terms of special sciences.

II. MOTIVATING CAUSAL THEORIES

The general approach to semantics into which causal theories fit is both well known and well defended, so I spend little space on it here. The approach is that defended in Field's classic 1972 paper on Tarski. Field argued that while Tarski (and others following him) have shown, for important fragments of natural language, how the semantics of complex expressions can be reduced to the semantics of simple expressions, he did not give any acceptable account of the semantics of simple expressions. In brief, Tarski reduced truth to reference, but his account of reference is no more than a list of word/thing pairs. Yet Field very plausibly argued that such a list is nothing like the genuine reductions found in science. But reduction is necessary, unless we are prepared either to accept that semantic facts are ontologically primitive, or to accept, with Davidson, some form of semantic instrumentalism.[1]

The framework for such a reduction is the causal theory of reference.[2] Hence, causal semantics is motivated by philosophical naturalism: semantics is part of a general science of human behavior. Causal theorists attempt to reduce semantics to psychology. Since, typically, they accept a functionalist account of the mental, semantic predicates come out as functional predicates, though not the "narrow" or "internal" functional predicates of Fodor's (1980). The inputs and outputs that help define psychological functions are not characterized abstractly or neurophysiologically, but rather in terms of the organism's insertion into his environment.

There are not just programmatic reasons for developing causal theories of NKTs. The rival, Fregean, approach is in serious trouble. On Fregean accounts reference is dependent on meaning or intension. Meaning, in turn, is understood in terms of a set of concepts analytically associated with the term giving necessary and sufficient conditions of a term falling in its extension. Understanding a term involves knowing or grasping this meaning, hence the reference of a particular token of an NKT depends on the psychological state of its user; on what intension he associates with the term.[3]

In a series of "Twin Earth" examples, Putnam demonstrated the failure of this approach. He constructed examples in which the psychological state of speakers was held constant, but the reference of kind terms they used varied. Hence reference could not be a function of psychological state. I will discuss this argument in some detail, since it has been attacked in Zemach (1976) and Mellor (1977).

To recapitulate. Suppose in 1750 Earth and its inhabitants had a *Doppelgänger,* Twin Earth, like it in every way save one. What passes for water on Twin Earth is not H_2O; it is XYZ. Now, uncontroversially, the inhabitants of Earth and Twin Earth associate with "water$_E$" and "water$_{TE}$" the same concepts. They are our physical twins, hence, by supervenience, they are our psychological twins. But we use "water" to refer to the stuff we drink, swim in, and so forth, while they use "water" to refer to the stuff *they* swim in, etc., i.e., XYZ.

It follows that reference is *not* determined by the psychological state of the speaker—in particular, not by the concepts a speaker associates with a kind term. So, Putnam suggests that we define kind terms by appeal to a common structural property of the kind's members. In this he is surely right. Componential analyses give the intension of a predicate in terms of a cluster of molar features. The point of this procedure is that we can suppose this analysis to be implicitly known by all competent speakers of the language. To understand "water" is to associate "water" with "colorless," "tasteless," and so on. For intension determines reference, and understanding intensions in this way allows them to be grasped by all speakers of the language, thus explaining how speakers succeed in referring to kinds. But if Putnam's argument goes through, reference cannot be explained by appeal to what speakers know about their language, hence the point of componential analysis is undercut. But componential analyses are not only without explanatory point; they also have further disadvantages.

Firstly, it is very difficult to define kind terms by appeal to molar features. Verificationists and operationalists tried and failed to give such definitions of magnitudes and theoretical kinds. Moreover, the molar features are a function of its inner structure *plus* environmental parameters, so standardly there is both variation within and atypical members of a kind.

Secondly, classifying kinds by appeal to molar features yields a bad taxonomy. Lawlike relations hold in virtue of microphysical, and, more generally, structural features of objects. So, an appropriate taxonomy for explanation and manipulation of our environment will sort particulars into groups not in terms of gross similarities; we do not co-classify dolphins and sharks. In stating laws, and in otherwise co-classifying our environment, we need to classify kinds structurally.

So, if Putnam's attack on Fregian semantics works, a causal theory of kinds is the natural alternative. But Zemach and Mellor reject Putnam's argument. For both deny that the extension of "water" excludes XYZ. Let's consider Zemach's position first. Zemach [(1975) pp. 117–19] tries to undercut the intuitions that make Putnam's claim plausible. He points out that had intercourse between Earth and Twin Earth become possible in 1750, Earth English speakers would have called XYZ, "water." I agree. For we are being called upon to imagine a situation in which the reference of "water" would change. "Water" would come to refer to both H_2O and XYZ; it would cease to be an NKT. There are examples of illegitimate extensions of NKTs—for instance, "rat" to cover rats like Australian marsupials. Zemach imagines a situation in which reference would change, though it is not clear how it would change. Perhaps "water" would partially refer to both H_2O and XYZ, but fully to neither, or perhaps "water" would fully refer to H_2O v XYZ. The case is indeterminate because underdescribed. Nonetheless, setting aside these indeterminacies, Zemach has described a changed situation where the extension of "water" includes both H_2O and XYZ. But that *is a change*. Water is H_2O. Our tokens of "water" connect systematically with H_2O and no other substance; "water$_E$" refers to H_2O. Since Zemach's speculations about what would have happened in 1750 are consistent with this claim, they do not undercut it.

Mellor [(1977) pp. 302–4] also points out that Putnam's Twin Earth/Earth examples depend on the claim that the extension of "water" on the two planets is distinct. In response, Mellor simply announces Fregian intuitions: in 1750 and 1950 "water" on Earth and Twin Earth had the same extensions, H_2O v XYZ.

I think it can be shown that this idea leads to trouble. It's true that if we had visited Twin Earth in 1750, we would have called XYZ water. But Mellor's idea has the consequence that we would still have done this if we had visited it in 1950. It further implies that if, in the complete absence of Twin Earthians, we had discovered XYZ we would still call it water. For the reference of "water" in our language does not depend on facts about other languages, so if its reference is H_2O v XYZ that, fact does not depend on the existence of Twin Earth English speakers. Both of these consequences are implausible: it is obvious that we would not now apply "water" to XYZ. But the only way to avoid these consequences is to suppose that the reference of "water" changed from 1750 to 1950; from H_2O v XYZ to H_2O. But since there is no reason to think this would happen, it would be *ad hoc* to make this claim.

Moreover, we can raise the cost of Fregean intuitions still further with a modified Twin Earth story. This story assumes that it is possible for two individuals to be in a biochemically different but psychologically identical state: an assumption uncontroversial in these days of functionalist supremacy. Putnam's stories assume this too, since my *Doppelgänger*'s body chemistry contains XYZ, not H_2O.

The story is the same as before, with this difference. H_2O, if any were to exist on Twin Earth, would be fatal and foul tasting to Twin Earthians. Conversely, if there were XYZ on Earth, it would be fatal and foul tasting to us. In these circumstances, surely not even the most stubborn could feel any temptation to say:

$$\text{extension of "water}_E\text{"} = \text{extension of "water}_{TE}\text{"} = H_2O \text{ v } XYZ$$

But if Putnam ever could plausibly claim that I and my Twin Earth counterpart had the same concept of water (were in the same psychological state in respect of "water"), he still can. This premise of Putnam's argument has not been challenged, but nothing essential to the Twin Earth tales has been changed. Psychological states, internally defined, do not determine reference.

Mellor gives a better reply to an alternative tale that focuses on kinds that standard speakers of the language do not recognize. Imagine that the Earthly roles of aluminum and molybdenum are switched on Twin Earth. So are the terms for them. Imagine further that laymen cannot tell the two metals apart. Consequently, laymen on Earth and Twin Earth are psychologically indistinguishable vis-à-vis "aluminum" and "molybdenum." But their extensions of their uses of these terms differ.

Mellor replies (p. 304) as follows. Let the laymen depend on experts while giving a Fregean account for the experts. One difficulty for this line of thought has already been highlighted. The H_2O–XYZ example shows that often *no one* in a speech community knows the necessary and sufficient conditions for a term's application. But there is another problem as well. Mellor cannot rely on an unexplained dependence of the lay on the experts. His account of these terms cannot be fully Fregean, I suggest, because no Fregean account of reference-borrowing is available. A Fregean theory requires the laymen to have true beliefs identifying the relevant kind. If this identification is via others, these beliefs will be of the form: the stuff x means by "aluminum." But in beliefs of this kind the reference of x must be determined causally. For recall the Twin Earth story. We have a *Doppelgänger* on Twin Earth. A layman on Twin Earth fixes the reference of "aluminum" by the belief. Aluminum is the stuff Max refers to by "aluminum." But what makes this belief about Max (Twin Earth) rather than Max (Earth)? *Ex hypothesi*, there is no description the layman knows that will distinguish the two. Our layman knows nothing about Twin Earthians that distinguishes them from their *Doppelgängers*. Qualitatively, his picture of one is a picture of the other.

The Twin Earth tales have *not* been met. Reference is not determined by psychological states, if psychological states are individuated from an internal standpoint. Of course, it does not thereby follow that predicates associated by a speaker with a term, or the speaker's beliefs about the reference of a term, play no role in a theory of reference. On the contrary, I shall suggest that they do. But it is clear that causal relations have a role to play too. It is causal relations with Twin Earth and Twin Earthians that make the Twin Earthians' beliefs about Twin Earth; similarly for us. I turn now to a theory of those causal relationships.

III. A CAUSAL THEORY OF NATURAL-KIND TERMS

In this section I intend to outline the basic ideas of a theory of NKTs. The theory must include two components. One concerns the *grounding* of NKTs. It explains how some tokens of an NKT are linked *directly* to their referent, for the link between some tokens of, for example, "platinum" and platinum is unmediated by other speakers. An account of grounding should, therefore explain how experts use the language: it should explain how jewelers and metallurgists can refer to platinum by "platinum."

But most uses of NKTs are mediated by other speakers. Putnam has pointed out the existence of a "division of linguistic labor." I can refer to an enormous number of natural kinds despite my innocence of the nature of most of these. In this I am typical. Clearly, this capacity of mine depends on my place in a linguistic community. In communities the ignorant depend on the knowledgeable; those not in contact with a kind depend for their semantic capacities on those who are. In other words, part of a semantic theory of NKTs is a theory of *reference-borrowing*. I shall have little to say about such a theory, for what Putnam and others have said seems right to me. Moreover, problems for causal theories arise in the theory of grounding. I shall concentrate on these.

As a first approximation, the grounding of an NKT will include both an ostensive component and a structural component. In the paradigm cases, NKTs are introduced into the language by ostensive contact with samples of the kind. The extension of the term is then the class of all objects that bear the relation "same kind as" to the ostensively given samples. A term like "gold" is introduced into our language by causal contact with local samples of the stuff. Gold is then all and only that stuff which bears the relation "same metal as" to those local samples. Crucially, the nature of this relation is discoverable only by scientific research. It follows that users of an NKT need not, and normally will not, know a necessary and sufficient condition for membership of that kind.

To illustrate the main idea, let's consider an apprentice jeweller being introduced to both "gold" and gold. He is shown various samples of gold and is told that they are gold. That stuff, gold, is then causally involved in the tokens of "gold" being produced. So, paradigmatically, the expert acquires the ability to refer to gold in perceptual contact both with gold and the language. Future tokens of "gold" in his speech refer to gold only if their immediate cause is that ability. Moreover, just as for a speaker a name can be multiply grounded in the object it names, so will be an NKT for an expert. For once our apprentice is introduced to both "gold" and gold, he will repeatedly reground the term. For many of his uses of that NKT both samples of the substance and his ability to refer will be immediately involved. Such tokens will be semantically linked to gold in the same way that his grounding use of "gold" is so linked. Such uses reground "gold." Through his work, the apprentice will reground the NKT, so that any token of the term he produces has its origins in an ability that has multiple links to the substance. This may be the case even if the apprentice knows no necessary and sufficient condition for goldhood.

This account of grounding is, however, oversimplified. It needs to be modified in two ways.

1) We need to give an account of kind terms that are introduced in the absence of samples.
2) We need to say more about the contact needed with examples: grounding requires more than the dubbing of a sample with a term.

1. The Role of Descriptions in Grounding

Kind terms can be introduced (or regrounded) in the absence of exemplars [see Mellor (1977)]. Exemplars may not be accessible (e.g., "black holes"), or the kind may not be composed of discrete members ("forces"). We therefore need to allow descriptions to play a role in grounding. We can incorporate descriptions into the theory in two ways.

(a) Referential Definite Descriptions

Terms can be introduced by descriptions that pick out the kind; for instance, by specifying the mass, charge, and spin of a new particle, or [as Putnam suggests in his article (1975b)] by specifying its causal powers. "By t, I shall mean the cause of effects $e_1 \ldots e_n$." But this move seems to pose a problem. For the most plausible candidates for introduction by description are theoretical predicates from science. Yet typically their introducers did not get their descriptions quite right. For instance, our account of protons has changed quite dramatically since the term was introduced. Must we then say that the reference of "proton" has changed from nothing to protons? This consequence can be avoided if the introducing descriptions are, in Donnellan's sense, referential rather than attributive. Devitt in his (1981) provides a causal theory of referential definite descriptions, showing how a definite description can pick out its reference without being uniquely true of it. Thus, a causal theory of singular terms will sustain a causal theory of NKTs by showing how descriptions can be involved in grounding within the context of a causal theory.

(b) Attributive Definite Descriptions

In his (1981), Devitt suggests that some perception-like epistemic link to the referent is required if a definite description is to be referential. So while we can suppose terms for kinds without discrete members to be introduced by referential definite descriptions, we have not yet given an account for terms like "neutrino." No experimental link to neutrinos was available when the term was introduced. So the introducing description for this term must have been attributive, not referential. So terms can be introduced without a causal link to the kind. But it does not follow that the term remains without causal links to the kind. Once a kind is named, its effects and interactions traced, we will be in a position to designate samples and/or give referential descriptions of the kind. The NKT will become causally grounded. This is important: for it is in virtue of such causal groundings that we are able to regard superceded theories as partly true, and their special vocabulary non-empty.[4] Of course, for one reason or another we may never be in a position to ground the kind term causally. If so, the terms are linked to the kind only by attributive description, and if the introducing description is not uniquely true of a kind term, it will fail to refer. Terms for some of the unsynthesized and not naturally occurring (near us) elements high in the periodic table may be like this. But I think such kind terms are rare.

2. Requirements on Grounding

It is central to causal theories that those who ground NKTs need not know necessary and sufficient conditions for membership of a kind. But I think those who ground a term by appeal to exemplars know *something* about the kinds they dub. Strengthening the conditions on grounding is theoretically productive, for it allows us to meet a number of objections to Putnam's formulation of the theory. I will show that a strengthened theory enables us to give a better account of reference failure and reference change. Moreover, we will be able to show why a *particular kind* is picked out when a kind term is introduced by a sample(s) that exemplify, as all do, many kinds.

(a) Knowledge of Causal Powers

Grounding an NKT requires knowledge about the causal powers of the kind. This knowledge need not be in the form of theoretical description. Rather, in many cases, the causal powers will be specified through beliefs about singular causal connection: beliefs about relations between members of the kind and instances of its effects. So grounding will require not just contact with samples of a kind, but also the assignment of causal powers to kinds. A putative grounding of a term will typically involve a cluster of beliefs, and the term will be grounded only if most of those beliefs, or perhaps certain central ones, are true.

For instance, consider someone grounding the term "cat" by reference to a cat. Any cat is a member of many kinds: cat, mammal, animal, and so on. Why will "cat" refer to the kind cat? I suggest that the grounded must have in mind a set of causal powers of the creature. If it has those powers in virtue of a structure common and peculiar to cathood, "cat" is grounded on the kind cat. This will be the case if the powers are mouse catcher, cockroach killer, and the like. If it has those powers in virtue of a structure common to all mammals (hairiness, for instance) "cat" will be grounded on the *kind* mammal. And so on.

Let me make this suggestion more explicit. Consider a sample a, which is a member of kinds F, G, and H, and with which we associate a variety of causal powers (or sets of causal powers), P1, P2, and P3.

We ground "F" in a by associating "F" with P1. Similarly, "G," with P2; "H" with P3. So "F" will apply to any object x which has a structure of the same kind as that in *a* responsible for *a*'s having P1. Of course, *x* need not have P1; it may be a nonstandard member of the kind. If *a* does not have all (or most) of P1, "F" is empty. If some object y has P1 in virtue of a different structure, "F" does not apply to y. So on this account "water$_E$" does not apply to the stuff on Twin Earth, XYZ, despite XYZ's possession of P1. XYZ has the causal powers a typical grounder associates with the wet stuff around here, but it does not have in virtue of the same structure.

Our semantic theory links P1 to "F" because the grounder did. But note that P1 typically will not constitute necessary and sufficient conditions of F-ness, nor need it include all the causal powers of *a*, but only the powers those who ground the term link with F-ness.

I will elaborate on this idea in the next section but before moving on to show the utility of this idea I shall suggest strengthening the conditions on grounding in an additional way.

(b) Recognitional Capacities

Grounding[5] a term involves the possession, or acquisition, of recognitional capacities. One can ground a term on a kind only if one has the ability to discriminate, reasonably reliably, members of the kind. This capacity may be limited: it will not matter if some members are not recognized as being members (diamonds not be recognized as carbon) so long as nonmembers are not systematically classified with members (under normal circumstances, etc.). This is a natural requirement: we credit our forebears with the capacity to refer to gold and many other kinds because, despite ignorance or error about the kinds, they had amongst them individuals with these capacities. Grounding "tiger" requires the ability, fallibly, to recognize tigers. I should point out that this capacity is *not* a psychological state individuated internally. It is a state constituted by the way an individual is embedded in his physical environment. It is how an individual *does* recognize and classify members of kinds, not how he would recognize members if inserted into a different environment. I have no capacities to recognize or classify XYZ.

For many theoretical kinds, the second condition will coalesce with the first. Recognition will be in virtue of the causal symptoms of kindhood. But for many other kind terms, the macroscopically observables, the recognitional capacity is not reduce to beliefs. It will simply be a learned perceptual capacity of the same kind as our ability to recognize shapes and smells: it will be knowledge *how*, not knowledge *that*.

Let me summarize my account of the grounding of NKTs. It is my view that terms can be both introduced and regrounded in the language in two ways:

(a) By face to face dubbing of samples. Such dubbing requires the introducer both to identify causal powers of the sample, and to acquire recognitional capacities about the kind.

(b) By descriptions of the kind. These descriptions may be referential or attributive. NKTs introduced by description may be regrounded by dubbing samples, and vice versa.

I shall now show that this account of grounding helps one to give an account of difficult cases for causal theories.

IV. THE POWER OF THE THEORY

The theory presented in the last section coheres with the idea of reducing semantics to more general psychological theory. More concretely, this theory obviously assigns "water$_E$" and "water$_{TE}$" their appropriate referents, H_2O and XYZ. For Twin Earthians will be causally connected to and will have both beliefs and recognitional capacities about XYZ. Similarly, for Earthians and H_2O. So the theory is not undercut by the reasons for developing causal theories. In this section I suggest that the theory has advantages over its cruder ancestors; advantages deriving from its making explicit provision for (a) regrounding, (b) a role for descriptions in grounding, (c) a role for knowledge in grounding.

(a) Reference Change and Reference Stability

One of the advantages of a causal theory is its ability to give an account of reference stability through theory and belief change. Devitt (1979) and Kitcher (1978) have exploited this advantage in defending realist accounts of science from attacks based on the incommensurability thesis. But it has been argued that causal theories make reference too stable: they make it impossible to give an account of reference change. Once a term is grounded on one object/kind of object, its reference cannot change. But reference does change; see for instance, Evans (1977), Field (1973), and Fine (1975) for examples. Hence, causal theories fail.

This conclusion is too strong. A causal theory incorporating regrounding can meet this problem. Devitt has shown that causal theories of singular terms must recognize that, for example, names are multiply grounded. That is, tokens of a name refer to the object they do because underlying that token's use is a causal network with multiple links to the object. The same will typically be true of NKTs. Underlying a jeweller's use of "platinum" is a causal network with many links to the kind, direct links from confrontation with the kind; indirect links through conversations. A typical NKT is multiply grounded.

Normally, then, one kind will play a quite special role in the groundings that link a term to the world. But with reference change, this is not the pattern. At one stage, before change starts, the causal network underlying the uses of a term is like the standard case, with the groundings basically on one kind. At a later stage, when reference change has started but is not complete, no kind plays this role, but two kinds play something like it: the kind to which the term originally referred and the kind to which it is coming to refer.[6] Much later, after reference change is complete, the later kind will play the central role in groundings in the network. Tokens will have numerous links with the new kind, and few or none with the old.

(b) Errors and Impurities

Regrounding NKTs helps solve other problems simpler theories face. Putnam is worried by mistakes made in grounding; errors of ostension: wanting to ground "water" and pointing to a glass of gin thinking it water. He tried to meet the problem [(1975a) p. 225] by claiming that the introducer of the term only intends his grounding to take, so to speak, if an empirical presupposition is met—namely, that the stuff the introducer points at is the stuff he thinks it is. But this solution is very unclear, hence is unpersuasive. Regrounding avoids this problem. For paradigm NKTs like "tiger," underlying each use is a causal network of borrowings and groundings. Such a network will have multiple links to one and only one kind. It is the unique kind that plays that distinguished role in the network that is the reference of the NKT, even if the network has links with nonmembers. Moreover, given the strengthened conditions on grounding, it's not obvious that the network will have even occasional links to non members. Samples of nonwater have often been dubbed "water," we may agree. But that is not sufficient to ground "water" on those other kinds.

The same approach works with another problem for causal theories. Both Putnam and Zemach mention the problem of impurities. For many kinds, confrontation with that kind is confrontation with other kinds as well. Point to a sample of platinum, and you point to its impurities. So why does "platinum" refer to platinum rather than its impurities. (Or to impure platinum.) Regrounding helps. The causal network underlying a typical use of the term will be multiply connected to platinum, and only peripherally, because occasionally, connected to various stray impurities. The strengthened conditions on grounding are also relevant. The causal powers assigned are causal powers of platinum, not its impurities. So platinum plays a distinguished role in the network underlying "platinum" both in the number and type of that term's connection to the kind.

(c) Reference Failure

Enc follows both Fine and Evans in arguing that causal theories of reference make reference too stable. For he argues that causal theories do not adequately account for reference failure. While Enc agrees that observational NKTs survive massive theory change, he denies that the theoretical do. More particularly, Enc argues that Putnam is committed to the highly counterintuitive claim that "phlogiston" refers to oxygen.

Enc says:

One possible . . . extension of the Kripke–Putnam thesis to the term "phlogiston" would be to assume that scientists meant to refer by that term to whatever it may be that was responsible for the phenomena they were trying to explain . . . the substance that is in fact responsible for calcination and combustion. [Enc (1976), p. 267]

Since that stuff is oxygen, "phlogiston" refers to oxygen. But Enc suggests that this cannot be right, since oxygen theorists discovered a new kind of stuff, not new facts about a known kind of stuff. "Phlogiston" is empty.

I think Enc has highlighted a difficult problem for causal theories, but one that can be met. He assumes that either "phlogiston" refers to oxygen or is empty. Confronting himself with this dichotomy, he plausibly plumps for the second alternative: "phlogiston," like "witch," fails to refer. But this dichotomy is false. We can opt for partial reference, partially to oxygen, partially to nothing,[7] as Field and Devitt have shown in the works already cited. Alternatively, following a suggestion of Kitcher, we might claim that oxygen is the referent of some tokens of "phlogiston" but that others are empty.

So a defender of the causal theory need only show that "phlogiston" does not fully refer to oxygen. This is possible: "phlogiston" does *not* meet the conditions on grounding defended in this paper. I will consider the three possibilities: that "phlogiston" is introduced by attributive descriptions, by dubbing samples, or by referential descriptions.

1. It is agreed that phlogiston theorists knew no necessary and sufficient condition for oxygen: they did not introduce the term by uniquely describing oxygen. I take it to be uncontroversial that "phlogiston" is not grounded on oxygen by attributive description.

2. "Phlogiston" is not grounded by dubbing samples. Even if we grant that phlogiston theorists were in a position to pick out samples of oxygen (which I doubt) they got oxygen's causal powers wrong. Oxygen does not suffocate mice, get expelled from metals, etc. Nor did they acquire any capacities to recognize oxygen.

3. "Phlogiston" is not grounded on oxygen by referential descriptions. The descriptions Enc offers are attributive, not referential. I have three grounds for this claim.

i. The referential/attributive distinction was introduced by an appeal to an intuitive dichotomy between having an object in mind in using a description and not so having. On this criterion, Enc's descriptions are attributive, for he suggests: phlogiston is whatever it is that is responsible for combustion and calcification. Such a description is close to the paradigm of an attributive description—namely someone hearing that Jones has been murdered saying that the murderer of Jones is insane (for whomever murdered Jones must be insane).

ii. On a less intuitive level, Devitt has suggested that quasi-perceptual contact with the referent is required if a description is to be grounded. Referential descriptions are used, he suggests, according to a convention which makes their reference dependent on perceptual or instrumental contact [(1981) pp. 46–53]. The descriptions involved in Enc's example meet no such conditions.

iii. Designating expressions—most names, demonstratives, and referential definite descriptions—are rigid. They refer in every possible world to the object they pick out in this world. But Enc's descriptions are *not* rigid: "whatever-descriptions" are paradigms of nonrigid descriptions.

So, "phlogiston" is not grounded on oxygen. Still, this case demonstrates the importance of elaborating the causal approach in the ways suggested in section III. Nor are examples of this kind restricted to theoretical NKTs. For consider the case of "witch." We think that there are no witches rather than regarding "witch" as coextensive with "woman." Why? There are plenty of ostended alleged witches with a genuine property, womanhood, in common. "Witch" is a problem for causal theories, especially since we need to contrast this case with Putnam's cats. Putnam has pointed out (1975a) that if we were to discover that cats had never been animals but were, and always have been, Martian spy robots, we would not conclude that "cat" was empty. Instead, we would conclude that cats were Martian spies.

How then would "cat" contrast with "witch"? Grounding the predicate "W" on a kind W through a sample *a* requires the individual to associate with *a* a set of causal powers. If *a* in fact lacks most of this set, "W" is empty. Precisely this is true of "witch." Those thought to be witches did not cause the events—plagues, pestilences, etc.—attributed to them. If they had, even by natural means, "witch" would refer; "witch" would pick out a certain class of criminal. By contrast Putnam's robot cats do have many of the causal powers commonly attributed to them, i.e. they kill rats, scratch dog's noses, support fleas, etc. Of course, we can imagine still more bizarre stories, when it would be much less clear that "cat" still referred. Imagine that instead of robocats there are immobile spies with a mechanical hypnosis device. When we think we see cats chasing mice, howling on roof tops, we are hallucinating. "Cat" would then be empty since the beliefs of causal connection would all be false: the cat-hallucinations do not cause the moving-mouse hallucinations, etc. Nor would we have an appropriate recognitional capacity.

Of course, only the *special* vocabulary of witch theory and its ilk is empty. So the special vocabulary of astrology—"ages," "quarters," "cusps"—is empty, but the terms, independently grounded by folk astronomy and folk navigation—"star," "planet," constellation names—are not.

It is possible to imagine various intermediate cases where we do not know what to say. But I think the theory as presented does justice to the clear cases of reference failure.

(d) The Qua Problem

When a kind term is introduced (or regrounded) by designating a sample, what kind is picked out? As, for example, Papineau (1979) and Dupre (1981) have pointed out, any object will be a member of many kinds. Suppose I go to Mars and come across a cat-like animal: I introduce the term "schmat." Schmats are animals bearing a certain relation to this paradigm local schmat I have just encountered. But what determines which relationship this is? For the schmat will be a member of many kinds. A nonexhaustive list would include: physical object, animate object, animate object of a certain biochemical kind, animate object with certain structural properties, schmats, schmats of a certain sex, schmats of a certain maturational state.

We must give an account of what determines the extension of "schmat." We cannot appeal to descriptive vocabulary, or schmat theory to solve the problem. For the descriptive vocabulary that would determine which kind is being picked out consists of NKTs, and we must suppose their extension to be fixed (calling this holism rather than circularity is unhelpful). More importantly, the descriptive vocabulary/theory associated with a term can be associated with it improperly, without overturning the reference of the kind term. This intuition gives causal theories their point.

It might be thought that anti-groundings ("That is not a schmat") can eliminate the ambiguity of groundings.[8] Not so: anti-groundings are no help with coextensive terms like "renate" and "cordate," yet these are semantically distinct in a way a causal theory should capture. More seriously, it must be groundings, not anti-groundings, that determine reference. Consider the example of carbon. One of the intuitions central to causal theories is that diamonds are in the extension of "carbon" whether or not that fact is recognized; even if it is denied.

The strengthened conditions on grounding help solve this problem. In addition to dubbing the sample, I must acquire various beliefs about its causal powers. It is thus that the kind is determined, for the sample will have its causal powers in virtue of a structural property. The paradigm schmat will have causal powers. It has these in the first instance in virtue of its biochemistry and anatomy; ultimately in virtue of its genetic code. So, in this case, it is the shared genetic code that determines the extension of "schmat." "Schmat" applies to all animals that have a structure that is the same as that in the paradigm schmat responsible for the causal powers associated with the exemplar. A similar story in terms of atomic structure works for kinds like gold and platinum.

Recognitional capacities converge on the structural property in the same way. It is not just that the exobiologist acquires the ability to recognize schmats, rather than schmat-sexes, or the genus that schmats exemplify, though this, too, is relevant to its being schmats that are picked out. But further, the recognitional capacity itself is one instance of the causal powers of the kind. I can recognize schmats because of certain of their macroscopic features though I may not know which or how. These features schmats have in virtue of a certain structural property that we therefore take to be extension-determining.

It is a consequence of this suggestion that NKTs, especially those not multiply grounded, may be indeterminate in their references.[9] For though reference to causal powers will reduce indeterminacy, it may not eliminate it. We may have more than one candidate for the "same kind as" relationship. The causal powers picked out may leave it indeterminate whether "schmat" refers to schmats of a given sex, or to schmats of a given sex/maturation stage. If so, "schmat" would partially refer to both kinds but fully to neither. Both natural language and the history of science exemplify this pattern. Dupre points out that many of the terms of folk biology do not pick out species but somewhat indeterminate larger groups. There are also examples from science. When elements were named before they were discovered to have different isotopes, these names partially referred to one isotope, and partially to the other isotope. Associating more causal powers when these terms are regrounded will help eliminate these indeterminacies, so one common form of reference change will be from term tokens partially referring to two kinds to term tokens fully referring to one kind.

V. CAUSAL THEORY AND THE SPECIAL SCIENCES

I have argued that developing causal theories along the lines suggested here helps solve difficult problems for such theories. In this section I consider whether the theory can be extended to give an account of the kind terms of the "special" sciences (the behavioral and social sciences).

In the natural sciences, all the members of a kind share a structure that can be defined physically. All samples of gold share an atomic number, all water is H_2O; all tigers have a common genetic structure.[10] The members of a kind bear a relationship to the exemplars of a kind because they share with exemplars a physical property or properties, though we saw in the last section that specifying this relationship is a nontrivial problem.

Notoriously, the same is not true of the predicates of the special sciences. There is no physical structure common to all samples of money. Very probably, the same is true of the kinds of psychology. It is not plausible to suppose that "is a pain" refers to whatever has the same physical/structural properties of exemplary pains. All the higher animals feel pain, despite differences in their neurophysiology. If there are extraterrestials we might take them to feel pain despite their different biochemistry.

It follows that our account of kinds—hence, kind terms—does not generalize to the special sciences. It seems that we cannot identify membership of a natural kind with possession of a physical property, or common physical structure, on pain of excluding the kinds of special sciences. Nor, of course, do we wish to recognize nonphysical essences of special science kinds. The solution seems to be to accept some kind of functionalist position. For instance, Field (1975) in discussing the kinds of semantics, suggests that we construe the properties constitutive of the kinds of special sciences as second order physical properties. These are defined by existential quantification over first-order physical properties.

Apparently, therefore, the causal theory extends to the special sciences. Everything is as before, except that the property common to all members of a kind of the special sciences is a second-order, not a first-order, physical property. Matters are, however, not that straightforward.

(i) If we can go functionalist for the kinds of the special sciences, why cannot we go functionalist for all kinds, and hence kind terms. Hence we would restore the theory to a fuller generality. Thus we could say that all water has a second-order physical property. Namely, the property of having some first-order physical property that plays a certain causal role, a role in virtue of which water boils at 100°C, is colorless, etc. But then it follows that XYZ is water, for XYZ has a first-order property in virtue of which it boils at 100°C, is colorless, etc. Since the intuition that XYZ is not water is a starting point of causal theories of general terms, we must bifurcate our treatment of general terms.

The difference is this. I have claimed that a predicate "F," grounded in object a with respect to a set of causal powers P1, applies to all objects with the *same structure* as that in a responsible for a's having P1 (or most of P1). Hence, "water," grounded on wet stuff around here, does not apply to XYZ. But the kind terms of special science differ. Apparently, a kind term of special science, grounded on an object b with respect to a set of powers P2, applies to all objects which have *any structure* in virtue of which the object has those powers.

(ii) This problem leads to another. On the assumption that kind terms of a special science are introduced and maintained in the language in the same way that a term like "tiger" is, it is difficult to explain how the bifurcation arises. Take "understands English" to be a kind term of psycholinguistics. According to the theory here outlined, this term is grounded by contact with an example(s) together with an association of the example with certain of its causal powers. But there is a problem. An object that is a member of this psycholinguistic kind is also a member of a neurophysical kind, defined by the state that (in functionalist parlance) realizes that capacity to understand English in that object, and which is responsible for the causal powers recognized of the example. The same point goes through for recognitional capacities. Hence a term for the neurophysical kind is grounded, not for the psycholinguistic kind.

So terms for the special science must be differently grounded. Any grounding that consists simply of associating causal powers (e.g., producing certain strings of phonemes) with exemplars will ground a term for whatever realizes the kind in that exemplar. A theoretical specification of the kind seems necessary, but this implies that special-science kind terms are attributive. But then such terms look to be vulnerable to reference failure through theory change. This in turn would make realism in the special sciences more vulnerable to skeptical arguments based on the incommensurability thesis and its relatives. Is there any way of blocking this skeptical conclusion about the special sciences? Two strategies are available.

Firstly, one might look for genuine causal groundings of special-science NKTs. Perhaps we could appeal to partial reference (regarding psychological terms as having divided reference to the physical kinds that are said to realize psychological states), or, alternatively, to multiple grounding since the psychological kind term can be linked to a range of physically distinct states.[11] Whether they can be so linked causally is however the problem.

The alternative is to show that though the terms of special science depend on general specifications of their reference, they are unlikely to be empty. The problem for realism is generated by the reasonable expectation of theory change. An expectation of theory change is an expectation that our current best descriptions of the kinds we take our terms to pick out are false. So if our kind terms depend on our descriptions being true, or mostly true, these terms will be empty.

I see no fully satisfactory resolution of this problem, but it can be made less acute. I have, for example, suggested a functionalist account of psychology. It follows that "pain" (to take the standard example) applies to an organism just in case *some* first-order physical property plays a certain role in that organism. Our problem is to specify that role.

A vague specification in terms of gross behavior—aversion, avoidance and the like—will protect "pain" from reference failure as psychology changes, but at too great a cost. For it will give "pain" too wide and indeterminate an extension for that term to be useful in developed psychology.

It is therefore better to give a detailed specification of the role of pain in the life of the organism, including its involvement in subtle behavioral and psychological conditions. "Pain" will then be a useful predicate in developed psychological theory. Moreover the problem of reference failure can be made less acute by grounding the term through a cluster of specifications of the role of pain in an organism. The term would then be empty only if we came to believe that most of those specifications picked out no (one) kind.

Thus, the theory defended in this paper does not extend straightforwardly to the special sciences though it is not, so far as I am aware, worse off in this respect than its rivals. But it does not clearly capture, in this domain, a standard advantage of causal theories. It may be, of course, an advantage it does not need in this domain. For this depends on just how damaging an argument against realism Putnam's "meta induction on the history of science" is, when applied to the special sciences. Does their history show dramatic theoretical shifts about (as the realist wants to say) the same subject matter? This is something very difficult to judge; fortunately, it is out of the scope of this paper.[12]

ENDNOTES

1. I discuss these issues in much more detail in Sterelny (1981).
2. See, for instance Field (1972), and (1975); Kripke (1972), Devitt (1974), (1976), and (1981).
3. Putnam discusses the most explicit form of this approach (Katz's) in his (1975e) and its set theoretic surrogates in his (1975).
4. See Devitt (1979); Kitcher (1978); Putnam (1975c).
5. This condition seems to me to be plausible, but I am not sure that it is required in addition to the knowledge criterion just discussed. For it is hard to think of a plausible case in which the knowledge criterion is met, but this condition is not. This makes me suspect that the two conditions are closely related.

6. At this stage of reference change, the term partially refers to one kind, and partially to the other. Partial reference is introduced and incorporated into truth theory in Field (1973) and defended in Devitt (1979) and (1980).

7. Or even more complexly, partially to hydrogen as well. Musgrave, in his (1976), points out that hydrogen was responsible for many of the effects attributed to phlogiston.

8. Michael Devitt and John Bigelow have both made this suggestion to me.

9. Field, in Field (1973), and Devitt, in Devitt (1979), have argued for the independent plausibility of this conclusion.

10. For an unconvincing argument to the contrary, see Dupre (1981).

11. I owe these suggestions to Robert Waldie.

12. Thanks to David Armstrong, John Bigelow, Alec Hyslop, Brian Loar, Hugh Mellor, Robert Pargetter, Robert Waldie, and especially Michael Devitt for their comments on earlier incarnations of this paper.

Part III
Mental Content and Mental Causation

Introduction

IN PART III, WE MOVE away from the philosophy of language and focus more directly on some of the implications of the Twin Earth stories for the philosophy of psychology. These fall into two main, related categories.

The first set of implications concern mental contents. Many mental states, such as beliefs, desires, and thoughts, have the interesting property of being *about* things. To believe that water quenches thirst is to be in a state that is, loosely, "about" at least water, thirst, and quenching; to desire that your spouse will be rewarded with a promotion is to be in a state that is "about" your spouse, promotions, and being rewarded. We typically ascribe such states (called "intentional states") to agents by using sentences of the form "X believes (desires, thinks, etc.) that *p*," where X is an agent and p is the proposition that X believes (desires, etc.). This proposition is known as the "content" of the state, and, according to many, is *essential* to that state: two agents (or one agent at two different times) will be in the same intentional state if and only if they are in states with the same content. The Twin Earth stories, then, raise many issues important for developing an understanding of the nature of that content.

Perhaps the most controversial issue is whether, or to what degree, the agent's external environment is relevant to the determination of the content of his intentional states. On the one hand, the environment is relevant in at least the sense that the entities that intentional states are about are frequently external to the agent; on the other hand, the environment is irrelevant in at least the sense that which mental state(s) an agent is in, including intentional state(s), seem to depend on nothing more than what is inside the agent's head. Given these competing constraints, many have found it necessary to distinguish different *kinds* of content. "Wide" (or "broad") content is highly sensitive to environmental context: one can change an agent's wide content by changing (in appropriate ways) only her external context. "Narrow" content, to the contrary, is sensitive to, or dependent on, only the agent's internal context: one can change an agent's narrow content only by changing, for example, her brain. Applied to the Twin

Earth stories, then, two Twins, each saying to herself, "I could use some water," will differ in wide mental contents and so in wide mental states (since, in their different external contexts, *what* the Twins desire is different, viz. H_2O v XYZ), while they will be identical in narrow mental contents and thus in narrow mental states (since the Twins are molecular duplicates and as such share all inner states). The key question, then, is this: Which of these competing views of content (if either) is most appropriate for psychology?

Those who answer in support of some version of narrow content are called "internalists" or "individualists," while those who support versions of wide content are called "externalists" or "anti-individualists." In the selections that follow, we will see much discussion of this key question (and its relatives) by members of both camps, as well as by at least one author who resists the very dichotomy itself. Must we indeed make the wide-narrow distinction, or can we get by without it? If we must make the distinction, how will we go about defining adequate notions of either kind? Are there, perhaps, different sorts of wide content, or of narrow content, each with its own merits and disadvantages? Does narrow content even qualify as "content"? How reliably do the "that-clauses" in sentences ascribing mental states track mental content? How do the different conceptions of content cohere with other important notions, including physicalism, supervenience, explanation, and especially, as we will see in a moment, causation? And what, if anything, does common-sense, "folk" psychology, have to say about all these issues?

The second set of Twin Earth's implications for the philosophy of psychology concerns the issue of mental causation. One common intuition is that mental states have causal powers. That is, many authors maintain that we typically behave as we do *because* we have the beliefs and desires we do. More specifically, we behave as we do in large measure because our beliefs and desires have the contents they do. The problem is, however, that it is no simple matter to make sense of *how* our mental states and their contents can have these causal powers in our seemingly very physical world.

The idea that they do have causal powers is problematic for a number of reasons. Foremost amongst these is the intuition that if we are to avoid an intolerable dualism, then there simply is no *room* for the mental to be causally efficacious since physical states and properties seem to do all the causing there is; the physical world is causally "closed." In other words, in what way can the content of an agent's intentional state be at all relevant to the state's causal powers when the neurons appear to do all the causing within the agent? Indeed, the problem of accounting for mental causation is even more imposing for externalists since wide content, with its sensitivity to external factors, invokes more than what is in the agent's head—and if mental states are to have any causal powers at all, it would seem, they could plausibly do so only as mediated by the agent's brain, which is comfortably nestled well *inside* the agent's head. In short, the problem for externalists isn't limited to merely the apparent superfluousness of mental content, but includes as well the fact that (wide) mental content is not exclusively dependent upon the neural.

In the selections below, then, we'll also see discussion of the following sorts of questions: What role, if any, should causal powers play in individuating mental states? How does the answer to this question bear on which notion of mental content is most appropriate for psychology? Is wide content even capable of being causally efficacious? How does the notion of causation cohere with those other notions mentioned above, i.e., physicalism, supervenience, and explanation? Is there any way to reconcile the causal relevance of the mental without merely identifying it with or reducing it to the physical? [For more on these and related issues, cf. Heil and Mele (1993).]

Having sketched some of the relevant general issues in Part III, we now turn to a brief overview of the articles.

In Tyler Burge's first selection in this volume, excerpted from his classic article "Individualism and the Mental" (1979), he argues against "individualism," here understood as the thesis that mental content depends on nothing more than what is inside the agent's head. At the heart of the argument is a three-step thought experiment. We are first asked to imagine an agent with a large number of beliefs about "arthritis," (as we would ascribe them), one of which is false—viz., his belief that he has developed arthritis in his thigh (since, in fact, arthritis is a disease of the joints only). Second, we are, asked to imagine a counterfactual situation in which we have just the same agent, with the same physical history and properties, but with a different social environment: in *his* community, "arthritis" is used to denote a disease that can occur not only in the joints, but also in the thigh. Finally, we are invited to join in an interpretation of these two steps, according to which the counterfactual agent lacks some or all of the arthritis beliefs of the original agent, due to his lack of the appropriate concept *arthritis*. (Although the counterfactual agent lacks the concept *arthritis*, note that he does possess a similar concept—say, *tharthritis*—of a disease that can occur in the joints and in the thigh.) If, as Burge argues, this interpretation is correct, then individualism must be false because "social context infects . . . mentalistic attributions."

While Burge's thought experiment has much in common with Putnam's Twin Earth thought experiments, Burge notes that his is more general. Putnam's analyses apply primarily to natural-kind terms (and concepts); Burge's apply also to artifact terms, color adjectives, social-role terms, abstract nouns, action verbs, legal terms, etc., and their corresponding concepts. Similarly, while Putnam is primarily concerned with differences between Twins' physical environments, Burge explores the implications of differences in social/linguistic environments as well. Putnam and Burge, in short, reach conclusions roughly similar in general externalist tone, but they do so via very different considerations and with very different emphases.

Burge addresses Putnam's Twin Earth analysis more directly in his "Other Bodies" (1982), our next selection, and in so doing further develops the anti-individualism sketched in "Individualism and the Mental." Burge notes that in "The Meaning of 'Meaning'," Putnam interprets the Twins' different uses of "water" purely as a difference in extension (cf. Crane's selection below—*eds.*);

further, he notes that Putnam ascribes the Twins the very same thoughts. On Burge's externalism, to the contrary, the Twins differ not merely in the extensions of their terms, but in their thoughts as well. Declining to speculate "why Putnam did not draw a conclusion so close to the source of his main argument," Burge instead criticizes those aspects of Putnam's discussion that obscure that conclusion. These include Putnam's claims that natural-kind terms are implicitly indexical and that mental states "narrowly individuated" do not "fix" the extensions of relevant agents' terms.

Regarding the first claim, Burge protests that the word "water" does not act like ordinary indexicals, such as "here." If it did, then just as "here" shifts its extension with context, so also would "water." But then when an Earthling visited Twin Earth and said of some XYZ that it was "water," he would be speaking truly—even though there is no water on Twin Earth! Thus, Burge concludes, any difference between the Twins is not due to the context-relativity of indexicals.

Regarding the second claim, Burge first suggests that Putnam's "narrow mental states"—those that don't presuppose the existence of anything other than the individual in that state—are equivalent to *de dicto*, nonrelational intentional states. But then on this construal, he argues, the Twin Earth examples fail to show that an agent's narrow states don't fix the extensions of his terms since (in effect) a distinct narrow state corresponds to each distinct extension. After further analysis, he concludes that the contents of *all* of an agent's intentional states involving natural kinds do indeed presuppose entities other than the agent. If to be narrow is not to so presuppose, then there just aren't any narrow intentional states.

Daniel Dennett, in a selection excerpted from his "Beyond Belief" (1982), disagrees with Burge's conclusion here. To "characterize psychological states 'in the narrow sense'," he writes, is to answer the question, "What is the organismic contribution to the fixation of propositional attitudes?" Inner syntax, he argues, can't be it because different syntactic states can support the same "contribution"; nor are propositional attitudes themselves basic since different propositional attitudes may *rest* on the same "contribution" (as in the case of indexical beliefs). Thus, something else is needed, something "halfway between syntax and semantics"—what Dennett calls "notional-attitude psychology."

Like phenomenology, such a psychology is concerned with the individual's subjective world; unlike phenomenology, it analyzes that world from outside, from a third-person perspective. This psychology tries to construct a model of the subject's representations, or, more accurately, of that which is represented thereby. This model, this notional world, is a fictional world, "but the inhabitants of the fictional world are treated as the notional referents of the subject's representations." After exploring constraints on the construction of notional worlds, Dennett observes that if notional attitudes are to play the intermediary roles described above, then it should follow that, roughly, notional attitudes plus environment yield propositional attitudes. But do they? In reply to the objection that they don't, he presents and analyzes a short tale called "The Ballad of Shakey's Pizza Parlor."

In the next selection, "Social Content and Psychological Content" (1985), Brian Loar observes that a strategy common to many of the authors arguing about "psychological" (i.e., mental) content is to criticize a given thesis about mental content by showing that the thesis fails to individuate intentional states in accordance with ordinary uses of that-clauses (such as "believes that p"). The thesis to be criticized might suggest, for example, that in a given case, two different beliefs are at play even though only a single that-clause applies to the believer. It might otherwise suggest that two individuals have the same belief even though we apply two different that-clauses to them. Loar notes that these two versions of the critical strategy share two assumptions: paraphrased roughly, that (A) sameness of that-clause application implies sameness of mental content; and (B) differences in that-clause application imply differences in mental content. Loar then argues that both (A) and (B) are false.

Regarding (A), Loar varies Kripke's well-known example about "Pierre," who grows up in France and comes to believe, via stories, a belief expressible by the sentence "Londres est jolie," and who later moves to London, not realizing it is also called "Londres," and comes to believe a belief expressible by the sentence "London is not pretty." In Loar's variation, Pierre's new belief is, in fact, one ascribable by "London is pretty." However, Loar argues, though "Londres est jolie" is synonymous with "London is pretty" (so that the corresponding that-clauses count as the same), Pierre actually has two different beliefs. This must be the case because those beliefs interact differently with Pierre's other beliefs. In France, for example, Pierre believed that if he ever lived in London ("Londres") he would live in the same city that Oscar Wilde once lived in. But though Pierre now believes he lives in London, he *doesn't* believe that he lives in the same city Oscar Wilde once lived in! Sameness of that-clause application, in short, does not imply sameness of belief.

Regarding (B), Loar argues that if we were to be given a diary and told that it belongs to either an Earthling or a Twin Earthling, but not told which, we would have no trouble providing adequate psychological explanations of the behaviors described therein, despite not knowing the proper referents (H_2O or XYZ) of the relevant terms—and, therefore, which that-clauses properly apply to the agent. This underscores the fact, Loar claims, that two Twins indeed share the relevant mental content even though different that-clauses apply to them. Differences in appropriate that-clauses do not, then, imply differences of belief.

Free of assumptions (A) and (B), the Twin Earth examples prove nothing more radical than that that-clauses don't perfectly map onto intentional states. This realization then allows us two different conceptions of mental content, each suitable for different purposes. "Psychological content" corresponds to the "narrow content" Twins share, which Loar characterizes in terms similar to Dennett's notional-attitude psychology. That-clauses, on the other hand, reflect "social content," which captures "certain extra-psychological relations of propositional attitudes to independent states of affairs. . . ."

A conception of narrow content different from Dennett's is offered by Jerry

Fodor in "Individualism and Supervenience," excerpted from his book *Psycho-semantics* (1987). The "Twin Earth Problem," Fodor argues in this selection, is "just a handful of intuitions together with a commentary on some immediate implications of accepting them." Nothing terribly radical results from them—such as the undermining of the notion of content central to scientific psychology—unless you accept a certain "Diagnosis" of them, viz., that the Twin Earth examples break the connection, for intentional states, between identity of extension and identity of content. But that Diagnosis, Fodor argues, is wrong. The Twin Earth examples don't *break* that connection; they just relativize it to context. Thus, Fodor provides an extensional identity criterion for mental contents: "Two thought contents are identical only if they effect the same mapping of thoughts and contexts onto truth conditions."

This mapping is the heart of Fodor's notion of "narrow content." While the Twins may not share broad contents, Fodor agrees, they do indeed share narrow contents. And indeed their so sharing is all a scientific psychology wants, he argues, since the narrow taxonomy (unlike the broad) doesn't violate such cherished scientific principles as: (1) the mental supervenes on the neural; and (2) taxonomy is guided by causal powers. Put alternatively, this latter principle suggests that states differing *only* in broad content don't differ in causal powers. As a result, they don't determine different kinds for scientific purposes. Furthermore, broad taxonomy isn't what science wants. To reconcile science's interest in mental causation with the idea that extensions are an important determiner of content, in short, requires one to rely on the notion of narrow content. (Fodor further develops the arguments in this selection in his article, "A Modal Argument for Narrow Content," which is also reprinted below.)

Addressing issues of explanation and causation, next, Frank Jackson and Philip Pettit defend, in "Functionalism and Broad Content" (1988), the simplest reply to the question: "What implications does the fact that certain intentional contents are broad (i.e., wide) have for the functionalist theory of mind?" The simplest reply is, merely, that the relevant functional states should themselves be specified broadly, in terms of causal relations to objects external to the agent. But, Jackson and Pettit note, this reply needs defending from two sorts of objections.

The first is that even a broad functionalism cannot capture the fact that mental states have their contents *essentially*. If, that is, a broadly specified functional state is an inner state of the agent, then just what it is causally related to, exactly, will be a contingent affair. In reply to this, Jackson and Pettit argue that it is in fact open to the functionalist to identify a mental state not with the state that plays the functional role, but rather with the state of *having* a state that plays this role. Construed thus, they explain, broad functionalism is perfectly compatible with mental states having their contents essentially.

The second objection to the "simple reply" above is that broad content, now accommodated by broad functionalism, is explanatorily redundant, providing nothing beyond what would be provided by narrow content together with the environment. This objection is typically made via Twin stories: How do we explain the core behavior we share with our Twins? Via our shared narrow contents. How do we explain the differences in our behaviors (e.g., you reach for H_2O, while he reaches for XYZ)? By the differences in environments. But then what is left over for broad content to explain?

In Jackson and Pettit's reply to this objection, they argue that it is not necessary that legitimate causal explanations cite some causally efficacious feature; all these explanations need to do is cite some feature that causally "programs" the effect. Thus, features that causally explain need not themselves cause. Jackson and Pettit's claim, then, is that broad-content explanations are, in fact, "program explanations." If so, the fact that broad properties are themselves not causally efficacious won't prevent them from a bona fide as well as a *distinct* role in psychological explanation. Jackson and Pettit then flesh out the notion of a program explanation, and defend its legitimacy, via the detailed analysis of a number of examples.

After reviewing the anti-individualistic conclusions of Putnam and Burge, Robert Stalnaker notes in the next selection, "On What's in the Head" (1989), that one common response to those conclusions is to grant them, but to limit their significance by revising our ordinary intentional concepts to accommodate them. This revision does not seem to be very radical: one merely needs to factor out the "organismic contribution" to an intentional state. Implicit in this response are two claims: (1) explanatory theories of behavior must be individualistic; and (2) ordinary intentional concepts can indeed be rendered individualistic while they preserve the basic structure of intentional explanation. Stalnaker argues first that (2) is much harder to realize than some think, and then, with regard to (1), that ordinary wide content is less mysterious than some assume.

Stalnaker's analysis of claim (2) consists largely of a critique of Jerry Fodor's and Daniel Dennett's separate attempts (as represented in this volume) to define a workable notion of narrow content. These attempts differ in this rather abstract way: "Fodor proposes to revise and narrow the folk concept of belief by changing the *kind* of thing that is the content of belief. Narrow contents are not propositions; they are functions from context to propositions. But for Dennett ['s notional-attitude psychology], in contrast, narrow contents are the same kind of thing as wide contents: both are propositions . . . What is changed . . . is the relation between a believer and a proposition in virtue of which that proposition correctly describes the believer's beliefs. . . ." Despite this difference, however, Stalnaker argues that both strategies are unsuccessful. Fodor's account neither indicates how to identify particular narrow contents, nor provides any reason to believe that an agent's internal states determine the proposed functions. Dennett's, on the other hand, unjustifiably accepts that an agent's internal dispositions sufficiently determine the agent's "notional world."

In the final part of the article, Stalnaker argues that those, (such as Fodor), who support claim (1) above in fact conflate the notions of individuation by causal powers and individuation by what *affects* causal powers. Distinguishing these enables one to preserve the causal relevance of "wide" properties in a way that makes ordinary wide content perfectly acceptable—not merely acceptable. Stalnaker provides several reasons why generalizations over wide properties may indeed be indispensable (cf. the Jackson and Pettit selection above). Stalnaker fleshes out all of this with some ideas from an informational account of mental representation.

Colin McGinn, in the brief selection "Twin Earth and Teleology" excerpted from his book *Mental Content* (1989), next argues that a teleological account of content explains very nicely the context-sensitivity of content demonstrated by the Twin Earth thought experiment. Biological functions, having evolved to cope with what is actually present in the environment, are clearly context-sensitive: the function of pigments in Earth skin includes that of protecting from sunburn, while the corresponding pigments in Twin Earth skin function to protect from Twin sunburn. But if one understands content as a "special case of function," as the teleology theorist does, then content will inherit the same context-sensitivity. "Twin Earth cases . . . are thus *predictable* from the teleological theory plus the context-dependence of functional specifications," McGinn writes, which amounts to "a pleasant confirmation of the teleological theory."

Jerry Fodor then returns in "A Modal Argument for Narrow Content" (1991) to have another go at defending individualism, presented here as the view that Twins should be treated as members of the same natural kind for purposes of psychological explanation. As he notes, he uses many of the same materials as in the selection from *Psychosemantics* summarized above, although he puts them together somewhat differently. The main objection Fodor addresses in this new version is the claim that two agents differing only in broad content may *indeed* differ in causal powers. After all, the objection goes, your water desire causes you to ask for water, while your Twin's twater desire causes him to ask for twater, and these would be the case even *if* you suddenly were to switch places. But then such differences in causal powers demand that the respective mental states be type-distinguished—and individualism is false.

In reply to this objection, Fodor first attempts to formulate and argue for a condition that "has to be satisfied if a property of a cause is a causal power in virtue of its responsibility for a certain property of an effect." He then argues that the sorts of properties that distinguish Twins don't satisfy this condition in the appropriate way. What is this condition? Basically this: for a difference in properties to count as a difference in causal powers, there must not only be a difference in effects due to those properties but, further, the difference between the effects must be *nonconceptually* related to the differences between the causes. It's this latter part the Twins cases fail, for the difference between asking for water and asking for twater is conceptually related to the difference between the mental states causing those behaviors. As Fodor explains, it is "conceptually necessary that water thinking leads to water behavior and twater thinking does not." In short, Fodor concludes again that a difference in broad content alone does *not* amount to a difference in causal powers, and individualism is preserved.

In "All the Difference in the World" (1991), Tim Crane observes that the general consensus about the Putnam and Burge thought experiments is that they force us one way or the other: we must be either for individualism or against it. In this selection, however, Crane takes issue with that consensus. In fact, he argues, Putnam's and Burge's externalist arguments *fail* to so force us. Not only are their conclusions at odds with other views we hold dear, but their arguments are unsound. As a result, there is no Twin Earth problem after all; those who have sought to solve the problem have sought needlessly for when looked at more carefully the problem *dissolves*.

With which other views is externalism at odds? As other authors in this volume note, externalism appears to be in conflict with basic principles about: (A) causation in general; and (B) the causal nature of intentional states in particular. (B) is just the relatively uncontroversial view that intentional states have causes and effects. (A) is the view that causal relations generally hold between instances of intrinsic properties. Together they are a problem for externalism since broad content as a nonintrinsic property seems according to (A) to be incapable of the causal role demanded by (B). This means that an externalist must give up at least one of the two principles. Since both (A) and (B) are very compelling, however, Crane concludes that we must look for ways to disarm the Twin Earth arguments.

What, then, is wrong with Putnam's arguments? (Note that Crane also addresses Burge's arguments.) In essence, the issue boils down to one premise: when Twins speak the same words, their sentences have different truth conditions (cf. Burge's "Other Bodies" selection above). Why should we believe this? In the cases of words like "water," and perhaps even more elemental natural-kind terms like "chlorine," it is plausible that, between Earth and Twin Earth, there are multiple types of the corresponding item. But then if twater is just a type of water, the Twins will mean the same thing by "water," and the "problem" dissolves. Similar considerations hold in the case of such substances as aluminum and molybdenum, where we have two genuinely different elements that are superficially indistinguishable. Why not just say that the Twins share a concept that happens to include in its extension both metals? If so, then, again, there is no longer an argument showing that intentional states are broad.

Should we then conclude that intentional states are narrow? No, Crane maintains, because narrow content was invented only in reply to the Twin Earth challenge. Without that challenge, there is no need to invoke it. Rather, intentional states simply have content "in the ordinary, truth-conditional sense"; what Twins share is a state with just this content, "nothing more, nothing less. All the differences are in the world."

Finally, in "Putnam on Mind and Meaning" (1992), our last selection in Part III, John McDowell examines Putnam's claim that the following two views do not cohere: (1) that extension is determined by meaning; and (2) that knowledge of meanings is wholly a matter of how things are in a subject's mind. Rather than argue this way, McDowell urges, "we should insist on making the two [views] cohere and conceive the mind in whatever way that requires." If, therefore, the Twin Earth examples show that meanings aren't in the head, then since knowledge of meanings is in the mind, we should conclude that the mind isn't in the head either. In this selection, McDowell suggests a reading of this latter claim that, he argues, should, in fact, to be congenial to Putnam.

McDowell's basic idea is this. To drop the idea that the mind is in the head is to drop the idea that mind is an "organ," i.e., that states and occurrences "in" the mind have an intrinsic nature independent of how the mind's possessor is placed in the environment. What follows from this is a radically nonsolipsistic conception of mind that undermines even the idea that Twins share at least some sort of underlying narrow mental state. But if this idea goes, so does another: that reference is some sort of external relation between an independently characterizable inner mental state and something in the world. In its place, McDowell suggests, should be the idea that mental states are *intrinsically* referential, that there is *nothing* in the mind characterizable independently of what that thing represents. In short, McDowell supports "the possibility of mental representing without representations."

But while these ideas seem to be opposed to Putnam's view, according to which the mind *is* an organ, McDowell observes that they follow from Putnam's own reflections on meaning. Indeed, McDowell's diagnosis of this situation is that while Putnam vigorously objects to (A) an "isolationist" conception of language, he fails to note his own (B) isolationist presuppositions about mind, as evident in his admitting even narrow (as opposed to wide) mental states. Putnam's attack on (A), McDowell notes, leaves (B) unquestioned. McDowell concludes: "Taking on the whole package would have yielded a deeper understanding of what underlies the 'isolationist' conception of language. . . . A general attack on 'isolationism' promises a satisfyingly cohesive and radical reorientation, very much in the spirit of Putnam's own best thinking, of philosophy's approach to the relations between the individual subject and the world."

7

From "Individualism and the Mental"

Tyler Burge

SINCE HEGEL'S *PHENOMENOLOGY OF SPIRIT*, a broad, inarticulate division of emphasis between the individual and his social environment has marked philosophical discussions of mind. On one hand, there is the traditional concern with the individual subject of mental states and events. In the elderly Cartesian tradition, the spotlight is on what exists or transpires "in" the individual—his secret cogitations, his innate cognitive structures, his private perceptions and introspections, his grasping of ideas, concepts, or forms. More evidentially oriented movements, such as behaviorism and its liberalized progeny, have highlighted the individual's publicly observable behavior—his input-output relations and the dispositions, states, or events that mediate them. But both Cartesian and behaviorist viewpoints tend to feature the individual subject. On the other hand, there is the Hegelian preoccupation with the role of social institutions in shaping the individual and the content of his thought. This tradition has dominated the continent since Hegel. But it has found echoes in English-speaking philosophy during this century in the form of a concentration on language. Much philosophical work on language and mind has been in the interests of Cartesian or behaviorist viewpoints that I shall term "individualistic." But many of Wittgenstein's remarks about mental representation point up a social orientation that is discernible from his flirtations with behaviorism. And more recent work on the theory of reference has provided glimpses of the role of social cooperation in determining what an individual thinks.

In many respects, of course, these emphases within philosophy—individualistic and social—are compatible. To an extent, they may be regarded simply as different currents in the turbulent stream of ideas that has washed the intellectual landscape during the last hundred and some odd years. But the role of the social environment has received considerably less clearheaded philosophical attention (though perhaps not less philosophical attention) than the role of the states, occurrences, or acts in, on, or by the individual. Philosophical discussions of social factors have tended to be obscure, evocative, metaphorical, or platitudinous, or to be bent on establishing some large thesis about the course of history and the destiny of man. There remains much room for sharp delineation. I shall offer some considerations that stress social factors in descriptions of an individual's mental phenomena. These considerations call into question

125

individualistic presuppositions of several traditional and modern treatments of mind. I shall conclude with some remarks about mental models.

I. TERMINOLOGICAL MATTERS

Our ordinary mentalistic discourse divides broadly into two sorts of idiom. One typically makes reference to mental states or events in terms of sentential expressions. The other does not. A clear case of the first kind of idiom is "Alfred thinks that his friends' sofa is ugly." A clear case of the second sort is "Alfred is in pain." Thoughts, beliefs, intentions, and so forth are typically specified in terms of subordinate sentential clauses, that-clauses, which may be judged as true or false. Pains, feels, tickles, and so forth have no special semantical relation to sentences or to truth or falsity. There are intentional idioms that fall in the second category on this characterization, but that share important semantical features with expressions in the first—idioms like "Al worships Buicks." But I shall not sort these out here. I shall discuss only the former kind of mentalistic idiom. The extension of the discussion to other intentional idioms will not be difficult.

In an ordinary sense, the noun phrases that embed sentential expressions in mentalistic idioms provide the *content* of the mental state or event. We shall call that-clauses and their grammatical variants "*content-clauses*." Thus, the expression "that sofas are more comfortable than pews" provides the content of Alfred's belief that sofas are more comfortable than pews. My phrase "provides the content" represents an attempt at remaining neutral, at least for present purposes, among various semantical and metaphysical accounts of precisely how that-clauses function and precisely what, if anything, contents are.

Although the notion of content is, for present purposes, ontologically neutral, I do think of it as holding a place in a systematic *theory* of mentalistic language. The question of when to count contents different, and when the same, is answerable to theoretical restrictions. It is often remarked that in a given context we may ascribe to a person two that-clauses that are only loosely equivalent and count them as attributions of the "same attitude." We may say that Al's intention to climb Mt. McKinley and his intention to climb the highest mountain in the United States are the "same intention." (I intend the terms for the mountain to occur obliquely here. See later discussion.) This sort of point extends even to content clauses with extensionally nonequivalent counterpart notions. For contextually relevant purposes, we might count a thought that the glass contains some water as "the same thought" as a thought that the glass contains some thirst-quenching liquid, particularly if we have no reason to attribute either content as opposed to the other, and distinctions between them are irrelevant. Nevertheless, in both these examples, every systematic theory I know of would want to represent the semantical contribution of the content-clauses in distinguishable ways—as "providing different contents."

One reason for doing so is that the person himself is capable of having different attitudes described by the different content-clauses, even if these differences are irrelevant in a particular context. (Al might have developed the intention to climb the highest mountain before developing the intention to climb Mt. McKinley—regardless of whether he, in fact, did so.) A second reason is that the counterpart components of the that-clauses allude to distinguishable elements in people's cognitive lives. "Mt. McKinley" and "the highest mountain in the U.S." serve, or might serve, to indicate cognitively different notions. This is a vague, informal way of generalizing Frege's point: the thought that Mt. McKinley is the highest mountain in the U.S. is potentially interesting or informative. The thought that Mt. McKinley is Mt. McKinley is not. Thus, when we say in a given context that attribution of different contents is attribution of the "same attitude," we use "same attitude" in a way similar to the way we use "same car" when we say that people who drive Fords (or green 1970 Ford Mavericks) drive the "same car." For contextual purposes different cars are counted as "amounting to the same."

Although this use of "content" is theoretical, it is not, I think, theoretically controversial. In cases where we shall be counting contents different, the cases will be uncontentious: in any systematic theory, differences in the *extension*—the actual denotation, referent, or application—of counterpart expressions in that-clauses will be semantically represented, and will, in our terms, make for differences in content. I shall be avoiding the more controversial, but interesting, questions about the general conditions under which sentences in that-clauses can be expected to provide the same content.

I should also warn of some subsidiary terms. I shall be (and have been) using the term "*notion*" to apply to components or elements of contents. Just as whole that-clauses provide the content of a person's attitude, semantically relevant components of that-clauses will be taken to indicate notions that enter into the attitude (or the attitude's content). The term is supposed to be just as ontologically neutral as its fellow. When I talk of understanding or mastering the notion of contract, I am not relying on any special epistemic or ontological theory, except insofar as the earlier-mentioned theoretical restrictions on the notion of content are inherited by the notion of notion. The expression, "*understanding (mastering) a notion*" is to be construed more or less intuitively. Understanding the notion of contract comes roughly to knowing what a contract is. One can master the notion of contract without mastering the term "contract"—at the very least if one speaks some language other than English that has a term roughly synonymous with "contract." (An analogous point holds for my use of "mastering a content.") Talk of notions is roughly similar to talk of concepts in an informal sense. "Notion" has the advantage of being easier to separate from traditional theoretical commitments.

I speak of *attributing* an attitude, content, or notion, and of *ascribing* a that-clause or other piece of language. Ascriptions are the linguistic analogs of attributions. This use of "ascribe" is nonstandard, but convenient and easily assimilated.

There are semantic complexities involving the behavior of expressions in content-clauses, most of which we can skirt. But some must be touched on. Basic to the subject is the observation that expressions in content-clauses are often not intersubstitutable with extensionally equivalent expressions in such a way as to maintain the truth value of the containing sentence. Thus, from the facts that water is H_2O and that Bertrand thought that water is not fit to drink, it does not follow that Bertrand thought that H_2O is not fit to drink. When an expression like "water" functions in a content-clause so that it is not freely exchangeable with all extensionally equivalent expressions, we shall say that it has *oblique occurrence*. Roughly speaking, the reason why "water" and "H_2O" are not interchangeable in our report of Bertrand's thought is that "water" plays a role in characterizing a different mental act or state from that which "H_2O" would play a role in characterizing. In this context at least, thinking that water is not fit to drink is different from thinking that H_2O is not fit to drink.

By contrast, there are nonoblique occurrences of expressions in content-clauses. One might say that some water—say, the water in the glass over there—is thought by Bertrand to be impure; or that Bertrand thought that *that* water is impure. And one might intend to make no distinction that would be lost by replacing "water" with "H_2O,"—or "that water" with "that H_2O" or "that common liquid," or any other expression extensionally equivalent with "that water." We might allow these exchanges even though Bertrand had never heard of, say, H_2O. In such purely nonoblique occurrences, "water" plays *no role* in providing the *content* of Bertrand's thought, *on our use of "content,"* or (in any narrow sense) in characterizing Bertrand or his mental state. Nor is the water part of Bertrand's thought content. We speak of Bertrand *thinking his content of* the water. At its nonoblique occurrence, the term "that water" simply isolates, in one of many equally good ways, a portion of wet stuff to which Bertrand or his thought is related or applied. In certain cases, it may also mark a context in which Bertrand's thought is applied. But it is expressions at oblique occurrences within content clauses that primarily do the job of providing the content of mental states or events, and in characterizing the person.

Mentalistic discourse containing obliquely occurring expressions has traditionally been called *intentional discourse*. The historical reasons for this nomenclature are complex and partly confused. But roughly speaking, grammatical contexts involving oblique occurrences have been fixed upon as specially relevant to the representational character (sometimes called "intentionality") of mental states and events. Clearly oblique occurrences in mentalistic discourse have something to do with characterizing a person's epistemic perspective—how things seem to him, or in an informal sense, how they are represented to him. So without endorsing all the commitments of this tradition, I shall take over its terminology.

The crucial point in the preceding discussion is the assumption that obliquely occurring expressions in content-clauses are a primary means of identifying a person's intentional mental states or events. A further point is worth remarking here. It is normal to suppose that those content clauses correctly ascribable to a person that are not in general intersubstitutable *salva veritate*—and certainly those that involve extensionally nonequivalent counterpart expressions—identify different mental states or events.

I have cited contextual exceptions to this normal supposition, at least in a manner of speaking. We sometimes count distinctions in content irrelevant for purposes of a given attribution, particularly where our evidence for the precise content of a person or animal's attitude is skimpy. Different contents may contextually identify (what amount to) the "same attitude." I have indicated that even in these contexts, I think it best, strictly speaking, to construe distinct contents as describing different mental states or events that are merely equivalent for the purposes at hand. I believe that this view is widely accepted. But nothing I say will depend on it. For any distinct contents, there will be imaginable contexts of attribution in which, even in the loosest, most informal ways of speaking, those contents would be said to describe different mental states or events. This is a consequence of the theoretical role of contents, discussed earlier. Since our discussion will have an "in principle" character, I shall take these contexts to be the relevant ones. Most of the cases we discuss will involve *extensional* differences between obliquely occurring counterpart expressions in that-clauses. In such cases, it is particularly natural and normal to take different contents as identifying different mental states or events.

II. A Thought Experiment

IIa. First Case

We now turn to a three-step thought experiment. Suppose first that:

A given person has a large number of attitudes commonly attributed with content-clauses containing "arthritis" in oblique occurrence. For example, he thinks (correctly) that he has had arthritis for years, that his arthritis in his wrists and fingers is more painful than his arthritis in his ankles, that it is better to have arthritis than cancer of the liver, that stiffening joints is a symptom of arthritis, that certain sorts of aches are characteristic of arthritis, that there are various kinds of arthritis, and so forth. In short, he has a wide range of such attitudes. In addition to these unsurprising attitudes, he thinks falsely that he has developed arthritis in the thigh.

Generally competent in English, rational and intelligent, the patient reports to his doctor his fear that his arthritis has now lodged in his thigh. The doctor replies by telling him that this cannot be so, since arthritis is specifically an inflammation of joints. Any dictionary could have told him the same. The patient is surprised, but relinquishes his view and goes on to ask what might be wrong with his thigh.

The second step of the thought experiment consists of a counterfactual supposition. We are to conceive of a situation in which the patient proceeds from birth through the same course of physical events that he actually does, right to and including the time at which he first reports his fear to his doctor. Precisely the same things (nonintentionally described) happen to him. He has the same physiological history, the same diseases, the same internal physical occurrences. He goes through the same motions, engages in the same behavior, has the same sensory intake (physiologically described). His dispositions to respond to stimuli are explained in physical theory as the effects of the same proximate causes. All of this extends to his interaction with linguistic expressions. He says and hears the same words (word forms) at the same time he actually does. He develops the disposition to assent to "Arthritis can occur in the thigh" and "I have arthritis in the thigh" as a result of the same physically described proximate causes. Such dispositions might have arisen in a number of ways. But we can suppose that in both actual and counterfactual situations, he acquires the word "arthritis" from casual conversation or reading, and never hearing anything to prejudice him for or against applying it in the way that he does, he applies the word to an ailment in his thigh (or to ailments in the limbs of others) which seems to produce pains or other symptoms roughly similar to the disease in his hands and ankles. In both actual and counterfactual cases, the disposition is never reinforced or extinguished up until the time when he expresses himself to his doctor. We further imagine that the patient's nonintentional, phenomenal experience is the same. He has the same pains, visual fields, images, and internal verbal rehearsals. The *counterfactuality* in the supposition touches only the patient's social environment. In actual fact, "arthritis," as used in his community, does not apply to ailments outside joints. Indeed, it fails to do so by a standard, nontechnical dictionary definition. But in our imagined case, physicians, lexicographers, and informed laymen apply "arthritis" not only to arthritis but to various other rheumatoid ailments. The standard use of the term is to be conceived to encompass the patient's actual misuse. We could imagine either that arthritis had not been singled out as a family of diseases, or that some other term besides "arthritis" were applied, though not commonly by laymen, specifically to arthritis. We may also suppose that this difference and those necessarily associated with it are the only differences between the counterfactual situation and the actual one. (Other people besides the patient will, of course, behave differently.) To summarize the second step:

> The person might have had the same physical history and nonintentional mental phenomena while the word "arthritis" was conventionally applied, and defined to apply, to various rheumatoid ailments, including the one in the person's thigh, as well as to arthritis.

The final step is an interpretation of the counterfactual case, or an addition to it as so far described. It is reasonable to suppose that:

> In the counterfactual situation, the patient lacks some—probably *all*—of the attitudes commonly attributed with content-clauses containing "ar-

thritis" in oblique occurrence. He lacks the occurrent thoughts or beliefs that he has arthritis in the thigh, that he has had arthritis for years, that stiffening joints and various sorts of aches are symptoms of arthritis, that his father had arthritis, and so on.

We suppose that in the counterfactual case we cannot correctly ascribe any content-clause containing an oblique occurrence of the term "arthritis." It is hard to see how the patient could have picked up the notion of arthritis. The word "arthritis" in the counterfactual community does not mean *arthritis*. It does not apply only to inflammations of the joints. We suppose that no other word in the patient's repertoire means *arthritis*. "Arthritis," in the counterfactual situation, differs both in dictionary definition and in extension from "arthritis" as we use it. Our ascriptions of content-clauses to the patient (and ascriptions within his community) would not constitute attributions of the same contents we actually attribute. For counterpart expressions in the content clauses that are actually counterfactually ascribable are not even extensionally equivalent. However we describe the patient's attitudes in the counterfactual situation, it will not be with a term or phrase extensionally equivalent with "arthritis." So the patient's counterfactual-attitudes contents differ from his actual ones.

The upshot of these reflections is that the patient's mental contents differ while his entire physical and nonintentional mental histories, considered in isolation from their social context, remain the same. (We could have supposed that he dropped dead at the time he first expressed his fear to the doctor.) The differences seem to stem from differences "outside" the patient considered as an isolated physical organism, causal mechanism, or seat of consciousness. The difference in his mental contents is attributable to differences in his social environment. In sum, the patient's internal qualitative experiences, his physiological states and events, his behaviorally described stimuli and responses, his dispositions to behave, and whatever sequences of states (nonintentionally described) mediated his input and output—all these remain constant, while his attitude contents differ, even in the extensions of counterpart notions. As we observed at the outset, such differences are ordinarily taken to spell differences in mental states and events.

IIB. FURTHER EXEMPLIFICATIONS

The argument has an extremely wide application. It does not depend, for example, on the kind of word "arthritis" is. We could have used an artifact term, an ordinary natural-kind word, a color adjective, a social-role term, a term for a historical style, an abstract noun, an action verb, a physical-movement verb, or any of various other sorts of words. I prefer to leave open precisely how far one can generalize the argument. But I think it has a very wide scope. The argument can get under way in any case where it is intuitively possible to attribute a mental state or event whose content involves a notion that the subject incompletely understands. As will become clear, this possibility is the key to the thought experiment. I want to give a more concrete sense of the possibility before going further.

It is useful to reflect on the number and variety of intuitively clear cases in which it is normal to attribute a content that the subject incompletely understands. One need only thumb through a dictionary for an hour or so to develop a sense of the extent to which one's beliefs are infected by incomplete understanding.[1] The phenomenon is rampant in our pluralistic age.

(a.) Most cases of incomplete understanding that support the thought experiment will be fairly idiosyncratic. There is a reason for this. Common linguistic errors, if entrenched, tend to become common usage. But a generally competent speaker is bound to have numerous words in his repertoire, possibly even common words, that he somewhat misconstrues. Many of these misconstruals will not be such as to deflect ordinary ascriptions of that-clauses involving the incompletely mastered term in oblique occurrence. For example, one can imagine a generally competent, rational adult having a large number of attitudes involving the notion of sofa—including beliefs that *those* (some sofas) are sofas, that some sofas are beige, that his neighbors have a new sofa, that he would rather sit in a sofa for an hour than on a church pew. In addition, he might think that sufficiently broad (but single-seat) overstuffed armchairs are sofas. With care, one can develop a thought experiment parallel to the one in section IIa, in which at least some of the person's attitude contents (particularly, in this case, contents of occurrent mental events) differ, while his physical history, dispositions to behavior, and phenomenal experience—non-intentionally and asocially described—remain the same.

(b.) Although most relevant misconstruals are fairly idiosyncratic, there do seem to be certain types of error which are relatively common—but not so common and uniform as to suggest that the relevant terms take on new sense. Much of our vocabulary is taken over from others who, being specialists, understand our terms better than we do.[2] The use of scientific terms by laymen is a rich source of cases. As the arthritis example illustrates, the thought experiment does not depend on specially technical terms. I shall leave it to the imagination of the reader to spin out further examples of this sort.

(c.) One need not look to the laymen's acquisitions from science for examples. People used to buying beef brisket in stores or ordering it in restaurants (and conversant with it in a general way) probably often develop mistaken beliefs (or uncertainties) about just what brisket is. For example, one might think that brisket is a cut from the flank or rump, or that it includes not only the lower part of the chest but also the upper part, or that it is specifically a cut of beef and not of, say, pork. No one hesitates to ascribe to such people content-clauses with "brisket" in oblique occurrence. For example, a person may believe that he is eating brisket under these circumstances (where "brisket" occurs in oblique position); or he may think that brisket tends to be tougher than loin. Some of these attitudes may be false; many will be true. We can imagine a counterfactual case in which the person's physical history, his dispositions, and his nonintentional mental life, are all the same, but in which "brisket" is commonly applied in a different way— perhaps in precisely the way the person thinks it applies. For example, it might apply only to beef and to the upper and lower parts of the chest. In such a case, as in the sofa and arthritis cases, it would seem that the person would (or might) lack some or all of the propositional attitudes that are actually attributed with content clauses involving "brisket" in oblique position.

(d.) Someone only generally versed in music history, or superficially acquainted with a few drawings of musical instruments, might naturally but mistakenly come to think that clavichords included harpsichords without legs. He may have many other beliefs involving the notion of clavichord, and many of these may be true. Again, with some care, a relevant thought experiment can be generated.

(e.) A fairly common mistake among lawyers' clients is to think that one cannot have a contract with someone unless there has been a written agreement. The client might be clear in intending "contract" (in the relevant sense) to apply to agreements, not to pieces of paper. Yet he may take it as part of the meaning of the word, or the essence of law, that a piece of formal writing is a necessary condition for establishing a contract. His only experiences with contracts might have involved formal documents, and he undergeneralizes. It is not terribly important here whether one says that the client misunderstands the term's meaning, or alternatively that the client makes a mistake about the essence of contracts. In either case, he misconceives what a contract is, yet ascriptions involving the term in oblique position are made anyway.

It is worth emphasizing here that I intend the misconception to involve the subject's attaching counterfactual consequences to his mistaken belief about contracts. Let me elaborate this a bit. A common dictionary definition of "contract" is "legally binding agreement." As I am imagining the case, the client does not explicitly define "contract" to himself in this way (though he might use this phrase in explicating the term). And he is not merely making a mistake about what the law happens to enforce. If asked why unwritten agreements are not contracts, he is likely to say something like, "They just aren't" or "It is part of the nature of the law and legal practice that they have no force." He is not disposed without prodding to answer, "It would be possible but impractical to give unwritten agreements legal force." He might concede this. But he would add that such agreements would not be contracts. He regards a document as inseparable from contractual obligation, regardless of whether he takes this to be a matter of meaning or a metaphysical essentialist truth about contracts.

Needless to say, these niceties are philosophers' distinctions. They are not something an ordinary man is likely to have strong opinions about. My point is that the thought experiment is independent of these distinctions. It does not depend on misunderstandings of dictionary meaning. One might say that the client understood the term's dictionary meaning, but misunderstood its essential application in the law—misconceived the nature of contracts. The thought experiment still flies. In a counterfactual case in which the law enforces both written and unwritten agreements and in which the subject's behavior and so forth are the same, but in which "contract" *means* "legally binding agreement based on written document," we would not attribute to him a mistaken belief that a contract requires written agreement, although the lawyer might have to point out that there are other legally binding agreements that do not require documents. Similarly, the client's other propositional attitudes would no longer involve the notion of contract, but another more restricted notion.

(f.) People sometimes make mistakes about color ranges. They may correctly apply a color term to a certain color, but also mistakenly apply it to shades of a neighboring color. When asked to explain the color term, they cite the standard cases (for "red," the color of blood, fire engines, and so forth). But they apply the term somewhat beyond its conventionally established range—beyond the reach of its vague borders. They think that fire engines, including *that* one, are red. They observe that red roses are covering the trellis. But they also think that *those* things are a shade of red (whereas they are not). Second looks do not change their opinion. But they give in when other speakers confidently correct them in unison.

This case extends the point of the contract example. The error is linguistic or conceptual in something like the way that the shopper's mistake involving the notion of brisket is. It is not an ordinary empirical error. But one may reasonably doubt that the subjects misunderstand the dictionary meaning of the color term. Holding their nonintentional phenomenal experience, physical history, and behavioral dispositions constant, we can imagine that "red" were applied as they mistakenly apply it. In such cases, we would no longer ascribe content-clauses involving the term "red" in oblique position. The attribution of the correct beliefs about fire engines and roses would be no less affected than the attribution of the beliefs that, in the actual case, display the misapplication. Cases bearing out the latter point are common in anthropological reports on communities whose color terms do not match ours. Attributions of content typically allow for the differences in conventionally established color ranges.

Here is not the place to refine our rough distinctions among the various kinds of misconceptions that serve the thought experiment. Our philosophical purposes do not depend on how these distinctions are drawn. Still, it is important to see what an array of conceptual errors is common among us. And it is important to note that such errors do not always or automatically prevent attribution of mental content provided by the very terms that are incompletely understood or misapplied. The thought experiment is nourished by this aspect of common practice.

IIC. EXPANSION AND DELINEATION OF THE THOUGHT EXPERIMENT

As I have tried to suggest in the preceding examples, the relevant attributions in the first step of the thought experiment need not display the subject's error. They may be attributions of a true content. We can begin with a propositional attitude that involved the misconceived notion, but in a true, unproblematic application of it: for example, the patient's belief that he, like his father, developed arthritis in the ankles and wrists at age 58 (where "arthritis" occurs obliquely).

One need not even rely on an underlying *misconception* in the thought experiment. One may pick a case in which the subject only partially understands an expression. He may apply it firmly and correctly in a range of cases, but be unclear or agnostic about certain of its applications or implications which, in fact, are fully established in common practice. Most of the examples we gave previously can be reinterpreted in this way. To take a new one, imagine that our protagonist is unsure whether his father has mortgages on the car and the house, or just one on the house. He is a little uncertain about exactly how the loan and collateral must be arranged in order for their to be a mortgage, and he is not clear about whether one may have mortgages on anything other than houses. He is sure, however, that Uncle Harry paid off his mortgage. Imagine our man constant in the ways previously indicated and that "mortgage" commonly applied only to mortgages on houses. But imagine banking practices themselves to be the same. Then the subject's uncertainty would plausibly not involve the notion of mortgage. Nor would his other propositional attitudes be correctly attributed with the term "mortgage" in oblique position. Partial understanding is as good as misunderstanding for our purposes.

On the other hand, the thought experiment does appear to depend on the possibility of someone's having a propositional attitude despite an incomplete mastery of some notion in its content. To see why this appears to be so, let us try to run through a thought experiment, attempting to avoid any imputation of incomplete understanding. Suppose the subject thinks falsely that all swans are white. One can certainly hold the features of swans and the subject's nonintentional phenomenal experience, physical history, and nonintentional dispositions constant, and imagine that "swan" meant "white swan" (and perhaps some other term, unfamiliar to the subject, meant what "swan" means). Could one reasonably interpret the subject as having different attitude contents without at some point invoking a misconception? The questions to be asked here are about the subject's dispositions. For example, in the actual case, if he were shown a black swan and told that he was wrong, would he fairly naturally concede his mistake? Or would he respond, "I'm doubtful that that's a swan" until we brought in dictionaries, encyclopedias, and other native speakers to correct his usage? In the latter case, his understanding of "swan" would be deviant. Suppose then that in the actual situation he would respond normally to the counterexample. Then there is reason to say that he understands the notion of swan correctly: and his error is not conceptual or linguistic, but empirical in an ordinary and narrow sense. (Of course, the line we are drawing here is pretty fuzzy.) When one comes to the counterfactual stage of the thought experiment, the subject has the same dispositions to respond pliably to the presentation of a black specimen. But such a response would suggest a misunderstanding of the term "swan" as counterfactually used. For in the counterfactual community what they call "swans" could not fail to be white. The mere presentation of a black swan would be irrelevant to the definitional truth "All swans are white." I have not set this case up as an example of the thought experiment's going through. Rather I have used it to support the conjecture that *if* the thought experiment is to work, one must at some stage find the subject believing (or having some attitude characterized by) a content, despite an incomplete understanding or misapplication. An ordinary empirical error appears not to be sufficient.

It would be a mistake, however, to think that incomplete understanding, in the sense that the argument requires, is in general an unusual or even deviant phenomenon. *What I have called "partial understanding" is common or even normal in the case of a large number of expressions in our vocabularies.* "Arthritis" is a case in point. Even if by the grace of circumstance a person does not fall into views that run counter to the term's meaning or application, it would not be the least deviant or "socially unacceptable" to have no clear attitude that would block such views. "Brisket," "contract," "recession," "sonata," "deer," "elm" (to borrow a well-known example), "ore-amplifier," "carburetor," "gothic," "fermentation" probably provide analogous cases. Continuing the list is largely a matter of patience. The sort of "incomplete understanding" required by the thought experiment includes quite ordinary, nondeviant phenomena.

It is worth remarking that the thought experiment as originally presented might be run in reverse. The idea would be to start with an ordinary belief or thought involving no incomplete understanding. Then we find the incomplete understanding in the second step. For example, properly understanding "arthritis," a patient may think (correctly) that he has arthritis. He happens to have heard of arthritis only occurring in joints, and he correctly believes that that is where arthritis always occurs. Holding his physical history, dispositions, and pain constant, we imagine that "arthritis" commonly applies to rheumatoid ailments of all sorts. Arthritis has not been singled out for special mention. If a patient were told by a doctor "You also have arthritis in the thigh," the patient would be disposed (as he is in the actual case) to respond, "Really? I didn't know that one could have arthritis except in joints." The doctor would answer, "No, arthritis occurs in muscles, tendons, bursas, and elsewhere." The patient would stand corrected. The notion that the doctor and patient would be operating with in such a case would not be that of arthritis.

My reasons for not having originally set out the thought experiment in this way are largely heuristic. As will be seen, discussion of the thought experiment will tend to center on the step involving incomplete understanding. And I wanted to encourage you, dear reader, to imagine actual cases of incomplete understanding in your own linguistic community. Ordinary intuitions in the domestic case are perhaps less subject to premature warping in the interests of theory. Cases involving not only mental-content attribution, but also translation of a foreign tongue, are more vulnerable to intrusion of side issues.

A secondary reason for not beginning with this "reversed" version of the thought experiment is that I find it doubtful whether the thought experiment always works in symmetric fashion. There may be special intuitive problems in certain cases—perhaps, for example, cases involving perceptual natural kinds. We may give special interpretations to individual misconceptions in imagined foreign communities, when those misconceptions seem to match our conceptions. In other words, there may be some systematic, intuitive bias in favor of at least certain of our notions for purposes of interpreting the misconceptions of imagined foreigners. I do not want to explore the point here. I think that any such bias is not always crucial, and that the thought experiment frequently works "symmetrically." We have to take account of a person's community in interpreting his words and describing his attitudes—and this holds in the foreign case as well as in the domestic case.

The reversal of the thought experiment brings home the important point that *even those propositional attitudes not infected by incomplete understanding* depend for their content on social factors that are independent of the individual, asocially and non-intentionally described. For if the social environment has been appropriately different, the contents of those attitudes would have been different.

Even *apart* from reversals of the thought experiment, it is plausible (in the light of its original versions) that our well-understood propositional attitudes depend partly for their content on social factors independent of the individual, asocially and nonintentionally construed. For each of us can reason as follows. Take a set of attitudes that involve a given notion and whose contents are well-understood by me. It is only contingent that I understand that notion as well as I do. Now holding my community's practices constant, imagine that I understand the given notion incompletely, but that the deficient understanding is such that it does not prevent my having attitude contents involving that notion. In fact, imagine that I am in the situation envisaged in the first step of one of the original thought experiments. In such a case, a proper subset of the original set of my actual attitude contents would, or might, remain the same—intuitively, at least those of my actual attitudes whose justification or point is untouched by my imagined deficient understanding. (In the arthritis case, an example would be a true belief that many old people have arthritis.) These attitude contents remain constant despite the fact that my understanding, inference patterns, behavior, dispositions, and so on would in important ways be different and partly inappropriate to applications of the given notion. What is it that enables these unaffected contents to remain applications of the relevant notion? It is not *just* that my understanding, inference patterns, behavior, and so forth are enough like my actual understanding, inference patterns, behavior, and so forth. For if communal practice had *also* varied so as to apply the relevant notion as I am imagining I misapply it, then my attitude contents would not involve the relevant notion at all. This argument suggests that communal practice is a factor (in addition to my understanding, inference patterns, and perhaps behavior, physical activity, and other features) in fixing the contents of my attitudes—even in cases where I fully understand the content.

IID. INDEPENDENCE FROM FACTIVE-VERB AND
INDEXICAL-REFERENCE PARADIGMS

The thought experiment does not play on psychological "success" verbs or "factive" verbs—verbs like "know," "regret," "realize," "remember," "foresee," "perceive." This point is important for our purposes because such verbs suggest an easy and clearcut distinction between the contribution of the individual subject and the object, "veridical" contribution of the environment to making the verbs applicable. (Actually the matter becomes more complicated on reflection, but we shall stay with the simple cases.) When a person knows that snow is common in Greenland, his knowledge obviously depends on more than the way the person is; it depends on there actually being a lot of snow in Greenland. His mental state (belief that snow is common in Greenland) must be successful in a certain way (true). By changing the environment, one could change the truth value of the content, so that the subject could no longer be said to know the content. It is part of the burden of our argument that even intentional mental states of the individual like beliefs, which carry no implication of veridicality or success, cannot be understood by focusing purely on the individual's acts, dispositions, and "inner" goings-on.

The thought experiment also does not rest on the phenomenon of indexicality, or on *de re* attitudes, in any direct way. When Alfred refers to an apple, saying to himself "That is wholesome," what he refers to depends not just on the content of what he says or thinks, but on what apple is before him. Without altering the meaning of Alfred's utterance, the nature of his perceptual experiences, or his physical acts or dispositions, we could conceive an exchange of the actual apple for another one that is indistinguishable to Alfred. We would thereby conceive him as referring to something different and even as saying something with a different truth value.

This rather obvious point about indexicality has come to be seen as providing a model for understanding a certain range of mental states or events—*de re* attitudes. The precise characterization of this range is no simple philosophical task. But the clearest cases involve nonobliquely occurring terms in content clauses. When we say that Bertrand thinks of some water that it would not slake his thirst (where "water" occurs in purely nonoblique position), we attribute a *de re* belief to Bertrand. We assume that Bertrand has something like an indexical relation to the water. The fact that Bertrand believes something of some water, rather than of a portion of some other liquid that is indistinguishable to him, depends partly on the fact that it is water to which Bertrand is contextually, "indexically" related. For intuitively we could have exchanged the liquids without changing Bertrand and thereby changed what Bertrand believed his belief content *of*—and even whether his belief was true of it.[3] It is easy to interpret such cases by holding that the subject's mental states and contents (with allowances for brute differences in the contexts in which he applies those contents) remain the same. The differences in the situations do not pertain in any fundamental way to the subject's mind or the nature of his mental content, but to how his mind or content is related to the world.

It seems to me clear that the thought experiment need not rely on *de re* attitudes at all. The subject need not have entered into special *en rapport* or quasi-indexical relations with objects that the misunderstood term applies to in order for the argument to work. We can appeal to attitudes that would usually be regarded as paradigmatic cases of *de dicto*, nonindexical, *non-de-re* mental attitudes or events. The primary mistake in the contract example is one such, but we could choose others to suit the reader's taste. To insist that such attitudes must all be indexically infected of *de re* would, I think, be to trivialize and emasculate these notions, making nearly all attitudes *de re*. All *de dicto* attitudes presuppose *de re* attitudes. But it does not follow that indexical or *de re* elements survive in every attitude (cf. notes 2 and 3).

I shall not, however, argue this point here. The claim that is crucial is not that our argument does not fix on *de re* attitudes. It is, rather, that the social differences between the actual and counterfactual situations affect the *content* of the subject's attitudes. That is, the difference affects standard cases of obliquely occurring, cognitive-content-conveying expressions in content-clauses. For example, still with his misunderstanding, the subject might think that this (referring to his disease in his hands) is arthritis. Or he might think *de re* of the disease in his ankle or of the disease in his thigh that his arthritis is painful. It does not really matter whether the relevant attitude is *de re* or purely *de dicto*. What is crucial to our argument is that the occurrence of "arthritis" is oblique and contributes to a characterization of the subject's mental content. One might even hold, implausibly I think, that all the subject's attitudes involving the notion of arthritis are *de re*, that "arthritis" in that-clauses *indexically* picks out the property of being arthritis, or something like that. The fact remains that the term occurs obliquely in the relevant cases and serves in characterizing the *dicta* or contents of the subject's attitudes. The thought experiment exploits this fact.

Approaches to the mental that I shall later criticize as excessively individualistic tend to assimilate environmental aspects of mental phenomena to either the factive-verb or indexical-reference paradigm (cf. note 2). This sort of assimilation suggests that one might maintain a relatively clearcut distinction between extra-mental and mental aspects of mentalistic attributions. And it may encourage the idea that the distinctively mental aspects can be understood fundamentally in terms of the individual's abilities, dispositions, states, and so forth, considered in isolation from his social surroundings. Our argument undermines this later suggestion. Social content infects even the distinctively mental features of mentalistic attributions. No man's intentional mental phenomena are insular. Every man is a piece of the social continent, a part of the social main.

ENDNOTES

1. Our examples suggest points about learning that need exploration. It would seem naive to think that we first attain a mastery of expressions or notions we use and then tackle the subject matters we speak and think about in using those expressions or notions. In most cases, the processes overlap. But while the subject's understanding is still partial, we sometimes attribute mental contents in the very terms the subject has yet to master. Traditional views take mastering a word to consist in matching it with an already mastered (or innate) concept. But it would seem, rather, that many concepts (or mental content components) are like words in that they may be employed before they are mastered. In both cases, employment appears to be an integral part of the process of mastery.

2. A development of a similar theme may be found in Hilary Putnam's notion of a division of linguistic labor [cf. "The Meaning of 'Meaning'," in Putnam (1975a), pp.227 ff.]. Putnam's imaginative work is in other ways congenial with points I have developed. Some of his examples can be adapted in fairly obvious ways so as to give an argument with different premises, but a conclusion complementary to the one I arrive at in Section IIa:

   Consider Alfred's belief contents involving the notion of water. Without changing Alfred's (or his fellows') nonintentional phenomenal experiences, internal physical occurrences, or dispositions to respond to stimuli on sensory surfaces, we can imagine that not water (H_2O), but a different liquid with different structure but similar macro-properties (and identical phenomenal properties) played the role in his environment that water does in ours. In such a case, we could ascribe no content clauses to Alfred with "water" in oblique position. His belief contents would differ. The conclusion (with which I am in sympathy) is that mental contents are affected not only by the physical and qualitatively mental way the person is, but by the nature of his *physical environment*.

   Putnam himself does not give quite this argument. He nowhere states the first and third steps, though he gives analogs of them for the meaning of "water." This is partly just a result of his concentration on meaning instead of propositional attitudes. But some of what he says even seems to oppose the argument's conclusion. He remarks in effect that the subject's *thoughts* remain constant between his actual and counterfactual cases (p. 224). In his own argument he explicates the difference between actual and counterfactual cases in terms of a difference in the extension of term, not a difference in those aspects of their meaning that play a role in the cognitive life of the subject. And he tries to explicate his examples in terms of indexicality—a mistake, I think, and one that tends to divert attention from major implications of the examples he gives (cf. Section IId). In my view, the examples do illustrate the fact that all attitudes involving natural-kind notions, including *de dicto* attitudes, presuppose *de re* attitudes. But the examples do not show that natural-kind linguistic expressions are in any ordinary sense indexical. Nor do they show that beliefs involving natural-kind notions are always *de re*. Even if they did, the change from actual to counterfactual cases would affect oblique occurrences of natural-kind terms in that-clauses—occurrences that are the key to attributions of cognitive content (cf. above and note 3). In the cited paper and earlier ones, much of what Putnam says about psychological states (and implies about mental states) has a distinctly individualistic ring. Below in Section IV (not reprinted here—

ed.), I criticize viewpoints about mental phenomena influenced by and at least strongly suggested in his earlier work on functionalism [cf. note 9 (not reprinted here—*ed.*)].

On the other hand, Putnam's articulation of social and environmental aspects of the meaning of natural-kind terms complements and supplements our viewpoint. For me, it has been a rich rewarder of reflection. More recent work of his seems to involve shifts in his viewpoint on psychological states. It may have somewhat more in common with our approach than the earlier work, but there is much that I do not understand about it.

The argument regarding the notion of water that I extracted from Putnam's paper is narrower in scope than our argument. The Putnam-derived argument seems to work only for natural-kind terms and close relatives. And it may seem not to provide as direct a threat to certain versions of functionalism that I discuss in Section IV: At least a few philosophers would claim that one could accommodate the Putnamian argument in terms of *non*intentional formulations of input-output relations (formulations that make reference to the specific nature of the physical environment). Our argument does not submit to this maneuver. In our thought experiment, the physical environment (sofas, arthritis, and so forth in our examples) and the subject's causal relations with it (at least as these are usually conceived) were held constant. The Putnamian argument, however, has fascinatingly different implications from our argument. I have not developed these comparisons and contrasts here because doing justice to Putnam's viewpoint would demand a distracting amount of space, as the ample girth of this footnote may suggest.

3. I have discussed *de re* mental phenomena in Burge (1977). There I argue that all attitudes with content presuppose *de re* attitudes. Our discussion here may be seen as bearing on the details of this presupposition. But for reasons I merely sketch in the next paragraph, I think it would be a superficial viewpoint that tried to utilize our present argument to support the view that nearly all intentional mental phenomena are covertly indexical or *de re*.

8

Other Bodies

Tyler Burge

I⊤ IS FAIRLY UNCONTROVERSIAL, I think, that we can conceive a person's behavior and behavioral dispositions, his physical acts and states, his qualitative feels and fields (all nonintentionally described) as remaining fixed, while his mental attitudes of a certain kind—his *de re* attitudes—vary.[1] Thus, we can imagine Alfred's believing of apple 1 that it is wholesome and holding a true belief. Without altering Alfred's dispositions, subjective experiences, and so forth, we can imagine having substituted an identically appearing but internally rotten apple 2. In such a case, Alfred's belief differs while his behavioral dispositions, inner causal states, and qualitative experiences remain constant.

This sort of point is important for understanding mentalistic notions and their role in our cognitive lives. But taken by itself, it tells us nothing very interesting about mental states. For it is easy (and I think appropriate) to phrase the point so as to strip it of immediate philosophical excitement. We may say that Alfred has the *same* belief-content in both situations.[2]

It is just that he would be making contextually different applications of that content to different entities. His belief is true of apple 1 and false of apple 2. The *nature* of his mental state is the same. He simply bears different relations to his environment. We do say in ordinary language that one belief is true and the other is false. But this is just another way of saying that what he believes is true of the first apple and would be false of the second. We may call these relational beliefs different beliefs if we want. But differences among such relational beliefs do not entail differences among mental states or contents, as these have traditionally been viewed.

This deflationary interpretation seems to me to be correct. But it suggests an oversimplified picture of the relation between a person's mental states or events and public or external objects and events. It suggests that it is possible to separate rather neatly what aspects of propositional attitudes depend on the person holding the attitudes and what aspects derive from matters external. There is no difference in the obliquely occurring expressions in the content-clauses we attribute to Alfred. It is these sorts of expressions that carry the load in characterizing the individual's mental states and processes. So it might be thought that we could explicate such states and processes by training our philosophical attention purely on the individual subject, explicating the differences in the physical objects that his content applies to in terms of facts about his environment.

To present the view from a different angle: *de re* belief-attributions are fundamentally predicational. They consist in applying or relating an incompletely interpreted content-clause, an open sentence, to an object or sequence of objects, which in effect completes the interpretation. What objects these open sentences apply to may vary with context. But, according to the picture, it remains possible to divide off contextual or environmental elements represented in the propositional attitude attributions from more specifically mentalistic elements. Only the constant features of the predication represent the latter. And the specifically mental features of the propositional attitude can, according to this picture, be understood purely in *individualistic* terms—in terms of the subject's internal acts and skills, his internal causal and functional relations, his surface stimulations, his behavior and behavioral dispositions, and his qualitative experiences, all nonintentionally characterized and specified without regard to the nature of his social or physical environment.

The aim of this paper is to bring out part of what is wrong with this picture and to make some suggestions about the complex relation between a person's mental states and his environment. Through a discussion of certain elements of Putnam's Twin Earth examples, I shall try to characterize ways in which identifying a person's mental states depends on the nature of his physical environment—or on specification, by his fellows, of the nature of that environment.[3]

Before entering into the details of Putnam's thought experiment, I want to sketch the general position that I shall be defending. What is right and what is wrong in the viewpoint I set out in the third and fourth paragraphs of this paper? I have already given some indication of what seems right: individual entities referred to by transparently occurring expressions, and, more generally, entities (however referred to or characterized) of which a person holds his beliefs do not in general play a direct role in characterizing the nature of the person's mental state or event. The difference between apples 1 and 2 does not bear on Alfred's mind in any sense that would immediately affect explanation of Alfred's behavior or assessment of the rationality of his mental activity. Identities of and differences among physical objects are crucial to these enterprises only insofar as those identities and differences affect Alfred's way of viewing such objects.[4] Moreover, it seems unexceptionable to claim that the obliquely occurring expressions in propositional attitude attributions are critical for characterizing a given person's mental state. Such occurrences are the stuff of which explanations of his actions and assessments of his rationality are made.

What I reject is the view that mental states and processes individuated by such obliquely occurring expressions can be understood (or "accounted for") purely in terms of nonintentional characterizations of the *individual subject's* acts, skills, dispositions, physical states, "functional states," and the effects of environmental stimuli on him, without regard to the nature of his physical environment or the activities of his fellows.[5]

In Burge (1979a) I presented a thought experiment in which one fixed nonintentional, individualistic descriptions of the physical, behavioral, phenomenalistic, and (on most formulations) functional histories of an individual. By varying the *uses of words* in his linguistic community we found that the contents of his propositional attitudes varied.[6] I shall draw a parallel conclusion from Putnam's Twin Earth thought experiment: We can fix an individual's physical, behavioral, phenomenalistic, and (on some formulations) functional histories; by varying the *physical environment* one finds that the contents of his propositional attitudes vary. It is to be re-emphasized that the variations in propositional attitudes envisaged are not exhausted by variations in the entities to which individuals' mental contents are related. The contents themselves vary. At any rate, I shall so argue.

I

In Putnam's thought experiment, we are to conceive of a near duplicate of our planet Earth, called "Twin Earth." Except for certain features about to be noted (and necessary consequences of these features), Twin Earth duplicates Earth in every detail. The physical environments look and largely are the same. Many of the inhabitants of one planet have duplicate counterparts on the other, with duplicate macrophysical, experiential, and dispositional histories.

One key difference between the two planets is that the liquid on Twin Earth that runs in rivers and faucets, and is called "water" by those who speak what is called "English" is not H_2O, but a different liquid with a radically different chemical formula, XYZ. I think it natural and obviously correct to say, with Putnam, that the stuff that runs in rivers and faucets on Twin Earth is thus not water. I shall not argue for this view because it is pretty obvious, pretty widely shared, and stronger than arguments that might be or have been brought to buttress it. I will just assume that XYZ is not water of any sort. Water is H_2O. What the Twin Earthians call "water" is XYZ. In translating into English occurrences of "water" in the mouths of Twin Earthians, we would do best to coin a new nonscientific word (say, "twater"), explicated as applying to stuff that looks and tastes like water, but with a fundamentally different chemistry.

It is worth bearing in mind that the thought experiment might apply to any relatively nontheoretical natural-kind word. One need not choose an expression as central to our everyday lives as "water" is. For example, we could (as Putnam in effect suggests) imagine the relevant difference between Earth and Twin Earth to involve the application of "aluminum," or "elm," or "mackerel."[7] A second key difference between Earth and Twin Earth—as we shall discuss the case—is that the scientific community on Earth has determined that the chemical structure of water is H_2O, whereas the scientific community on Twin Earth knows that the structure of twater is XYZ. These pieces of knowledge have spread into the respective lay communities but have not saturated them. In particular, there are numerous scattered individuals on Earth and Twin Earth untouched by the scientific developments. It is these latter individuals who have duplicate counterparts.

We now suppose that Adam is an English speaker and that Adam$_{te}$ is his counterpart on Twin Earth. Neither knows the chemical properties of what he calls "water." This gap in their knowledge is probably not atypical of uneducated members of their communities.[8] But similar gaps are clearly to be expected of users of terms like "aluminum," "elm," "mackerel." (Perhaps not in the case of water, but in the other cases, we could even imagine that Adam and Adam$_{te}$, have no clear idea of what the relevant entities in their respective environments look like or how they feel, smell, or taste.) We further suppose that both have the same qualitative perceptual intake and qualitative streams of consciousness, the same movements, the same behavioral dispositions and inner functional states (nonintentionally and individualistically described). Insofar as they do not ingest, say, aluminum or its counterpart, we might even fix their physical states as identical.

When Adam says or consciously thinks the words, "There is some water within twenty miles, I hope," Adam$_{te}$ says or consciously thinks the same word forms. But there are differences. As Putnam, in effect, points out, Adam's occurrences of "water" apply to water and mean *water*, whereas Adam$_{te}$'s apply to twater and mean *twater*. And, as Putnam does not note, the differences affect *oblique* occurrences in that-clauses that provide the contents of their mental states and events. Adam hopes that there is some water (oblique occurrence) within twenty miles. Adam$_{te}$ hopes that there is some twater within twenty miles. That is, even as we suppose that "water" and "twater" are not logically exchangeable with coextensive expressions *salva veritate*, we have a difference between their thoughts (thought contents).

Laying aside the indexical implicit in "within twenty miles," the propositional attitudes involved are not even *de re*. But I need not argue this point. Someone might wish to claim that these are *de re* attitudes about the relevant *properties* of water (being water? waterhood?) in one case and of twater (etc.) in the other. I need not dispute this claim here. It is enough to note that even if the relevant sentences relate Adam and his counterpart to *res*, those sentences also specify how Adam and Adam$_{te}$ think about the *res*. In the sentence applied to Adam, "water" is, by hypothesis, not exchangeable with coextensive expressions. It is not exchangeable with "H_2O," or with "liquid which covers two-thirds of the face of the earth," or with "liquid said by the Bible to flow from a rock when Moses struck it with a rod." "Water" occurs obliquely in the relevant attribution. And it is expressions in oblique occurrence that play the role of specifying a person's mental contents, what his thoughts are.

In sum, mental states and events like beliefs and thoughts are individuated partly by reference to the constant, or obliquely occurring elements in content clauses. But the contents of Adam and Adam$_{te}$'s beliefs and thoughts differ while every feature of their nonintentionally and individualistically described physical, behavioral, dispositional, and phenomenal histories remains the same. Exact identity of physical states is implausible in the case of water. But this point is irrelevant to the force of the example—and could be circumvented by using a word, such as "aluminum," "elm," etc., that does not apply to something Adam ingests. The difference in their mental states and events seems to be a product primarily of differences in their physical environments, mediated by differences in their social environments—in the mental states of their fellows and conventional meanings of words they and their fellows employ.

II

The preceding argument and its conclusion are not to be found in Putnam's paper. Indeed, the conclusion appears to be incompatible with some of what he says. For example, Putnam interprets the difference between Earth and Twin Earth uses of "water" purely as a difference in extension. And he states that the relevant Earthian and Twin Earthian are "exact duplicates in . . . feelings, thoughts, interior monologue etc." (1975b, p. 224) On our version of the argument the two are in no sense exact duplicates in their thoughts. The differences show up in oblique occurrences in true attributions of propositional attitudes. I shall not speculate about why Putnam did not draw a conclusion so close to the source of his main argument. Instead, I will criticize aspects of his discussion that tend to obscure the conclusion (and have certainly done so for others).

Chief among these aspects is the claim that natural kind words like "water" are indexical (ibid., pp. 229–35). This view tends to suggest that Earth and Twin Earth occurrences of "water" can be assimilated simply to occurrences of indexical expressions like "this" or "I." Adam and Adam$_{te}$'s propositional attitudes would then be further examples of the kind of *de re* attitudes mentioned at the outset of this paper. Their contents would be the same, but would be applied to different *res*.[9] If this were so, it might appear that there would remain a convenient and natural means of segregating those features of propositional attitudes that derive from the nature of a person's social and physical context, on one hand, from those features that derive from the organism's nature, and palpable effects of the environment on it, on the other. The trouble is that there is no appropriate sense in which natural kind terms like "water" are indexical.

Putnam gives the customary explication of the notion of indexicality: "Words like 'now', 'this', 'here', have long been recognized to be *indexical* or *token-reflexive*—i.e., to have an extension which varied from context to context or token to token" (ibid., pp. 233–4). I think that it is clear that "water," *interpreted as it is in English,* or as we English speakers standardly interpret it, does not shift extension from context to context in this way. (One must, of course, hold the language, or linguistic construal, fixed. Otherwise, every word will trivially count as indexical. For by the very conventionality of language, we can always imagine some context in which our word—word form—has a different extension.) The extension of "water," as interpreted in English in all non-oblique contexts, is (roughly) the set of all aggregates of H_2O molecules, together, probably, with the individual molecules. There is nothing at all indexical about "water" in the customary sense of "indexical."

Putnam suggests several grounds for calling natural kind words indexical. I shall not try to criticize all of these, but will deal with a sampling:

(a) Now then, we have maintained that indexicality extends beyond the *obviously* indexical words. . . . Our theory can be summarized as saying that words like "water" have an unnoticed indexical component: "water" is stuff that bears a certain similarity relation to the water *around here*. Water at another time or in another place or even in another possible world has to bear the relation [same-liquid] to *our* "water" in order to be water. [(1975b), p. 234]

(b) "Water" is indexical. What do I mean by that? If it is indexical, if what I am saying is right, then "water" means "whatever is like water, bears some equivalence relation, say the liquid relation, to *our* water." Where "our" is, of course, an indexical word. If that's how the extension of "water" is determined, then the environment determines the extension of "water." Whether "our" water is in fact XYZ or H_2O.[10]

These remarks are hard to interpret with any exactness because of the *prima facie* circularity, or perhaps ellipticality, of the explications. Water around here, or our water, is just water. Nobody else's water, and no water anywhere else, is any different. Water is simply H_2O (give or take some isotopes and impurities). These points show the superfluousness of the indexical expressions. No shift of extension with shift in context needs to be provided for.

Narrower consideration of these "meaning explanations" of "water" brings out the same point. One might extrapolate from (a) the notion that "water" means (a') "stuff that bears the same-liquid relation to the stuff we call 'water' around here." But this cannot be right. (I pass over the fact that there is no reason to believe that the meaning of "water" involves reference to the linguistic expression "water." Such reference could be eliminated.) For if Adam and his colleagues visited Twin Earth and (still speaking English) called XYZ "water," it would follow on this meaning explication that their uses of the sentence "Water flows in that stream" would be true. They would make no mistake in speaking English and calling XYZ "water." For since the extension of "here" would shift, occurrences on Twin Earth of "stuff that bears the same-liquid relation to the stuff we call 'water' around here flows in that stream" would be true. But by Putnam's own account, which is clearly right on this point, there is no water on Twin Earth. And there is no reason why an English speaker should not be held to this account when he visits Twin Earth. The problem is that although "here" shifts its extension with context, "water" does not. "Water" lacks the indexicality of "here."

A similar objection would apply to extrapolating from (b) the notion that "water" means (b') "whatever bears the same-liquid relation to what we call 'water'," or (b") "whatever bears the same-liquid relation to this stuff." "Water" *interpreted as it is in English* does not shift its extension with shifts of speakers, as (b') and (b") do. The fact that the Twin Earthians apply "water" to XYZ is not a reflection of a shift in extension of an indexical expression with a fixed linguistic (English) meaning, but of a shift in meaning between one language, and linguistic community, and another. Any expression, indexical or not, can undergo such "shifts," as a mere consequence of the conventionality of language. The relevant meaning equivalence to (b') is no more plausible than saying that "bachelor" is indexical because it means "whatever social role the speaker applies 'bachelor' " to where "the speaker" is allowed to shift in its application to speakers of different linguistic communities according to context. If Indians applied "bachelor" to all and only male hogs, it would not follow that "bachelor" as it is used in English is indexical. Similar points apply to (b").

At best, the term "water" and a given occurrence or token of, (b') or (a'), say an introducing token, have some sort of deep or necessary equivalence. But there is no reason to conclude that the indexicality of (a'), (b'), or (b")—which is a feature governing *general use*, not particular occurrences—infects the meaning of the *expression* "water", as it is used in English.

Much of what Putnam says suggests that the appeal to indexicality is supposed to serve other desiderata. One is a desire to defend a certain view of the role of the natural-kind terms in talk about necessity. Roughly, the idea is that "water" applies to water in all discourse about necessity. Putnam expresses this idea by calling natural kind terms rigid, and seems to equate indexicality and rigidity [(1975b), p. 234]. These points raise a morass of complex issues that I want to avoid getting into. It is enough here to point out that a term can be rigid without being indexical. Structural, descriptive, syntactical names are examples. Denying that natural kind terms are indexical is fully compatible with holding that they play any given role in discourse about necessity.

Another purpose that the appeal to indexicality seems to serve is that of accounting for the way natural-kind terms are introduced, or the way their reference is fixed [cf. (1975b), p. 234; and (b) above]. It may well be that indexicals frequently play a part in the (reconstructed) introduction or reference-fixing of natural-kind terms. But this clearly does not imply that the natural-kind terms partake in the indexicality of their introducers or reference-fixers. With some stage setting, one could introduce natural-kind terms, with all their putative modal properties, by using nonindexical terms. Thus a more general rational reconstruction of the introduction, reference-fixing, and modal behavior of natural kind terms is needed. The claim that natural kind terms are themselves indexical is neither a needed nor a plausible account of these matters.

It does seem to me that there is a grain of truth encased within the claim that natural kind terms are indexical. It is this. *De re* beliefs usually enter into the reference-fixing of natural kind terms. The application of such terms seems to be typically fixed partly by *de re* beliefs we have of particular individuals, or quantities of stuff, or physical magnitudes or properties—beliefs that establish a semantical relation between term and object. (Sometimes the *de re* beliefs are about evidence that the terms are introduced to explain.) Having such beliefs requires that one be in not-purely-context-free conceptual relations to the relevant entities [cf. Burge 1977]. That is, one must be in the sort of relation to the entities that someone who indexically refers to them would be. One can grant the role of such beliefs in establishing the application and function of natural-kind terms without granting that all beliefs and statements involving terms whose use is so established are indexical. There seems to be no justification for the latter view, and clear evidence against it.

I have belabored this criticism not because I think that the claim about indexicality is crucial to Putnam's primary aims in "The Meaning of 'Meaning'." Rather, my purpose has been to clear an obstacle to properly evaluating the importance of the Twin Earth example for a philosophical understanding of belief and thought. The difference between mistaking natural-kind words for indexicals and not doing so—rather a small linguistic point in itself—has large implications for our understanding of mentalistic notions. Simply assimilating the Twin Earth example to the example of indexical attitudes I gave at the outset trivializes its bearing on philosophical understanding of the mental. Seen aright, the example suggests a picture in which the individuation of a given individual's mental *contents* depends partly on the nature (or what his fellows think to be the nature) of entities about which he or his fellows have *de re* beliefs. The identity of one's mental contents, states, and events is not independent of the nature of one's physical and social environment.

To summarize our view: The differences between Earth and Twin Earth will affect the attributions of propositional attitudes to inhabitants of the two planets, including Adam and $Adam_{te}$. The differences are not to be assimilated to differences in the extensions of indexical expressions with the same constant, linguistic meaning. For the relevant terms are not indexical. The differences, rather, involve the constant context-free interpretation of the terms. Propositional-attitude attributions which put the terms in oblique occurrence will thus affect the content of the propositional attitudes. Since mental acts and states are individuated (partly) in terms of their contents, the differences between Earth and Twin Earth include differences in the mental acts and states of their inhabitants.

III

Let us step back now and scrutinize Putnam's interpretation of his thought experiment in the light of the fact that natural kind terms are not indexical. Putnam's primary thesis is that a person's psychological states—in what Putnam calls the "narrow sense" of this expression—do not "fix" the extensions of the terms the person uses. A psychological state in the "narrow sense" is said to be one which does not "presuppose" the existence of any individual other than the person who is in that state [(1975b), p. 220]. The term "presuppose" is, of course, notoriously open to a variety of uses. But Putnam's glosses seem to indicate that a person's being in a psychological state does not presuppose a proposition P if it does not logically entail P.[11]

Now we are in a position to explore a first guess about what psychological states are such in the "narrow sense."[12] According to this interpretation, being in a psychological state in the narrow sense (at least as far as propositional attitudes are concerned) is to be in a state correctly ascribable in terms of a content-clause which contains no expressions in a position (in the surface grammar) which admits of existential generalization and which is not in any sense *de re*. *De dicto*, nonrelational propositional attitudes would thus be psychological states in the narrow sense. They entail by existential generalization the existence of no entities other than the subject (and his thought contents). *De re* propositional attitudes—at least those *de re*, propositional attitudes in which the subject is characterized as being in relation to something other than himself and his thought contents—appear to be psychological states in the "wide sense." Having *de re* attitudes of (*de*) objects other than oneself entails the existence of objects other than oneself.

Granted this provisional interpretation, the question arises whether Putnam's Twin Earth examples show that a person's psychological states in the narrow sense fail to "fix" the extensions of the terms he uses. It would seem that to show this, the examples would have to be interpreted in such a way that Adam and Adam$_{te}$ would have the same *de dicto* propositional attitudes while the extensions of their terms differed. This objective would suggest an even stronger interpretation of the thought experiment. Expressions in oblique position in true attributions of attitudes to Adam and Adam$_{te}$ would be held constant while the extensions of their terms varied. But neither of these interpretations is plausible.[13]

Let us see why. To begin with, it is clear that Adam and Adam$_{te}$ will (or might) have numerous propositional attitudes correctly attributable with the relevant natural-kind terms in oblique position. The point of such attributions is to characterize a subject's mental states and events in such a way as to take into account the *way* he views or thinks about objects in his environment. We thus describe his perspective on his environment and utilize such descriptions in predicting, explaining, and assessing the rationality and the correctness or success of his mental processes and overt acts. These enterprises of explanation and assessment provide much of the point of attributing propositional attitudes. And the way a subject thinks about natural kinds of stuffs and things is, of course, as relevant to these enterprises as the way he thinks about anything else. Moreover, there is no intuitive reason to doubt that the relevant natural-kind terms can express and characterize his way of thinking about the relevant stuffs and things—water, aluminum, elms, mackerel. The relevant subjects meet socially accepted standards for using the terms. At worst, they lack a specialist's knowledge about the structure of the stuffs and things to which their terms apply.

We now consider whether the same natural-kind terms should occur obliquely in attributions of propositional attitudes to Adam and Adam$_{te}$. Let us assume, what seems obvious, that Adam has propositional attitudes correctly attributed in English with his own (English) natural-kind terms in oblique position. He hopes that there is some water within twenty miles; he believes that sailboat masts are often made of aluminum, that elms are deciduous trees distinct from beeches, that shrimp are smaller than mackerel. Does Adam$_{te}$ have these same attitudes or at least attitudes with these same contents? As the case has been described, I think it intuitively obvious that he does not.

At least two broad types of consideration back the intuition. One is that it is hard to see how Adam$_{te}$ could have acquired thoughts involving the concept of water (aluminum, elm, mackerel).[14] There is no water on Twin Earth, so he has never had any contact with water. Nor has he had contact with anyone else who has had contact with water. Further, no one on Twin Earth so much as uses a word which means *water*. It is not just that water does not fall in the extension of any of the Twin Earthians' terms. The point is that none of their terms even translates into our (nonindexical) word "water." No English$_{te}$-to-English dictionary would give "water" as the entry for the Twin Earthians' word. It would thus be a mystery how a Twin Earthian could share any of Adam's attitudes that involve the notion of water. They have not had any of the normal means of acquiring the concept. The correct view is that they have acquired, by entirely normal means, a concept expressed in their language that bears some striking, superficial similarities to ours. But it is different. Many people in each community could articulate things about the respective concepts that would make the difference obvious.

There is a second consideration—one that concerns truth—that backs the intuition that Adam$_{te}$ lacks attitudes involving the notion of water (aluminum, elm, mackerel). There is no water on Twin Earth. If Adam$_{te}$ expresses attitudes that involve the concept of water (as opposed to twater), a large number of his ordinary beliefs will be false—that *that* is water, that there is water within twenty miles, that chemists in his country know the structure of water, and so forth. But there seems no reason to count his beliefs false and Adam's beliefs true (or vice versa). Their beliefs were acquired and relate to their environments in exactly parallel and equally successful ways.

The differences between the attitudes of Adam and Adam$_{te}$ derive not from differences in truth-value, but from differences in their respective environments and social contexts. They give different sorts of entities as paradigm cases of instances of the term. Their uses of the term are embedded in different communal usages and scientific traditions that give the term different constant, conventional meanings. In normal contexts, they can explicate and use the term in ways that are informative and acceptable within their respective communities. In doing so, they express different notions and different thoughts with these words. Their thoughts and statements have different truth-conditions and are true of different sorts of entities.

Of course, Adam$_{te}$ believes of XYZ everything Adam believes of water—*if* we

delete all belief-attributions that involve "water" and "twater" in oblique position, and assume that there are no relevant differences between uses of others
among their natural-kind terms. In a sense, they would explicate the terms in the
same way. But this would show that they have the same concept only on the
assumption that each must have *verbal means besides "water"* of expressing his
concept—means that suffice in every outlandish context to distinguish that
concept from others. I see no reason to accept this assumption. Nor does it seem
antecedently plausible.

So far I have argued that Adam and Adam$_{te}$ differ as regards the *contents* of
their attitudes. This suffices to show that their mental states, ordinarily so-called,
as well as the extensions of their terms differ. But the examples we used involved
relational propositional attitudes: belief that *that* is water (twater), that some
water (twater) is within twenty miles of *this place*, that chemists in *this country*
know the structure of water (twater), and so on. Although these do not involve
"water" as an indexical expression and some are not even of *(de)* water (twater),
they are, plausibly, propositional attitudes in the wide sense. Thus, these examples
do not strictly show that Adam and Adam$_{te}$ differ in their *de dicto* attitudes—
attitudes in the narrow sense.

But other examples do. Adam might believe that some glasses somewhere
sometime contain some water, or that some animals are smaller than all mackerel.
Adam$_{te}$ lacks these beliefs. Yet these ascriptions may be interpreted so as not to
admit of ordinary existential generalization on positions in the "that"-clauses,
and not to be *de re* in any sense. We can even imagine differences in their *de dicto*
beliefs that correspond to differences in truth-value. Adam may believe what he is
falsely told when someone mischievously says, "Water lacks oxygen." When
Adam$_{te}$ hears the same words and believes what *he* is told, he acquires (let us
suppose) a true belief: twater does lack oxygen.[15]

I shall henceforth take it that Adam and Adam$_{te}$ have relevant propositional
attitudes from whose content ascriptions no application of existential generalization is admissible. None of these contents need be applied by the subjects—*de
re*—to objects in the external world. That is, the relevant attitudes are purely *de
dicto* attitudes. Yet the attitude contents of Adam and Adam$_{te}$ differ.

IV

Thus it would seem that on the construal of "narrow sense" we have been
exploring, the Twin Earth examples fail to show that psychological states in the
narrow sense (or the contents of such states) do not "fix" the extensions of terms
that Adam and Adam$_{te}$ use. For different contents and different propositional
attitudes correspond to the different extensions. This conclusion rests, however,
on a fairly narrow interpretation of "fix" and—what is equally important—on a
plausible, but restrictive application of "narrow sense." Let me explain these
points in turn.

Propositional attitudes involving non-indexical notions like that of water do "fix" an extension for the term that expresses the notion. But they do so in a purely semantical sense: (necessarily) the notion of water is true of all and only water. There is, however, a deeper and vaguer sense in which nonrelational propositional attitudes do not fix the extensions of terms people use. This point concerns explication rather than purely formal relationships. The Twin Earth examples (like the examples from "Individualism and the Mental") indicate that the order of explication does not run in a straight line from propositional attitudes in the "narrow sense" (even as we have been applying this expression) to the extensions of terms.[16] Rather, to know and explicate what a person believes *de dicto*, one must typically know something about what he believes *de re*, about what his fellows believe *de re* (and *de dicto*), about what entities they ostend, about what he and his fellows' words mean, and about what entities fall in the extensions of their terms.

A corollary of this point is that one cannot explicate what propositional-attitude *contents* a person has by taking into account only facts about him that are nonintentional and individualistic. There is a still flourishing tradition in the philosophy of mind to the contrary. This tradition claims to explain psychological states in terms of nonintentional, functional features of the individual—with no reference to the nature of the environment or the character of the actions, attitudes, and conventions of individuals.[17] Although there is perhaps something to be said for taking nonintentional, individualistic research strategies as one reasonable approach to explaining the behavior of individuals, the view is hopelessly oversimplified as a philosophical explication of ordinary mentalistic notions.

Even insofar as individualism is seen as a research strategy, like the "methodological solipsism" advocated by Jerry Fodor, it is subject to limitations. Such strategies, contrary to Fodor's presumptions, cannot be seen as providing a means of individuating ordinary ("nontransparent") attributions of content. Indeed, it is highly doubtful that a psychological theory can treat psychological states as representational at all and at the same time individuate them in a strictly individualistic, formal, or "syntactic" way. One could, I suppose, have a theory of behavior that individuated internal states "syntactically". Or one could have a representational theory (like most of the cognitive theories we have) which abstracts, in particular attributions to individuals, from the question of whether or not the attributed contents are true. But the latter type of theory, in every version that has had genuine use in psychological theory, relies on individuation of the contents, individuation which involves complex reference to entities other than the individual. Putnam's examples, interpreted in the way I have urged, constitute one striking illustration of this fact.

These remarks invite a reconsideration of the expression "psychological state in the narrow sense." Putnam originally characterized such states as those that do not "presuppose" (entail) the existence of entities other than the subject. And we have been taking the lack of presupposition to be coextensive with a failure of existential generalization and an absence of *de re* attitudes. Thus, we have been taking psychological states in the "narrow sense" to be those whose standard "that"-clause specification does not admit of existential generalization on any of its expressions, and is not in any sense *de re*. But our weakened construal of "fix" suggests a correction in the application of the notion of presupposition. One might say that Adam's *de dicto* attitudes involving the notion of water do presuppose the existence of other entities. The conditions for individuating them make essential reference to the nature of entities in their environment or to the actions and attitudes of others in the community. Even purely *de dicto* propositional attitudes presuppose the existence of entities other than the subject in this sense of presupposition. On this construal, *none* of the relevant attitudes, *de re* or *de dicto*, are psychological states in the narrow sense.

I want to spend the remainder of the section exploring this broadened application of the notion of presupposition. The question is what sorts of relations hold between an individual's mental states and other entities in his environment by virtue of the fact that the conditions for individuating his attitude contents—and thus his mental states and events—make reference to the nature of entities in his environment, or at least to what his fellows consider to be the nature of those entities.

We want to say that it is logically possible for an individual to have beliefs involving the concept of water (aluminum, elm, mackerel) even though there is no water (and so on) of which the individual holds these beliefs. This case seems relatively unproblematic. The individual believer might simply not be in an appropriately direct epistemic relation to any of the relevant entities. This is why existential generalization can fail, and the relevant attitudes can be purely *de dicto*, even though our method of individuating attitude contents makes reference to the entities.

I think we also want to say something stronger. It is logically possible for an individual to have beliefs involving the concept of water (aluminum, and so on), even though there exists no water. An individual or community might (logically speaking) have been wrong in thinking that there was such a thing as water. It is epistemically possible—it might have turned out—that contrary to an individual's beliefs, water did not exist.

Part of what we do when we conceive of such cases is to rely on actual circumstances in which these illusions do not hold—rely on the actual existence of water—in order to individuate the notions we cite in specifying the propositional attitudes. We utilize—must utilize, I think—the actual existence of physical stuffs and things, or of other speakers or thinkers, in making sense of counterfactual projections in which we think at least some of these surroundings away.

But these projections are not unproblematic. One must be very careful in carrying them out. For the sake of argument, let us try to conceive of a set of circumstances in which Adam holds beliefs he actually holds involving the notion of water (aluminum, etc.), but in which there is no water and no community of other speakers to which Adam belongs. Adam may be deluded about these matters: he may live in a solipsistic world. What is problematic about these alleged circumstances is that they raise the question of how Adam *could* have propositional attitudes involving the notion of water. How are they distinguished from attitudes involving the notion of twater, or any of an indefinitely large number of other notions?

In pressing this question, we return to considerations regarding concept acquisition and truth. How, under the imagined circumstances, did Adam acquire the concept of water? There is no water in his environment, and he has contact with no one who has contact with water. There seems no reason derivable from the imagined circumstances (as opposed to arbitrary stipulation) to suppose that Adam's words bear English interpretations instead of English$_{re}$ interpretations, since there are no other speakers in his environment. Nothing in Adam's own repertoire serves to make "water" mean *water* instead of *twater* or numerous other possibilities. So there seems no ground for saying that Adam has acquired the concept of water.

Considerations from truth-conditions point in the same direction. When Adam's beliefs (as held in the putative solipsistic world) are carried over to and evaluated in a "possible world" in which twater (and not water) exists, why should some of the relevant beliefs be false in this world and true in a world in which water exists, or vice versa? Nothing in the solipsistic world seems to ground any such distinction. For these reasons, it seems to me that one cannot credibly imagine that Adam, with his physical and dispositional life history, could have beliefs involving the notion of water, even though there were no other entities (besides his attitude contents) in the world.

We have now supported the view that the point about explication and individuation brings with it, in this case, a point about entailment. Adam's psychological states in the narrow sense (those that do not entail the existence of other entities) do not fix (in either sense of "fix") the extensions of his terms. This is so not because Adam's beliefs involving the notion of water are indexical or *de re*, and not because he has the same propositional attitudes as Adam$_{re}$ while the extensions of his terms differ. Rather, it is because all of Adam's attitude contents involving relevant natural-kind notions—and, thus, all his relevant attitudes (whether *de re* or *de dicto*)—are individuated by reference to other entities. His having these attitudes in the relevant circumstances entails (and thus presupposes in Putnam's sense) the existence of other entities.

The exact nature of the relevant entailment deserves more discussion than I can give it here. As I previously indicated, I think that Adam's having attitudes whose contents involve the notion of water does not entail the existence of water. If by some wild communal illusion, no one had ever really seen a relevant liquid in the lakes and rivers, nor had drunk such a liquid, there might still be enough in the community's talk to distinguish the notion of water from that of twater and from other candidate notions. We would still have our chemical analyses despite the illusoriness of their object. (I assume here that not all of the community's beliefs involve similar illusions.)[18] I think that Adam's having the relevant attitudes probably does not entail the existence of other speakers. *Prima facie*, at least, it would seem that if he did interact with water and held a few elementary true beliefs about it, we would have enough to explain how he acquired the notion of water—enough to distinguish his having that notion from his having the notion of twater. What seems incredible is to suppose that Adam, in his relative ignorance and indifference about the nature of water, holds beliefs whose contents involve the notion, even though neither water nor communal cohorts exist.

V

It should be clear that this general line promises to have a bearing on some of the most radical traditional skeptical positions. (I think that the bearing of the argument in "Individualism and the Mental" is complementary and more comprehensive.) The line provides fuel for the Kantian strategy of showing that at least some formulations of traditional skepticism accept certain elements of our ordinary viewpoint while rejecting others that are not really separable. Exploring the epistemic side of these issues, however, has not been our present task.

Our main concern has been the bearing of these ideas on the philosophy of mind. What attitudes a person has, what mental events and states occur in him, depends on the character of his physical and social environment. In some instances, an individual's having certain *de dicto* attitudes *entails* the existence of entities other than himself and his attitude contents. The Twin Earth thought experiment may work only for certain propositional attitudes. Certainly its clearest applications are to those whose contents involve nontheoretical natural-kind notions. But the arguments of "Individualism and the Mental" suggest that virtually no propositional attitudes can be explicated in individualistic terms. Since the intentional notions in terms of which propositional attitudes are described are irreducibly nonindividualistic, no purely individualistic account of these notions can possibly be adequate.

Although most formulations of the lessons to be learned from Twin Earth thought experiments have seemed to me to be vague or misleading in various ways, many of them indicate a broad appreciation of the general drift of the argument just presented. In fact, as I indicated earlier, the general drift is just beneath the surface of Putnam's paper. A common reaction, however, is that if our ordinary concept of mind is nonindividualistic, so much the worse for our ordinary concept.

This reaction is largely based on the view that if mentalistic notions do not explain "behavior" individualistically, in something like the way chemical or perhaps physiological notions do, they are not respectable, at least for "cognitive" or "theoretical" as opposed to "practical" purposes. I cannot discuss this view in the detail it deserves here. But it has serious weaknesses. It presupposes that the only cognitively valuable point of applying mentalistic notions is to explain individual "behavior." It assumes that the primary similarities in "behavior" that mentalistic explanations should capture are illustrated by Adam's and Adam$_{re}$'s similarity of physical movement. It assumes that there are no "respectable" nonindividualistic theories. (I think evolutionary biology is a counterexample—not to appeal to much of cognitive psychology and the social sciences.) And it assumes an unexplicated and highly problematic distinction between theoretical and practical purposes. *All* of these assumptions are questionable and, in my view, probably mistaken.

The nonindividualistic character of our mentalistic notions suggests that they are fitted to purposes other than (or in addition to) individualistic explanation. The arguments I have presented, here and earlier, challenge us to achieve a deeper understanding of the complex system of propositional-attitude attribution. The purposes of this system include describing, explaining, and assessing people and their historically and socially characterized activity against a background of objective norms—norms of truth, rationality, right. Some form of fruitful explanation that might reasonably be called "psychological" could, conceivably, ignore such purposes in the interests of individualistic explanation. But animus against mentalistic notions because they do not meet a borrowed ideal seems to me misplaced. That, however, is a point for sharpening on other occasions.

ENDNOTES

1. It is difficult to avoid at least a limited amount of philosophical jargon in discussing this subject. Since much of this jargon is subjected to a variety of uses and abuses, I will try to give brief explications of the most important special terms as they arise. An ordinary-language discourse is *intentional* if it contains oblique occurrences of expressions. (Traditionally, the term "intentional" is limited to mentalistic discourse containing obliquely occurring expressions, but we can ignore this fine point.) An oblique [sometimes "indirect" and less appropriately, "opaque" (or "nontransparent"] occurrence of an expression is one on which *either* substitution of co-extensive expressions may affect the truth-value of the whole containing sentence, or existential generalization isn't a straightforwardly valid transformation. For example, "Al believes that many masts are made of aluminum" is intentional discourse (as we are reading the sentence) because "aluminum" occurs obliquely. If one substituted "the thirteenth element in the periodic table" for "aluminum," one might alter the truth-value of the containing sentence.

   The characterization of *de re attitudes* (sometimes "relational attitudes") is at bottom a complex and controversial matter. For a detailed discussion, see my (1977, pp. 338–62), especially section 1. For present purposes, we shall say that *de re* attitudes are those where the subject or person is unavoidably characterized as being in a not-purely-conceptual, contextual relation to an object (*re*), of which he holds his attitude. Typically, though not always, a term or quantified pronoun in nonoblique position will denote the object, and the person having the attitude will be said to believe (think, etc.)

that object be ∅ (where "∅" stands for oblique occurrences of predicative expressions). *De re* attitudes may equivalently, and equally well, be characterized as those whose content involves an ineliminable indexical element which is applied to some entity. *De dicto* attitudes (sometimes "notional attitudes") are those that are not *de re*.

2. An attitude *content* is the semantic value associated with oblique occurrences of expressions in attributions of propositional attitudes. Actually, there may be more to the content than what is attributed, but I shall be ignoring this point in order not to complicate the discussion unduly. Thus, the content is, roughly speaking, the conceptual aspect of what a person believes or thinks. If we exclude the *res* in *de re* attitudes, we may say that the content is what a person believes (thinks, etc.) in *de re* or *de dicto* attitudes. We remain neutral here about what, ontologically speaking, contents are.

3. Putnam (1975).

4. This point is entirely analogous to the familiar point that *knowing* is not a mental state. For knowledge depends not only on one's mental state, but on whether its content is true. The point above about indexicals and mental states is the analogue for predication of this traditional point about the relation between the mind and (complete) propositions. Neither the truth or falsity of a content, enters directly into the individuation of a mental state. For more discussion of these points, see Burge [(1979a), section IId].

5. This rejection is logically independent of rejecting the view that the intentional can be accounted for in terms of the nonintentional. I reject this view also. But here is not the place to discuss it.

6. Burge (1979a). Much of the present paper constitutes an elaboration of remarks in footnote 2 of that paper.

7. Anyone who wishes to resist our conclusions merely by claiming that XYZ is water will have to make parallel claims for aluminum, helium, and so forth. Such claims, I think, would be completely implausible.

8. I am omitting a significant extension of Putnam's ideas. Putnam considers "rolling back the clock" to a time when everyone in each community would be as ignorant of the structure of water and twater as Adam and Adam$_{te}$ are now. I omit this element from the thought experiment, partly because arriving at a reasonable interpretation of this case is more complicated and partly because it is not necessary for my primary purposes. Thus, as far as we are concerned, one is free to see differences in Adam and Adam$_{te}$'s mental states as deriving necessarily from differences in the actions and attitudes of other members in their respective communities.

9. This view and the one described in the following sentence were anticipated and criticized in Burge [(1979a), section IId and note 2]. Both views have been adopted by Jerry Fodor [(1980), pp. 63–73]. I believe that these views have been informally held by various others. Colin McGinn [(1977), pp. 521–35], criticizes Putnam (correctly, I think) for not extending his theses about meaning to propositional attitudes. But McGinn's argument is limited to claiming that the *res* in relational propositional attitudes differ between Earth and Twin Earth and that these *res* enter into individuating mental states. (The congeniality of this view with Putnam's claim that natural-kind terms are indexical is explicitly noted.) Thus, the argument supports only the position articulated in the first paragraphs of this paper and is subject to the deflationary interpretation that followed (cf. also note 4). McGinn's argument neither explicitly accepts nor explicitly rejects the position subsequently adopted by Fodor and cited above.

10. Putnam [(1974), p. 451]. Cf. also "Language and Reality," in Putnam [(1975a), p. 277].

11. In explaining the traditional assumption of "methodological solipsism," Putnam writes: "This assumption is the assumption that no psychological state, properly so-called, presupposes the existence of any individual other than the subject to whom that state is ascribed. (In fact, the assumption was that no psychological state presupposes the existence of the subject's *body* even: if P is a psychological state, properly so-called, then it must be *logically possible* for a 'disembodied mind' to be in P.)" [(1975), p. 220, the second italics added]. He also gives examples of psychological states in the "wide sense" and characterizes these as entailing the existence of other entities besides the subject of the state (ibid., p. 220). Although there is little reason to construe Putnam as identifying entailment and presupposition, these two passages taken together suggest that for his purposes, no difference between them is of great importance. I shall proceed on this assumption.

12. This guess is Fodor's (1980). As far as I can see, the interpretation is not excluded by anything Putnam says. It is encouraged by some of what he says—especially his remarks regarding indexicality and his theory about the normal form for specifying the meaning of "water."

13. Jerry Fodor (1980) states that inhabitants of Twin Earth harbor the thought that water is wet—even granted the assumption that there is no water on Twin Earth and the assumption that their thought is not "about" water (H_2O), but about XYZ. Fodor provides no defense at all for this implausible view.

14. More jargon. I shall use the terms *"concept"* and *"notion"* interchangeably to signify the semantical values of obliquely occurring parts of content-clauses, parts that are not themselves sentential. Thus, a concept is a nonpropositional part of a content. The expressions "concept" and "notion" are, like "content," intended to be ontologically neutral. Intuitively, a concept is a context-free way a person thinks about a stuff, a thing, or a group of things.

15. As I mentioned earlier, one might hold that "water" names an abstract property or kind and that attitude attributions typically attribute *de re* attitudes *of* the kind. I do not accept this view, or see any strong reasons for it. But let us examine its consequences briefly. I shall assume that "kind" is used in such a way that water is the same kind as H_2O. To be minimally plausible, the view must distinguish between kind and concept (cf. note 14)—between the kind that is thought of and the person's way of thinking of it. "Water" may express or indicate one way of thinking of the kind "H_2O" another. Given this distinction, previous considerations will show that Adam and Adam$_{te}$ apply different concepts (and contents) to the different kinds. So even though their attitudes are not "narrow," they still have different mental states and events. For mental states and events are individuated partly in terms of contents.

16. I am tempted to characterize this as Putnam's own primary point. What counts against yielding to the temptation is his interpretation of natural kind terms as indexical, his focus on meaning, and his statement that those on Twin Earth have the same thoughts [(1975), p. 224] as those on Earth. Still, what follows is strongly suggested by much that he says.

17. Works more or less explicitly in this tradition are Putnam, "The Nature of Mental States" in Putnam [(1975a), p. 437]; Harman [(1973), pp. 43–6, 56–65]; Lewis [(1972b), pp. 249–50; (1974), pp. 331ff]; Fodor [(1975), chapter 1; and (1980)].

18. Thus I am inclined to think that, if one is sufficiently precise, one could introduce a

"natural-kind" notion, like water, without having had any causal contact with instances of it. This seems to happen when chemical or other kinds are anticipated in science before their discovery "in nature." The point places a *prima facie* limitation on antiskeptical uses of our argument. Thus . . . I have been careful to emphasize Adam's relative ignorance in our criticism of solipsistic thought experiments.

9

From "Beyond Belief": Notional Attitudes[1]

Daniel Dennett

In the face of the objections of Putnam and others to "classical" propositional attitudes, we adverted to the question: what is the organismic contribution to the fixation of propositional attitudes? The answer would characterize psychological states "in the narrow sense." The attempt to capture these narrow psychological state types as sentential attitudes ran into a variety of problems, chief of which was that any sentential-attitude characterization, being essentially a syntactical typecasting, would cut too fine. In Putnam's thought experiment we grant that *physical* replicahood is sufficient but not necessary for identity of organismic contribution; we could also grant that the weaker similarity captured by *syntactic* replicahood (at some level of abstraction) would be sufficient for identity of organismic contribution, but even though identity of organismic contribution— narrow-psychological twinhood—is a very stringent condition, it would not seem to require syntactic twinhood at any level of description. Consider the somewhat analogous question: Do all Turing machines that compute the same function share a syntactic (i.e., machine table) description? No, unless we adjust our levels of description of the machine table and the input-output behavior so that they coalesce trivially. What should count as equivalence for Turing machines (or computer programs) is a vexed question; it would not be if it weren't for the fact that nontrivially different descriptions in terms of internal "syntax" can yield the same "contribution"—at some useful level of description.

The analogy is imperfect, no doubt, and other considerations—e.g., biological considerations—might weigh in favor of supposing that complete narrow-psychological Twinhood required syntactic twinhood at some level, but even if that were granted, it would not at all follow that *partial* psychological similarity can always be described in some general system of syntactic description applicable to all who share the psychological trait. People who are vain, or paranoid, for instance, are surely psychologically similar; a large part of the similarity in each case would seem well captured by talking of similar or shared beliefs. Even if one takes a self-defeatingly stringent line on belief-identity (according to which no two people ever really share a belief), these *similarities* in belief cry out for capturing within psychology. They could not plausibly be held to depend on monolingualism—vain people's brains all speaking the same Mentalese. Nor can we capture these similarities in belief-state via *propositional* attitudes, because of

161

the indexicality of many of the crucial beliefs: "People admire *me*," "People are trying to ruin *me*."

These considerations suggest that what we are looking to characterize is an intermediate position—halfway between syntax and semantics you might say. Let us call it *notional-attitude psychology*. We want it to work out that I and my *Doppelgänger*—and any other narrow psychological twins—have exactly the same notional attitudes, so that our differences in propositional attitudes are due entirely to the different environmental contributions. But we also want it to work out that you and I, no psychological Twins but "of like mind" on several topics, share a variety of notional attitudes.

A familiar idea that has occurred in many guises can be adapted for our purposes here: the idea of a person's subjective world, Helen Keller's *The World I Live In* or John Irving's *The World According to Garp*, for instance. Let us try to characterize the *notional world* of a psychological subject so that, for instance, although my *Doppelgänger* and I live in different real worlds—Twin Earth and Earth—we have the same notional world. You and I live in the same real world, but have different notional worlds, though there is a considerable overlap between them.

A notional world should be viewed as a sort of *fictional* world devised by a theorist, a third-party observer, in order to characterize the narrow-psychological states of a subject. A notional world can be supposed to be full of notional objects, and the scene of notional events—all the objects and events the subject believes in, you might say. If we relax our methodological solipsism for a moment, we will note that some objects in the real world inhabited by a subject match objects in the subject's notional world, but others do not. The real world contains many things and events having no counterparts in any subject's notional world (excluding the notional world of an omniscient God), and the notional worlds of gullible or confused or ontologically profligate subjects will contain notional objects having no counterparts in the real world. The task of describing the relations that may exist between things in the real world and things in someone's notional world is notoriously puzzle-ridden—that is one reason to retreat to methodological solipsism: to factor out those troublesome issues temporarily.

Our retreat has landed us in very familiar territory: What are notional objects but the *intentional objects* of Brentano? Methodological solipsism is apparently a version of Husserl's *époché*, or bracketing. Can it be that the alternative to both propositional-attitude psychology and sentential-attitude psychology is . . . Phenomenology? Not quite. There is one major difference between the approach to be sketched here and the traditional approaches associated with Phenomenology. Whereas Phenomenologists propose that one can get to one's own notional world by some special somewhat introspectionist bit of mental gymnastics—called, by some, the phenomenological reduction—we are concerned with determining the notional world of *another*, from the outside. The tradition of Brentano and Husserl is *auto-phenomenology*; I am proposing *hetero-phenomenology* [see "Two Approaches to Mental Images" in Dennett (1978)].

Although the results might bear a striking resemblance, the enabling assumptions are very different.

The difference can best be seen with the aid of a distinction recently resurrected by Fodor (1980) between what he calls, following James, *naturalistic* and *rational* psychology. Fodor quotes James:

> On the whole, few recent formulas have done more service of a rough sort in psychology than the Spencerian one that the essence of mental life and of bodily life are one, namely, "the adjustment of inner to outer relations." Such a formula is vagueness incarnate; but because it takes into account the fact that minds inhabit environments which act on them and on which they in turn react; because, in short, it takes mind in the midst of all its concrete relations, it is immensely more fertile than the old-fashioned "rational psychology" which treated the soul as a detached existent, sufficient unto itself, and assumed to consider only its nature and its properties. [James (1890), p. 6]

James sings the praises of naturalistic psychology, psychology in the *wide* sense, but the moral from Twin Earth, drawn explicitly by Fodor, is that naturalistic psychology casts its net too wide to be doable. The Phenomenologists draw the same conclusion, apparently, and both turn to different versions of methodological solipsism: concern for the psychological subject "as a detached existent, sufficient unto itself," but when they "consider its nature and its properties," what do they find? The Phenomenologists, using some sort of introspection, claim to find a *given* in experience, which becomes the raw material for their construction of their notional worlds. If Fodor, using some sort of (imagined) internal inspection of the machinery, claimed to find a Mentalese text *given* in the hardware (which would become the raw material for construction of the notional attitudes of the subject) we would have as much reason to doubt the existence of the given in this case as in the case of Phenomenology (see chapter 8 of *The Intentional Stance*). James is right: you cannot do *psychology* (as opposed to, say, neurophysiology) without determining the *semantic* properties of the internal events and structures under examination, and you cannot uncover the semantic properties without looking at the relations of those internal events or structures to things in the subject's environment. But nowhere is it written that the environment relative to which we fix such a system's semantic properties must be a real environment, or the actual environment in which the system has grown up. A fictional environment, an idealized or imaginary environment, might do as well. The idea is that in order to do "mental-representation" theory, you need to do the semantics of the representations from the beginning. (You can't first do the syntax, then the semantics.) But that means you need a model, in the sense of Tarskian semantics. A fictional model, however, might permit enough Tarskian semantics to get under way for us to determine the partial semantics, or protosemantics, we need to characterize the organismic contribution.

The idea of a notional world, then, is the idea of a model—but not necessarily the actual, real, true model—of one's internal representations. *It does not consist itself of representations but of representeds*. It is the world "I live in," not the world of representations *in me*. [So far, this is pure Brentano, at least as I understand him. See Aquila (1977)]. The theorist wishing to characterize the narrow-psychological states of a creature, or, in other words, the organismic contribution of that creature to its propositional attitudes, *describes* a fictional world; the description exists on paper, the fictional world does not exist, but the inhabitants of the fictional world are treated as the notional referents of the subject's representations, as the intentional objects of that subject. It is hoped that by this ploy the theorist can get the benefits of James and Spencer's naturalism without the difficulties raised by Putnam and the rest.

Now the question is: What guides our construction of an organism's notional world? Suppose, to dramatize the problem, we receive a box containing an organism from we know not where, alive but frozen (or comatose)—and hence cut off from any environment. We have a Laplacean snapshot of the organism's complete description of its internal structure and composition—and we can suppose that this enables us to determine exactly how it would respond to any new environmental impacts were we to release it from its state of suspended animation and isolation. Our task is like the problem posed when we are shown some alien or antique gadget and asked: What is it for? Is it a needle-making machine or a device for measuring the height of distant objects or a weapon? What can we learn from studying the object? We can determine how the parts mesh, what happens under various conditions, and so forth. We can also look for telltale scars and dents, wear and tear. Once we have compiled these facts we try to imagine a setting in which given these facts it would *excellently* perform some imaginably useful function. If the object would be an equally good sail mender or cherry pitter we won't be able to tell what it *really* is—what it is for—without learning where it came from, who made it, and why. Those facts could have vanished without a trace. Such an object's true identity, or essence, could then be utterly undeterminable by us, no matter how assiduously we studied the object. That would not mean that there was no fact of the matter about whether the thing was a cherry pitter or a sail mender, but that the truth, whichever it was, no longer made a difference. It would be one of those idle or inert historical facts, like the fact that some of the gold in my teeth once belonged to Julius Caesar—or didn't.

Faced with our novel organism, we can easily enough determine what it is for—it is for surviving and flourishing and reproducing its kind—and we should have little trouble identifying its sense organs and modes of action and biological needs. Since *ex hypothesi* we can figure out what it would do if . . . (for all fillings in of the antecedent), we can determine, for instance, that it will eat apples but not fish, tends to avoid brightly lit places, is disposed to make certain noises under certain conditions, etc. Now what kind of an environment would these talents and proclivities fit it for? The more we learn about the internal structure, behavioral dispositions, and systemic needs of the organism, the more particular becomes our hypothetical ideal environment. By "ideal environment" I do not mean the best of all possible worlds for this organism ("with the lemonade spring where the bluebirds sing"), but the environment (or class of environments) for which the organism as currently constituted is best fitted. It might be a downright nasty world, but at least the organism is prepared to cope with its nastiness. We can learn something about the organism's enemies—real or only notional—by noting its protective coloration or its escape behavior or . . . how it would answer certain questions.

So long as the organism we are dealing with is very simple and has, for instance, little or no plasticity in its nervous system (so it cannot learn), the limit of specificity for the imagined ideal environment may fail to distinguish radically different but equally well-fitted environments, as in the case of the gadget. As the capacity to learn and remember grows, and as the richness and complexity of the possible relations with environmental conditions grows (see chapter 2 of *The Intentional Stance*), the class of equally acceptable models (hypothetical ideal environments) shrinks. Moreover, in creatures with the capacity to learn and store information about their world in memory, a new and more powerful exegetical principle comes into play. The scars and dents on the cherry pitter (or was it a sail mender?) may on occasion prove to be telltale, but the scars and dents on a learning creature's memory are *designed* to be telltale, to record with high fidelity both particular encounters and general lessons, for future use. Since the scars and dents of memory are for future use, we can hope to "read" them by exploiting our knowledge of the dispositions that depend on them, so long as we assume the dispositions so attached are in general appropriate. Such interpretations of "memory traces" yield more specific information about the world in which the creature lived and to which it had accommodated itself. But we will not be able to tell information about this world from misinformation, and thus the world we extrapolate as *constituted* by the organism's current state will be an ideal world, not in the sense of *best*, but in the sense of *unreal*.

The naturalists will rightly insist that the actual environment as encountered has left its mark on the organism and intricately shaped it; the organism is in its current state *because of the history it has had,* and only such a history could in fact have put it into its present state. But in a thought-experimental mood we can imagine creating a duplicate whose *apparent* history was not its actual history (as in the case of a faked antique, with its simulated "distress" marks and wear and tear). Such a complete duplication (which is only logically, thought-experimentally, possible) is the limiting case of something actual and familiar: any particular feature of current state may be misbegotten, so that the way the world ought to have been for the creature now to be in this state is not quite the way the world was. The notional world we describe by extrapolation from current state is thus not exactly the world we take to have created that state, even if we know that actual world, but rather the apparent world of the creature, the world apparent *to* the creature as manifested in the creature's current total dispositional state.

Suppose we apply this imaginary exercise in notional world formation to highly adaptive organisms like ourselves. Such organisms have internal structure and dispositional traits so rich in information about the environment in which they grew up that we could in principle say: this organism is best fitted to an environment in which there is a city called Boston, in which the organism spent its youth, in the company of organisms named . . . and so forth. We would not be able to distinguish Boston from Twin Earth Boston, of course, but except for such virtually indistinguishable variations on a theme, our exercise in notional world formation would end in a unique solution.

That, at any rate, is the myth. It is a practically useless myth, of course, but theoretically important, for it reveals the fundamental assumptions that are being made about the ultimate dependence of the organismic contribution on the physical constitution of the organism. [This dependence is otherwise known as the supervenience of (narrow) psychological traits on physical traits; see, e.g., Stich (1978a).] At the same time, the myth preserves the underdetermination of ultimate reference that was the acclaimed moral of the Putnamian considerations. If there is a language of thought, this is how you would have to bootstrap your way to discovering it and translating it—without so much as the benefit of bilingual interpreters or circumstantial evidence about the source of the text. If there is any third-person alternative to the dubious introspectionist (*genuinely* solipsistic) method of the Phenomenologists, if hetero-phenomenology is possible at all, it will have to be by this method.

In principle, then, the ultimate fruits of the method, applied to a human being under the constraints of methodological solipsism, would be an exhaustive description of that person's notional world, complete with its mistaken identities, chimeras and personal bogeymen, factual errors and distortions.[2] We may think of it as *the* notional world of the individual, but of course the most exhaustive description possible would fail to specify a unique world. For instance, variations in a world entirely beyond the ken, or interests, of a person would generate different possible worlds equally consistent with the maximal determination provided by the constitution of the person.

The situation is analogous to that of more familiar fictional worlds, such as the world of Sherlock Holmes or Dickens's London. Lewis (1978) provides an account of "truth in fiction," the semantics of the interpretation of fiction, that develops the idea we need: "the" world of Sherlock Holmes is formally better conceived of as a *set* of possible worlds, roughly: all the possible worlds consistent with the entire corpus of Sherlock Holmes texts by Conan Doyle.[3] Similarly, "the" notional world we describe might better be viewed formally as the set of possible worlds consistent with the maximal description [see Hintikka (1962); Stalnaker (1984)]. Note that the description is the *theorist's* description; we do not *assume* that the structural features of the organism on which the theorist bases his description include elements which themselves are descriptions. (The features of the cherry pitter that lead us to describe a cherry (rather than a peach or an olive) are not themselves descriptions of cherries.) From this perspective, we can see that Putnam has devised Twin Earth and Earth both to be members of the set of possible worlds that *is* the notional world I share with my *Doppelgänger*. XYZ slakes thirst, dissolves wallpaper paste, and produces rainbows as well as H_2O does; its difference from H_2O is beneath all the thresholds of discrimination of both me and my *Doppelgänger*—provided, presumably, that neither of us is, or consults with, a wily chemist or microphysicist.

Given a notional world for a subject, we can talk about what the subject's beliefs are *about*, in a peculiar, but familiar, sense of "about." Goodman (1961) discusses sentences of Dickens that are "Pickwickabout," a semantic feature of these sentences that is not genuinely relational, there being no Mr. Pickwick for them to be about in the strong, relational sense. In a similar spirit, Brentano discusses the "relation*like*" status of mental phenomena whose intentional objects are nonexistent [see Aquila (1977)]. An enabling assumption of notional-attitude psychology is that the theorist can use Pickwickaboutness and its kin as the semantic properties one heeds for the foundations of any theory of mental representation.

The strategy is not untried. Although no notional-attitude psychology has been concocted here as a response to the philosophical problems encountered in propositional attitude and sentential-attitude psychology, it can be easily discerned to be the tacit methodology and ideology of a major branch of Artificial Intelligence. Consider, for instance, the now famous SHRDLU system of Winograd (1972). SHRDLU is a "robot" that "lives in" a world consisting of a table on which there are blocks of various colors and shapes. It perceives these and moves them about in response to typed commands (in English) and can answer questions (in English) about its activities and the state of its world. The scare-quotes above are crucial, for SHRDLU isn't really a robot, and there is no table with blocks on it for SHRDLU to manipulate. That world, and SHRDLU's actions in it, are merely simulated in the computer program of which SHRDLU the robot *simulation* is a part. Fodor (1980) makes the point we want, even anticipating our terminology:

> In effect, the machine lives in an entirely notional world; all its beliefs are false. Of course, it doesn't matter to the machine that its beliefs are false since falsity is a semantic property and, qua computer, the device satisfies the formality conditions; viz., it has access only to formal (non-semantic) properties of the representation that it manipulates. In effect, the device is in precisely the situation that Descartes dreads: it's a mere computer which dreams that it's a robot.

To some critics, the fact that SHRDLU does not really perceive things in the world, touch them, and otherwise enter into causal relations with them, suffices to show that whatever else SHRDLU may have, SHRDLU certainly has no *beliefs* at all. What beliefs could SHRDLU have? What could their content be? What could they be about? SHRDLU is a purely formal system quite unattached to the world by bonds of perception, action, or indeed interest. The idea that such merely formal, merely syntactical states and processes, utterly lacking all semantic properties, could provide us with a model of belief is preposterous! (SHRDLU brings out the bluster in people.)

The gentle reply available in principle runs as follows. Indeed, as the critics proclaim, a genuine believer must be richly and intimately attached by perception and action to things in the world, the objects of his beliefs, but providing those bonds for SHRDLU by providing it with real TV-camera eyes, a real robotic arm, and a real table of blocks on which to live, would have been expensive, time-consuming, and *of little psychological interest*. Clothed in a transducer-effector overcoat of robotics hardware, SHRDLU would have a notional world of blocks on a tabletop—which is to say, plunked into that real environment SHRDLU would make out very well; a blocks world is a good niche for SHRDLU. Stripped of the robotics overcoat, SHRDLU has a vastly less-specific notional world; many more possible worlds are indistinguishable to it, but still, the functional structure of the core is the locus of the interesting psychological problems and their proposed solutions, so choosing the blocks world as an *admissible* notional world (it is in the set of Tarski models for the core system) is an innocent way of clothing the system in a bit of verisimilitude.

In the actual case of SHRDLU, this defense would be optimistic; SHRDLU is not that good. It would not be trivial, or even an expensive but straightforward bit of engineering, to clothe SHRDLU in robotics, and the reasons why it would not are of psychological interest. By keeping SHRDLU's world merely notional, Winograd neatly excused himself from providing solutions to a wealth of difficult, deep, and important problems in psychology. It is far from clear that any improvements on SHRDLU, conceived in the same spirit within the same research program, could more justly avail themselves of this line of defense. But that it is the assumed ideal line of defense of such research is, I think, unquestionable. To Husserl's claim that bracketing the real world leaves you with the essence of the mental, Winograd and AI can add: Yes, and besides, bracketing saves you time and money.

The Husserlian themes in this AI research program are unmistakable, but it is important to remind ourselves as well of the differences. To the auto-phenomenologist, the relative inaccessibility of the real referents of one's beliefs—and hence, as Putnam argues, the relative inaccessibility of one's *propositional* attitudes—is presented as a point about the limits of introspective privileged access, a very Cartesian result: *I* cannot discriminate *for sure*; *I* am not *authoritative* about which proposition I am now entertaining, which real object I am now thinking about. But SHRDLU's "introspections" play no privileged role in hetero-phenomenology: SHRDLU's notional world is fixed from the outside by appeal to objective and publicly accessible facts about the capacities and dispositions of the system, and hence its fate in various imagined environments. The counterpart to the Cartesian claim is that even the totality of these public facts underdetermines propositional attitudes. Even though the environments appealed to are imaginary, the appeal places hetero-phenomenology squarely on the naturalistic side of the Jamesian division.

The elaboration of imaginary ideal environments for purposes of comparison of internally different systems is a strategy of some currency, in engineering for instance. We can compare the power of different automobile engines by imagining them in pulling contests against a certain fictional horse, or we can compare their fuel efficiency by seeing how far they will push a car in a certain simulated environment. The use of an ideal environment permits one to describe *functional* similarities or competences independently of details of implementation or performance. Utilizing the strategy in psychology to elaborate notional worlds is just a particularly complex case. It enables us to describe partial similarities in the psychological "competences" of different subjects—for instance, their representational *powers*—in ways that are neutral about their implementation—for instance, their representational means.

The analogy with fiction is again useful in making this point. What exactly is the similarity between Shakespeare's *Romeo and Juliet* and Bernstein's *West Side Story?* The latter was "based on" the former, we know, but what do they actually have in common? Are they about the same people? No, for they are both fictions. Do they contain the same or similar representations? What could this mean? The same words or sentences or descriptions? The scripts of both happen to be written in English, but this is clearly irrelevant, for the similarity we are after survives translation into other languages, and—more dramatically—is evident in the film of *West Side Story* and in Gounod's opera. The similarity is independent of any particular means of representation—scripts, sketches, descriptions, actors on stages or before cameras—and concerns *what is represented*. It is not any kind of syntactic similarity. Since such similarities are as evident in fiction as in factual reporting, we must understand "what is represented" to take us to elements of a notional world, not necessarily the real world. We can compare different notional or fictional worlds with regard to matters large and small, just as we can compare different parts of the real world. We can compare a notional world with the real world. (The nearsighted Mr. Magoo's notional world only intermittently and partially resembles the real world, but just enough, miraculously, to save him from disaster.)

When, then, shall we say that two different people share a notional attitude or set of notional attitudes? When their notional worlds have a point or region of similarity. Notional worlds are agent-centered or egocentric [Perry (1977); Lewis (1979)]; when comparing notional worlds for psychological similarity it will typically be useful, therefore, to "superimpose" the centers—so that the origins, the intersection of the axes, coincide—before testing for similarity. In this way the psychological similarities between two paranoids will emerge, while the psychological difference between the masochist and his sadistic partner stands out in spite of the great similarity in the *dramatis personae* of their notional worlds viewed uncentered.[4]

The prospect of a rigorous method of notional-world comparison—a decision procedure for finding and rating points of coincidence, for instance—is dim. But we have always known that, for the prospects of setting conditions for propositional-attitude identity are equally dim. I believe that salt is sodium chloride, but my knowledge of chemistry is abysmal; the chemist believes that salt is sodium chloride as well, but there is not going to be any crisp way of capturing the common core of our beliefs Dennett (1969). The comparability of beliefs, viewed either as notional attitudes or as propositional attitudes, is not going to be rendered routine by any theoretical stroke. The *gain in precision* one might misguidedly have hoped to obtain by isolating and translating "the language of thought"—if it exists—would not improve the comparability of *beliefs*, such as mine and the chemist's about salt, but only the comparability of a certain novel kind of sentence—sentences in the head. But sentences are already nicely comparable. The English-speaking chemist and I use exactly the same words to express our belief about salt, and if, perchance, our brains do as well, we will still have the problem of comparability for our beliefs.

A language of thought would give no more leverage in the vexed case of irrational—and especially contradictory—beliefs, and for the same reason. Sup-pose the hypothesis is bruited that Bill has a particular pair of contradictory beliefs: he believes both that Tom is to be trusted and that Tom is not to be trusted. In any language worth its salt nothing is more cut-and-dried than determining when one sentence contradicts another, so knowing Bill's language of thought, we search in his brain for the relevant pair of sentences. And we find them! What would this show? The question would still remain: Which (if either) does he believe? We might find, on further investigation, that one of these sentences was vestigial and nonfunctional—never erased from the cerebral blackboard, but never consulted either. Or we might find that one sentence (the Mentalese for "Tom is not to be trusted") was intermittently consulted (and acted upon)—good evidence that Bill believes Tom is not to be trusted, but it keeps slipping his mind. He forgets, and then his natural *bonhomie* takes over and, believing that people in general are to be trusted, he behaves as if he believes Tom is to be trusted. Or perhaps we find truly conflicting behavior in Bill; he goes on and on in conversation about Tom's trustworthiness, but we note he never turns his back on Tom. One can multiply the cases, filling gaps and extending the extremes, but in none of the cases does the presence or absence of explicit contradiction in the Mentalese play more than a peripheral supporting role in our decision to characterize Bill as vacillating, forgetful, indecisive, or truly irrational. Bill's behavior counts for more, but behavior will not *settle* the matter either (see chapter 4 of *The Intentional Stance* and its reflections).

People certainly do get confused and worse; sometimes they go quite mad. To say that someone is irrational is to say (in part) that in some regard he is ill-equipped to deal with the world he inhabits; he ill fits his niche. In bad cases we may be unable to devise any notional world for him; no possible world would be a place where he fits right in. One could leave the issue there, or one could attempt to be more descriptive of the person's confusion.[5] One could compose an avowedly inconsistent description, citing chapter and verse from the subject's behavioral propensities and internal constitution in support of the various parts of the description. Such an inconsistent description could not be of a notional world, since notional worlds, as sets of *possible* worlds, cannot have contradictory properties, but nothing guarantees that a subject has a single coherent notional world. His notional world may be shattered into fragmentary, overlapping, competing worlds.[6] When the theorist, the hetero-phenomenologist or notional world psychologist, takes the course of offering an admittedly inconsistent description of a notional world, it counts not as a settled, positive characterization of a notional world, but as a surrender in the face of confusion—giving up the attempt at (complete) interpretation. It is analogous to lapsing into direct quotation when conveying someone's remarks. "Well, what he *said* was: 'Nothing noths.' "

Notional-world hetero-phenomenology does not, then, settle the disputes and indeterminacies, or even sharpen the boundaries of everyday-folks' thinking about belief; it inherits the problems and simply recasts them in a slightly new format. One might well wonder what resources it has to recommend it. The prospect of constructing the notional world of an actual creature from an examination of its physical constitution is as remote as can be, so what value can there be in conceiving of a creature's notional world? Working in the other direction: starting with a description of a notional world and then asking how to design a "creature" with that notional world. Part of the allure of AI is that it provides a way of starting with what are essentially phenomenological categories and distinctions—features of notional worlds—and working backward to hypotheses about how to implement those competences. One starts with representational *powers* and works toward *means*. Philosophers have also toyed with this strategy.

The recent philosophical literature on the distinction between *de re* and *de dicto* beliefs and other attitudes is replete with sketchy suggestions for various sorts of mental machinery that might play a crucial role in drawing that distinction: Kaplan's (1968) *vivid names*, the *modes of presentation* of Schiffer (1978) and various other authors, and Searle's (1979a) *aspects*, to name a few. These are typically supposed to be definable purely in terms of narrow psychology,[7] so notional-attitude psychology should, in principle, be able to capture them. When we turn to that literature in the next section, we will explore the prospects for such machinery, but first there are some more grounds for skepticism about notional worlds to bring into the open.

The theme of a notional world, a world *constituted* by the mind or experience of a subject, has been a recurrent *leitmotif* in philosophy at least since Descartes. In various forms it has haunted idealism, phenomenalism, verificationism, and the coherence theory of truth, and in spite of the drubbing it typically takes, it keeps getting resurrected in new, improved versions: in Goodman's (1978) *Ways of Worldmaking* and in Putnam's (1978) recent revaluation of realism, for instance. The ubiquity of the theme is no proof of its soundness in any guise; it may be nothing more than an eternally tempting mistake. In its present guise it runs headlong into an equally compelling intuition about reference. If notional attitudes are to play the intermediary role assigned to them, if they are to be the counterpart for psychology of Kaplan's concept of the character of a linguistic expression, then it should follow that when a psychological subject or creature, with its notional world fixed by its internal constitution, is placed in different contexts, different real environments, this should determine different propositional attitudes for the subject:

notional attitude + environment → propositional attitude.

That means that if I and my *Doppelgänger* were to be switched, instantaneously (or in any case without permitting any change of internal state to occur during the transition—the interchange could take a long time so long as I and my *Doppelgänger* were comatose throughout), I would wake up with propositional attitudes *about the things on Twin Earth,* and my *Doppelgänger* would have propositional attitudes *about things on Earth.*[8] But that is highly counterintuitive (to many people, I discover, but not to all). For instance, I have many beliefs and other attitudes about my wife, a person on Earth. When my *Doppelgänger* first wakes up on Earth after the switch and thinks, "I wonder if Susan has made the coffee yet," *surely* he isn't thinking thoughts about *my wife*—he has never met her or heard of her! His thoughts, surely, are about his Susan, light years away, though he hasn't an inkling of the distance, of course. The fact that he'd never know the difference, nor would anyone else except the Evil Demon that pulled off the switch, is irrelevant; what no one could verify would nevertheless be true; his thoughts are not about my wife—at least not until he has had some causal commerce with her.

That is the essence of the causal theory of reference [see, e.g., Kripke (1972); Evans (1973); Donnellan (1966), (1970), (1974)] and the thought experiment nicely isolates it. But intuitions provoked in such wildly science-fictional circumstances are a poor test. Consider the same issue as it could arise in a perfectly possible train of events right here on Earth. In Costa Mesa, California, there is, or at any rate used to be, an establishment called Shakey's Pizza Parlor, a garish place featuring an ill-tuned player piano with fluorescent keys and with various "funny" handpainted signs on the walls: "Shakey's has made a deal with the bank: we don't cash checks, and the bank doesn't make pizza," and so forth. Oddly enough, very oddly in fact, in Westwood Village, California, some fifty miles away, there was another Shakey's Pizza Parlor, and it was eerily similar: built to the same blueprint, same ill-tuned player piano, same signs, same parking lot, same menu, same tables and benches. The obvious practical joke occurred to me when first I noticed this, but sad to say I never carried it out. It could easily have been done, however, so let me tell you the tale as if it actually happened.

The Ballad of Shakey's Pizza Parlor

Once upon a time, Tom, Dick, and Harry went to Shakey's in Costa Mesa for beer and pizza, and Dick and Harry played a trick on Tom, who was new to the area. After they had ordered their food and begun eating, Tom went to the men's room, whereupon Dick slipped a mickey into Tom's beer. Tom returned to the table, drained his mug, and soon fell sound asleep at the table. Dick gathered up the uneaten pizzas, Harry got Tom's hat off the peg behind his head, and then they dragged Tom out to the car and sped to Westwood Village, where they reestablished themselves, with a new pitcher of beer and some mugs, at the counterpart table. Then Tom woke up. "I must have dozed off," he commented, and the evening proceeded, noisily, as before. The conversation turned to the signs and other decorations, and then to graffiti; to the delight of Dick and Harry, Tom pointed toward the men's room and confessed that although he isn't really that sort of guy, tonight he was inspired to carve his initials on the door of the leftmost stall in that men's room. Dick and Harry doubted his word, whereupon Tom offered a wager. He announced he was prepared to bet that his initials were carved on that door. Dick took the wager, with Harry to referee, and a paper and pencil were produced, on which the explicit expression of the proposition at issue was to be written. At this point, the suspense was high, for whether or not Dick won the wager depended on the exact wording. If Tom wrote "I wager $5 that on the leftmost stall door in the men's room in the Costa Mesa Shakey's my initials appear," Tom would win the wager. But if Tom wrote "I wager $5 that my initials appear on the leftmost stall of the men's room of the pizza parlor in which we currently are seated"—or words to that effect—Dick would win. A third possibility was that Tom would compose a sentence that *failed to express a proposition* because it contained a vacuous name or vacuous description: "the Costa Mesa Shakey's, in which we are now sitting" or "the men's room of the place wherein I bought and entirely consumed an anchovy pizza on the night of February 11, 1968." In that case Harry would be forced to declare the wager ill-formed and return the stakes. (If Harry is a strict Russellian about definite descriptions, he may declare Tom's sentence false in these instances, and award the money to Dick.)

But Tom played into their hands, committed himself on paper to the Westwood Village door (though not under that description, of course), and lost the bet. The practical joke was explained to him, and Tom, though he admitted he'd been tricked, agreed that he had committed himself to a false proposition and had fairly lost the bet. But which door had he "had in mind"? Well, in some regards, he could rightly insist, he'd had the Costa Mesa door in mind. He'd vividly recalled the episode of his penknife digging into that door. But also he'd vividly "pictured" the door as being just a few feet away and eagerly anticipated, in his imagination, the triumph to ensue when the three of them walked into the adjacent men's room to settle the bet. So there was also a lot to be said in favor of his having had the Westwood Village door in mind. Such a puzzle! Clearly this was a job for sober philosophers with a technical vocabulary at their disposal!

There is a distinction, the philosophers say, between belief *de re* and belief *de dicto*. Everyone knows this distinction in his heart, but like many important philosophical distinctions, it is hard to characterize precisely and uncontroversially. We're working on it. In the meantime, we mark the distinction, which tends to get lost in the ambiguities of casual talk, by always using the awkward but at least arguably grammatical "of" style of attribution, when speaking of beliefs *de re*, reserving the "that" style for attributions of belief *de dicto*.[9] Thus

(1) Bill believes *that* the captain of the Soviet Ice Hockey team is a man

but it is not the case that

(2) Bill believes *of* the captain of the Soviet Ice Hockey Team that he is a man

since Bill is utterly unacquainted with that stalwart Russian, whoever he is. In contrast,

(3) Bill believes *of* his own father that he is a man.

Surely we all know *that* distinction, the distinction ostended by the example, so now we can proceed to apply it in the case of Shakey's Pizza Parlor. In virtue of Tom's rich causal intercourse with the Costa Mesa Shakey's and the things within it, Tom is entitled to *de re* beliefs relating him to those things. When he wakes up in Westwood Village, as his eyes dart about the room he swiftly picks up the obligatory causal relations with many of the objects in Westwood Village as well, including the Westwood Village Shakey's itself. Thus we can catalogue some of the true and false *de re* beliefs on Tom shortly after waking.

Tom believes *of* the Costa Mesa Shakey's:

True	False
that he bought a pizza in it tonight	that he is in it now
that he dozed off in it	that he woke up in it
that he put his hat on a peg in it	that his hat is on a peg in it

Tom believes *of* the Westwood Village Shakey's:

True	False
that he is in it now	that he bought a pizza in it tonight
that he woke up in it	that he dozed off in it
that his hat is on a peg in it	that he put his hat on a peg in it

Where in the normal course of things a person would have a single beliefs, Tom, because of the trick dislocation we have produced, has a dual list of *de re* beliefs; every true *de re* belief has a false twin about a different object. Of course this doubling up of Tom's beliefs is entirely unrecognized by Tom; there is still *something unitary* about his *psychological state*. (We could say: there is unity in his notional world, where there is duality in the real world. Each single, notional attitude of his spawns a pair of propositional attitudes, given his peculiar circumstances.)

But problems emerge when we attempt to continue the list of Tom's *de re* beliefs. Tom presumably believes of his hat both that it is on a peg in Costa Mesa and that it is on a peg right behind his head. Having noticed the Costa Mesa peg, however casually, Tom can also be said to believe *of* the Costa Mesa peg that his hat is on it (or, putting the two together: he believes of his hat and that peg that the former is on the latter). But can he believe of the peg behind his head, with which his only causal interaction to date has been an infinitesimally weak mutual gravitational attraction, that his hat is on it? The causal theorist must deny it. One would think that Tom's psychological state *vis-à-vis* his hat and its location was quite simple (and so it seems to Tom), but in fact it is quite wonderfully complex, when subjected to philosophical analysis. Tom believes *that* his hat is on a peg behind his head (and that is a true belief); he also believes truly *that* the peg behind his head on which his hat is resting is made of wood. He does not believe *of* that peg, however, that it is made of wood or behind his head. Moreover, Tom believes truly *that* there is a leftmost stall door in the adjacent men's room and believes falsely *that* the leftmost stall door in the adjacent men's room has his initials carved on it. So he believes that the leftmost stall door has his initials on it, but he does not believe of the leftmost stall door that it has his initials on it.

Some philosophers would disagree. Some [e.g., Kaplan (1968)] would say Tom's rapport with the Costa Mesa peg was too *casual* (though causal) to qualify Tom for *de re* beliefs about it. Pushing in the other direction, some [e.g., Kaplan (1978)] would hope to weaken the causal requirement (and replace it with something else, still to be determined) so that Tom could have *de re* beliefs about the unseen peg and the unmarked door. And some would stick to their guns and claim that the admittedly bizarre distinctions drawn in the preceding paragraph were nothing more than the tolerable implications of a good theory put *in extremis* by highly unusual conditions.

The point of pursuing these disagreements, of settling the philosophical dispute, might well be lost on a psychologist. It is tempting to hold that the *philosophical* problems encountered here, even if they are serious, real problems whose solution is worth pursuing, are not problems for psychology at all. For note that the different schools of thought about Tom's *de re* beliefs fail to differ in the predictions they would make of Tom's behavior under various circumstances. Which sentences he can be enticed to bet on, for instance, does not depend on which *de re* beliefs he *really* has. No school can claim predictive superiority based on its more accurate catalogue of Tom's beliefs. Those who hold he does not have any *de re* beliefs about the unseen door will *retrospectively* describe those cases in which Tom makes a losing bet as cases in which he willy-nilly asserts something he does not mean to assert, while those of the opposite persuasion will count him on those occasions as having (willy-nilly) expressed exactly what he believed. In the imagined case, if not perhaps in other, more normal cases, the presence or absence of a particular *de re* belief plays no predictive, hence no explanatory, role. But if in the imagined case it plays no role, should we not abandon the concept in favor of some concept which can characterize the crucial variables in both the normal and the abnormal cases?

The apparent failure of the philosophical distinctions to mesh with any useful psychological distinction may be due, however, to our looking in the wrong place, focusing too narrowly on a contrived local indiscernibility and thus missing an important psychological difference that emerges somehow in a broader context. The family of outlandish cases concocted by participants in the literature, involving elaborate practical jokes, tricks with mirrors, people dressed up like gorillas, identical twins, and the rest of the theatrical gimmicks designed to produce cases of *mistaken identity*, succeed in producing only momentary or at best unstable effects of the desired sort. One cannot easily sustain the sort of illusion required to ground the anomalous verdicts or other puzzles. Drawing verdicts based on shortlived anomalies in a person's psychological state provides a seriously distorted picture of the way people are related to things in the world; our capacity to keep track of things through time is not well described by any theory that atomizes psychological processes into successive moments with certain characteristics.[10] This is all, I think, very plausible, but what conclusion should be drawn from it? Perhaps this: formal semantics requires us to *fix* an object to be evaluated, at a particular time and in a particular context, for truth-value or reference, and while overt linguistic behavior provides the theorist with candidate objects—utterances—for such a role, *moving the game inside* and positing analogous "mental" objects or states for such fixing must do violence to the psychological situation. Anyone who imports the categories required for a formal semantic theory and presses them into service in a psychological theory is bound to create a monster. Such a conclusion is, as James might say, "vagueness incarnate." In particular, it is not yet clear whether it might be so strong a conclusion as to threaten all versions of "mental representation" theory, all theories that suppose there are syntactic objects in the head for which a principled semantic interpretation can be given.

I find it very difficult to put a crisper expression to this worry, but can for the moment render it more vivid with the aid of an analogy. One of the most inspired skits featured regularly on the television show *Laugh-In* was "Robot Theater," in which Arte Johnson and Judy Carne played a pair of newlywed robots. They would appear in some mundane circumstance, making breakfast or hubby-home-from-the-office, and would move about in a slightly jerky simulacrum of human action. But things never worked quite right; Arte would reach out to open a door, grasp just short of the knob, turn wrist, swing arm, and crash headlong into the still closed door; Judy would pour coffee for Arte, but the coffee would miss the cup—no matter, since Arte would not notice, and would "drain" the cup, turn lovingly to Judy and say "Delicious!" And so forth. The "problem," one saw, was that their *notional worlds didn't quite "match" the real world;* one had the impression that if they had been moved over about a half an inch before they were "started," everything would have gone swimmingly; then their beliefs would have had a chance of being *about* the things in the world around them. Their behavior was to be explained, presumably, by the fact that each of them contained an internal representation of the world, by consultation with which they governed their behavior. That's how robots work. This internal representation was constantly updated, of course, *but not continuously*. Their perceptual machinery (and their internal records of their actions) provided them with a succession of snapshots, as it were, of reality, which provoked revisions in their internal representations, but not fast enough or accurately enough to sustain a proper match of their notional world, their world-as-represented, and the real world.[11] Hence the behavioral infelicity. The "joke" is that *we are not at all like that.*

Well, are we or aren't we? The hope of cognitive science is that we *are* like that, only much, much better. In support of this conviction, cognitive science can point to precisely the anomalous cases envisaged in the literature on *de re* and *de dicto* beliefs: these are nothing more than experiments, in effect, that induce pathology in the machinery, and hence are rich sources of clues about the design principles of that machinery. That one must work so hard to contrive cases of actual pathology just shows how very good we are at updating our internal representations. The process of keeping track of things is practically continuous, but it will still have a perspicuous description in terms of swift revision of an internal model. Besides, as the pathological cases often show, when one adds *verbal* informing to purely *perceptual* informing of the system, the possibilities of serious dislocation, the creating of notional objects with no real counterparts, and the like, are dramatically increased. Beliefs acquired through the medium of language create problems when they must be meshed with perceptually induced beliefs, but these are problems soluble within the domain of cognitive science (Dennett, forthcoming c).

This suggests that the problems encountered in the story of Shakey's Pizza Parlor come from the attempt to apply a single set of categories to two (or more) very different styles of cognitive operation. In one of these styles, we do have internal representations of things in the world, the content of which in some way guides our behavior. In the other style we have something like procedures for keeping track of things in the world, which permit us to minimize our *representations* of those things by letting us consult the things themselves, rather than their representatives, when we need more information about them. Reflections on this theme are to be found in the literature of philosophy [e.g., Burge (1977); Kaplan (1968), (1978), (1980); Morton (1975); Nelson (1978)], psychology [e.g., Gibson (1969); Neisser (1976)] and Artificial Intelligence [e.g., Pylyshyn (1979)], but no one has yet succeeded in disentangling the goals and assumptions of the various different theoretical enterprises that converge on the topic: the semantics of natural language, the semantics and metaphysics of modal logic, the narrow cognitive psychology of individuals in environments and social groups. Armed, tentatively, with the idea of notional worlds, which provides at least a picturesque, if not demonstrably sound way of describing those matters that belong within the domain of narrow psychology and distinguishing them from matters requiring a different perspective, perhaps some progress can be made by considering the origins of the problematic distinctions in the context of the theoretical problems that gave birth to them.

ENDNOTES

1. This chapter is excerpted from Dennett's essay "Beyond Belief," in Woodfield (1982).
2. What about the objects of its fears, hopes, and desires? Are they denizens of the subject's notional world, or must we add a desire world, a fear world, and so forth to the subject's belief world? (Joe Camp and others have pressed this worry.) When something the subject believes to exist is also feared, or desired, by him, there is no problem: some denizen of his notional world is simply colored with desire or fear or admiration or whatever. How to treat "the dream house I hope someday to build" is another matter. Postponing the details to another occasion, I will venture some incautious general claims. My dream house is not a denizen of my notional world on a par with my house or even the house I will end my days in; thinking about *it* (my dream house) is not, for instance, to be analyzed in the same fashion as thinking about my house or thinking about the house I will end my days in. (More on this theme in the following section.) My dream house gets constituted indirectly in my notional world via what we might call my *specifications*, which are perfectly ordinary denizens of my notional world, and my general beliefs and other attitudes. I believe in my specifications, which already exist in the world as items of mental furniture created by my thinking, and then there are general beliefs and desires and the like involving those specifications: to say my dream house is built of cedar is not to say my specification is made of cedar, but to say that any house built to my specification would be made of cedar. To say I plan to build it next year is to say that I plan to build a house to my specs next year.
3. Special features of (literary) fiction lead Lewis to make substantial ingenious modifications to this idea in order to account for the role of background assumptions, narrator knowledge, and the like in the normal interpretation of fiction. For instance, we assume that the map of Holmes's London is that of Victorian London except where overridden by Conan Doyle's inventions; the texts neither assert nor strictly imply that Holmes did not have a third nostril, but the possible worlds in which this is the case are excluded.
4. The issues surrounding "I" and indexicality are much more complicated than this hurried acknowledgement reveals. See not only Perry and Lewis, but also Castaneda [(1966), (1967), (1968)]. For illuminating reflections on a similar theme, see Hofstadter [1979], pp. 373–76].
5. "A man may think that he believes *p*, while his behavior can only be explained by the hypothesis that he believes not-*p*, given that it is known that he wants *z*. Perhaps the

confusion in his mind cannot be conveyed by any simple (or complex—D. C. D.) account of what he believes: perhaps only a reproduction of the complexity and confusion will be accurate" [Hampshire (1975), p. 123].

6. See the discussion of phenomenology and "Feenomanology" in "Two Approaches to Mental Images," in Dennett (1978). See also Lewis's (1978) remarks on how to deal with inconsistency in a work of fiction.

7. Kaplan (1968) is explicit: "The crucial feature of this notion (Ralph's vivid names) is that it depends only on Ralph's current mental state, and ignores all links whether by resemblance or genesis with the actual world. . . . It is intended to go to the purely internal aspects of individuation" (p. 201).

8. My Doppelgänger would not, however, have thoughts *about me* when he thought, "I'm sleepy," and so forth. The reference of the first-person pronoun is not affected by world-switching, of course [see Putnam (1975); Perry (1977), (1979); Lewis (1979)]. But one must be careful not to inflate this point into a metaphysical doctrine about personal identity. Consider this variation on a familiar science-fiction theme in philosophy. Your spaceship crashes on Mars, and you want to return to Earth. Fortunately, a Teleporter is available. You step into the booth on Mars and it does a complete microphysical analysis of you, which requires dissolving you into your component atoms, of course. It beams the information to Earth, where the receiver, stocked with lots of atoms the way a photocopier is stocked with fresh white paper, creates an exact duplicate of you, which steps out and "continues" your life on Earth with your family and friends. Does the Teleporter "murder to dissect," or has it transported you home? When the newly arrived Earth-you says "I had a nasty accident on Mars," is what he says true? Suppose the Teleporter can obtain its information about you without dissolving you, so that you continue a solitary life on Mars. On your mark, get set, go. . . . [Some who have taken up this philosophical party game: Hofstadter & Dennett (1981); Nozick (1981); Parfit (1984); Nagel (1986).]

9. Connoisseurs of the literature will note that this sentence delicately reproduces a familiar equivocation that marks the *genre*: Does *"de re"* modify "speaking" or "beliefs"; does *"de dicto"* modify "attributions" or "belief"?

10. Evans, in lectures in Oxford in 1979, developed the theme of the *process* of keeping track of things in the world [see Evans (1980)]. It echoes a central theme in Neisser's (1976) apostatic renunciation of two-dimensional, tachistoscopic experiments in the psychology of perception, in favor of a Gibsonian "ecological" approach to perception.

11. The problem of preserving that match has as its core the "frame problem" of Artificial Intelligence which arises for planning systems that must reason about the effects of contemplated actions. See McCarthy and Hayes (1969); Dennett [(1978a) chapter 7; and (1984c)]. It is either the most difficult problem AI must—and can eventually— solve, or the *reductio ad absurdum* of mental representation theory.

10

Social Content and Psychological Content

Brian Loar

BY PSYCHOLOGICAL CONTENT I SHALL mean whatever individuates beliefs and other propositional attitudes in commonsense psychological explanation so that they explanatorily interact with each other and with other factors such as perception in familiar ways. In discussions of what appropriately individuates propositional attitudes there occurs the following kind of argument. Some thesis about psychological content is proposed, about, say, what constitutes it in general or constitutes some aspect of it. The reply is made that the thesis fails to capture the correct individuation conditions because correct ascriptions of attitudes using *that-clauses* count them the same when the proposed thesis distinguishes them or vice versa. Here are some examples.

1. There is the idea that the perceptual ability to discriminate objects of a given kind, cats say, may constitute a concept of that kind of object. Think of "concept" here as meaning a certain abstraction from the individuation conditions of certain beliefs and other attitudes, about cats, say. Then the capacity to have certain beliefs about cats, beliefs that have certain psychological contents, would involve the ability perceptually to discriminate cats. Variants of this idea have seemed natural to empiricists and recently to certain functionalists: What better criterion for having certain ordinary concepts than the ability systematically to pick out their instances?

But there is a problem when we consider how apparently we individuate beliefs, as Stephen Stich points out:

> Suppose I tell a blind person and a sighted person that there is a cat in the next room, and they believe my report. It seems natural to say that they both come to have the same belief: the belief that there is a cat in the next room. Our intuitions remain the same if we change the example by replacing the merely blind subject with a person like Helen Keller whose perceptual deficiencies are staggering.[1]

On these grounds Stich regards as false any theory that implies that the sighted and the blind person's beliefs have distinct contents.

The premise appears correct, for "believes that there is a cat in the next room" does seem univocally assertible of both the sighted person and Helen Keller. For if each were sincerely to assert, "There is a cat in the next room," their words conventionally would *mean* the same, and so by ordinary criteria the belief ascription would be true of each on an *oblique* or *de dicto* univocal reading. (The sameness of belief ascription is not then merely a function of a common *de re* reference to the kind *cat*.)

2. There is the very general thesis that the psychological content of a person's attitudes consists in their conceptual or cognitive-functional roles, thus presupposing that our commonsense system of psychological explanation individuates attitudes along nonsocial, individualistic lines. Tyler Burge has mounted an imposing counterargument.[2] He has two objections: that the individualist conceptual role theory counts beliefs as different which common sense counts the same; and that the conceptual role theory counts beliefs as the same which common sense counts different. Both objections rest on the following well-known example of Burge's.

Suppose that a person who is otherwise a normal English speaker believes that he has arthritis in his thigh, and that he also has many true beliefs about arthritis, for example, that he has it in his wrists and ankles. When a doctor tells him that arthritis cannot occur in the thigh ("arthritis means an ailment of the joints"), he is surprised but takes the doctor's word for it. Now consider that earlier belief which he would have expressed as "I have arthritis in my ankles." On the conceptual role theory, that belief should count as distinct from the doctor's belief that his patient has arthritis in his ankles. For the two have, or had, crucially different ideas about what "arthritis" means, and consequently the two beliefs have (should on a conceptual-role theory be counted as having) crucially different conceptual links to other beliefs. But as Burge argues, common sense ascribes the same belief to both: the belief that the patient has arthritis in his ankles. Thus, sameness of conceptual role is not *necessary* for sameness of psychological content.[3] Now it seems clear that Burge is right that the belief ascription applies both to the doctor and to the patient in his uncorrected state on a univocal reading, one that is, moreover, oblique or *de dicto*.

That sameness of conceptual role is not *sufficient* for sameness of content is argued as follows. Suppose the patient (whom we'll now call Bert) had lived in a world much like this one, but one in which doctors apply "arthritis" not to a disease specifically of joints but to a broader class of rheumatoid ailments including one that can occur in thighs. Suppose that Bert's history in that world had from an individualistic point of view been identical with what it is in the real world and that, therefore, before visiting the doctor Bert had had a belief he would have expressed as "I have arthritis in my thigh." As we see things, would that have been a belief that he had *arthritis* in his thigh? Burge says no, and again I believe he is right. In that world Bert may have had a belief that he had *tharthritis* (as we may choose to say) in his thigh, for there "arthritis" does not mean what it means among us. So in the actual and the counterfactual situations, the individualistic facts at out the conceptual roles of Bert's beliefs are the same, but distinct belief ascriptions are true of him. Burge draws the strong conclusion that the content of a person's beliefs depends in part on social facts that are independent of his cognitive makeup, social facts of which he may not be aware.

Stich's point and the first of Burge's points have a common structure: it is said to be false that discriminative abilities are partially constitutive of psychological contents, and that individual conceptual roles are constitutive of psychological contents, because those theses would count beliefs as distinct to which the same *de dicto* or oblique ascription univocally applies.

3. Metalinguistic contents have often been invoked for beliefs that normally would not be expressed metalinguistically. Thus, suppose a person asserts "there are elms in Spain" but knows of no non-metalinguistic distinguishing features of elms among trees or of Spain among countries. It could he said that the content of this person's belief involves the conception of elms as "those trees which among us are called 'elms' " and of Spain as "that country which among us is called 'Spain'."

One objection (there are others I shall not discuss) is the following. Suppose an Italian who would assert "Ci sono olmi in Spagna" is in the same situation as our English speaker; he does not know elms ("olmi") from other trees or Spain ("Spagna") from other countries. To be consistent we then say that his beliefs involve metalinguistic reference to those Italian nouns. But of course if everything else is normal we should rather say that the two speakers believe the same thing, namely that there are elms in Spain. This holds of them *de dicto* and univocally. They have the same belief while the metalinguistic analysis counts them as having distinct beliefs. Once again, I find the premise about the oblique or *de dicto* ascription correct, not open to an unforced denial; it would be misguided to insist that we must throw out the univocal that-clause and substitute a pair of metal-inguistic that-clauses in order to describe those beliefs correctly.

The question then to be addressed is the relation between *de dicto* or oblique ascriptions of beliefs and their psychological contents, between such ascriptions and their individuation in commonsense psychological explanation. I shall argue that psychological content is not in general identical with what is captured by oblique that-clauses, that commonsense constraints on individuation induce only a loose fit between contents and that-clauses, and that this does not make contents ineffable or even especially elusive. Let me emphasize that the topic is not some theoretical refinement of commonsense psychology, but ordinary every-day psychological explanation.

Behind the three arguments—against recognitional concept theories, conceptual role theories, and metalinguistic concept analyses—lies something like the following assumption:

(*) Sameness of *de dicto* or oblique ascription implies sameness of psychological content.

Perhaps there are facts about the occurrence of indexicals and demonstratives which would generally be perceived nowadays as counterexamples to (*) in its unqualified form. But it is pretty evident, I think, that the above arguments presuppose a version of (*) restricted to general terms (including also proper names; cf. "Spain"). So we have something like:

(A) Sameness of the *de dicto* or oblique occurrence of a general term in two belief ascriptions implies, if everything else is the same, sameness of the psychological content of the two beliefs thus ascribed.

My reply to the above arguments involves denying (A): sameness of the general terms in a pair of belief ascriptions does not (even though all else is equal) ensure that the ascribed beliefs are individuated as the same belief in commonsense psychological explanation.

I shall also argue the falsity of the converse of (A), viz.

(B) Differences in *de dicto* or oblique ascription imply differences in psychological content.

This is important again in connection with Burge's anti-individualism, for it seems to be required for his argument that sameness in the conceptual roles of thoughts is not sufficient for their sameness in psychological content.

A variant of a well-known example of Kripke's may serve to introduce the reason for rejecting (A). In the original example[4] Pierre grew up monolingual in France, where he had heard of a pretty city called "Londres"; he was moreover disposed to assert "Londres est jolie." Subsequently he was taken to live in London, not knowing it to be the Londres he had heard of; the part he lived in was unattractive and he was disposed to assert "London is not pretty." Our ordinary principles of belief ascription lead us then to say, as Kripke points out, both that Pierre believes that London is pretty, and that Pierre believes that London is not pretty. These ascriptions are true on an oblique reading,[5] and "London" is univocal as we use it.

Now Pierre might have been more fortunate; he might have been taken to an attractive part of London and thus been happy to assert "London is pretty," still unaware that this was the Londres he had heard of. The upshot is interesting: "Pierre believes that London is pretty" is true by virtue of the earlier facts about Pierre, and it is true by virtue of the later facts. And its double truth is on a univocal oblique reading. The point does not depend on translation; parallel cases arise in which someone mistakenly thinks a name names two things and ascribes the same predicate twice.

But how many beliefs does Pierre have? In other words, how many belief types are involved, as that is individuated by commonsense psychology? Clearly there are two beliefs, and they are as distinct as my beliefs that Paris is pretty and that Rio is pretty. Those beliefs would interact differently with other beliefs in ordinary psychological explanation. Perhaps in France Pierre came to believe that were he ever to live in "Londres" he would live in the same city as Oscar Wilde, and he retains this belief. But he does not draw from the conjunction of this belief and his later beliefs the conclusion that he now lives in a pretty city also inhabited by Oscar Wilde; and this is not because he has not bothered to put them together.

These beliefs not only are individuated by commonsense psychology as distinct in their psychological roles; it also seems quite appropriate to regard them as distinct in *content*. The differences in their interactive properties flow from differences in how Pierre conceives things, in how he takes the world to be, in what he regards the facts as being—that is, differences in some semantic or intentional dimension. And yet one and the same oblique belief description is true of Pierre univocally; by virtue of these beliefs that are distinct in their psychological content.

Let us now look at some beliefs involving general terms. Suppose that Paul, an English speaker, has been raised by a French nanny in a sheltered way. She speaks English with Paul, but amuses herself by referring to the cats around them as "chats" (she says "shahs," pronouncing the "s") and never as "cats." Paul acquires thereby a perfectly good recognitional acquaintance with cats and many beliefs about them, but he does not know that in English they are properly called "cats." Suppose he forms the belief he would express as "All chats have tails"; it seems we are then justified in asserting that Paul believes that all cats have tails, on an oblique reading.[6] As it happens, he occasionally sees his parents, who speak of animals called "cats." Because no cats are ever present, nor any pictures of cats, Paul does not realize that cats are his familiar "chats." Now Paul's parents tell him various things about cats, in particular that they all have tails. On this basis it is again true of Paul that he believes that all cats have tails. And it seems clear that Paul has two beliefs, with distinct psychological contents. For they interact potentially with other beliefs in different ways despite their common univocal ascription.

Had Paul's parents told him of Manx cats, it would have been true that Paul believes that all cats have tails and believes that not all cats have tails, on oblique unequivocal readings. But we should say that those beliefs are not inconsistent in their psychological contents,[7] and this means that these oblique ascriptions do not individuate Paul's beliefs in a way that reflects their psychological relations.

Stephen Stich's reply to the general thesis that recognitional abilities may be crucial to the individuation of beliefs was that Helen Keller and a sighted person both may believe that there is a cat in the next room. Now suppose that Paul had had a slightly different phonological history. His nanny used the English "cat," but somehow Paul got the idea that there are two different meanings of "cat," each referring to a distinct kind of animal (cf. "crab"), the kind he recognizes at a glance and the kind his parents speak of. This idea is so entrenched that when his nanny and his parents, on one of their rare joint appearances, both say, "there's a cat in the next room," Paul believes that there are two animals in the next room and is interested to see finally one of the unfamiliar "cats." Now Helen Keller has conveniently dropped by, and she overhears Paul's parents' remark. It seems that she thereby acquires only one belief that there's a cat in the next room, but that Paul has two such beliefs, distinct as types in their psychological individuation. Helen Keller's belief is then identical in type with at most one of Paul's beliefs. And so it is left open that the content of the other belief is constituted in part by Paul's ability to recognize cats. Naturally (A) is thereby falsified.

Now consider again Tyler Burge's first thesis, that two beliefs may differ in their conceptual roles (by virtue of different understandings of some concept) and nevertheless have the same content. Suppose that when Paul leaves home he lives in France for a while, learns about a rheumatoid ailment called "arthrite," and comes to believe that he has it both in his thigh and in his ankles. He would be surprised to learn that you can't have "arthrite" in your thigh. As it happens Paul has a perfectly good understanding of the English "arthritis," which he does not realize is renderable in French as "arthrite" (perhaps he never sees them written down). He is unfortunately given to hypochondria, and comes to believe that he has two problems with his ankles, in his words "arthrite" and "arthritis." It seems that "believes that he has arthritis in his ankles" is doubly but univocally true of Paul, by virtue of beliefs with distinct psychological contents. Had he been less inclined to hypochondria, his English belief could have instead been that he does not have arthritis in his ankles. Now that belief would clearly have been psychologically consistent with his French belief that he has arthritis in his ankles, but not with his *actual* English belief. The latter two therefore must be distinct in psychological content—unless, that is, you want to deny that the relevant sort of consistency is consistency in content.[8]

So Burge's observation that "believes that Bert has arthritis in his ankles" is true of the doctor and Bert on an oblique univocal reading, which I have agreed is correct, does not imply that their beliefs have the same content as that is individuated in commonsense psychological explanation.

I shall not go into the third argument, the one against metalinguistic analyses. But it should by now be clear that it does not follow from the fact that "believes that there are elms in Spain" is univocally true of those English and Italian speakers that their beliefs are not metalinguistic with regard to their respective languages and therefore distinct in their psychological contents.

It may be useful to distinguish two theses in what I have been arguing, namely, a thesis about how beliefs are *individuated* in commonsense psychological explanation, and a thesis about *content*, the former being more minimal than the latter.

Commonsense psychological explanation appeals to various elementary *structures* in the relations among beliefs, wants and so on. There are motivational structures: x's believing something, x's believing something else to the effect that given the first thing doing A would have a certain result, and x's desire for that result may explain x's doing A. There are inferential structures: x's believing something and x's believing something else to the effect that the first thing is sufficient for a certain further thing may explain x's believing that further thing. There are structures of irrationality: x's believing something, x's desire for a certain thing and x's belief to the effect that the first thing could rule out the second may conjointly explain x's compartmentalizing or suppressing the first belief. And so on.[9]

These structures apply to beliefs and desires only as they are appropriately individuated. The simple cases I have been discussing can be spun out in obvious ways to show that the appropriate individuation conditions are not captured by oblique readings of ordinary belief ascriptions. For example, imagine Paul's English belief that he has arthritis in his ankles interacting with a French belief of his that if he has arthritis in his ankles he should apply heat: not much happens as a result. The correct individuation transcends, in some crucial respects at least, what ordinary ascriptions capture. And I am speaking always of commonsense explanation.

As for psychological *content*, if it is not captured by that-clauses, what constitutes it? Are we entitled to regard my alleged underlying psychological individuation as determining a kind of content? I shall return to this question.

Let us take up the second strong Burgean thesis. Suppose "arthritis" had meant *tharthritis*: even if Bert's nonsocially described ruminations remained the same, it would not have been true that Bert believed that he had arthritis in his ankles and thigh. *Therefore* sameness of individualist conceptual role is not sufficient for sameness of psychological content.

Now Burge's premise, that our old belief ascription would not then be true of Bert, is correct; and it is an important discovery that belief ascriptions are thus sensitive to social facts which may not be reflected in believers' own versions of things. But the further thesis, that content as it is individuated in psychological explanation depends on independent social factors, is I think not correct.

The anti-individualist conclusion depends on (B), that differences in oblique ascription imply differences in psychological content. But the intuitions which in the cases of Paul and Pierre led us to reject (A) ought also to bring us to reject (B). We should hold that despite their different ascriptions Bert's belief that he has arthritis in his ankles and his belief that he has tharthritis in his ankles have the same psychological content, because they have the same potential for explanatory interaction with other beliefs; what intuitively appeared to determine that potential in the case of Paul and Pierre was how they, as it were, personally conceived things. But let me give some new arguments directed specifically against (B) and the Burgean thesis that sameness of individualist conceptual role is not sufficient for sameness of psychological content.

That (B) is false is already accepted by whomever takes a certain widespread view of Twin Earth cases. Although those Twin Earthling thoughts which they express using "water" are, as the story goes,[10] like ours in their personal conceptual roles, we cannot ascribe to them the thought that, say, they bathe in water. Twin Earthlings have referential contact not with H_2O, but with a chemically distinct if phenomenally indistinguishable substance, and so we cannot translate their "water" into English as "water" and hence cannot assert of them anything of the form "believes that . . . water. . . ." Conceding these facts about belief *ascriptions*, many have found it intuitive, indeed have taken it to be the point of Twin

Earth cases, that Twin Earthlings' thoughts have the same content as ours as that is individuated in psychological explanation, the same "narrow content."

Such intuitions appear to be vindicated by two rather different thought experiments. (1) Suppose Bert is a full member of two English-speaking communities that differ linguistically in small ways of which he is unaware. The first is ours, where "arthritis" means arthritis; but in the second "arthritis" means tharthritis. Let the individual facts about Bert be as in Burge's case. How are we to describe him? If there is no reason to choose just one of the languages as his language, then apparently the best thing for us to say is that Bert believes that he has arthritis in his ankles and believes that he has tharthritis in his ankles. But in explaining Bert psychologically the natural thing to say is that he has just one belief, one way of conceiving what is wrong with his ankles. Similarly, we may imagine a commuter between Earth and Twin Earth who is biworldly in his language without knowing of the systematic referential differences between English and Twin English. He would assert "Water quenches thirst." Again it seems that two belief ascriptions are in order, but that they should be seen as merely different extrinsic descriptions of what is, as regards psychological explanation, the commuter's one way of conceiving things.

2. Here is a different thought experiment. One is given a diary and told that it is by either an Earthling or a Twin Earthling but not which. An entry says, "No swimming today; we think the water is too rough." This reports a psychological explanation, one that loses nothing from our ignorance of the diary's provenance, that is, from our ignorance of whether it would be correct, in reporting that thought obliquely in a that-clause, to use "water" or "Twin water." It is not that we switch rapidly back and forth between two explanations, one in terms of water and the other in terms of Twin water; all we have to have been told is that the diary was written in one of a class of worlds that resemble Earth in the relevant respects. Or, again, suppose that I do not know whether in Bert's linguistic community "arthritis" means arthritis or tharthritis, but that I know all the relevant individualist facts about Bert. I read in his diary: "I fear I have arthritis, and so today I have made an appointment with a specialist." It is difficult to accept that we do not fully understand the psychological explanation given here, despite our not being in a position to produce the correct that-clause. We understand the diarists' explanations because we know how they conceive things.

What is there to be said against these intuitions in favor of "narrow content"? Two objections could be thought to have force. The first is that so-called narrow content cannot capture an *intentional* property; for the two beliefs in the Burge case and those in the Twin Earth case do not share *truth-conditions*. "Content" should mean intentionality, and intentionality is a certain *directedness* of thoughts onto things, properties, states of affairs—in short, truth-conditions and the components of truth-conditions. The second objection is that there is no appropriate way to *specify* the common content in those pairs of beliefs; and thus the notion of narrow content is just hand-waving.

I shall not say in response to either objection that there are that-clauses which do not contain "water" or "arthritis" and which capture the common content of those pairs of beliefs. I am quite prepared to concede that that-clauses are so generally shot through with social and causal presuppositions that narrow content cannot in general be captured thus.

There is a kind of reply to the objection concerning intentionality and truth conditions which I believe is important but shall not develop at length here. Put sketchily the idea is that the conceptual roles of thoughts are distinct from their truth conditions, and in more than one sense do not determine truth-conditions (except perhaps for certain demonstrative judgments involving perceptual discriminative concepts).[11] But commonsense psychological explanation of the sort we have intuitively appealed to in discussing Paul and Pierre individuates attitudes according to their conceptual roles, the specification of truth-conditions having some further function—on which more anon. How can there be *content* without truth conditions? This is, I think not merely a terminological question, for it involves intuitions about the apparent intentionality of one's own thoughts as judged from a first-person perspective. The point is that the conceptual roles of one's thoughts determine *how* one *conceives* things, and it is difficult to see how one conceives things without that in some sense involving what one's thoughts are "about." And that is appropriately called content by a Principle of the Transparency of Content: If something from an unconfused perspective appears to be content then it is a kind of content. As I say, this is sketchy, but I mention it to register that the defender of "narrow content" has more than one line of defense. It would not matter that narrow content does not determine truth-conditions if there is a kind of content that does not involve truth conditions.

Furthermore the demand for a narrow or individualist account of intentionality, in the sense of the outward directedness of thoughts onto states of affairs, is not unanswerable. Consider Bert's diary again. I do not know whether Bert's use of "arthritis" involves a misconception because I do not know the social facts about it. But I do know this: how the world *would* be if Bert's conceptions are or were not misconceptions. How Bert thinks of things—as that is described from an individualist perspective—appears to determine a set of possible worlds, namely, those in which Bert's thoughts are or would be true if they are or were not misconceptions. Call that set of worlds the *realization conditions* of Bert's beliefs. If my ability to explain Bert psychologically presupposes a grasp of something "intentional," something like truth-conditions, then it would seem that my grasp of the realization conditions of Bert's beliefs is sufficient. The diary thought experiment supports this.

Realization-conditions are, of course, not truth conditions in our official sense. The truth-conditions of a belief depend on some that-clause which correctly ascribes it, and as Burge has shown that is not in general determined by individualist facts. Thus, I am not saying that the *real* truth conditions of thoughts are their realization conditions. I am not proposing a redefinition of anything. Rather, I am saying that if psychological explanation involves a mapping of thoughts onto possible states of affairs, then realization-conditions are there for the taking.

There is nothing recondite in the idea; our commonsense understanding of others delivers the realization conditions of their beliefs without our having a name for them.[12]

An adjustment to this suggestion is needed. Suppose I find a diary with the entry "Hot and sunny today; phoned Maria to invite her to the beach." Now, the date has been torn off the page. Still I appear to understand the diarist's explanation of his/her phoning Maria, despite not knowing the truth-conditions (in one sense) of the thought expressed by "hot and sunny today." Is there not, however a sense in which I do know the truth-conditions? Suppose on Tuesday one thinks, "it is hot and sunny today" and on Friday one thinks, "it is hot and sunny today." They have the same truth conditions in the sense of conditions of truth in abstraction from context. Call them *context-indeterminate*, by contrast with the context-determinate truth-conditions that determine sets of possible worlds. Then if understanding the psychological explanation given in the diary requires in some sense knowing truth-conditions, they need merely be context-indeterminate.

To put this together with the former point, we may say this: if psychological explanation involves intentionality, then *context-indeterminate realization-conditions* are all the intentionality required.[13]

There is still the objection that we cannot in general *specify* the narrow content of thoughts. Now if this means merely that narrow content is not in general captured by ordinary that-clauses, it is difficult to see why it is an objection. We have perfectly sound intuitions about when to distinguish the beliefs of Paul, Pierre, and Bert, despite the fact that that-clauses do not make the right distinctions. If we then lack specifications of narrow content in the sense in which we have specifications of wide, social content, that must mean that psychological explanation does not require such specifications. We get along perfectly well without them; we individuate beliefs and understand their realization-conditions without an official system of generating such specifications. Narrow contents are not ineffable, we get at them in context via various devices. (a) We use that-clauses with one eye on the background facts: different narrow contents are implied by "Paul believes that cats have tails" in the "chat" context and in the "cat" context. (b) We report a person's words, or approximations thereto, together with other utterances which help us to interpret his words: Bert says "I have arthritis in my ankles," but he also says, "I have arthritis in my thigh." The second helps one to understand the narrow content expressed by the first. (c) We ascribe narrow content by producing words that have the same narrow content for us. Imagine a Twin Earthling whose language is Twin German; it may help to render one of his beliefs as "I bathe in water" even though there is no water there and those are not the words he would utter. Not that we have much opportunity for interpreting Twin Earthlings, but interpretation by approximately matching narrow contents is one of our fundamental techniques in psychological explanation.

It now seems to me somewhat extraordinary that we should have thought that psychological states are captured by a neat set of content specifications. But what then are that-clauses for? Of course they play a central role in psychological explanation, given suitable background information; but we have been misconceiving that role in thinking that they define precisely the individuation-conditions of psychological states. That-clauses on their oblique readings are sensitive, either directly or indirectly via translation, to how beliefs would linguistically be expressed, and that is, as the examples of Paul and Pierre show, only loosely related to psychological content. Now, as Burge's cases show, that-clauses capture how a belief would be expressed by exhibiting something that is equivalent in *social content* (as we might say) to what the subject would utter, given his deference to the usage of his linguistic community. This enables that-clauses to capture certain extra-psychological relations of propositional attitudes to independent states of affairs, what we may think of as their *socially determined truth-conditions*. The fundamental usefulness of this is that we may then describe people as conveyors of more or less determinate information, which remains constant even when the psychological contents of their states vary. That-clauses enable us to impose a grid of socially regularized information on the vagaries of individual psychology. Presumably the system of propositional-attitude ascription is part of a larger framework of *restraints*, even, on the centrifugal tendencies of the thoughts of each of us.

ENDNOTES

1. Stich [(1983), pp. 66–67].
2. Burge (1979a).
3. It is fair to say that many have taken this to be the message of Burge's paper—that is, that beliefs are not individuated in commonsense explanation by their conceptual roles. Of course, Burge's direct point is about the presuppositions of *ascriptions* of beliefs. But because of the widespread supposition that the significance of this point lies in the stronger point, I am taking the stronger point to be the consequential burden of Burge's paper. He writes: "It is expressions at oblique occurrences within content clauses that primarily do the job of providing the content of mental states or events, and in characterizing the person" [Burge (1979a), p. 76]. And again he writes of "the idea that the distinctively mental aspects can be understood fundamentally in terms of the individual's abilities, dispositions, state, and so forth, considered in isolation from his social surroundings" as follows: "our argument undermines this latter suggestion. Social context infects even the distinctively mental features of mentalistic attributions. No man's intentional mental phenomena are insular [(1979a), p. 87]. More recently, Burge has argued for an apparently less stringent position, namely, that even though there *might* be a level of scientific psychology which is individualist, (a) there are important examples of scientific psychology which cannot be construed individualistically, (b) such nonindividualist explanation is legitimate as regards scientific methodology, and (c) commonsense psychological explanation is nonindividualist. In this paper I am concerned to argue that Burge's observations about belief ascriptions may be accepted while denying (c).
4. Kripke (1979).

5. This assumes that when we ascribe beliefs obliquely to speakers of other languages, the correct way to do so is (roughly) to translate how they would be expressed.

6. How else to represent the belief obliquely than by translating "chats" as "cats"? Keep in mind that the point does not depend on translation.

7. In Loar (1987), I discuss the significance of the phenomenon in connection with Saul Kripke's "puzzle about belief."

8. Perhaps it is some sort of "formal" consistency. But then beliefs would not be individuated in commonsense psychological explanation by their *content*, which seems implausible.

9. The circumlocutory wording is meant to avoid propositional variables which appear to presuppose that-clauses. For a way of understanding these structures of irrationality, see sections 4 and 6 of my accompanying paper "A New Kind of Content" (not reprinted here—*ed.*).

10. Putnam (1975).

11. See Loar (1982).

12. This is perhaps similar to what David Lewis proposes in Lewis (1981).

    As several people have pointed out to me, my "context-independent realization conditions" are quite similar, including their detachment from that-clauses, to Daniel Dennett's *notional worlds* [see Dennett (1982)]. I discuss the relation between my account, as that is elaborated in section 6 of "A New Kind of Content," and Dennett's theory in footnote 6 of that paper.

13. Jerry Fodor has recently proposed that narrow content be construed in terms of functions from contexts to sets of possible worlds (in a paper given at UCLA, Spring 1985). [See also Chapter 2 in Fodor (1987), reprinted here—*ed.*]. And in correspondence he has suggested that this would preclude the need for the realization conditions I propose here. But I do not think that Kaplanesque characters will in fact do the job of capturing the narrow content of general terms, or not unless I am missing something. The reason is that, if you treat natural-kind terms as if they are pure indexicals whose semantic values are determined by context, then "water" and "alcohol" would count as having the same narrow content—viz., that function which maps a natural-kind term onto a natural-kind in accordance with certain causal facts in its history of use. A Kaplanesque "character," a function of that kind, may well individuate the narrow content of a very special feature of thought, such as the first-person pronoun, for it can be argued that self-ascription is the only aspect of narrow content whose reference-function always maps the belief onto the believer. But in the narrow individuation of beliefs involving "water" and "alcohol," we want their contributions to be different, in accordance with their conceptual roles. That combination of indexicality and substantive conceptual content is what context-indeterminate realization conditions are supposed to capture.

11

From *Psychosemantics*: Individualism and Supervenience

Jerry Fodor

After the Beardsley exhibit at the V&A, walking along that endless tunnel to South Kensington Station, I thought, why this is "behavior"—and I had said, perhaps even written: "where does 'behavior' begin and end?"

—BARBARA PYM

I BEG YOUR INDULGENCE. I am about to tell you two stories that you've very probably heard before. Having once told you the stories, I will then spend most of this chapter trying to puzzle out what, if anything, they have to do either with commonsense belief/desire explanation or with the Representational Theory of Mind (RTM). The conclusion will be: not much. That may sound pretty dreary, but I've been to parties that were worse; and there's a sort of excuse in the following consideration: the two stories I'm about to tell you have been at the center of a great lot of recent philosophical discussion. Indeed, contrary to the conclusion that I am driving toward, it is widely held that one or both stories have morals that tend to undermine the notion of content and thereby raise problems for propositional-attitude-based theories of mind.

Since these stories are so well known, I shall tell them in abbreviated form, entirely omitting the bits about the shaggy dog.

The Putnam story. Is there anyone who hasn't heard? There's this place, you see, that's just like here except that they've got XYZ where we've got H_2O. (XYZ is indistinguishable from H_2O by any casual test, though of course one could tell them apart in the chemical laboratory.) Now, in this place where they have XYZ, there's someone who's just like me down to and including his neurological microstructure. Call this guy Twin Me. The intuition we're invited to share is that, in virtue of the chemical facts and in spite of the neurological ones, the form of words "water is wet" means something different in his mouth from what it does in mine. And, similarly, the content of the thought that Twin Me has when he thinks (*in re* XYZ, as one might say) that water is wet is different from the content of the thought that I have when I think that water is wet *in re* H_2O. Indeed, the

192

intuition we're invited to share is that, strictly speaking, Twin Me can't have the thought that water is wet at all.

The Burge story. The English word "brisket," according to the Funk & Wagnalls *Standard Desk Dictionary* and other usually reliable authorities, means "the breast of an animal, esp. of one used as food" (from the Old French "bruschet," in case you were wondering). Imagine a guy—call him Oscar—who speaks English all right but who suffers from a ghastly misapprehension: Oscar believes that only certain food animals—only beef, say—have brisket; pork, according to Oscar's mistaken world view, is *ipso facto* brisketless.

First intuition: Oscar, despite his misapprehension, can perfectly well have brisket-beliefs, brisket-desires, brisket-fears, brisket-doubts, brisket-qualms, and so forth. In general: If the butcher can bear attitude *A* toward the proposition that brisket is *F*, so too can Oscar. Of course, Oscar differs from the butcher—and other speakers of the prestige dialect—in that much of what Oscar believes about brisket is false. The point, however, is that Oscar's false belief that pork isn't brisket is nevertheless a brisket-belief; it is *brisket* that Oscar believes that pork brisket isn't (if you see what I mean). From which it follows that Oscar "has the concept" BRISKET—whatever exactly that amounts to.

Now imagine an Oscar Twin. Oscar2 is molecularly identical to Oscar but lives in a language community (and talks a language) which differs from English in the following way. In that language the phonetic form "brisket" does apply only to breast of beef; so whereas what Oscar believes about brisket is false, what Oscar2 believes about brisket2 is true.

Second intuition: Oscar2 doesn't have brisket attitudes; it would be wrong for us—us speakers of English, that is—to say of Oscar2 that his wants, beliefs, yearnings, or whatever are ever directed toward a proposition of the form: ". . . brisket. . . ." For Oscar2, unlike his molecularly identical twin Oscar, doesn't have the concept *brisket*; he has the concept *brisket2* (= brisket of beef, as *we* would say).

So much for the stories. Now for the ground rules. Some philosophers are inclined to claim about the Putnam story that Twin-Me actually is just like Me; that it's wrong to think that Twin-Me hasn't got the concept *water*. Analogously, some philosophers are inclined to say that Oscar actually is just like Oscar2; that it's wrong to think that Oscar has the concept *brisket*. (Indeed, if your theory of language is at all "criteriological," you quite likely won't be prepared to have the intuitions that Putnam and Burge want you to have. Criteriological theories of language aren't fashionable at present, but I've noticed that the fashions tend to change.) Anyhow, for purposes of discussion I propose simply to grant the intuitions. If they're real and reliable, they're *worth* discussing; and if they're not, there's no great harm done.

Second, I will assume that the Burge story shows that whatever exactly the moral of the Putnam story is, it isn't specific to terms (/concepts) that denote "natural kinds." In fact, I'll assume that the Burge story shows that if the Putnam story raises *any* problems for the notion of content, then the problems that it raises are completely general and affect all content-bearing mental states.

Third, I will assume that what's at issue in the Putnam and Burge stories is something about how propositional attitudes are individuated; and that the intuitions Putnam and Burge appeal to suggest that the attitudes are in some sense individuated with respect to their *relational* properties. (Thus, my Twin's water2-beliefs are supposed to differ in content from my water-beliefs, and what's supposed to account for the difference is the chemical composition of the stuff *in our respective environments*. Analogously, Oscar's brisket-beliefs are supposed to differ in content from Oscar2's brisket2-beliefs, and what's supposed to account for the difference is what the form of words "is brisket" applies to *in their respective language communities*.)

Brian Loar, in a recent, important paper (1988), has argued that these concessions may be too generous. Loar points out that the standard interpretation of the Twin cases takes for granted that if, for example, the predicate "believes that water is . . ." applies to me but not to my Twin, and the predicate "believes that water2 is . . ." applies to my Twin but not to me, then it follows that the content of my belief differs in some respect from the content of my Twin's. In effect, according to Loar, Putnam and Burge assume that you can infer identities and differences in beliefs from corresponding identities and differences in the "that . . ." clauses that are used to ascribe them; and Loar gives grounds for doubting that such inferences are invariably sound. I think Loar may well be right about this, but I propose to ignore it. It's interesting to see what would follow from assuming that people situated the way that the Twins and the Oscars are *ipso facto* believe different things, whether or not the Burge/Putnam intuitions actually show that they do.

In aid of which, I shall talk as follows: Standards of individuation according to which my beliefs differ in content from my Twin's (and Oscar's differ from Oscar2's) I'll call "relational." Conversely, if attitudes are individuated in such fashion that my beliefs and my Twin's are identical in content, then I'll say that the operative standards are "nonrelational." It's going to turn out, however, that this terminology is a little coarse and that relational individuation per se isn't really the heart of the matter. So when more precision is wanted, I'll borrow a term from Burge; standards of individuation according to which my Twin and I are in the same mental state are "individualistic."

OK, now: What do the Burge and Putnam stories show about the attitudes?

SUPERVENIENCE

Here's a plausible answer. At a minimum they show that propositional attitudes, as common sense understands them, don't supervene on brain states. To put it roughly: States of type X supervene on states of type Y iff there is no difference among X states without a corresponding difference among Y states. So, in particular, the psychological states of organisms supervene on their brain states iff their brains differ whenever their minds differ. Now, the point about Me and Twin Me (and about Oscar and Oscar2) is that although we have different propositional attitudes, our brains are identical molecule-for-molecule; so it looks like it just follows that our attitudes don't supervene upon our brain states. But it's arguable that any scientifically useful notion of psychological state ought to respect supervenience; mind/brain supervenience (and/or mind/brain identity) is, after all, the best idea that anyone has had so far about how mental causation is possible. The moral would appear to be that you can't make respectable science out of the attitudes as commonsensically individuated.

I'm actually rather sympathetic to this line of thought; I think there is an issue about supervenience and that it does come out that we need, when doing psychology, other identity conditions for mental states than those that common sense prefers. This doesn't bother me much, because (a) redrawing these boundaries doesn't jeopardize the major claim on which the vindication of the attitudes as explanatory constructs depends—viz., that scientific psychological explanation, like commonsense belief/desire explanation, is committed to states to which semantic and causal properties are simultaneously ascribable; and (b) I think it's quite easy to see how the required principles of individuation should be formulated.

All that will take some going into. For starters, however, there's this: It needs to be argued that there *is* any problem about supervenience to be solved. Contrary to first impressions, that doesn't just fall out of the Burge and Putnam stories. Here's why: to get a violation of supervenience, you need not just the relational individuation of mental states; you also need *the nonrelational individuation of brain states.* And the Twin examples imply only the former.

To put the same point minutely differently: My brain states are type-identical to my Twin's only if you assume that such relational properties as, for example, *being a brain that lives in a body that lives in a world where there is* XYZ *rather than* H_2O *in the puddles,* do *not* count for the individuation of brain states. But why should we assume that? And, of course, if we *don't* assume it, then it's just not true that my Twin and I (or, *mutatis mutandis,* Oscar1 and Oscar2) are in identical brain states; and it's therefore not true that they offer counterexamples to the supervenience of the attitudes.

("Fiddlesticks! For if brain states are individuated relationally, then they will themselves fail to supervene on states at the next level down; on molecular states, as it might be."

"Fiddlesticks back again! You beg the question by assuming that *molecular* states are nonrelationally individuated. Why shouldn't it be relational individuation all the way down to quantum mechanics?")

You will be pleased to hear that I am not endorsing this way out of the supervenience problem. On the contrary, I hope the suggestion that brain states should be relationally individuated strikes you as plain silly. Why, then, did I suggest it?

Well, the standard picture in the recent philosophical literature on cognitive science is the one that I outlined above: The Burge and Putnam stories show that the commonsense way of individuating the attitudes violates supervenience; by contrast, the psychologist individuates the attitudes nonrelationally ("narrowly," as one sometimes says), thereby preserving supervenience but at the cost of requiring an individualistic (/"nonrelational"/"narrow") notion of content. Philosophers are then free to disagree about whether such a notion of content actually can be constructed. Which they do. Vehemently.

This standard understanding of the difference between the way that common sense construes the attitudes and the way that psychology does is summarized as follows:

Commonsense Taxonomy (Pattern A)
1. Individuates the attitudes relationally; hence, assumes a nonindividualistic notion of content.
2. Distinguishes: my beliefs from my Twin's, Oscar's beliefs from Oscar2's.
3. Individuates brain states nonrelationally; therefore:
4. Violates supervenience.[1]

Psychological Taxonomy (Pattern B)
1. Individuates the attitudes nonrelationally; hence, assumes a narrow notion of content.
2. Identifies: my beliefs with my Twin's, Oscar's beliefs with Oscar2's.
3. Individuates brain states nonrelationally; therefore:
4. Preserves supervenience.

One can imagine quite a different reaction to the Twin examples, however. According to this revisionist account, psychology taxonomizes the attitudes precisely the same way that common sense does. Both follow pattern A; both assume principles of individuation that violate supervenience. And so much the worse for supervenience. This, if I understand him right, is the line that Burge himself takes;[2] in any event, it's a line that merits close consideration. If psychology individuates the attitudes relationally, then it is no more in need of a narrow notion of content than common sense is. It would save a lot of nuisance if this were true, since we would not then have the bother of cooking up some narrow notion of content for psychologists to play with. It would also disarm philosophers who argue that cognitive science is in trouble because it needs a notion of narrow content *and can't have one*, the very idea of narrow content being somehow incoherent.

Alas, there is always as much bother as possible; the revisionist reading cannot be sustained. It turns out that the considerations that militate for the nonrelational individuation of mental states (hence, for preserving supervenience at the cost of violating the commonsense taxonomy) are no different from the ones that militate for the nonrelational individuation of brain states, molecular states, and such. This becomes evident as soon as one understands the source of our commitment to nonrelational taxonomy in these latter cases.

All this takes some proving. I propose to proceed as follows. First, we'll consider why we think that brain states and the like should be individuated nonrelationally. This involves developing a sort of metaphysical argument that individuation in science is *always individualistic*. It follows, of course, that the scientific constructs of psychology must be individualistic too, and we'll pause to consider how the contrary opinion could ever have become prevalent. (It's here that the distinction between "nonrelational" and "individualistic" individuation is going to have some bite.) We will then be back exactly where we started. Common sense postulates a relational taxonomy for the attitudes; psychology postulates states that have content but are individualistic; so the question arises what notion of content survives this shift in criteria of individuation. It will turn out— contrary to much recent advertisement—that this question is not really very hard to answer. The discussion will therefore close on an uncharacteristic note of optimism- The prospects for a scientifically defensible intentional psychology are, in any event, no worse now than they were before the discovery of XYZ; and brisket is a red herring.

CAUSAL POWERS

I have before me this *gen-u-ine* United States ten cent piece. It has precisely two stable configurations; call them "heads" and "tails." (I ignore dimes that stand on their edges; no theory is perfect.) What, in a time of permanent inflation, will this dime buy for me? Nothing less than control over the state of every physical particle in the universe.

I define "is an H-particle at t" so that it's satisfied by a particle at t iff my dime is heads-up at t. Correspondingly, I define "is a t-particle at t" so that it's satisfied by a particle at t iff my dime is tails-up at t. By facing my dime heads-up, I now bring it about that every particle in the universe is an H-particle . . . thus! And then, by reversing my dime, I change every particle in the universe into a T-particle . . . thus! And back again . . . thus! (Notice that by defining H and T predicates over objects at an appropriately higher level, I can obtain corresponding control over the state of every *brain* the universe, changing H-brain states into T-brain states and back again just as the fancy takes me.) With great power comes great responsibility. It must be a comfort for you to know that it is a trained philosopher whose finger is on the button.

What is wrong with this egomaniacal fantasy? Well, in a certain sense, nothing; barring whatever problems there may be about simultaneity, "is H at t" and "is T at t" are perfectly well defined predicates and they pick out perfectly well defined (relational) properties of physical particles. Anybody who can get at my dime can, indeed, affect the distribution of these properties throughout the universe. It's a matter of temperament whether one finds it fun to do so.

What *would* be simply mad, however, would be to try to construct a particle physics that acknowledges *being an H-particle* or *being a T-particle* as part of its explanatory apparatus. *Why* would that be mad? Because particle physics, like every other branch of science, is in the business of causal explanation; and whether something is an *H*-(*T*-) particle *is irrelevant to its causal powers*. I don't know exactly what that means; but whatever it means, I'm morally certain that it's true. I propose to wade around in it a bit.

Here are some things it seems to me safe to assume about science. We want science to give causal explanations of such things (events, whatever) in nature as can be causally explained.[3] Giving such explanations essentially involves projecting and confirming causal generalizations. And causal generalizations subsume the things they apply to in virtue of the causal properties of the things they apply to. Of course.

In short, what you need in order to do science is a taxonomic apparatus that distinguishes between things insofar as they have *different* causal properties, and that groups things together insofar as they have the *same* causal properties. So now we can see why it would be mad to embrace a taxonomy that takes seriously the difference between *H*-particles and *T*-particles. All else being equal, *H*-particles and *T*-particles have identical causal properties; whether something is an *H*-(*T*-)particle is irrelevant to its causal powers. To put it a little more tersely, if an event *e* is caused by *H*-particle *p*, then that same event *e* is also caused by *p* in the nearest nomologically possible world in which *p* is *T* rather than *H*. (If you prefer some other way of construing counterfactuals, you are welcome to substitute it here. I have no axes to grind.) So the properties of being *H* (/*T*) are taxonomically irrelevant for purposes of scientific causal explanation.

But similarly, *mutatis mutandis*, for the properties of being *H* and *T* *brain states*. And similarly, *mutatis mutandis*, for the properties of being *H* and *T* *mental states*. And similarly, *mutatis mutandis*, for the property of being a mental state of a person who lives in a world where there is XYZ rather than H_2O in the puddles. These sorts of differences in the relational properties of psychological (/brain/particle) states are irrelevant to their causal powers; hence, irrelevant to scientific taxonomy.

So, to summarize, if you're interested in causal explanation, it would be mad to distinguish between Oscar's brain states and Oscar2's; their brain states have identical causal powers. That's why we individuate brain states individualistically. And if you are interested in causal explanation, it would be mad to distinguish between Oscar's *mental* states and Oscar2's; their mental states have identical causal powers. But common sense deploys a taxonomy that *does* distinguish between the mental states of Oscar and Oscar2. So the commonsense taxonomy won't do for the purposes of psychology. Q.E.D.[4]

I can, however, imagine somebody not being convinced by this argument. For the argument depends on assuming that the mental states of Twins do in fact have the same causal powers, and I can imagine somebody denying that this is so. Along either of the two following lines:

First line: "Consider the effects of my utterances of the form of words 'Bring water!' Such utterances normally eventuate in somebody bringing me water—

viz., in somebody bringing me H_2O. Whereas, by contrast, when my Twin utters 'Bring water!' what he normally gets is water2 — viz., XYZ. So the causal powers of my water-utterances do, after all, differ from the causal powers of my Twin's 'water'-utterances. And similarly, *mutatis mutandis*, for the causal powers of the mental states that such utterances express. And similarly, *mutatis mutandis*, for the mental states of the Oscars in respect of brisket and brisket2."

Reply: This will not do; identity of causal powers has to be assessed *across* contexts, not *within* contexts.

Consider, if you will, the causal powers of your biceps and of mine. Roughly, our biceps have the *same* causal powers if the following is true: *For any thing x and any context C, if you can lift x in C, then so can I; and if I can lift x in C, then so can you.* What is, however, *not* in general relevant to comparisons between the causal powers of our biceps is this: that there is a thing x and a pair of contexts C and C' such that you can lift x in C and I cannot lift x in C'. Thus suppose, for example, that in C (a context in which this chair is not nailed to the floor) you can lift it; and in C' (a context in which this chair *is* nailed to the floor) I cannot lift it. That eventuality would give your biceps nothing to crow about. Your biceps — to repeat the moral — have cause for celebration only if they can lift x's *in contexts in which my biceps can't.*

Well, to return to the causal powers of the water-utterances (/water-thoughts) of Twins: It's true that when I say "water" I get water and when my Twin says "water" he gets XYZ. But that's irrelevant to the question about identity of causal powers, *because these utterances (/thoughts) are being imagined to occur in different contexts* (mine occur in a context in which the local potable is H_2O, his occur in a context in which the local potable is XYZ). What *is* relevant to the question of identity of causal powers is the following pair of counterfactuals: (a) if his utterance (/thought) had occurred in my context, it *would have had* the effects that my utterance (/thought) did have; and (b) if my utterance (/thought) had occurred in his context, it *would have had* the effects that his utterance (/thought) did have. For our utterances (/thoughts) to have the same causal powers, both of those counterfactuals have to be true. But both of those counterfactuals *are* true, since (for example) if I had said "Bring water!" on Twin-Earth, it's XYZ that my interlocutors would have brought; and if he had said "Bring water!" here, his interlocutors would have brought him H_2O.

This line of argument no doubt assumes that I *can* say "Bring water!" on Twin Earth — that my being on Twin Earth doesn't *ipso facto* change my dialect to English2 (and, *mutatis mutandis*, convert my concept *water* into the concept *water2*). But although I've heard it suggested that mental states construed nonindividualistically are easily bruised and don't "travel," the contrary assumption would in fact seem to be secure. The standard intuition about "visiting" cases is that if, standing on Twin Earth, I say "That's water" about a puddle of XYZ, then what I say is *false*. Which it wouldn't be if I were speaking English2.

So, OK so far; we have, so far, no reason to suppose that the causal powers of my Twin's mental states are different from the causal powers of mine. On the contrary, since the causal subjunctives about the two states are the same, it must be that they have the same causal powers and thus count as the same state by what we're taking to be the relevant typological criteria.

Second line: "Maybe the causal powers of the mental states of Twins are always the same when their effects are *non*intentionally individuated. But consider their effects as intentionally described; consider, in particular, the *behavioral* consequences of the mental states of Oscar and Oscar2. (I assume, here and throughout, that the interesting relations between behaviors and states of mind are typically causal. Philosophers have denied this, but they were wrong to do so.) Oscar's thoughts and desires sometimes eventuate in his *saying* such things as that he prefers brisket to, as it might be, hamburger; Oscar's thoughts sometimes lead to his evincing brisket-eating preferences and brisket-purchasing behavior; and so forth. Whereas Oscar2 never does any of these things. Oscar2 may, of course, say that he likes brisket2; and he may evince brisket2 preferences; and he may, when appropriately stimulated (by, for example, a meat counter), behave brisket2-purchasingly.[5] And, of course, when he says and does these things with brisket2 in mind, he may produce precisely the same bodily *motions* as his counterpart produces when he says and does the corresponding things with brisket in mind. But all that shows is that behaving isn't to be identified with moving one's body; a lesson we ought to have learned long ago."

There's another aspect of this line of reply that's worth noticing: Independent of the present metaphysical issues, anybody who takes the Burge/Putnam intuitions to be decisive for the individuation of the attitudes has a strong motive for denying that Oscar's and Oscar2's behaviors (or Mine and My Twin's) are, in general, type-identical. After all, behavior is supposed to be the result of mental causes, and you would generally expect different mental causes to eventuate in correspondingly different behavioral effects. By assumption the Twins' attitudes (and the two Oscars') differ a lot, so if these very different sorts of mental causes nevertheless invariably converge on identical behavioral effects, that would seem to be an accident on a very big scale. The way out is obviously to deny that the behavioral effects *are* identical; to insist that the commonsense way of identifying behaviors, like the commonsense way of identifying the attitudes, goes out into the world for its principles of individuation; that it depends essentially on the relational properties of the behavior. (Burge—who would, of course, accept this conclusion on independent grounds—nevertheless objects that the present sort of argument misunderstands the function of his and Putnam's thought experiments: Since the examples concern the description of circumstances presumed to be counterfactual, the likelihood or otherwise of such circumstances *actually occurring* is not, according to Burge, a relevant consideration. (See Burge (1986a).) But this misses a point of methodology. We do, of course, want to tell the right story about how counterfactual circumstances should be described qua counterfactual. But we *also* want to tell the right story about how such circumstances should be described if they were real. The present intuition is that, were we actually to encounter Twins, what we should want to say of them is not that their quite different mental states have somehow managed to converge on the same behaviors; we *can* imagine examples that we'd want to describe that way, but Twins aren't among them. Rather, what we'd want to say about Twins is just that the (putative) differences between their minds are reflected, in the usual way, by corresponding differences between their behaviors. But we *can* say this only if we *are* prepared to describe their behaviors as different. So again it turns out that anyone who counts in a way that distinguishes the minds of Twins should also count in a way that distinguishes their acts.)

In short, Barbara Pym's question "Where does 'behavior' begin and end?" is one that needs to be taken seriously in a discussion of the causal powers of mental states. Claiming, as indeed I have been doing, that my mental states and My Twin's are identical in causal powers begs that question—or so, in any event, the objection might go.

First reply: If this argument shows that my mental state differs from my Twin's, it's hard to see why it doesn't show that our brain states differ too. My Twin is in a brain state that eventuates in his uttering the form of words "Bring water." I am in a brain state that eventuates in my uttering the form of words "Bring water." If our uttering these forms of words counts as our behaving differently, then it looks as though our brain states differ in their behavioral consequences, hence in their causal powers, hence in the state types of which they are tokens. (Similarly, *mutatis mutandis*, for our quantum-mechanical states.) But I thought we agreed a while back that it would be grotesque to suppose that brain states that live on Twin Earth are *ipso facto* typologically distinct from brain states that live around here.

Second reply: Notice that corresponding to the present argument for a taxonomic distinction between my mental state and my Twin's, there is the analogous argument for distinguishing H-particles from T-particles. Here's how it would sound: "Being H rather than T does affect causal powers after all; for H-particles enter into H-particle interactions, and no T-particle does. H-particle interactions may, of course, look a lot like T-particle interactions—just as Oscar2's brisket2-eating behaviors look a lot like Oscar's brisket-eating behaviors, and just as my water-requests sound a lot like my Twin's requests for XYZ. Philosophers are not, however, misled by mere appearances; we see where the eye does not."

The least that all this shows is how taxonomic and ontological decisions intertwine. You can save classification by causal powers, come what may, by fiddling the criteria for event identity. To classify by causal powers is to count no property as taxonomically relevant unless it affects causal powers. But x's having property P affects x's causal powers just in case x wouldn't have caused the same events had it not been P. But of course, whether x would have caused the same events had it not been P depends a lot on which events you count as the same and which you count as different. In the present case, whether the difference between being H and being T affects a particle's causal powers depends on whether the very same event that *was* an interaction of H-particles *could have been* an interaction of T particles. (Perhaps it goes without saying that the principle that events are individuated by their causes and effects is perfectly useless here; we can't apply it unless we already know whether an event that *was* caused by an H-particle could have had *the same cause* even if it had been the effect of a T-particle.)

Could it be that this is a dead end? It looked like the notion of taxonomy by causal powers gave us a sort of *a priori* argument for individualism and thus put some teeth into the idea that a conception of mental state suitable for the psychologist's purposes would have to be interestingly different from the commonsense conception of a propositional attitude. But now it appears that the requirement that states with identical causal powers ought *ipso facto* to be taxonomically identical can be met *trivially* by anyone prepared to make the appropriate ontological adjustments. Yet surely there has to be something wrong here; because it's false that two events could differ just in that one involves H-particles and the other involves T-particles, and it's false that H-particles and T-particles differ in their causal powers; and—as previously noted—it would be *mad* to suggest saving the supervenience of the propositional attitudes by individuating brain states relationally. Moreover, it is very plausible that all these intuitions hang together. The question is: What on earth do they hang *on*?

I hope I have managed to make this all seem very puzzling; otherwise you won't be impressed when I tell you the answer. But in fact the mystery is hardly bigger than a bread box, and certainly no deeper. Let's go back to the clear case and trace it through.

If H-particle interactions are *ipso facto* different events from T-particle interactions, then H-particles and T-particles have different causal powers. But if H-particles and T-particles have different causal powers, then the causal powers—not just certain of the relational properties, mind you, but *the causal powers*—of every physical particle in the universe depend on the orientation of my *gen-u-ine* United States ten cent piece. That includes, of course, physical particles that are a long way away; physical particles on Alpha Centauri, for example. And *that's* what's crazy, because while such relational properties as being H or being T can depend on the orientation of my dime *by stipulation*, how on Earth could the *causal powers* of particles on Alpha Centauri depend on the orientation of my dime? Either there would have to be a causal mechanism to mediate this dependency, or it would have to be mediated by a fundamental law of nature; and there aren't any such mechanisms and there aren't any such laws. *Of course* there aren't.

So, then, to avoid postulating impossible causal mechanisms and/or impossible natural laws, we will have to say that, all else being equal, H-particle interactions are *not* distinct events from T-particle interactions; hence, that H-particles and T-particles do *not* differ in their causal powers; hence, that the difference between being an H-particle and being a T-particle does *not* count as taxonomic for purposes of causal explanation. Which is, of course, just what intuition tells you that you *ought* to say.

Exactly the same considerations apply, however, to the individuation of mental states.[6] If every instance of brisket-chewing behavior *ipso facto* counts as an event distinct in kind from any instance of brisket2-chewing behavior, then, since brisket-cravings cause brisket-chewings and brisket2-cravings don't, Oscar's mental state differs in its causal powers from Oscar2's. But then there must be some mechanism that connects the causal powers of Oscar's mental states with the character of the speech community he lives in *and that does so without affecting Oscar's physiology* (remember, Oscar and Oscar2 are molecularly identical). But there is no such mechanism; you *can't* affect the causal powers of a person's mental states without affecting his physiology. That's not a conceptual claim or a metaphysical claim, of course. It's a contingent fact about how God made the world. God made the world such that the mechanisms by which environmental variables affect organic behaviors run via their effects on the organism's nervous system. Or so, at least, all the physiologists I know assure me.

Well then, in order to avoid postulating crazy causal mechanisms, we shall have to assume that brisket chewings are not ipso facto events distinct from chewings of brisket2; hence, that brisket cravings do not *ipso facto* have different causal powers from brisket2 cravings; hence, that for purposes of causal explanation Oscar's cravings count as mental states of the same kind as Oscar2's.

There is, I think, no doubt that we do count that way when we do psychology. Ned Block has a pretty example that makes this clear. He imagines a psychologist (call her Psyche—the P is silent, as in Psmith) who is studying the etiology of food preferences, and who happens to have both Oscar and Oscar2 in her subject population. Now, on the intuitions that Burge invites us to share, Oscar and Oscar2 have different food preferences; what Oscar prefers to gruel is brisket, but what Oscar2 prefers to gruel is brisket2. Psyche, being a proper psychologist, is of course interested in sources of variance; so the present case puts Psyche in a pickle. If she discounts Oscar and Oscar2, she'll be able to say—as it might be— that there are two determinants of food preference: 27.3 percent of the variance is genetic and the remaining 72.7 percent is the result of early training. If, however, she counts Oscar and Oscar2 in, and if she counts their food preferences the way Burge wants her to, then she has to say that there are *three* sources of variance: genetic endowment, early training, *and linguistic affiliation.* But surely it's *mad* to say that linguistic affiliation is per se a determinant of food preference; how *could* it be?[7]

I think it's perfectly clear how Psyche ought to jump: she ought to say that Oscar and Oscar2 count as having *the same* food preferences and therefore do not constitute counterexamples to her claim that the determinants of food preference are exhausted by genes and early training. And the previous discussion makes clear just *why* she ought to say this: if Oscar and Oscar2 have different food preferences, then there must be some difference in the causal powers of their mental states—psychological taxonomy is taxonomy *by* causal powers. But if there is such a difference, then there must be some mechanism which can connect the causal powers of Oscar's mental states with the character of his linguistic affiliation *without affecting his physiological constitution.* But there is no such mechanism; the causal powers of Oscar's mental states supervene on his physiology, just like the causal powers of your mental states and mine.

So, then, to bring this all together: You can affect the relational properties of things in all sorts of ways—including by stipulation. But for one thing to affect the causal powers of another, there must be a mediating law or mechanism. It's a mystery what this could be in the Twin (or Oscar) cases; not surprisingly, since it's surely plausible that the only mechanisms that *can* mediate environmental effects on the causal powers of mental states are neurological. The way to avoid making this mystery is to count the mental states—and, *mutatis mutandis*, the behaviors—of Twins (Oscars) as having the same causal powers, hence, as taxonomically identical.

So much for the main line of the argument for individualism. Now just a word to bring the reader up to date on the literature.

In a recent paper (1986a), Burge says that reasoning of the sort I've been pursuing "is confused. The confusion is abetted by careless use of the term "affect," conflating causation with individuation. Variations in the environment that do not vary the impacts that causally "affect" the subject's body may "affect" the individuation of the . . . intentional processes he or she is undergoing. . . . It does not follow that the environment causally affects the subject in any way that circumvents its having effects on the subject's body" [(1986a), p. 16]. But it looks to me like that's precisely what *does* follow, assuming that by "causally affecting" the subject Burge means to include determining the causal powers of the subject's psychological states. You can't both individuate behaviors Burge's way (viz., *non*locally) and hold that the causal powers of mental states are locally supervenient. When individuation is *by* causal powers, questions of individuation and causation don't divide in the way that Burge wants them to.

Consider the case where my Twin and I both spy some water (viz., some H_2O). My seeing the stuff causes me to say (correctly) "That's water!" His seeing the stuff causes him to say (incorrectly) "That's water2!" (His saying this sounds just like my saying "That's water!" of course.) These sayings count as *different behaviors* when you individuate behaviors Burge's way; so the behavioral effects of seeing water are different for the two of us; so the causal powers of the state of seeing water are different depending on which of us is in it. And this difference is uniquely attributable to differences in the contextual background; aside from the contextual background, my Twin and I are identical for present purposes. So if you individuate behavior Burge's way, differences in contextual background effect differences in the causal powers of mental states without having correspondingly different "effects on the subject's body"; specifically, on his neural structure. But is Burge seriously prepared to give up the local supervenience of causal powers? *How could* differences of context affect the causal powers of one's mental states without affecting the states of one's brain?

Burge can say, if he likes, that mind/brain supervenience be damned; though, as I keep pointing out, if mind/brain supervenience goes, the intelligibility of mental causation goes with it. Or he can save mind/brain supervenience by going contextual on *neurological* individuation [as, indeed, he appears to be tempted to do; see his footnote 18 in (1986a). Here both intuition and scientific practice clearly run against him, however.] But what he can't do is split the difference. If supervenience be damned for individuation, it can't be saved for causation. Burge says that "local causation does not make more plausible local individuation" (p. 16), but he's wrong if, as it would seem, "local causation" implies local supervenience of causal powers. Local causation *requires* local individuation when so construed. You can have contextual individuation if you insist on it. But you can't have it for free. Etiology suffers.

Well, if all this is as patent as I'm making it out to be, how could anyone ever have supposed that the standards of individuation appropriate to the psychologist's purposes are other than individualistic? I cast no aspersions, but I have a dark suspicion; I think people get confused between methodological *individualism* and methodological *solipsism*. A brief excursus on this topic, therefore, will round off this part of the discussion.

Methodological individualism is the doctrine that psychological states are individuated *with respect to their causal powers*. Methodological solipsism is the doctrine that psychological states are individuated *without respect to their semantic evaluation*.[8]

Now, the semantic evaluation of a mental state depends on certain of its relational properties (in effect, on how the state corresponds to the world). So we could say, as a rough way of talking, that solipsistic individuation is *nonrelational*. But if we are going to talk that way, then *it is very important* to distinguish between solipsism and individualism. In particular, though it's a point of definition that solipsistic individuation is nonrelational, there is nothing to stop principles of individuation from being simultaneously relational and individualistic. *Individualism does not prohibit the relational individuation of mental states*; it just says that no property of mental states, relational or otherwise, counts taxonomically unless it affects causal powers.

Indeed, individualism couldn't rule out relational individuation per se if any of what I've been arguing for up till now is true. I've taken it that individualism is a completely general methodological principle in science; one which follows simply from the scientist's goal of causal explanation and which, therefore, all scientific taxonomies must obey. By contrast, it's patent that taxonomic categories in science are *often* relational. Just as you'd expect, relational properties can count taxonomically whenever they affect causal powers. Thus "being a planet" is a relational property par excellence, but it's one that individualism permits to operate in astronomical taxonomy. For whether you are a planet affects your trajectory, and your trajectory determines what you can bump into; so whether you're a planet affects your causal powers, which is all the individualism asks for. Equivalently, the property of being a planet is taxonomic because there are causal laws that things satisfy in virtue of being planets. By contrast, the property of living in a world in which there is XYZ in the puddles is *not* taxonomic because there are *no* causal laws that things satisfy in virtue of having *that* property. And similarly for the property of living in a speech community in which people use "brisket" to refer to brisket of beef. The operative consideration is, of course, that where there are no causal laws about a property, having the property—or failing to have it—has no effect on causal powers.[9]

To put the point the other way around, solipsism (construed as prohibiting the relational taxonomy of mental states) is unlike individualism in that it couldn't *conceivably* follow from any *general* considerations about scientific goals or practices. "Methodological solipsism" is, in fact, an empirical theory about the mind: it's the theory that mental processes are computational, hence syntactic. I think this theory is defensible; in fact, I think it's true. But its defense can't be conducted on a priori or metaphysical grounds, and its truth depends simply on the facts about how the mind works. Methodological solipsism differs from methodological individualism in both these respects.

Well, to come to the point: If you happen to have confused individualism with solipsism (and if you take solipsism to be the doctrine that psychological taxonomy is nonrelational), then you might try arguing against individualism by remarking that the psychologist's taxonomic apparatus is, often enough, non-solipsistic (viz., that it's often relational). As, indeed, it is. Even computational ("information-flow") psychologists are professionally interested in such questions as, "Why does this organism have the computational capacities that it has?"; "Why does its brain compute this algorithm rather than some other?"; or even, "Why is this mental process generally truth preserving?" Such questions often get answered by reference to relational properties of the organism's mental state. See for example, Ullman (1979), where you get lovely arguments that run like this: *This perceptual algorithm is generally truth preserving because the organism that computes it lives in a world where most spatial transformations of objects are rigid. If the same algorithm were run in a world in which most spatial transformations were not rigid, it wouldn't be truth preserving, and the ability to compute it would be without survival value. So, presumably, the organism wouldn't have this ability in such a world.* These sorts of explanations square with individualism, because the relational facts they advert to affect the causal powers of mental states; indeed, they affect their very existence. But naturally, explanations of this sort—for that matter, *all* teleological explanations— are ipso facto nonsolipsistic. So *if* you have confused solipsistic (viz., nonrelational) taxonomies with individualistic taxonomies (viz., taxonomies by causal powers), then you *might* wrongly suppose that the affection psychologists have for teleological explanation argues that they—like the laity—are prone to individuate mental states nonindividualistically. But it doesn't. And they aren't.

I repeat the main points in a spirit of recapitulation. There are two of them; one is about the methodology of science, and one is about its metaphysics.

Methodological point: Categorization in science is characteristically taxonomy by causal powers. Identity of causal powers is identity of causal consequences across nomologically possible contexts.

Metaphysical point: Causal powers supervene on local microstructure. In the psychological case, they supervene on local neural structure. We abandon this principle at our peril; mind/brain supervenience (/identity) is our only plausible account of how mental states could have the causal powers that they do have. On the other hand, given what causal *powers* are, preserving the principle constrains the way that we individuate causal *consequences*. In the case of the behavioral consequences of the attitudes, it requires us to individuate them in ways that violate the commonsense taxonomy. So be it.

Well, I've gotten us where I promised to: back to where we started. There is a difference between the way psychology individuates behaviors and mental states and the way common sense does. At least there is if you assume that the Burge/Putnam intuitions are reliable.[10] But this fact isn't, in and of itself, really very interesting; scientific taxonomy is forever cross-cutting categories of everyday employment. For that matter, the sciences are forever cross-cutting one another's taxonomies. Chemistry doesn't care about the distinction between streams and lakes; but geology does. Physics doesn't care about the distinction between bankers and butchers; but sociology does. (For that matter, physics doesn't care about the distinction between the Sun and Alpha Centauri either; sublime indifference!)

None of this is surprising; things in Nature overlap in their causal powers to various degrees and in various respects; the sciences play these overlaps, each in its own way.

And, for nonscientific purposes, we are often interested in taxonomies that cross-cut causal powers. Causal explanation is just one human preoccupation among many; individualism is a constitutive principle of science, not of rational taxonomy per se. Or, to put it a little differently—more in the material mode—God could make a genuine electron, or diamond, or tiger, or person, because being an electron or a diamond or a tiger or a person isn't a matter of being the effect of the right kind of causes; rather, it's a matter of being the cause of the right kind of effects. And similarly, I think, for all the other natural kinds. Causal powers are decisively relevant to a taxonomy of natural kinds because such taxonomies are organized in behalf of causal explanation. Not all taxonomies have that end in view, however, so not all taxonomies classify by causal powers. Even God couldn't make a *gen-u-ine* United States ten cent piece; only the U.S. Treasury Department can do that.

You can't, in short, make skepticism just out of the fact that the commonsense way of taxonomizing the mental differs from the psychologist's way. You might, however, try the idea that disagreement between the commonsense taxonomy and the scientific one matters more in psychology than it does elsewhere *because psychology needs the commonsense notion of mental content*. In particular, you might try the idea that the notion of mental content doesn't survive the transition from the layman's categories to the scientist's. I know of at least one argument that runs that way. Let's have a look at it.

What we have—though only by assumption, to be sure—is a typology for mental states according to which my thoughts and my Twin's (and Oscar's thoughts and Oscar2's) have identical contents. More generally, we have assumed a typology according to which the physiological identity of organisms guarantees the identity of their mental states (and, *a fortiori*, the identity of the contents of their mental states). All this is entailed by the principle—now taken to be operative—that the mental supervenes upon the physiological (together with the assumption—which I suppose to be untendentious—that mental states have their contents essentially, so that typological identity of the former guarantees typological identity of the latter). All right so far.

But now it appears that even if the physiological identity of organisms ensures the identity of their mental states and the identity of mental states ensures the identity of contents, *the identity of the contents of mental states does not ensure the identity of their extensions*: my thoughts and my Twin's—like Oscar's and Oscar2's—*differ in their truth conditions*, so it's an accident if they happen to have the same truth values. Whereas what makes my water-thoughts true is the facts about H_2O, what makes my Twin's "water"-thoughts true is the facts about XYZ. Whereas the thought that I have—when it runs through my head that water is wet—is true iff H_2O is wet, the thought that he has—when it runs through his head that "water" is wet—is true iff XYZ is wet. And it's an accident (that is, it's just contingent) that H_2O is wet iff XYZ is. (Similarly, what I'm thinking about when I think: *water*, is different from what he's thinking about when he thinks: "*water*"; he's thinking about XYZ, but I'm thinking about H_2O. So the denotations of our thoughts differ.) Hence the classical—Putnamian—formulation of the puzzle about Twins: If mental state supervenes upon physiology, then thoughts don't have their truth conditions essentially; two tokens of the *same* thought can have *different* truth conditions, hence different truth values. If thoughts are in the head, then content doesn't determine extension.

That, then, is the "Twin-Earth Problem." Except that so far it *isn't* a problem; it's just a handful of intuitions together with a commentary on some immediate implications of accepting them. If that were *all*, the right response would surely be "so what?" What connects the intuitions and their implications with the proposal that we give up on propositional-attitude psychology is a certain *Diagnosis*. And while a lot has been written about the intuitions and their implications, the diagnosis has gone largely unexamined. I propose now to examine it.

Here's the Diagnosis: "Look, on *anybody's* story, the notion of content has got to be at least a little problematic. For one thing, it seems to be a notion proprietary to the information sciences, and *soi-disant* "emergents" bear the burden of proof. At a minimum, if you're going to have mental contents, you owe us some sort of account of their individuation.

"Now, prior to the Twin Earth Problem, there *was* some sort of account of their individuation; you could say, to a first approximation, that identity of content depends on identity of extension. No doubt that story leaked a bit: Morning-Star thoughts look to be different in content from the corresponding Evening-Star thoughts, even though their truth-conditions are arguably the same. But at least one could hold firmly to this: "Extension supervenes on content; no difference in extension without some difference in content." Conversely, it was a test for identity of content that the extensions had to come out to be the same. And that was the *best* test we had; it was the one source of evidence about content identity that seemed surely reliable. Compare the notorious wobbliness of intuitions about synonymy, analyticity, and the like.

"But now we see that *it's not true after all* that difference of extension implies difference of content; so unclear are we now about what content-identity comes to—hence, about what identity of propositional attitudes comes to—that we can't even assume that typologically identical thoughts will always be true and false together. The consequence of the psychologist's insistence on preserving supervenience is that we now have no idea at all what criteria of individuation for propositional attitudes might be like; hence, we have no idea at all what counts as *evidence* for the identity of propositional attitudes.

"Short form: Inferences from difference of extension to difference of content used to bear almost all the weight of propositional-attitude attribution. That was, however, a frail reed, and now it has broken. The Twin Earth Problem *is* a problem, *because it breaks the connection between extensional identity and content identity*."

Now, the Twin Earth intuitions are fascinating, and if you care about semantics you will, no doubt, do well to attend to them. But, as I've taken pains to emphasize, you need the Diagnosis to connect the intuitions about Twins to the issues about the status of belief/desire psychology, and—fortunately for those of us who envision a psychology of propositional attitudes—the Diagnosis rests on a quite trivial mistake: *The Twin Earth examples don't break the connection between content and extension; they just relativize it to context.*

Suppose that what you used to think, prior to Twin-Earth, is that contents are something like functions from thoughts to truth-conditions: given the content of a thought, you know the conditions under which that thought would be true. (Presumably, a truth-condition would itself then be a function from worlds to truth-values: a thought that has the truth-condition TC takes the value T in world W iff TC is satisfied in W. Thus, for example, in virtue of its content the thought that it's raining has the truth condition *that it's raining* and is thus true in a world iff it's raining in that world.) I hasten to emphasize that if you don't—or didn't—like that story, it's quite all right for you to choose some other; my point is going to be that if you liked any story of even remotely that kind before Twin Earth, you're perfectly free to go on liking it now. For even if all the intuitions about Twin Earth are right, and even if they have all the implications that they are said to have, extensional identity still constrains intentional identity because *contents still determine extensions relative to a context.* If you like, contents are functions from contexts and thoughts onto truth conditions.

What, if anything, does that mean? Well, it's presumably common ground that there's something about the relation between Twin Earth and Twin Me in virtue of which his "water"-thoughts are about XYZ even though my water-thoughts are not. Call this condition that's satisfied by (Twin Me, Twin Earth) condition C (because it determines the *Context* of his "water"-thoughts). Similarly, there must be something about the relation between me and Earth in virtue of which my water-thoughts are about H_2O even though my Twin's "water"-thoughts are not. Call this condition that is satisfied by (me, Earth) condition C'. I don't want to worry, just now, about the problem of how to articulate conditions C and C'. Some story about constraints on the causal relations between H_2O tokenings and water-thought tokenings (and between XYZ tokenings and "water"-thought to-kenings) would be the obvious proposal; but it doesn't matter much for the purposes now at hand. Because we *do* know this: Short of a miracle, it must be true that if an organism shares the neurophysical constitution of my Twin *and satisfies* C, it follows that its thoughts and my Twin's thoughts share their truth condi-tions. For example, short of a miracle the following counterfactual must be true: Given the neurological identity between us, in a world where I am in my Twin's context my "water"-thoughts are about XYZ iff his are. (And, of course, vice versa: In a world in which my Twin is in my context, given the neurological identity between us, it must be that his water-thoughts are about H_2O iff mine are.)

But now we have an extensional identity criterion for mental contents: Two thought contents are identical only if they effect the same mapping of thoughts and contexts onto truth conditions. Specifically, your thought is content-identical to mine only if in every context in which your thought has truth condition T, mine has truth condition T and vice versa.

It's worth reemphasizing that, by this criterion, my Twin's "water" thoughts are intentionally identical to my water-thoughts; they have the same contents even though, since their contexts are *de facto* different, they differ, *de facto*, in their truth-conditions. In effect, what we have here is an extensional criterion for "narrow" content. The "broad content" of a thought, by contrast, is what you can semantically evaluate; it's what you get when you specify a narrow content *and fix a context.*

We can now see why we ought to reject both of the following two suggestions found in Putnam (1975): that we consider the extension of a term (/concept/ thought) to be an independent component of its "meaning vector"; and that we make do, in our psychology, with stereotypes *instead of* contents. The first proposal is redundant, since, as we've just seen, contents (meanings) determine extensions given a context. The second proposal is unacceptable, because unlike contents, stereotypes *don't* determine extensions. (Since it's untendentious that stereotypes supervene on physiology, the stereotypes for real water and Twin water must be identical; so if stereotypes did fix extensions, my Twin's "water"-thoughts would have the same extension as mine.) But, as the Diagnosis rightly says, we need an extension determiner as a component of the meaning vector, because we rely on "different extension → different content" for the individuation of concepts.

"Stop, stop! I have an objection."

Oh, good! Do proceed.

"Well, since on your view your water-thoughts are content-identical to your Twin's, I suppose we may infer that the English word 'water' has the same intension as its Tw-English homonym (hereinafter spelled 'water2')."

We may.

"But if 'water' and 'water2' have the same intensions, they must apply to the same things. So since 'water2' applies to XYZ, 'water' applies to XYZ too. It follows that XYZ must *be* water (what else could it mean to say that 'water' applies to it?). But, as a matter of fact, XYZ *isn't* water; only H_2O is water. Scientists discover essences."

I don't know whether scientists discover essences. It may be that philosophers make them up. In either event, the present problem doesn't exist. The denotation of "water" is determined not just by its meaning but by its context. But the context for English 'anchors' "water" to H_2O just as, *mutatis mutandis*, the context for Tw-English anchors "water2" to XYZ. (I learned "anchors" at Stanford; it is a very useful term despite—or maybe because of—not being very well defined. For present purposes, an expression is anchored iff it has a determinate semantic value.) So then, the condition for "x is water" to be true requires that x be H_2O. Which, by assumption, XYZ isn't. So English "water" doesn't apply to XYZ (though, of course, Tw-English "water" does). OK so far.

And yet . . . and yet! One seems to hear a Still Small Voice (SSV)—could it be the voice of conscience?—crying out as follows: "You say that 'water' and its Tw-English homonym mean the same thing; well then, what do they mean?"

How like the voice of conscience to insist upon the formal mode. It might equally have put its problem this way: "What *is* the thought such that when I have it its truth condition is that H_2O is wet and when my Twin has it its truth condition is that XYZ is wet? What is the concept *water* such that it denotes H_2O in this world and XYZ in the next?" I suspect that this—and not Putnam's puzzle about individuation—is what *really* bugs people about narrow content. The construct invites a question which—so it appears—we simply don't have a way of answering.

But conscience be hanged; it's not the construct but the question that is ill advised. What the Still Small Voice wants me to do is utter an English sentence which expresses just what my "water"-thoughts have in common with my Twin's. Unsurprisingly, I can't do it. That's because the content that an English sentence expresses is *ipso facto anchored* content, hence *ipso facto not* narrow.

So, in particular, qua expression of English "water is wet" is anchored to the wetness of water (i.e., of H_2O) just as, *qua* expression of Tw-English, "water2 is wet" is anchored to the wetness of water2 (i.e., of XYZ). And of course, since it is anchored to water, "water is wet" doesn't—can't—express the narrow content that my water-thoughts share with my Twin's. Indeed, if you mean by content what can be semantically evaluated, then what my water-thoughts share with Twin "water"-thoughts *isn't* content. Narrow content is radically inexpressible, because it's only content *potentially*; it's what gets to be content when—and only when—it gets to be anchored. We can't—to put it in a nutshell—*say* what Twin thoughts have in common. This is because what can be said is *ipso facto* semantically evaluable; and what Twin-thoughts have in common is *ipso facto* not.

Here is another way to put what is much the same point: You have to be sort of careful if you propose to co-opt the notion of narrow content for service in a "Griceian" theory of meaning. According to Griceian theories, the meaning of a sentence is inherited from the content of the propositional attitude(s) that the sentence is conventionally used to express. Well, that's fine so long as you remember that it's *anchored* content (that is, it's the content of anchored attitudes), and hence not narrow content, that sentences inherit. Looked at the other way around, when we use the content of a sentence to specify the content of a mental state (viz., by embedding the sentence to a verb of propositional attitude), the best we can do—in principle, *all* we can do—is avail ourselves of the content of the sentence qua anchored; for it's only qua anchored that sentences *have* content. The corresponding consideration is relatively transparent in the case of demonstratives. Suppose the thought "I've got a sore toe" runs through your head and also runs through mine; what's the content that these thoughts share? Well, you can't say what it is by using the sentence "I've got a sore toe," since, whenever you use that sentence, the "I" automatically gets anchored to you. You can, however, sneak up on the shared content by *mentioning* that sentence, as I did just above. In such cases, mentioning a sentence is a way of abstracting a form of words from the consequences of its being anchored.

One wants, above all, to avoid a sort of fallacy of subtraction: "Start with anchored content; take the anchoring conditions away, and you end up with a *new sort of content*, an unanchored content; a *narrow* content, as we say." (Compare: "Start with a bachelor; take the unmarriedness away, and you end up with a *new sort of bachelor*, a married bachelor; a *narrow* bachelor, as we say.") Or rather, there's nothing wrong with talking that way, so long as you don't then start to wonder *what the narrow content of—for example—the thought that water is wet could be*. Such questions can't be answered in the nature of things; so, in the nature of things, they shouldn't be asked.[11] People who positively *insist* on asking them generally get what they deserve: phenomenalism, verificationism, "procedural" semantics, or skepticism, depending on temperament and circumstance.

"But look," the SSV replies, "if narrow content isn't really content, then in what sense do you and your Twin have any water-thoughts in common at all? And if the form of words 'water is wet' doesn't express the narrow content of Twin water-thoughts, how can the form of words 'the thought that water is wet' succeed in picking out a thought that you share with your Twin?"

Answer: What I share with my Twin—what supervenience *guarantees* that we share—is a mental state that is semantically evaluable relative to a context. Referring expressions of English can therefore be used to pick out narrow contents via their *hypothetical* semantic properties. So, for example, the English expression "the thought that water is wet" can be used to specify the narrow content of a mental state that my Twin and I share (even though, qua anchored to H_2O, it doesn't, of course, *express* that content). In particular, it can be used to pick out the content of my Twin's "water"-thought via the truth conditions that it *would have had* if my Twin had been plugged into my world. Roughly speaking, this tactic works because the narrow thought that water is wet is the *unique* narrow thought that yields the truth condition H_2O *is wet* when anchored to my context and the truth condition XYZ *is wet* when anchored to his. You can't, in absolute strictness, express narrow content; but as we've seen, there are ways of sneaking up on it.

SSV: "By that logic, why don't you call the narrow thought you share with your Twin 'the thought that water2 is wet'? After all, that's the 'water thought' that you would have had if you had been plugged into your Twin's context (and that he *does* have in virtue of the fact that he *has* been plugged into his context). Turn about is fair play."

Answer: (a) "The thought that water2 is wet" is an expression of Tw-English; I don't speak Tw-English. (b) The home team gets to name the intention; the actual world has privileges that merely counterfactual worlds don't share.

SSV: "What about if you are a brain in a vat? What about then?"

Answer: If you are a brain in a vat, then you have, no doubt, got serious cause for complaint. But it may be some consolation that brains in vats have no special *semantical* difficulties according to the present account. They are, in fact, just special cases of Twins.

On the one hand, a brain in a vat instantiates the same function from contexts to truth conditions that the corresponding brain in a head does; being in a vat does not, therefore, affect the narrow content of one's thoughts. On the other hand, it *may* affect the *broad* content of one's thoughts; it may, for example, affect their truth-conditions. That would depend on just which kind of brain-in-a-vat you have in mind; for example, on just what sorts of connections you imagine there are between the brain, the vat, and the world. If you imagine a brain in a vat that's hooked up to *this* world, and hooked up *just* the same way one's own brain is, then—of course—that brain shares one's thought-contents *both* narrow *and* broad. Broad content supervenes on neural state together with connections to context. It had better, after all; a skull is a kind of vat too.

SSV: "But if a brain is a function from contexts to truth conditions, and if a vat can be a context, then when a brain in a vat thinks 'water is wet' the truth condition of its thought will be (not something about H_2O or XYZ but) something about its vat. So it will be thinking something *true*. Which violates the intuition that the thoughts of brains in vats have to be *false* thoughts."

Answer: You're confused about your intuitions. What they really tell you isn't that the thoughts of brains in vats have to be false; it's that being in a vat wouldn't stop a brain from having the very thoughts that you have now. And that intuition is *true*, so long as you individuate thoughts narrowly. It's tempting to infer that if a brain has your thoughts, and has them under conditions that would make your thoughts false, then the thoughts that the brain is having must be false too. But to argue this way is exactly to equivocate between the narrow way of individuating thoughts and the broad way.

SSV: "Mental states are supposed to cause behavior. How can a function cause anything?"

Answer: Some functions are implemented in brains; and brains cause things. You can think of a narrow mental state as determining an equivalence class of mechanisms, where the criterion for being in the class is *semantic*.

SSV: "I do believe you've gone over to Steve Stich. Have you no conscience? Do you take me for a mere expository convention?"

Answer: There, there; don't fret! What is emerging here is, in a certain sense, a "no content" account of narrow content; but it is nevertheless also a fully intentionalist account. According to the present story, a narrow content is *essentially* a function from contexts onto truth conditions; different functions from contexts onto truth conditions are ipso facto different narrow contents. It's hard to see what more you could want of an intentional state than that it should have semantic properties that are intrinsic to its individuation. In effect, I'm prepared to give Stich everything except what he wants. [See Stich (1983)].

Now, sleep conscience!

What I hope this chapter has shown is this: Given the causal explanation of behavior as the psychologist's end in view, he has motivation for adopting a taxonomy of mental states that respects supervenience. However, the psychologist needs a way to reconcile his respect for supervenience with the idea that the extension of a mental state constrains its content; for he needs to hold onto the argument from *difference* of extension to *difference* of content. When it comes to individuating mental states, that's the best kind of argument he's got, just as Putnam says. It turns out, however, that it's not hard to reconcile respecting supervenience with observing extensional constraints on content, because you can relativize the constraints to context: given a context, contents are different if extensions are. There isn't a shred of evidence to suggest that this principle is untrue—surely the Twin cases provide no such evidence—or that it constrains content attributions any less well than the old, unrelativized account used to do. The point to bear in mind is that if "difference in extension → difference in intension" substantively constrains the attribution of propositional attitudes, then so too does this same principle when it is relativized to context. *The Moral*: If the worry about propositional attitudes is that Twin-Earth shows that contents don't determine extensions, the right thing to do is to *stop worrying*.

So it looks as though everything is all right. Super; Let, you might suppose, rejoicing be unconstrained. But if you do suppose that, that's only because you've let the Twin problems distract you from the hard problems. The hard problems start in chapter 3 (not reprinted here—*ed.*).[12]

ENDNOTES

1. If, however, Loar (1985) is right, then the commonsense taxonomy actually fits pattern B; i.e., common sense and psychology both individuate the attitudes narrowly and both respect supervenience. So far as I know, nobody has explicitly endorsed the fourth logically possible option—viz., that commonsense taxonomy is narrow and psychological taxonomy relational—though I suppose Skinner and his followers may implicitly hold some such view.

2. Notice that taking this line wouldn't commit Burge to a violation of *physicalism*; the differences between the attitudes of Twins and Oscars supervene on the (inter alia, physical) differences between their worlds. Or rather, they do assuming that the relevant differences between the linguistic practices in Oscar's speech community and Oscar2's are physicalistically specifiable. (I owe this caveat to James Higgenbotham.)

3. No need to dogmatize, however. There may be scientific enterprises that are not—or not primarily—interested in causal explanation; natural history, for example. And in these sciences it is perhaps not identity and difference of causal powers that provide the criterion for taxonomic identity. But either propositional-attitude psychology is in the business of causal explanation or it is out of work.

    To put it at a minimum, if there is so much as a presumption of scientific utility in favor of a taxonomy by causal powers, then if—as I'm arguing—the causal powers of the mental states of the Twins are ipso facto identical, then there is a corresponding presumption in favor of the utility of narrow individuation in psychology.

4. The implication is that commonsense attitude attributions aren't—or rather, aren't *solely*—in aid of causal explanation; and this appears to be true. One reason why you might want to know what Psmith believes is in order to predict how he will behave. But another reason is that beliefs are often true, so if you know what Psmith believes, you have some basis for inferring how the world is. The relevant property of Psmith's beliefs for this latter purpose, however, is not their causal powers but something like *what information they transmit* [see Dretske (1981)]. And, quite generally, what information a thing transmits depends on relational properties of the thing which may not affect its causal powers. My utterance "water is wet" has, let's say, the same causal powers as my Twin's; but—assuming that both utterances are true—one transmits the information that H_2O is wet and the other transmits the information that XYZ is.

It is, I think, the fact that attitude ascriptions serve both masters that is at the bottom of many of their logical peculiarities; of the pervasiveness of the opacity/transparency ambiguities, for example.

5. Since all brisket2 is brisket (though not vice versa), every brisket2 purchase is a brisket purchase. This, however, is a consideration not profoundly relevant to the point at issue.

6. This is a little unfair—but, I think, *only* a little. There is, after all, *no causal relation at all* between my coin and the particles on Alpha Centauri whose causal powers its orientation is alleged to affect. Whereas, by contrast, there is supposed to be a causal relation between my Twin's "water"-thoughts and XYZ puddles (mutatis mutandis, between my water-thoughts and H_2O puddles) in virtue of which the thoughts refer to the stuff that they do. Similarly, it might be supposed that the semantic effects of linguistic coaffiliation require causal relations among the members of the language community so affected. (Though maybe not; it's sometimes suggested that the mere existence of experts in my language community shapes the contents of my mental states, whether or not there's a causal chain that connects us.)

But this hardly seems enough to meet the present worry, which isn't that my coin affect particles "at a distance," but that such relations as there are between the coin and the particles *aren't the right kind* to affect the causal powers of the latter. The point is that just specifying that *some causal relation or other* obtains isn't enough to plug this hole. Effects on causal powers require mediation by laws and/or mechanisms; and, in the Twin cases, there are no such mechanisms and no such laws.

If you are inclined to doubt this, notice that for any causal relation that holds between my mental states and the local water puddles, there must be a corresponding relation that holds between my *neurological* states and the local water puddles; a sort of causal relation into which, by assumption, my Twin's neurological states do not enter. Despite which, the intuition persists that my neurological states and my Twin's are taxonomically identical. Why? Because the difference in the causal *histories* of our brain states is not of the right sort to effect a difference in the causal *powers* of our brains. And qua scientific, neurological taxonomy groups *by* causal powers. Parallelism of argument surely requires us to hold that the differences between the causal histories of the mental states of Twins are not of the right sort to effect differences in the causal powers of their minds. And, qua scientific, *psychological* taxonomy groups by causal powers too.

7. Burge points out (personal communication) that Oscars' food preferences *don't* differ if you individuate *de re*; i.e., that brisket and gruel are such that *both Oscars* prefer the former to the latter (a fact that Psyche could establish by testing them on samples). But I don't see that this helps, since it seems to me thoroughly implausible that linguistic affiliation per se determines food preferences de dicto.

If it does, that opens up new vistas in nonintrusive therapy. For example, it looks as though we can relieve Oscar's unnatural craving for brisket just by changing the linguistic background—viz., by getting his colinguals to talk English2 instead of English. Whereas it used to seem that we'd be required to operate on *Oscar*: desensitization training, depth therapy, Lord knows what all else.

Psyche and I find this sort of consequence preposterous, but no doubt intuitions differ. That's why it's nice to have a principle or two to hone them on.

8. More precisely, methodological solipsism is a doctrine not about individuation in psychology at large but about individuation in aid of the psychology of mental

processes. Methodological solipsism constrains the ways mental processes can specify their ranges and domains: They can't apply differently to mental states just in virtue of the truth or falsity of the propositions that the mental states express. And they can't apply differently to concepts depending on whether or not the concepts denote. [See Fodor (1980).] This is, however, a nicety that is almost always ignored in the literature, and I shan't bother about it here.

9. In published comments on an earlier version of this chapter, Martin Davies (1986) remarks that what I say about being a planet "seems to be in tension with the insistence that causal powers must be compared across contexts or environments. For it cannot be the case *both* that a planet has characteristic causal powers and not merely those of a physically similar chunk of matter that is not a planet, *and* that causal powers have to be compared across contexts or environments quite generally." But—to put it roughly—this confuses the question whether *being a planet* is taxonomic (which it is; two things that differ in *that* ipso facts differ in their effects in many contexts) with the question whether *being this piece of rock* is taxonomic (which it isn't; two things that differ in *that* property do not thereby differ in their effects in *any* context).

Once again: A difference between properties P and $P1$ can affect causal powers (can be taxonomic) only when there is a situation S such that the instantiation of P is S has, ipso facto, different effects from the instantiation of $P1$ in S. By this criterion, the difference between *being a planet* and *not being a planet* affects causal powers because there are situations in which something that's a planet has, ipso facto, different effects from something that isn't. By contrast, the difference (in content) between the thought that water is wet and the thought that water2 is wet does *not* affect the causal powers of tokens of these thoughts: there are *no* situations in which one thought has, ipso facto, different effects than the other. So, in particular, if I am transported to Twin Earth, all else being left unchanged, then if I have the thought that water is wet in a situation where my Twin's thought that water2 is wet has consequence C, then my thought has consequence C in that situation too. (Compare a real—taxonomically relevant—difference in content; e.g., the difference between my thought that water is toxic and your thought that it's potable. Tokens of these thoughts differ in their consequences in *all sorts* of situations.)

10. It is, however, worth echoing an important point that Burge makes; the differences between the way that these taxonomies carve things up only show in funny cases. In practically all the cases that anybody actually encounters outside philosophical fantasies, the states that one is tempted to count as token beliefs that P share not just the causal powers that psychologists care about but also the relational background to which the commonsense taxonomy is sensitive. This enormous de facto coextension is part of the argument that the psychologists's story really is a vindication of the commonsense belief/desire theory.

11. Since you buy the narrow content construct at the cost of acknowledging a certain amount of inexpressibility, it may be some consolation that *not* buying the narrow content construct also has a certain cost in inexpressibility (though for a quite different sort of reason, to be sure). So, suppose you think that Twin-Earth shows that content doesn't determine extension and/or that content doesn't supervene on physiology. So, you have no use for narrow content. Still there's the following question: When my Twin thinks "water2 is wet," how do you say, in English, what he is thinking? Not by saying "water2 is wet," since, on the present assumptions, whatever "water2" means, it's something different from what "water" means; not by saying "XYZ

is wet," since my Twin will presumably take "water2 is XYZ" to say something informative; something, indeed, which he might wish to deny. And not, for sure, by saying "H_2O is wet," since there isn't any H_2O on Twin-Earth, and my Twin has never so much as heard of the stuff. It looks like the meaning of "water2 is wet" is *inexpressible* in English. And, of course, the same thing goes—only the other way 'round—for expressing the meaning of "water" in Tw-English.

12. Much the same treatment of Twin examples as the one I propose here was independently suggested to White (1982).

My indebtedness to the spirit of David Kaplan's treatment of demonstratives will be clear to readers familiar with his work. However, the current proposal is *not* that kind terms and the like are indexicals. You have to relativize narrow contents to contexts—roughly, to a world—to get *anything* that's semantically evaluable. But in the case of true indexicals you require *further* relativization—roughly, to an occasion of utterance. So, according to this analysis, "water" isn't an indexical, but "I" and the like are. Which is just as it should be.

12

Functionalism and Broad Content

Frank Jackson and Philip Pettit

THE CONTENTS OF CERTAIN INTENTIONAL states are broad or context-bound. The contents of some beliefs (and desires and hopes . . .) depend on how things are outside the subject in addition to depending on how things are inside the subject.[1] What implications does this have for the functionalist theory of mind? In this paper we defend the simplest reply to this question.

Functionalism is the doctrine that, for very many kinds of psychological states, to be in a psychological state of that kind is to have in one a state playing a certain role between inputs, outputs, and other internal states. It is the nature of the role, not the nature of the occupant of the role, which matters. The simplest functionalist response to states with broad contents is to analyze them in terms of broad roles, that is in terms of roles which are specified as having some inputs or outputs that are happenings outside the skin. When functionalists give an account of a belief with broad content, this response requires them to include outside happenings in their specification of the functional role definitive of having a belief with that content. The response, therefore, ensures that having a belief with that content involves how things are outside the subject as well as how they are inside.[2]

It has seemed to many that this simple, minimally disruptive response on behalf of functionalism to the fact of broad content cannot be right. Sometimes the argument turns on the claim that because an intentional state's content is an essential property of it, states with broad content are essentially broad, and essential broadness is alleged to be incompatible with functionalism, or at least incompatible with the functionalism just sketched. The idea is that broad content presents a much more radical challenge to functionalism's whole perspective on the mind than our tinkering acknowledges. As it is sometimes put, broad content shows the failure of the view that mental processes are essentially inner processes, and it is alleged that functionalism is wedded to the inner picture.[3]

Other times the objection comes from the functionalist camp itself. It is claimed that a certain argument, which we will call the *Doppelgänger* challenge, shows that the ascription of broad content does not play an appropriate role in the explanation of behavior. It is argued that it is the ascription of narrow content, content which does not depend on how things are outside the subject, which plays the appropriate role in explaining behavior.[4] Accordingly, we should be dualists about content. There is narrow content, which plays the right kind of

219

explanatory role with respect to behavior to fall within the purview of functionalism, and there is broad content, which plays a distinct role, perhaps that of representing the world, or perhaps that of being denigrated as a relic of folk psychology. The most plausible version of the dualist response casts states with broad content as mixed states. They are in part properly psychological—this part has narrow content and is given a functionalist account; and they are in part not psychological at all—this part is constituted by the relations between a subject and his environment and is no business of psychology, and so no business of functionalism.[5]

Call a functionalism which insists that the inputs or outputs in its functional roles sometimes include external happenings "broad," and one that confines the inputs and outputs to happenings at or inside the skin "narrow." Our position is that functionalists should respond to broad contents by moving to broad functionalism, analyzing such contents by broad roles. The first objection is then that broad functionalism cannot accommodate the fact that broad content is essential, and the second objection is that broad functionalism cannot accommodate the fact that, as it is argued, broad content is not suitably explanatory.

We reply to the first objection in part I where we argue that broad functionalism is neutral on the question of whether broad content is essential or accidental. In part II we reply to the second objection by arguing that the ascription of broad content is explanatory of behavior in a way fully in accord with the motivation of functionalism and with a properly scientific attitude towards psychology. The bulk of this part is concerned with what we will call the *Doppelgänger* challenge to broad content's explanatory value.

I. FUNCTIONALISM AND ESSENTIAL BROADNESS

WHY ESSENTIALLY BROAD CONTENT IS THOUGHT A PROBLEM

Broad content is content which does not supervene on how things are inside me. When I am in an intentional state with broad content, things must be thus and so around me as well as being thus and so inside me. For later purposes, particularly in part II, it is helpful to put the distinction between narrow and broad content in terms of the notion of a *Doppelgänger*. A *Doppelgänger* of mine is a subject of experience exactly like me as far as what goes on inside the skin is concerned. He is an internal molecule for internal molecule duplicate of me. Narrow content is content subjects share with all their *Doppelgängers*; broad content is content subjects do not share with all their *Doppelgängers*.

[There is a certain degree of arbitrariness about drawing the boundary at the skin. Why not count a brain in a vat which duplicates everything that goes on in my brain while differing profoundly in respect of what goes on between my brain and my skin, as one of my *Doppelgängers*? It is, however, a little easier to conduct the discussion in terms of the narrower definition, for it means that the similarities in outputs between me and my *Doppelgängers* can be described (roughly, anyway) in familiar behavioral terms rather than in neurophysiological ones.]

We are going to take for granted the familiar and persuasive arguments for the existence of broad content; and, in order to focus the discussion, we are going to take as our standard illustration of an intentional state with broad content my belief that that cup contains water. We will suppose that the content which the sentence "that cup contains water" assigns to my belief is such that two conditions need to be fulfilled. First, I could not have a belief with that content unless it was that very cup which I was causally affected by—say, by seeing it. Thus, my *Doppelgänger* viewing an exactly similar but numerically distinct cup, has a belief with a different content (whether he knows it or not). And, secondly, I could not have a belief with that content unless I had causal commerce, even if only through a baptismal chain, with water. This is why my Twin Earth *Doppelgänger* does not have a belief with that content (he may use the same word "water" in characterizing his belief, but the content he ascribes will nevertheless be different). This kind of position on intentional states like my belief that that cup contains water is very widely accepted, and general agreement with a position of this overall kind is all that we need for the paper.[6]

Many hold that a psychological state's content—be it broad or narrow—is an essential property of it. Consider our sample state, my belief that that cup contains water. Had it been a different cup or had I been on Twin Earth, I could not have been in that state, not just in the sense that the description "is a belief that that cup contains water" would not have been true of my state—that is, not just in the sense that my state might have had a different content—but in the sense that I could not have been in that very state, however described. This view has the consequence that some mental states, in particular those with broad content, are essentially broad, and it lies at the heart of much of the controversy over broad psychology. For it is the view that had the world around me been different in various ways, I would *have* to have been in different mental states—not merely in the sense of states satisfying different descriptions but in the sense of numerically different states. It is this view which challenges the "inner life" view of psychology, for it makes the very identity of my mental states a matter of my surroundings.[7]

A natural thought is that broad functionalism is incompatible with the existence of essentially broad states. If there are essentially broad psychological states, then functionalism (broad or narrow) is false, or at least false as a theory of those states. We will argue, on the contrary, that functionalism *per se* is neutral on the existence of essentially broad states. It is functionalism as it is usually characterized which is incompatible with the essentially broad, and the relevant part of this characterization is entirely optional for functionalists.

TWO POSSIBLE METAPHYSICS FOR FUNCTIONALISTS

Functionalism *per se* is a thesis about the truth-conditions of psychological attributions. It says that I am in mental state M when I have in me a state which is playing the causally intermediate role between inputs, outputs, and other states definitive of M. For short, I am in M if and only if I have in me a state playing the M role. The metaphysical question of which state *is* the psychological state is a further matter. Thus functionalism *per se* says that to be in pain is to have in one a state playing the pain role, where the pain role is defined in terms of being causally intermediate between inputs, outputs, and other states in one. And this means that there are *two* candidates to be one's pain: the state which plays the role, and the state of having the state which plays the role. Suppose that it is having C fibers firing which plays the pain role in me on some occasion, then the essence of the functionalist view is that I am in pain precisely because this state is playing that role in me. This leaves open which of two states are my pain: my having C fibers firing or my having in me the state—which is, as it happens, C fibers firing—which plays the pain role.

Consider the following parallel. To be sky-colored is to have the same color as the sky. That gives us the conditions under which "My house is sky-colored" is true, namely, that it is true if and only if "My house is the same color as the sky" is true. Suppose that my house is in fact the same color as the sky, which state of my house is its state of being sky-colored? Its state of being blue, or its state of being the same in color as the sky? There are two states here, for had the sky and my house both been red, my house would not have been in the first state but would still have been in the second state. But although there are two states, it does not follow that one answer or the other is definitely correct as to which state is my house's being sky-colored. Perhaps, "my house being sky-colored" is variable and ambiguous in its reference: in some contexts it refers to one state, in some contexts to the other, and in still other contexts there is no fact of the matter as to which of the two states it refers to. For suppose someone expresses surprise at my house being sky-colored, what are they expressing surprise at? The fact that my house is blue, or the fact that my house is the same color as the sky? Clearly there are two distinct possibilities here, but stipulation as to the intended reference of "my house being sky-colored" is called for in order to know which possibility is being remarked upon.

The truth-conditional essence of functionalism leaves open the metaphysical question of which state—my having my C fibers firing, or my having the state playing the pain role—is my state of pain. The usual option taken is to make my having C fibers firing be my pain, and in general to make the state playing, realizing, or occupying the role, call it "the realizer state," be the psychological state; the less usual option is to make my having the state playing the pain role be my pain, and in general to make what we will call "the role state," the *having* of a state occupying the role, be the psychological state. The role state is a second-order state, namely, that of having a state of a certain kind, just as having the same color as the sky is a second-order property. The distinction between the role state and the realizer state is a subtle one, and surely it is plausible—from a functionalist perspective anyway—that the natural language terms we use for denoting the various psychological states are ambiguous and variable as regards which of the two is being referred to. A decision between the two is a matter of stipulation, not discovery. In any case, whatever should be said about linguistic usage, functional-ists may properly count either role states or realizer states as being what psycho-logical states are. There is nothing in functionalism *per se* which rules out either option.

REPLY TO THE OBJECTION FROM ESSENTIAL BROADNESS

If we take the usual option of identifying psychological states with realizer states, it is quite correct that functionalism is incompatible with essential broadness, though it easily and naturally accommodates what we might call accidental broadness. Take any mental state with a broad content. On the broad functional-ist account, the broadness of that state is captured simply by making the inputs or outputs associated with its role include happenings outside the skin. For instance, the functionalist story about my belief that that cup contains water will include the proviso that the state be caused (in the right way) by that cup and by water. But, on the realizer option for functionalism, the broadness secured by including this proviso will be an accidental broadness. For the very same state might of course have stood in different causal relations: the functional role a state plays is not an essential property of it. Thus, the broad functionalist who takes the realizer state option must say that my belief that that cup contains water, that very state, might not have been caused by that cup, but by, say, a duplicate of that cup, and might not have had the causal links to water, that is, to H_2O, which are responsible for it being, on the account in question, the belief that it is water and not XYZ which the cup contains.

Suppose, however, that a broad functionalist takes the less usual option of identifying my belief that that cup contains water with the role state instead of with the realizer state. My belief then will be, not the state which plays the belief-that-that-cup-contains-water role, but the state of having a state which plays the belief-that-that-cup-contains-water role. Now for this second-order state, though not for the realizer state, individuation goes by role: different role, numerically different state. Although the very same realizer state might have been caused by this cup or instead by that one, or by XYZ instead of by H_2O, my being in a realizer state caused by this cup rather than by that one or in a realizer state caused by H_2O rather than by XYZ are different role states. Replace water then by XYZ, or that cup by another, no matter how similar, and it will no longer be true that I believe that that cup contains water. Why? Because the functional role realized is different; but that is to say that I am in a numerically different role state, though I may be in numerically the same realizer state. The upshot is that, compatibly with functionalism, we may take my belief that that cup contains water to be essen-tially broad, for we may take my belief to be the role state, and the role state's identity—which state it *is*, not just which descriptions it satisfies—depends on how things are outside of me, in particular, on whether or not it is water and that cup which do the causing of the realizer state.[8]

ON TWO OBJECTIONS TO OUR METAPHYSICAL NEUTRALITY

Our claim is that functionalists, and in particular broad functionalists, have a choice between identifying mental states with realizer states or with role states, and that therefore broad functionalism is neutral as between whether my belief that that cup contains water is accidentally or essentially broad. There is, however, one consideration which suggests that functionalists ought to take the realizer state option, and another which suggests that they ought to take the role state option. If either is correct, our neutrality is misconceived.

If we want psychological states to be causes of behavior, then we must regard them as realizer states. It is the state that fills the functional role, not the state of having a state that fills the role, which does the causing of behavior. And this looks like a powerful consideration in favour of identifying mental states with realizer states. Was not the explanatory role of the mental a major reason for moving from behaviorism to functionalism?

What, exactly, is the datum concerning psychological states and causality? Perhaps in the case of the bodily sensations there is introspective evidence that they themselves cause behavior, though even there this sort of evidence should be treated with extreme circumspection. In the case of beliefs and other intentional states, however, the only clear datum is that we invoke them in causal explanations of behavior, not that they are causes of behavior; beliefs are not inner feelings whose causal links are available to introspection. Now the role state conception of belief is perfectly compatible with, indeed entails, that ascribing a belief of a certain kind explains behavior, for on that conception to ascribe a belief is to say that there is a cause of a certain kind in one who has the belief, even though the belief is not itself the cause. I may explain why an object moves in a certain way by saying that there is a force of a certain kind acting on it, even though it is the force itself, not the existential state of affairs of there being a force of the certain kind, which does the causing.

The consideration that appears to favor the role state option relates to a point made at the very beginning. We observed that if, as many hold, an intentional state's content is an essential property of it, then to admit broad content is to admit that some states are essentially broad. Thus Tyler Burge argues that we individuate beliefs by content, so that different content means, not just different description of belief state, but numerically different belief state.[9] Suppose that the links to that cup and to water are broken, so that the content of the belief changes and the belief I have is no longer correctly described as the belief that that cup contains water. Burge would say that to suggest that we might still be dealing with the same state is as absurd as the suggestion that by changing the membership of a set we might change the descriptions true of the set but not change the set that is being described. If Burge is right, functionalists cannot take the realizer state option, at least for states with functionally specified content, for that option makes content a contingent feature.

The appeal of this argument rests on conflating the two senses in which we talk about beliefs, thoughts, and the propositional attitudes in general. It is often observed—for instance in discussing the bad objection to the identity theory that thoughts are not located whereas brain states are—that we sometimes use the term "thought" to denote what is thought, the content, and sometimes the thought itself, the state located in space-time. The claim that beliefs are individuated by content is beyond question if meant as a claim about what is thought; indeed, it is then a tautology. But this claim is very much in question if it is meant as a claim about the state of belief, the state with the content. Functionalists of the realizer state persuasion are entitled to reply that they have provided a plausible account of what a belief is, and that this account has the consequence that content does not individuate: that is, that a belief's content is not an essential property of it. This reply turns on the point that which properties of a thing are essential may be an a *posteriori* question. But this is hardly controversial: orphans do not refute the necessity of origin.

We hope to have defused the issue about the compatibility of essentially broad mental states with broad functionalism. Essential broadness is a free option for broad functionalists. To take it, formulate your functionalism with role states being the psychological states. To decline it, formulate your functionalism in the more usual way so that realizer states are the psychological states. The states with broad content will then be accidentally broad and you need a reply (we have suggested one immediately above) to those who hold that content is essential.

II. THE EXPLANATORY VALUE OF BROAD CONTENT

The ascription of content to an intentional state is part of the project of explaining a subject's behavior. The broad functionalist accepts this, adding that the point applies as much to broad as to narrow content. Given that I desire water, my belief that that cup contains water explains why I reach for that cup in the same general way that my belief that the only white cup in the room contains stuff that goes under the name of "water"—supposing for the purposes of exposition that the latter is indeed a belief with narrow content—explains why I reach for the only white cup in the room. In this part we reply to the familiar challenge, the *Doppelgänger* challenge, to the explanatory value of broad content. We start with some clarificatory remarks about the nature of the challenge before explaining the notion central to our reply to it, that of a distinction between those causal explanations we will call program explanations and those we will call process explanations.

We will frame our discussion in terms of a functionalism which identifies intentional states with realizer states, this being the more familiar way of thinking of functionalism. However nothing we say about the explanatory value of broad content turns on this choice—as had better be the case given our relaxed stance on the decision between the role and realizer state options for functionalism. The metaphysics of broad content is a separate matter from the explanatory value of broad content. Our question is whether the ascription of certain connections between an agent's internal goings on and external happenings can be explanatory of his behavior in the way required by the functionalist perspective. The nature of this question is not affected by whether we hold that those goings on are the states with broad content, or whether it is the second-order states of having states with such connections which are the states with broad content. Either way the internal states are there and are so connected with external affairs, and it is the explanatory significance of this fact which concerns us.

THE *DOPPELGÄNGER* CHALLENGE

The *Doppelgänger* challenge to the explanatory value of broad content is sometimes put rather tersely, somewhat as follows.[10] I and my *Doppelgängers* behave exactly alike. That is, we agree in behavior. Also we agree in narrow states while disagreeing in broad states. Mill's method of agreement leads immediately to the conclusion that my narrow states explain my behavior, and that my broad states are explanatorily idle. (And the same goes, of course, for each of my *Doppelgängers*.)

This is wrong in two ways. First, I and my *Doppelgängers* do not behave exactly alike. I reach for that cup and drink water, my *Doppelgänger* on Twin Earth reaches for a different cup and drinks XYZ. Secondly, we have here a highly dubious application of the method of agreement. Suppose my pulling the trigger of a gun explains someone's death. Consider the bullet as it enters the body and imagine it replaced by a *Doppelgänger* bullet moving with the same velocity, entering at the same point, at the same angle, and so on, but issuing from another source: your gun, not mine. The death will be exactly the same in every detail, yet this in no way shows that my pulling the trigger was not part of the explanation of the death. I cannot get off the hook with a thought experiment! The reason the argument goes wrong here is that my pulling the trigger is part of the explanation of why the bullet was as it was when it entered the body. Similarly, broad content and narrow content are not independent in the way required for the method of agreement to show that broad content is idle. What makes it true that I am in a state with broad content is in part my causal past, and that causal past will be part of the explanation of my being in a state with a certain narrow content. What that cup and various samples of water did to me in the past is in part responsible for those narrow states which lead me to reach for that cup.

The substantial *Doppelgänger* challenge, the one that calls for a detailed reply in terms, as we will argue, of the notion of a program explanation is not designed to show that broad content is explanatorily idle, but rather that it is explanatorily redundant: that is, that it plays no distinctive role, the explaining it does being best done by a combination of narrow psychological states together with environment.[11] Although my behavior is not exactly the same as that of my *Doppelgängers*, it is similar in an important respect. When I reach for that cup and drink the water in it, many of my *Doppelgängers* will be reaching for a different cup and drinking XYZ. This is different behavior, but obviously not that different. We all reach out and we all swallow, while differing in what we reach out towards and in what we swallow. There is, that is, a set of core behaviors in common between me and all my *Doppelgängers*. Our bodies gyrate in the same way, as we might put it. How is this fact to be explained? Obviously, in terms of the fact that I and my *Doppelgängers* are similar in a very important way; but that way does not include sharing psychological states with broad content. It is only narrow psychological states that we share. Hence, runs the substantial *Doppelgänger* challenge, as far as explanation in psychological terms goes, we only need narrow content to explain that aspect of my behavior which I share with my *Doppelgängers*.

If we call this shared aspect of behavior, pure behavior, the point is that narrow content is all we need to explain pure behavior. How then is impure behavior to be explained, how is my reaching for *that cup* or my swallowing *water* to be explained? The answer seems clear. What needs to be added to swallowing to get swallowing water is water, what needs to be added to reaching to get reaching for that cup is that cup. In general, then, the suggestion is that we can explain impure behavior by adding to our explanation of pure behavior facts about the environment. But then we can explain behavior, be it pure or impure (or, perhaps better, be it described in pure or impure terms) in terms of psychological states with narrow content together with, if needed, facts about the subject's environment. The conclusion is that broad content is redundant, that it plays no distinctive role in explaining behavior.

We can reinforce the point that the substantial *Doppelgänger* challenge is not that broad content plays no explanatory role at all, only that it plays no distinctive one. The line of thought which underlies the *Doppelgänger* challenge naturally suggests a picture which *entails* that broad content explains behavior. Suppose that, on some given occasion, I believe that that cup contains water. And suppose we accept, as we did in expounding the challenge, that though my *Doppelgängers* do not share this belief, there is some mental state which we do all share, call it the belief that <that cup contains water>, which together with the appropriate environmental details entails that I believe that that cup contains water. That is, I both believe that <that cup contains water> and that that cup contains water, and what makes the former up into the latter is my environment.[12]

It may be that we did not need to introduce the special "<>" notation here and that ordinary English will do. Perhaps the underlying narrow belief of mine is that there is a white cup, and only one white cup, which contains stuff known as "water" in my speech community. Or perhaps not even this belief is narrow in content and we need the language of thought instead of English. Or perhaps it is not really a belief, but a proto thought or belief, which is the psychological state underlying my belief that that cup contains water.[13] None of this matters here. The crucial point is that on this natural way of fleshing out the *Doppelgänger* challenge, it follows from that challenge that broad content has explanatory value. For to ascribe broad content is to commit oneself to there being a psychological state with narrow content which, according to the challenge itself, is what does the explaining. Hence, by this very fact, the ascription of broad content is explanatory. If to ascribe broad content is *inter alia* to ascribe narrow content and narrow content is explanatory of behavior, then so is broad content.

The *Doppelgänger* challenge, then, should be seen as seeking to induce, not skepticism about the explanatory value of broad content, but skepticism about the *distinctive* explanatory value of broad content. What explanatory work does it do that is not done by the correlative narrow content (however exactly we pick out that narrow content)? We now seek to answer this question, and so the doppelgänger challenge, via the idea of a program explanation.

PROGRAM EXPLANATIONS

The *Doppelgänger* challenge is only one way of raising the problem of how the ascription of broad content explains. Sometimes the problem is raised by drawing on a distinction between those properties which are causally efficacious or productive and those which do nothing. (Sometimes the term "causally explanatory" is used in place of "causally efficacious," but as we will see shortly this obscures a crucial distinction.) It is observed that this coin landing heads rather than tails does not affect the rising of the sun tomorrow. True, it changes that event in the sense that had the coin not landed heads, the rising of the sun would not have had the property of occurring after the coin landed heads, but that is a "Cambridge" change in the rising of the sun. The fact remains that we have here a good example of an inefficacious property, however difficult it may be to give a philosophically precise account of the notion.[14]

Similarly, what makes a psychological state broad is a good example of a causally inefficacious property, for what makes it broad is irrelevant to its effect on other states, and so to its effect on behavior. What makes a state my belief that that cup contains water is, in part, its causal connection with that cup and with water. We include that cup and water among the inputs in the broad functionalist story, as opposed, for instance, to including a duplicate of that cup and XYZ. Now these causal connections will be quite invisible to the other states of mine which link my belief to behavior. For example, if my belief is my having B-fibers firing, then the effect of my belief on other states of mine along the causal path to behavior will simply be the effect of B-fibers' firing. The fact that the B-fibers' firing was caused in a certain way will be quite invisible to the other states.

Raised in this way, the problem concerns narrow functionalism as much as broad functionalism. The argument turns on the highly relational nature of broad content, not on its nonindividualistic nature, and narrow content, though individualistic, is highly relational. For the effect that one neurophysiological state has on another in the causal path to behavior is a function of the states' relatively intrinsic properties, not of their highly relational ones. What one neurophysiological state does to another neurophysiological state is a function of their relatively intrinsic characters, not of their relations to more remote states, regardless of whether those more remote states are inside or outside the skin. How then can the possession of a certain narrow content by an agent's intentional state—a highly relational matter according to functionalism—explain the agent's behavior?

Our argument will be that this sort of argument, be it deployed against broad or narrow content, is misconceived, and that seeing why it is misconceived shows the mistake in the *Doppelgänger* challenge. The argument embodies a plausible but quite mistaken view about causal explanation, namely that causal explanations that proceed by citing some feature must cite a causally efficacious or productive feature. On the contrary, we can and often do explain by citing a feature which causally *programs* without causing. Features which causally explain need not cause. This is typically what happens when we explain in terms of highly relational properties. We will introduce the idea of causally programming through some everyday examples of explanations.

Electrons A and B are acted on by independent forces F_A and F_B respectively, and electron A then accelerates at the same rate as electron B. The explanation of this fact is that the magnitude of the two forces is the same. This is a perfectly acceptable explanation, and yet the same points that are made against broad psychological explanation can be made about it. We explain the fact that electron A accelerates at the same rate as B in terms of the force acting on A being the same in magnitude as that acting on B. But this sameness in magnitude is quite invisible to A and is not shared by A's *Doppelgängers*. This sameness does not make A move off more or less briskly; what determines the rate at which A accelerates is the magnitude of F_A not that magnitude's relationship to another force altogether. The two electron-force pairs may indeed be sufficiently separated to be quite independent of each other. What happens to one does not causally affect what happens to the other. Or, in other words, the equality *per se* of the forces acting on the electrons does not do any causal work. The work is all done by the individual forces acting on the electrons. (And if the equality *per se* did do some work, how remarkable that it arranges to do exactly the right amount so as not to conflict with the result produced by the individual forces.)

There is nothing particularly special about the electron example. It is typical of many cases where a present fact is explained in terms of a highly relational past fact. "Why was the price of a lamb at the Portland auction the same as the price at the Ballarat auction? Because the relationship between supply and demand was the same at both places." "Why did the Bourbons last longer than the Windsors? Because they had more male offspring. "Why do trees grow faster in Melbourne than in Canberra? Because there are fewer frosts in Melbourne." In each of these cases, remarks similar to those we made about the electron case apply. For example it is the number of frosts that slows down the trees in Canberra, not the fact that there are fewer than in Melbourne. The trees in Canberra would grow at exactly the same rate whether or not there was a single frost in Melbourne.

How is it that in these examples the instantiation of a property causally explains a certain result without actually producing it? The answer is that we have in these examples a range of possible situations, any one of which would be equally able to produce the result, and one of which actually does produce the result. The impressed forces on the electrons are, say, each of magnitude five, causing an acceleration in each electron of magnitude ten, say. Thus, in this case what actually produces the result that the accelerations are the same is both forces being of magnitude five. But both forces being of magnitude six, or seven, or . . . instead would equally have produced the result that the electrons' accelerations were the same. The property we cite as explaining the result is the relevant property in common between the various members of the range of possible situations, each member of which would have produced the result and one of which did in fact produce the result. We will describe such a common property as causally programming the result, and call explanations in terms of properties which program without producing, program explanations, as opposed to process explanations which do cite the productive features.

We can express the basic idea behind a program explanation in terms of what remains constant under variation. Suppose state A caused state B. Variations on A, say, A', A", . . . would have caused variations on B, say B', B", . . . , respectively. It may be that if the A^i share a property P, the B^i would share a property Q: keep P constant among the actual and possible causes, and Q remains constant among the actual and possible effects. If you like, Q *tracks* P.[15] Our point is that in such a case P causally explains Q by programming it, even though it may be that P does not produce Q.[16]

Explanations in terms of highly disjunctive states are typically program explanations. It is not the disjunctive state per se which produces the result but rather the state corresponding to one or other of the disjuncts. But we accept the explanation stated in the disjunctive terms provided any state, or any state within limits, corresponding to one of the disjuncts would have produced the result. We may explain the conductor's annoyance at a concert by the fact that someone coughed. What will have actually caused the conductor's annoyance will be the coughing of some particular person, Fred, say; but when we say that it was someone's coughing that explains why the conductor was annoyed, we are thinking of someone's coughing as Fred's coughing or Mary's coughing or Harry's coughing or . . . , and saying that any one of these disjuncts would have caused the conductor's annoyance—it did not have to be Fred.

Explanation by properties which causally program rather than produce what is to be explained is very common. Take Hilary Putnam's famous example where the failure of a one inch peg to go into a one inch round hole is explained by the fact that the peg is square. As Putnam observes, the causal interactions will all be between particular submicroscopic particles, and that story will not involve squareness as such. The squareness of the peg and the roundness of the hole will enter the picture only indirectly, namely by virtue of the fact that there is a whole range of possible situations constituting a square one inch peg interacting with a round one inch hole; in all of them (barring the extremely unlikely) the peg will not fit into the hole. As we say it, the squareness of the peg together with the roundness of the hole programs the failure of the peg to fit into the hole, or the failure of the peg to fit in the hole tracks the fact that the peg is square and the hole round through a whole set of variations elsewhere in the circumstances. In no particular case will the squareness and the roundness as such figure in the full story of the multitude of interactions which stop the peg from fitting into the hole, but the fact of squareness and roundness ensures, though not causally, that there is some very complex set of interactions which stops the peg from fitting into the hole.

Or take the case where we explain the shattering of a glass vessel in terms of the increase in temperature of the gas inside it. The increase of temperature is just the increase in the result of adding up the kinetic energy of all the molecules and dividing by the number of molecules, and clearly that increase does not itself cause the shattering. It is the impact of a relatively very small number of molecules on the walls of the vessel which actually breaks the glass. Nevertheless, we properly count citing the increase in temperature as explaining the shattering, for the increase programs the shattering. There are many ways the increase in temperature might have been realized. All of them (again barring extremely implausible ones) would have caused the shattering, and one actually did cause it.[17]

Functional state explanations are a species of program explanations. Take the simplest (and least informative) kind of functional state explanation. A glass's breaking is explained in terms of its being fragile. A familiar puzzle about this explanation has been that it is the categorical basis of the glass, not its fragility, that causes the breaking (along with the impact on the floor or whatever). Our answer to this puzzle is that when we explain the glass's breaking in terms of its being fragile, we are abstracting away from the particular basis of its fragility. We are saying that any basis for fragility would have combined with the impact to cause breaking. One basis did the work—the basis which was in fact the state which played the fragility role in the glass—but also a whole range of bases could have done the work of combining with the impact to cause breaking: it is like the explanation of the conductor's annoyance in terms of someone coughing. That explanation says more than that it was Fred's coughing, if it was indeed Fred who coughed, that caused the annoyance. It says that any of a whole range of members of the audience coughing would have caused annoyance in the conductor. If it turned out that it was crucial that it was Fred—he always coughs, and that was what really got the conductor's goat—then we would have to replace someone's coughing by *Fred's* coughing as the explanation of the conductor's annoyance.

Functional state explanations, then, are program explanations. They give us a highly relational property, the property corresponding to the specification, which picks out a range of states satisfying the functional specification such that one state in the range did the causing, but the others would have had they been realized. The result is explained as a feature that tracks the satisfying of the functional specification. Our point here is a natural corollary of the familiar point about multiple realizability and functionalism. What matters for being in a certain mental state is not what realizes the functional role but the fact that the role is realized in one of the many ways that it might have been. In the same way, what matters for the causing of a certain result may be, in one sense, the functional role filled, not what fills it. Of course, in another sense, what matters is what causally produces the result; but in the sense at issue it is what does or would have produced the result, and functional state explanations, like program explanations in general, tell us about the range of states that do or would produce the result without telling us which state in fact did the job. Just as the functional-ist theory of mind tells us that what matters for being in mental state M is the fact that role F(M) is filled, not what fills it; so program explanations tell us that what matters for some result R is the fact that some highly relational state of affairs is satisfied, not what satisfies it.

There can be more and less informative ways of picking out the range of states which would have produced a certain result, and so more and less informative program explanations, and, in particular, more and less informative functional state explanations. Explaining breaking on being knocked in terms of fragility is a good example of a less informative functional state explanation. For in the explanation, the range of states that would have produced a certain result is specified as the states satisfying the functional role definitive of fragility, and that role is specified in terms of being knocked as input and breaking as output. But we already know that knocking led to breaking. All we are getting by way of additional information is that a range of categorical bases would have caused the breaking; it was not, that is, a peculiarity of the basis that actually did the causing which was crucial for the breaking. This is not no information, which is why we count dispositional explanations as explanations, but it is not a lot of information, which is why we count them as marginal explanations.[18]

However, the specification of functional role need not always be so close to what we already know. I observe that Fred's sighting of that cup causes him to reach for it, and explain his behavior in terms of his belief that it contains water. This explana-tion says that a range of states playing the belief that-that-cup-contains-water role would have caused him to reach for it, and that one of them did cause him to. This is considerable additional information over and above what I know merely from the fact that he reaches for the cup and does so because of how things are with him. The functional role definitive of that content is highly complex, is consistent with his not reaching for the cup (as, for instance, in the case where he does not want water), and involves the causal antecedents of the internal state. Hence, although the glass which breaks because, in part, of how it is constituted is by that very fact fragile, the agent who reaches for the cup because, in part, of how he is need not have the belief that that cup contains water.

We introduced program explanations as our response to the concern that it is not having a certain content (broad or narrow) that enables a belief to drive behavior: that it is instead the neurophysiological properties of beliefs which are causally efficacious, being the "visible" properties in the chain of states mediating input and output. We now apply the distinction between program and process explanations to the diagnosis of where the *Doppelgänger* challenge goes wrong. Thus, though that challenge is directed to broad content only, if we are right, the one notion—that of a program explanation—is the key to how the ascription of content explains behavior, quite independently of whether the content is broad or narrow. There is nothing especially problematic about the explanatory value of broad content.

The Mistake in the *Doppelgänger* Challenge

The challenge is to say what—in view of the similarity in behavior of *Doppelgängers*—an explanation by broad content could add to an explanation by correlative narrow content plus environmental detail. Our answer turns on the point that explanations by broad content are program explanations.

We will introduce the crucial idea with an example. An object X is pressed into damp clay. The clay is allowed to harden with the impression of X's shape recorded in it. Object Y is then placed in the impression and fits perfectly. How should we explain this fact? One explanation might run somewhat as follows. X left a certain impression, say, a round one of five centimeters in diameter, in the clay. Y fitted snugly because it too is round and five centimeters in diameter. This is in terms of a narrow state of the clay, that of having a round, five centimeters impression in it, an impression our piece of clay shares with all its *Doppelgängers*. Another explanation might be that the impression was caused by an object, as it happens X, which is the same shape as Y. Having an impression caused by an object which is the same shape as Y is a broad state of the clay, because it is not one it shares with all its *Doppelgängers*, and hence this second explanation is one in broad terms.

It would clearly be a mistake to hold that the second (broad) explanation was redundant in the presence of the first (narrow) one. The second gives us explanatory information not contained in the first. It tells us that the particular shapes and sizes were not important, it was their all being the same that mattered. Had X and Y both been ten centimeters square instead of both being five centimeters round, we still would have had a snug fit. Of course, it is also true that the first contains information not in the second, for the first tells us which particular shapes and sizes were causally involved. Neither explanation makes the other redundant; each has its own distinctive explanatory role. A *Doppelgänger* challenge here would emphasize the fact that Y will fit just as snugly into all the duplicates of our piece of clay as it does in the original piece, despite the fact that the impressions in the duplicates do not all have the property of being caused by an object which is the same shape as Y. But this is simply irrelevant in the context of a program explanation. The *Doppelgänger* point—which is perfectly correct as far as it goes—tells us that if we keep constant the particular shape of both Y and the impression, we will get that same result of a snug fit, but clearly this in no way undermines the fact that if we vary the particular shape of Y and of the object causing the impression but keep constant their relationship, it is also true that we will get the same result of a snug fit. The crucial point is that the explanation in terms of the impression being caused by an object of the same shape as Y tells us the sense in which the particular shapes do not matter. The *Doppelgänger* point draws our attention to the (different) sense in which the particular shapes do matter.

We say the same about explanation by the ascription of broad content. Although the environment will have caused some narrow state in me—let us suppose, for convenience of reference, that it is a belief with a narrow content expressible in English—which will in turn have caused a piece of behavior by me, the particular narrow state does not matter, in the following sense. There will be an aspect of my behavior, say, it's being a reaching for that cup, which remains constant under a whole range of possibilities concerning which narrow state does the causing, provided the cup acts on me in the right way for me to have a belief described as being about the cup. The cup will be a certain color and shape, a certain distance from me, in a certain direction, illuminated in a certain way, and so on and so forth. All in all, the cup will present itself as, say, the F. These facts together will cause me to believe that the F is desirable under some aspect, and so to reach for the F, and, as the F is that cup, to reach for that cup. But equally had the cup been a different color and shape, a different distance and direction from me and so on, in short, the G and not the F, I still would have reached for it. For I would in that case have believed that the G is desirable and, consequently, have reached for the G; but in that case the G would have been that cup, and so it still would have been true that I reached for that cup.

The distinctive explanatory role of broad content can be brought out in terms of the multiple realizability of broad content by narrow content and environment. For a given broad content B there will be a number of ways of realizing that content by the appropriate combination of narrow content N and environment E, say: N_1 & E_1, N_2 & E_2, ... One of these ways, say Na & Ea, will be the actual way B is realized. Now each of the N_i & E_i will explain and predict different behavior in the subject, but it may be that there is a common thread T running through these different pieces of behavior. In this case ascribing B explains and predicts T just as well as ascribing Na & Ea, and does something distinctive besides—it tells us that it did not matter as far as getting T goes that it was Na & Ea that was actual instead of, say, N_2 & E_2. It might be objected that to say that Na & Ea in fact realizes B is to say that Na & Ea constitutes (as things in fact are) B. So how can ascribing Na & Ea not explain all, and possibly more besides, that ascribing B does? Our answer should by now be clear. Fred's coughing may, as things in fact are, constitute someone's coughing, and yet explaining the conductor's annoyance in terms of the fact that someone coughed is not subsumed in an explanation in terms of the fact that Fred coughed. Similarly, Na & Ea may as it happens constitute B, yet an explanation in terms of B is not subsumed in an explanation in terms of Na & Ea.

In sum, program explanations are explanations that give a range of states which would have produced the result we want explained. Explanation in terms of broad content picks out the range of states via *inter alia* the role of the environment in causing the states. The causally efficacious properties of the states will be neurophysiological properties, and different environmental stimuli will produce neuro-physiologically different states, and so different behaviors. However, it may be that if we keep fixed some feature of the environment, then the different behaviors display a common feature despite variations elsewhere. In such a case, the feature of the environment may be part of a program explanation of the behavioral constancy. Our claim is that explanations in terms of broad content employ a relationship to the environment—thus, the context-bound nature of broad content—as part of what singles out the range of narrow states that would produce, and one of which does produce, behavior manifesting the feature the broad content explains. We said earlier that program explanations concern what remains constant under variation. The explanatory point of ascribing broad content is that keeping a relationship of agents to external factors constant through variations inside those agents may preserve as a constant some feature of their otherwise varying behavior. Some feature of their behavior may track the relationship to external factors.[19]

CONCLUSION

We started from the fact of broad content, from the fact that some intentional states have the content they do have in virtue of how things are around their subjects in combination with how things are inside their subjects. Our question was how functionalists should respond to this fact. Our answer was that they should respond in the least disruptive fashion possible, namely, by sometimes including outside factors in the inputs and outputs that figure in their story. We defended this answer against two widely entertained objections. The first is that the fact of broad content undermines the whole picture of the mind as something internal (a picture which brings functionalist and Cartesian into unholy alliance). Our reply was that functionalists at least can be neutral on whether the mind is internal in the relevant sense. For, by choosing what we called the role state option, they can make an intentional state's content an essential property of it, and so make a state with broad content to be such that its very identity, not just how it may be described, is linked to the surroundings of the subject which has the state.

The second objection is that broad content does not play the kind of explanatory role needed to justify incorporating it into the functionalist story in our simple (minded?) way. It is, as the *Doppelgänger* challenge shows, narrow content which plays that kind of role, and accordingly we should be dualists about content. Narrow content does the explaining of behavior in a way right for inclusion in the (narrow) functionalist story. Our reply to this objection was to argue that properties may be causally explanatory properties without being causally productive or efficacious ones. These properties program the result to be explained, rather than actually bringing it about, and are the properties appealed to in what we called program explanations. We argued that program explanations are very common, being the kind of explanations offered when we explain in terms of highly relational properties, and that explanations in terms of content, be it narrow or broad content, are program explanations. This fact enabled us to identify a distinctive explanatory role for broad content, a role not filled by the correlative narrow content, and so to justify broad content's inclusion in its own right in the functionalist story about content.[20]

ENDNOTES

1. This thesis is (now) widely accepted. Mostly, its defense turns on the role of natural kind terms in sentential characterizations of content, on the singular or *de re* nature of some beliefs, or on the communal aspects of belief characterizations. See, respectively, e.g., Putnam (1975), Evans (1982), ch. 6, and Burge (1979a). For further references and a survey of the various considerations advanced in support of the existence of broad content, see the editors' introduction to Pettit & McDowell (1986), and Owens (1987).

2. Outside happenings are included in two of functionalism's ancestors: Gilbert Ryle's version of logical behaviourism and J. J. C. Smart's topic neutral analyses. As Hornsby (1986) notes, Ryle, unlike many contemporary functionalists, explicitly allows as behavioral outputs events outside the body; and Smart (1959) analyzes having a yellowish-orange image as having something going on in one like what goes on when an *orange* is before one.

3. See, e.g., McDowell (1986).

4. For a recent forceful presentation, see Fodor (1986). We're using "narrow content" here in a catch-all way to include for instance John Perry's senses, see n. 11.

5. See Fodor (1986), and, for a particularly detailed account of a dualist view, McGinn (1982). For further dualist accounts see the references in Owens (1987).

6. See, e.g., the papers cited in n. 1.

7. See, e.g., McDowell (1986), and Burge (1979a) and (1982).

8. Our argument that broad functionalism can allow essentially broad states rests on the claim that role states are individuated in part by role. If you are unhappy about this claim—perhaps because it is token states which we are talking about, and you take a coarse-grained view on the individuation of token states, even when they are second-order states—replace role states in the above by aggregations of realizer states with the relevant external happenings. As aggregations with different members are necessarily distinct this makes broadness an essential feature.

9. See the papers by Burge cited in n. 7. The view that content is essential cuts across many differences in doctrine elsewhere, thus Fodor, op. cit., endorses it.

10. See, e.g., Devitt & Sterelny [(1987), p. 166].

11. Although some of the phrasings in McGinn (1982) suggest that he holds that broad content is idle, we take his considered view to be that it is redundant.

12. In the terminology of Perry (1977), the *sense* of what I believe is common to me and my *Doppelgängers*, though we have different *thoughts*. Perry argues that it is the sense of what I believe and not the thought, that is important for psychological explanation.

13. For a view of this kind see Dennett (1982).

14. Cf. Fodor, op. cit., p. 43.

15. This sense of "tracking" is weaker than Robert Nozick's in his [(1981), p. 178]. It

involves an analogue of his sufficiency condition but not of his necessity clause. On related matters see Dretske (1986).

16. For earlier and less transparent accounts of the idea of distinguishing program from process explanations, see the distinction between normalizing nd regularizing explanations in Pettit (1986), and Jackson & Pargetter (forthcoming). We are indebted here to number of discussions with Robert Pargetter.

17. We believe that some of the puzzles about teleological and evolutionary explanations can be illuminated by seeing them in terms of program explanations, but that is another story.

18. Our discussion of program explanations is designed to be relatively neutral as between various views about causal explanation, but here is one place where the influence of Lewis (1986) shows.

19. *Ceteribus paribus* and within limits as always, but particularly where psychological explanation is concerned.

20. We are much indebted to comments by various readers and audiences on earlier versions, especially from Martin Davies, David Lewis, Robert Pargetter, and Kim Sterelny.

13

On What's in the Head

Robert Stalnaker

"Cut the pie any way you like, meanings just ain't in the head!"[1] So Hilary Putnam taught us some years ago. He made the point with some compelling examples all fitting a now familiar pattern: first we are asked to imagine a counterfactual person exactly like some actual person with respect to all purely internal psychological and physical properties, but situated in a counterfactual environment which differs from ours in some subtle way. For example, where we have aluminum, they have a metal that resembles aluminum superficially, but that has a different chemical structure. We are then invited to note that despite the intrinsic similarities of the two *Doppelgängers*, their utterances have different semantic properties. When the Earthling says "Aluminum is used in the construction of airplanes," she says something that differs in content from what her Twin says when she utters the same sounds. Since what is in the heads of the two is the same, while what they mean when they use certain words is different, the meanings of those words must depend on something other than what is in those heads. Tyler Burge developed this kind of example in more detail and extended the point in several ways.[2] First he argued that it is not just meaning and other semantical properties, but also intentional psychological properties that are shown to depend on external conditions: beliefs, desires, hopes and fears ain't in the head either. Second, he argued that social conditions—facts about the linguistic practices of members of the agent's community—were among the external conditions on which intentional mental states depend. Third, he emphasized that the dependence on external conditions was a pervasive phenomenon, one not restricted to some narrow range of concepts and expressions. It applies not just to de re attitudes or to attitudes expressed with proper names, indexical expressions and natural kind terms, but to de dicto attitudes and to all kinds of concepts and expressions. Burge called the thesis he was attacking—the thesis that intentional mental states are intrinsic properties of the individuals who are in those states—*individualism.*

In retrospect, it seems that we should not have been surprised by the conclusions of Putnam and Burge. Isn't it obvious that semantic properties, and intentional properties generally, are *relational* properties: properties defined in terms of relations between a speaker or agent and what he or she talks or thinks about. And isn't it obvious that relations depend, in all but degenerate cases, on more than the intrinsic properties of one of the things related. This, it seems, is not just a consequence of some new and controversial theory of reference, but should follow from any account of representation that holds that we can talk and think, not just about our own inner states, but also about things and properties outside of ourselves. But the conclusions were surprising, and they remain controversial. One reason is that the anti-individualistic thesis seems to have some paradoxical consequences. If what we mean or think is not in the head, it would seem that we cannot know, or at least cannot be authoritative about, what we mean or think.[3] Another reason is that this thesis seems to be incompatible with the explanatory role that intentional mental states are thought to play. We explain why people behave the way they do in terms of what they believe and want. In fact, it is often assumed that belief and desire states are to be defined in terms of the behavior they dispose the agents in those states to engage in. But how can such states be causally relevant if they are relational states—states that depend on things outside of the agent?

One response to the anti-individualist thesis is to grant it, but to deny its significance. If our ordinary concepts of belief, desire, and meaning are relational concepts that individuate mental states in a non individualistic way, this only shows that our ordinary concepts are inappropriate for the purpose of the explanation of behavior. But, this response suggests, the revisions needed to render intentional concepts individualistic are not very radical. What such a revision must do is to factor out the "organismic contribution" to an intentional mental state—that component of the state that is dependent or supervenient or the internal states of the agent.

The revisionist response makes a negative and a positive claim. The negative claim is that no systematic explanatory theory of behavior will be tenable unless it is individualistic. The positive claim is that although ordinary intentional psychological concepts are not individualistic as they stand, they can he revised in a way that renders them individualistic while preserving the basic structure of intentional explanation. Jerry Fodor has defended both claims; Daniel Dennett has proposed ways to defend the positive thesis. and Stephen Stich and P. M. and P. S. Churchland have defended the negative thesis while rejecting the positive claim. In this paper, I want to explore both parts of the revisionist doctrine, beginning with the positive side. After trying to get clear about what is required in general to define an individualistic analogue of a relational concept, I will look at two proposals for defining narrow content—a kind of content that is intended to render intentional states purely internal. Then I will turn to the negative side of the case, discussing a number of formulations of the negative thesis and a number of arguments in its defense. I will be arguing, first, that it is harder than some have assumed to define narrow content, and second that ordinary wide content is less mysterious than some have assumed.

A number of quite different issues are involved in the revisionist doctrine: some are relatively abstract questions concerning concept formation, methodology, and the distinction between intrinsic and relational properties; others are more specific questions concerning the nature of intentional concepts and the psychological mechanisms that underlie their application. To help separate these different issues from each other, I will begin by exploring an analogy: I will look at a very simple causal relational concept—a concept that should be relatively transparent and uncontroversial—and consider what is involved in the attempt to define a narrow or purely intrinsic version of it. Then I will look back at the intentional concepts themselves and at the proposals for carving out narrow content.

Consider the concept of a *footprint*. This is a causal-relational concept: something is a footprint in virtue of the way it was caused. One might make the point that a footprint is not intrinsic to the sand or mud in which it is located by telling a Twin Earth story: imagine a beach on Twin Earth which is, at a certain moment on July 4, 1985, exactly like Jones Beach in every intrinsic detail. The difference is that the counterpart on Twin Earth of a certain footprint on Jones Beach was caused, not by a foot, but by the way the waves happened to fall some hours earlier. So something on Twin Earth that is intrinsically indistinguishable from a footprint is not a footprint. A philosopher with a gift for coining slogans might sum up the lesson of this thought experiment this way: *Cut the pie any way you like, footprints just ain't in the sand!*

The revisionist replies that this may be true of our ordinary folk concept of a footprint, but explanatory science is interested only in states that are intrinsic to the sand. So let us define a new concept that individuates the relevant state of the sand in a way that is independent of its causal history and environment: let us say that a *narrow footprint* is a foot-shaped indentation, whatever its cause. Can't we, in this way, isolate that component of the state of containing a footprint that is intrinsic to the medium that is in that state? The anti-individualist will note that the new concept is still a relational one. Footprints in the new sense no longer depend on the *particular* cause of the indentation, but they still depend on general facts that are extrinsic to the sand. An elaboration of the Twin Earth story makes the point: Suppose that on Twin Earth feet have a different normal shape. If this is true, the indentation in the sand there will not only fail to be an ordinary footprint because of its different causal history, it will also fail to be a *narrow* footprint because normal footprints are differently shaped there, and so the indentation on the beach is not even shaped like a foot.

This pattern of conceptual revision—replacing a dependence on a specific causal interaction with dependence on a general regularity in the environment—is exemplified in less artificial cases. It seems reasonable to say that in defining dispositional properties, for example, we begin with a kind of causal interaction (a substance dissolves, or an object is observed). We then use suitably hedged counterfactuals to get at a stable property of one of the things involved in the interaction—a property that the thing has independently of the fact that the interaction took place. A sugar cube is soluble if it would dissolve if put in water (under normal conditions). An object is observable if it would be observed if a normal observer were suitably placed. Some such dispositional properties (such as solubility in water) may be purely intrinsic, but others will not be. Whether something is observable may depend on the capacities of normal observers, perhaps also on the lighting conditions that in fact obtain, or at least on the lighting conditions that normally obtain. The concept of belief may be this kind of narrowed version of the concept of knowledge, replacing a dependence on more specific causal relations between the fact known and a state of the knower with more general patterns of causal relations between facts and internal states.

One might further narrow our revised concept of footprint by taking the phrase "foot-shaped indentation" in a reference-fixing way. That is, by a narrow footprint we mean an indentation that is shaped the way feet are *actually* shaped. So whatever shape feet have on Twin Earth, the counterpart on Twin Earth of the footprint on Jones Beach is still a narrow footprint. Now, it seems, we have succeeded in isolating a purely internal state of the sand.

The pattern of concept formation now looks like this: we begin with a concept that classifies states of a thing in terms of a relational property—specifically, in terms of the way those states are caused. We then focus on the intrinsic properties of the states the concept picks out, classifying them in a new way: as states that share those intrinsic properties. This pattern too seems to be exemplified in less artificial cases. Consider, for example, the concepts of *mass* and *weight*. Weight is the quantity that is closer to the surface—more directly observed and measured. But it is a relational concept: what you weigh depends on the gravitational field you are in. Mass is the quantity that a body has, independently of its gravitational field, that explains why it weighs what it does in different gravitational fields. Even at an initial stage of inquiry when we may not know very much about the relevant intrinsic properties, we can still use this strategy of concept formation to point at the properties, whatever they are, that play a certain role in the explanation of a thing's behavior.[4]

Our definition of narrow footprint may make use of a sound strategy of concept formation, but the success of this kind of definition will always depend on a substantive presupposition: that the things picked out by the relational property are similar to each other in an appropriate way. The substantive presupposition will never be plausible unless one idealizes a bit: there are deformed feet, and distorting conditions that may give rise to footprints of an unusual shape. These will certainly be footprints, but if our definition of narrow footprint is to succeed, they, and other indentations shaped like them, must be excluded. By foot-shaped indentations we mean indentations that have the *normal* or *characteristic* shape that feet make under *normal* conditions. This kind of qualification is a familiar part of characterizations of dispositional properties: a thing is soluble in water if it would dissolve if put in water *under normal conditions*. The point of the qualification is to insure that what is defined is a stable property that we can generalize about. It might be that a thing would not dissolve if put in water in a particular situation because of anomalous environmental conditions even though the thing is intrinsically similar to soluble things. But we don't want to say that the thing loses its solubility under the abnormal external conditions. The qualification allows us to say that the thing remains soluble even though, in this case, it would not dissolve if put in water.

Even given such qualifications, a definition of this kind may fail. If the concept of footprint we begin with is the concept of a print made by a human bare foot, then the concept of a narrow footprint is perhaps well defined, since there is a relatively well defined shape that prints have, in normal cases, when they are made by such feet. But suppose we start with a more general notion: by "footprint" we mean a print made by a foot of some animal or other. This concept includes prints made by cloven hooves, webbed feet, and the paws of dogs as well as human feet, and it is not clear that these footprints have any one characteristic shape at all. If they do not, then our concept will collapse when we try to abstract away from the causal origin of the indentations we want to pick out. Or at best we will be left with a wildly disjunctive concept that will be of no interest.[5]

The moral of the story is that the narrowing of causal relational concepts exemplifies a legitimate pattern of concept formation, but not a pattern that will in all cases yield a well-defined purely internal property. First, the pattern may succeed in eliminating a dependence of a property on specific interactions with other things, while leaving a dependence on general facts about the environment. Second, whether the pattern succeeds at all will depend on substantive presuppositions about the intrinsic similarities of things that share the causal-relational property. To evaluate the positive part of the revisionist thesis we need to see just what the presuppositions are in the case of intentional mental concepts, and to consider whether we have good reason to accept them.

The defense of the positive part of the revisionist thesis requires more than just the definition of narrow analogues for particular belief properties such as the property of believing that aluminum is used in the construction of airplanes; what is needed is a narrow analogue of belief in general. Like ordinary belief, narrow belief must be expressed as a relation between the believer and some kind of *content*. This is essential since the project is to explain mental states as internal states *while preserving the structure of intentional explanations*. The strategy is to change the notion of content in a way that makes belief states purely internal. But however content is explained, how is it possible for belief to be both a relation between a person and a content and also a purely internal state? To answer this we need to distinguish two ways in which a concept can be relational. Consider again the quantities weight and mass: a Twin Earth thought experiment will show that weight is a relational property. William weighs three hundred pounds, but his Twin on the less massive Twin Earth weighs less. Mass, in contrast, is intrinsic; Twin William is equally massive. But both weight and mass are relational in another sense: they are both *semantically* relational concepts. There is a relation—weight (or mass) in pounds—that William bears to the number three hundred and that Wilma bears to one hundred and two. Both weight and mass are concepts expressed by using a relational *predicate* together with a number to pick out a property. It is the fact that the family of properties—weight or mass properties—has a certain structure that makes it possible for them to be expressed in this way. But this is compatible with the properties being intrinsic in the sense that whether a thing has one of them is not contingent on anything external to the thing. The revisionist project requires a concept of belief that is semantically relational, but that expresses belief properties that are ontologically intrinsic; it proposes to accomplish this by changing or restricting the contents that are used to pick out the properties. Belief is to be narrowed by narrowing content.

So how is narrow content to be explained? The first answer I will consider is Jerry Fodor's.[6] Let me sketch, first Fodor's diagnosis of the problem—his explanation of the fact that content, in the ordinary wide sense, is not in the head—and then say how he proposes to revise the notion of content to get it back into the head where it belongs. The problem, Fodor says, derives from the following constraint on the identity conditions for content: beliefs that are true under different conditions have different contents. It is because the Earthling's thought or statement, "Aluminum is used in the construction of airplanes" could be true in possible circumstances in which her Twin's corresponding statement or thought is false that we are required to conclude that the two have different content. Narrow contents cannot differ in this way, but if narrow content is not constrained by truth conditions, how can it be a notion of content at all? The solution, Fodor proposes, is not to give up the connection between content and truth conditions, but rather to relativize this connection to context. Narrow content will be something that determines the truth conditions of a belief or utterance as a function of the external environment of the believer or speaker. The model for this account of narrow content is David Kaplan's account of the semantics for demonstratives and indexicals. Kaplan makes a distinction between *meaning* (or what he calls *character*) and *content*, and this distinction provides the model for Fodor's distinction between narrow and wide content. According to Kaplan's account, when Daniels and O'Leary both say "I am bald," they say something with the same *character*, but with different *content*. Daniels's statement says that Daniels is bald, whereas O'Leary's says that O'Leary is. Character is explained as a function from context to content. The pronoun "I" has a constant character: it always refers to the speaker. But because different speakers use that pronoun, the same sentences containing it may be used to say different things. In general, the character of a sentence of the form "I am F" will be a function taking a context in which x is the speaker into the proposition that is true if and only if x has the property expressed by "F." Narrow content, on Fodor's account of it, is a generalization of character in Kaplan's sense, where the context includes any fact external to the believer that is relevant to the determination of wide content.[7]

Fodor suggests that once we are clear about the general nature of narrow content, "it's quite easy to see how the required principles of individuation should be formulated."[8] Here is his explanation of the "extensional identity criterion" for narrow content:

There is presumably something about the relation between Twin Earth and Twin Me in virtue of which his "water"-thoughts are about XYZ even though my water-thoughts are not. Call this condition that's satisfied by [Twin Me, Twin Earth] condition C. . . . Similarly, there must be something about the relation between Me and Earth in virtue of which my water-thoughts are about H_2O even though my Twin's "water"-thoughts are not. Call this condition that is satisfied by [Me, Earth] condition C'. . . . Short of a miracle, it must be true that if an organism shares the neurophysiological constitution of my Twin *and satisfies* C, it follows that its thoughts and my Twin's thoughts share their truth conditions. . . . But now we have an extensional identity criterion for mental contents: two thought contents are identical only if they effect the same mapping of thoughts and contexts onto truth conditions.[9]

This argument tells us what kind of thing narrow content should be: a mapping from context into truth conditions; and it shows that *if* we succeeded in specifying such a mapping, it would have the right properties: it would be *narrow* (intrinsic) and it would be like *content* in the crucial way: it would determine the semantic or intentional properties of the thought (relative to context). But the argument tells us less than it seems about how such mappings are to be specified, and it obscures the fact that it is a substantive hypothesis that the internal states of believers contain thoughts that determine such mappings.

It is surely right that if the context (C or C') includes all information external to the believer that may be relevant to the determination of truth conditions, then context, together with the internal states of the believer, will determine truth conditions. That is only to say that truth conditions are determined by the conditions that are relevant to determining them. But pointing this out does not tell us what function from context to content narrow content is supposed to be, or explain how it is that the relevant function is determined by what is in the believer's head. If the abstract procedure outlined in the argument could, by itself, show how to narrow content, then it could be used to define a narrow analogue of any relational property.

Consider this parody of Fodor's characterization of the criterion for narrow content: Take the property of being exactly three miles from a burning barn. Suppose I have this property, even though my counterpart who is located at exactly the same place in a certain counterfactual situation does not. He, let us suppose, is instead exactly three miles from a snow-covered chicken coop. Now there is presumably something about the relation between my counterpart and his world in virtue of which he is three miles from a snow-covered chicken coop even though I am not. Call this condition C. Similarly, there is something about the relation between me and my world in virtue of which I am three miles from a burning barn, even though my counterpart is not. Call it C'. Whatever these conditions are, we *do* know this: short of a miracle, it must be true that anyone in the location that both I and my counterpart are in in our respective worlds would be three miles from a snow-covered chicken coop if condition C obtained, and three miles from a burning barn if instead C' obtained. But this does not help us identify a specific function that takes condition C' into the property of being three miles from a snow-covered chicken coop and also takes C into the property of being three miles from a burning barn—a function that is supposed to represent the contribution that an individual's location makes to the relational property. There are many such functions, and no reason to identify any of them with the contribution that my intrinsic location makes to the specific relational property. My counterpart cannot reasonably say, "I did my part toward being three miles from a burning barn by going to a place where, if conditions C' had obtained instead of C, I would have been three miles from a burning barn." *Every* location is such that for some external conditions, if those conditions obtain, then anything in that location is three miles from a burning barn.

The exclusive focus on Twin Earth situations makes it look easier than it is to factor out the contribution that the external environment makes to the possession of some relational property. In a Twin Earth story, we are asked to consider a possible situation in which an individual shares *every* intrinsic property with its actual counterpart. So if the actual individual has the relational property in question, we can be sure that its Twin Earth counterpart will have whatever property is supposed to be the purely intrinsic component of that relational property. But the story does not help us to identify the relevant intrinsic property. If we were to consider, not *Twin* Earths, but, say, *Cousin* Earth stories in which an individual resembles its counterpart in some but not all internal ways, it would be clearer that this strategy for defining intrinsic properties in terms of relations may leave many questions unanswered. Suppose, for example, that Cousin Earth contains both H_2O and XYZ. In this world the two substances are easily distinguished. Their superficial properties are somewhat different from the superficial properties that H_2O has on Earth, and that XYZ has on Twin Earth, and also somewhat different from each other. But both substances are somewhat like water in fact is. Suppose also that Cousin English has different (non-scientific) words for the two substances, neither one of which is spelled or pronounced like "water," but that otherwise Cousin English is a lot like English. Now suppose my counterpart on Cousin Earth believes that salt is soluble in water, but does not believe that salt is soluble in the other stuff. Does his belief have the same narrow content as my belief that salt is soluble in water (and so the same narrow content as my Twin's belief that salt is soluble in the other stuff)? Fodor's abstract account, by itself, gives no guidance about how to answer this question.[10]

There are several disanalogies between Kaplan's notion of character and Fodor's proposed account of narrow content—disanalogies that suggest that Fodor's project is much more ambitious, and much more speculative. First, Kaplan's notion of context is not designed to include everything external to the individual, and the character of an utterance is not something determined by the purely internal properties of the speaker. As a result, characters are not required to have the counterfactual power that narrow contents must have. That the pronoun "I" has the character it has is a fact about a social practice—the practice of speaking English. The functions from context to content that Kaplan calls characters are not intended to tell us what speakers would be saying if they were speaking some other language. Kaplan's notion need not tell us this since the aim of his theory is not to isolate the purely internal component of what determines the content of speech acts, but simply to explain how some languages in fact work. The practice of speech is more efficient if speakers can exploit information about the environment—information available to all the participants in a conversation—in communicating. So languages make this possible by including rules that make what is said a function of that kind of information. That a language contains such rules (rather than, say, just lots of unsystematic ambiguity) is a substantive hypothesis, though in this case an obviously correct one. That our minds contain much more general systematic procedures for determining content as a function of context in a more general sense is a much more ambitious and speculative hypothesis.

Second, because Kaplan's theory is a theory of speech rather than a theory of thought we can identify, more or less independently of theory, the objects that the theory is interpreting: the objects that *have* character and content. A speech act can be described in terms of its content (O'Leary said that salt is soluble in water), but it also may be described in more neutral ways (O'Leary uttered the sentence, or the sounds, "Salt is soluble in water") But in the case of thought it is much less clear what it is that has a particular content or narrow content. As with a speech act, we can describe a particular belief in terms of its content (O'Leary believes that salt is soluble in water), but in this case there is no easily identifiable mental state, describable independently of its content, that constitutes that person's having that belief. Of course a psychological theory might turn up such a mental state or object. It might be that what it is to believe that salt is soluble in water is to be storing in a certain location a mental sentence that says that salt is soluble in water. If this were true, then we could identify the thing that has the content independently of the content that it has. But it also might be that states of belief are more holistic. Suppose a total belief state were a complex cluster of dispositions to behave in various ways under various conditions. One might be able to use particular belief contents such as the belief that salt is soluble in water to describe such a state without it being possible to match up those contents with particular dispositions in the cluster. On this kind of account, the question "what makes it true (given the facts about the external context) that O'Leary believes that salt is soluble in water?" will be answered by describing how O'Leary is disposed to behave under various conditions. But the same behavioral dispositions that constitute O'Leary's total belief state will also make it true that he believes various other nonequivalent propositions. Compare: the question "what makes it true (given the facts about the external context) that O'Leary is three miles from a burning barn?" will be answered by describing O'Leary's location. But this same location will also make it true that O'Leary has various other nonequivalent relational properties (being more than two thousand miles from Los Angeles, being closer to Istanbul than to New Delhi, etc.). Even if we could find a narrow, purely internal characterization of the belief state as a whole, it wouldn't follow that we could find narrow analogues of the (relational) facts about the belief state that are expressed by ordinary attributions of belief.[11]

Fodor's abstract account of narrow content is motivated by a particular picture of belief and other mental states, a picture that he has made explicit and vigorously defended. Beliefs are internal sentences stored in the mind. The particular contents of those sentences depend on the believer's environment, but the sentences themselves can be identified as sentences, and as *beliefs*, independently of the particular environmental conditions that determine their interpretation. The sentences are beliefs in virtue of their internal functional role— the way they are affected by sensory inputs, interact with other internal states, and determine behavioral outputs. Their semantic properties will depend in part on what is going on outside—beyond the periphery—but the way they depend on what is going on outside is determined by the purely internal state. This is a very attractive picture, but it is not inevitable; it has strong, highly speculative, empirical presuppositions. Fodor's abstract account of narrow content as a function from context (in a very broad sense) to truth-conditional content may seem plausible given this picture, but it does not contribute much to defending the picture, or to explaining how it is to be developed. It does not, by itself, tell us how to identify narrow contents, and it does not give us reason to believe that internal states determine functions of this kind that will do any explanatory work. No general *a priori* argument will show that this is the way that things must be.

Is there a way to define narrow content that does not depend on the language of thought picture? Daniel Dennett, after criticizing the sententialist approach, makes some suggestions about how we might isolate what he calls the "organismic contribution" to the content of belief in a way that is neutral as to how that contribution is represented in the believer.[12] He calls his approach "*notional attitude psychology*," and contrasts it both with *propositional attitude psychology*, which describes attitudes in terms of the ordinary wide conception of content, and *sentential attitude psychology*, which takes the contents of attitudes to be syntactic objects—sentences of an inner language. The contents of notional attitudes are explained in terms of a kind of possible world, which Dennett calls a "notional world." "A notional world should be viewed as a sort of *fictional* world devised by a theorist, a third party observer, in order to characterize the narrow psychological states of a subject."[13] Notional worlds are supposed to be defined so that, "although my *Doppelgänger* and I live in different real worlds—Twin Earth and Earth—we have the *same* notional world."[14] The set of notional worlds that define the narrow contents of a person's beliefs is something like the worlds that are the way that the person takes the real world to be.

Notional worlds, it seems, are just the possible worlds that have been used to characterize ordinary wide contents in *propositional* attitude psychology. Possible worlds—at least all but one of them—are also fictional worlds in the sense that they are not actual. So how are notional attitudes different from propositional attitudes, characterized in this way? What difference explains why the contents of notional attitudes are narrow, while the contents of propositional attitudes are wide? The difference will not be found in the nature of the worlds themselves, or in the nature of the contents, which in both cases are just sets of worlds. So far as I can see, narrow contents, on Dennett's account, are just propositions. The difference between notional and propositional content is to be found in the different answers that the two theories give to the question, "in virtue of what facts do a believer's beliefs have the (notional or propositional) contents that they have?" According to propositional attitude psychology, the contents of an organism's attitudes are picked out as a function of relations between the organism and its actual environment. Just what relations do the job is a difficult and controversial question, but the Twin Earth thought experiments show that the content of a belief, as ordinarily conceived, is not a function of purely internal properties of the believer. The task of narrow, notional attitude psychology is to explain how purely internal properties of an organism can be used to pick out a set of possible worlds—a perhaps different set that will characterize the organism's attitudes in a way that is different from the way it is characterized by an ordinary propositional attitude attribution. The idea is roughly this: O'Leary believes (correctly) that there is water in the basement. The proposition he believes is true in the actual world, but false in the counterfactual world where there is no water, but only XYZ in the basement. There is, however, a different proposition that does not distinguish the actual world from this counterfactual world—a proposition that we might roughly describe as the proposition that there is some water like stuff in the basement. The first proposition is the wide content of O'Leary's belief; the aim of Dennett's project is to define narrow content so that the second of these propositions is the narrow content.

One can contrast Fodor's strategy with Dennett's in the following very abstract way: Fodor proposes to revise and narrow the folk concept of belief by changing the *kind* of thing that is the content of belief. Narrow contents are not propositions; they are functions from context to propositions. But for Dennett, in contrast, narrow contents are the same kind of thing as wide contents: both are propositions—functions from possible worlds (= notional worlds) into truth values. What is changed in the move to narrow content is the relation between a believer and a proposition in virtue of which that proposition correctly describes the believer's beliefs. To accomplish that change, Dennett needs to tell us just how the purely internal properties of individuals determine the narrow propositional content of their beliefs.

Here is Dennett's strategy for answering this question: suppose we know about an organism everything there is to know about its capacities and dispositions, but nothing about how it got that way: nothing about its historical properties, or about the environment that it came from. The problem is to say how to go from this limited information about the organism to a characterization of its notional world. "Our task," Dennett says, "is like the problem posed when we are shown some novel or antique gadget, and asked: what is it for?" We can't know, Dennett supposes, what it was actually designed for, but we could try to figure out, from its internal properties, what functions it is ideally suited to perform. "We *try to imagine a setting* in which . . . it would *excellently* perform some imaginably useful function."[15] In the same way, to find an organism's notional world—the world according to it—we try to imagine "the environment (or a class of environments) for which the organism as currently constituted is best fitted."[16] Propositions true in those possible environments will be the narrow contents of the organism's beliefs.

On the face of it, this doesn't look like what we want at all. Possible worlds picked out in this way look more like worlds in which the organisms needs or wants are satisfied than like worlds in which its beliefs are true. The antelope, for example, is aware of lions in its environment, and equipped to detect and escape from them. But it is not clear that it is better fitted for a lion-filled environment than for one that is lion-free. The antelope would have some useless defense mechanisms in certain lion-free environments, but it might still do a better job of "surviving and flourishing and reproducing its kind"[17] in such an environment. But, Dennett says, we are not supposed to understand "ideal environments" in a straightforward way: "By 'ideal environment' I do not mean the best of all possible worlds for this organism. . . . It might be a downright nasty world, but at least the organism is prepared to cope with its nastiness."[18] So ideal environments, in the intended sense, are environments for which the organism is prepared to cope. This is better: we do try to cope with the world as we believe it to be, and so worlds that are that way are presumably among the ones that our behavior is best fitted to cope with. But something essential still seems to be left out. Many features of organisms that help them cope with their environments seem intuitively to have nothing to do with their beliefs, and the fact that we have some feature that *would* help us cope with some counterfactual environment is surely not sufficient to say that such a counterfactual possibility is compatible with the world as we take it to be.

Consider the porcupine whose quills protect it from predators. It is best fitted, in Dennett's sense, for an environment containing animals that would attack and eat it if it weren't for the quills, and this will be true even if the porcupine's *only* defense mechanism is this passive one that does not require the porcupine to perceive or respond in any way to the presence of such predators. If the porcupine goes through life oblivious to the potential predators that its quills protect it against, it would surely be unreasonable to populate its notional world—the world according to it—with them.

The dangers that the porcupine's quills protect it from are real ones. The problem gets even worse if one considers, as Dennett's procedure requires, merely possible dangers that some actual feature we have might help to guard against. For example, consider a possible world containing fierce and powerful beasts that would love to eat human beings if it weren't for the fact that these beasts are repelled by the distinctive smell that humans in fact give off. We humans, as we actually are, are ideally fitted to cope with such predators, but I don't think worlds containing them can be used to characterize our beliefs.

It seems to me right that states of belief are states that help the believer to cope with an environment, and that the contents of those states are essentially connected with the kind of environment they help the believer to cope with. But to be a belief state, a feature of an organism must contribute in a particular way to the fitness of the organism to cope with its environment. At the very least, a belief state must involve the reception of information from the environment, and a role for this information in the determination of the behavior of the organism. While Dennett's general account of his procedure for identifying narrow content is not restricted to this kind of case, the examples he uses focus on it, and we can consider how his strategy fares if we apply it only to states of an organism that help it cope by receiving and storing information in a form that makes it available to help determine the organism's behavior.

Understood in this way, Dennett's procedure is a variation of one kind of naturalistic account of wide content that has been proposed. According to this kind of account, a representational system is a system that is capable of being in a range of alternative internal states that tend to be causally dependent on the environment in a systematic way. Suppose that an organism is capable of being in internal states, $S_1, S_2, \ldots, S_n$, and that which of these states it is in normally depends on which of a corresponding range of alternative states the environment is in. Normally, for each i, the organism is in state S_i if (and because) the environment is in state E_i. Whenever a structure of causal dependencies of this kind obtains, it is appropriate to say that the organism *represents* the environment as being in state E_i in virtue of the fact that it is in state S_i, and that the organism's states contain *information* about the environment. Suppose further that the states of the organism are, or determine, behavioral dispositions, and that for each i, the behavior that state S_i disposes the organism to engage in is behavior that would be appropriate (given its needs or wants) in environment E_i. Then those representational states will be of the right general kind to be belief states.

This account of representation is like Dennett's account of narrow content in that it identifies content with a set of possible states of the environment. This account, like Dennett's, treats the descriptions of the relevant environments as the theorist's way of classifying internal states: the descriptions are not attributed to the organism. And like Dennett's, it does not distinguish information from misinformation. If the organism is in state S_i, then it represents the world as being in state E_i, whatever state the environment is actually in. But the notion of content that results from the causal account of representation will be a notion of *wide* content since the structure of causal relations in virtue of which the internal states are representational states will depend not just on the internal structure of the organism, but on general features of the environment. If the environment were radically different in certain ways, then the same states of the organism might tend to be sensitive to different features of the environment, or might not be sensitive to the environment at all. Content ascriptions, on this kind of account, are descriptions of internal states, but they describe them in terms of the organism's capacity to distinguish between a limited range of alternative possibilities, a range of possibilities that is constrained by certain facts about the organism's actual environment.

But even if our ordinary concept of content depends on facts about the actual environment in this way, might we apply this sort of procedure without relying on such facts? If we knew enough about the purely internal dispositional properties of a believer, might we be able to determine, from this information alone, a set of possible environments meeting this condition: if the believer were in such an environment it would tend to behave in ways that are appropriate (that tend to satisfy its needs better than alternative actions available in that environment), and it would do so *because* it is in such an environment? Dennett claims that if the believers were sophisticated enough we could, and that the resulting notion of content would be just the notion of narrow content we want.

> Highly adaptive organisms like ourselves . . . have internal structure and dispositional traits so rich in information about the environment in which they grew up that we could in principle say: this organism is best fitted to an environment in which there is a city called Boston, in which the organism spent its youth, in the company of organisms named . . . and so forth. We would not be able to distinguish Boston from Twin Earth Boston, of course, but except for such virtually indistinguishable variations on a theme, our exercise in notional world formation would end in a unique solution.[19]

I see no basis for this optimism. I suspect that the attempt to recover information about a virtual environment without making any assumptions at all about the actual environment is just too unconstrained to work. Imagine a purely internal description of the movements that I am disposed to make under various internal conditions, as I walk down the streets of Boston going places to satisfy my wants and needs, a description that makes no reference to what is going on either specifically or in general beyond my skin. How could anything about *Boston*, or about Boston-like cities, be recovered from such a description? With a little imagination, one should be able to tell all kinds of wild fairy tales about environments in which the movements I am disposed to make are appropriate, but that are not anything like the way the world seems to me. The world beyond myself *could* be wired up so that the actions whose actual appropriateness depends on facts about Boston instead depended for their appropriateness on some totally different set of facts, say facts about the social organization of termite colonies. If the organism's internal structure and dispositional traits are rich and complex, then we will have to tell a long fairy tale. The world described by such a tale will perhaps have to share an abstract structure of some kind with the worlds that define the ordinary wide content of the organism's beliefs, but I don't see why they would have to share any content.

In normal everyday ascriptions of content we usually ignore not only fairy tale possibilities, but all possibilities except those that differ from the actual world only in very limited ways. When I say that O'Leary believes there is water in his basement, I may be saying only that O'Leary's conception of the world distinguishes the possibility that there is water in the basement from the possibility that his basement is dry. What this means, on the causal-informational account of representation, is that O'Leary is in a state that he would normally be in only if there were water in his basement. Further, that state is one that would normally cause O'Leary to behave in ways that would better serve his needs and wants if there were water in his basement than if the basement were dry: it disposes him to get out the mop, or call the plumber. But does O'Leary really believe that the liquid on his basement floor is *water*? Well, he certainly knows, or assumes, that it is not gasoline or olive oil. If it were any of a range of familiar alternative liquids, O'Leary's states and behavior would normally be different. But what about the possibility that it is a substance just like water in its superficial properties, but different from water in its underlying chemical structure? Does O'Leary's internal state contain information that distinguishes the actual situation from this one? Is there anything about him that would dispose him to behave differently (under normal conditions) if that situation were actual? In the usual context, that possibility is not relevant. When we claim that O'Leary thinks there is water in the basement, we are not claiming that he has ruled out the possibility that the stuff down there is really not water, but XYZ. We can, however, raise the question, and in this way change the range of relevant alternatives. The question will then shift, focusing on O'Leary's knowledge and beliefs about the chemical composition of water. If O'Leary is innocent of even the most elementary knowledge of chemistry, then nothing in his mind or behavioral dispositions will distinguish Earth from Twin Earth, but that won't make it wrong to say, in a normal context in which Twin Earth possibilities are ignored,that O'Leary believes that the stuff on his basement floor is water. That ascription of content distinguishes, in the right way, the relevant alternative possibilities that are compatible with O'Leary's conception of the world from the relevant possibilities that are not.

The revisionist may argue that it is this context-dependence of ordinary wide content ascriptions that makes them inappropriate for the purposes of theoretical explanation in cognitive science. Dennett's project might be seen as an attempt to eliminate the context-dependence by defining content relative to an absolutely neutral context that is free of all presuppositions about the external environment. But on the causal-informational account of representation, informational content is *essentially* relative to a range of alternative possibilities that are determined by general facts about the causal structure of the world in which the organism functions. It is internal states of the representor, on this kind of account, that contain information (or misinformation), but the system of causal relationships in virtue of which those internal states contain information cannot itself be something internal to the representor. The theorist, in describing the internal states of a representor in terms of informational content, has some choice in the range of alternatives relative to which content is defined. It may even be that for any possibility we can describe, there is a context in which we can ask whether the representor's beliefs distinguish that possibility from certain others. But this does not imply that there is an absolutely neutral context, a context free of all presuppositions about the environment, relative to which content ascriptions make sense.

In his attempt to characterize narrow content, Dennett has tied one hand behind his back. He proposes to extract a kind of content from facts about the believer while ignoring certain information that is available and that is used to determine ordinary wide content—information about the believer's historical properties and relation to the actual environment. I have argued that no reasonable notion of content will result from this procedure; one might also question the point of the exercise. Why bother? Why shouldn't an explanatory theory make use of historical and environmental information in defining content? To answer this we need to look at the other half of the revisionist's project: the arguments for the negative thesis.

The negative side of the revisionist doctrine has been formulated in various ways and given various labels: *methodological solipsism*,[20] *individualism*,[21] *the principle of autonomy*.[22] These different theses are sometimes distinguished from each other, but the general idea of all of them is that the states and properties that are described and expressed in an explanatory psychological theory should be intrinsic states and properties of the organism whose behavior is being explained. A number of similar arguments for this thesis have been advanced; they go roughly like this: an explanatory theory of human behavior, or of the behavior of anything else for that matter, should concern itself only with properties that are relevant to the causal powers of the thing whose behavior is being explained. Things that are intrinsically indistinguishable are indistinguishable with respect to causal powers, and so should not be distinguished by an explanatory theory. The Putnam-Burge thought experiments help to bring this point out: it is clear that people on Earth and their *Doppelgängers* on Twin Earth will behave in exactly the same ways when put into the same environments. No tenable theory will explain their behavior in different ways, and so no tenable theory needs concepts that distinguish them.[23]

Before turning to this argument, we need to look more closely at the theses it is intended to support. First, here is Fodor's formulation of what he calls *individualism*: "Methodological individualism is the doctrine that psychological states are individuated *with respect to their causal powers*."[24] This doctrine is, Fodor says, a special case of a completely general methodological principle that all scientific taxonomies should conform to, a principle that can be defended on *a priori* metaphysical grounds. He emphasizes that individualism, in his sense, does not by itself rule out the individuation of mental states by relational properties.

Relational properties can count taxonomically whenever they affect causal powers. Thus, "being a planet" is a relational property par excellence, but it's one that individualism permits to operate in astronomical taxonomy. For whether you are a planet affects your trajectory and your trajectory determines what you can bump into; so whether you're a planet affects your causal powers.[25]

There is a shift in this characterization of individualism from a stronger to a weaker claim: it is one thing to individuate by causal powers, another to individuate by what *affects* causal powers. The fact that a planet is a planet is a fact about the configuration of its environment. This configuration plays a role in causing the planet to have the causal powers it has, for example its velocity. But the environmental facts do not *constitute* causal powers. Does individualism really require only that mental states be individuated by what causally affects causal powers? If so, then individualism in Fodor's sense is a much weaker doctrine than the individualism that Burge has argued against. On this interpretation, individuation by ordinary wide content will be compatible with Fodor's individualism since, for example, the fact that it is *water* in O'Leary's basement—or at least the fact that there is water in his environment generally—surely plays a role in putting him into the internal state that disposes him to behave as he does. Of course as the Twin Earth story shows, there are alternative causal histories that could have put O'Leary into the same internal state, but an analogous claim will be true for the planets. Imagine a Twin Earth that is not a planet but is in a field of forces exactly like the one the Earth is in.

The defense of the negative thesis by Fodor and others trades on a conflation of the weaker and the stronger thesis. If the thesis is to have any bite—if it is to be a thesis that rules out the individuation of psychological states by ordinary wide content—it must be the stronger thesis. But the arguments and examples used to support individualism often count only against the weaker thesis. Fodor, for example, illustrates his version of individualism and defends its plausibility with an example of a causally irrelevant relational property: call a particle an h-particle if a certain coin is heads up, and a t-particle if the coin is tails up. No plausible theory, Fodor argues, will use this distinction to explain the behavior of particles. No one will disagree with this; it should be clear and uncontroversial that facts that are causally irrelevant to the internal states of a particle or an organism should play no role in characterizing its theoretically important physical or psychological states. But it does not follow from this that such states must be purely internal.

The same shift between a weaker and a stronger version of the negative thesis is evident in other discussions. Consider, for example Stephen Stich's principle of autonomy: "The basic idea of the principle is that the states and processes that ought to be of concern to the psychologist are those that supervene on the current, internal, physical states of the organism." This is clearly the strong thesis, restricting the psychologist to purely internal states. But causal language creeps into Stich's subsequent discussion of the principle: historical and environmental facts, he says, will be irrelevant to psychological theory except when they "make a difference" to the organism's internal state; such facts "will be psychologically relevant only when they *influence* an organism's current, internal, physical state." The facts about distant causal histories of a term that determine its reference are said to be psychologically irrelevant because they need not "leave their trace" on the current internal state of the subject using the term.[26]

Stich argues for his principle of autonomy with what he calls the *replacement argument*:

> Suppose that someone were to succeed in building an exact physical replica of me—a living human body whose current internal physical states at a given moment were identical to mine at that moment.... The replica, being an exact physical copy, would behave just as I would in all circumstances.... But now, the argument continues, since psychology is the science which aspires to explain behavior, any states or processes or properties which are not shared by Stich and his identically behaving replica must surely be irrelevant to psychology.[27]

Stich illustrates his point with an example of an industrial robot. Suppose we describe the robot by saying that it is successfully performing its millionth weld. This is, in Stich's terminology, a nonautonomous behavioral description. An exact physical replica behaving in a way that is, in a reasonable sense, exactly the same, might not satisfy it. The description is a "conceptual hybrid" of an autonomous description—"successfully performing a weld"[28] and a purely historical description—"having performed 999,999 other welds." "If we are seeking a set of generalizations to explain robot behavior, it would be perverse to expect them to explain the latter fact or the hybrid into which it enters."[29]

The argument and the example seem compelling, I think, only if we assume that the historical property is causally irrelevant to the current state of the robot. But if we keep in mind that those first 999,999 welds must surely have taken their toll, then it may not seem so perverse to look for generalizations that explain the fact that the robot satisfies the hybrid description. Suppose that, because of metal fatigue, robots of this kind almost always break down soon after about nine hundred thousand welds. If the robot failed to break down, we might ask for an explanation: how was this particular robot able to perform its millionth weld? We might call robots "old" after their nine hundred thousandth weld, and generalize about the behavior of old robots. We certainly generalize about the behavior of human beings on the basis of historical properties such as age and experience.

If we replace our robots with new ones after 900,000 welds, they won't break down as often, but, Stich might point out, this is because real replacements won't be the exact replicas required by the replacement argument. If the new robots were really physically exactly like the ones they replace, then of course they would be similarly unreliable. If an eighty-year-old woman were physically exactly like a seven-year-old child, then she would behave like a seven-year-old child, falsifying biological and psychological generalizations about eighty-year-old women. But this counterfactual possibility does not, by itself, threaten the truth, or even the explanatory power, of such generalizations.

There may be a sense in which certain nonautonomous properties are causally irrelevant. Consider a simple causal chain: A causes B, which in turn causes C. Suppose that B is sufficient, in the circumstances, for C: that is, B would have caused C even if it had been caused by something other than A. So this causal chain contrasts with a more complex one where A is doing some additional work, perhaps not only causing B but also causing other things that enable B to cause C. To rule out this contrasting case, we might say that A is causally irrelevant to the fact that B causes C. But in another sense, A is causally relevant to this fact, since without A, B would not have happened, and so would not have caused C. Suppose we have a pair of alternative causal chains: alternative inputs A_1 or A_2 will cause a device to be in one of two alternative internal states, B_1 or B_2, which in turn will cause the device to produce outputs C_1 or C_2. If we ask why the internal state B_1 produces output C_1, it is not relevant to mention A. But if we ask why the device produces output C_1, it would be correct and informative to say, "because it is in the B-state caused by A_1." It is one thing to explain why a particular internal state has the causal powers it has; it is another to explain why something is in an internal state that has those causal powers.

Does the internal state of the device contain *information* about how it came to be in that state? If there are alternative causes of B_1, then the fact that the device is in state B_1 does not distinguish them: the device does not "know" that A_1 causes B_1, as contrasted with a counterfactual possibility in which A_2 causes B_1. But since it is A_1 that in fact causes the device to be in state B_1, and since the device would not have been in that state if A_1 hadn't happened, it "knows," in virtue of being in state B_1, that A_1 happened.

In light of these distinctions, consider the following argument in defense of methodological solipsism from a paper by P. M. and P. S. Churchland:

> A neuron cannot know the distant causal ancestry . . . of its input. . . . An activated neuron causes a creature to withdraw into its shell not because such activation represents the presence of a predator—though it may indeed represent this—but because that neuron is connected to the withdrawal muscles, and because its activation is of the kind that causes them to contract. The *"semantic" content of the state, if any, is causally irrelevant.*[30]

One cannot explain why the neuron's being activated causes the creature to withdraw by citing the fact that the activation represents the presence of a predator. But this does not prevent us from explaining why the creature withdraws by citing the presence of a predator, or by citing the fact that the creature is in a state that represents the presence of a predator. The semantic content is causally relevant to the behavior of the creature since if the creature had not been in a state with that semantic content, it would not have withdrawn into its shell. Can a neuron know the distant causal ancestry of its input? It cannot distinguish the situation in which its activation is caused by the presence of a predator from the situation in which it is caused by something else. But if in fact the neuron was activated by the presence of a predator, and would not have been activated if a predator had not been present, then it "knows," in virtue of being activated, that a predator is present.

The critic of wide content might respond to these general considerations as follows: even if a theory *can* generalize about properties and states that are individuated by their causes, wouldn't it better, methodologically, to try to find a theory that individuates them more narrowly? Won't generalizations in terms of the internal properties be deeper and more accurate? Generalizations about the causal powers or behavioral dispositions of old robots, creatures that are representing the presence of a predator, or footprints will inevitably have exceptions; to the extent that they are true, they must hold in virtue of internal properties of those things, and we won't understand why the generalizations hold until we are clear about the relevant internal properties.

It is right that *one* explanatory task is the task of characterizing the mechanisms that underlie certain causal regularities. We want to know how the creature represents the presence of a predator, and how that representation causes it to withdraw into its shell. But there are at least three reasons why we may still want to generalize about causal and historical properties. First, we need to refer to such properties, and to generalizations about them, in order to pose the explanatory questions about the mechanisms. The creature has certain capacities: it can recognize predators and protect itself from them. The reason we are interested in the neurophysiological processes in the creature is that they explain how it is able to do such things. Second, we may not know enough to be able to generalize in terms of internal properties. Suppose our device is a black box and that all we know about the states B_1 and B_2 is that they are the states caused (or normally caused) by A_1 and A_2, respectively. Often we know something about the mechanisms that explain why a device has certain capacities or incapacities, but not enough to describe them in purely autonomous terms. We may have to wait for the completion of science before we are able to describe things in purely internal terms, if there are such terms. As Fodor said in another context, and in defense of the opposite conclusion, "No doubt it's all right to have a research strategy that says 'wait a while,' but who wants to wait *forever?*"[31] Third, there may be generalizations that can be stated only in terms of non-individualistic states and properties. Different mechanisms explain how different creatures recognize predators, but we may still be able to generalize about the recognition of predators. Suppose there are lots of black boxes that take inputs A_1 and A_2 into outputs C_1 and C_2, but that they do it in different ways. It is, of course, the idea of functionalism that it is possible and useful to generalize about causal roles independently of the specific mechanisms by which those causal roles are realized. Functional theories are theories that characterize the internal states of individuals in nonautonomous terms in order to generalize at a certain level of abstraction. It is not a mysterious coincidence that such generalizations hold. There may be general causal pressures, such as evolutionary pressures, that tend to favor situations in which A causes C but that leave open the question of the means or intervening process by which this is accomplished. In such a case there may be two different questions about why A causes C. If the question is about the mechanism, one cites B. If it is about the general pattern, then one cites the general pressures. Why do chameleons change color to match their background? Because this provides camouflage and in this way helps them survive, or because certain chemical processes take place in the chameleon's skin.

Any psychological theory, folk or scientific, that understands mental states in terms of intentional states is a theory that sees a person or other organism as a receiver and user of information. The real lesson of Twin Earth is that the fact that we are receivers and users of information is a fact, not just about us, but about the way we relate to our environments. In different environments, the internal states that in fact carry certain information would carry different information, or would not carry information at all. Ironically, the Twin Earth stories that make this point so vividly also serve to obscure its significance in at least two ways: they make the dependence of intentional states on the environment seem, first, easier to avoid, and second, more mysterious, than it is. In the special case of Twin Earth, it is easy to match up O'Leary's beliefs with corresponding beliefs of his Twin, and to identify the narrow content with what these corresponding beliefs have in common. It is less easy to say, in general, how to factor out the purely internal component of a belief. I have argued that it is a highly speculative substantive hypothesis that there is any narrow notion of content that can be used to individuate intentional states autonomously. The special case of Twin Earth also makes the dependence of intentional states on environment seem stranger than it is. Since the internal states of O'Leary's Twin are exactly the same as O'Leary's, there is a sense in which the environmental differences between the two worlds make no difference to the internal states of the two Twins, and so one is tempted to conclude that the environmental facts on which intentional states depend are therefore causally irrelevant. But the fact that a state might have had different causes does not show that the causes it does have are causally irrelevant.

Is O'Leary's belief that there is water in his basement an internal state of O'Leary? Is it in his head? Of course it is, in the same way that the mosquito bite on his nose is on his nose, and the footprint in the sand is in the sand. We can appeal to that belief to explain the fact that he is looking for the mop, just as we can appeal to the mosquito bite to explain why he is scratching his nose. We commonly individuate states and properties in terms of the way things interact with their environments, and use them to explain why things behave as they do. It is not easy to see how we could get along without doing this, or why we should try.[32]

ENDNOTES

1. Putnam [(1975b), p. 144].
2. Burge (1979a).
3. It is not clear that this is right. What does follow is that the intrinsic state of the head is not authoritative: that is, it does not follow from the head's being in the intrinsic state it is in that it has certain beliefs. But unless we assume the kind of individualism that is being denied, this does not imply that we are not authoritative.

4. There is a rough but useful analogy between this strategy of concept formation and a popular account of the way natural kind terms acquire their content. According to that account, one kind of property—a cluster of superficial properties—determines a set of things—say a set of animals—and then this extension is used to determine a different type of property-structural or explanatory or essential properties. The relevant properties of this type are the ones shared by the things in the extension.

5. One might argue that concepts, such as the general concept of footprint, that collapse when we try to abstract away from causal origins are just the concepts that are of no interest to science. But this need not be true. It is conceivable, for example, that there be ecological generalizations about the role of footprints in the behavior of certain kinds of predators and their prey even if there were no interesting generalizations about the shapes of the relevant footprints. If there can be functional theories at all, then there can be theories that generalize about causal roles in abstraction from the intrinsic properties of the states that realize those roles.

6. Fodor (1987), ch. 2.

7. An explanation of narrow content based on this analogy was developed in some detail in White (1982).

8. Fodor [(1987), p. 30].

9. Ibid., p. 48.

10. The point of my Cousin Earth story is not just that narrow content may in some cases be indeterminate. That, I would argue and many would agree, is true of wide content as well. The point is that once we go beyond the Twin Earth scenario, it becomes clear that we have been told nothing at all about how to identify narrow content. That there is such a thing to be identified is a substantive hypothesis.

11. The point is that it doesn't follow that one could find *interesting* purely internal analogues of the relational properties of belief-states that are expressed by ordinary attributions of belief—internal properties that might be expected to play a role in an explanatory theory of behavior. One could always, by brute force, define some sort of internal property. Consider the location analogy: there is a set of absolute locations that are (in fact, at a certain moment) three miles from a burning barn. The property of being in one of those locations is (assuming, as we have been for purposes of the analogy, absolute space) independent of the external environment, and it is distinct from the property of being in one of the locations in the set that is in fact at least two thousand miles from Los Angeles. But such properties will have no interest; at other times or in counterfactual situations where barns are burning at different places, there will be no point in distinguishing the locations where, at this time and in this situation, a barn is burning three miles away.

12. Dennett (1982).

13. Ibid., p. 38.

14. Ibid.

15. Ibid., p. 41.

16. Ibid., p. 42.

17. Ibid., p. 41.

18. Ibid., p. 42.

19. Ibid., p. 43.

20. This term is first used for this doctrine in Putnam (1975b). Jerry Fodor defends the doctrine in Fodor (1981a).

21. This is Burge's term. Fodor distinguishes methodological solipsism from individualism

in chapter 2 of Fodor (1987) (reprinted here—*ed.*), though I think it is not clear that Fodor and Burge are using the term in the same sense.

22. This is Stephen Stich's term. Stich distinguishes the principle of autonomy from methodological solipsism. See Stich (1983).

23. Fodor's chapter 2 of (1987) contains a clear development of this argument. See also Stich's replacement argument in Stich, 165ff.

24. Fodor [(1987) p. 42]. Fodor's emphasis.

25. Ibid., p. 43.

26. Stich [(1983), pp. 164–165].

27. Ibid., p. 167.

28. Paul Teller has pointed out that "successfully performing a weld" is not really an autonomous description, since its application depends on a social and technological context. With a little imagination, one could tell a Twin Earth story in which what Twin Robot was doing did not count as performing a weld.

29. Stich [(1983), p. 168].

30. P. S. Churchland & P. M. Churchland (1983).

31. Fodor [(1981a), p. 248].

32. Many people provided me with helpful comments on an earlier version of this paper. I want to thank Kathleen Akins, Ned Block, Richard Boyd, Dan Dennett, Hartry Field, Sydney Shoemaker, Paul Teller, J. D. Trout, and Paul Weirich.

14

From *Mental Content:* Twin Earth and Teleology[1]

Colin McGinn

Consider the skin of the organisms populating Twin Earth. Suppose it contains pigments chemically just like those of organisms on earth: these pigments cause the skin to darken under the impact of light and so forth. On earth we would say that the function of these pigments is (roughly) to protect organisms from light rays emanating from the sun—to prevent sunburn, we would say. But now suppose that Twin Earth orbits, not around the sun, but around a *twin sun*. The skin of organisms on Twin Earth has never been exposed to light rays from the sun, only to rays from the twin sun. Nevertheless, what happens locally at the skin—the causal mechanism that operates there—is indistinguishable from what happens at the skin of Earthlings. Question: what is the function of these pigments on Twin Earth? I think we would naturally say that their function is to protect the organisms from rays emanating from the twin sun—to prevent twin sunburn, we would say. We would say this because the relation implicated in the function is a relation between the organisms and their environment—which contains the twin sun, not the sun.[2] In other words, function is environment-dependent; these functions are individuated by reference to the surrounding world. As we might put it, such functions are not "in the body"—they are strongly external.[3] You cannot then be an "individualist" about relational functions like these. Teleology, here, is a contextual matter.

It is the same with functions that relate to natural kinds. The function of Earth kidneys is to process water (H_2O); the function of Twin Earth kidneys is to process retaw (XYZ). The function of Earth bee dances is to indicate the whereabouts of nectar; the function of Twin Earth bee dances is to indicate the whereabouts of ratcen. And so on. The relevant traits have in fact evolved to cope with what is actually there in the environment, not with qualitative doubles of what is there. The actual environment does the selecting, so it gets to individuate the function selected.[4]

But now we can hardly fail to be struck by this structural parallel between function and content: they both seem context-sensitive in the same sort of way. The teleological theory offers a neat explanation of this parallel; content just is a special case of function. The desire for water, say, is associated with the function

261

of obtaining water; but the desire for retaw is associated with the function of obtaining retaw. The content differs because the function differs. And so for the other propositional attitudes in which the concept water features. Twin Earth cases for this kind of content are thus *predictable* from the teleological theory plus the context-dependence of functional specifications. This seems like a pleasant confirmation of the teleological theory.

It might be objected that I am describing functions in too fine-grained a way. Instead of saying that the function of skin pigments is to prevent sunburn (or twin sunburn), I should say that their function is to prevent burns from *any* fiery celestial body that sends down light rays of the kind organisms need to be protected from. And similarly for the other cases mentioned. Then we could say that the functions are invariant between Earth and Twin Earth. But if we did that, then we obviously could not explain the agreed differences of content in terms of functional differences. I would make two replies to this objection. First, I think we do in fact naturally employ the more specific mode of functional description, and that there seems nothing particularly objectionable in this practice—indeed it seems rather well motivated in view of our general conception of how natural selection works.[5] We can, of course, though perhaps with some contrivance, fashion less specific descriptions of function, but these need not be taken to oust the more specific descriptions: what we in effect have is a sort of nesting of increasingly specific functional descriptions. It is an interesting question what general principles govern this sort of nesting, but I do not see that any reason has been given to distrust or extrude the specific functional descriptions naturally evoked by my Twin Earth cases. Second, it seems to me that the availability of the less specific functional descriptions comports with a feature of Twin Earth cases that we *want* registered, so that the teleological theory is in fact doubly confirmed. For it is also clear that there is *a* level of psychological description with respect to which thinkers on Earth and Twin Earth *are* indiscernible: that level which makes us want to say that things *seem* the same to the two groups of subjects. Beliefs about water and beliefs about retaw present themselves to their subjects in phenomenologically similar ways, despite the difference of content. We can account for the difference in terms of specific function; and we can account for the similarity in terms of less specific function. The specific function of the belief is to combine with the desire for water to obtain *water*; the less specific function is to combine with the desire for water to obtain *whatever nourishes as water does*— this including retaw. Thus the teleological theory can capture the commonalities as well as the divergences of content.

ENDNOTES

1. Excerpted from McGinn (1989), pp. 157–9.
2. If you find it more natural to say that the function is to protect the skin from light rays of certain sorts, so that no mention is made of the specific celestial source of these rays,

thus picking out the same function on Earth and Twin Earth, then change the example so that the proximate natural kind is varied between the two planets—suppose that on Twin Earth *twight* rays are what cause the pigments to operate.

3. ["Weak externalism . . . is the thesis that a given mental state requires the *existence* of some item belonging to the nonmental world, and that its identity turns on that item. Strong externalism . . . is the thesis that a given mental state requires the existence *in the environment of the subject* of some item belonging to the nonmental world, and that its identity turns on that item" (McGinn (1989), p. 7).]

4. The detailed principles controlling the way function ascription is dependent upon the environment will no doubt be fairly subtle, and different kinds of function may be tied more or less strongly to the actual environment. We need, in particular, to allow for weakly external functional descriptions in order to deal with cases in which the function fails to be fulfilled in the organism's actual environment. As a conceptual point, indeed, we need to allow for functions that exist and yet never succeed in being fulfilled, even for the ancestors of a given organism. (God could equip a species with an organ designed to melt ice into liquid water but then never let the temperature fall below zero. (He finds it a bit hard to keep track of everything He does.) There is no reason in general to believe that the individuation of functions is going to be any simpler than the individuation of contents—which is one reason why function is a good way of thinking about content. The difficulties match.

5. It is part of our unreflective folk biology, how we actually operate with the notion of function. Of course, we may find reasons for doing it differently in scientific biology— we might prefer a notion of "narrow function" there. And so we have the question whether folk biology provides a sound starting point for scientific biology—specifically, with respect to its individuative predilections. I can see the journal papers now: "Methodological Solipsism Considered as a Research Strategy in Evolutionary Biology," "A Syntactic Theory of Biological Function," "Wide Function: Does Biology Need It?"

15

A Modal Argument for Narrow Content[1]

Jerry Fodor

HERE IS A MODERN ANTINOMY. On the one hand, there is argument A:

Argument A:
1. My Twin and I are molecular duplicates.
2. Therefore our (actual and counterfactual) behaviors are identical in relevant respects.
3. Therefore the causal powers of our mental states are identical in relevant respects.
4. Therefore my Twin and I belong to the same natural kind for purposes of psychological explanation and "individualism" is true.

But, on the other hand, there is argument B:

Argument B:
1. My Twin and I are molecular duplicates.
2. Nevertheless, our (actual and counterfactual) behaviors are different in relevant respects.
3. Therefore the causal powers of our mental states are different in relevant respects.
4. Therefore my Twin and I belong to different natural kinds for purposes of psychological explanation and "individualism" is false.

At least one of these arguments must be unsound. Which one? And what is wrong with it?

In chapter 2 of Fodor [(1987), reprinted here—*ed.*], I offered some considerations intended to advance the cause of argument A. They were supposed to show that mental states that differ only in "broad" intentional properties (the sorts of intentional properties that the mental states of molecular Twins may fail to share) *ipso facto* do not differ in causal powers; hence that mere differences in broad intentional content do not determine differences in natural kinds for purposes of psychological explanation. The arguments I offered in Fodor (1987) were not, however, greeted with unequivocal enthusiasm. Such was their subtlety, in fact, that I am not, myself, always quite sure how they were supposed to go. In the present paper, I propose to have another try at bolstering argument A.

I shall use many of the same materials that I did in Fodor (1987), but I shall put the pieces together somewhat differently. In passing I shall have a word or two to say about some of the comments that the Fodor (1987) arguments have provoked.

A preliminary remark, however, before we are under way. For most philosophical purposes, it may not really matter much how the individualism issue turns out. For example, I do not think that a resolution in favor of argument A (that is, in favor of individualism) would affect the status of "externalism" in semantics. Externalism is independent of individualism because, whatever the *explanatory* status of broad content, it is not in dispute (anyhow, it is not in *this* dispute) that the content of my Twin's *water* thoughts differs from the content of mine; or that "water" means something different in my mouth and in his; or that these semantical differences derive from differences in our respective head/world relations. (Presumably they derive from the fact that, whereas the causal history of my *water* thoughts connects them to samples of H_2O, the causal history of his connects them to samples of XYZ.) If, in short, the intuitions about Twins make a case for content externalism at all, then that case stands whether or not broad intentional states determine natural kinds for the purposes of causal explanation in psychology.

Similarly—and *pace,* for example, Stich (1983)—it is by no means obvious that the scientific vindication of intentional realism depends on how the issues about individualism are resolved. Suppose that there is some metaphysical argument to show that causal explanation in psychology requires the individuation of mental states to be individualistic (so that the mental states of molecular Twins are ipso facto type-identical, as in argument A.) It would follow that psychological explanation is not, strictly speaking, a species of belief/desire explanation since it is common ground that beliefs and desires are individuated broadly. But it would still be open whether psychological explanations are species of *intentional* explanations. That would depend on whether an individualistic notion of "intentional state" suitable for the purposes of psychological explanation can be constructed. [For more on this, see Fodor (1987).]

In short, you can do quite a lot of business in semantics and the philosophy of mind while benignly neglecting the issues about individualism. Still, I think it is worth trying to get these issues straight. We are about to see that they raise some interesting questions about the family of notions that include causal explanation, causal power, type identity, and natural kind. Getting some of this stuff sorted out may therefore be of use to metaphysics and the philosophy of science, even if it leaves things more or less unaltered in semantics and the philosophy of mind. So here we go.

Argument A says that, in virtue of our molecular identity, my Twin's behavior and my behavior are identical *in all relevant respects*. Not, of course, that they are identical *tout court*. On the contrary, just as it is common ground in this discussion that the *mental states* of Twins can differ in certain of their intentional properties, so it is common ground that Twin *behaviors* can differ under some of their intentional descriptions. Indeed, it may be that the second concession is entailed by the first, since it is plausible that the intentional properties of behaviors are inherited from the intentional contents of their mental causes. Thus, it is plausibly because I can think about water and my Twin cannot that I but not my Twin can reach for water, drill for water, or recommend water to a thirsty friend. A committed individualist might wish to argue that none of these is really, *strictu dictu*, an example of *behavioral* description; but that is not a tack that I propose to take.

So then: Twins can differ in the contents of their mental states; and, in consequence of these mental state differences, the behaviors of Twins can differ in certain of their intentional properties. I shall take for granted (what is not, however, uncontested) that these differences in intentional properties are the *only* (relevant) differences between the Twins' behaviors. That is, I am taking it for granted that the behaviors of Twins are *ipso facto* identical in all nonintentional properties that are relevant to psychological taxonomy. That is, of course, stronger than assuming what, I think, literally everybody agrees about, namely, that our behaviors are identical under *physical* descriptions, i.e., identical qua motions.

Here is an apparent exception to the stronger claim: if I utter "Gimme water," then, if all goes well, I get water; but if my Twin utters "Gimme water," then, if all goes well, he gets twater. So maybe there are nonintentional descriptions under which our behaviors are relevantly different after all. Second thoughts, however, make this difference go away; it is an artifact of the boring consideration that, whereas my utterance happened on earth, his happened on Twin Earth. The salient consideration is that, if Twin-me had uttered "Gimme water" here, he would have gotten water; and if I had uttered "Gimme water" on Twin-earth, I would have gotten twater. To put it slightly differently, my "Gimme water" does not get water *come what may*; at best it gets water *in certain circumstances*. But in *those* circumstances, his "Gimme water" gets water, too.[2]

The moral is that you have to judge identity and difference of causal powers in a way that bears the counterfactuals in mind, namely, *across* contexts rather than *within* contexts.[3] That does not get us out of the woods, however. For notice that, in the case where I utter "Gimme water" on Earth$_2$ and my Twin utters it here, neither of us gets what he asks for. That is, whatever the context of utterance, my utterance is a water request and his utterance is a twater request. So our behaviors remain relevantly different under these intentional descriptions *even by the across-context test*. It is this residual difference between the behaviors—their cross-context difference under certain intentional descriptions—which is the challenge to individualism and local supervenience.

So then, the question about individualism is: Do the Twins' mental states belong to different natural kinds (do they have different causal powers) in virtue of differences in the intentional properties of the Twins' behavior for which they are responsible? Since "causal power", "natural kind," and the like are, of course, technical terms, this question is not possessed of the highest degree of clarity. We shall see, however, that there are some clear intuitions about cases, and they will do for the purposes at hand.

It should be evident that the kind of question we are raising about the intentional states of Twins can also arise in cases that have nothing in particular to do with intentionality. Suppose we have a pair of causes $C1$, $C2$, together with their respective effects $E1$, $E2$. Assume that:

C1 differs from C2 in that C1 has cause property CP1 where C2 has cause property CP2.
E1 differs from E2 in that E1 has effect property EP1 and E2 has effect property EP2.
The difference between C1 and C2 is responsible for the difference between E1 and E2 in the sense that, if C1 had had CP2 rather than CP1, then E1 would have EP2 rather than EP1; and if C2 had had CP1 rather than CP2, E2 would have had EP1 rather than EP2.[4]

Call this *schema S*.[5] And now, what we want to know is: Which instances of schema S are cases where the difference between having CP1 and having CP2 is a difference in causal power in virtue of its responsibility for the difference between E1 and E2? (I shall often abbreviate this to "When is having CP1 rather than CP2 a causal power?") If we knew the answer to this general question, then we would know whether, in particular, the difference between having water thoughts and having twater thoughts is a difference in causal power in virtue of its being responsible for the difference between my producing water behaviors and my Twin's producing twater behaviors.[6] And, if we knew *that* we would know whether individualism is true; which is what we started out wanting to know, as the patient reader may recall.

Now, a plausible first reaction to this is that it is just not a philosophical issue. For, one might say, the question being raised is when the fact that a generalization supports counterfactuals shows that it has explanatory status. And the answer will depend, in the usual way, on systematic questions about the simplicity, plausibility, power, and so forth of the explanations, and on whether alternative counterfactual supporting generalizations are available. Some of the things that Burge (1989) says about the desirability of not apriorizing about the taxonomy that psychological explanation requires suggest that he would approve of this line of thought; for example:

It is a mistake ... to allow ontological preconceptions that have only philosophical underpinning to affect one's interpretation of scientific enterprises. It is a larger mistake to allow them to dictate the sorts of explanatory kinds that are deemed admissible for explanation (*ibid.*).

But though I would not have thought that apriorism is among my major methodological vices, still this does strike me as perhaps a little prim. It would be surprising if we could give interesting *a priori sufficient* conditions for when a difference in the properties of causes constitutes a difference in their causal powers. But it seems likely that we can give *a priori* arguments for some *necessary* conditions. After all, the commitment to causal explanation presumably has *some* methodological consequences qua commitment to causal explanation; and it ought to be possible to tease these out by reflecting on what kinds of things causal explanations are.

And, in fact, it does seem reasonably clear, *a priori*, that some instances of schema S are not bona fide. Consider, for a thoroughly trivial example, the case where EP1 is the property of being the effect of C1, and EP2 is the property of being the effect of C2. There is, of course, a property of C1 in virtue of which its effects are effects of C1, namely, the property of being C1. Correspondingly, there is a property of C2 in virtue of which its effects are effects of C2, namely, the property of being C2. Counterfactual support goes through in the required way; if the cause of E1 had had the property of being C2 rather than C1, then E1 would have had the property EP2 rather than the property EP1. But it seems *a priori* obvious that this is not a case where having CP1 is a causal power of C's in virtue of its responsibility for E's having EP1. One of the properties of my effects that your effects cannot have, however hard you try, is *the property of being caused by me*. But I take it to be simply obvious that this difference in our effects does not make the property of *being me rather than you* a causal power. I am not a unit natural kind in virtue of my unique power to cause effects that are effects of me.

It seems clear *a priori*, then, that not every case in which a difference between causes is responsible for a difference in effects is a case where the difference in causes is a difference in their causal powers. There are, in fact, plenty of examples. I can define a property *being an H-particle* that is satisfied by any x at time t if [(x is a physical particle at t) & (the coin in my hand at t is heads up)]. And correspondingly for T-particles. So a difference between properties of coins in my hand (namely, the difference between being heads up and being tails up) is responsible for the difference between the state of affairs in which all the particles in the universe are H-particles and the state of affairs in which all the particles in the universe are T-particles. But, of course, the difference between being heads up and being tails up does not count as a causal power in virtue of its responsibility for this difference in the particles.

Or again: in virtue of my having siblings, I am able to have sons who are nephews. A molecular Twin who did not have siblings would *ipso facto* fail to have nephews among his children. But I take it to be *a priori* obvious that the difference between having siblings and not having siblings does not constitute a difference in the causal powers of parents in virtue of its responsibility for this difference among the properties of their offspring.[7]

While we are on the topic of what is *a priori* obvious: the preceding three examples might suggest that the difference between CP1 and CP2 in instances of schema S does not constitute a difference of causal powers when CP1 and CP2 are *relational* properties. But a moment's reflection shows that this cannot be right [as, indeed, Fodor (1987) was at some pains to point out]. Taxonomy by relational properties is ubiquitous in the sciences, and it is not in dispute that properties like *being a meteor* or *being a planet*—properties which could, notice, distinguish molecularly identical chunks of rock—constitute causal powers. It is because *this* rock-Twin is a planet and *that* rock-Twin is not that this rock-Twin has a Keplerian orbit and that rock-Twin does not; it is because this rock-Twin is a meteor and that rock-Twin is not that this rock-Twin's effects include craters and that rock-Twin's effects do not. But, patently, *being a planet* and *being a meteor* are relational properties in good standing. To be a planet is to be a rock (or whatever) that is revolving around a star; to be a meteor is to be a rock (or whatever) that is falling, or has fallen, into collision with another rock.

Since the intuitions are pretty strong in all these cases, there is *prima facie* reason to suppose that there are some conditions on cause properties being causal powers which can be recognized from the armchair: not all cause properties are causal powers; not all relational properties fail to be, for two examples. I shall presently state a condition that, I claim, has to be satisfied if a property of a cause is a causal power in virtue of its responsibility for a certain property of an effect; and I shall claim that properties that distinguish Twins (like being causally connected to water rather than twater; or having water thoughts rather than twater thoughts) do not satisfy this condition in virtue of their responsibility for differences between the intentional properties of the Twins' behaviors. My evidence for the acceptability of this condition will be largely that it sorts examples like the ones I have just run through in an intuitively satisfactory way.

We need, however, some more ground clearing before we get down to it. (I solicit the reader's forbearance; once the ground is all clear, we shall be able to move very fast.) To begin with, I want to call your attention to what turns out to be a critical property of schema S: the question we are raising is not whether the difference between having $CP1$ and having $CP2$ is a difference in causal powers; rather, it is whether the difference between having $CP1$ and having $CP2$ is a difference in causal powers *in virtue of its being responsible for a certain difference between $E1$ and $E2$*, namely, in virtue of its being responsible for $E1$'s having $EP1$ rather than $EP2$ and for $E2$'s having $EP2$ rather than $EP1$. The point I am wanting to emphasize is that a cause property might fail to count as a causal power in virtue of its responsibility for one effect property, but still might constitute a causal power in virtue of its responsibility for some other effect property.

My coin's being heads up (rather than tails up) does not constitute a causal power in virtue of its responsibility for the universe being populated with H-particles; but it might constitute a causal power in virtue of its being responsible for my coin's reflecting light the way it does rather than some other way (e.g., rather than the way it would if it were tails up). Similarly, my having siblings does not constitute a causal power in virtue of its enabling me to have sons who are nephews. But suppose there is such a thing as sibling's disease; it causes people who have siblings to break out in a rash. Having a sibling might then be a causal power in virtue of being responsible for people coming down with sibling's disease. I stress this point because, if you do not relativize the issue about causal powers in this way, it turns out on a weak assumption that every contingent property is a causal power. The weak assumption is that it is (nomologically) possible to build a detector for any contingent property.

Consider, for example, the property of having had a Bulgarian grandmother who once plucked a daffodil as she went trippingly on her way to market. This is the sort of property that can distinguish between you and your molecular Twin. And, no doubt, your effects have properties because of your having had such a grandmother which his do not have because he did not, e.g., your effects have one and all got the property of being the effects of someone who had a Bulgarian grandmother who . . . , etc. But, intuitively, that is not sufficient for making the possession of a Bulgarian G who . . . —or the lack of a Bulgarian G who . . . —a causal power. Indeed, you would not have thought that *any* of the Bulgarian-grandmother-dependent properties of your effects—any of the properties that distinguish the effects of the molecular Twin with the Bulgarian G . . . from the effects of the molecular Twin without one—would be of the right kind to make having a Bulgarian grandmother a causal power.

And yet, it would surely be possible to build (more precisely, it would surely have been possible to have built) a machine which exhaustively examines the piece of space-time that starts with the birth of your grandmother and ends with your birth and which goes into one state if it detects somebody who was your grandmother and was Bulgarian and once plucked a daffodil as she went trippingly on her way to market, but which goes into a different state in case it detects no such person. I assume that it is possible (in principle) to build a machine that reliably detects this property. I am prepared to assume that it is possible (in principle) to build such a machine for any contingent property at all. If this assumption is true, then the Bulgarian grandmother detector can distinguish between you and your molecular Twin, and having a Bulgarian grandmother is having a causal power *in virtue of the (actual or possible) effects that instantiations of this property have on Bulgarian G . . . detectors.* (Quite generally, if any contingent property can be detected then any contingent property is a causal power in virtue of the effects of its instantiations on its detectors.) What does not follow, however, is that having had a Bulgarian G . . . is a causal power *in virtue of its effects on your behavior*; or, indeed, in virtue of its responsibility *for any property of yours.*

I am going through this song and dance by way of replying to an argument that Burge suggested (but does *not* endorse) that might lead one to think that having a water thought (rather than a twater thought) *must* be a causal power. After all, this argument says, it must be possible, in principle, to build a machine which looks through the chunk of space-time that starts with my birth and ends up with now, and which goes into one state if I am connected (in the right way) to water but goes into another state if I am connected (in the right way) to twater. This machine responds differently to me and my molecular Twin, and does so in virtue of the fact that I am connected to water in the way that my Twin is connected to

XYZ. So my Twin and I differ in our power to effect the states of this machine. So having water thoughts rather than twater thoughts (namely, having the kind of thoughts that you have if you are connected to water rather than twater) is a causal power in virtue of its responsibility for the machine's being in the state it is. So, if individualism says that having water thoughts rather than twater thoughts is *not* a causal power, then individualism is false.

Individualism does *not* say, however, that having water thoughts rather than twater thoughts is not a causal power. What it says is that having water thoughts rather than twater thoughts is not a causal power *in virtue of its being responsible for your producing water behaviors rather than twater behaviors*. (And similarly, being connected to water rather than twater is not a causal power in virtue of its being responsible for your having water thoughts rather than twater thoughts.) This is to say that the difference between having water thoughts and having twater thoughts is not a causal power in virtue of its responsibility for those of your properties *which are relevant to what psychological natural kinds your thoughts belong to*, e.g., it is not a causal power in virtue of its responsibility for the properties of your behavior.

That is all that an individualist has to show; to ask him to show more would be to make individualism false if there can be detectors for broad content properties. But that would be to trivialize the issue about individualism[8] since, as remarked above, it is plausible that there can be detectors for *any* contingent property (and, up to the limits of Turing machines, for quite a lot of noncontingent properties, too.)

So now: two causes differ in a certain property, and their effects differ in a certain property in virtue of this difference in the causes, and we want to know when the difference between the effects makes the difference between the causes a causal power. I shall tell you in just a moment. But it may be worth emphasizing that the cases we are interested in are not ones where the property that distinguishes the causes is *itself* the property of having a certain causal power.

Consider the case where CP1 just is the property of having the causal power to produce events that have EP1. Then, of course, the difference between having CP1 and not having it is the difference between having a certain causal power and not having it. This sort of case is easy because *it is noncontingent* that having CP1 is having a causal power. There are other, slightly less transparent, cases of this kind. For example, it is noncontingent that *being soluble in water* is having a causal power, because it is noncontingent that things that have that property have the power of dissolving in water; and the property of *being a camshaft* is a causal power because it is noncontingent that things that have that property have the power to lift the valves in a certain kind of engine (given conditions of optimal functioning . . . , etc.). There are, of course, scientifically interesting questions about properties that are noncontingently causal powers; for example, there are interesting questions about the supervenience bases of these properties and about their proper analysis into microfunctions. But there are not any interesting questions about whether things that have these properties have causal powers in virtue of having them. That question answers itself.

Compare, however, the properties of being a planet, being a meteor, and the like. These are causal powers in virtue of, for example, their respective abilities to produce Keplerian orbits and craters. But, insofar as being a planet is a causal power in virtue of the ability of planets to produce Keplerian orbits, it is contingent that being a planet is a causal power (for it is contingent that planets have Keplerian orbits); and insofar as being a meteor is a causal power in virtue of the ability of meteors to make craters, it is contingent that being a meteor is a causal power (for it is contingent that meteors make craters).

Notice that the broad content cases are like the meteor and planet cases and unlike the dispositional and functional cases. It may be that being connected to water rather than twater (hence having water thoughts rather than twater thoughts) is having a causal power; but if it is, it is contingent that it is. The property of being connected to water is not *identical* to the property of having a certain causal power, though it may be that there are causal powers that one has if one is connected to water that one would not have if one were not.

I draw two morals. First [contrary to some suggestions of Van Gulick (1989)], the fact that having a functional property is ipso facto having a certain causal power throws no particular light, one way or the other, on the question whether having a broad-content property is having a causal power. This conclusion may seem paradoxical since, after all, it is supposed to be that psychological properties *are* functional; so, if functional properties are noncontingently causal powers, and if psychological properties are functional, how could water thoughts and twater thoughts fail to be causal powers?

The answer is that it is actually not in dispute whether water thoughts and twater thoughts are causal powers. On the contrary, *of course* they are: my water thoughts are causally responsible for my reaching for water, my Twin's twater thoughts are causally responsible for his reaching for twater . . . , and so on. The question on which local supervenience—hence individualism—turns, however, is whether the *difference* between water thoughts and twater thoughts is a difference in causal powers. The anti-individualist says "yes, it is, in virtue of the intentional difference between the behaviors that water thoughts and twater thoughts cause." The individualist says "no it isn't. Water thoughts and twater thoughts are the same causal powers, only they're instantiated in people with different causal histories." The idea that mental states are functional roles resolves this dispute only on the question-begging assumption that water behaviors and twater behaviors are behaviors of different kinds.

Imagine that we had different words for *being thirsty and born in the Bronx* and *being thirsty and born in Queens*. There would then be no question but that being Bronx-thirsty and being Queens-thirsty are causal powers; being Bronx-thirsty and being Queens-thirsty both make people drink, for example. But a question might arise whether being Bronx-thirsty and being Queens-thirsty are *different* causal powers.[9] My point is that this issue would still be open *even though* there is no question but that being Bronx-thirsty and being Queens-thirsty are causal powers.

A functionalist might undertake to argue that they are different causal powers because, on the one hand, psychological states are functionally individuated, and, on the other hand, Bronx thirst and Queens thirst lead to different behavioral consequences, namely, to Bronx thirst-quenching behaviors in the one case and Queens thirst-quenching behaviors in the other. But, clearly, to argue this way would be to beg the question. For, anybody who denies that Queens thirst and Bronx thirst are different causal powers, will also deny and for the same reason that Bronx thirst-quenching behavior and Queens thirst-quenching behavior are behaviors of different kinds. So, the principle that psychological states are functionally individuated does not settle questions about identity and difference of causal powers in this sort of case. And, of course, for an individualist, "wants water" *is* this sort of case; for an individualist, "wants water" means something like "thirsty and born *here*."

What distinguishes Twins and threatens local supervenience is the property of *having water thoughts rather than twater thoughts*. No doubt, if functionalism is true, then mental states are one and all causal powers. But of course it does not follow from functionalism that differences between mental states are one and all functional differences; so it does not follow that differences between mental states are one and all differences of causal power. In fact, so far as I can tell, the only relevant connection between functionalism and the present issues about individualism is this: if, as I have claimed, the difference between the mental states of Twins is at best *contingently* a difference of causal powers, it follows that it *cannot* be a difference of functional role, since differences of functional role are differences of causal powers *non*contingently.[10] Compare being water soluble rather than twater soluble. It is *not* contingent that having *this* property is having a causal power; to be soluble in water but not in twater just is to have the power to dissolve in the first but not in the second. So it is all right to allow that *being water soluble rather than twater soluble* is a functional property, as, indeed, intuition demands.

My impression is that this is all reasonably untendentious. In general, friends of broad content argue that it perfectly well *could turn out*—that there is no metaphysical reason why it should not turn out—that having mental states that differ in their broad content is having mental states that differ in their causal powers. (For example, it could turn out that there are causal laws that distinguish between Twins.) But I do not remember hearing anyone argue that having mental states that differ in the way that the mental states of Twins do just is having mental states that differ in their causal powers. On the contrary, according to the usual understanding, it is their causal histories that distinguish the mental states of Twins. And the intuition about features of causal history is that some of them are causal powers (e.g., *having been dropped in transit; having been inoculated for smallpox*) and some of them are not (e.g., *having had a Bulgarian grandmother; having been born on a Tuesday*) and it is contingent which are which.

So, then, the second moral that I draw is that, in our hunt for a useful condition on what makes a difference in causal properties a difference in causal powers, we can restrict ourselves to cases where it's *contingent* whether the difference in the properties constitutes a difference between powers. We are, finally, getting to where you can smell blood.

I am now, at last, going to tell you a story about why being a planet (for example) is a causal power and having siblings (for example) is not. I propose to do this in two steps. First, I shall tell you a simplified version of the story; it has the virtue of making the basic idea relatively transparent, but it has the disadvantage that it does not work. I shall then make the technical moves required to plug the leak; the complicated version that emerges will be a motivated condition upon a property of a cause being a causal power; one which, I claim, broad-content properties fail to meet.[11]

So, then: here is me and here is my molecular Twin; and I have siblings and he does not; and in virtue of my having siblings my sons are nephews, and in virtue of his not having siblings his sons are not nephews; and what we want to know is: Why is *having siblings* not a causal power in virtue of its being responsible for this difference in our offspring? Here is a first fling at the answer: it is because having siblings is *conceptually* connected to having sons who are nephews; to be a nephew *just is* to be a son whose parents have siblings. And, to put it roughly, your causal powers are a function of your *contingent* connections, not of your conceptual connections. As, indeed, Uncle Hume taught us.

Similarly: though it is a fact that all the world's particles become H-particles when my coin is heads up, that fact does not make being heads up a causal power of my coin. That is again because the connection between all the world's particles becoming H-particles at t and my coin's being heads up at t is conceptual. To be an H-particle at t *just is* to be a particle at a time when my coin is heads up.

Compare cases of relational properties that really are causal powers, like *being a planet*. Being a planet is a causal power in virtue of, for example, its contingent (*a fortiori*, nonconceptual) connection with having a Keplerian orbit. That is, being a planet is a causal power because it is true and contingent that, if you have molecularly identical chunks of rock, one of which is a planet and the other of which is not, then, *ceteris paribus*, the one which is a planet will have a Keplerian orbit, and *ceteris paribus*, the one which is not a planet will not.

Here is the general form of the proposed solution.[12] Consider an instance of schema S. C1 has CP1, C2 has CP2, E1 has EP1, E2 has EP2, and the difference between the causes is responsible for the difference between the effects in the sense that E1 would not have had EP1 (rather than EP2) but that C1 had CP1 (rather than CP2). And what we want to know is: When does the fact that this difference in the causes is responsible for this difference in the effects make CP1 and CP2 causal powers? The answer, which I shall call *condition C*, is:

> Only when it is not a conceptual truth that causes that which differ in that one has CP1 where the other has CP2 have effects that differ in that one has EP1 where the other has EP2.[13]

So, for example, it is all right with condition C for *being a meteor* to be a causal power in virtue of the fact that meteors are responsible for craters. Take a pair of rock-Twins such that one is a meteor and the other is not. Then (*ceteris paribus*) craters will be among the effects of the first but not among the effects of the second. And the relation between the difference between the rock-Twins and the difference between their effects is nonconceptual. So it is all right for being a meteor (rather than a meteor Twin) to be a causal power in virtue of the fact that meteors cause craters and meteor Twins do not.[14]

Notice that the moral is that it is all right for being a meteor to be a causal power in virtue of this fact; not that being a meteor *is* a causal power in virtue of this fact. Satisfying condition C is, I suppose, necessary but not sufficient for being a causal power. As we are about to see, however, broad-content properties *fail* to satisfy this necessary condition, and that is enough to vindicate individualism.

Consider, first, the property of having water in your history (the property of being connected to water in whatever way it is that I am and my Twin is not). The difference between being so connected and not being so connected is responsible for a certain difference between the broad contents of my thoughts and the broad contents of my Twin's, namely, that I have water thoughts and he has twater thoughts. What we want to know is: Does this difference between our histories count as a causal power in virtue of the difference between the contents of our thoughts for which it is responsible? And the answer is: "No, because it is *conceptually necessary* that if you are connected to water in the right way then you have water thoughts (rather than twater thoughts) and it is again conceptually necessary that if you are connected to twater in the right way then you have twater thoughts (rather than water thoughts)." To have a water thought *just is* to have a thought that is connected to water in the right way, and to have a twater thought *just is* to have a thought that is connected to twater in the right way.[15] So it is not the case that my being connected to water rather than to twater is a difference in my causal powers in virtue of its responsibility for my having water thoughts rather than twater thoughts.

Now consider the difference between having water thoughts and having twater thoughts. Water thoughts cause water behavior (drilling for water and the like); twater thoughts cause twater behavior (drilling for twater and the like). What we want to know is: Does the difference between having water thoughts and having twater thoughts count as a causal power in virtue of the fact that it is responsible for this difference in the intentional properties of the behavior of the thinker? And the answer is: "No, because it is conceptually necessary that people who have water thoughts (rather than twater thoughts) produce water behavior (rather than twater behavior)." Being water behavior (rather than twater behavior) *just is* being behavior that is caused by water thoughts (rather than twater thoughts). So, though it is true that water thoughts are responsible for water behavior and twater thoughts are not, it does not follow that water thoughts have a causal power that twater thoughts lack. On the contrary, being a water thinker is the same causal power as being a twater thinker, only instantiated in a person with a different causal history.

I have been saying that it is only when the difference between the causes is not conceptually connected to the corresponding differences in the effects that the difference in the causes counts as a difference in causal powers. I think this really is the heart of the matter; it is why being responsible for particles being H-particles, being responsible for sons' being nephews, being responsible for behavior's being water behavior, and the like do not count as causal powers. But alas, the proposal does not work as stated and I shall have to do some patching.

Suppose that water is Bush's favorite thing to drink. Then, we have both:

1. If I am connected to water in the right way then my thoughts are water thoughts.

and

2. If I am connected to water in the right way, then my thoughts are thoughts about Bush's favorite drink.

Notice that both 1 and 2 distinguish me from my Twin: because he is not connected to water in the right way, it is false of him that he has water thoughts, and it is also false of him that his thoughts are about B's favorite drink. And, though 1 is conceptually necessary, 2 is contingent. That is, even though the difference between being water-connected and being twater-connected does not satisfy condition C in virtue of its being responsible for the difference between having water thoughts and having twater thoughts, it *does* satisfy condition C in virtue of its responsibility for the difference between having thoughts that are about Bush's favorite drink and having thoughts that are not. Hence, it satisfies condition C in virtue of making some *prima facie psychological* difference, some difference that is *prima facie* relevant to psychological taxonomy. So, even if, as I claim, condition C has its heart in the right place, still, as stated it has no teeth. Damn![16]

Everything is going to be all right, however. Let G be a property that nephews have, and let it be as contingent as you like that nephews have it. (G might be the property of glowing in the dark if it turns out that nephews do that.) Then the following is necessary:

3. If G is a property that nephews have, then if I have siblings then my sons have G.

So, for example, it is necessary that (if nephews glow in the dark, then if I have siblings, then my sons glow in the dark). The reason that this is necessary is, roughly, that it is conceptually necessary that the sons of people with siblings are nephews, so it is conceptually necessary that if you have a sibling then your sons have whatever properties nephews have. Notice, to repeat, that this is true even of properties that nephews have contingently: it is conceptually necessary that if *P* is a property that nephews have contingently then if you have siblings then your sons have *P*. (What is not true, of course, is 3′, the variant of 3 that has the modal operator imported. 3′ is false in the cases where *P* is a property that nephews have contingently.)

3′. If *P* is a property of nephews, then if you have siblings then it is necessary that your sons have *P*.

Now compare 4, which I take to be clearly contingent.

4. If *E* is a property that Keplerian orbits have then, if I am a planet, then my orbit has *E*.

(You might wish to try out 4 reading *E* as the property of being eliptical.)

The reason that 4 is contingent is, roughly, that it is contingent that planets have Keplerian orbits, so it is contingent that if I am a planet then my orbit has whatever properties Keplerian orbits do. This is true even if *E* is a property that Keplerian orbits have necessarily (like being a Keplerian orbit).[17]

Now we can do the case that was bothering us before. Consider 5, where *B* might be the property of being a thought about Bush's favorite drink:

5. If *B* is a property that water thoughts have, then if I am connected to water in the right way, then *B* is a property that my thoughts have.

I take it that 5 is obviously conceptually necessary. The reason is, roughly, that it is conceptually necessary that if I am connected to water in the right way then my thoughts are water thoughts, and it is a truism that if something is a property of water thoughts then it is a property of my thoughts if my thoughts *are* water thoughts.[18] Similarly, *mutatis mutandis*, with 6.

6. If *B* is a property that water behaviors have, then if my thoughts are water thoughts then my behaviors have *B*.

6 is conceptually necessary because, roughly, it is conceptually necessary that the behaviors that water thoughts cause are water behaviors, so it is conceptually necessary that if something is a property of water behaviors then it is a property of the behaviors of water thinkers. This is true even if *B* is a property that water behaviors have contingently, like being behaviors that are concerned with Bush's favorite drink.

Compare these cases with ones where thoughts have bona fide causal powers. Suppose that thinking about topology gives one headaches. Then we have 7:

7. If B is a property of headaches then if I have topology thoughts then my mental state has B.

7 is clearly contingent, and it is so because of the contingency of the (putative) relation between something's being a topology thought and its having headaches among its effects. Notice that 7 is contingent even if B is a property that headaches have necessarily (like being headaches).

So, here is the story. For the difference between being CP1 and being CP2 to be a difference of causal powers, it must at least be that the effects of being CP1 differ from the effects of being CP2. But, I claim, it is further required that this difference between the effects be *nonconceptually* related to the difference between the causes. This further condition is motivated both by our intuitions about the examples and by the Humean consideration that causal powers are, after all, powers to enter into nonconceptual relations. Broad-content differences, per se, do not satisfy this condition, however. There are differences between my behavior and my Twin's which are due, in the first instance, to the difference between the intentional contents of our thoughts, and, in the second instance, to my being connected to water in a way that he is not. But these differences among the effects are conceptually related to the differences between the causes; it is conceptually necessary that being connected to water rather than twater leads to water thinking rather than twater thinking; and it is again conceptually necessary that water thinking leads to water behaving and twater thinking does not.

So, then, the difference between the mental states of Twins does not count as a difference in causal power in virtue of its responsibility for the intentional differences among Twin behaviors. So argument B is no good; what is wrong with it is that the inference from 2′ to 3′ is unsound.[19] Finally, since it is assumed that the effects of mental states that differ only in broad content are (relevantly) different *only* under intentional description, it follows that there are *no* taxonomically relevant differences consequent upon broad-content differences as such. From the point of view of psychological taxonomy, my mental states must therefore belong to the same natural kind as those of my molecular Twin. So individualism is true and local supervenience is preserved. End of story.

—Oi! Halt thief! Stop that person.
—What's the matter?
—You promised me an argument *for* narrow content. But all you've given me is an argument *against* arguments against individualism. I want my money back.
—Sorry.

We have seen that twater thoughts and water thoughts are not different causal powers. So, for the psychologist's purposes, they are the same intentional state.[20] But they cannot be the same intentional state unless they have the same intentional content. And they cannot have the same intentional content unless intentional content is individuated narrowly. Now it is an argument for narrow content.

—Much obliged.
—My pleasure.

APPENDIX: A NOTE ON THE CROSS-CONTEXT TEST FOR IDENTITY OF CAUSAL POWERS

Suppose that my Twin and I are both green, but I live in red world (where everything except me is red) and he lives in green world (where everything including him is green). So then, he has a property of *being adapted to the color of his environment* which I lack. And, intuitively, this property is a causal power: because he has it, he can sneak up on things; because I lack it, I cannot. But this appears to make trouble for the idea that identity of causal powers has to be assessed *across* contexts. The cross-context test implies that there cannot be a difference in our causal powers unless there are counterfactuals that are true of one of us but not of the other; but, in the present case, it looks like the counterfactuals come out the same for him as they do for me. If he were in my world, he could not sneak up on things; if I were in his world, I could. So our causal powers are the same according to the cross-context test. So there must be something wrong with the idea that identity of causal powers should be assessed across contexts. (For elaboration of what I take to be essentially this line of argument, see Van Gulick, *op. cit.*)

But this argument is fallacious; it rests on a confusion between, to put it roughly, an attributive and a referential way of reading the definite description in "the color of his environment," with a consequent confusion about how the across-context test applies. This will only take a minute to sort out. If you read "the color of his environment" referentially, then my Twin's being adapted to the color of his environment is his being green. Read that way, then, *I too am adapted to the color of his environment* (I am green, too); so being adapted to the color of his environment is a causal power that we *share*. As, indeed, the cross-context test for causal powers properly predicts: if I were in his environment, I would be able to sneak up on things; if he were in mine, he would not. It is just that, since I am *not* in his environment and he is, being adapted to the color of his environment does him a lot more good than it does me.

If, however, you read "the color of his environment" attributively, then his being adapted to the color of his environment consists in his being the *same color as the environment that he is in*. So, if you move *that* property across contexts, then when he is in my environment his being adapted to the color of his environment consists in his being (not green like me but) *red*. So, if he is adapted to the color of his environment in *that* sense, then when we are both in my environment, he can sneak up on things and I cannot. So, according to the across-context test, being adapted to the color of his environment is a causal power that my Twin has and I lack, which is, again, the intuitively correct result.

So there is nothing wrong with the test.

(—Well, but what about the property of *being-adapted-to-the-color-of-red-world-and-in-red-world*. Is *that* not a causal power that defies the cross-context test?

—Answer: It does not *defy* the cross-context test; it merely satisfies it trivially. Red-world is the only context in which one *can* have that property.)

ENDNOTES

1. This paper is deeply indebted to conversations with Georges Rey and Steve Stich. Help from Ned Block, Anne Jacobson, Tim Maudlin, Colin McGinn, Brian McLaughlin, and Stephen Schiffer is also gratefully acknowledged, as are edifying emails from Fred Adams, Joe Levine, and David Rosenthal.

2. Here is a related case—suggested by an example of Colin McGinn's—that I take to be susceptible to the same sort of treatment. Suppose on Earth$_2$, there is not only Twin water, but also Twin salt (it is LCaN rather than NaCl). And suppose the fact is that thinking about salt makes you want water (whereas thinking about LCaN makes your Twin want XYZ). So, would there not then be a difference between the causal powers of salt thoughts and Twin salt thoughts in virtue of these differences between the contents of the wants that they cause? No, because salt thoughts do not have the power to cause water wants *come what may*; what they have is the power to cause water wants *in somebody who has the concept water*. (That is, in somebody who has the appropriate causal/historical—or whatever—connections to H$_2$O.) But, of course, Twin salt thoughts have *that* power too (just as salt thoughts have the power to cause twater wants in somebody who has the appropriate causal/historical connections to XYZ.) Here as elsewhere, one applies the cross-context test by asking whether A would have the same effects as B does have if A were to interact with the same things (in the present case, with the same mental things) with which B does interact.

   The box score is: the cross-context test shows that *certain differences that their effects have under intentional description* (namely, causing NaCl wants versus causing LCaN wants) and *certain differences that their effects have under nonintentional description* (see text) do *not* make the difference between having water thoughts and having twater thoughts a difference of causal power. We are about to see, however, that there are differences between the effects that Twin mental states exhibit under intentional description which *survive* the cross-context test. These are the ones that, *prima facie*, make trouble for individualism.

3. This, surely, is the intuitively natural way to compare causal powers. Consider:
   —"Cats raised in Manhattan unable to climb trees," top scientist says.
   —Why, that's rather disturbing. How do you explain it?
   —There aren't any trees in Manhattan for them to climb.
   —Oh.
   (For more on this, see the Appendix.)

4. It is important, in order that relevant questions not be begged, that this is all that is required for the fact that C1 has CP1 to be "responsible for" the fact that E1 has EP1 (and similarly, *mutatis mutandis*, for the fact that C2 has CP2 to be responsible for the fact that E2 has EP2.) In like spirit, nothing in the examples will depend on stressing the requirement that the Cs and the Es be related as causes and effects, so long as it is assumed that the difference between the Cs is responsible for the difference between Es in the sense just specified.

5. It will ease the exposition if we think of schema S sometimes as relating events and sometimes as relating event types. I shall exploit this ambiguity in what follows; but nothing in the argument turns on it.

6. Reminder: "Water behavior" means not *behavior that has to do with water* but *behavior that has a reference to water in its intentional description*. We are assuming (see above) that the only relevant descriptions under which the behaviors of Twins differ are intentional.

7. Another *a priori* taxonomic intuition that cries out to be taken seriously, it is [as Fodor (1988) urged] preposterous to suggest that neurological (or biochemical; or molecular) states should be taxonomized by reference to the sorts of properties that distinguish Twins in the standard examples—by whether there is water or twater in the local puddles, for example. Burge remarks that perhaps all this shows is that psychological taxonomy is more contextually sensitive than neurological taxonomy. But surely that will not run: if someone were to discover (for example) that living near high-tension wires turns your dendrites green, you can bet the neurologists would pay attention. So: what is the difference between living near high-tension wires and living near puddles of twater such that one, but not the other, is a candidate for a neurological causal power? (See below.)

8. Even being an H-particle would be a causal power in virtue of the nomological possibility of building H-particle detectors. Particle detecting is notoriously expensive and tricky; but once you have got a particle detector, it is trivial to convert it to detect H-particles. An H-particle detector is a particle detector that is hooked up to any gadget that is sensitive to which face of my coin is up. A particle detector that is hooked up to a Bulgarian grandmother would do.

9. This might well turn out to be the same question as whether "is Bronx-thirsty" and "is Queens-thirsty" are projectible; whether, for example, psychological generalizations about Bronx-thirsty people as such are confirmed by their instances.

10. This comports with the idea that, whereas *having a belief* (desire, whatever) is being in the right functional state, having a belief *that P* is a matter of having the right head-to-world relations. So the difference between having a belief that P and a belief that Q is *not* a functional difference. For more on this, see *Psychosemantics*.

11. Perhaps I had best reiterate that this is short for: ". . . a motivated condition for a difference between properties of causes being a difference in their causal powers" and that the claim is not that being a water (/twater) thought is not a causal power, but rather that the difference between having a water thought and having a twater thought is not a difference in causal power. More generally, the claim is that no two states differ in their causal powers *just* in virtue of differing in their broad contents.

12. But please, *please* keep it in mind that this solution applies in cases where, if the properties under consideration are causal powers, then they are causal powers contingently. In particular, it is *not* supposed to apply to properties that are causal powers necessarily, like dispositions. See above.

13. I want to emphasize that condition C does not impugn the Davidsonian doctrine that the necessity/contingency of relations among *events* is description-relative. Suppose *e*1 causes *e*2, so that "*e*1 causes *e*2" is contingently true. Still, there will be descriptions satisfied by *e*1 which entail (/presuppose) that *e*1 causes *e*2 (for example, such descriptions as "the cause of *e*2"; "the cause of *e*2 caused *e*2" is, of course, necessarily true). But none of this implies that there is anything description-relative about whether the instantiation of one property entails the instantiation of another (about whether, for example, it is conceptually necessary that whatever instantiates bachelorhood instantiates unmarriedness; or whether it is conceptually necessary that whatever instantiates *water-thinker-hood* instantiates *causally-connected-to-water-hood*. It is these latter sort of claims, not the former sort, which are at issue in respect of condition C.

14. By contrast, I take it that their ability to produce *meteor* craters (where a meteor crater just is a crater that is caused by a meteor) is not a causal power that meteors have over and above their power to produce craters *tout court*. This is for the now familiar sort of reason: it is conceptually necessary that, whereas a crater caused (in the right way) by a meteor is a meteor crater, a crater caused (in whatever way) by a molecularly identical nonmeteor is not. Analogously, its ability to produce sunburns is not a causal power that the sun has over and above its power to produce burns.

15. More precisely (and assuming that functionalism is right about what beliefs, desires, and the like are) to have a water thought is to have a thought that (a) is connected to water in the right way; and (b) has whatever functional properties water thoughts and twater thoughts share. I leave out (b) in the text to simplify the exposition. No doubt, the exposition could do with some of that.

16. I am indebted to Stich for this line of argument. I suppose he thinks I should be grateful.

17. 4 is necessary, however, if you choose E as some property that *everything* has necessarily; like being self-identical. This does not, of course, prejudice the present point.

18. For those following the technicalities: in effect, my original line of argument depended on there being a conceptual relation between water connectedness and water thoughts construed *de dicto*. Stich gets a *contingent* relation between water connectedness and water thoughts *de re* by invoking such contingent premises as, for example, that water is Bush's favorite drink; and thus trivially satisfies condition C. In effect, 5 provides a substantive version of C by conditionalizing on these contingent premises.

19. I can imagine that someone might now want to say: "All this follows from my conceding that the intentional properties that distinguish twins are causal powers contingently if they're causal powers at all. Well, I was wrong; those sorts of differences among broad content states are *non*contingently differences of causal powers. For example, the property of having water thoughts (rather than twater thoughts) is *identical* to the property of being able to produce water behaviors (rather than twater behaviors); the property of being connected to water (rather than twater) is *identical* to the property of being able to have water thoughts (rather than twater thoughts), etc. Notice that being soluble is a causal power even though the difference between being soluble and not is conceptually connected to the difference between dissolving and not."

   All right, but it really does not help; if having water thoughts (rather than twater thoughts) is identical to having (*inter alia*) the power to drill for water (rather than twater), then the broad-content psychological generalizations that distinguish Twins [like, "if you have water wants (rather than twater wants) then you drill for water (rather than twater)"] themselves all come out conceptually necessary (a kind of point to which Ryleans were, of course, entirely alert). So, if the assumption is that intentional states are noncontingently causal powers, then the appropriate form for the individualist's supervenience claim is that no *contingent* intentional generalization can distinguish twins (no contingent intentional generalization can be such that one but not the other of the twins satisfies its antecedent or consequent). The moral would then be: no causal laws about broad intentional states as such (in fact, just the sort of moral that Ryleans used to draw).

It is true that being soluble is a causal power even though it is conceptually connected to dissolving. But the price for thus evading condition C is the "quasilogical" status of "if soluble then dissolves."

20. —But why can this putative psychologist not allow them to be *different* states but with the *same* causal powers?

—Because, if he does, his theory misses generalizations, namely, all the generalizations that subsume me and my twin. Good taxonomy is about *not* missing generalizations.

16

All the Difference in the World

Tim Crane

I. Introduction

The celebrated "Twin Earth" arguments of Hilary Putnam (1975a) and Tyler Burge (1979a) aim to establish that some intentional states logically depend on facts external to the subjects of those states. Ascriptions of states of these kinds to a thinker entail that the thinker's environment is a certain way. It is not possible that the thinker could be in those very intentional states unless the environment is that way.

Those who accept this result are called variously "broad minded," "externalists," or "anti-individualists"; those who reject it "narrow minded," "internalists," "individualists" or "methodological solipsists." There are many subtle differences in the positions that can be taken on this issue,[1] but there is a general consensus on the significance of the Putnam/Burge arguments. The consensus is that these arguments do succeed in forcing us one way or the other: for broad mindedness or against.

My purpose in this paper is to dispute this consensus. The Putnam/Burge arguments do not, I think, force us to opt for broad or narrow mindedness. I will argue not only that their conclusions are fundamentally opposed to crucial assumptions we are obliged to make about causation and the causal role of mental states, but also that the arguments for these conclusions are unsound. There is no Twin Earth problem of the kind Putnam, Burge and many others think there is. So there is no need to respond to it with broad or narrow mindedness.

A slightly different form of broad mindedness, has been articulated and defended by Gareth Evans, (1982) and John McDowell ((1984), (1986)). This position does not use Putnam/Burge-style Twin Earth examples to generate its conclusions, and for this reason I will not discuss it here. My concern in this paper is to refute the Putnam/Burge *arguments* for broad mindedness, not broad mindedness in every form.[2]

Why another paper on Twin Earth? My approach is, I think, different from that of most writers in the field. Most writers have accepted the Twin Earth arguments as sound, and have either developed theories of the mind to account for their conclusions, or altered their theories to accommodate them. But here I shall return to Putnam's and Burge's original arguments, and dispute them. My excuse for adding another paper to the already vast literature is that if my arguments are right, they will help not just to solve, but to *dissolve* the Twin Earth problem.

II. Putnam's Thought Experiment

Putnam's original aim in "The Meaning of 'Meaning' " (1975a) was to dispute certain "grotesquely mistaken" views of language [(1975a), p. 271] which arise from philosophers' tendency to ignore the contribution made by our natural and social environment to the meanings of our words. Putnam claimed that these views depend on two incompatible assumptions about meaning. The first assumption is that knowing the meaning of a term is a matter of being in a certain psychological state—in general, the meanings of words are fixed by the psychological states of those who use them. I shall call this "MPS." The second is that meaning determines reference: a difference in reference is sufficient for a difference in meaning. I shall call this "MDR."

Putnam uses the Twin Earth story to show that these two assumptions can be true of no notion—of meaning, Fregean Sinn, Carnapian intension or whatever. (I apologize to the reader for repeating the details of this familiar story, but it is necessary, I think, in order to disentangle some of the issues involved.) Putnam asks us to suppose that "somewhere in the galaxy" there is a planet, Twin Earth, as similar as can be to Earth, except that on Twin Earth, the substance people call "water" is not made up of H_2O, but has a complex chemical constitution whose description we may abbreviate to "XYZ." XYZ feels and tastes like H_2O, and the people on Twin Earth do the same things with it. He also supposes that each of us has a duplicate "Twin" or *Doppelgänger* on Twin Earth, type-identical to each of us down to the last atom.

Now suppose that on Earth I say "Water, water everywhere, nor any drop to drink" and my Twin makes the same noises. Do we utter two sentences with the same meaning? Putnam argues that we do not, since the references of our words are different: H_2O and XYZ on Earth and Twin Earth respectively. Since the reference of the two utterances of "water" is different on each planet, then by MDR, their meanings differ. But what each speaker "has in mind" (sensations, beliefs about the superficial properties of water, etc.) is the same.

Putnam insists that this difference in meaning between Earth and Twin Earth does not depend on the fact that some scientists on each planet could *tell* that H_2O is not XYZ. To illustrate this he describes Earth and Twin Earth in 1750, before the development of adequate chemistry. In this case no one could tell the difference between the two substances; but the reference of "water" on each planet differs, according to Putnam. And since the reference differs, so does the meaning, "in the intuitive, preanalytic use of that term" [(1975a), p. 224]. This is so on the plausible assumption that the meaning of "water" does not change between 1750 and (say) 1950, simply because scientists found out more about water.

Putnam concludes that MPS is false. The psychological states of twins do not determine the reference of their utterances of "water." So if we keep MDR, as he urges we should, then certain meanings aren't determined by psychological states. Meanings aren't "in the head" [(1975a), p. 223].[3]

The argument only establishes that MPS is false if my Twin and I are in the same psychological states. So the nature of what is being referred to (H_2O or XYZ) should not affect our psychological states in this sense. These are what Putnam calls psychological states "in the narrow sense" [(1975a), p. 221], states which are permitted by "the assumption of methodological solipsism":

> that no psychological state, properly so called, presupposes the existence of any individual other than the subject to whom these states are ascribed. [(1975a), p. 220].

Psychological states which do not meet this condition are psychological states in the "wide" or "broad" sense: my Twin and I share our narrow psychological states, but differ in our broad psychological states. So what MPS really says is that the *narrow* psychological states of a language-user do not determine meaning.[4]

It is now obvious that there is an extension of Putnam's argument to intentional states in general [Colin McGinn (1977) was the first to point this out]. Assume that the contents of intentional states have truth conditions. Then if the truth conditions of my Twin's and my states differ, so do their contents; and so do the intentional states we are in. (This is what it means to say that intentional states are "individuated by their contents.") And this can happen, it is urged, without any change in our narrow states: so Putnam's argument seems to show that intentional states, like meanings, are broad.

III. WHAT IS THE PROBLEM?

Why did Putnam's argument create such a stir? He claimed that we should jettison MPS, but why did anyone believe it in the first place? After all, most philosophers of language were aware that reference—and hence meaning—had something to do with the relations between language-users and their environment, "it takes two to make a reference" as David Lewis [(1983) p. 371] has put it. So, since Putnam has done them the service of picking out some of these relations, why should anyone object to his conclusion?

One answer, which I do not endorse, comes from a "Cartesian" conviction that narrow psychological states are the only ones that matter.[5] The relevant Cartesian thesis is not substance dualism, but the idea that our states of mind are the way they are regardless of what the external world is like. How things seem to us is something to which we have immediate and authoritative "access," and can be the way it is whatever the external facts are. This thesis can then be supported by some form of physicalism: being in an intentional state is a matter of being in a certain brain state, and one's brain could exist no matter what else exists. So, since I could have all the thoughts I now have in a world in which my brain is the only object, how could I have any mental states that entail the existence of something outside my brain? Thus Searle:

> the brain is all we have for the purpose of representing the world to ourselves and everything we can use must be inside the brain. Each of our beliefs must be possible for a being who is a brain in a vat because each of us is precisely a brain in a vat; the vat is a skull and the "messages" coming in by way of impacts on the nervous system. [(1983), p. 230]

But this is precisely the picture Putnam is urging us to abandon. So it is no good to bring Cartesian "intuitions" to bear in saying why the Twin Earth case is so problematic. For it is notorious that such "intuitions" are often either deeply theory laden or as controversial as the thesis they are supposed to support. And since this Cartesian thesis is indeed extremely controversial, it will be best not to assume it in saying what is wrong with Twin Earth.

The problem with the Twin Earth result arises not from Cartesianism, nor indeed from physicalism, but from its conflict with two fundamental principles about causation and the causal nature of intentional states. The first principle is that intentional states have causes and effects. I take it as uncontroversial that beliefs, for example, are caused by perceptions and other beliefs, and combinations of beliefs and desires cause actions. This principle is crucial to the naturalistic aspirations of contemporary philosophy of mind. Naturalism is the view that mental states are as much part of the natural world as physical, chemical, biological and other natural states. There is nothing about the mental that *prohibits* it from being described and explained in principle by a science of the mental, a science that invokes laws in much the same way that other sciences do. And if the natural is in some sense the causal, we have to believe that a naturalistic theory of the mental will, in part, be a theory of how mental states have causes and effects, and under which laws they fall.

It is worth saying that naturalism is not *physicalism*, the doctrine that "chemical facts, biological facts, psychological facts and semantical facts are all explicable (in principle) in terms of physical facts" [Field (1972), p. 357]. To think that mental facts are part of the natural world, and that they participate in causal interactions which may be explained by laws, in no way entails that they must be reducible to or "explicable in terms of" physical facts. One can be a naturalist, and still believe that theories can define their own laws and concepts in their own terms, without them having to obtain a seal of approval from [see Crane & Mellor (1990)].

There is of course much opposition to naturalistic theories of the mind. But I shall not argue for naturalism here, since my aim here is to address those philosophers who are naturalistic, but who also see Twin Earth as a problem to which they have to respond. I shall argue that, properly understood, Twin Earth provides no threat to naturalism; so naturalists can rest easy. However, my argument against Putnam will be of interest to non-naturalists too, if they think that Twin Earth shows that naturalism is doomed to failure [as Putnam himself does—see Putnam (1988), ch. 1].

The second principle is about which properties of things are involved in causal interactions between them. Suppose we assume, following Lewis (1983) and many others, that a property is the semantic value of a predicate. We need to make a distinction between two kinds of properties, thus liberally conceived.[6] We should distinguish between those properties whose acquisition or loss by a particular is a *real change* in that particular, and those whose acquisition or loss is not. When I grow an inch and become six feet tall, there is a change in me. But when my brother becomes shorter than me by my growth, there is no change in him. His becoming shorter than me is a mere "Cambridge change" [see Geach (1969), p. 71, and Shoemaker (1984), pp. 207–8]. Properties of the first kind are, uncontroversially, *intrinsic* properties; and properties of the second kind are non-intrinsic.

This distinction is important because when we look for causes, we look for intrinsic properties. (Whether these are properties of particular events or of particular objects is immaterial here). My brother's becoming smaller than me when I grew was not *caused* by my growth, and neither can the fact that my brother is smaller than me have any effects. But my becoming six feet tall was caused, and it can have effects: it can, for example, cause me to knock my head on a small door frame. My height, one of my intrinsic properties, is one of my *causally efficacious* properties; while my brother's being smaller than me, one of his non-intrinsic properties, is not one of his.

I admit that the intrinsic/non-intrinsic distinction is a problematic one, and I do not claim to define it in detail here. This is because all I need is the claim that there are clear cases of intrinsic properties and clear cases of non-intrinsic properties, and that a particular's causally efficacious properties are its intrinsic properties. The second principle relevant to Twin Earth, then, is that causation generally holds between instances of intrinsic properties.

Now the worry about Twin Earth is that broad intentional states are not, and do not systematically depend on, intrinsic properties of thinkers. Being in a world that contains H_2O is plainly not an intrinsic property of mine, and nor is being in a world that contains XYZ an intrinsic property of my Twin's.[7] Yet according to Putnam, this difference *alone* gives our relevant intentional states different contents. What we are asked to believe is that my Twin's and my intentional states are different in virtue of a difference that does not depend on our intrinsic properties.

This would not matter if intentional states were not supposed to have causes and effects. There is nothing wrong with properties like being taller than my brother, or living in a world that contains XYZ. It is just that they are not causally efficacious properties. But believing that water is thirst-quenching should be, according to our naturalistic principle, a causally efficacious property. And on Putnam's account, the differences in the molecular constitution of water on Earth and Twin Earth make it the case that my Twin and I are caused to do different things—he drinks XYZ, I drink H$_2$O. In virtue of inhabiting worlds containing different watery stuff, our thoughts have different causal powers. But, if causally efficacious properties must be intrinsic, we must ask: how can there be such a difference in the causal powers of our states of mind without any mediating difference in our intrinsic properties?

This line of thought is implicit in Chapter Two of Fodor's *Psychosemantics* (1987). Unlike Putnam, Fodor wants to defend methodological solipsism—though he uses the term in a slightly different way from Putnam. Fodor distinguishes between Methodological *Solipsism* and Methodological *Individualism* [(1987), p. 42]. The latter is, for Fodor, the empirical principle that sciences individuate kinds of entities by their causal powers. The former is the psychological claim that the contents of intentional states supervene on "formal" properties of representations, items in a hypothesized "language of thought."[8] Methodological Solipsism, on this construal, is equivalent to Fodor's "formality condition" [(1980), p. 227], the claim that mental processes only have "access" to formal properties of mental representations: no mental difference without a "formal" difference.

The route from Fodor's definition of methodological solipsism to Putnam's is quite straightforward if you assume, as Fodor does, that formal properties of representations supervene on intrinsic properties of the brains of thinkers. Since *ex hypothesi*, my Twin and I do not differ in our intrinsic properties, we do not differ in the formal properties of our representations either. And since we do not differ in these properties, methodological solipsism entails that our intentional states do not differ. My Twin and I therefore share all our intentional states if we share all our intrinsic properties: so intentional states must be narrow.

In my opinion, however, Fodor weakens his case by making the dependence on intrinsic properties a high-level generalization of scientific practice. This is a weakness because it is open for the broad theorist to respond that since the science of content is as yet waiting in the wings, we should not assume that it will not individuate content broadly [this seems to be Burge's (1986) view]. This response can be blocked by showing how the assumptions that Twin Earth challenges are not just generalizations about the current practice of science, but assumptions about causation and the causal status of states of mind.

This is not of course a knock-down argument against broad mindedness. For the whole point of the broad minded argument is that it is supposed to force a *revision* in our concept of an intentional state. What Twin Earth is supposed to show is that our intentional states depend on our environment in a much more radical way than was previously thought. So obviously some of our previous assumptions are to be challenged.

But my exposition of the problem makes it clear exactly what broad mindedness must deny in holding this. It must deny either that intentional states as such have causes and effects, or that relational properties like inhabiting a world in which water is XYZ cannot have immediate effects.[9] That is, to be broad minded, you must give up one or both of the principles I outlined above. But both principles are, I think, extremely compelling. So if the Twin Earth argument were sound, it would undermine much of what we think about causation and the causal status of mental states. This is why it matters.

IV. WHAT IS WRONG WITH PUTNAM'S ARGUMENT?

I now turn to the assessment of Putnam's argument. Despite its influence, I think that reflection shows that it is inadequate, and that his positive claims are either implausible or largely irrelevant to the problems of intentionality and mental representation. However, to be fair to Putnam, I am only interested in his argument in so far as it bears on intentional states and their contents. I think some of the points he makes about language and its social character are well taken, but part of what I shall argue is that we should not be hasty in reading off claims about intentional states from claims about the use of language.

Putnam's argument rests on the following three premises:

(1) MDR—meaning determines reference.
(2) My Twin and I are atom-for-atom identical, and so (by definition) share all our narrow states.
(3) When I say "water is wet" and my Twin says the same, our sentences do not have the same truth conditions, since his water is XYZ and mine is H_2O.

From these he concludes that narrow states—the states my Twin and I share—do not determine the meanings of our words.

The argument is valid, so we must look at the premises. Premise (1) is just the assumption MDR, which we should accept (*pace*, perhaps, the case of indexicals[10]). Premise (2) is part of the story, and although it is rather irritatingly undermined by the fact that our bodies are composed of water, this is just a feature of the example. There is certainly nothing incoherent in supposing that there can be two people atom-for-atom indistinguishable.

So all the interest rests with (3). Why should we believe it? Why should a difference in the chemical structure of water affect the truth conditions of "water is wet"? Why should we not say, for instance, that if there were such a substance as XYZ, all this would show is that "not all water has the same microstructure" (Mellor (1977), p. 303). And indeed, we knew this already, since it would surely be stipulative to deny that heavy water (D_2O) is really *water*. So why does the fact that most of our water is H_2O entail that the truth conditions of "water is wet" differ across Earth and Twin Earth?

Perhaps a defender of Putnam could respond that "water" is not really a natural kind term. Perhaps we should accept that there are other kinds of water, because of the different chemical structures that can have similar superficial properties. But when you get to the names of elements you get "real" natural-kind terms—there cannot be different kinds of gold, or lead or helium.

But what about isotopes? Which isotopes of elements are the substances referred to by the "real" natural-kind terms? Which of the two isotopes of chlorine is really chlorine? Maybe they both are—but in that case "chlorine" like "water" is not a real natural-kind term either, for the same reasons. And this seems to restrict the range of real natural terms to such an extent as to make them a trivial category for metaphysics and the philosophy of science: terms that pick out elements that do not have isotopes. The obvious lesson is that the idea of a natural-kind term, as used by essentialists like Putnam, is not very well defined.[11]

It may be responded that when there is a clear case of two genuinely different elements—not isotopes of the same element—that are superficially indistinguishable, then Putnam's argument will work. This does somewhat reduce the force of the argument, but it is worth looking at such a case in some detail to see exactly what is wrong with it.

Take aluminum and molybdenum, two practically indistinguishable metals whose names (and relative scarcity) are switched on Earth and Twin Earth. And suppose my Twin and I are atom-for-atom identical. Putnam says that the meaning of "aluminum" spoken by my Twin and me is underdetermined by our narrow states—the states we share. Our narrow states determine molybdenum and aluminum as the extension of our uses of the word "aluminum." But why not therefore say that neither of us has a full understanding of the meanings of our words? Why not say that we have the same concept (call it *"molyminum"*) that applies to aluminum and molybdenum alike? The concept *molyminum* will distinguish less "finely" between substances than the concepts *aluminum* and *molybdenum*.

That there can be incomplete understanding of the meanings of words in natural language is indisputable. Indeed, it must be a premise in Putnam's own argument for the "division of linguistic labor" [(1975a), p. 227] which I will discuss briefly below. But Putnam may respond that my "common concept" response forces us to give up MDR. Since the extensions of my Twin's and my use of "aluminum" are different, then the common meaning of our utterances—the concept *molyminum*—does not determine the extensions of our uses.

I agree that the concept *molyminum* does not determine the exact extension of the Earthly word "aluminum," and nor does it determine the exact extension of the Twin Earthly word. But it still determines an extension: the extension that includes both aluminum and molybdenum. Since my Twin and I have an incomplete understanding of the word "aluminum," our concept *molyminum* does not determine the extension of "aluminum" as the concept of someone who does have a complete understanding does. Such a person, someone "in the know," has the more precise concept, and is thus in a position to correct the uses of the word "aluminum" of those speakers who do not distinguish sufficiently between aluminum and molybdenum. This is just Putnam's division of linguistic labor—but it gives us no reason to think that my Twin and I do not share our concepts. Indeed, it gives us a reason for thinking that we must share them.

The reason for this is that we should distinguish between the conventionally assigned meaning of a word in a public language, and the concept intended to be expressed by the user of that word. This distinction should not be controversial—it is needed, for instance, to make sense of ambiguity and punning. The sentence "The ship is veering to port" has at least two meanings in standard English, but a sincere competent assertion of it could only be the expression of one content [the example is from Evans (1982), p. 68]. There can be unclarity in thought, but not ambiguity.

This point is actually very important if we believe, as I think we should, that thought can be independent of public language. For after all, incomplete understanding is still understanding—there is the world of difference between my utterance of "Planes are made of aluminum," even when I cannot distinguish between aluminum and molybdenum, and the same sounds made by a monolingual Chinese speaker or a parrot. As we say, the Chinese speaker and the parrot have "no idea what they are talking about." But I do have an idea—and my Twin has the same idea—it is just not as precise an idea as that of someone in the know.

So my concept *molyminum* is not the same as the concept of someone in the know—even when the same word is used by him and me. When I say "Planes are made of aluminum" on Earth, those in the know will take me as talking about aluminum. So I will have succeeded in referring to aluminum—after all, my concept *molyminum* does include aluminum in its extension. But since there is nothing in my mind that enables me to distinguish between aluminum and molybdenum, my concept includes molybdenum in its extension as well. Similarly with my Twin—except he succeeds in talking about molybdenum, since this is how those in the know on Twin Earth would take his words. So on a number of plausible assumptions, the "aluminum" example does not show that my Twin's and my intentional states differ purely in virtue of the difference in the relative scarcity of aluminum and molybdenum, and the difference in the use of a word. So it does not show that intentional states are broad.

But what if no one is in the know? Putnam's claim about the difference in the meaning of "water" on Earth and Twin Earth in 1750 is intended to show that this does not matter. The meaning of "water" depends on its microstructure, and since H_2O is not XYZ, the meanings of utterances of "water" vary across the planets no matter who is in the know.

This cannot be right. Even if we ignore the largely unsupported assumption that the microstructure of a substance gives the meaning of a word for that substance, the point falls foul of the principle, mentioned in III, that immediate causation must go via intrinsic properties. Consider a "visiting case" when a pre-1750 Earthian travels—without his knowledge—to Twin Earth. On Putnam's view, his intentional states that are about water will be changed purely in virtue of the fact that he is now related to XYZ. But if our causal principle is right, then this cannot be a real change unless there is some change in his intrinsic properties, which *ex hypothesi* there is not. So Putnam must say that the change in his intentional states is not caused by the presence of XYZ—but there is surely little reason to accept this conclusion, given the availability of the "common concept" strategy.[12]

I conclude that Putnam's argument fails. If there are people in the know, then the public meaning of my words can "float free" of my concept, as Putnam himself admits. But this does not prevent me and my Twin having the same concept. But if no one is in the know, the concept expressed on Earth and Twin Earth by "water" applies to H_2O, XYZ, D_2O and anything else that is—how shall we put it?—*water*.

What about Putnam's positive proposals? The two major claims made about meaning are that natural-kind terms like "water" are indexical, and that there is a division of linguistic labor (a thesis I mentioned above). These two claims are intended to compensate for philosophers' lack of concern for the roles of "the world" and "other people" respectively in determining meaning. However, I think that the first claim is both false and inconsistent with other claims of Putnam's, while the second is true but irrelevant to this paper.

First, the Twin Earth cases are meant to demonstrate that the world itself can, as it were, fix the meanings of some of our words. To show how this might work, Putnam introduced the idea that natural kind words have an "unnoticed indexical component: 'water' is stuff that bears a certain similarity relation to the water round here" [(1975a), p.234]. The idea seems to be that once the reference of "water" has been fixed (perhaps by saying "This is water"; (Putnam (1975a), p.231) then the word can only refer to the substance which is relevantly similar in constitution to the substance referred to. So if meaning still determines reference, then the meaning of a term must be sensitive to the context of the use of that term. "Context" is often a vague term in this debate—a catch-all label for those things we do not understand—but in the "water" case, it is fairly clear that for Putnam, the relevant features of the context are the microstructure of water, and where the utterance is made.

It is a commonplace that indexical terms fix reference by sensitivity to context. "I," "here" and "now" refer to different speakers, places and times in different contexts of utterance. This is clearly what makes Putnam say that natural-kind terms are indexical. And he also sees a connection between this idea and Kripke's thesis that natural-kind terms are "rigid designator": they refer to the same substance in all possible worlds in which that substance exists [see Kripke (1980) pp. 3–5; Putnam says that Kripke's doctrine and his are "two ways of making the same point"; (1975a), p. 234]. So, since the Twin Earth cases are supposed to show that there is no water on Twin Earth, Putnam concludes that "water" works something like "I" in picking out different substances in relevantly different contexts.

However, even if we accept that XYZ is not water, this claim is incorrect. For if "water" is a rigid designator, then "water" as used on Twin Earth is a mere homonym of "water" as used on Earth. But indexicals are not homonyms—indexical type-expressions have a constant meaning. For example, since the work of Kaplan (1977) and Perry (1979), many accept that the constant meaning of (say) the type "here" is a function which maps contexts (places of utterance) on to a contribution to truth conditions.[13] But Putnam should hold that there is *no* constant meaning in the uses of "water" across Earth and Twin Earth, since he believes that meaning determines extension. [This is a point made by Burge (1982), p. 102.]

So if "water" is genuinely indexical, then all tokens of "water" must have a constant meaning. But this is inconsistent with the conclusion of the Twin Earth argument. On the other hand, if the Twin Earth argument is sound, then tokens of "water" spoken on both planets are mere homonyms. But this is inconsistent with the claim that "water" is an indexical. So if Putnam is to keep the conclusion of the Twin Earth argument, then he ought to abandon the claim that "water" is indexical.[14]

Putnam's second positive claim is based on his suspicion that the *communal* aspect of meaning has been ignored by philosophers of language. As I said above, it is plain that for many of the words we use, we would be unable to say exactly how to apply them. Scientific words which have passed into everyday usage, like "protein," "gene," or "evolution" would be good examples. According to Putnam, our ability to use these terms depends on a "division of linguistic labor" [(1975a), p. 227]. The users of certain terms—Putnam talks only of natural kind terms—are divided into "producers" and "consumers": there are those who have a precise grasp on how to apply a particular term, and there are those who use the term without having such a grasp. In using such terms, the consumers "defer to the experts," who have authority on what the meaning of the term is.

I think this is right, but it does not tell us much about intentional states. The division of labor is a consequence of the communal nature of language and inquiry. Consider the Quine–Neurath metaphor of the community of enquirers as sailors on a ship: some of us replace the planks in the hull, some of us weave new sails, some of us navigate, some of us repaint the figurehead and some of us cook. No one sailor can do everything on such a large ship and still keep it seaworthy— hence the division of epistemic and linguistic labor. If you are mending the sails, wait for the cook to provide your meals. But don't waste your time wondering what that fish soup is made of—or what the words "Clam Chowder" really *mean*—we have a ship to keep afloat!

This whole picture depends on the idea that there can be incomplete under-standing of the meaning of words. But as I said above, where there is incomplete understanding, there is still *some* understanding—and it is this we are interested in when analyzing intentionality. The meanings of words in a communal language can float free of the beliefs of individual speakers—but this uncontroversial description of the division of labor *presupposes* the very distinction between public meaning and belief that shows the thesis to be about public linguistic meaning, not about the contents of individuals' intentional states. In stating the thesis we have to *assume* that it is not simply about the contents of intentional states; this is why, though true, it is irrelevant to this paper.

So Putnam's main claims in "The Meaning of 'Meaning' " are either implausible or largely irrelevant to intentionality. In particular, they do not show anything about the broadness of intentional states unless implausible assumptions (e.g., essentialism about natural kinds) are made. It has been worth spelling this out, since many writers, on both broad and narrow sides, simply assume that Putnam has shown that the "ordinary notion" of an intentional state is a broad notion [e.g., Fodor (1980), Butterfield (1986), and Jackson & Pettit (1988)]. If I am right, the argument does not begin to set up the problem to which so many writers have felt the need to respond. However, perhaps Burge's version of Twin Earth fares better.

V. BURGE'S THOUGHT EXPERIMENT

Burge has used a version of Putnam's Twin Earth story to argue against "individualism," the view that "there is no necessary or deep individuative relation between the individual's being in [intentional] states . . . and the nature of the individual's physical or social environment" [(1986), p. 4]. Burge is clearly using the term "individualism" in a different way from Fodor (see section II above). For it may be that individualism in his sense is false while in Fodor's sense it is true, and vice versa. This would be so if the nature of an individual's physical or social environment had a "necessary or deep" effect on the causal powers of a thinker's thoughts.

Burge seems not to believe that intentional states must be individuated by causal powers [(1986), p. 16], but this is not the same as denying individualism in his sense. The real issue between Burge and Fodor is rather over the truth of Fodor's methodological *solipsism*: the claim that intentional states supervene on formal (i.e., intrinsic) properties. For once this "formality condition" is accepted, then differences in intentional states can only come about through differences in intrinsic properties. Burge's thought experiment is intended to show why this is false.

Here is Burge's familiar story.[15] Suppose that Alf has a large number of beliefs and desires about arthritis. Many of Alf's beliefs about arthritis are true, but he also has the false belief that he has arthritis in his thigh. His belief is false because although he "grasps" the concept of arthritis, he misapplies it in this particular case: arthritis can only occur in the joints. Now imagine a counterfactual situation in which all Alf's physical and nonintentional psychological states are the same, but in which the word "arthritis" is applied by Alf's community to many different types of rheumatoid ailments, including the disease Alf has in his thigh. In this case, Alf's belief would be true. Burge's conclusion is that in the counterfactual situation, Alf lacks some—perhaps all—of the "attitudes commonly attributed in the actual situation with content clauses containing the word 'arthritis' in oblique occurrence" [(1979a), p. 75]. In other words, in the counterfactual situation Alf has no beliefs (or desires, etc.) about arthritis. This is because he does not have the *concept* of arthritis in the counterfactual situation. He has a different concept, which he expresses by using the word "arthritis." Yet *ex hypothesi* Alf's intrinsic properties have not changed in both situations.

Burge's thought experiment differs from Putnam's in two significant ways. First, it is concerned directly with the contents of intentional states, not just with word-meaning; an extension which, as we saw, Putnam could have made himself. And second, it does not just apply to "natural kind" terms, but it can be applied to any term that someone could mistakenly misuse [see Burge (1986b)]. The general point of the argument is that we can conceive of counterfactual situations in which all the physical and nonintentional psychological states of a thinker are the same as in an actual case, but in which the thinker's intentional states vary because of a difference in some feature of his or her linguistic environment.

VI. WHAT IS WRONG WITH BURGE'S ARGUMENT?

Burge's argument raises the same worry as Putnam's. If immediate causation acts only via intrinsic properties of things, how can a difference in the contents of two subjects' intentional states have any causal manifestation if there is no intrinsic difference between the subjects? Burge thinks that the intentional states of actual and counterfactual Alf are different, and that this difference is due simply to a difference in the uses of words in their linguistic communities. It has no reflection in their intrinsic properties. Of course, there are many links between thinkers' thoughts and the linguistic practice of their communities—and many of the links are surely causal. The problem for Burge is to say how this can happen without affecting thinkers' intrinsic properties.

In his most recent criticism of Burge, Fodor (1987) has a similar objection. He wants to defend mind/brain supervenience, which he thinks is "the best idea that anyone has had so far about how mental causation is possible" [(1987), p. 30]. Burge (1986) rejects supervenience, though he does believe that intentional states supervene on physical properties of the brain-plus-environment. Fodor objects, in effect, that Burge's thesis provides no way of accounting for the fact that causal relations hold between intrinsic properties of things:

> you can't affect the causal powers of a person's mental state without affecting his physiology. That's not a conceptual claim or a metaphysical claim of course. It's a contingent fact about how God made the world. God made the world such that the mechanisms by which environmental variables affect organic [sic.] behaviors run via their effects on the organism's nervous system. Or so, at least, all the physiologists I know assure me. [(1987a), pp. 39–40]

Burge will respond that Fodor's objection begs the question by simply assuming the truth of supervenience; after all, part of what Burge wants to establish is that there is a way in which thinkers' intentional states can be "affected" without affecting their physiology. But as we saw in section III, Fodor's objection can be made more powerful, and more general, by recognizing that the point about the causally mediating properties is not so much that they should be physiological, but that they should be *intrinsic*. (And I suppose this is a "conceptual or meta-physical claim.")[16]

Burge responds to the Fodorean objection by saying that it confuses "causation with individuation" [(1986), p. 16]. Indeed it does associate causation with individuation; but there is no confusion. Fodor is absolutely right to say that theories do, and should, individuate properties by their causal powers or dispositions. There will always be other ways of describing and picking out properties, but when our concern is with what happens and why, we should look for causal powers.

Given this objection, it will be instructive to analyze the stages in Burge's actual argument, to see what is wrong with it. In doing so, we will learn something about the relation between thought and language, just as we did when discussing Putnam.

As we saw, Burge's thought experiment is supposed to work using any concept that a thinker could mistakenly apply. To begin with, we should distinguish between what I shall call Burge's *linguistic* and his *non-linguistic* thought experiments. Although he emphasizes the role of the linguistic community in shaping content, Burge does not want to argue that one needs to have a language in order to have intentional states. Indeed, in his more recent papers, he has tried to formulate his thought experiment in such a way that it applies to all types of content, not just that expressed or expressible by language-users [(1986); (1986a)]. But for this purpose he has to introduce a different set of considerations, to play an analogous role to the one played by the practice of the linguistic community in the original thought experiment. So we should consider the linguistic and non-linguistic cases separately.

To see what is wrong with Burge's linguistic thought experiment, I suggest that we should look more closely at the source of the alleged error in actual Alf's belief. In order for Alf to express his belief with the sentence "I have arthritis in my thigh," not only does he have to believe that the disease he has in his thigh is arthritis, but also that the sentence "I have arthritis in my thigh" is the right one to express this belief. For beliefs to be expressed in words, they have to go via second-order beliefs about which words are the right ones for expressing which beliefs: sentences do not, as it were, just "squirt out" beliefs.

So Alf's error is introduced either by the belief (1) that *I have arthritis in my thigh*, or by his belief that "*I have arthritis in my thigh*" *is the right sentence to express this belief*, or by both. [In (2), "this belief" refers not to (1) but to whatever first-order belief Alf is having about the disease in his thigh.] Clearly, the latter belief (2) is false. But what about the former? To describe Alf's beliefs correctly, we have to choose between: first, attributing to him a concept *tharthritis* which applies to both arthritis and whatever is the disease he has in his thigh; and second, attributing to him the public concept *arthritis*. The first attribution would entail that his first-order belief is really *I have tharthritis in my thigh* and is true; the second would entail that it is belief (1) and false.[17] Which attribution is right?

Linguistic evidence is not enough to decide this. For as we saw, the falsity of Alf's belief that "*I have arthritis in my thigh*" *is the right sentence to express this belief* is enough to explain why his utterance of "I have arthritis in my thigh" is false. So the utterance's falsity cannot be used as evidence in deciding between the first and the second attributions. What about non-linguistic evidence? It has been persuasively argued by Ned Block that a problem with Burge's thesis is presented by the fact that a psychologist would not be able to distinguish between the non-verbal behavior (e.g., food preferences, in the "brisket" example) of two Burgean twins in certain experimental situations [Block is referred to by Fodor (1987), p. 40]. This would seem to be so in our case too: up to the time described by the thought experiment, Alf has *(ex hypothesi)* all the same dispositions to (non-verbal) behavior in the actual and the counterfactual situations. This suggests that we should attribute the concept *tharthritis* to him.

And indeed this does seem to be the right thing to do. For until actual Alf is able to correct his belief about the meaning of the word "arthritis," there is no reason as yet to suppose that he can discriminate between arthritis and tharthritis. So his concept—which at the very least must reflect an ability to discriminate—will apply to arthritis and tharthritis alike.

On this diagnosis, then, Alf has a true belief, *I have tharthritis in my thigh,* a false belief to the effect that *"I have arthritis in my thigh" is the right sentence to express this belief,* and thus makes a false statement, "I have arthritis in my thigh." This means that though his belief is true, he says something false when he attempts to express it. This sounds paradoxical, but it becomes clear when we distinguish, as we did when discussing Putnam, between the meanings of sentences in public languages and the contents of beliefs.

As we saw above, once words in a language are endowed with meaning, there "opens up the possibility of a gap between what a speaker means to say by uttering certain words—what [content] he wishes to express—on the one hand, and what he strictly, and literally says, according to the conventional meanings of the words he utters, on the other" [Evans (1982), p. 67]. As we saw, the existence of ambiguity and punning clearly show the need for postulating such a gap. Also, I can say something by uttering "p" without knowing the precise meaning of "p" and thus without expressing a belief of mine by my utterance. It is therefore quite unsurprising that there should be cases, like Burge's, where a thinker may have a true belief, *p,* but yet utter a falsehood because of a mistaken belief about which words are the right ones to express *p.*

The key idea here is that the expression of beliefs in language is mediated by beliefs about which words to use. And this is a point which I think Burge does not sufficiently appreciate. In his paper, "Belief and Synonymy," he argues that we can quite easily make sense of someone who says

> For years I believed that a fortnight was ten days, not fourteen, though of course I never believed that fourteen days were ten days. [(1978), p. 126]

without having to attribute him any "metalinguistic" beliefs about the meanings of his words. Now indeed this remark makes perfectly good sense, and one who utters it does not say something contradictory. But surely this is only because we should construe the speaker's previous erroneous belief as involving a mistaken belief about the meaning of "fortnight." What the speaker believed was that "fortnight" means a period of *ten days*. What else could his belief be? There is nothing more to being a fortnight than being a period of fourteen days; there would be nothing *about fortnights* for the speaker's beliefs to latch on to, apart from the definition of "fortnight."

Burge considers this response but dismisses it, chiefly on the grounds that (a) thinkers need have no beliefs about meanings in order to think a fortnight is ten days [see, e.g., (1978), p. 126]; and (b) this way of construing the belief "does not accord with our ordinary attributions of belief" [(1978), p. 132]. Neither point is persuasive. It is true that one needs no beliefs about meaning, truth or reference in order to think; but to express one's thoughts in words, it is not possible that one should lack beliefs about these things. Imagine asking a speaker, "Do you believe that the word 'fortnight' means a period of ten days?" The speaker will answer "Yes," "No" or "I'm not sure" in each case, expressing a belief about the meaning of a word.

As for (b), this is simply debatable. Burge seems to treat the particular sentence used by a thinker to express a belief as a transparent medium, through which the ascriber of a belief can simply gaze and read off its content.[18] But surely the business of ascribing beliefs is rarely like this. In working out what others think, we often need to question them further, translate their use of words into our "idiolects," and redescribe their attitudes as evidence accumulates. We do not, as Burge urges we should [(1978), p. 132], take utterances like the one above at face value, any more than we would take a speaker's sincere utterance of "I have a hippopotamus in my refrigerator" at face value [Davidson (1984), pp. 100–1].[19]

So this is why I think it plausible to say that in our *arthritis* example, Alf has one true belief, one false one and makes a false (public language) statement. Of course there are, as a matter of fact, concepts whose possession requires knowing a public language. But this does not yield Burge's conclusion, since it is consistent with holding that the relations between a community's linguistic practice and an individual's behavior have to be mediated by their intrinsic properties—a thesis Burge implicitly denies.

However, it appears that if this analysis of Burge's case is right, then thinkers cannot make certain sorts of mistake.[20] I said that it was more plausible to treat Alf and counterfactual Alf as having the same concept, *tharthritis*, with the result that they both have true beliefs about tharthritis while actual Alf has a false belief about what "arthritis" means. But, it may be said, it seems that if this procedure is generalized, we can always explain away the appearance of an error in a thinker's belief, when that belief is not about the meaning of a word, by attributing to him a different concept. So when someone mistakenly thinks that *a is F*, we can explain away this error by attributing to him a non-standard concept *F**, which has *a* in its extension. No one should doubt that thinkers can have non-standard concepts; but it is equally undeniable that thinkers make simple mistakes. It might appear that my analysis of Burge's case assimilates the second sort of case to the first:

there can be mistakes in perception, and in beliefs about what words mean, but there cannot be mistakes in the beliefs in between.

This would be an unacceptable result. We often make mistakes in thought, and a theory of thought must explain this. But in fact my analysis of Burge's case can cope with this, as long as the right distinctions are made. When working out what thinkers believe, we have to take into account not only the evidence of what they say or do at a particular time, but what they *would* say or do under other circumstances. That is, we have to consider which counterfactuals are true of them. Taking only the evidence of one utterance or one action will, of course, radically underdetermine the correct ascription of the thinker's beliefs.

Such limited evidence will also underdetermine whether a thinker makes a genuine mistake or has a non-standard concept. Suppose we have *prima facie* evidence that a thinker, T, believes that an object, *a*, has a certain property, F, when it does not. What settles whether T falsely believes that *a is F* or truly believes that *a is F** is just which counterfactuals are true of T. If T would apparently believe, when confronted with *a* on another occasion, that it is F, then we might be tempted to think that he has a concept F*. If T would (apparently) believe, for instance, that some things that are similar to *a* are also F (when they are not), then this would support the attribution of F*. If T is a sophisticated thinker, T may, under questioning, offer other beliefs of his about *a*, connected in more or less consistent ways. This would again support the attribution to T of the belief that *a is F**. We may be thereby entitled to attribute to T a slightly off-beat *theory*, in which the concept F* figures, and applies to *a* and things similar to it.

If, on the other hand, T would not be disposed to believe that some things similar to *a* are F, and would not have many other beliefs to call upon in support of his (apparent) belief that *a is F*, then T's belief that *a is F* is a mere "slip of the mind"—a mistake, but one that does not infect the identity of the concept. It is hard, without a theory of concepts and of error, to say here exactly which counterfactuals are essential to having the belief that *a is F* at all. But what matters here is that if it is granted, as it should be, that the two sorts of case are different, then my analysis of Burge's thought experiment will go through. This is because Burge's "arthritis" case is much more like the first case than the second. We are told that actual Alf has lots of true beliefs "about arthritis." He thinks he has a disease of the joints, that it is very painful, and that he has the same disease in his thigh. So he thinks the disease he has in his thigh can occur in muscles. He has an off-beat theory of the various ailments he has—not a very well-informed theory, but a theory none the less. This is why I say he has the concept *tharthritis*, one that he shares with his counterfactual "twin." Of course, since this concept does not fit the usage of actual Alf's community, it is the wrong concept for him to have: he is wrong to think that there is such a disease as tharthritis. But what I am urging is the importance of distinguishing this belief from the belief that he has arthritis in his thigh—a belief that neither Alf nor his counterfactual twin has.[21]

Much more needs to be said: about how, in general, error comes about, about how to distinguish, in a principled way, between errors and nonstandard concepts, and about how to individuate concepts. None of these questions have easy answers, but all I need for the purposes of this paper is to show why my analysis of Burge's cases does not rule out the possibility of any error. And this much, I claim, can be done.

So that is how I deal with Burge's linguistic thought experiment. But Burge also wants to show that even intentional states which are not essentially expressible in a public language are non-individualistic. However, I shall not deal with Burge's non-linguistic thought experiment, and its ingenious application to Marr's theory of vision, since I think these arguments have been refuted by Gabriel Segal (1989b) and I refer the reader to the details of Segal's paper. My target in this paper has been Burge's linguistic thought experiment.

VII. NEITHER BROAD NOR NARROW

So Burge and Putnam fail to provide good arguments for the conclusion that intentional states are broad. Nor do they show that the constitution of natural kinds or the linguistic practice of a community affects the identity of intentional states in the way their thought experiments say. But this does not mean that we should retreat from broad mindedness into a narrow minded position. In particular, we should not suppose that what my Twin and I (or Alf and counterfactual Alf) have in common is an attitude to a *"narrow content"* [see Fodor (1987), ch. 2; Block (1987)]. Nor should we be thereby committed to a "Two Component" theory of content which says that intentional states are composite states, involving a broad "component" which, as Twin Earth shows, determines the reference and truth condition of the state's content, and a narrow, "internal" component which is responsible for the causation of behavior [see McGinn (1982), pp. 208–16].

The reason why narrow mindedness is not the alternative to the Putnam/Burge thesis is that narrow mindedness, and the notion of narrow content, were only introduced in response to the challenge of Twin Earth. So if I am right that Twin Earth presents no real challenge, then there is no need to define a notion of narrow content in response. So neither Fodor nor anyone else needs narrow content. Narrow content is a specious notion constructed only out of a desperate need to solve the Twin Earth problem—but this problem can be dissolved before we need to postulate narrow content.

Of course, if narrow states are just, by definition, states that any pair of "Twins" share, then I accept that intentional states are narrow states. But this does not mean that these states do not have content in the ordinary, truth-conditional sense. It is just that any difference in the contents of these states must be mediated by a difference in their intrinsic properties. To put it in terms reminiscent of Fodor's formality condition: there is no difference in content without some intervening difference in intrinsic properties.

So if intentional states are to be the causes of behavior, they have to cause behavior indirectly, via some intrinsic property of the thinker. Fodor agrees [e.g., (1981), pp. 201–2], and he also agrees that these intrinsic properties—"mental representations"—must be *correlated* with the contents of these states, to give them the right causes and effects. For instance, the intrinsic properties of my belief that water is wet must be correlated (somehow!) with the content *water is wet* in order for it to cause me to ask for water and not whiskey at the bar. And the intrinsic properties of my desire for water must be correlated (somehow!) with the content *I drink some water* in order for my action—asking for water—to result in the satisfaction (or not) of *this* desire.

To say how thinkers' intrinsic properties are correlated with the contents of their thoughts would be to solve the problem of intentionality. Unfortunately, I do not have a solution to this problem. But if what I say here is right, then the Twin Earth argument has to be dissolved before the problem of intentionality is solved. This is because the Twin Earth argument entails either that intentional states are not the causes of behavior; or that the contents of intentional states can affect what they cause without any intrinsic causal mechanism. If the first of these is true, then there really is no problem of intentionality; and if the second is true, then the problem of intentionality is solved by something like an appeal to magic. I think neither of these are satisfactory solutions to the problem: dissolving Twin Earth is the only option.

So Putnam and Burge have not shown intentional states to be broad. Burge's twins differ only in the truth values of their beliefs about the right word to use in their communities; Putnam's twins may differ in this way too (cf. "aluminum") or they only differ according to an essentialist redescription of the contents of their thoughts (cf. "water"), a description that tells us nothing about psychological reality, since the alleged difference in no way affects their relevant intrinsic properties. The first difference depends on a difference in communal linguistic practice, but does not show much about intentional states; the second alleged difference is the consequence of an undefended and implausible essentialism. So the path is cleared for the natural, obvious conclusion: what the twins have in common is a state with ordinary, truth-conditional content: nothing more, nothing less. All the differences are in the world.[22]

ENDNOTES

1. In addition to Putnam's (1988) and Burge's (Burge (1982), (1986), (1986a), (1986b)) other work, three collections of papers stand out: Woodfield (1982), Butterfield (1986b) (both largely narrow minded) and McDowell & Pettit (1986) (the broad minded backlash). For elaboration of some of the varieties of broad and narrow mindedness, see Blackburn (1984), ch.9, Butterfield (1986) and McGinn (1989), ch. 1, esp. pp. 3ff.
2. But see Segal (1989a) for criticism of McDowell. For criticism of Evans, see Blackburn (1984), ch.9, Noonan (1986), and Carruthers (1987).

3. The "in the head" locution has come in for a lot of criticism. As Davidson (1987) points out: to say that a certain condition of my skin is sunburn is to identify it by its cause. A twin with a type-identical skin condition which was not caused by the sun would not be sunburned. But this fact does not prevent my sunburn from being "in" me. So it does not follow from the fact that a thinker's state (e.g., knowing the meaning of "water") is identified in terms of its causal history that the state is not properly a state of the thinker—not "in" that thinker's head. For this reason, I will refrain from talking about states being in or outside the head. There are clearer ways to put the broad/narrow distinction.

4. In order for Putnam's definition of methodological solipsism to fit his story, narrow psychological states should fail to presuppose not just the existence of particular objects, but facts about the (e.g.,) chemical makeup of the substances they are about. For more on the definition of methodological solipsism, see Burge [(1986a), pp. 112–14]; Noonan (1984); Butterfield [(1986) pp.99–100]. However, Twin Earth arguments can be used to support the thesis that some thoughts entail the existence of particular *objects* (see e.g., McCulloch [(1986), pp. 62–3]) but I think it is important to keep this thesis distinct from the precise claims of Putnam (1975a).

5. See for instance Bach [(1982), p. 127]; and McGinn [(1989) p. 33]. Many broad minded philosophers have brought the charge of Cartesianism against narrow theorists [see, in particular, McDowell (1986)].

6. Some writers have a causal test for real properties—e.g., Mellor (1981), and Shoemaker (1984)—and so would rule out being taller than my brother as a real property on these grounds. I am sympathetic to this approach, but it suits my expository purposes to begin by treating properties as the semantic values of predicates.

7. We now come up against an irritating kink in Putnam's original story: our intrinsic properties *are* different, because most of our bodies are composed of water! I will follow most writers in treating this fact as irrelevant [see Dennett (1982), p. 11; McDowell & Pettit (1986), p. 2] so I hope the reader will bear with me in what follows.

8. For the idea of a language of thought, see Fodor (1975), (1981), (1987) appendix; and Field (1978). I defend the coherence of the language of thought hypothesis in Crane (1990).

9. It is clear what Putnam thinks: "Only if we assume that psychological states in the narrow sense have a significant degree of causal closure . . . is there any point in . . . making the assumption of Methodological Solipsism. But three centuries of failure of mentalistic psychology is tremendous evidence against this procedure, in my opinion" [(1975a), p. 221]. Putnam (1988) develops this line of thought in a critique of functionalism.

10. The idea being, of course, that for an indexical, meaning-plus-context determines reference [see Kaplan (1977), Perry (1979)]. See below on Putnam's application of the semantics of indexicals to the "water" case. Fodor has attempted to generalize this feature of indexicals to all contents to account for Twin Earth: "narrow" content, he says, is a function from context to truth-conditions [(1987), ch. 2]. The difficulties for this proposal are many—but if my approach to Twin Earth is taken, there will be no need to introduce the notion of narrow content, as we shall see.

11. For a refutation of the Kripke/Putnam view of natural kinds, see Mellor (1977). I am indebted to this paper, and to Dupré (1981).

12. Colin McGinn has argued that Putnam's argument depends on the "highly compelling and intuitive thesis" that "perceptual seemings are not necessarily as fine-grained as

the reality that causes them" [(1989), p. 32]. For him, the argument is a special case of the plausible claim that how things seem to us does not determine how they are: for a thinker's thoughts about the superficial properties of water (the "seemings") do not alone determine the reference of those thoughts (the "reality"). But Putnam's argument needs more than this. To hold that XYZ and H_2O are both water—and therefore to say that my Twin and I share our water-thoughts—is consistent with holding that the relevant seemings can be mistaken—my Twin and I can both be wrong about whether what we have before us is indeed water. To get to Putnam's conclusion, we have to add the tendentious assumption, which I deny, that the relevant feature of the reality in question is the microstructure of water.

13. I am not denying that it is a difficult task to explain how a token indexical refers in a context—for some discussion, see Perry (1979), Kaplan (1977), Evans (1982) and Mellor (1989).

14. The fact that the reference of "water" may be fixed by a "baptism" *using* an indexical is irrelevant, since Putnam will surely agree with Kripke [(1980), pp. 55–8] that fixing the reference of a term does not amount to giving its meaning.

15. Burge has given many versions of his story, some more elaborate than others [(1986b) gives the most recent and elaborate version]. For my purposes, these differences do not matter, since I want to capture the essentials of his argument.

16. Putting the point this way isolates Fodor's objection from the commitment to mind-brain supervenience—which may make it more acceptable to some. For doubts about supervenience, see Crane & Mellor (1990), 5.

17. I claim no great originality for the "tharthritis" move; it is a natural response to Burge, and one that he has not, I think, adequately refuted.

18. Here I agree with Kent Bach, who challenges Burge's "assumption that when we use a term in the 'that'-clause of an attitude attribution literally and correctly, we must be ascribing the notion [concept] expressed by the term to the content of the attitude" [Bach (1988), p. 88].

19. The point derives from Quine: "Assertions startlingly false on the face of them are likely to turn on hidden differences of language. The maxim is strong enough in all of us to swerve us even from the homophonic method that is so fundamental to the very acquisition and use of one's mother tongue" [(1960), p. 59].

20. Here I am grateful to Mark Sainsbury.

21. Again, my sympathies are with the letter, though not the spirit, of some of Davidson's remarks on interpretation. Davidson says that he does "not find Burge's thought-experiment as persuasive as Burge does; they seem to me at best to encourage us to consider what principles we use in (correctly) interpreting the thoughts and words of others" [(1988), p. 665].

22. I am grateful to the participants at a meeting of the Wolfson Philosophy Society in Oxford, and to Tom Baldwin, Jeremy Butterfield, Naomi Eilan, Melinda Hogan, Greg McCulloch, Hugh Mellor, Mark Sainsbury and especially Gabriel Segal for discussions that have helped me with this paper.

17

Putnam on Mind and Meaning

John McDowell

1. TO BEGIN WITH IN "The Meaning of 'Meaning',"[1] and in a number of writings since then, Hilary Putnam has argued trenchantly, and I think convincingly, that in the case of at least certain sorts of words, the environment of those who use them enters into determining their extension. We cannot understand what constitutes the fact that a natural-kind word like "water," as used by ordinarily competent speakers of English, has the extension it does without appealing to the actual scientifically discoverable nature of a stuff that figures in their lives in a way that has an appropriate connection to the correct use of the word, and to facts of a broadly sociological kind about relations within the community of English speakers. Now it seems plausible that the extension of a word as a speaker uses it should be a function of its meaning; otherwise we lose some links that seem to be simply common sense—not part of some possibly contentious philosophical theory—between what words mean on speakers' lips, what those speakers say when they utter those words, and how things have to be for what they say to be true.[2] If we keep those links, Putnam's thesis about extension carries over to meaning: that a speaker means what she does by "water" must be constituted at least in part by her physical and social environment. As Putnam memorably puts it: "Cut the pie anyway you like, 'meanings' just ain't in the *head*!"[3]

I have rehearsed this basic thesis of Putnam's in a deliberately unspecific way. The question I want to raise in this paper does not require going into possibly disputable details about how the physical and social environments serve to determine extension, or how the roles of the physical and social environments might be related.[4] Nor do I need to go into the question of how far similar theses can be made out to apply beyond the original case of words for natural kinds.[5] I am going to take it for granted that, however such details are to be spelled out, Putnam is right in this basic thesis: at least some meanings are at least in part environmentally constituted. My question is at a more abstract level. I want to ask what significance the basic thesis has for how we ought to conceive the nature of the mind.

2. One might take it to be another simply intuitive idea, not a bit of possibly contentious philosophical theory, that command of a word's meaning is a mental capacity, and exercise of such command is a mental act—an act of the intellect and therefore, surely, of the mind. In that case the moral of Putnam's basic

305

thought for the nature of the mental might be, to put it in his terms, that the mind—the locus of our manipulations of meanings—is not in the head either. Meanings are in the mind, but, as the argument establishes, they cannot be in the head; therefore, we ought to conclude, the mind is not in the head. Rather than arguing, as Putnam does, that the assumption that extension is determined by meanings will not cohere with the assumption that knowledge of meanings is wholly a matter of how things are in a subject's mind, we should insist on making the two assumptions cohere and conceive the mind in whatever way that requires.

I want to pursue this line, and urge a reading of the claim that the mind is not in the head that ought, I believe, to be congenial to Putnam, although as far as I can tell it goes missing from the space of possibilities as he considers things, which is organized by the idea that the two assumptions cannot be made out to be compatible.

3. Putnam's argument works against the theory that he sets up as its target, just because the theory is stipulated to include the claim that the mind is in the head. Another way of putting that claim is to say that states of mind in some strict or proper sense, are what Putnam calls "psychological states in the narrow sense": that is, states whose attribution to a subject entails nothing about her environment.[6] The idea of "psychological states in the narrow sense" contrasts with the idea of "psychological states in the wide sense": these are attributed by intuitively psychological attributions that involve the attributor in commitments about the attributee's environment, as for instance "x is jealous of y" commits the attributor to the existence of y. The conception of meaning that Putnam attacks embodies the claim that knowledge of a meaning is exhausted by a certain psychological state, with "psychological state" stipulated to mean "psychological state in the narrow sense."

Now if we try to preserve the thought that knowledge of a meaning is a psychological state, consistently with Putnam's basic thesis that meanings are environmentally constituted, we have to suppose that knowledge of a meaning (at least the kind that Putnam's thesis applies to) is a "psychological state in the wide sense." And if we try to make sense of that while maintaining the idea that the mental in a strict or proper sense is characterized by "narrow" psychological attributions, we have to suppose that knowledge of a meaning (of the relevant kind), qua mental, is, in itself, a "narrow" psychological state, which, however, can be characterized as knowledge of a physical and social environment. On this picture, knowledge of a meaning is, in itself, in the head; the moral of Putnam's basic thought is that we need to be looking at relations between what is in the head and what is not, if it is to be available to us that knowledge of a meaning (at least if it is a meaning of the relevant kind) is what some state, in itself in the head, is.

According to this picture, then, there is a sense in which the mind is in the head: that is where the relevant states and occurrences are. But this picture does yield a sense in which we might say that the mind is (at least partly) not in the head: the characterizations that display the relevant states and occurrences as ("wide") content-involving states and occurrences are characterizations, in terms of meanings of sorts to which Putnam's argument applies, and hence characterizations that get a grip on the states and occurrences only on the basis of relations between the subject and the environment. At least some distinctively mental truths cannot come into view except in an inquiry that takes account of how the mind in question is related to its environment.

The conclusion of this line of thought is that the concept of command of a meaning (at least of the kind that Putnam's argument applies to) is constitutively "duplex," as Colin McGinn puts it: it is the concept of something that is, in itself, in the head, but conceived in terms of its relations to what is outside the head. And this line of thought obviously extends from knowledge of the meaning of "water" (and whatever other meanings Putnam's argument, or something of similar effect, applies to) to, say, beliefs or occurrent thoughts about water (and similarly for whatever other meanings are relevant). It is widely supposed that Putnam's considerations compel a "duplex" conception of at least large tracts of our thought and talk about the mental. The idea is that part of the complete truth about the mind is the truth about something wholly in the head; another part of the complete truth about the mind is the truth about how the subject matter of the first part is related to things outside the head.[7]

4. This reading of the idea that the mind is not in the head is not what I meant when I suggested that the idea ought to be congenial to Putnam.

This reading preserves a role for what is in the head, in the constitution of knowledge of meanings, or more generally in the constitution of psychological states and occurrences such as beliefs or thoughts about water, to which Putnam's claim of environmental determination clearly extends. What is the attraction of this? I think the answer is that, on this "duplex" conception, at least one component of the constitutive truth about the psychological in the "wide" sense looks like an unquestionably suitable topic for a straightforwardly natural science, a science that would investigate how states and occurrences in the head are responsive to impacts from the environment, interact with one another, and figure in the generation of behavior. In his *Representation and Reality*[8] and elsewhere, Putnam argues that the role played by interpretation, in a proper account of the import of psychological characterizations in terms of ("wide") content, ensures that psychology *in general* cannot be within the scope of natural science. But, however convinced we might be by such arguments, there would still be some comfort for a scientistic orientation to the mental in the idea that, all the same, science can in principle be done, and indeed is already being done, about the intrinsic natures of the states and occurrences—in themselves in the head—that those "wide" characterizations get a grip on, in ways that, according to such arguments, are not amenable to scientific treatment.

On this account, what makes the "duplex" reading of the thesis that the mind is not in the head attractive is that, by leaving part of the truth about the mind wholly in the head, it offers comfort to a possibly residual scientism about how our understanding of the mental works.[9] But at least since his conversion from scientific realism, Putnam's explicit attitude towards scientism has been one of staunch opposition. When I suggested that the thesis could be read in a way that ought to be congenial to Putnam, I had in mind a reading that would not make even this residual concession to scientism. I had in mind a reading that would place our talk about knowledge of meanings, thoughts about water, and so forth entirely out of the reach of a scientistic conception of the role played by our mental lives in our understanding of ourselves and others.

5. It will be helpful to distinguish a second possible reading of the thesis that the mind is not in the head from the one I mean.

This reading is like the one I mean in that it focuses on the literal meaning of "in the head." We might begin explaining the point of denying that the mind is in the head by saying that the mind is not spatially located at all, except perhaps unspecifically, where its owner is. The mind is not somewhere in particular in the literal, spatial, interior of its owner; it is not to be equated with a materially constituted and space-occupying organ, such as the brain.

But on the conception I am considering now, the mind is still conceived as an organ: it is just that it is not the brain but an immaterial organ. (A well-placed embarrassment might induce one to add "so to speak.") What I mean by saying that the mind is conceived as an organ is that states of affairs and occurrences in a mind are, on this view no less than on the view that the mind is literally in the head, taken to have an intrinsic nature that is independent of how the mind's possessor is placed in the environment. It is just that this intrinsic nature is not conceived as capturable in the terms of any science that deals with matter, for instance, neurophysiological terms.

This reading of the thesis that the mind is not in the head clearly cannot serve my purpose, because it is obvious that this conception of the mind, as an immaterial organ of psychological activity, does not open up a possibility of evading Putnam's argument, so that we could after all locate knowledge of meanings wholly in the mind. Characterizations of the mind, as it is in itself, are no less "narrow" on this picture than they are if conceived as characterizations of what is literally in the head. And Putnam's point is obviously not just that what is literally in the head cannot amount to knowledge of meanings, to the extent to which knowledge of meanings is environmentally constituted. *Nothing* "narrow," whether material or (supposing we believed in such things) immaterial, can amount to something that is environmentally constituted. We can put the point by saying that the phrase "in the head," in Putnam's formulation of his basic thesis, is already not restricted to a literal, spatial reading. When Putnam says that meanings are not in the head, that is a vivid way of saying that no "narrow" psychological attribution can amount to knowledge of a meaning of the relevant sort, whether it is a material or an immaterial organ of thought in virtue of whose internal arrangements such attributions are conceived as true.

6. I can now sketch the interpretation I mean for the thesis that the mind is not in the head. On this interpretation, the point of the thesis is not just to reject a

more specific spatial location for someone's mind than that it is where its possessor is. It is to reject the whole idea that the mind can appropriately be
conceived as an organ: if not a materially constituted organ, then an immaterially
constituted organ. As I said, the cash value of this talk of organs is the idea that
states and occurrences "in" the mind have an intrinsic nature that is independent
of how the mind's possessor is placed in the environment. So the point of the
different interpretation is to reject that idea altogether. Talk of minds is talk of
subjects of mental life, insofar as they are subjects of mental life; and, on the
interpretation I mean, it is only a prejudice, which we should discard, that mental
life must be conceived as taking place in an organ, so that its states and occurrences are intrinsically independent of relations to what is outside the organism.

Of course there is an organ, the brain, whose proper functioning is necessary to
mental life. But that is not to say that the proper functioning of that organ is what
mental life, in itself, is. And if we deny that, we need not be suggesting instead
that mental life is, in itself, the functioning of a mysteriously immaterial para-
organ (an organ "so to speak"). Mental life is an aspect of *our* lives, and the idea
that it takes place in the mind can, and should, be detached from the idea that
there is a part of us, whether material or (supposing this made sense) immaterial,
in which it takes place. Where mental life takes place need not be pinpointed any
more precisely than by saying that it takes place where our lives take place. And
then its states and occurrences can be no less intrinsically related to our environment than our lives are.

7. Putnam himself expresses skepticism about whether there is any point in
reconstructing the intuitive or pre-theoretical conception of the mental, which
counts "wide" states like jealousy as psychological, in the way that is prescribed by
"methodological solipsism": that is, the thesis that psychological states in a strict
and proper sense are "narrow."[10] That skepticism seems to recommend pushing
his reflections about terms like "water" in the direction that I am suggesting.
What is to be learned from those reflections is not, as Putnam himself argues, that
it cannot be true both that "knowing the meaning of a term is just a matter of
being in a certain psychological state" and that "the meaning of a term determines its extension"; so that if we retain the second of these assumptions, we must
renounce the first. This presupposes that anyone who embraces the first assumption must be restricting psychological states to "narrow" states. Rather, the moral
of Putnam's considerations is that the idea of a psychological state, as it figures in
the first assumption, cannot be the idea of a "narrow" state. That is: we should not
leave in place an idea of the mind that is shaped by the tenets of "methodological
solipsism," and conclude that meanings are not in the mind, since they are not in
the head. Rather, we should read the two assumptions in such a way that they *can*
be true together and exploit such a reading to force us into explicit consideration
of a different conception of the mind.

At one point in "The Meaning of 'Meaning'," Putnam concedes that "it may be
trivially true that, say, *knowing the meaning of the word 'water'* is a 'psychological
state'."[11] The idea that this concession is trivial points to an accommodation of

the basic thesis on the lines of the "duplex" conception of the mental. The concession is trivial, on this account, because it does not undermine the view that the two assumptions cannot be true together; given that psychological states in the strict and proper sense are "narrow," knowing a meaning (of the appropriate sort) would not be "*just* a matter of being in a certain psychological state," any more than, on that view, any "wide" psychological state would be. What Putnam never seems to consider is the possibility of a position that holds that command of a meaning is wholly a matter of how it is with someone's mind (the first assumption), and combines that with the determination of extension by meaning so as to force a radically non-solipsistic conception of the mind to come to explicit expression. Instead, he assumes that anyone who wants to conceive knowledge of a meaning as wholly a matter of how it is with someone's mind must be already committed to a theoretical conception of the mind—a conception of the mind as in the head—which, in conjunction with Putnam's reflections about meaning, guarantees that the wish cannot be fulfilled.[12]

There may be some temptation to deny that the idea that the mind is in the head is a bit of theory, on the ground of evidently untheoretical usages like "I did the calculation in my head, not on paper." But that idiom does not mesh with the sense that "in the head" bears in Putnam's argument. One might equally take in one's stride, say, "It came into my head that I wanted a drink of water"; here the meaning of "water" is "in the head" in the sense of the idiom, and the possibility of talking like this obviously poses no threat to what Putnam means by saying that meanings are not in the head.[13]

The radically non-solipsistic conception of the mental that I am urging would dictate a way of talking about Twin Earth cases that contrasts with Putnam's. In one of Putnam's cases, the correct extensions of "beech" and "elm" are reversed on Twin Earth, where Putnam has a *Doppelgänger* who is as unable to tell the two kinds of trees apart as Putnam blushingly confesses he is. The words are nevertheless secured their differed extensions, on the lips of Putnam and his *Doppelgänger*, by the fact that each defers to a different set of experts.[14] Putnam says, about himself and his *Doppelgänger* when each is in a psychological state, that he would express using one of those terms: "It is absurd to think *his* psychological state is one bit different from mine." On the conception I am urging, this is not absurd at all. Putnam's psychological state involves his mind's being directed towards, say, beeches (if beeches constitute the extension of the word that he is disposed to use in order to give expression to his psychological state); his *Doppelgänger's* psychological state involves his mind's being directed towards elms. The psychological state of each as it were expands in accordance with the determination of the extensions of their terms, in a way that is compelled if we are to maintain both of the two assumptions.

The possibility of talking like this would be merely trivial, in a sense like the one involved in Putnam's concession that we can count knowing a meaning as a psychological state, if the divergent psychological attributions ("thinking of elms" and "thinking of beeches") had to be seen as applying in virtue of some

shared underlying psychological state, with the divergence resulting from different ways in which that shared underlying state is embedded in its environment.
That is how the "duplex" conception would see things; on this view, Putnam and
his *Doppelgänger* do not differ in fundamental psychological properties. But we
need not see things this way. It is certainly true that Putnam and his *Doppelgänger*,
in the case described, have something psychological in common. (We can make
this vivid by noting that if Putnam were transported to Twin Earth without
knowing it, he would not be able to tell the difference.) But it is perfectly possible
to hold that the psychological common property holds of each in virtue of his
"wide" state, rather than that the "wide" state is constituted by the common
property, together with facts about how each is embedded in his environment.
The common property need not be fundamental.

Compare the psychological feature that is unsurprisingly shared between someone who sees that such-and-such is the case and someone to whom it merely looks
as if such-and-such is the case. (Again, if one were switched without knowing it
between possible worlds that differ in that way, one would not be able to tell the
difference.) It is not compulsory to conceive seeing that such-and-such is the case
as constituted by this common feature together with favorable facts about embedding in the environment. We can understand things the other way round: the
common feature—its being to all intents as if one sees that such-and-such is the
case—intelligibly supervenes on each of the divergent "wide" states. And it is
better to understand things this way round. It is very common for philosophers to
suppose that Twin Earth comparisons compel the idea that "wide" attributions
bear on states that are in themselves "narrow," with the "wide" attributions
coming out differently by virtue of the different ways in which those supposedly
fundamental psychological states are embedded in extra-psychological reality.
But this idea is closely parallel to the Argument from Illusion, and that by itself
should be enough to make us suspicious of it.[15]

8. Putnam does not seem to consider the possibility that his reflections about
meaning might be brought to bear against the idea that the mind is the organ of
psychological activity. In fact much of his own thinking seems to presuppose just
such a conception of the mind.

In *Representation and Reality* (7), he describes Jerry Fodor's "mentalism" as "just
the latest form taken by a more general tendency in the history of thought, the
tendency to think of concepts as scientifically describable ('psychologically real')
entities in the mind or brain." There is an equivalence implied here between
"psychologically real" and "scientifically describable," which cries out to be ques-
tioned: it looks like simply an expression of scientism about what it might be for
something to by psychologically real. (We do not need to surrender the term
"psychological" to *scientific* psychology.) But as far as I can see Putnam leaves the
equivalence unchallenged, even though a great deal of his point in that book is to
attack the effects of scientism on how philosophers conceive the mental. The term
"mentalism" has a perfectly good interpretation as a label for the view that the
mental is a genuine range of reality. (We do not need to accept that the nature of

reality is *scientifically* determined.) But Putnam, without demur, lets "mentalism" be commandeered for the view that the topic of mental discourse can appropriately be specified as "the mind/brain." Talk of the main/brain embodies the assumption that the mind is appropriately conceived as an organ, together, or course, with the idea—which is in itself perfectly sensible—that *if* the mind is an organ, the brain is the only organ it can sensibly be supposed to be. The assumption that the mind is an organ is one that Putnam does not challenge.[16]

An assumption to the same effect seems to underlie Putnam's argument, in *Reason, Truth and History*,[17] that one cannot suppose that mental states or occurrences are intrinsically referential—intrinsically directed at the world— without falling into a magical conception of reference. Putnam's governing assumption here is that a mental state or occurrence that is representational, say an occurrence in which one is struck by the thought that one hears the sound of water dripping, must in itself consist in the presence in the mind of an item with an intrinsic nature characterizable independently of considering what it repre-sent. (Such a state of affairs would be what an internal arrangement in an organ of thought would have to amount to.) It clearly follows, from such a conception of that which is strictly speaking present in the mind, that such items cannot be intrinsically endowed with referential properties; to suppose that they might be would be to appeal to magic, just as Putnam argues. What never comes into view is this possibility: that being, say, struck by a thought is not, in itself, the presence in the mind of an item with a non-representational intrinsic nature. The argu-ment is controlled by the assumption that occurrences in the mind are, in themselves, "narrow."

Am I suggesting that being struck by a thought might not involve mental representation? It seems truistic that a thought that such-and-such is the case is a representation that such-and-such is the case. But this is not the notion of mental representation as it figures in Putnam's argument.

In Putnam's argument, mental representations are representations in the sense in which, say, drawings or sentences are representations. A representation is an item whose intrinsic nature is characterizable independently of its representa-tional properties: a symbol. The nerve of Putnam's argument is that symbols are not intrinsically endowed with their representational properties, and that claim seems beyond question. But from the fact that thinking, say, that one hears the sound of water dripping is representing that one hears the sound of water drip-ping, it does not follow that thinking that one hears the sound of water dripping must in itself consist in the presence in the mind of a symbol: something into which the significance that one hears the sound of water dripping can be read, as it can be read into the sign-design "I hear the sound of water dripping," although in both cases the symbol's bearing that significance is extraneous to its intrinsic nature. Putnam's solid point cannot dislodge the possibility that thinking that one hears the sound of water dripping is a mental representation, in the sense of a mental representing, that intrinsically represents what it represents.

What this means is that being struck by that thought, say, would not be the mental occurrence that it is if it were not *that* that one found oneself thinking. What the mental occurrence is in itself already involves that referential directed-ness at the world. The firm point in Putnam's argument is that this could not be so, except by magic, if the intrinsic nature of the mental occurrence were constituted by the presence in the mind of a representation, in Putnam's sense. So the possibility that goes missing in Putnam's argument could be described as the possibility of mental representing without representations.

Putnam would dispute something I have been suggesting, that it is just an assumption on his part that the contents of the mind when we think are represen-tations in his sense. His claim is that this thesis is established by introspection. "Stop the stream of thought when or where we will, what we catch are words, images, sensations, feelings."[18] (This is meant to be a list of kinds of items that are not intrinsically representational.) But to me it seems wildly inaccurate to suggest that when I am struck by the thought that I hear the sound of water dripping, the fact that my thought is, say, about *water* is not part of what I find in my stream of consciousness, but has to be read into what I find there. Putnam's phenome-nological claim is not an unprejudiced introspective report. It is theory-driven; he tells us not what he finds in his stream of consciousness but what *must* be there, given the pre-conceived theory that the contents of representing consciousness are representations in his sense. I think an unprejudiced phenomenology would find it more accurate to say that the contents of consciousness, when we have occurrent thoughts, are thoughts themselves, on something like Frege's usage for "thought" (or "*Gedanke*"): sense potentially expressed by assertoric sentences, not vehicles for such senses. Similarly with imagery: if I close my eyes and visualize, say, my wife's face, it seems wildly wrong to suggest that the fact that what I am visualizing is my wife's face—a fact that relates my mental state to the extra-psychological environment—is extraneous to the contents of my con-sciousness, extraneous to what I find when I "stop the stream of thought." So far from supporting the apparatus of his argument, Putnam's phenomenological claim here is unconvincing enough to give us reason to raise questions about the theory that underlies the argument.[19]

9. Putnam has often expressed suspicion of the idea that there is good philoso-phy to be done by grappling with questions like "How does language hook on to the world?"[20] It ought to be similar with questions like "How does thinking hook on to the world?" Such a question looks like a pressing one if we saddle ourselves with a conception of what thinking is, considered in itself, that deprives thinking of its characteristic bearing on the world—its being about this or that object in the world, and its being to the effect that this or that state of affairs obtains in the world. If we start from a conception of thinking as in itself without referential bearing on the world, we shall seem to be confronted with a genuine and urgent task, that of reinstating into our picture the way thinking is directed at the world. But if we do not accept the assumption that what thinking is, considered in itself, is a mental manipulation of representations in Putnam's sense, no such task confronts us. The need to construct a theoretical "hook" to link thinking to the

world does not arise, because if it is thinking that we have in view at all—say being struck by the thought that one hears the sound of water dripping—then what we have in view is *already* hooked on to the world; it is already in view as possessing referential directedness at reality.[21]

It would be a mistake to suppose that what I am doing here is what Putnam describes as "just postulating mysterious powers of mind"; as Putnam says, surely rightly, that "solves nothing."[22] The proper target of that accusation is a way of thinking in which we try to combine conceiving the mind as an organ of thought, so that what an episode of thinking is in itself is a mental manipulation of a representation, with supposing that an episode of thinking has its determinate referential bearing on the world intrinsically. Putnam's cogent point is that this combination pushes us into a magical picture of the reference of the supposed mental symbols, and hence into a magical picture of the powers of the mind. But the conception I am urging needs no appeal to a magical theory of reference, precisely because it rejects the supposed mental symbols. My aim is not to postulate mysterious powers of mind; rather, my aim is to restore us to a conception of thinking as the exercise of powers possessed, not mysteriously by some part of a thinking being, a part whose internal arrangements are characterizable independently of how the thinking being is placed in its environment, but unmysteriously by a thinking being itself, an animal that lives its life in cognitive and practical relations to the world. "Just postulating mysterious powers of mind" would be an appropriate description for a misguided attempt to respond to a supposed problem that I aim to join Putnam in rejecting.

It would equally be a mistake to suppose that what I have said about the phenomenology of thinking is merely a version of what Putnam calls "the attempt to understand thought by what is called 'phenomenological' investigation."[23] Putnam's objection to this is that any such attempt must miss the point that understanding, or more generally the possession of a concept, is an ability rather than an occurrence. "The attempt to understand thought" is the attempt to respond to a philosophical puzzlement about how thought "hooks on to the world." But my aim is to bring out a way of conceiving thought in which there is no need to try to embark on such a project at all.

It is true that understanding, or more generally the possession of a concept, is an ability rather than an occurrence. But it does not follow that there cannot be occurrences that are intrinsically directed at reality in the way that I have suggested is characteristic of occurrent thought. If the concept of water is an ability that is exercised in thinking about water, we can conceive its exercises as, precisely, occurrences that are intrinsically episodes of thinking about water.[24]

10. What is the attraction for Putnam of the idea that "the stream of thought" is populated by representations in his sense, rather than representings? Any answer must be speculative; an answer that seems to me to have some plausibility is that Putnam is himself swayed by the residual influence of a scientism like the one I mentioned in connection with the "duplex" conception of "wide" psychological attributions. Without the idea of intrinsic structurings in some inner

medium, it is hard to see how we could picture a mapping of our psychological talk into a subject matter susceptible of scientific treatment. In particular, mental representings occupy a position in the causal order; and if we want to be able to integrate that fact into a natural-scientific conception of the causal order, it is very tempting to suppose that representings must owe their causal character to the causal character of structures in a medium that is ultimately susceptible of physical description.[25] Putnam's phenomenological claim reflects a plausible conception of the most that could be available to introspection, if we understand introspection as a capacity to scan or monitor such inner structures.[26]

What is missing here is the thought that mentalistic talk can be intellectually respectable without any such mapping being needed. I do not suggest that this is an easy thought for us to get our minds around, subject as we are to intelligible pressures to scientize our conception of the causal order. But we ought to ensure that we are fully conscious of the effects of such pressures on our thinking, and we ought to be alive to the possibility that it is not compulsory to succumb to them.

The suggestion that Putnam's thinking is partly shaped by a residual scientism will surely provoke from some people the response "So what? What's so bad about scientism?" In another context, I should feel obliged to say something in answer to that. Here, though, I shall not even begin to do so, since I am confident that that response will not be Putnam's own.

Putnam ends "The Meaning of 'Meaning' " with this remark: "Traditional philosophy of language, like much traditional philosophy, leaves out other people and the world; a better philosophy and a better science of language must encompass both."[27] I am not sure how "traditional" the approach to language that Putnam attacks really is, but I do not want to make anything of that here. My point in this paper is that the "isolationist" conception of language that Putnam objects to is all of a piece with a similarly "isolationist" conception of the mind—at least of the mind as it is in itself. And Putnam's attack on the "isolationist" conception of language leaves the counterpart conception of the mind unquestioned. Taking on the whole package would have yielded a deeper understanding of what underlies the "isolationist" conception of language. I think this broader project would have been better suited than Putnam's partial move is to his admirable aim of showing us what "a better philosophy" would be like. A general attack on "isolationism" promises a satisfyingly cohesive and radical reorientation, very much in the spirit of Putnam's own best thinking, of philosophy's approach to the relations between the individual subject and the world.

ENDNOTES

1. Reprinted in Putnam (1975a) (and here—*ed.*).
2. That the extension of a term is determined by its meaning is one of the two assumptions that Putnam plays off against each other in "The Meaning of 'Meaning'." (The other is that "knowing the meaning of a term is just a matter of being in a certain

psychological state." [Putnam (1975), 219].) What Putnam argues in the first instance is that the assumptions cannot be true together, and he registers the possibility that one might respond by discarding the assumption that meaning determines extension (e.g., at 266). But his own thinking (much more attractively) leaves that assumption in place. So he directs the argument against the other assumption.

3. Putnam (1975), 227.
4. For some discussion of such details, see the introduction to Pettit & McDowell (1986).
5. Putnam considers this at (1975), 242–5.
6. Putnam (1975), 220. I have slightly altered Putnam's gloss on "the narrow sense" in line with some remarks of Fodor (1981a), 225–53. I think the alteration captures what Putnam intended.
7. See McGinn (1982), 207–58. Other considerations are thought to conspire with Putnam's to necessitate this picture, but in this paper I am restricting myself to the significance of Putnam's basic thesis.
8. Putnam (1988).
9. I say "possibly residual" because of the attraction that this conception has for someone of a fundamentally scientistic cast of mind who accept, perhaps on the basis of an argument like Putnam's about interpretation, that ("wide") content is not available to a scientific psychology. Of course there are people who have a less defensive scientism than that, because they are not persuaded by such arguments, or ignore them.
10. Putnam (1975), 220–21.
11. Putnam (1975), 220.
12. Given a Principle of Charity, this raises a question (which is made all the more pressing by Putnam's own lack of sympathy with "methodological solipsism") whether Putnam may have misinterpreted at least some of the philosophers against whom he directs his basic thesis. I am particularly doubtful about the case of Frege. But I do not want to go into questions about Putnam's reading of his targets here.
13. On the ordinary idiomatic use of "in the head," compare Wittgenstein (1953), section 427.
14. Putnam (1975), 226–7.
15. There is some discussion of issues in this vicinity in my "Singular Thought and the Extent of Inner Space," in Pettit and McDowell, eds., op. cit., 137–68.
16. It is only in connection with mentalism on this interpretation that Putnam considers Gareth Evans's views in Evans (1982); see Putnam (1988), 129 n.4. Evans's thinking actually opens up the possibility of a satisfactory understanding of thought (a mental phenomenon, surely) and meaning as environmentally constituted: an understanding that ought to be welcome to Putnam. But Putnam restricts himself to finding it puzzling how Evans could conceive his thinking as a kind of mentalism, since Evans obviously does not equate thoughts with "representations inside the mind/brain."
17. Putnam (1981).
18. Putnam (1981), 17; see also 27 for a parallel appeal to introspective evidence.
19. For a "cry of disbelief" (69) against similar phenomenological falsifications, forced on philosophers by the theory that "an occurrent conscious thought bears its 'intention' or content in the same way as a bit of language bears it significance" (86), see Ayers (1972), 69–96. One of Ayers's targets is Wittgenstein; I suggest a rather different reading of Wittgenstein (although I would not dispute that there are passages that fit Ayers's reading) in my (1991), 148–69.
20. His suspicions are expressed in several of the essays in his (1990).

21. And the world that it is already hooked on to is not The World as contemplated by the metaphysical realism that Putnam has attacked. My thought that I hear the sound of water dripping has its point of contact with reality in the fact that I hear the sound of water dripping, or perhaps in the fact that I do not hear the sound of water dripping. I use my conceptual capacities (I just did) in pinpointing which possible facts these are; the world (which is all the facts, as Wittgenstein said in the *Tractatus*) is not here pictured as beyond the reach of concepts.

22. Putnam (1981), 2.

23. Putnam (1981), 20.

24. These remarks are directed against the close of chapter 1 of Putnam (1981), where Putnam suggests that the perfectly correct point that concepts are not mental occurrences, combined with the phenomenological claim about which I have already expressed doubts, demolishes the very idea that there can be mental episodes with an intrinsic referential bearing on the world. By claiming that concepts are "signs used in a certain way" (18), Putnam makes it look as if exercises of concepts would have to be occurrences (tokenings) of signs. He thereby forces on us a "narrow" conception of what exercises of concepts must be in themselves. This obliterates a perfectly workable conception according to which exercises of concepts are, for instance, acts of judgment, intrinsically possessed of referential bearing on the world.

25. See John Haugeland's suggestive discussion of "the paradox of mechanical reason," in his (1985), 365–41.

26. For an unusually explicit expression of such a view of introspection, see McGinn (1982), 253–54.

27. Putnam (1975), 271.

Part IV
Self-Knowledge

Introduction

THE AUTHORS IN PART III debated the implications of the Twin Earth stories for theories about the nature of mental content. In part IV we now turn towards Twin Earth's implications for theories about a thinker's authoritative *knowledge* of her own mental contents or thoughts. In general, the discussions which follow center on two questions. First, just what does self-knowledge amount to? Here reference is typically made to various traditional doctrines about the mental: first-person authority, privileged access, or authoritative self-knowledge (to name the most popular). The second question is, how do Putnam's reflections bear on these doctrines? The answers vary widely.

Some philosophers hold that the Twin Earth stories, together with Putnam's externalist (or "anti-individualist") conclusions, imply that such doctrines apply to many fewer of our mental contents (if they even apply at all) than pretheoretical intuition would have us believe. Theorists who argue in such a way differ over *the extent to which* such doctrines fail, or the *sorts of contents* for which failure is most to be expected. But in general they agree that (1) Twin Earth sorts of considerations pose a "problem" for any views that involve the above doctrines about self-knowledge, and (2) that the problem itself forces the conclusion that our grip on our own mental contents is not as secure as these doctrines would have it.

It is in response to these philosophers that we may locate the Davidson and Burge selections in part IV.

In his "Knowing One's Own Mind" (1987), Davidson develops a line of argument he first presented in his "First Person Authority" (1984a). His thesis is that "attention to how we attribute thoughts and meanings to others . . . explain[s] first-person authority without inviting skeptical doubts." He begins by noting that first person authority falls out of the fact that a thinker generally knows what she believes before she speaks or acts. Given this latter, the (self-ascribed) belief that one has a thought "is enough to justify that belief." The

319

problem of first person authority, for Davidson, is the need to explain why this should be so.

Davidson's proposed solution is based on his view that meanings (contents) are whatever is yielded by correct interpretation of the utterances of others. The assumption that others generally know what they mean and think—in other words, the assumption of first person authority—is a crucial part of this process of interpretation. Davidson writes,

> unless there is a presumption that the speaker knows what she means, i.e., is getting her own language right, there would be nothing for an interpreter to interpret. To put the matter another way, nothing could count as someone regularly misapplying her own words.

He concludes, contrary to those who have argued that externalism and first-person authority are incompatible, that "first-person authority, the social character of language, and the external determinants of thought and meaning go naturally together."

Davidson, however, is not satisfied with merely having presented a solution to the problem of authority. He also proposes a diagnosis of what has led so many other thinkers to (what for him is) the *unsubstantiated conclusion* that externalism about content is incompatible with first-person authority. Developed in greater detail in his "What Is Present to the Mind?" (1991), his idea is that the incompatibility claim appears forced on us *only if* we accept the "dogma" that "to have a thought is to have an object before the mind." He explains this diagnosis:

> if to have a thought is to have an object "before the mind," and the identity of the object determines what the thought is, then it must always be possible to be mistaken about what one is thinking. For unless one knows *everything* about the object, there will always be senses in which one does not know what object it is.

But, as he argues below and in his (1991), there is no reason to accept this dogma. And it is by seeing this, he thinks, that one paves the way to a clearheaded acceptance of his response to the problem of first-person authority.

In "Individualism and Self-Knowledge" (1988), Tyler Burge too is anxious to show that a rejection of individualism does not undermine independently motivated views about self-knowledge. However, he sets up the "problem" in rather different terms. He begins by acknowledging the phenomenon of *basic self-knowledge*, judgments that he claims are "self-verifying." He explains that they are the class of first-person judgments that (1) "constitute knowledge", (2) "are not the by-products of ordinary empirical investigation," and (3) "are peculiarly direct and authoritative." It is this phenomenon, Burge thinks, that must be accommodated by any acceptable theory of content. The central problem for Burge, then, is:

that of understanding how we can know some of our mental events in a direct, nonempirical manner, when those events depend for their identities on our relations to the environment.

Burge's response to this problem involves an appeal to one crucial distinction. He distinguishes between the knowledge involved when you know a given thought, from that involved when you know "the complex conditions that must obtain if one is to think that thought." The latter conditions he calls the thought's "enabling conditions," and he urges that knowledge of a given thought does not presuppose that one has knowledge of the enabling conditions. Instead, "it is enough that [such conditions] actually be satisfied."

On the basis of this distinction, he erects an account of basic self-knowledge that squares with the anti-individualist view that thoughts are individuated in part by appeal to things beyond the thinker herself. He suggests that basic self-knowledge is a matter of having immediate and authoritative *second*-order beliefs about one's own *first*-order thoughts. Since the ability to form the relevant second-order belief accompanies the having of an occurrent first-order thought, we possess this knowledge. What is more to the present point, Burge insists that anti-individualism about content does not jeopardize the authority or the immediacy of such second-order beliefs, for the simple reason that the second-order belief *inherits the content* of the first-order one. Burge explains:

> Any conditions that are necessary to thinking that *p* will be equally necessary to the relevant knowledge that one is thinking that *p*. . . . The reflexive judgment simply inherits the content of the first-order thought.

And since knowing the first-order thought that *p* does not involve knowing the "enabling conditions" of the thought that *p*, one can have the knowledge that one is thinking that *p* in an immediate and noninferential way.

McKinsey's "Anti-Individualism and Privileged Access" (1991) is a reply to both Burge and Davidson. Against both, he maintains that anti-individualism and privileged access—the idea that "it is possible to have *a priori* knowledge of one's own neutral cognitive attitude states" like thought, belief, intention, and desire—are incompatible "as standardly understood," and so "something has to give."

The problem with Davidson's solution, according to McKinsey, is that it does not appear to have preserved privileged access to *content*. Davidson

> wishes to claim, apparently, that one could have privileged access to an episode of thought independently of having privileged access to any particular descriptions that the episode might satisfy. But then what would one have privileged access *to* in such a case?

And the problem with Burge's account, according to McKinsey, is that he preserves the compatibility of anti-individualism and privileged access only by tacitly making an illegitimate assumption, at the heart of his compatibilist account, concerning what it is for a content to be wide. Burge holds that content-attributing statements *necessarily depend* on "external propositions"—i.e., propositions whose presuppositions make the content wide—in the sense that the former "metaphysically entail" the latter. But metaphysical entailment will not do, since on such an understanding of wide content, anti-individualism becomes "a trivial consequence of (token) materialism." In short, McKinsey argues that neither Burge nor Davidson succeeds in defending the compatibility of external-ism and self-knowledge.

In the final article in part IV, "Can Externalism Be Reconciled with Self-Knowledge?" (1992), Akeel Bilgrami argues that (1) both Davidson and Burge have misidentified the *prima facie* problem about self-knowledge to which the doctrine of externalism gives rise, (2) as a result at least Burge's "solution" fails, and (3) nonetheless externalism and self-knowledge can be reconciled.

Bilgrami raises the problem in the context of belief attribution, and character-izes it as a sort of trilemma. *Either* we insist (with Putnam) on a scientific essentialist view of natural-kind terms, in which case we are going to attribute patent inconsistencies to a thinker whenever she lacks the relevant scientific knowledge; *or else* we avoid such uncharitable attributions at the price of attribut-ing a lack of self-knowledge; *or else* we unhappily "bifurcate" content into two components, one of which is not externalist and so "does not have any problem with self-knowledge." If *this* is the problem, Davidson's diagnosis in terms of "inner objects of thought" is not to the point; this claim Bilgrami argues for in greater detail in his (1991). And, against Burge, Bilgrami argues that Burge's response must ultimately impale him on one of the three horns.

Bilgrami's own proposed reconciliation depends on his distinction between externalism, understood in a *general* way as the denial of methodological solips-ism, and what he calls "orthodox externalism," understood as wedded to particu-lar views of reference and meaning—including the "new theories of reference" of Kripke and Putnam, as well as Burge's own views. He claims that externalism on its more general construal need not jeopardize self-knowledge, so long as we impose the following constraint on content attribution:

(C): When fixing an externally determined concept of an agent, one must do so by looking to indexically formulated utterances of the agent which express indexical contents containing that concept and then picking that external determinant of the concept which is in consonance with other contents that have been fixed for the agent.

The remainder of Bilgrami's article attempts to defend this version of externalism against several objections that it appears to invite. [A more detailed presentation is found in Bilgrami (1992).]

18

Knowing One's Own Mind

Donald Davidson

THERE IS NO SECRET ABOUT the nature of the evidence we use to decide what other people think: we observe their acts, read their letters, study their expressions, listen to their words, learn their histories, and note their relations to society. How we are able to assemble such material into a convincing picture of a mind is another matter; we know how to do it without necessarily knowing how we do it. Sometimes I learn what I believe in much the same way someone else does, by noticing what I say and do. There may be times when this is my only access to my own thoughts. According to Graham Wallas,

> The little girl had the making of a poet in her who, being told to be sure of her meaning before she spoke, said "How can I know what I think till I see what I say?"[1]

A similar thought was expressed by Robert Motherwell: "I would say that most good painters don't know what they think until they paint it."

Gilbert Ryle was with the poet and the painter all the way in this matter; he stoutly maintained that we know our own minds in exactly the same way we know the minds of others, by observing what we say, do, and paint. Ryle was wrong. It is seldom the case that I need or appeal to evidence or observation in order to find out what I believe; normally I know what I think before I speak or act. Even when I have evidence, I seldom make use of it. I can be wrong about my own thoughts, and the appeal to what can be publicly determined is not irrelevant. But the possibility that one may be mistaken about one's own thoughts cannot defeat the overriding presumption that a person knows what he or she believes; in general, the belief that one has a thought is enough to justify that belief. But though this is true, and even obvious to most of us, the fact has, so far as I can see, no easy explanation. While it is clear enough, at least in outline, what we have to go on in trying to fathom the thoughts of others, it is obscure why, in our own case, we can so often know what we think without appeal to evidence or recourse to observation.

Because we usually know what we believe (and desire and doubt and intend) without needing or using evidence (even when it is available), our sincere avowals concerning our present states of mind are not subject to the failings of conclusions based on evidence. Thus sincere first-person present-tense claims about thoughts, while neither infallible nor incorrigible, have an authority no second- or third-person claim, or first-person other-tense claim, can have. To recognize this fact is not, however, to explain it.

Since Wittgenstein it has become routine to try to relieve worries about "our knowledge of other minds" by remarking that it is an essential aspect of our use of certain mental predicates that we apply them to others on the basis of behavioral evidence but to ourselves without benefit of such aid. The remark is true, and when properly elaborated, it ought to answer someone who wonders how we can know the minds of others. But as a response to the skeptic, Wittgenstein's insight (if it is Wittgenstein's) should give little satisfaction. For, first, it is a strange idea that claims made without evidential or observational support should be favored over claims with such support. Of course, if evidence is not cited in support of a claim, the claim cannot be impugned by questioning the truth or relevance of the evidence. But these points hardly suffice to suggest that in general claims without evidential support are more trustworthy than those with. The second, and chief, difficulty is this. One would normally say that what counts as evidence for the application of a concept helps define the concept, or at least places constraints on its identification. If two concepts regularly depend for their application on different criteria or ranges of evidential support, they must be different concepts. So if what is apparently the same expression is sometimes correctly employed on the basis of a certain range of evidential support and sometimes on the basis of another range of evidential support (or none), the obvious conclusion would seem to be that the expression is ambiguous. Why then should we suppose that a predicate like "x believes that Ras Dashan is the highest mountain in Ethiopia," which is applied sometimes on the basis of behavioral evidence and sometimes not, is unambiguous? If it is ambiguous, then there is no reason to suppose it has the same meaning when applied to oneself that it has when applied to another. If we grant (as we should) that the necessarily public and interpersonal character of language guarantees that we often correctly apply these predicates to others, and that therefore we often do know what *others* think, then the question must be raised what grounds each of us has for thinking he knows what (in the same sense) *he* thinks. The Wittgensteinian style of answer may solve the problem of other minds, but it creates a corresponding problem about knowledge of one's own mind. The correspondence is not quite complete, however. The original problem of other minds invited the question how one knows others have minds at all. The problem we now face must be put this way: I know what to look for in attributing thoughts to others. Using quite different criteria (or none), I apply the same predicates to myself; so the skeptical question arises why I should think it is *thoughts* I am attributing to myself. But since the evidence I use in the case of others is open to the public, there is no reason why I shouldn't attribute thoughts to myself in the same way I do to others, in the mode of Graham Wallas, Robert Motherwell, and Gilbert Ryle. In other words, I don't, but I could, treat my own mental states in the same way I do those of others. No such strategy is available to someone who seeks the same sort of authority with respect to the thoughts of others as he apparently has in dealing with his own thoughts. So the asymmetry between the cases remains a problem, and it is first person authority, that creates the problem.

I have suggested an answer to this problem in another paper.[2] In that paper I argued that attention to how we attribute thoughts and meanings to others would explain first person authority without inviting skeptical doubts. In recent years, however, some of the very facts about the attribution of attitudes on which I relied to defend first person authority have been employed to attack that authority: it has been argued, on what are thought to be new grounds, that while the methods of the third person interpreter determine what we usually deem to be the contents of an agent's mind, the contents so determined may be unknown to the agent. In the present paper I consider some of these arguments, and urge that they do not constitute a genuine threat to first person authority. The explanation I offered in my earlier paper of the asymmetry between first and other-person attributions of attitudes seems to me if anything to be strengthened by the new considerations, or those of them that seem valid.

It should be stressed again that the problem I am concerned with does not require that our beliefs about our own contemporary states of mind be infallible or incorrigible. We can and do make mistakes about what we believe, desire, approve, and intend; there is also the possibility of self-deceit. But such cases, though not infrequent, are not and could not be standard; I do not argue for this now, but take it as one of the facts to be explained.

Setting aside, then, self-deception and other anomalous or borderline phenomena, the question is whether we can, without irrationality, inconsistency, or confusion, simply and straightforwardly think we have a belief we do not have, or think we do not have a belief we do have. A number of philosophers and philosophically minded psychologists have recently entertained views that entail or suggest that this could easily happen—indeed, that it must happen all the time.

The threat was there in Russell's idea of propositions that could be known to be true even though they contained "ingredients" with which the mind of the knower was not acquainted; and as the study of the *de re* attitudes evolved the peril grew more acute.

But it was Hilary Putnam who pulled the plug. Consider Putnam's 1975 argument to show that meanings, as he put it, "just ain't in the head."[3] Putnam argues persuasively that what words mean depends on more than "what is in the head." He tells a number of stories the moral of which is that aspects of the natural history of how someone learned the use of a word necessarily make a difference to what the word means. It seems to follow that two people might be in physically identical states, and yet mean different things by the same words.

The consequences are far-reaching. For if people can (usually) express their thoughts correctly in words, then their thoughts—their beliefs, desires, intentions, hopes, expectations—also must in part be identified by events and objects outside the person. If meanings ain't in the head, then neither, it would seem, are beliefs and desires and the rest.

Since some of you may be a little weary of Putnam's *Doppelgänger* on Twin

Earth, let me tell my own science fiction story—if that is what it is. My story avoids some irrelevant difficulties in Putnam's story, though it introduces some new problems of its own.[4] (I'll come back to Earth, and Twin Earth, a little later.) Suppose lightning strikes a dead tree in a swamp; I am standing nearby. My body is reduced to its elements, while entirely by coincidence (and out of different molecules) the tree is turned into my physical replica. My replica, The Swamp-man, moves exactly as I did; according to its nature it departs the swamp, encounters and seems to recognize my friends, and appears to return their greetings in English. It moves into my house and seems to write articles on radical interpretation. No one can tell the difference.

But there is a difference. My replica can't recognize my friends; it can't recognize anything, since it never cognized anything in the first place. It can't know my friends' names (though of course it seems to), it can't remember my house. It can't mean what I do by the word "house," for example, since the sound "house" it makes was not learned in a context that would give it the right meaning—or any meaning at all. Indeed, I don't see how my replica can be said to mean anything by the sounds it makes, nor to have any thoughts.

Putnam might not go along with this last claim, for he says that if two people (or objects) are in relevantly similar physical states, it is "absurd" to think their psychological states are "one bit different."[5] It would be a mistake to be sure that Putnam and I disagree on this point, however, since it is not yet clear how the phrase "psychological state" is being used.

Putnam holds that many philosophers have wrongly assumed that psychological states like belief and knowing the meaning of a word are both (I) "inner" in the sense that they do not presuppose the existence of any individual other than the subject to whom the state is ascribed, and (II) that these are the very states which we normally identify and individuate as we do beliefs and the other propositional attitudes. Since we normally identify and individuate mental states and meanings in terms partly of relations to objects and events other than the subject, Putnam believes (I) and (II) come apart: in his opinion, no states can satisfy both conditions.

Putnam calls psychological states satisfying condition (I) "narrow." He thinks of such states as solipsistic, and associates them with Descartes' view of the mental. Putnam may consider these states to be the only "true" psychological states; in much of his paper he omits the qualifier "narrow," despite the fact that narrow psychological states (so called) do not correspond to the propositional attitudes as normally identified. Not everyone has been persuaded that there is an intelligible distinction to be drawn between narrow (or inner, or Cartesian, or individualistic—all these terms are current) psychological states and psychological states identified (if any are) in terms of external facts (social or otherwise). Thus John Searle has claimed that our ordinary propositional attitudes satisfy condition (I), and so there is no need of states satisfying condition (II), while Tyler Burge has denied that there are, in any interesting sense, propositional attitudes that satisfy condition (I).[6] But there seems to be universal agreement that no states satisfy both conditions.

The thesis of this paper is that there is no reason to suppose that ordinary mental states do not satisfy both conditions (I) and (II): I think such states are "inner," in the sense of being identical with states of the body, and so identifiable without reference to objects or events outside the body; they are at the same time "non-individualistic" in the sense that they can be, and usually are, identified in part by their causal relations to events and objects outside the subject whose states they are. A corollary of this thesis will turn out to be that contrary to what is often assumed, first person authority can without contradiction apply to states that are regularly identified by their relations to events and objects outside the person.

I begin with the corollary. Why is it natural to assume that states that satisfy condition (II) may not be known to the person who is in those states?

Now I must talk about Putnam's Twin Earth. He asks us to imagine two people exactly alike physically and (therefore) alike with respect to all "narrow" psychological states. One of the two people, an inhabitant of Earth, has learned to use the word "water" by being shown water, reading and hearing about it, etc. The other, an inhabitant of Twin Earth, has learned to use the word "water" under conditions not observably different, but the substance to which she has been exposed is not water but a lookalike substance we may call "twater." Under the circumstances, Putnam claims, the first speaker refers to water when she uses the word "water"; her twin refers to twater when *she* uses the word "water." So we seem to have a case where "narrow" psychological states are identical, and yet the speakers mean different things by the same word.

How about the thoughts of these two speakers? The first says to herself, when facing a glass of water, "Here's a glass of water"; the second mutters exactly the same sounds to herself when facing a glass of twater. Each speaks the truth, since their words mean different things. And since each is sincere, it is natural to suppose they believe different things, the first believing there is a glass of water in front of her, the second believing there is a glass of twater in front of *her*. But do they know what they believe? If the meanings of their words, and thus the beliefs expressed by using those words, are partly determined by external factors about which the agents are ignorant, their beliefs and meanings are not narrow in Putnam's sense. There is therefore nothing on the basis of which either speaker can tell which state she is in, for there is no internal or external clue to the difference available. We ought, it seems, to conclude that neither speaker knows what she means or thinks. The conclusion has been drawn explicitly by a number of philosophers, among them Putnam. Putnam declares that he ". . . totally abandons the idea that if there is a difference in meaning . . . then there *must* be some difference in our concepts (or in our psychological state)." What determines meaning and extension " . . . is not, in general, fully known to the speaker."[7] Here "psychological state" means *narrow* psychological state, and it is assumed that only such states are "fully known." Jerry Fodor believes that ordinary propositional attitudes are (pretty nearly) "in the head," but he agrees with Putnam that if propositional attitudes were partly identified by factors outside the agent, they would not be in the head, and would not necessarily be known to the agent.[8] John Searle also, though his reasons are not Fodor's, holds that meanings are in the head ("there is nowhere else for them to be"), but seems to accept the inference that if this were not the case, first person authority would be lost.[9] Perhaps the plainest statement of the position appears in Andrew Woodfield's introduction to a book of essays on the objects of thought. Referring to the claim that the contents of the mind are often determined by facts external to and perhaps unknown to the person whose mind it is, he says:

> Because the external relation is not determined subjectively, the subject is not authoritative about that. A third person might well be in a better position than the subject to know which object the subject is thinking about, hence be better placed to know which thought it was.[10]

Those who accept the thesis that the contents of propositional attitudes are partly identified in terms of external factors seem to have a problem similar to the problem of the skeptic who finds we may be altogether mistaken about the "outside" world. In the present case ordinary skepticism of the senses is avoided by supposing the world itself more or less correctly determines the contents of thoughts about the world. (The speaker who thinks it is water is probably right, for he learned the use of the word "water" in a watery environment; the speaker who thinks twater is probably right, for he learned the word "water" in a twatery environment.) But skepticism is not defeated; it is only displaced onto knowledge of our own minds. Our ordinary beliefs about the external world are (on this view) directed onto the world, but we don't know what we believe.

There is, of course, a difference between water and twater, and it can be discovered by normal means, whether it is discovered or not. So a person might find out what he believes by discovering the difference between water and twater, and finding out enough about his own relations to both to determine which one his talk and beliefs are about. The skeptical conclusion we seem to have reached concerns the extent of first person authority: it is far more limited than we supposed. Our beliefs about the world are mostly true, but we may easily be wrong about what we think. It is a transposed image of Cartesian skepticism.

Those who hold that the contents of our thoughts and the meanings of our words are often fixed by factors of which we are ignorant have not been much concerned with the apparent consequence of their views which I have been emphasizing. They have, of course, realized that if they were right, the Cartesian idea that the one thing we can be certain of is the contents of our own minds, and the Fregean notion of meanings fully "grasped," must be wrong. But they have not made much of an attempt, so far as I know, to resolve the seeming conflict between their views and the strong intuition that first person authority exists.

One reason for the lack of concern may be that some seem to see the problem as confined to a fairly limited range of cases, cases where concepts or words latch on to objects that are picked out or referred to using proper names, indexicals, and words for natural kinds. Others, though, argue that the ties between language and thought on the one hand and external affairs on the other are so pervasive that no aspect of thought as usually conceived is untouched. In this vein Daniel Dennett remarks that " . . . one must be richly informed about, intimately connected with, the world at large, its occupants and properties, in order to be said with any propriety to have beliefs."[11] He goes on to claim that the identification of all beliefs is infected by the outside, non-subjective factors that are recognized to operate in the sort of case we have been discussing. Burge also emphasizes the extent to which our beliefs are affected by external factors, though for reasons he does not explain, he apparently does not view this as a threat to first person authority.[12]

The subject has taken a disquieting turn. At one time behaviorism was invoked to show how it was possible for one person to know what was in another's mind; behaviorism was then rejected in part because it could not explain one of the most obvious aspects of mental states: the fact that they are in general known to the person who has them without appeal to behavioristic evidence. The recent fashion, though not strictly behavioristic, once more identifies mental states partly in terms of social and other external factors, thus making them to that extent publicly discoverable. But at the same time it reinstates the problem of accounting for first person authority.

Those who are convinced of the external dimension of the contents of thoughts as ordinarily identified and individuated have reacted in different ways. One response has been to make a distinction between the contents of the mind as subjectively and internally determined, on the one hand, and ordinary beliefs, desires, and intentions, as we normally attribute them on the basis of social and other outward connections, on the other. This is clearly the trend of Putnam's argument (although the word "water" has different meanings, and is used to express different beliefs when it is used to refer to water and to twater, people using the word for these different purposes may be in "the same psychological state"). Jerry Fodor accepts the distinction for certain purposes, but argues that psychology should adopt the stance of "methodological solipsism" (Putnam's phrase)—that is, it should deal exclusively with inner states, the truly subjective psychological states which owe nothing to their relations to the outside world.[13]

Stephen Stich makes essentially the same distinction, but draws a sterner moral: where Fodor thinks we merely need to tinker a bit with propositional attitudes as usually conceived to separate out the purely subjective element, Stich holds that psychological states as we now think of them belong to a crude and confused "folk psychology" which must be replaced by a yet to be invented "cognitive science." The subtitle of his recent book is "The Case Against Belief."[14]

Clearly those who draw such a distinction have insured that the problem of first person authority, at least as I have posed it, cannot be solved. For the problem I have set is how to explain the asymmetry between the way in which a person knows about his contemporary mental states and the way in which others know about them. The mental states in question are beliefs, desires, intentions, and so on, as ordinarily conceived. Those who accept something like Putnam's distinction do not even try to explain first person authority with respect to these states; if there is first person authority at all, it attaches to quite different states. (In Stich's case, it is not obvious that it can attach to anything.)

I think Putnam, Burge, Dennett, Fodor, Stich, and others are right in calling attention to the fact that ordinary mental states, at least the propositional attitudes, are partly identified by relations to society and the rest of the environment, relations which may in some respects not be known to the person in those states. They are also right, in my opinion, in holding that for this reason (if for no other), the concepts of "folk psychology" cannot be incorporated into a coherent and comprehensive system of laws of the sort for which physics strives. These concepts are part of a common-sense theory for describing, interpreting, and explaining human behavior which is a bit freestyle, but (so I think) indispensable. I can imagine a science concerned with people and purged of "folk psychology," but I cannot think in what its interest would consist. This is not, however, the topic of this paper.

I am here concerned with the puzzling discovery that we apparently do not know what we think—at least in the way we think we do. This is a real puzzle if, like me, you believe it is true that external factors partly determine the contents of thoughts, and also believe that in general we do know, and in a way others do not, what we think. The problem arises because admitting the identifying and individuating role of external factors seems to lead to the conclusion that our thoughts may not be known to us.

But does this conclusion follow? The answer depends, I believe, on the way in which one thinks the identification of mental contents depends on external factors.

The conclusion does follow, for example, for any theory which holds that propositional attitudes are identified by objects (such as propositions, tokens of propositions, or representations) which are in or "before" the mind, and which contain or incorporate (as "ingredients") objects or events outside the agent; for it is obvious that everyone is ignorant of endless features of every external object. That the conclusion follows from these assumptions is generally conceded.[15] However, for reasons I shall mention below, I reject the assumptions on which the conclusion is in this case based.

Tyler Burge has suggested that there is another way in which external factors enter into the determination of the contents of speech and thought. One of his "thought experiments" happens pretty well to fit me. Until recently I believed arthritis was an inflammation of the joints caused by calcium deposits; I did not know that any inflammation of the joints, for example gout, also counted as arthritis. So when a doctor told me (falsely as it turned out) that I had gout, I believed I had gout but I did not believe I had arthritis. At this point Burge asks us to imagine a world in which I was physically the same but in which the word "arthritis" happened actually to apply only to inflammation of the joints caused by calcium deposits. Then the sentence "Gout is not a form of arthritis" would have been true, not false, and the belief that I expressed by this sentence would not have been the false belief that gout is not a form of arthritis but a true belief about some disease other than arthritis. Yet in the imagined world all my physical states, my "internal qualitative experiences," my behavior and dispositions to behave, are the same as they are in this world. My *belief* would have changed, but I would have no reason to suppose that it had, and so could not be said to know what I believed.

Burge stresses the fact that his argument depends on

> . . . the possibility of someone's having a propositional attitude despite an incomplete mastery of some notion in its content . . . *if* the thought experiment is to work, one must at some stage find the subject believing (or having some attitude characterized by) a content, despite an incomplete understanding or misapplication.[16]

It seems to follow that if Burge is right, whenever a person is wrong, confused, or partially misinformed about the meaning of a word, he is wrong, confused, or partially misinformed about any of his beliefs that is (or would be?) expressed by using that word. Since such "partial understanding" is "common or even normal in the case of a large number of expressions in our vocabularies" according to Burge, it must be equally common or normal for us to be wrong about what we believe (and, of course, fear, hope for, wish were the case, doubt, and so on).

Burge apparently accepts this conclusion; at least so I interpret his denial that ". . . full understanding of a content is in general a necessary condition for believing the content." He explicitly rejects

> . . . the old model according to which a person must be directly acquainted with, or must immediately apprehend, the contents of his thoughts . . . a person's thought *content* is not fixed by what goes on in him, or by what is accessible to him simply by careful reflection.[17]

I am uncertain how to understand these claims, since I am uncertain how seriously to take the talk of "direct acquaintance" with, and of "immediately apprehending," a content. But in any case I am convinced that if what we mean and think is determined by the linguistic habits of those around us in the way Burge believes they are, then first person authority is very seriously compromised. Since the degree and character of the compromise seem to me incompatible with what we know about the kind of knowledge we have of our own minds, I must reject some premise of Burge's. I agree that what I mean and think is not "fixed" (exclusively) by what goes on in me, so what I must reject is Burge's account of how social and other external factors control the contents of a person's mind.

For a number of reasons, I am inclined to discount the importance of the features of our attributions of attitudes to which Burge points. Suppose that I, who think the word "arthritis" applies to inflammation of the joints only if caused by calcium deposits, and my friend Arthur, who knows better, both sincerely utter to Smith the words "Carl has arthritis." According to Burge, if other things are more or less equal (Arthur and I are both generally competent speakers of English, both have often applied the word "arthritis" to genuine cases of arthritis, etc.) then our words on this occasion mean the same thing, Arthur and I mean the same thing by our words, and we express the same belief. My error about the dictionary meaning of the word (or about what arthritis is) makes no difference to what I meant or thought on this occasion. Burge's evidence for this claim seems to rest on his conviction that this is what anyone (unspoiled by philosophy) would report about Arthur and me. I doubt that Burge is right about this, but even if he is, I don't think it proves his claim. Ordinary attributions of meanings and attitudes rest on vast and vague assumptions about what is and is not shared (linguistically and otherwise) by the attributer, the person to whom the attribution is made, and the attributer's intended audience. When some of these assumptions prove false, we may alter the words we use to make the report, often in substantial ways. When nothing much hinges on it, we tend to choose the lazy way: we take someone at his word, even if this does not quite reflect some aspect of the speaker's thought or meaning. But this is not because we are bound (outside of a law court, anyway) to be legalistic about it. And often we aren't. If Smith (unspoiled by philosophy) reports to still another party (perhaps a distant doctor attempting a diagnosis on the basis of a telephone report) that Arthur and I both have said, and believe, that Carl has arthritis, he may actively mislead *his* hearer. If this danger were to arise, Smith, alert to the facts, would not simply say "Arthur and Davidson both believe Carl has arthritis"; he would add something like, "But Davidson thinks arthritis must be caused by calcium deposits." The need to make this addition I take to show that the simple attribution was not quite right; there was a relevant difference in the thoughts Arthur and I expressed when we said "Carl has arthritis." Burge does not have to be budged by this argument, of course, since he can insist that the report is literally correct, but could, like any report, be misleading. I think, on the other hand, that this reply would overlook the extent to which the contents of one belief necessarily depend on the contents of others. Thoughts are not independent atoms, and so there can be no simple, rigid rule for the correct attribution of a single thought.[18]

Though I reject Burge's insistence that we are bound to give a person's words the meaning they have in his linguistic community, and to interpret his propositional attitudes on the same basis, I think there is a somewhat different, but very important, sense in which social factors do control what a speaker can mean by his words. If a speaker wishes to be understood, he must intend his words to be interpreted in a certain way, and so must intend to provide his audience with the clues they need to arrive at the intended interpretation. This holds whether the hearer is sophisticated in the use of a language the speaker knows or is the learner of a first language. It is the requirement of learnability, interpretability, that provides the irreducible social factor, and that shows why someone can't mean something by his words that can't be correctly deciphered by another. (Burge seems to make this point himself in a later paper.)[19]

Now I would like to return to Putnam's Twin Earth example, which does not depend on the idea that social linguistic usage dictates (under more or less standard conditions) what speakers mean by their words, nor, of course, what their (narrow) psychological states are. I am, as I said, persuaded that Putnam is right; what our words mean is fixed in part by the circumstances in which we learned, and used, the words. Putnam's single example (water) is not enough, perhaps, to nail down this point, since it is possible to insist that "water" doesn't apply just to stuff with the same molecular structure as water but also to stuff enough like water in structure to be odorless, potable, to support swimming and sailing, etc. (I realize that this remark, like many others in this piece, may show that I don't know a rigid designator when I see one. I don't.) The issue does not depend on such special cases nor on how we do or should resolve them. The issue depends simply on how the basic connection between words and things, or thoughts and things, is established. I hold, along with Burge and Putnam if I understand them, that it is established by causal interactions between people and parts and aspects of the world. The dispositions to react differentially to objects and events thus set up are central to the correct interpretation of a person's thoughts and speech. If this were not the case, we would have no way of discovering what others think, or what they mean by their words. The principle is as simple and obvious as this: a sentence someone is inspired (caused) to hold true by and only by sightings of the moon is apt to mean something like "There's the moon"; the thought expressed is apt to be that the moon is there; the thought inspired by and only by sightings of the moon is apt to be the thought that the moon is there. Apt to be, allowing for intelligible error, second hand reports, and so on. Not that all words and sentences are this directly conditioned to what they are about; we can perfectly well learn to use the word "moon" without ever seeing it. The claim is that all thought and language must have a foundation in such direct historical connections, and these connections constrain the interpretation of thoughts and speech. Perhaps I should stress that the arguments for this claim do not rest on intuitions concerning what we would say if certain counterfactuals were true. No science fiction or thought experiments are required.[20]

I agree with Putnam and Burge, then, that

> . . . the intentional content of ordinary propositional attitudes . . . cannot be accounted for in terms of physical, phenomenal, causal-functional, computational, or syntactical states or processes that are specified nonintentionally and are defined purely on the individual in isolation from his physical and social environment.[21]

The question remains whether this fact is a threat to first person authority, as Burge seems to think, and Putnam and others certainly think. I have rejected one of Burge's arguments which, if it were right, would pose such a threat. But there is the position described in the previous paragraph, and which I hold whether or not others do, since I think this much "externalism" is required to explain how language can be learned, and how words and attitudes can be identified by an interpreter.

Why does Putnam think that if the reference of a word is (sometimes) fixed by the natural history of how the word was acquired, a user of the word may lose first person authority? Putnam claims (correctly, in my view) that two people can be in all relevant physical (chemical, physiological, etc.) respects the same and yet mean different things by their words and have different propositional attitudes (as these are normally identified). The differences are due to environmental differences about which the two agents may, in some respects, be ignorant. Why, under these circumstances, should we suppose these agents may not know what they mean and think? Talking with them will not easily show this. As we have noted, each, when faced with a glass of water or twater says honestly, "Here's a glass of water." If they are in their home environments, each is right; if they have switched earths, each is wrong. If we ask each one what he means by the word "water," he gives the right answer, using the same words, of course. If we ask each one what he believes, he gives the right answer. These answers are right because though verbally identical, they must be interpreted differently. And what is it that they do not know (in the usual authoritative way) about their own states? As we have seen, Putnam distinguishes the states we have just been discussing from "narrow" psychological states which do not presuppose the existence of any individual other than the subject in that state. We may now start to wonder why Putnam is interested in narrow psychological states. Part of the answer is, of course, that it is these states that he thinks have the "Cartesian" property of being known in a special way by the person who is in them. (The other part of the answer has to do with constructing a "scientific psychology"; this does not concern us here.)

The reasoning depends, I think, on two largely unquestioned assumptions. These are:

(1) If a thought is identified by a relation to something outside the head, it isn't wholly in the head. (It ain't in the head.)
(2) If a thought isn't wholly in the head, it can't be "grasped" by the mind in the way required by first person authority.

That this is Putnam's reasoning is suggested by his claim that if two heads are the same, narrow psychological states must be the same. Thus if we suppose two people are "molecule for molecule" the same ("in the sense in which two neckties can be 'identical' "; you may add, if you wish, that each of the two people "thinks the same verbalized thoughts . . ., has the same sense data, the same dispositions, etc."), then "it is absurd to think [one] psychological state is one bit different from" the other. These are, of course, narrow psychological states, not the ones we normally attribute, which ain't in the head.[22]

It is not easy to say in exactly what way the verbalized thoughts, sense data, and dispositions can be identical without reverting to the neckties, so let us revert. Then the idea is this: the narrow psychological states of two people are identical when their physical states cannot be distinguished. There would be no point in disputing this, since narrow psychological states are Putnam's to define; what I wish to question is assumption (1) above which led to the conclusion that ordinary propositional attitudes aren't in the head, and that therefore first person authority doesn't apply to them.

It should be clear that it doesn't follow, simply from the fact that meanings are identified in part by relations to objects outside the head, that meanings aren't in the head To suppose this would be as bad as to argue that because my being sunburned presupposes the existence of the sun, my sunburn isn't a condition of my skin. My sunburned skin may be indistinguishable from someone else's skin that achieved its burn by other means (our skins may be identical in "the necktie sense"); yet one of us is really sunburned and the other not. This is enough to show that an appreciation of the external factors that enter into our common ways of identifying mental states does not discredit an identity theory of the mental and the physical. Andrew Woodfield seems to think it does. He writes:

> No *de re* state about an object that is external to the person's brain can possibly be identical with a state of that brain, since no brain state presupposes the existence of an external object.[23]

Individual states and events don't *conceptually* presuppose anything in themselves; some of their *descriptions* may, however. My paternal grandfather didn't presuppose me, but if someone can be described as my paternal grandfather, several people besides my grandfather, including me, must exist.

Burge may make a similar mistake in the following passage:

> . . . no occurrence of a thought . . . could have a different content and be the very same token event . . . [T]hen . . . a person's thought event is not *identical* with any event in him that is described by physiology, biology, chemistry, or physics. For let *b* be any given event described in terms of one of the physical sciences that occurs in the subject while he thinks the relevant thought. Let "*b*" be such that it denotes the same physical event occurring in the subject in our counterfactual situation . . . *b* need not be affected by counterfactual differences [that do not change the contents of the thought event]. Thus . . . *b* [the physical event] is not identical with the subject's occurrent thought.[24]

Burge does not claim to have established the premise of this argument, and so not its conclusion. But he holds that the denial of the premise is "intuitively very implausible." He goes on, ". . . materialist identity theories have schooled the imagination to picture the content of a mental event as varying while the event remains fixed. But whether such imaginings are possible fact or just philosophical fancy is a separate question." It is because he thinks the denial of the premise to be very improbable that he holds that "materialist identity theories" are themselves "rendered implausible by the non-individualistic thought experiments."[25]

I accept Burge's premise; I think its denial not merely implausible but absurd. If two mental events have different contents they are surely different events. What I take Burge's and Putnam's imagined cases to show (and what I think The Swampman example shows more directly) is that people who are in all relevant physical respects similar (or "identical" in the necktie sense) can differ in what they mean or think, just as they can differ in being grandfathers or being sunburned. But of course there is *something* different about them, even in the physical world; their causal histories are different.

I conclude that the mere fact that ordinary mental states and events are individuated in terms of relations to the outside world has no tendency to discredit mental-physical identity theories as such. In conjunction with a number of further (plausible) assumptions, the "externalism" of certain mental states and events can be used, I think, to discredit type-type identity theories; but if anything it supports token-token identity theories. (I see no good reason for calling all identity theories "materialist"; if some mental events are physical events, this makes them no more physical than mental. Identity is a symmetrical relation.)

Putnam and Woodfield are wrong, then, in claiming that it is "absurd" to think two people could be physically identical (in the "necktie" sense) and yet differ in their ordinary psychological states. Burge, unless he is willing to make far stronger play than he has with essentialist assumptions, is wrong in thinking he has shown all identity theories implausible. We are therefore free to hold that people can be in all relevant physical respects identical while differing psychologically: this is in fact the position of "anomalous monism" for which I have argued elsewhere.[26]

One obstacle to non-evidential knowledge of our own ordinary propositional attitudes has now been removed. For if ordinary beliefs and the other attitudes can be "in the head" even though they are identified as the attitudes they are partly in terms of what is not in the head, then the threat to first person authority cannot come simply from the fact that external factors are relevant to the identification of the attitudes.

But an apparent difficulty remains. True, my sunburn, though describable as such only in relation to the sun, is identical with a condition of my skin which can (I assume) be described without reference to such "external" factors. Still, if, as a scientist skilled in all the physical sciences, I have access only to my skin, and am denied knowledge of the history of its condition, then by hypothesis there is no way for me to tell that I am sunburned. Perhaps, then, someone has first person authority with respect to the contents of his mind only as those contents can be described or discovered without reference to external factors. In so far as the contents are identified in terms of external factors, first person authority necessarily lapses. I can tell by examining my skin what my private or "narrow" condition is, but nothing I can learn in this restricted realm will tell me that I am sunburned. The difference between referring to and thinking of water and refer-ring to and thinking of twater is like the difference between being sunburned and one's skin being in exactly the same condition through another cause. The semantic difference lies in the outside world, beyond the reach of subjective or sublunar knowledge. So the argument might run.

This analogy, between the limited view of the skin doctor and the tunnel vision of the mind's eye, is fundamentally flawed. It depends for its appeal on a faulty picture of the mind, a picture which those who have been attacking the subjective character of ordinary psychological states share with those they attack. If we can bring ourselves to give up this picture, first person authority will no longer be seen as a problem; indeed, it will turn out that first person authority is dependent on, and ex-plained by, the social and public factors that were supposed to undermine that authority.

There is a picture of the mind which has become so ingrained in our philosoph-ical tradition that it is almost impossible to escape its influence even when its worst faults are recognized and repudiated. In one crude, but familiar, version, it goes like this: the mind is a theater in which the conscious self watches a passing show (the shadows on the wall). The show consists of "appearances," sense data, qualia, what is given in experience. What appear on the stage are not the ordinary objects of the world that the outer eye registers and the heart loves, but their purported representatives. Whatever we know about the world outside depends on what we can glean from the inner clues.

The difficulty that has been apparent from the start with this description of the mental is to see how it is possible to beat a track from the inside to the outside. Another conspicuous, though perhaps less appreciated, difficulty is to locate the self in the picture. For the self seems on the one hand to include theater, stage, actors, and audience; on the other hand, what is known and registered pertains to the audience alone. This second problem could be as well stated as the problem of the location of the objects of the mind: are they in the mind, or simply viewed by it?

I am not now concerned with such (now largely disavowed) objects of the mind as sense-data, but with their judgmental cousins, the supposed objects of the propositional attitudes, whether thought of as propositions, tokens of proposi-tions, representations, or fragments of "mentalese." The central idea I wish to attack is that these are entities that the mind can "entertain," "grasp," "have before it," or be "acquainted" with. (These metaphors are probably instructive: voyeurs merely want to have representations before the mind's eye, while the more aggressive grasp them; the English may be merely acquainted with the contents of the mind, while more friendly types will actually entertain them.)

It is easy to see how the discovery that external facts enter into the individua-tion of states of mind disturbs the picture of the mind I have been describing. For if to be in a state of mind is for the mind to be in some relation like grasping to a object, then whatever helps determine what object it is must equally be grasped if the mind is to know what state it is in. This is particularly evident if an external object is an "ingredient" in the object before the mind. But in either case, the person who is in the state of mind may not know what state of mind he is in.

It is at this point that the concept of the subjective—of a state of mind—seems to come apart. On the one hand, there are the true inner states, with respect to which the mind retains its authority; on the other hand there are the ordinary states of belief, desire, intention and meaning, which are polluted by their necessary connections with the social and public world.

In analogy, there is the problem of the sunburn expert who cannot tell by inspecting the skin whether it is a case of sunburn or merely an identical condition with another cause. We can solve the sunburn problem by distinguishing between sunburn and sunnishburn; sunnishburn is just like sunburn except that the sun need not be involved. The expert can spot a case of sunnishburn just by looking, but not a case of sunburn. This solution works because skin conditions, unlike objects of the mind, are not required to be such that there be a special someone who can tell, just by looking, whether or not the condition obtains.

The solution in the case of mental states is different, and simpler; it is to get rid of the metaphor of objects before the mind. Most of us long ago gave up the idea of perceptions, sense data, the flow of experience, as things "given" to the mind; we should treat propositional objects in the same way. Of course people have beliefs, wishes, doubts, and so forth; but to allow this is not to suggest that beliefs, wishes and doubts are *entities* in or before the mind, or that being in such states requires there to be corresponding mental objects.

This has been said before, in various tones of voice, but for different reasons. Ontological scruples, for example, are no part of my interest. We will always need an infinite supply of objects to help describe and identify attitudes like belief; I am not suggesting for a moment that belief sentences, and sentences that attribute the other attitudes, are not relational in nature. What I am suggesting is that the objects to which we relate people in order to describe their attitudes need not in any sense be *psychological* objects, objects to be grasped, known, or entertained by the person whose attitudes are described.

This point, too, is familiar; Quine makes it when he suggests that we may use our own sentences to keep track of the thoughts of people who do not know our language. Quine's interest is semantical, and he says nothing in this context about epistemological and psychological aspects of the attitudes. We need to bring these various concerns together. Sentences about the attitudes are relational; for semantic reasons there must therefore be objects to which to relate those who have attitudes. But having an attitude is not having an entity before the mind; for compelling *psychological* and *epistemological* reasons we should deny that there are objects of the mind.

The source of the trouble is the dogma that to have a thought is to have an object before the mind. Putnam and Fodor (and many others) have distinguished two sorts of objects, those that are truly inner and thus "before the mind" or "grasped" by it, and those that identify the thought in the usual way. I agree that no objects can serve these two purposes. Putnam (and some of the other philosophers I have mentioned) think the difficulty springs from the fact that an object partly identified in terms of external relations cannot be counted on to coincide with an object before the mind because the mind may be ignorant of the external relation. Perhaps this is so. But it does not follow that we can find other objects which will insure the desired coincidence. For if the object isn't connected with the world, we can never learn about the world by having that object before the mind; and for reciprocal reasons, it would be impossible to detect such a thought in another. So it seems that what is before the mind cannot include its outside connections—its semantics. On the other hand, if the object is connected with the world, then it cannot be fully "before the mind" in the relevant sense. Yet unless a *semantic* object can be before the mind *in its* *semantic aspect,* thought, conceived in terms of such objects, cannot escape the fate of sense data.

The basic difficulty is simple: if to have a thought is to have an object "before the mind," and the identity of the object determines what the thought is, then it must always be possible to be mistaken about what one is thinking. For unless one knows *everything* about the object, there will always be senses in which one does not know what object it is. Many attempts have been made to find a relation between a person and an object which will in all contexts hold if and only if the person can intuitively be said to know what object it is. But none of these attempts has succeeded, and I think the reason is clear. The only object that would satisfy the twin requirements of being "before the mind" and also such that it determines what the content of a thought must, like Hume's ideas and impressions, "be what it seems and seem what it is." There are no such objects, public or private, abstract or concrete.

The arguments of Burge, Putnam, Dennett, Fodor, Stich, Kaplan, Evans and many others to show that propositions can't *both* determine the contents of our thoughts and be subjectively assured are, in my opinion, so many variants on the simple and general argument I have just sketched. It is not just propositions that can't do the job; no objects could.

When we have freed ourselves from the assumption that thoughts must have mysterious objects, we can see how the fact that mental states as we commonly conceive them are identified in part by their natural history not only fails to touch the internal character of such states or to threaten first person authority; it also opens the way to an explanation of first person authority. The explanation comes with the realization that what a person's words mean depends in the most basic cases on the kinds of objects and events that have caused the person to hold the words to be applicable; similarly for what the person's thoughts are about. An interpreter of another's words and thoughts must depend on scattered information, fortunate training, and imaginative surmise in coming to understand the other. The agent herself, however, is not in a position to wonder whether she is generally using her own words to apply to the right objects and events, since whatever she regularly does apply them to gives her words the meaning they have and her thoughts the contents they have. Of course, in any particular case, she may be wrong in what she believes about the world; what is impossible is that she should be wrong most of the time. The reason is apparent: unless there is a presumption that the speaker knows what she means, i.e., is getting her own language right, there would be nothing for an interpreter to interpret. To put the matter another way, nothing could count as someone regularly misapplying her own words. First person authority, the social character of language, and the external determinants of thought and meaning go naturally together, once we give up the myth of the subjective, the idea that thoughts require mental objects.[27]

ENDNOTES

1. Graham Wallas, *The Art of Thought*.
2. Davidson [(1984a), pp. 101–11].
3. Putnam [(1975), p. 227].
4. I make no claim for originality here; Stephen Stich has used a very similar example in his [(1978a), p. 573 ff]. I should emphasize that I am not suggesting that an object accidentally or artificially created could not think; The Swampman simply needs time in which to acquire a causal history that would make sense of the claim that he is speaking of, remembering, identifying, or thinking of items in the world. (I return to this point later.)
5. Putnam [(1975), p. 144].
6. See Searle (1983) and Burge [(1986), pp. 3–45].
7. Putnam [(1975), pp. 164–5].
8. Fodor [(1982), p. 103]. Also see his (1980).
9. Searle (1983), ch. 8.
10. Woodfield [(1982), p. viii].
11. Dennett [(1982), p. 76].
12. Burge, in Woodfield (1982); Burge (1979a); Burge [(1982a), pp. 284–93]; Burge (1986).
13. Fodor (1980).
14. Stich (1983).
15. See, for example, Gareth Evans (1982).
16. Burge [(1979a), p. 83].
17. Burge [(1979a), pp. 90, 102, 104].
18. Burge suggests that the reason we normally take a person to mean by his words what others in his linguistic community mean, whether or not the speaker knows what others mean, is that "People are frequently held, and hold themselves, to the standards of the community when misuse or misunderstanding are at issue." He also says such cases ". . . depend on a certain responsibility to communal practice" [(1979a), p. 90]. I don't doubt the phenomenon, but its bearing on what it is supposed to show. (a) It is often reasonable to hold people responsible for knowing what their words mean; in such cases we may treat them as committed to positions they did not know or believe they were committed to. This has nothing (directly) to do with what they meant by their words, nor what they believed. (b) As good citizens and parents we want to encourage practices that enhance the chances for communication; using words as we think others do may enhance communication. This thought (whether or not justified) may help explain why some people tend to attribute meanings and beliefs in a legalistic

way; they hope to encourage conformity. (c) A speaker who wishes to be understood must intend his words to be interpreted (and hence interpretable) along certain lines; this intention may be served by using words as others do (though often this is not the case). Similarly, a hearer who wishes to understand a speaker must intend to interpret the speaker's words as the speaker intended (whether or not the interpretation is "standard"). These reciprocal intentions become morally important in endless situations which have no necessary connection with the determination of what someone had in mind.

19. See, for example, Burge [(1982a), p. 289].
20. Burge has described "thought experiments" which do not involve language at all; one of these experiments prompts him to claim that someone brought up in an environment without aluminum could not have "aluminum thoughts" [(1986), p. 5.]. Burge does not say why he thinks this, but it is by no means obvious that counterfactual assumptions are needed to make the point. In any case, the new thought experiments seem to rest on intuitions quite different from the intuitions invoked in Burge (1979a); it is not clear how social norms feature in the new experiments, and the linguistic habits of the community are apparently irrelevant. At this point it may be that Burge's position is close to mine.
21. Burge [(1982a), p. 288].
22. Putnam [(1975), p. 227].
23. Woodfield [(1982), p. viii].
24. Burge [(1979a), p. 111].
25. Burge [(1986), p. 15, note 7]. Cf. Burge [(1979a), p. 111].
26. Davidson (1970).
27. I am greatly indebted to Akeel Bilgrami and Ernie LePore for criticism and advice. Tyler Burge generously tried to correct my understanding of his work.

19

Individualism and Self-Knowledge

Tyler Burge

THE PROBLEM I WANT TO DISCUSS derives from the juxtaposition of a restricted Cartesian conception of knowledge of one's own thoughts and a nonindividualistic conception of the individuation of thoughts. Both conceptions are complex and controversial. But I shall not explain them in detail, much less defend them. I shall explicate them just enough to make the shape of the problem vivid. Then I shall say something about solving the problem.

Descartes held that we know some of our propositional mental events in a direct, authoritative, and not merely empirical manner. I believe that this view is correct. Of course, much of our self-knowledge is similar to the knowledge of others' mental events. It depends on observation of our own behavior and reliance on others' perceptions of us. And there is much that we do not know, or even misconstrue, about our minds. Descartes tended to underrate these points. He tended to overrate the power of authoritative self-knowledge and its potential for yielding metaphysical conclusions. Characterizing the phenomenon that interested Descartes is a substantial task. I shall not take on this task here. I think, however, that Descartes was right to be impressed with the directness and certainty of some of our self-knowledge. This is the point I shall rely on.

Descartes's paradigm for this sort of knowledge was the cogito. The paradigm includes not only this famous thought, but fuller versions of it—not merely "I am now thinking," but "I think (with this very thought) that writing requires concentration" and "I judge (or doubt) that water is more common than mercury." This paradigm goes further toward illuminating knowledge of our propositional attitudes than has generally been thought. But I note it here only to emphasize that Descartes's views about the specialness of some self-knowledge are not merely abstract philosophical doctrine. It is certainly plausible that these sorts of judgements or thoughts constitute knowledge, that they are not products of ordinary empirical investigation, and that they are peculiarly direct and authoritative. Indeed, these sorts of judgments are self-verifying in an obvious way: making these judgments itself makes them true. For mnemonic purposes, I shall call such judgments *basic self-knowledge*.

Let us turn from knowledge of one's thoughts to individuation of one's thoughts. My view on this matter is that many thoughts are individuated nonindividualistically: individuating many of a person or animal's mental kinds— certainly including thoughts about physical objects and properties—is necessarily

342

dependent on relations that the person bears to the physical, or in some cases social, environment. This view is founded on a series of thought experiments, which I shall assume are familiar.[1] Their common strategy is to hold constant the history of the person's bodily motion, surface stimulations, and internal chemistry. Then, by varying the environment with which the person interacts while still holding constant the molecular effects on the person's body, one can show that some of the person's thoughts vary. The details of the thought experiments make it clear that the variation of thoughts is indicative of underlying principles for individuating mental kinds. The upshot is that which thoughts one has—indeed, which thoughts one can have—is dependent on relations one bears to one's environment.

Our problem is that of understanding how we can know some of our mental events in a direct, nonempirical manner, when those events depend for their identities on our relations to the environment. A person need not investigate the environment to know what his thoughts are. A person does have to investigate the environment to know what the environment is like. Does this not indicate that the mental events are what they are independently of the environment?

By laying aside certain contrary elements in Descartes's views, one can reconstruct a tempting inference to an affirmative answer from his conception of self-knowledge.

In reflecting on the demon thought experiment, one might think that, since we can know our thoughts authoritatively, while doubting whether there is any physical world at all, the natures of our thoughts—our thought kinds—must be independent of any relation to a physical world. A parallel inference is presupposed in Descartes' discussion of the real distinction between mind and body. In *Meditations* IV, he argues that the mind can exist independently of any physical entity. He does so by claiming that he has a "clear and distinct idea" of himself as only a thinking and unextended thing, and a "clear and distinct idea" of body as only an extended and unthinking thing. He claims that it follows that the mind that makes him what he is can exist independently of any physical body. The argument also occurs in *Principles* I, LX:

> . . . because each one of us is conscious [through clear and distinct ideas] that he thinks, and that in thinking he can shut off from himself all other substance, either thinking or extended, we may conclude that each of us . . . is really distinct from every other thinking substance and from every corporeal substance.[2]

Descartes also believed that he had "clear and distinct ideas" of his thoughts. One might argue by analogy that, since one can "shut off" these thoughts from all corporeal substance, they are independent for their natures from physical bodies in the environment, and presumably from other thinkers. This line of argument implies that knowledge of one's own thoughts guarantees the truth of individualism.[3]

The root mistake here has been familiar since Arnaud's reply. It is that there is no reason to think that Descartes's intuitions or self-knowledge give him sufficient clarity about the nature of mental events to justify him in claiming that their natures are independent of relations to physical objects. Usually, this point has been made against Descartes's claim to have shown that mental events are independent of a person's body. But it applies equally to the view that mental kinds are independent of the physical environment. One can know what one's mental events are and yet not know relevant general facts about the conditions for individuating those events. It is simply not true that the cogito gives us knowledge of the individuation conditions of our thoughts which enables us to "shut off" their individuation conditions from the physical environment. Our thought experiments, which have directly to do with conditions for individuation, refute the independence claim.[4]

It is one thing to point out gaps in inferences from self-knowledge to individualism. It is another to rid oneself of the feeling that there is a puzzle here. Why is our having nonempirical knowledge of our thoughts not impugned by the fact that such thoughts are individuated through relations to an environment that we know only empirically?

Let us assume that our thoughts about the environment are what they are because of the nature of entities to which those thoughts are causally linked. According to our thought experiments, a person with the same individualistic physical history could have different thoughts if the environment were appropriately different. One senses that such a person could not, by introspection, tell the difference between the actual situation (having one set of thoughts) and the counterfactual situation (having another).

This intuition must be articulated carefully. What do we mean by "introspection"? In each situation, the person knows what his thoughts are; and in each situation the thoughts are different. If "introspection" were explicated in terms of self-knowledge, there would be an introspectible difference.

Certainly, if one were stealthily shifted back and forth between actual situations that modeled the counterfactual situations, one would not notice some feature in the world or in one's consciousness which would tell one whether one was in the "home" or the "foreign" situation. But this remark does not capture the idea that the two lives would feel the same. The thoughts would not switch as one is switched from one actual situation to another Twin actual situation. The thoughts would switch only if one remained long enough in the other situation to establish environmental relations necessary for new thoughts. So quick switching would not be a case in which thoughts switched but the introspection remained the same.

But slow switching could be such a case. Suppose that one underwent a series of switches between actual Earth and actual Twin Earth so that one remained in each situation long enough to acquire concepts and perceptions appropriate to that situation. Suppose occasions where one is definitely thinking one thought, and other occasions where one is definitely thinking its Twin.[5] Suppose also that the switches are carried out so that one is not aware that a switch is occurring. The continuity of one's life is not obviously disrupted. So, for example, one goes to sleep one night at home and wakes up in Twin home in Twin bed—and so on. (Your standard California fantasy). Now suppose that, after decades of such switches, one is told about them and asked to identify when the switches take place. The idea is that one could not, by making comparisons, pick out the Twin periods from the "home" periods.

I grant these ideas. The person would have no signs of the differences in his thoughts, no difference in the way things "feel." The root idea is that at least some aspects of one's mental life are fixed by the chemical composition of one's body. One might call these aspects *pure phenomenological feels*. If one were uncomfortable with this notion, one could explicate or replace it in terms of an abstraction from the person's inability to discriminate between different mental events under the stated switching situations.

The upshot of all this is that the person would have different thoughts under the switches, but the person would not be able to compare the situations and note when and where the differences occurred. This point, easily, though I think mistakenly, suggests the further point that such a person could not know what thoughts he had unless he undertook an empirical investigation of the environment which would bring out the environmental differences. But this is absurd. It is absurd to think that, to know which thoughts we think, we must investigate the empirical environment in such a way as to distinguish our actual environment from various Twin environments.

In basic self-knowledge, a person does individuate his thoughts in the sense that he knows the thought tokens as the thought tokens, and types, that they are. We know which thoughts we think. When I currently and consciously think that water is a liquid, I typically know that I think that water is a liquid. So much is clear.

How can one individuate one's thoughts when one has not, by empirical methods, discriminated the empirical conditions that determine those thoughts from empirical conditions that would determine other thoughts?

It is uncontroversial that the conditions for thinking a certain thought must be presupposed in the thinking. Among the conditions that determine the contents of first-order empirical thoughts are some that can be known only by empirical means. To think of something as water, for example, one must be in some causal relation to water—or at least in some causal relation to other particular substances that enable one to theorize accurately about water. In the normal cases, one sees and touches water. Such relations illustrate the sort of conditions that make possible thinking of something as water. To know that such conditions obtain, one must rely on empirical methods. To know that water exists, or that what one is touching is water, one cannot circumvent empirical procedures. But to *think* that water is a liquid, one need not *know* the complex conditions that must obtain if one is to think that thought. Such conditions need only be presupposed.

Now let us turn to knowledge of one's thoughts. Knowing what one is thinking when one has thoughts about physical entities presupposes some of the same conditions that determine the contents of the empirical thoughts one knows one is thinking. This is a result of the second-order character of the thoughts. A knowledgeable judgment that one is thinking that water is a liquid must be grounded in an ability to think that water is a liquid.

When one knows that one is thinking that p, one is not taking one's thought (or thinking) that p merely as an object. One is thinking that p in the very event of thinking knowledgeably that one is thinking it. It is thought and thought about in the same mental act. So any conditions that are necessary to thinking that p will be equally necessary to the relevant knowledge that one is thinking that p. Here again, to think the thought, one need not know the enabling conditions. It is enough that they actually be satisfied.

Both empirical thoughts and thinking that one is thinking such thoughts presuppose conditions that determine their contents. In both cases, some of these conditions can be known to be satisfied only by empirical means. Why do these points not entail that one cannot know that one is thinking that such and such unless one makes an empirical investigation that shows that the conditions for thinking such and such are satisfied? The answer is complex, but it can be seen as a series of variations on the point that one must start somewhere.

It is helpful in understanding self-knowledge to consider parallel issues regarding perceptual knowledge. It is a fundamental mistake to think that perceptual knowledge of physical entities requires, as a precondition, knowledge of the conditions that make such knowledge possible. Our epistemic right to our perceptual judgments does not rest on some prior justified belief that certain enabling conditions are satisfied. In saying that a person knows, by looking, that there is food there, we are not required to assume that the person knows the causal conditions that make his perception possible. We certainly do not, in general, require that the person has first checked that the light coming from the food is not bent through mirrors, or that there is not counterfeit food in the vicinity. We also do not require that the person be able to recognize the difference between food and every imaginable counterfeit that could have been substituted.

In fact, it is part of our common conception of the objectivity of perception that there is no general guarantee that the perceiver's beliefs, dispositions, and perceptions could in every context suffice to discriminate the perceived object from every possible counterfeit. The possibility of unforeseeable misperceptions and illusions is fundamental to objectivity. So the very nature of objective perception insures that the perceiver need not have a perfect, prior mastery over the conditions for his perceptual success.

This point is obvious as applied to common practice. But it is the business of philosophy and the pleasure of skepticism to question common practice. My discussion of knowledge and individualism has proceeded on the unargued assumption that skepticism is mistaken. Granted this assumption, the point that perceptual knowledge does not require knowledge of its enabling conditions is obvious.

I shall not overburden this essay with an attempt to disarm skepticism. But it is worth noting that nearly all currently defended responses to skepticism, other than transcendental ones, agree in denying that perceptual knowledge must be justified by separately insuring that the enabling conditions hold and the skeptic's defeating conditions do not hold.[6] And since transcendental responses provide at most general guarantees against skepticism, the only tenable responses, which I know of, that attempt to justify particular perceptual knowledge claims in the face of skepticism take this route. I think that it is the right route.

I have maintained that perceptual knowledge of physical objects does not presuppose that one has first checked to insure that the background enabling conditions are fulfilled. The same point applies to knowledge of one's own mental events, particularly knowledge of the sort that interested Descartes. Such knowledge consists in a reflexive judgment which involves thing a first-order thought that the judgment itself is about. The reflexive judgment simply inherits the content of the first-order thought.

Consider the thought, "I hereby judge that water is a liquid." What one needs in order to think this thought knowledgeably is to be able to think the first-order, empirical thought (that water is a liquid) and to ascribe it to oneself, simultaneously. Knowing one's thoughts no more requires separate investigation of the conditions that make the judgment possible than knowing what one perceives.

One knows one's thought to be what it is simply by thinking it while exercising second-order, self-ascriptive powers. One has no "criterion," or test, or procedure for identifying the thought, and one need not exercise comparisons between it and other thoughts in order to know it as the thought one is thinking. Getting the "right" one is simply a matter of thinking the thought in the relevant reflexive way. The fact that we cannot use phenomenological signs or empirical investigation to discriminate our thoughts from other thoughts that we might have been thinking if we had been in a different environment in no way undermines our ability to know what our thoughts are. We "individuate" our thoughts, or discriminate them from others, by thinking those and not the others, self-ascriptively. Crudely put, our knowledge of our own thoughts is immediate, not discursive. Our epistemic right rests on this immediacy, as does our epistemic right to perceptual beliefs. For its justification, basic self-knowledge in no way needs supplementation from discursive investigations or comparisons.[7]

So far I have stressed analogies between basic self-knowledge and perceptual belief. But there are fundamental differences. A requirement that, to know what thoughts we are thinking, we must be able first to discriminate our thoughts from Twin thoughts is, in my view, even less plausible than the analogous position with regard to perceptual knowledge.

Why? In developing an answer to this question, I want to dwell on some fundamental ways in which perceptual knowledge of physical entities differs from the sort of self-knowledge that we have been featuring. We commonly regard perceptual knowledge as *objective*. For our purposes, there are two relevant notions of objectivity. One has to do with the relation between our perceptions and the physical entities that are their objects. We commonly think that there is no necessary relation between any one person's abilities, actions, thoughts, and perceptions up to and including the time of a particular perception, on one hand, and the natures of those entities which that person perceptually interacts with at that time, on the other. On any given occasion, our perceptions could have been misperceptions. The individual physical item that one perceptually interacts with at any given time is fundamentally independent from any one person's perceptions—and conceptions. The nature of the physical entity could have been different even while one's perceptual states, and other mental states, remained the same.

This fact underlies a normative point about perception. We are subject to certain sorts of possible errors about empirical objects—misperceptions and hallucinations that are "brute." Brute errors do no result from any sort of carelessness, malfunction, or irrationality on our part. A person can be perceptually wrong without there being anything wrong with him. Brute errors depend on the independence of physical objects' natures from how we conceive or perceive them, and on the contingency of our causal relations to them. The possibility of such errors follows from the fact that no matter what one's cognitive state is like (so, no matter how rational or well-functioning one is) one's perceptual states could in individual instances fail to be veridical—if physical circumstances were sufficiently unfortunate.

There is a second sense in which perceptual knowledge is objective. This sense bears on the relation between one person's perceptions of an object and other persons' perception of the same object. The idea is that perceptual knowledge, like all other empirical knowledge, is impersonal. Any observer could have been equally well placed to make an observation. Others could have made an observation with the same type of presentation of the scene, if they had been in the same position at the relevant time. And this possible observation could have had the same justificatory status as the original observation. Even though empirical commitments must be made by persons, nothing relevant to the justification of any empirical commitment regarding the physical world has anything essentially to do with any particular person's making the commitment.

The paradigmatic cases of self-knowledge differ from perceptual knowledge in both these respects. To take the first: in the case of cogito-like judgments, the object, or subject matter, of one's thoughts is not contingently related to the thoughts one thinks about it. The thoughts are self-referential and self-verifying. An error based on a gap between one's thoughts and the subject matter is simply not possible in these cases. When I judge: I am thinking that writing requires concentration, the cognitive content that I am making a judgment about is self-referentially fixed by the judgment itself; and the judgment is self-verifying. There is a range of cases of self-knowledge which extend out from this paradigm. I think that, in all cases of authoritative knowledge, brute mistakes are impossible.

All errors in matters where people have special authority about themselves are errors which indicate something wrong with the thinker. Dealing with the whole range requires subtlety. But the point as applied to what I take to be the basic cases is straightforward. No errors at all are possible in strict cogito judgments; they are self-verifying.[8]

The paradigmatic cases of self-knowledge also differ from perceptual knowledge in that they are essentially personal. The special epistemic status of these cases depends on the judgments' being made simultaneously from and about one's first-person point of view. The point of view and time of the judgment must be the same as that of the thought being judged to occur. When I judge: I am thinking that writing requires concentration, the time of the judgment and that of the thought being judged about are the same; and the identity of the first-person pronouns signals an identity of point of view between the judge and the thought being judged about. In all cases of authoritative self-knowledge, even in those cases which are not "basic" in our sense, it is clear that their first-person character is fundamental to their epistemic status.

These differences between perceptual knowledge and authoritative self-knowledge ground my claim that it is even less plausible than it is in the case of perceptual knowledge to think that basic self-knowledge requires, as a precondition, knowledge of the conditions that make such knowledge possible.

Let us think about the difference as regards objectivity in the relation to an object. In the case of perceptual knowledge, one's perception can be mistaken because some counterfeit has been substituted. It is this possibility which tempts one into the (mistaken) view that, to have perceptual knowledge, one must first know something that rules out the possibility of a counterfeit. But in the cases of the cogito-like self-verifying judgments there is no possibility of counterfeits. No abnormal background condition could substitute some other object in such a way as to create a gap between what we think and what we think about. Basic self-knowledge is self-referential in a way that insures that the object of reference just is the thought being thought. If background conditions are different enough so that there is another object of reference in one's self-referential thinking, they are also different enough so that there is another thought. The person would remain in the same reflexive position with respect to this thought, and would again know, in the authoritative way, what he is thinking.

For example, imagine a case of slow switching between actual home and actual Twin home situations. In the former situation, the person may think "I am thinking that water is a liquid." In the latter situation, the person may think "I am thinking that twater is a liquid." In both cases, the person is right and as fully justified as ever. The fact that the person does not know that a switch has occurred is irrelevant to the truth and justified character of these judgments. Of course, the person may learn about the switches and ask, "Was I thinking yesterday about water or twater?"—and not know the answer. Here knowing the answer may sometimes indeed depend on knowing empirical background conditions. But such sophisticated questions about memory require a more complex story. If a person, aware of the fact that switching has occurred, were to ask, "Am I now thinking about water or twater?", the answer is obviously "both." Both concepts are used. Given that the thought is fixed and that the person is thinking it self-consciously, no new knowledge about the thought could undermine the self-ascription—or therefore its justification or authority.

In basic self-knowledge, one simultaneously thinks through a first-order thought (that water is a liquid) and thinks about it as one's own. The content of the first-order (contained) thought is fixed by nonindividualistic background conditions. And by its reflexive, self-referential character, the content of the second-order judgment is logically locked (self-referentially) onto the first-order content which it both contains and takes as its subject matter. Since counterfeit contents logically cannot undermine such self-knowledge, there should be not temptation to think that, in order to have such knowledge, one needs to master its enabling conditions.

The view I constructed on Descartes runs contrary. On that view, since basic self-knowledge is more certain than perceptual knowledge, it is more imperative that one be master of all its enabling conditions. One temptation toward this sort of reasoning may derive from construing self-knowledge as a perfected perceptual knowledge. If one thinks of one's relation to the subject matter of basic self-knowledge on an analogy to one's relation to objects of empirical investigation, then the view that one's thoughts (the subject matter) are dependent for their natures on relations to the environment will make it appear that one's knowledge of one's thoughts cannot be any more direct or certain than one's knowledge of the environment. If one begins by thinking of one's thoughts as objects like physical objects, except that one cannot misperceive or have illusions about them, then to explicate authoritative self-knowledge, one makes one of two moves. Either one adds further capacities for ruling out the possible sources of misperception or illusion in empirical perception, or one postulates objects of knowledge whose very nature is such that they cannot be misconstrued or misconceived. In the first instance, one grants oneself an omniscient faculty for discerning background conditions whose independence from us, in the case of perceptual knowledge, is the source or error. In the second instance, one imagines objects of thought (propositions that can be thought only if they are completely understood, or ideas whose *esse* is their *percipi*) whose natures are such that one cannot make any mistakes about them—objects of thought which one can "see" from all sides at once. In either case, one takes oneself to have ultimate insight into the natures of one's thoughts.

This line of reasoning is deeply misconceived. One need only make it explicit to sense its implausibility. The source of our strong epistemic right, our justification, in our basic self-knowledge is not that we know a lot about each thought we know we have. It is not that we can explicate its nature and its enabling conditions. It is that we are in the position of thinking those thoughts in the second-order, self-verifying way. Justification lies not in the having of supplemental background knowledge, but in the character and function of the self-evaluating judgments.

Let us turn to the point that self-knowledge is personal. The view that anti-individualism is incompatible with authoritative self-knowledge is easily engendered by forgetting the essentially first-person character of self-knowledge. We switch back and forth between thinking our thoughts and thinking about ourselves from the point of view of another person who knows more about our environment than we do. This is a key to Descartes's skeptical thought experiments. And it would not be surprising if he tended to think about self-knowledge in such a way as to give it a sort of omniscience from the third-person point of view—in order to protect the first person point of view from the fallibilities to which impersonal or third-person judgments (especially empirical judgments) are prone. Since we are not omniscient about empirical matters, it is natural to reduce the scope of the relevant third-person perspective so that the character of one's thoughts is independent of an environment about which we cannot be omniscient. Individualism ensues.

To illustrate the train of thought in a more concrete way: we think that we are thinking that water is a liquid. But then, switching to a third-person perspective, we imagine a situation in which the world is not as we currently think it is—a situation, say, in which there is no water for us to interact with. We take up a perspective on ourselves from the outside. Having done this, we are easily but illegitimately seduced into the worry that our original first-person judgment is poorly justified unless it can somehow encompass the third-person perspective, or unless the third-person perspective on empirical matters is irrelevant to the character of the first-person judgment. In this fallen state, we are left with little else but a distorted conception of self-knowledge and a return to individualism.[9]

As one thinks a thought reflexively, it is an object of reference and knowledge, but simultaneously a constituent of one's point of view. The essential role that the first-person singular plays in the epistemic status of authoritative self-knowledge differentiates this knowledge not only from empirical knowledge, but also from most *a priori* knowledge, the justification of which does not depend on the first-person point of view in the same way.

The tendency to blur distinctions between *a priori* knowledge (or equally, knowledge involved in explication of one's concepts) and authoritative self-knowledge is, I think, an instance of Descartes's central mistake: exaggerating the implications of authoritative self-knowledge for impersonal knowledge of necessary truths. One clearly does not have first-person authority about whether one of one's thoughts is to be explicated or individuated in such and such a way. Nor is there any apparent reason to assume that, in general, one must be able to explicate one's thoughts correctly in order to know that one is thinking them.

Thus, I can know that I have arthritis, and know I think I have arthritis, even though I do not have a proper criterion for what arthritis is. It is a truism that to think one's thoughts, and thus to think cogito-like thoughts, one must understand what one is thinking well enough to think it. But it does not follow that such understanding carries with it an ability to explicate correctly one's thoughts or concepts via other thoughts and concepts; nor does it carry an immunity to failures of explication. So one can know what one's thoughts are even while one understands one's thoughts only partially, in the sense that one gives incomplete or mistaken explications of one's thoughts or concepts. One should not assimilate "knowing what one's thoughts are" in the sense of basic self-knowledge to "knowing what one's thoughts are" in the sense of being able to explicate them correctly—being able to delineate their constitutive relations to other thoughts.[10]

For its justification, basic self-knowledge requires only that one think one's thoughts in the self-referential, self-ascriptive manner. It neither requires nor by itself yields a general account of the mental kinds that it specifies. Conceptual explication—knowledge of how one's thought kinds relate to other thought kinds—typically requires more objectification: reasoning from empirical observation or reflection on general principles. It requires a conceptual mastery of the conditions underlying one's thoughts and a conceptual mastery of the rules one is following. These masteries are clearly beyond anything required to think thoughts in the second-order, self-ascriptive way. Explicative knowledge is neither self-verifying nor so closely tied to particular mental events or particular persons' points of view.[11]

Despite, or better because of, its directness and certainty, basic self-knowledge is limited in its metaphysical implications. It is nonetheless epistemically self-reliant. By itself it yields little of metaphysical interest; but its epistemic credentials do not rest on knowledge of general principles, or on investigation of the world.

ENDNOTES

1. Cf. Burge (1979a), (1982), (1986), (1986a), and (1986b).
2. Haldane & Ross (1955), pp. 243–4.
3. Cf. *ibid.*, p. 190.
4. I have discussed this and other features of the inference in Burge (1986a). See also Burge (1988). I now think that Descartes's views have more anti-individualistic elements than I realized in writing those articles. I hope to discuss these matters elsewhere.
5. Of course, there can arise difficult questions about whether one is still employing thoughts from the departed situation or taking over the thoughts appropriate to the new situation. I think that general principles govern such transitions, but such principles need not sharply settle all borderline cases. Insofar as one finds problems associated with actual switches distracting, one could carry out the objection I am articulating in terms of counterfactual situations.
6. This remark applies to reliabilist theories, Moorean theories that insist on the directness of perception, Quinean theories that attempt to show that the skeptic's doubt is

covertly a bad empirical doubt, and Carnapian theories that attempt to show that the skeptic's question is somehow irrelevant to actual empirical claims. The words "first" and "separately" are crucial in my formulations. As against some reliabilist views that try to block skepticism by denying closure principles, I think that we can know that no demon is fooling us. But we know this by inferring it from our perceptual knowledge.

Several philosophers have thought that anti-individualism, combined with the view that we are authoritative about what thoughts we think, provides a "transcendental" response to skepticism. Cf. Hilary Putnam (1981). Putnam's argument is criticized by Brueckner (1986). I agree with Brueckner that Putnam's arguments do not do much to undermine skepticism. But Brueckner seems to hold that, if anti-individualism and the authority of self-knowledge are accepted, one would have an antiskeptical argument. He suggests that the assumption of anti-individualism undercuts the assumption of authoritative self-knowledge. I do not accept this suggestion. I believe, however, that there is no easy argument against skepticism from anti-individualism and authoritative self-knowledge. This is a complicated matter best reserved for other occasions.

7. I shall not develop the issue of one's epistemic right to one's authoritative self-ascriptions here. It is an extremely complex issue, which deserves separate attention.

8. Mistakes about the *res* in *de res* judgments are not counterexamples to the claim that basic cogito-like judgments are self-verifying (hence infallible). Suppose I judge: I am thinking that my aunt is charming; and suppose that the person that I am judging to be charming is not my aunt (I have some particular person in mind). It is true that I am making a mistake about the identity of the person thought about; I have no particular authority about that, or even about her existence. But I am not making a mistake about what I am thinking about that person; there is no mistake about the intentional act and intentional content of the act. Authority concerns those aspects of the thought which have intentional (aboutness) properties. For me, those are the only aspects of the content of a thought.

9. My knowledge that I am thinking that mercury is an element depends on an ability to think—not explicate—the thought that mercury is an element. Compare my knowledge that my words "mercury is an element" are true if and only if mercury is an element. This knowledge depends on understanding the words "mercury is an element" well enough to say with them, or think with them, that mercury is an element. It is this ability which distinguishes this knowledge from mere knowledge that the disquotation principle as applied to "mercury is an element" is true (mere knowledge that the sentence " 'mercury is an element' is true if and only if mercury is an element" is true). I know that my word "mercury" applies to mercury (if to anything), not by being able to provide an explication that distinguishes mercury from every conceivable Twin mercury, but by being a competent user of the word, whose meaning and reference are grounded in this environment rather than in some environment where the meaning of the word form would be different. The fact that one may not be able to explicate the difference between mercury and every possible Twin mercury should not lead one to assimilate one's use of "mercury" to knowledge of purely formal relationships (e.g., knowledge that all instances of the disquotation principle are true).

One other comparison: I know that I am here (compare: on Earth) rather than somewhere else (compare: Twin Earth). My knowledge amounts to more than knowing I am wherever I am. I have normal ability to perceive and think about my surroundings. I have this knowledge because I perceive my surroundings and not other conceivable surroundings, and I have it even though other places that I could not distinguish by perception or description from here are conceivable. For a variety of reasons, one should not assimilate terms like "water" to indexicals like "here." Cf. Burge (1982). But these analogies may be helpful here.

10. Davidson's views about self-knowledge have some crucial points in common with mine. But he may be making this mistake when he writes that, if one concedes the possibility of partial understanding as I do, one must concede that anti-individualism undermines the authority of self-knowledge. Cf. Davidson (1987) and (1984a). It is unclear to me why Davidson says this. I have discussed the distinction between the sort of understanding necessary to think and the sort of understanding necessary to explicate one's thoughts, in Burge (1979a), (1986b), (forthcoming), and (1989a).

11. As I indicated earlier, basic self-knowledge is at most an illuminating paradigm for understanding a significant range of phenomena that count as self-knowledge. Thus, the whole discussion has been carried out under a major simplifying assumption. A full discussion of authoritative self-knowledge must explicate our special authority, or epistemic right, even in numerous cases where our judgments are not self-verifying or immune to error. I think, however, that reflection on the way that errors can occur in such cases gives not the slightest encouragement to the view that anti-individualism (as regards either the physical or social environments) is a threat to the authority of our knowledge of the contents of our thoughts.

20

Anti-Individualism and Privileged Access

Michael McKinsey

IT HAS BEEN A PHILOSOPHICAL commonplace, at least since Descartes, to hold that each of us can know the existence and content of his own mental states in a privileged way that is available to no one else. This has at least seemed true with respect to those "neutral" cognitive attitudes such as thought, belief, intention, and desire, whose propositional contents may be false. The crucial idea is not that one's knowledge of these states in oneself is incorrigible, for surely one can make mistakes about what one believes, intends, or desires. Rather, the idea is that we can in principle find out about these states in ourselves "just by thinking," without launching an empirical investigation or making any assumptions about the external physical world. I will call knowledge obtained independently of empirical investigation *a priori* knowledge. And I will call the principle that it is possible to have *a priori* knowledge of one's own neutral cognitive attitude states, the Principle of Privileged Access, or just "privileged access" for short.

Although many philosophers would insist that privileged access is undeniable, a series of recent discoveries and arguments in the philosophy of language has, I believe, convinced a perhaps equally large number of philosophers that privileged access is a complete illusion. One of the most persuasive of these arguments was proposed by Tyler Burge (1982) as an application of Putnam's (1975) famous Twin Earth case. Oscar, a resident of Earth, believes that water is wet. On Twin Earth, there is no water; rather there is a qualitatively similar liquid with a different chemical composition, a liquid that we may call "twater." Toscar, who is Oscar's identical twin and a denizen of Twin Earth, does not believe that water is wet. For Toscar has no beliefs about water at all; rather, he believes that twater is wet, that twater fills the oceans, etc. Yet Oscar and Toscar, being absolutely identical twins, would certainly seem to be internally the same. In Putnam's terminology, Oscar and Toscar would share all the same "narrow" psychological states. Thus, Burge concludes, Oscar's belief that water is wet must be a *wide* state: it must, that is, "presuppose" or "depend upon" the relations that Oscar bears to other speakers or objects in his external environment.

In general, Burge endorses a conclusion something like

(B) Some neutral cognitive states that are ascribed by *de dicto* attitude sentences (e.g., "Oscar is thinking that water is wet") necessarily depend upon or presuppose the existence of objects external to the person to whom the state is ascribed.

Now (B) might certainly *appear* to conflict with privileged access. For (B) implies that sometimes, whether or not a person is in a given cognitive state is determined by external facts that the person himself could only know by empirical investigation. In such cases, it would seem, the person would therefore not be able to know *a priori* that he is in the cognitive state in question.

But interestingly enough, Burge (1988a) has recently urged that despite appearances, his anti-individualism [that is, his conclusion (B)] is perfectly compatible with privileged access. And a similar point of view had earlier been expressed by Davidson (1987). I want to argue here that Burge and Davidson are wrong. Anti-individualism and privileged access as standardly understood are incompatible, and something has to give.[1]

I will first briefly discuss Davidson's defense of compatibilism. Davidson clearly accepts anti-individualism as formulated by (B), and like Burge he accepts (B) in part on the basis of Burge's persuasive application of Putnam's Twin Earth case. But Davidson insists that anti-individualism does not undermine first person authority about one's own mental states. He agrees with the anti-individualist thesis that some *de dicto* attitude ascriptions "identify thoughts by relating them to things outside the head" [(1987), p. 451]. But he suggests that philosophers like Putnam who find a difficulty for privileged access in this thesis are in effect confusing thoughts with their descriptions. Such philosophers make the mistake, Davidson says, of inferring from the fact that a thought is identified or *described* by relating it to something outside the head, that the thought itself must therefore *be* outside the head and hence must be unavailable to privileged access [(1987), p. 451].

Now I do not myself see any reason to believe that Putnam or anyone else has actually made this mistake. Certainly, as we shall see below, the most cogent reason for endorsing incompatibilism does not involve this mistake at all, so that Davidson's diagnosis is inconclusive at best. But what is most disconcerting about Davidson's remarks is the version of privileged access that he apparently takes himself to be defending. He explicitly accepts anti-individualism, understanding it as the thesis that thoughts are often *described* (in attitude ascriptions) by relating them to objects outside the head. Then he (quite correctly) points out that it does not follow from this thesis that the thoughts so described are *themselves* outside the head. But what is the relevance of this point to the issue at hand? Apparently Davidson is saying that since the thoughts in question are inner episodes that exist independently of our means of describing them, we can have privileged access to these episodes, whatever the external implications of our descriptions of the episodes might be.

But if this is what Davidson has in mind, then the version of privileged access that he is defending is too weak to be of much philosophical interest. He wishes to claim, apparently, that one could have privileged access to an episode of thought independently of having privileged access to any particular descriptions that the episode might satisfy. But then what would one have privileged access to in such a case? Perhaps one would be privileged to know only that the episode exists; given what Davidson says, there is no reason to suppose that the agent would have privileged access even to the fact that the episode is an episode of *thought*, as opposed to being, say, an episode of indigestion.

But surely, having access of this sort to one's thoughts is not much of a privilege. The traditional view, I should think, is not just that we have privileged access to the fact that our thoughts occur, rather the view is that we have privileged access to our thoughts *as satisfying certain descriptions*. In particular, the traditional view is that we have privileged access to our thoughts as having certain contents, or as satisfying certain *de dicto* cognitive attitude predicates. Thus, if Oscar is thinking that water is wet, the traditional view would be that Oscar has privileged access, not just to the fact that some episode or other is occurring in him, but to the fact that he is thinking that water is wet. Now apparently, Davidson would just *deny* that Oscar has privileged access to the latter sort of fact, since as he says, the fact relates Oscar to objects outside his head. But if he would deny this, then Davidson's claim to be defending first person authority seems misleading at best.[2]

In contrast to Davidson, Burge clearly means to defend privileged access in its traditional guise. Given what he says in "Individualism and Self-Knowledge" (1988a), Burge would maintain that the following three propositions are consistent:

(1) Oscar knows *a priori* that he is thinking that water is wet.
(2) The proposition that Oscar is thinking that water is wet necessarily depends upon E.
(3) The proposition E cannot be known *a priori* but only by empirical investigation.

(Here I assume that E is the "external proposition" whose presupposition makes Oscar's thought that water is wet a wide state.)

Whether (1)-(3) are consistent is determined by the sense that the phrase "necessarily depends upon" is taken to have in (2). Unfortunately, Burge never explains or clarifies the concept of necessary dependency that he invokes throughout his paper. I will now argue that Burge is able to make his compatibility thesis appear plausible only by tacitly identifying the dependency relation with *metaphysical* necessity. But this identification is illegitimate in the present context, for a reason that I will explain below.

A clue to what Burge has in mind by dependency is provided by the analogy he chooses to undermine the incompatibilist's reasoning. One who reasons from the assumption that we can know our own mental states *a priori* to the conclusion that these states must be independent of any empirical propositions about physical objects is, says Burge, making the same mistake as was once made by Descartes and diagnosed by Arnaud [(1988a), pp. 650–51].

From the fact that he could know directly and incorrigibly the existence of himself and his own thoughts, while consistently doubting the existence of his body and the rest of the physical world, Descartes inferred that it was possible for him to exist as a disembodied mind in a nonphysical universe. But this inference is illegitimate. The fact that Descartes could not correctly *deduce* the existence of the physical world from the existence of himself and his thoughts may show something significant about Descartes' *concepts* of himself and his thoughts. But as Arnaud pointed out, this failure of deduction shows nothing about the nature of either Descartes or his thoughts. It is perfectly consistent with this failure of deduction to suppose that both Descartes and his thoughts have an essentially physical nature, and that neither Descartes nor his thoughts could possibly have existed unless certain physical objects, including perhaps Descartes' body, Descartes' parents, and the sperm and egg cells from which Descartes developed, had also existed. For the fact, if it is a fact, that Descartes' existence is dependent upon the existence of these other physical objects would not be something that is knowable *a priori*. It would be a fact that is necessary but only knowable *a posteriori*. [As Kripke (1980) pointed out]. Thus the dependency would be a fact that is not deducible *a priori* from Descartes' incorrigible knowledge of himself and his thoughts.

Since metaphysical dependencies are often only knowable *a priori*, propositions that are knowable *a priori* might metaphysically depend upon other propositions that are only knowable *a posteriori*. Thus Oscar might know *a priori* that he exists, and his existence might metaphysically depend upon the existence of his mother, even though Oscar cannot know *a priori* that his mother exists.

The upshot of this discussion is that (1), (2), and (3) are all clearly consistent, provided that "depends upon" in (2) is interpreted as meaning *metaphysical* dependency. When the material conditional "if p then q" is metaphysically necessary, let us say that *p metaphysically entails q*. Then our result so far is that (1) and (3) are consistent with

(2a) The proposition that Oscar is thinking that water is wet metaphysically entails E.

Burge's main point in defense of the compatibility of antiindividualism and privileged access, then, seems to be that such triads as (1), (2a) and (3) are consistent. In other words, his point is that our having privileged access to our own mental states is compatible with those states being metaphysically dependent upon facts to which we have no privileged access.

But this point, though correct, is quite irrelevant to the main issue. For antiindividualism is the thesis that some neutral *de dicto* cognitive attitude states are wide states, and to say that a state is wide (not narrow) cannot mean *merely* that the state metaphysically entails the existence of external objects.[3] For if it did, then given certain materialistic assumptions that are pretty widely held, it would follow that probably *all* psychological states of *any* kind would be wide, so that the concept of a narrow state would have no application at all, and anti-individualism would be merely a trivial consequence of (token) materialism.

For instance, it is plausible to suppose that no human could (metaphysically) have existed without biological parents, and that no human could (metaphysically) have had biological parents other than the ones she in fact had. [See Kripke (1980), pp. 312–314]. If this is so, then Oscar's thinking that water is wet metaphysically entails that Oscar's mother exists. In fact, Oscar's having any psychological property (or any property at all) would metaphysically entail the existence of Oscar's mother. Thus if metaphysical entailment of external objects were what made a psychological state wide, then probably all of Oscar's—and everyone else's—psychological states would be wide.

But this is obviously *not* the sense of "wide psychological state" that philosophers like Putnam and Burge have had in mind. While it may well be true that Oscar's thinking that water is wet entails the existence of Oscar's mother or the existence of the egg from which Oscar developed, it would nevertheless not be for *this* kind of reason that Oscar's mental state is wide! Clearly, to say that the state in question is wide is not to say something that is true by virtue of Oscar's *nature* or the *nature* of the particular event that is Oscar's thought that water is wet. Rather it is to say something about the *concept,* or property, that is expressed by the English predicate "x is thinking that water is wet"; it is to say something about what it *means* to say that a given person is thinking that water is wet.

Let us say that a proposition *p* conceptually *implies* a proposition *q* if and only if there is a correct deduction of *q* from *p*, a deduction whose only premises other than *p* are necessary or conceptual truths that are knowable *a priori*, and each of whose steps follows from previous lines by a self-evident inference rule of some adequate system of natural deduction. I intend the relation of conceptual implication to be an appropriately logical, as opposed to a metaphysical, relation.

Our discussion shows, I believe, that the thesis of anti-individualism should be stated in terms of conceptual implication rather than metaphysical entailment.[4] In this connection, it is worth noting that when Putnam originally introduced the notions of narrow and wide psychological states, he did so in terms of logical possibility [(1975), p. 141]. Moreover, he introduced these notions as explicitly Cartesian concepts. Thus a narrow state should be (roughly) a state from which the existence of external objects cannot be *deduced,* and a wide state would be one from which the existence of external objects *can* be deduced.

On my proposal, Burge's thesis of anti-individualism should be understood as

(Ba) Some neutral cognitive states that are ascribed by *de dicto* attitude sentences (e.g., "Oscar is thinking that water is wet") conceptually imply the existence of objects external to the person to whom the state is ascribed.

But, of course, now that we have made anti-individualism into the conceptual thesis that it should be, we also have our contradiction with privileged access back again.

For instance, (2) must now be understood as

(2b) The proposition that Oscar is thinking that water is wet conceptually implies E,

and it is easy to see that (1), (2b), and (3) form an inconsistent triad. The argument is this. Suppose (1) that Oscar knows *a priori* that he is thinking that water is wet. Then by (2b), Oscar can simply *deduce* E, using only premises that are knowable *a priori*, including the premise that he is thinking that water is wet. Since Oscar can deduce E from premises that are knowable *a priori*, Oscar can know E itself *a priori*. But this contradicts (3), the assumption that E *cannot* be known *a priori*. Hence (1), (2b), and (3) are inconsistent. And so in general, it seems, anti-individualism is inconsistent with privileged access.

It is worth keeping the structure of this simple argument in mind, so as not to confuse it with another (bad) argument that Burge frequently alludes to in his (1988a). Burge sometimes characterizes the person who thinks that anti-individualism is inconsistent with privileged access as reasoning on the basis of the following sort of assumption [see for instance (1988a), p. 653]:

(4) Since the proposition that Oscar is thinking that water is wet necessarily depends upon E, no one, including Oscar, could know that Oscar is thinking that water is wet without first knowing E.

One who assumes (4) could then reason that (1), (2), and (3) are inconsistent, as follows. (2) and (4) imply that Oscar could not know that he is thinking that water is wet without first knowing E. But by (3), E is not knowable *a priori*. Hence, Oscar could also not know *a priori* that he is thinking that water is wet. But this contradicts (1). Hence, (1), (2), and (3) are inconsistent.

Burge is certainly right when he objects to this line of reasoning. The reasoning is obviously bad when necessary dependency is interpreted as metaphysical entailment. For then, one would be assuming (4) on the basis of the principle that

(5) If p metaphysically entails q, then no one could know that p without first knowing that q.

But (5) is obviously false. For instance, even if Oscar's existence metaphysically entails the existence of Oscar's mother, Oscar can surely know that he exists without first knowing that his mother does!

Even when necessary dependency is interpreted as conceptual implication, the reasoning is bad. In this case, (4) would be assumed on the basis of

(6) If p conceptually implies q, then no one could know that p without first knowing that q.

But, of course, it is a well known fact that closure principles like (6) are false: certainly with respect to any proposition p that can be known at all, it is possible to know p without first knowing each of (the infinite number of) p's logical consequences.

So Burge was certainly right to object to the kind of reason he imagined one might have for believing that anti-individualism and privileged access are incompatible. But, of course, this does not show that no good reason for the incompatibility can be given. The simple argument I gave above is in fact such a good reason, and it does not depend on any suspicious closure principles like (5) and (6).

Rather, the argument is much more straightforward. In effect it says, look, if you could know *a priori* that you are in a given mental state, and your being in that state conceptually or logically implies the existence of external objects, then you could know *a priori* that the external world exists. Since you obviously can't know *a priori* that the external world exists, you also can't know *a priori* that you are in the mental state in question. It's just that simple. I myself find it hard to understand why Burge and Davidson will not just accept this obvious and compelling line of reasoning.

ENDNOTES

1. I have elsewhere discussed at length the problems for particular forms of anti-individualism that arise from these theses' apparent incompatibility with privileged access. See McKinsey (1978) and (1987).
2. It is, of course, possible that Davidson would be prepared to defend a view on which all our thoughts that fall under wide *de dicto* descriptions also fall under *other* descriptions of some important kind to which we have privileged access. Perhaps, for instance, he might be willing to say that every thought with a "wide" content would also have another "narrow" content to which we have privileged access. [I suggest such a "two-content" view in my (1986).] But as far as I know, Davidson nowhere spells out or defends such a view. And, of course, the mere hypothetical fact that Davidson *might* be willing to develop a view on which privileged access is compatible with anti-individualism does not by itself provide us with any *argument* in favor of this compatibility.
3. Here I assume that, for Burge, metaphysical entailment of external objects must be a logically sufficient condition for a state to be wide. Perhaps it might be objected that this is unfair to Burge, since all he really needs is the assumption that metaphysical entailment of external objects is a *necessary* condition of wideness. But this objection is misconceived. Burge is trying to show that such triads as (1), (2), and (3) are consistent. His argument is that this is so because (1), (2a), and (3) are consistent. But this argument requires the assumption that (2a)—the claim concerning metaphysical entailment—is logically *sufficient* for (2)—the claim concerning wideness, or necessary dependency. For unless (2a) is sufficient for (2), the fact that (1), (2a), and (3) are consistent is quite irrelevant to the conclusion that (1), (2), and (3) are consistent. (The correct general principle for proving consistency is that, if p and q are consistent, and q logically implies r, then p and r are consistent. Note the difference between this principle and the false principle that if p and q are consistent and q is logically implied by r, then p and r are consistent: this is wrong, since r might for instance be an explicit contradiction that logically implies the consistent q.)
4. In McKinsey (1991) I give a more thorough and detailed defense of the thesis that the concepts of narrow and wide psychological states must be understood in terms of conceptual implication rather than metaphysical necessity.

21

Can Externalism Be Reconciled with Self-Knowledge?

Akeel Bilgrami

I. IT ALL STARTED WITH PUTNAM

It is a tribute not just to his impressive originality as a philosopher but to the systematic range of his thought that Hilary Putnam, who—along with Kripke, Marcus, Chastain, and no doubt some others—founded a certain conception of the nature of reference and meaning, was the first to then go on to draw the consequences it has for the nature of intentionality. The conception I have in mind is, of course, the so-called "causal" conception of reference and meaning, sometimes also called "direct reference." The consequences I have in mind have amounted to a view of intentionality which is often called the "externalist" account of intentional content.

My concern in this paper is with the latter and, in particular, with one very important and problematic theme that emerges from this externalist view of intentional content. This is the theme of self-knowledge of our intentional contents, sometimes also described as a "first-person authority" that agents have over their intentional contents. (I will use the expressions "self-knowledge" and "first-person authority" more or less interchangeably throughout the paper except at one crucial point, where the latter will mark a special non-inferentiality of much of our self-knowledge. For this see note 22 and the text to which it attaches.) It is widely thought that there is at the very least a *prima facie* difficulty that externalism raises for the idea that we have self-knowledge, in cases where we would otherwise think it intuitive that we do have it. Even those who deny that it poses a difficulty have tended to acknowledge that there is at least a *prima facie* problem that they must remove.

I won't pause to sketch in detail Putnam's causal views of reference and meaning, nor to spell out the details by which it comes to have the externalist consequences it has in the philosophy of mind. These are well known and have been extensively elaborated in the voluminous commentary that Putnam has inspired. Let me simply begin with a general definition of externalism as one finds it in his paper "The Meaning of 'Meaning'."[1] Externalism is a denial of the following thesis: Intentional states, in the ordinary non-scientific sense that Aristotle intended when he devised the "practical syllogism," that is, states such as beliefs and desires which we invoke to make sense of or "rationalize" people's various doings, "do not presuppose the existence of any thing external to the agent who possesses such states" (136). The denied thesis may and has been called "internalism" or, in Putnam's own phrase, "methodological solipsism"; its denial has been called "externalism." I will call this externalism (G.E.) to mark the perfectly general definition of externalism just given. I believe that external-ism, so generally and minimally defined, is an extremely important truth about intentionality.

However, here is something well worth noting. Though (G.E.) is indeed a consequence of Putnam's causal conception of reference and meaning, there is no entailment in the opposite direction. That is, it is perfectly possible to accept externalism, *generally* defined as above (and as Putnam himself defines it) and *not* go on to embrace Putnam's views of reference and meaning nor the *specific* externalist picture of intentionality that these views have as a conse-quence. I have, elsewhere, proposed a specific externalism which falls under (G.E.) and which makes no appeal to those views of reference and meaning.[2] I say this at this point only to draw attention to the fact that we need to distinguish between a general characterization of externalism and specific externalist proposals which may fall under it. Putnam's views of reference and meaning give rise to a specific externalism, but it is quite uncompulsory for externalists, that is for those who subscribe to (G.E.), to adopt these views and the externalism it gives rise to. (From now on, my use of the expression "Putnam's externalism" will be restricted to talk of his specific thesis rather than to his general definition.) This fact has gone more or less unnoticed, and almost everyone in the large class of contemporary philosophers of mind and language who thinks that there is something worthwhile in externalism takes it for granted that externalism must be cashed out in terms of these views. Since this amounts to such an orthodoxy today, I will call this specific version of externalism that falls under (G.E.), (O.E.).[3] Because it is such an ortho-doxy, (O.E.) is often simply conflated with (G.E.); being an orthodoxy, its adherents cannot imagine any other specific externalist proposal than their own, and so they proceed as if their proposal is equivalent to the general thesis. I will argue that we would do well to guard against this conflation. For one of my principal and eventual claims in this paper will be that on the theme of self-knowledge of intentional states, externalists, that is, anyone who subscribes to (G.E.), would do better to shun (O.E.) for some alternative externalism which does not raise the difficult problems that (O.E.) raises for self-knowledge. I briefly sketch such an alternative externalism towards the end of the paper.

But first, let me say something about why it is thought that externalism poses even a *prima facie* problem for self-knowledge.

II. THE *PRIMA FACIE* PROBLEM EXTERNALISM POSES FOR SELF-KNOWLEDGE

Before raising the problem, I should point out that here too not only was Putnam the first to point out what this problem is, but that Putnam accepted defeat in the face of the problem, and was the first to propose a highly influential way of living with it. However, some other externalists have been more defiant on Putnam's behalf and have tried to argue that the problem is only *prima facie* and that, on scrutiny, it is illusory. Let me explain all this.

Why is it natural to assume, at least *prima facie*, that states which are constituted, in part, by things external to a person may sometimes not be known to the person who is in these states? In some recent papers Davidson asks exactly this question and answers it by invoking Putnam's Twin Earth example.[4] The idea is that a pair of internally identical twins on Earth and Twin Earth respectively have different but, as far as *they* can tell, indistinguishable substances, which they both call "water," in their environments; so, given externalism, they have different "water"-concepts and "water"-thoughts. Since they have different thoughts without really being able to tell the difference, they do not fully know what their own thoughts are. The example and its general point have been widely discussed, so I will not pause over details. The particular point that Davidson's discussion is intended to bring out is that if the contents of our thoughts are not constituted only by things internal to us in some suitably Cartesian sense, then it may seem at least *prima facie* natural to think that we will often not know what our thoughts are, since we may often not know crucial things about items external to us. He points out that Putnam grants this *initially* natural point as *in the end* undeniably true, and he criticizes Putnam for giving in to it too easily. Tyler Burge also raises this problem for externalism and he too thinks that we should hold out for a way of reconciling externalism and self-knowledge.[5]

Putnam, of course, despite his concession, does not *rest content* with the conclusion that because of externalism we very often do not know the contents of our thoughts. To do so would be foolish, even in a thoroughly post-Freudian climate. I say "foolish" and mean it. However widespread psychological phenomena such as self-deception, self-censorship, inattention . . . might be, these are *psychological* phenomena, which psychologists such as Freud, and many others, have studied; and though there may be some quarreling at the margins about the extent of their sway, we are intuitively willing to grant that such phenomena obstruct self-knowledge. What is foolish and unintuitive is to grant that a wholly non-psychological phenomenon, i.e., an entirely abstract philosophical doctrine about reference, should be seen as raising an obstruction to self-knowledge. At any rate it is foolish and unintuitive to see it as obstructing the very same sort of (or the very same sense of) knowledge state that the psychological phenomena just listed obstructs. And to see it as obstructing some other kind of (or sense of) state of self-knowledge would be to make equivocal the notion of self-knowledge in a way that adds unnecessary complication and brings no illumination.

So, as I was saying, Putnam, laudably, does not rest content with a denial of self-knowledge of our thoughts and goes on, in effect, to claim that there are two notions of a thought's content, one internal and one external, and it is only the latter which raises a problem for self-knowledge; the former is always available to the agent (unless, of course, it is obstructed by one of the psychological phenomena listed above). Thus we find that Putnam, after conceding lack of self-knowledge, bifurcates the intentional aspect of the mind into two, a distinction now routinely described as a distinction between "narrow" (internal) intentional content and "wide" (external) intentional content.

But Davidson and Burge eschew this bifurcation because they think that it arises, in part, from an unnecessary surrender in the face of the problem raised only *prima facie* by externalism for self-knowledge.

I will argue that Putnam is right in thinking that the problem is crippling for the idea of a unified or unbifurcated mind, and that Davidson and Burge do not see this only because they do not raise the problem for self-knowledge that Putnam's externalism poses in an appropriately specific way. The right way of raising the problem reveals the problem to be an insuperable one. But my defense of Putnam will only be partial. It will only be a defense against Davidson and Burge. The eventual point of my criticisms of Davidson and Burge will not be that all externalists are stuck with Putnam's bifurcated conception of intentionality. My solution, as I said, will rather be that we need to abandon orthodox externalism (O.E.), and fashion a new and alternative kind of specific position which satisfies (G.E.) but for which the problem regarding self-knowledge does not arise even *prima facie*.

III. DAVIDSON'S WAY OF RECONCILING EXTERNALISM WITH SELF-KNOWLEDGE

Davidson's criticisms of Putnam depend crucially on a particular diagnosis he offers for why philosophers have thought first-person authority is possible in the first place. He first points out that there is a long tradition of post-Cartesian thinking which persists today in which it is taken for granted that there are *objects of thoughts*. In Descartes and various traditional and modern empiricists these were usually taken to be objects in consciousness, available in an authoritative and complete way to the subject of the thoughts and unavailable in such a way to any other subject. Davidson says that though contemporary philosophers like Searle still cling to the Cartesian version of such objects of thought, others have moved them some distance from their Cartesian moorings in inner consciousness and have taken them to be either propositions, or sentences in the head, or sometimes even (as in the somewhat exceptional case of Gareth Evans's and John McDowell's Russellian version of singular thoughts) external objects with which we are directly acquainted.[6] But despite these differences between them, they all share the common idea that there are such objects of thought and, according to Davidson, it is this idea which they all assume makes self-knowledge possible. If, after all, the contents of our thought are defined in terms of special kinds of object authoritatively and completely available to us, then there is no problem regarding our knowledge of them.

Davidson then goes on to say that Putnam, in shunning internalism (for his wide contents, anyway), gives up on the internalist idea that there are such objects of thought.[7] But having given up on the idea, he immediately concludes that with it he must also give up on first-person authority over such contents, for it is the idea which is supposed to account for such authority. So Davidson charges Putnam with having retained the traditional and longstanding internalist assumption that objects of thought alone can explain first-person authority. That is to say, though Putnam, in giving up on internalism, gives up on there *being* such objects of thought (for wide content) he does *not* take the radical step of giving up on the assumption that it is these internalist objects of thought alone which account for our self-knowledge of such contents. This combination of retaining the assumption while giving up on the objects forces him to give up on self-knowledge for those contents.

Having diagnosed, to his own satisfaction, why it is that Putnam gives up on a reconciliation between self-knowledge and externalism, Davidson then goes on to say that the reconciliation should not be hard to achieve, if we *do* take the radical step of also giving up on the assumption that objects of thought account for self-knowledge. He too denies that there are such objects of thought which have any such epistemological standing. He does not deny that when we attribute thoughts we use our interpreted sentences or utterances to specify the thoughts. But he denies that to do this amounts in any way to attributing anything which is within the epistemological or psychological ken of the agent to whom the thoughts are being attributed. And, since he gives up not only on the objects themselves but *also* on the assumption that we need any such epistemic intermediaries to account for self-knowledge, he concludes the following: If with Putnam we reject internalism, and therefore give up on such objects of thought, we may nevertheless now not follow him in giving up on self-knowledge for those externally constituted thoughts.

It only remains for Davidson to give some alternative account of self-knowledge from the one he attributes to the tradition, an account which makes no appeal to the traditional idea of objects of thought. The account he offers is, roughly and crudely, that interpreting another person and attributing thoughts to her requires the assumption that she has direct and non-inferential knowledge of her own thoughts. If we did not do so, we would not have anything to interpret. Thus the very idea of interpretation requires that the interpretee has authority over her own thoughts. And since, for Davidson, to be a thinker is to be the object of interpretation, all thinkers have first-person authority. I will not spend time discussing this alternative explanation at this point, since this is not primarily a paper on Davidson's positive views.[8] Since my present concern is only in his criticism of Putnam's handling of the problem that externalism poses for self-knowledge, it is enough to just record that Davidson's alternative account of self-knowledge does not invoke objects of thought, and can therefore live with externalism in a way that Putnam could not.

IV. BURGE'S WAY OF RECONCILING EXTERNALISM WITH SELF-KNOWLEDGE

Burge suggests a slightly different way of avoiding the *prima facie* problem by pointing to a feature of what he calls "basic cases" of self-knowledge. These are the cases expressed in sincere, first-person, present-tense, judgments about thoughts. In these basic cases, in knowing or thinking that one is thinking that *p*, one is also thinking that *p*. This is the feature he then exploits as follows. An agent's thought that *p* has certain necessary constitutive conditions, and since when one knows that one is thinking that *p*, one is also thinking that *p*, it follows that those constitutive conditions carry over to the self-knowledge too. Therefore these constitutive conditions cannot possibly obstruct self-knowledge. If the constitutive conditions are external to the agent, that makes no difference.

This point is correct. It assumes self-knowledge and shows that, if one has self-knowledge of one's thought that *p*, then (in the form of the basic cases, at least), what goes into the individuation of *p* carries over to the iterated thought that expresses the self-knowledge. It is true that he only has shown it for the basic cases, but that is quite enough to show that, in itself, externalism poses no, *in principle*, obstacle to self-knowledge.

One might protest that his argument assumes that we have self-knowledge, where that is exactly what needs to be shown in the face of his externalism. But the protest is missing the point of Burge's strategy. He is really claiming that the *prima facie* objection does not really get off the ground because, given his argument, there is no reason to think that externalism poses a problem for self-knowledge in the first place. One does not have to know all the constitutive conditions that go into the thought that p being the thought it is in order to have that thought. And so if one is unaware of the various external factors that go into its being that thought, it neither follows that one doesn't have that thought nor, given their common necessary conditions, that one doesn't have the iterated thought that expresses self-knowledge of the thought.

By this strategy, it looks as if Burge is going to insist that one can never argue directly from externalism to a threat to self-knowledge. So far as I can see, the strategy, as it stands, looks reasonable and anybody who argues simply that Burge's (or Putnam's) externalism leads *directly* to absence of self-knowledge has not said enough to resist the strategy.

All the same, I think there is a common flaw in the way that Davidson and Burge approach Putnam's externalism, and this allows them to run away with the impression that they have in their different ways reconciled it with the fact of first-person authority. The flaw lies in the way that the problem for self-knowledge is posed by them.

Let me consider Burge first.

V. WHAT'S WRONG WITH BURGE'S RECONCILIATION?

We concluded our exposition of Burge's reconciliation by pointing out that Burge had satisfactorily answered the *prima facie* objection (from considerations about self-knowledge) to externalism: he did so with his strategy of appealing to the unique feature of his basic cases which blocked any *direct* route from externalism to a denial of self-knowledge.

But all this shows is that the *prima facie* objection is a badly posed objection, and that one needs to chart a more indirect route from externalism to lack of self-knowledge. One needs to raise the objection in a more roundabout way than is done by the *prima facie* objection.

In order to do so, let's put aside the question of self-knowledge for just a moment and notice once again that Putnam's externalism gives rise to a quite *different prima facie* problem. The indirect strategy says that self-knowledge is threatened not directly by the fact of externalism but by the fact that there is no way to avoid this other *prima facie* problem except by surrendering self-knowledge.

The other *prima facie* problem is this. Because (as the Twin Earth example above makes clear) Putnam is committed to an externalism that comes from a certain scientific essentialist view of natural-kind terms and concepts, his view is, on the face of it, sometimes going to attribute *inconsistent* thoughts to agents. It is sometimes going to attribute inconsistent thoughts when the agents are ignorant of the objective natures and the scientific essences, as for example, when an ignorant agent says "I have arthritis in my thigh" or "Water is not H_2O."[9] If such an agent's concept of the disease or the substance is determined by its objective nature, the scientific essence, these predications amount to blatant inconsistency. That is, it is tantamount to attributing to him the belief that he has a disease of the joints only in his thigh (a blatant inconsistency, if we assume, as we may, that he knows that a thigh is not a joint), or attributing to him the belief that a substance with the chemical composition H_2O is not H_2O. But these agents are not logical idiots. However, the only way to avoid the false and uncharitable conclusion that they are logically incompetent is to say that though they believe those things, as these externalisms require, they need not know that they believe them. Their ignorance of the full meaning of the terms or concepts sometimes makes them unaware of their own thoughts in which those concepts figure. And if they don't know that they believe these blatantly inconsistent things then they can't be accused of logical idiocy. But now we have avoided this accusation of attributing logical idiocy at the price of attributing lack of self-knowledge. So: we have arrived at the denial of self-knowledge in a somewhat more indirect way.

This indirect way of posing the problem for Burge makes his remarks and his strategy for how externalism can accommodate self-knowledge unsatisfyingly general. They do not address the specific *dilemma* we have posed for Putnam's specific externalism: either agents must often be falsely accused of logical idiocy, or, and this brings us to our subject, they must often be denied self-knowledge of their contents (for instance in the examples just mentioned) when intuitively there is no reason to deny it.[10] Actually, strictly speaking it is a *trilemma* since there is a third option, which is simply to opt for a bifurcation of content into two, one of which is not externalist (in Putnam's sense of externalism) and therefore does not have any problem with self-knowledge. This is, as I said, Putnam's own solution, but, as I also said, it amounts to accepting that self-knowledge cannot be reconciled with his externalism. Since Burge has explicitly resisted accepting this and has denied the wisdom in bifurcation,[11] we may see the bifurcatory way out of the problems created by the first two horns of the dilemma as the third horn of a trilemma for him.

It would be surprising if the case against Burge were so simple. So let me consider various responses one could make on his behalf in order to avoid the trilemma.[12]

FIRST RESPONSE

In the reasoning which led to making the charge about inconsistent attributions (the first horn), there was one very important step. This step consisted in rewriting the occurrence of "arthritis" and "water" in the inconsistent belief attributions with "a disease of the joints only" and "a substance with the chemical composition H_2O." Without this step we could not attribute the blatantly inconsistent thoughts. Blatant inconsistency only arises if we claim that the ignorant agent thinks that it is this sort of substance which is not H_2O, or this sort of disease which has afflicted his thigh.

Now someone may resist this "rewrite" interpretation of Putnam's externalism, and in a recent paper Burge himself has introduced certain distinctions which someone may invoke in this resistance.[13] Here is the passage with the distinction:

> I distinguish between a lexical item and the explication of its meaning that articulates what the individual would give, under some reflection, as his understanding of the word. Call the former "the word" and the latter "the entry for the word." I also distinguish between the concept associated with the word and the concept(s) associated with the entry. Call the former "the concept" and the latter "the conceptual explication." Finally, I distinguish between a type of meaning associated with the word, "translational meaning," and the meaning associated with its entry, "explicational meaning." For our purposes, the explicational meaning is the semantical analogue of

the conceptual explication. The translational meaning of a word can be articulated through exact translation and sometimes through such trivial thoughts as my word "tiger" applies to tigers, but need not be exhaustively expressible in other terms in an idiolect. (181)

He goes on to criticize the view (he calls it the "traditional" view) which claims that:

> . . . a word's explicational meaning and its translational meaning are, for purposes of characterizing the individual's idiolect, always interchangeable; and that the individual's conceptual explication always completely exhausts his or her concept. This view is incorrect. It is incorrect because of the role that the referent plays in individuating the concept and translational meaning, and because of the role that non-explicational abilities play in the individual's application of the word and concept. Accounting for a person's lexical entry or conceptual explication is relevant to determining the nature of a person's meaning or concept. But the two enterprises are not the same. (181)

Now all this is relevant because someone may think that in the crucial step above, my insistence that Putnam's externalist view amounts to taking the agent's concept of arthritis as involving an attribution of the concept of a disease of the joints only, is a running together of the agent's "concept" with the "conceptual explication"—just what Burge warns us against in the traditional view. An inconsistency is only attributed if the agent can exhaustively articulate (recall the definition of "conceptual explication" in the first quotation) the concept of arthritis, in particular articulate that it is a disease of the joints only, which, being ignorant, he cannot. Thus the rewrite description is not part of his conceptual explication. Clearly since we want to avoid the first horn, that is, clearly since we are in advance convinced by considerations of charity that the agent is not being blatantly inconsistent, we may, armed now with these distinctions, attribute to him only the explicatory portion of the concept of arthritis and thereby ensure that no inconsistency is being attributed. In short, someone may want to defend Putnam against the charge of attributing inconsistencies to agents, such as in the arthritis example above, by saying that it involves a case of the conceptual explication not exhausting the concept.

The trouble with this response, however, is that it has surreptitiously, that is to say with other words and labels, conceded that there is a second notion of content. Contents are composed of concepts. And now we are being told that there are two notions of concepts: 1) concepts proper, given by externalist reference and 2) concepts in the sense of conceptual explications that the agent can, on reflection, articulate. It is only when the second of these is attributed that an attribution of inconsistency is avoided. Contents composed of the former will often harbor internal inconsistencies when the agent is seriously misinformed about the reference, as in the examples above.

The conceptual explication of "arthritis" in this example of an ignorant agent will consist, say, of the agent's belief that it is a disease, that it is a painful disease, that it occurs more often in older people, etc., but *not* that it is a disease of the joints only. And it is this conceptual explication that avoids the first horn. This explication, of course, does not get us to the reference of "arthritis" (in any official sense of "reference") nor does it coincide with the explication of the experts. It is concepts proper which are tied to reference and to experts' explications. If one attributes contents composed of concepts proper to this agent, as Burge says we must, and if we want to avoid an intentional psychology for him that uncharitably and quite wrongly attributes blatant inconsistencies, we had better also attribute the other kind of content to him. We had better attribute contents with concepts in the sense of conceptual explications.

Hence an appeal to these distinctions to save Burge against the first horn succeeds only by accepting a bifurcation of content into two. It can only avoid the first horn by impaling him on the third horn.

SECOND RESPONSE

Burge may resist my talk of the explicatory portions of concepts as forming the basis of a second notion of content. He may deny that it is necessary to talk that way in order to avoid the first horn and the charge of attributing inconsistencies. Recall again that the problem about attributions of inconsistent beliefs arose for externalism because we allowed ourselves to rewrite "arthritis" in the representation of the agent's belief with, among other things, "a disease of the joints only." Only thus the inconsistency in his thinking, "I have arthritis in my thigh" (assuming still that he knows that the thigh is not a joint). Our justification for doing so was just Putnam's claim that the concept determined in terms of the scientific essences and objective natures of the external items must be attributed to the agent. That rewrite just *is* the concept which is so determined.

It is this substitution or rewrite that the distinctions invoked by the first response were trying to finesse. Here is another, somewhat related, but not identical, reason why the inconsistency-inducing rewrites might be resisted. It might be said that the rewrite is only permissible if one believes in something like the analytic-synthetic distinction. Only if one thought that concepts or terms, such as "arthritis," have definite meanings which include "a disease of the joints only", is it permitted. But why, it will be protested, should we hitch this old cart horse of a distinction to a shiny new buggy like Putnam's externalism? Indeed Burge has explicitly denied that he embraces the distinction in another recent paper[14] (and Putnam himself has, famously, opposed the distinction for a long time). It is unfair to him, then, to interpret his idea of the external element's constitutive relevance to concepts and contents as the idea that we take any definite belief or set of beliefs defining "arthritis" and plug them into the representations of individual agents' beliefs whenever we might have said "arthritis." But without plugging it in we cannot have the first horn, we cannot have our inconsistent belief attributed.

This response is fair enough only if we are told of an alternative way of saying what the agent's notion is than the one which is specified by the substitution of some set of beliefs capturing the objective natures. What, according to Putnam's externalism, are we attributing to the agent when we say that he believes that he has arthritis in his thigh, if it is not, among other things, the belief that he has a disease, which afflicts the joints only, in his thigh? The experts and most other people who are scientifically knowledgeable do, after all, think that that is what arthritis is, i.e., that is what it refers to; so what is left of Putnam's externalism, with its appeal to scientific essences, if the substitution is not allowed? How can we retain the relevance of this external element (the objective natures that the experts are tracking) to this agent's concepts and contents and fail to specify things this way?

The only alternative specification of his concept of arthritis, which retains the relevance of the scientific essences, is one which appeals to a very much more general belief *of the agent himself*, something like the belief: "arthritis is whatever the experts, call 'arthritis'." This metalinguistic specification is a convenient way of bringing in the scientific essentialist element without saying anything specific by way of a definition of "arthritis," and it thus avoids saying anything that smacks of a commitment to the analytic-synthetic distinction. And because it does not say anything very specific it does not involve the agent in any inconsistency. But notice that this way of retaining the external element retains the wrong thing. The external now enters in a way that abandons Putnam's externalism. It, after all, enters mediated by a belief or description of the agent's, even if the belief is metalinguistically specified. It now is indistinguishable from a view of the external and referential element which is mediated by the descriptions of the agent. It is no longer an externalism based on the causal-theoretic view of reference which is familiar from Putnam.

It is interesting to note that if someone, on Burge's behalf, accepted these metalinguistic ways of bringing in the external,[15] Putnam's externalism would collapse with a much weaker and much more general thesis than his externalism: the thesis about the linguistic division of labor. This latter thesis plausibly emphasizes the fact that there is no specifying many of our concepts and many of the meanings of our terms except by noting that they are determined in part by our reliance on others in the society in which we live. But the thesis does not amount to Putnam's specific externalism at all since reliance can be captured by *beliefs or descriptions of the relying agent*—metalinguistically specified—such as the one mentioned in the last paragraph. It does not amount to a referential external-ism because it does not attribute the same concept (of, say, arthritis or, to take a famous example from Putnam, of elm) to the relying agent as it does to the expert, the relied-upon agent. The latter's concept, since it does *not* turn on similar metalinguistically specified beliefs, but on more purely medical or botanical beliefs, is quite different from the relying agent's concept. The reference is no longer crucial in the specification of concepts, it is the *differing* beliefs or descriptions of the relied-upon and the relying agent which are doing the work, so the concepts attributed to them will be quite different.[16]

I conclude then that Burge can only endorse this second line of response by abandoning the externalist thesis in Putnam that the response was supposed to defend.

THIRD RESPONSE

It may still seem that I have not allowed Burge the most sympathetic exposition of his position so that he can make Putnam avoid the problem of having to attribute an inconsistency and, thus, avoid the first horn. Someone may deny that the only way for a social externalist to avoid a commitment to the analytic-synthetic distinction is to rewrite "arthritis" along the metalinguistic lines suggested in my reply to the second response. Someone might say that there is no reason to plug in for "arthritis," in the specification of the agent's content, either the metalinguistic rewrite ("whatever the experts call 'arthritis'") or the inconsistency-inducing rewrite ("a disease of the joints only"). There is no need for any rewrite. Rather what is needed, it might be said, is simply the concept of *arthritis*. There is nothing else to say. So to the question: what does he think he has in his thigh, the answer simply is: arthritis. He is able to think this because he thinks, falsely, that one can have arthritis in one's thigh. That the concept is the concept of *arthritis* (which is a disease one can only have in the joints) allows us to say no more, Burge might say, than something harmless such as "He thinks, *of* a disease which one can (in fact) only have in one's joints, that he has it in his thigh." No need to rewrite things at all, neither as the belief that he has a disease which is among other things a disease of the joints only, in his thigh, nor as the belief that he has the disease, which is called "arthritis" by the experts, in his thigh.

This third response, I believe, leaves things with a mystery. One is being left with what is sometimes called a purely "disquotational" specification of the concept. If I were to persist, well what is it that you are attributing when you say that he has arthritis in his thigh, what does "arthritis" *in the de dicto specification of the content* tell us?—the answer will simply be that "arthritis" refers to arthritis."[17] To the question, what's *that?*, what does the right hand occurrence of the term convey, the protest will be that I am insisting on definitions, an insistence from the dark ages when the analytic-synthetic distinction was still in currency. Notice, though, that I am asking for what "arthritis" in the specification tells us, I am not asking for *further* information about something which has already been conveyed by the disquotational specification. The protest, then, has got to be that even this minimal and initial demand smacks of a commitment to definitions and therefore to the analytic-synthetic distinction.

This protest against my rewrite is not the same as another more clearly mistaken protest. It is not the protest which says that I am missing the obvious point that *de dicto* attributions do not allow of substitutions. Such a protest would itself be missing the obvious point that it cannot be that *de dicto* attributions allow of no substitutions. The prohibition of substitutions in *de dicto* attributions turn on the attributee *not knowing* of the co-extensiveness of the expressions involved; and I am precisely protesting that there must be some, at the minimum one, and often more, expressions that can be substituted, or else it is not clear that any concept of arthritis should be attributed to him. And moreover if we admit that "a disease of the joints only" is not one of the expressions to be substituted for "arthritis" because the attributee does not know of the co-extensiveness, then, as I said in my reply to the second response, that puts into doubt the relevance of Putnam's externalist concept of arthritis to *de dicto* attributions.

The more serious protest under consideration charges my insistence on rewrites with the more specific charge of being committed to the idea of analyticity.

I have no particular wish to defend the analytic-synthetic distinction and toward the end of the paper I will say something to make it absolutely clear that my view does not require any commitment to it. But even on the face of it, it does seem to me quite wrong to think that if one persists with the question (what is it that the reference-giving assertion "'arthritis' refers to arthritis" is really saying?) one must be doing so because of a desire for definitions. All that the persistence reflects is a dissatisfaction with a trivially conceived disquotational specification of the term "arthritis" when one is asking for the concept being specified in the content attribution. Disquotation cannot be a merely syntactic device, for if it were, it could never specify the concept of arthritis in content attributions. Indeed it could never specify any meaning of anything at all. Disquotation, if it is to be in the service of an account of meaning, is not a wholly trivial idea. It must be anchored in something which is not made explicit in the disquotational clause itself. The right hand side occurrence of "arthritis," after all, is a *use* of the term. It expresses something.

And so if disquotation is not a mere syntactic device, one *does*, if not explicitly at least implicitly,[18] get an answer to the question one is persisting with, the question what is it that one is saying when one says that an agent thinks that he has *arthritis* in his thigh. And then one wants to know, if the right hand side of the reference-giving statement expresses something, why—*for Putnam's externalism*—it does not express the inconsistency-inducing "a disease of the joints only," since that is what the scientific experts think arthritis is. What remains of his externalism, with its appeal to scientific essences, if that is not what the right hand side occurrence expresses?

One answer to this criticism might be that the appeal to the idea that "arthritis" refers to arthritis in specifying the concept is not an appeal to disquotation as a syntactic device at all. Rather the disquoted term conveys that the term "arthritis" hooks up with something in the world by a causal relation which is unmediated by any description. It is hooked up with an *object*, and is not to be elaborated, as I am insisting, by the specification of an *object under some beliefs or descriptions*, which descriptions can then be plugged in.

Here again I must confess, along with many others, that it is hard for me to understand how terms like reference (and truth) can possibly have a theoretical role to play in the study of concepts (and contents) if the right hand sides of the statements attributing reference (and truth-conditions) reduce us to utter ineffability about what the concept is. This way of avoiding the triviality of disquotation as a syntactic device makes things trivial not by making something syntactic out of something semantic, but rather by making semantics ineffable and mysterious. The highly metaphysical nature of the hook-up has the same trivializing effect. Both the syntactic move and this move appealing to such an ulterior metaphysics of reference have the same consequence: they convey no information at all as to what the concept being attributed is.

Here is a way of bringing this out more vividly. Nobody can deny that there is, at least, a *prima facie* difference between the sentence "Vermeer's *View of the Delft* is beautiful" and "Vermeer's *View of the Delft* is painted on a canvas," between "Nehru was a good man" and "Nehru was born in Allahabad." Nobody can deny that predicates like "is beautiful" and "is good" are, *prima facie*, different from predicates like "is painted on canvas" and "is born in Allahabad." The difference consists in the fact that, at least *prima facie*, there is a difference in the way we think of how they stand in relation to concepts like truth and reference. The application of concepts like reference and truth is, at least *prima facie*, problematic when we are dealing with evaluative predicates and sentences. No doubt many will eventually want to say that evaluative predicates like "is good" and "is beautiful" are susceptible to a naturalistic or an intuitionistic treatment and so there is not a serious difference between them and the other predicates, as far as applying the concept of reference and truth to them goes. But that is something we might *eventually* say, so it does not spoil the observation that there is a *prima facie* difference. That is, it takes a lot of philosophical work to put oneself in an eventual naturalistic or intuitionistic position of being able to say that there is no serious difference. But if one took reference and truth in a disquotational way in either of the two senses we are considering (the syntactic or the highly metaphysical causal hook-up with objects), we will not be able even to acknowledge that there is a *prima facie* difference between these two sorts of sentences and predicates. We will not be in a position to acknowledge that there is even a *prima facie* problem in thinking of truth-conditions and reference as applying to the evaluative sentences and evaluative predicates respectively.

If disquotation is a purely syntactic device then it is indifferent to the *prima facie* distinction we are marking between these two sorts of sentences and predicates. That is, it merely removes the quotes with no particular care about the meaning of what is inside of them, so it does not care if there are evaluative sentences inside of the quotes, for which "is true" might, at least *prima facie*, be inappropriate. Equally, if descriptions and beliefs are wholly irrelevant to the hook-up with objects which these disquotational assertions are supposed to convey, then there are no resources to state the problem that evaluative predicates might *prima facie* raise for the application of notions like truth and reference. For all we have said and can say, these predicates hook-up with objects (Goodness,

Beauty) just like any other predicate, so there cannot even be a *prima facie* problem of this kind. But we started by saying that there is, undeniably, a *prima facie* problem; so there is nothing else to conclude but that this highly metaphysical way of thinking of the specification of our agent's concept, "'arthritis' refers to arthritis," is just as unsatisfactory as the syntactic treatment of the disquotation involved in it. It papers over a genuine *prima facie* problem and distinction. It does not even allow us to raise the problem or to make the distinction in a tentative, preliminary way.

I have heard it said that concepts are "primitive" things about which one can say no more than what this pure notion of disquotation allows. The disquotation does not convey any further explication because if it did it would deny the primitiveness of concepts. But "primitive" here merely labels what I am finding mysterious.

Some may object that surely *some* concepts have to be primitive. Not all concepts can be such that they get a rewritable explication, because explications themselves invoke other concepts and it would make things circular or infinitely regressive unless some concepts did not get explications. I think this view comes from an altogether uncompulsory foundationalist picture of a bedrock of concepts on which others are founded. No doubt, we hold some concepts steady in the background in order to explicate what others mean in the foreground. But that does not mean that the ones we held steady are primitive in the sense of not themselves susceptible to explication, holding *other* concepts steady. Illumination about concepts comes from this shifting dialectic between background and explication, and not from some foundationalist bedrock.

Someone may be tempted to say that my complaint about how there is a mystery at the heart of the orthodox externalist's appeal to disquotation is unfair because such a mystery arises for my own view as well. They may say that I just assume that there is no mystery about how the beliefs or descriptions (which form the agent's conception of the disease and which I insist on plugging in for the term "arthritis") get us the meaning of "arthritis." Why should we find agents' conceptions less mysterious than direct unmediated reference? In short, as I have often heard it said, if direct "reference" is mysterious why is "sense" any the less mysterious? It is just as mysterious to say that words get meaning via sense as it is to say that they get it via reference.

First of all, my view is not committed to any orthodox notion of sense, as will become clear later (see note 29 and the text to which it attaches). But that apart, I would deny that mystery also attaches to my view. What I find mysterious about the claim that there are in principle no beliefs or descriptions which can get substituted for concepts is perfectly easy to state, and state precisely; and, once stated, it is obvious that it is not to be found in my view.

Following Wittgenstein, I find mystery in these matters if something is altogether and, by its very nature, inexpressible. Whereof one cannot speak, thereof one is mystery-mongering. By inexpressibility here I don't mean merely that something cannot be explicitly listed because it would take longer than we have, but something which is by its very nature not the sort of thing which is expressible, something for which descriptions are the wrong sort of things to demand. (I admit that there are some very special and unusual contexts in which demonstratives are used which are an exception to my insistence that there be some descriptions available to the speaker; in these cases it is wordless, nonconceptualized skills by which we fasten and focus on particular referents—but I think it is possible to treat these as limiting and degenerate instances, and they do not affect the point I am making against inexpressibility. Being degenerate there is no lesson to be learned from them for terms like "arthritis" or "water" or, for that matter, for all the *other* contexts in which demonstratives are used.) The principled inexpressibility I am opposing is implied by the appeal to disquotation and primitiveness in the third response. It is said that Wittgenstein himself took a rather glamorous view of the inexpressible at the end of the *Tractatus*. That may or may not be so. I don't think we should take such a view. In not allowing that there is anything to be said in answer to the question: what does the right hand side of the occurrence of "arthritis" in a reference-giving statement convey? the orthodox externalist is being mysterious, by this criterion of what is mysterious. But by the same criterion my insistence on beliefs or descriptions being brought in to answer the question precisely eschews this mysteriousness.

Of course, I grant that for any term in any of the descriptions given to answer such questions, more such questions can be raised. And the point is that more such answers appealing to further descriptions will be given. There is no reason to admit to inexpressibility and reduce oneself to silence. Therefore there is no mystery, at least as defined above. It is true that I have traded mystery for other things such as a seemingly infinitely regressive appeal to descriptions. But I have already said that that difficulty is inherent in anti-foundationalism, a difficulty which can be overcome in routine pragmatist ways by *tentatively* holding some descriptions unquestioned in the background while answering questions about others in the foreground. This is all of course much messier than the view that concepts are primitive and that they must be purely disquotationally characterized. But life is a mess, and theoretical and philosophical reflection on these matters would do well to acknowledge the mess and keep faith with it, rather than produce an artificially tidy theory with a mystery at its very core.

I have stated clearly what I mean by "mysterious" and I have found the view I am opposing—the view that permits no rewrite— guilty of it, in precisely the way that my own view—which demands a rewrite—is not. If someone is going to turn on me and say that I too am being mysterious in insisting on descriptions and beliefs, they must have in mind another sense of what is mysterious. And I don't know what that is, so I cannot answer the charge.

I conclude, then, that this third response on behalf of Burge, which tries to deal with the first horn of the dilemma by invoking purely disquotational specifications of concepts, and which thereby avoids any kind of rewrite of the concept of arthritis, won't work either. It avoids the first horn at the cost of making it wholly mysterious what concept, and, therefore, what content is being attributed to the ignorant agent in our trilemma.

It remains for me to say something about why my insistence that there must be some form of implicit rewrite in order to specify a concept, does not, at least on my view of intentional content, bring with it any commitment to an analytic-synthetic distinction. I cannot do so right away, since I need to present my own externalist conception of intentionality before I have the resources to do so. I will do that at the end of the paper.

To sum up this section on Burge: I have criticized his strategy for solving the problem for self-knowledge, raised by externalism, by showing that the strategy is only effective against a much too direct way of raising the problem. I then presented a more indirect way of raising the problem against which his strategy does not work because it is too general. And then I spent some time defending my indirect way of raising the problem against three responses which claimed that raising it that way was unjustified. I now turn to Davidson's way of denying that externalism raises a crippling problem for self-knowledge.

VI. WHAT'S WRONG WITH DAVIDSON'S RECONCILIATION?

Davidson, recall, says that Putnam's repudiation of internalism in turn repudiates the idea of objects of thought. And, given an assumption that he says Putnam shares with internalists (that only such objects will account for self-knowledge), he says Putnam gives up on self-knowledge for externally constituted contents.

The trouble with the criticism is that it takes Putnam to be saying that a *mere* denial of internalism is sufficient to give up on first-person authority. But it does not seem to me that Putnam's idea that we may often not know what we believe turns on just simply repudiating the internalist position with its commitment to internal objects of thought. Rather it turns on the *specific* externalist commitments which flow from his (and Kripke's and Burge's) views on reference and meaning.

Putnam is committed to an externalism that comes from a certain scientific essentialist view of natural-kind terms and concepts. And it is this, when it is extended to a thesis about concepts and intentional contents, that gives rise to the problem for self-knowledge. If many of my concepts—say, the concept of water—are fixed by the objective natures of kinds in the environment, then my intentional contents which are composed of these concepts—say, the belief that water will quench thirst—will not be something that I will have (full) self-knowledge of, if I have no knowledge (or only partial knowledge) of their objective natures. That is, if I do not have the appropriate knowledge (of chemistry) in this case, and the chemical facts about water at least partly determine my concept of water, then—if my indirect strategy against Burge is effective—it follows as a consequence that I will at best have only partial knowledge of the contents which contain my concept of water.

The assumption about objects of thought accounting for self-knowledge is irrelevant to this consequence. If Putnam were to *join* Davidson in denying that objects of thought account for self-knowledge, could he avoid this consequence of his externalist view? I don't see how he can. Here again I must invoke my indirect strategy to show that he cannot. Suppose a chemical ignoramus on Earth believes that water is not H_2O. It would seem that if we take Putnam's externalist view this person believes in something blatantly inconsistent. But, to repeat, that is an absurdly uncharitable conclusion to come to. A chemically ignorant person is chemically ignorant, not logically deficient. How can Putnam, then, get out of this absurd conclusion that seems to follow from his externalism? Only, I suggest, by saying that this person does not know (or does not know fully) what he believes. If he does not know what he believes then attributing a blatantly inconsistent belief is not absurdly uncharitable. But this has landed Putnam with just the rejection of self-knowledge which we had advertised as unavoidable. No amount of denying that objects of thought account for self-knowledge is going to help Putnam avoid this conclusion.

I also think that Putnam's specific externalist commitments better explain why it is that, for Putnam, self-knowledge fails to hold only in *some* cases (cases where an agent does not know the right chemistry or some other of nature's essences). If one gave Davidson's explanation for why Putnam gives up on self-knowledge, then self-knowledge should fail to hold much more comprehensively than Putnam seems to want to say; more comprehensively, because if one believed that self-knowledge of thoughts was a result of thoughts having inner objects and one also thought that there are no inner objects of thought, then presumably one would not restrict one's denial of self-knowledge to the sorts of cases (involving natural kinds) Putnam discusses.[19]

The final proof of the point that Putnam's denial of self-knowledge turns on his specific externalist thesis (rather than on an assumption he shares with internalists) will be that one can formulate a specific externalist view of content that is an alternative to Putnam's externalism and which does not deny self-knowledge in this way. I will briefly sketch such an externalism below, an externalism in which the external world constitutes concepts without having any truck with the scientific essentialism or rigid designation that is essential to Putnam's view of certain terms and concepts that go into the specification of contents. My point for now is that there are externalisms which threaten self-knowledge and there are externalisms which do not. Davidson's diagnosis for why an externalist need not abandon self-knowledge does not distinguish between these externalisms and is, as a result, an unsatisfyingly general diagnosis for a problem that has a much more specific source.[20]

This unsatisfyingly unspecific diagnosis in Davidson feeds into the similarly unsatisfying positive suggestion he goes on to make about how to make Putnam compatible with self-knowledge, once we give up on objects of thoughts. His suggestion is that there can be no denying the presumption of first-person authority or self-knowledge because without it agents could not be said to be "interpretable at all." In one of his papers,[21] he says:

When we have freed ourselves from the assumption that thoughts must have mysterious objects, we can see how the fact that mental states as we commonly conceive them are identified in part by their natural history not only fails to touch the internal character of such states or to threaten first person authority; it also opens the way to an explanation of first person authority. The explanation comes with the realization that what a person's words mean depends in the most basic cases on the kinds of external objects and events that have caused the person to hold the words to be applicable; similarly for what the person's thoughts are about. *An interpreter of another's words and thoughts must depend on scattered information, fortunate training, and imaginative surmise in coming to understand the other. The agent herself, however, is not in a position to wonder whether she is generally using her own words to apply to the right objects and events, since whatever she regularly applies them to gives her words the meaning they have and her thoughts the contents they have* [my emphasis]. Of course, in any particular case, she may be wrong about what she believes about the world; what is impossible is that she should be wrong most of the time. The reason is apparent: unless there is a presumption that the speaker knows what she means, i.e., is getting her own language right, there would be nothing for an interpreter to interpret. To put the matter another way, nothing could count as someone regularly misapplying her own words. First person authority, the social character of language, and the external determinants of thought and meaning go naturally together, once we give up the myth of the subjective, the idea that thoughts require mental objects. (455–56)

This positive suggestion manifestly fails to answer the difficulty that Putnam's externalism poses for self-knowledge, because Davidson's description of the difficulty ushers out the real underlying source of the difficulty. Because Davidson nowhere mentions the relevance of the specific sorts of referential commitments in Putnam's externalism, the question he addresses in his positive explanation is something quite else than the question Putnam's externalism generates.

Davidson's positive remarks answer a question that has nothing specifically to do with Putnam's externalism: what, in general, explains the undeniable fact that agents whom we are interpreting by and large have *non-inferential* self-knowledge (first-person authority) of their own thoughts, given that in our interpretations we are not specifying objects of thought within their epistemological ken, but looking instead to external objects in their environments? And it answers this question, as the passage I emphasized makes clear, by saying that if there are going to be meanings for the interpreter to interpret it is only because the interpretee knows her own thoughts in ways that are quite different from the way the interpreter comes to know them, i.e., directly and not via interpretation. Putting aside for a moment whether this answers the new question adequately, the relevant point for now is that the question itself, though it does focus on the interpreter and the agent's environment rather than on the internal objects of the agent's thought, is nevertheless a quite different question from the *initial* question we were interested in (and which Davidson himself posed), which was: how is self-knowledge compatible with Putnam's externalism? Notice that this initial question is not particularly about the non-inferential nature of self-knowledge. It is about whether one has full self-knowledge (whether inferential or non-inferential is not the point) of what one thinks, even when, as in the case of the chemically or medically ignorant agent, one's thoughts are composed of concepts (arthritis, water) which one may not have full knowledge of.[22]

I think that Davidson is under the impression that because his explanation is given from the point of view of what even the *third person* or interpreter must acknowledge about the first person or interpretee's authority over his own states, it is an explanation which *does* answer the initial question. But Putnam's externalism—that is, (O.E.)—is a much more specific doctrine than an externalism which says that contents are constituted by the deliverances of a third person or interpreter who looks to an agent's environment. Putnam's externalism, in the initial question we are interested in, claims that the interpreter makes essential appeal to the *objective natures* of natural kinds in the agent's external environment as constituting his contents. Davidson's positive explanation of self-knowledge makes no mention of this appeal at all. The question which his positive explanation does address is a more general question: how can *any kind of externalist— anyone* who gives up on internalism and thereby believes in something very general like (G.E.)—avoid making self-knowledge inferential from knowledge of the external world and, therefore, how can he avoid giving up on the special non-inferential authority that attaches to self-knowledge? In other words, how can we show that just because what we think is constituted partly by external things, it does not follow that we *know what we think* partly by way of inferences from knowledge of those external things. But Putnam's externalism is, as I have been saying, much more specific and much less minimal than (G.E.) and it raises instead our initial question which has no particular focus on the non-inferential character of self-knowledge. Davidson offers no help with this question, and that is not surprising because, as my indirect strategy demonstrates, once one adopts Putnam's externalism there *is no* help against the threat to self-knowledge (except for the unwelcome help offered by the other two horns of the trilemma).

I have tried to display how both Burge and Davidson's efforts at dealing with this initial question, how Burge and Davidson's reconciliation between Putnam's externalism and self-knowledge, fail to see the precise way in which Putnam's externalism makes it natural and right for Putnam to abandon self-knowledge (of wide, or externally constituted, contents). If I'm right, anyone who adopts Putnam's externalism has no way to avoid the threat to self-knowledge. But now the question remains whether it is compulsory for all externalists,—i.e., all those who subscribe to (G.E.), which is Putnam's own general characterization of externalism,—to adopt Putnam's specific externalist proposal which has such widespread currency today. That is, is it compulsory for them to adopt (O.E.)? In the next and last section I will deny that that is compulsory by sketching an externalism about intentional content which is quite different from (O.E.). My externalism raises no problem, not even *prima facie*, about self-knowledge.

VII. How to Reconcile Externalism with Self-Knowledge

The challenge to be met is: how shall we appeal to the external elements in an agent's environment in the determination of his intentional contents without giving up on the natural and intuitive assumption that he or she has knowledge of those contents? My answer, for reasons of space, will have to be very crude and smudged, and I will have to leave the refinements and qualifications to another place.[23] In my externalist account, this challenge is met by imposing a crucial constraint on the way the externalist element determines content and, I claim, that there is no chance that the challenge can be met without constraining the external element in this way. The constraint can be stated thus:

(C): *When fixing an externally determined concept of an agent, one must do so by looking to indexically formulated utterances of the agent which express indexical contents containing that concept and then picking that external determinant of the concept which is in consonance with other contents that have been fixed for the agent.*

The emphasis in (C) is the heart of the constraint but some other rather basic things need to be clarified before I come to it.

First of all let me say at the very outset that though I formulate the constraint and the whole question of externalism in the context of how we fix an agent's concepts and contents, this does not mean that I am interested only or even primarily in the epistemological question: how do we find out about another's concepts and contents? That would be to get things the wrong way round. If we assume that meanings and concepts and intentional contents are public then we may assume that whatever it is that goes into their constitution is publicly available, i.e., available to another. So looking at how these are fixed by another does not by any means amount to a mere question about how we find about them as opposed to a question about what is their nature. It is because their nature is such that it is partly constituted by external things that this external constitution should emerge in the answering of the question: what goes into the fixing of concepts by another? So one should not be misled by my talk of concept-fixing and content-attribution to get things the wrong way round.

Second, let me say what is meant by "concepts." Assuming a certain close relation between intentionality and meaning, I use "concept" to talk of the counterpart to "term" in just the way that "content" is thought of as the counterpart to "sentence." Just as the content of an agent's belief that arthritis is painful is cashed out in terms of the meaning of the sentence "arthritis is painful," so also the concept of arthritis which, in part, composes that content is cashed out in terms of the meaning of the term "arthritis" which, in part, composes that sentence. In assuming this close relation between intentionality and meaning I follow most others who write on this subject.[24]

Third, the fixing of externally determined concepts takes place, as one might expect, by looking at the indexical contents (and the utterances expressing them) in which they occur. One should expect this because it is indexical contents and utterances ("It's cold," "Here comes Maggie," "That's a Bosendorfer," "This is a gazelle") which can be correlated most obviously with saliencies in the external world that are supposed to be determining the concepts they contain. It is with these that one can most easily identify the external determinants. Indexical contents and utterances are, therefore, the points of entry into another's mind, since they are the first clear clues to the external (and public) sources of another's meanings. One fixes concepts first by correlating them, or at any rate, by correlating the terms in the utterances in which they are expressed, with items in the environment of the agent who thinks and expresses them. Thus these correlations consist in finding some sort of salient item regularly present in the environment when indexical utterances with a given term expressing some concept are uttered. The centrality of indexical utterances and thoughts, however, should not give the impression of any commitment to anything like "direct reference." Indexicals are central to externalism because they are essential clues to an agent's perceptions of and responses to things and events around him. This centrality is not lost if it is unaccompanied by doctrines of direct reference.

Fourth, clearly one has to distinguish between those indexical utterances which are sincere and literal and those which are not, else we will not correlate them with the right item in the environment or perhaps we will not find any sort of item regularly present. Only the former must be correlated with external saliencies. If I were uttering a lie or a metaphor when I said "He's a beast" the correlated external salience would not help much in fixing the concept correctly. There is, however, no algorithm for sifting out the sincere and literal utterances from the lies, the metaphors, the stage performances, etc. Nor is there any reason to assume that a concept or term occurs more frequently in sincere and literal utterances than in this vast variety of other uses. But one may assume that the lies and metaphors and so on, even if more frequent, will bring no single item in the environment to the fore since they will be used with an indefinite variety of motives; so over time if there *is* a correlation at all with something in the environment then we can proceed on the assumption that we *had* got hold of the sincere utterances and, therefore, have the right external determinant. All this is, of course, a dynamic process of theory building (of concept attribution or fixing) and as with all theories one may revise earlier attributions if they turn out to fail to provide a coherent theoretical picture due to having fastened on some non-literal or insincere indexical utterances in the early phases.

Fifth, obviously, not all concepts will be externally determined. Not, for example, the concept of a unicorn nor the concept of the number five. But these concepts will in one way or another be related to others which will be determined externally. In the case of the concept of the unicorn, it will be related by *composition* to other concepts which are externally determined—the concept of a horse, the concept of a horn, etc.; not so in the case of a concept of the number five, which will not be composed of externally determined concepts but rather related to externally determined concepts by more complicated relations.

Finally, the heart of the externalism, the constraint itself.

What makes one an externalist at all is that in looking to fix concepts one looks to correlations with *external* things. But that is just externalism in the very general sense defined as (G.E.).

My constraint on externalism gives rise to a more specific version of this externalism. It asserts that in selecting the item in the environment which is supposed to fix the concept that is being expressed, one has not only to pick what is salient and is correlated with that term but one has to be very careful how one *describes* this external determinant of the concept. One has to describe it in a way that fits in with the other *contents* one has attributed to the agent. Expressions such as "fits in with" or, as in the original formulation, "in consonance with" are vague, so let me give a sharper intuitive sense to what I have in mind, by way of an example.

Finding the right gross external item to correlate an agent's concept with requires no more than a) shared similarity standards, presumably wired into us all, so that what is grossly salient to him is not wholly at odds with what to us, and b) Mill's methods. These two things, however, will only get us the relevant gross and regular saliencies in the environment and no more. But it is the selection, not of the regular gross salience in the environment, but the right description of it, which the constraint is meant to address; and its claim is that the right description turns on looking to other beliefs attributed to the agent.

So, to give a very crude example, let us suppose that, by an application of Mill's methods and by shared similarity standards, we have noticed that there is a pedal regularly present under the left foot of an agent when he utters indexical utterances with a certain term. Then the constraint says not to describe this external determinant of his concept expressed by that term as a "clutch" if one has no confidence that he has other beliefs, however rudimentary, regarding the inner workings of an automobile. If, by this method in which external items determine concepts, one could not describe the determinant that way, one would not end up attributing the determined concept of a clutch to the agent and so no contents relating to clutches. For some agents we may find ourselves, for similar sorts of reasons, withholding from the external determinant even the description "pedal" (i.e., in such a case the regular gross salience will not even get the initial description "pedal") with similar consequences for concepts and contents.

Notice that there is a strong element of anti-foundationalism built into this constraint. One may have thought otherwise, misled by my insistence that there is something basic about the indexical utterances which correlate with saliencies in the environment. One may have thought that this insistence on seeing the indexical utterances as a starting point makes for an externalist foundational-ism.[25] The thought is not intended at all and the constraint makes that clear. Even for this basic level, this ground floor of indexically formulated utterances and beliefs by which one enters another's mind, the external determinants we pick out and correlate them with have to be described only as they cohere with the other beliefs. Hence the method at the ground floor is a convenient starting point in the building of a theoretical structure of another's beliefs and concepts, but it is built like Neurath's boat, and conclusions about the ground floor are just as mediated by belief, and just as revisable as we proceed with the theorizing if they will not lend themselves to a coherent theoretical picture. There are no Archimedean points in this externalism. Some links with the external world may be more direct than others, i.e., less mediated by surrounding beliefs than others—for instance those that determine the concept of a pedal rather than those that determine the concept of a clutch. But there are no unmediated causal links. There is no getting away from this mediation and the appeal to external causality is not intended to stop or interrupt a holistic (by which I only mean anti-foundationalist[26]) pattern. Anti-foundationalist holism and externalism are both absolutely essential features of content and they are perfectly compatible.

My constraint's appeal to the agents' other beliefs in fastening on an appropriate description of the external determinant is bound to give the impression that I am, after all, an internalist. For it will seem that I am insisting on an internalist filter upon the external. This impression would be quite wrong. There is, to begin with, something misleading, in fact downright false, in thinking of the filter as internal since the belief contents of an agent which provide the filter will contain concepts, which are themselves externally determined. There is nothing internal about the filter at all, if it is defined in contrast with externally constituted content. But, that apart, I think the impression comes from a tedious and misguided oscillation between a false pair of choices: a highly direct externalism and internalism. The plain fact is that if we take the definition of externalism with which we started at the beginning of the paper, i.e., (G.E.), seriously and if we refuse to fall for the uncritical conflation of externalism, generally defined, with (O.E.), then any position which is incompatible with the scenario enter-tained in Descartes's First Meditation is "externalist" in a perfectly clear sense of that term. And my position is certainly incompatible with that scenario since it explicitly entails a denial of the claim that one could have the thoughts one has if there were no external world. That is, it explicitly denies something entailed by that scenario. In short my position is not internalist because it satisfies the minimal definition for externalism in (G.E).

There is one more crucial element in my overall account of content which needs to be briefly summarized. I will call it the "locality" of content. It is an element forced by one of the effects of my constraint. As I described it, the constraint requires that no concept be attributed along externalist lines, unless it is in consonance with the other contents of the agent to whom it is being attributed. This leads to a rather alarmingly fine-grained concept. After all, the beliefs of an agent that are relevant to (and that he associates with) the concept or term "clutch" or "water" or "arthritis" or "lemon" might be very numerous and very diverse.

In my picture of things this does not matter. The reason why it does not matter is that these attributions of concepts are attributions of things that *do not go directly* into the attribution of specific contents to explain behavior. All that these attributions do is to provide a pool of resources which one uses in a selective way in order to attribute specific contents in the explanation of behavior. Let me explain with an example. Suppose you know a fair amount of chemistry and I know none, i.e., you have various chemical beliefs and I don't. The concept of water attributed to you in accord with the constraint requires that it be different from the concept attributed to me. Your beliefs which constrain the description of the external substance with which your "water"-utterances are correlated will be different from mine since you have beliefs about water's chemical composition which I do not. The case is exactly like the one about the concept of clutch and pedal for two agents who respectively do and do not have beliefs about the workings of automobiles. At this level—what we might call the "aggregative" level of concept attribution—it is unlikely that any two people will have the same concept of anything since it is unlikely that they have *all* the same beliefs associated with the term which expresses that concept. This is the level at which theories of meaning do their work: they specify the concepts or the term-meanings of an agent along the lines of this constrained externalist method. At the meaning-theoretic level, as I've been saying, the concepts are very fine-grained and they are hardly ever shared by people.

But this does not matter since it is not *these* concepts, so thought of, which go into the contents that explain action. Action explanation always takes place at another level than this meaning-theoretic level. It takes place at a more local level. Here the entire aggregate of beliefs that an agent associates with "water" are not all relevant. One distills out of the aggregate of resources provided by the meaning theory only those beliefs that are relevant to the action explanation at the local level. Thus if you and I are both drinking some substance from the kitchen tap because we want to quench our thirst with the cheapest available drink, we may *in this locality* both be attributed the *same* content: ". . . that water will quench thirst." In this locality of explanation, your chemical beliefs are simply not among the beliefs selected from the specifications for "water" in the meaning theory (for your idiolect) for use in the local explanation of your behavior. That is to say, the local concept of water, which goes into the specification of the content which explains your behavior in this locality, is to be thought of as a small selection of beliefs from the aggregate of beliefs you associate with "water." In the locality, one selects only what is needed to make the explanation: and the chemical beliefs are not needed for the concept of water in your belief that water quenches thirst, which explains your drinking water. Thus the whole aggregate of beliefs that makes up a concept at the meaning-theoretic level is usually not needed in localities, only selections from them which make up local concepts are needed. So although our idiolects are never likely to be the same for any single concept, in many localities—for instance in the locality being considered in the example—we may nevertheless share many concepts, and therefore contents. There will obviously be other localities in which we will not share contents because in those localities we will find it necessary to use your chemical beliefs from the overall pool in order to capture your local concept of water which composes the content which explains your action.

I call this thesis the "locality" of content.

(It should be obvious to the reader that one of the implications of this thesis is that the great importance that has been give to the "theory of meaning" in the last few decades is highly exaggerated. Content is attributed and behavior is explained only in localities, and the aggregative deliverances of a theory of meaning have no direct role to play in them.[27] The deliverances of such theories, then, have no psychological reality since the concepts they specify do not pull their weight in any explanation of an agent's behavior. Only local concepts compose contents, so only local concepts pull their weight in explanations. The meaning-theoretic specifications have no other function than to summarize aggregates of beliefs associated with each concept, from which to make local selections of concepts.)

It should be obvious from this brief sketch why my externalism does not entail a threat to self-knowledge in the way that orthodox externalism does, so I will be very brief.

First of all notice how my constraint immediately distinguishes my externalism from those I reject. Putnam and Kripke would look to the external paradigmatic samples with their "objective," scientifically revealed, "natures" (the right chemical composition for "water," the right DNA for "lemon" . . .) in fastening on the right external determinant; Burge would look at the external determinant as it is mediated by the beliefs of the expert in that community; but my constraint instead insists that we look to the external determinant only as it is mediated by the beliefs of the agent whose concepts are being fixed. For my externalism, a concept is not fixed by correlating it with an external item as God sees that item, or as the expert in given societies sees it, or as the expert at the end of inquiry sees it, or even as the radical interpreter sees it. It is quite wrong to think that externalism must adopt any of these ulterior methods, since to do so entails among other things an insuperable problem for self-knowledge which can only be solved by Putnam's bifurcation of content, i.e., by the introduction of a supplementary internalist notion of content to handle the problem of self-knowledge which such ulterior notions manifestly cannot handle. Without surrender to internalism, my constraint does not allow this problem to arise in the first place.

To see this clearly, think again of my indirect strategy for raising the problem for self-knowledge against Burge's and Davidson's efforts at reconciling Putnam's externalism with self-knowledge. Self-knowledge, by this indirect strategy, was only under threat because threatening it is the only way which will allow Putnam's externalism to refrain from attributing certain blatant inconsistencies to agents. But my externalism, unlike these others, has no problems with inconsistent attributions in the first place. There is no first horn, so the trilemma I raised for orthodox externalisms like Putnam's never gets going for my view. My constraint sees to it that external items which determine concepts do not determine concepts that are at such odds with an agent's other beliefs that she will fall into the situation of uttering or thinking inconsistent thoughts just on the basis of the concepts attributed to her. Agents, on my view, may think thoughts that we specify as "water is not H_2O" or "I have arthritis in my thigh," but the concept of water or arthritis in these cases will not be determined by the experts' beliefs or by scientific essences. The sorts of inconsistency, which follow upon these other externalist views of concepts, therefore, are simply not entailed if one applies my constraint. If the agent lacks certain chemical or medical beliefs he will not be attributed the same concept of arthritis or water as the society's and its experts. Thus if he goes on to say things like "I have arthritis in my thigh," etc., this will not amount, even *prima facie*, to inconsistency. My constraint has the effect of bringing in the external determining item under descriptions, or more properly under beliefs, of the agent.

We have already seen in countering the second response made on behalf of Burge to the trilemma I posed for him that if the external items (in that case it was the *social* external items, i.e., the community's expert's knowledge) enter routed through an ignorant agent's own beliefs (specified, in that case, by metalinguistic specifications such as "water is whatever the experts call 'water' " . . .) then the threat of inconsistent attributions to the ignorant agent and the eventual threat of attributing absence of self-knowledge to him is avoided. The social enters into the concept without losing respect for the fact that the relevant individual agent himself knows very little about the chemical composition of various substances. Where the external items are *not* taken to be social, then the beliefs will not be metalinguistically specified, they will just be ordinary beliefs of the chemically ignorant agent, beliefs such as, for example, "water is the substance that comes out of the kitchen tap," etc. The point is that for chemically ignorant agents the concept of water will not be determined by an external substance under any chemical descriptions or beliefs. So if such an agent were to brashly think that water is not H_2O, he would not be thinking something inconsistent. If he is not thinking something inconsistent, then the first horn in the indirect strategy which leads eventually, in the second horn, to a threat to self-knowledge, is unavailable. Neither, therefore, is the second horn available. There just is no threat to self-knowledge.

This way of avoiding the threat to self-knowledge within externalism is, of course, very different from Burge's and Davidson's. It is different because it addresses a problem that arises specifically for orthodox externalism in a way that their solutions do not. They run away with the impression that they have avoided the threat because in discussing self-knowledge they raise the threat in a way that does not bring out why the specific orthodox externalist position really gives rise to the threat. Once one sees via the indirect strategy why orthodox externalism gives rise to the threat in a very specific way, then only does one see clearly why my constraint on externalism alone will provide for the compatibility of external-ism with self-knowledge.

Only one issue remains. Does my constraint's insistence that beliefs of an agent must enter into the constitutive work the external items do smack of definitions and analyticity. This was an issue that I promised to deal with in my reply to the third response on behalf of Burge. And quite apart from that response, any insistence that concepts are to be conceived in terms of descriptions or beliefs must address the charge of a commitment to analyticity. The so-called "cluster" version of the descriptive theory of terms was an early response to a roughly similar charge made in a slightly different setting. But my response is quite different. My response makes vital use of what I just called the thesis of the locality of content, which is an essential aspect of the overall externalist concep-tion of intentionality that I am offering as an alternative to orthodox externalism.

The charge of analyticity was made against my claim that Putnam's externalism is obliged to rewrite some description such as "the disease which afflicts joints only" or "the substance which has the chemical composition H_2O," for "arthritis" and "water" respectively in various judgements (with those terms or concepts) that individuals make in our physical and social environments. The charge was that to insist that there be such a rewrite was to hanker for analytic definitions of these terms.

My insistence on the rewrite flowed merely from the fact that I think that the alternative which denies all rewrites leaves unexplained and mysterious what the concept in question is. Now, it is *only* if one holds Putnam's externalism with its view of natural kinds and their scientific essences (or if one holds Burge's social externalism) that the insistence on the rewrite looks as if it will lead to defini-tions, and therefore to what looks like a commitment to the analytic-synthetic distinction. This is because on Burge's view, or on the scientific-essentialist view, there is some privileged belief or beliefs of the expert, or some paradigm instance of a natural kind, which fixes the reference and meaning of agents' concepts and terms. Thus I am claiming that the insistence on the rewrite (an insistence forced by the mystery attaching to any view that denies it) *by itself* does not commit one to the analytic-synthetic distinction. It is only if one combines the insistence with certain accounts of concepts or the meaning of terms that one is committed to analyticity.[28]

If instead one combines the insistence on rewrites with an externalist account committed to the locality thesis like the one I just sketched, there is no such commitment. For me a concept, at the level at which concepts are attributed by a theory of meaning, is nothing but an indiscriminate and aggregative carrier of all the beliefs an agent associates with the term which expresses the concept. There are no weights placed on some beliefs over others which might give the impres-sion of definitional status or of the notion of criteria (versus merely symptom) or anything like that. There is, of course, another level over and above the meaning-theoretic level, the local level. But the whole point of distinguishing between the aggregative, meaning-theoretic level and the local level was to allow that there can be lots of different localities at the local level. This means that there is no single rewrite because there is no single locality. There is, therefore, no definition. Different localities, different explanatory contexts, dictate different selections or distillations from these aggregates, but there is no fixed concept, no canonical selection or distillation, at the local level. Different localities will distill out different beliefs and thus sanction different rewrites. Though there might be overlap and coincidence in what is distilled in different localities there is no saying *in advance* what these are. Thus there are no weights imposed on any of the beliefs within the aggregate of beliefs at the meaning-theoretic level such that some beliefs are more important than others and must be distilled out in all localities. So the rewrites I insist on will have no fixed criteria, if one adopts my picture of concepts and contents. They cannot, therefore, count as a commitment to analyticity.[29]

By contrast, once one forces the need for rewrites, as I have via my charge of mystery, the orthodox accounts I oppose are bound to provide the more rigid definitional rewrites which give rise to analyticity. Given their accounts, the rewrites *will* be canonical—e.g., the scientific essences, the expert's beliefs, etc. No wonder they worry about and resist having to allow rewrites.

So, my response to those who charge my demand for a rewrite with a commitment to analyticity is simply this. There is nothing in the demand itself which makes that commitment. The demand merely flows from the inability to specify what a concept is if one did not meet the demand. Only if one were already given to certain specific views on meaning and concepts, would the commitment be made with the rewrites. My view of meaning and concepts makes no such commitment, but the view of meaning of the externalisms I am opposing, given the need to rewrite, does.

I have had two aims in this paper. The first was to show—by way of defense of Putnam against Burge and Davidson—that Putnam's specific externalism (and others like it) which I called orthodox externalism, pose an insuperable problem for self-knowledge. The second was to show that Putnam's specific externalism was not the only specific proposal which satisfied his general characterization of externalist doctrine, which I called (G.E.). I offered an alternative specific proposal which posed no problem to self-knowledge.

I have restricted myself to the question of self-knowledge and externalism and tried to show how Putnam's externalism cannot be reconciled with self-knowledge, while the externalism I offer can. That in itself does not amount to a decisive repudiation of Putnam's externalism since there are many other things that motivate philosophers to adopt externalism which I have not considered here and which might favor Putnam's more orthodox externalist view. So various questions remain: what are the motivations that have led Putnam and others to adopt orthodox externalism, are these good motivations, and if good can they not also be fulfilled by my own externalism?[30] These questions must await an answer elsewhere.[31]

ENDNOTES

1. Putnam (1975b).
2. See Bilgrami (1992), chapter 1. See also Bilgrami (1987).
3. Putnam's externalism is not the only orthodox externalism. Burge in Burge (1979a) has given a more socially oriented version of Putnam's views of reference, and drawn consequences for a more socially oriented externalist view of intentional content. Fodor in chapter 4 of Fodor (1987) has given a more information-theoretic version of externalism. Despite these differences between them, all these externalisms raise at least a *prima facie* problem for self-knowledge. In this and other respects they all stand in contrast to the externalism I propose in the last section of this paper. There are other externalists, such as McDowell and Davidson, whose externalisms I oppose because I believe they too contain an implicit and hidden bifurcation of content. But I will not discuss them here since they cannot really be classified with the orthodox externalisms I am primarily discussing. I discuss McDowell's and Davidson's externalisms in detail in chapter 4 of Bilgrami (1992).
4. See Davidson (1987). Also Davidson (1991).
5. See Burge (1988a).
6. See the caveat about Evans and McDowell in the next note. For Evans's Russellian view see Evans (1982). See also McDowell (1984) and Searle (1983).
7. We need to record here that the case of Evans's and McDowell's commitment to external objects of thought is a very exceptional case. But for them, the objects of thoughts idea is an internalist idea. Most externalists who follow Putnam do give up on objects of thought for their externalist contents, and it is they that Davidson has in mind when he says that to adopt externalism is to give up on objects of thought.
8. I have written on the subject of objects of thought, and on Davidson's views on it, in Bilgrami (1991).
9. It must be admitted that arthritis will not be counted a natural kind in the blue-chip sense that water is; it will seem to be somewhat more constructed. Since this difference does not affect the point I am making in any really deep way I shall ignore it.
10. For my reason for saying that it is intuitive not to deny it in these cases, see the point above of the foolishness and unintuitiveness of denying it unless *psychological* obstructions are involved.
11. Burge denies it by denying the need or the coherence of the idea of a second notion of internal or narrow content in his (1986).
12. In earlier papers such as Bilgrami (1985) and also in Bilgrami (1987) I had raised the problem for self-knowledge via this indirect strategy but had failed to fortify it with replies to the responses which follow. Loar (1985), the paper I was commenting on in (Bilgrami 1985), offers a different indirect strategy which *implicitly* raises a very similar problem for self-knowledge. By invoking the intentional states of Kripke's Pierre who travels from Paris to London with a different conception of London in each place, he shows how inferences involving relations between these states which involve the different conceptions of London can fail to be made by him. Given certain intuitive connections between self-knowledge and inference (for which see note 10), we can easily raise a similar problem about self-knowledge, though Loar himself does not.

13. Burge (1989a).
14. Burge (1986b).
15. Burge himself does not accept this metalinguistic ploy. In Burge (1979a) he very explicitly rejects these metalinguistic specifications (96–97) as a way of avoiding his externalist conclusion.
16. It is interesting that Putnam who first formulated the thesis of the "linguistic division of labor" did not notice and still has not claimed that the thesis can be given this reading, which makes it much weaker than his externalism and Burge's anti-individualism. For more on this way of accommodating reliance and the division of linguistic labor with individualism about content, see Bilgrami (1987).
17. Recall that this is rather like what Burge explicitly says about "tiger" when he is talking of the "translational" concept in the first long quotation cited during the discussion of the first response.
18. The implication here is that disquotational truth may be exploited in meaning specification only if somewhere *implicitly* in the overall theory in which such specifications are lodged, there is something being conveyed about what the right hand side of disquotational clauses express. In Davidson's use of such clauses in his truth-theoretic conception of meaning, for instance, this implicit information emerges in the recesses of the radical interpretation process.
19. Putnam casts his externalist net a little wider than I am indicating here. It is more than natural-kind terms that will raise a problem for self-knowledge. Since he shares Kripke's causal views of reference about proper names, judgments with proper names or singular concepts could raise a similar problem. Burge casts the net even wider by bringing in a social externalism over and above a scientific essentialist one, thereby including terms and concepts for artificial kinds as well, such as "sofa," "aluminum", etc.
20. This is a common flaw in discussions of this subject. See, for instance, Wright [(1989): 630], especially his long footnote 6. Here Wright moves unconsciously from a discussion of the specific externalisms of Putnam and Burge to remarks about why externalism need not threaten self-knowledge, remarks which talk much more generally about externalism rather than about Putnam and Burge's specific externalist views. A genuine defense of their externalisms against the charge that they threaten self-knowledge must take up *their specific* externalisms in detail and must respond to them.
21. See Davidson (1987).
22. Sometimes the term "first-person authority" is restricted to describing the special non-inferential character of much of our self-knowledge, and it may be wise therefore not to use it as roughly equivalent to the term "self-knowledge" as I have been doing in this paper. My only excuse for doing so is that this paper is not primarily concerned with the problem of reconciling the *non-inferential* nature of self-knowledge with externalism. This paper is primarily concerned rather with a prior and harder problem raised by the indirect strategy, which is the problem of reconciling self-knowledge *at all* with externalism. The indirect strategy makes it clear that the latter reconciliation must be had first before the question of the former reconciliation even arises, because the strategy puts into doubt that we know what we think at all (whether inferentially or non-inferentially). Philosophers who have discussed the question of self-knowledge and externalism have failed to keep these two issues apart. And, in particular, I'm saying that Davidson, who raises both issues, fails to keep them apart and fails to see that his positive remarks address only the former issue, not the latter. I'm not neces-

sarily denying that Davidson (and Burge), if they are allowed to pretend that there is no prior and harder problem raised by the indirect strategy, would have given satisfactory solutions to the less hard problem about non-inferentiality. I'm only insisting that they have not correctly addressed the prior and harder problem. I have discussed the question of non-inferentiality of self-knowledge in the appendix to Bilgrami (1992).

23. See Bilgrami (1992).

24. The close relation is not intended to convey the obvious falsehood that an agent's utterances of sentences always express the contents that the meanings of those sentences cash out. But the close relation is conveyed by the fact that a sincere, non-self-deceived etc., utterance of (or assent to) a sentence by an agent is an utterance of something whose meaning gives the content of the intentional state that is expressed by that utterance. The fact that sentences are often not asserted this way does not spoil the connection, though it obviously gives those who believe in the connection the task of producing an appropriately nuanced formulation of the connection.

25. The impression may come from such superficial things as my use of expressions like "ground floor" and "points of entry into another's mind," and less superficially from the fact that more traditional internalist foundationalist views, such as Russell's Logical Atomism, also stress the indexical utterances, but with an accompanying stress on correlations with inner experiential items rather than with external items in the environment.

26. I stress this qualification to distinguish the holism I intend by my constraint from other well-known doctrines such as Davidson's.

27. In case such a suspicion has been created, this should make it clear that I am not surreptitiously committing myself to two notions of content, one local and the other aggregative or meaning-theoretic. As I just said, there is only one notion of content and that occurs at the local level. There are, to be sure, two notions of concepts, but one of them does not play any role in contents and therefore, as I say below, has no psychological reality. It is merely an aggregate pool of resources from which to select concepts which do play a role in composing contents and which therefore do have psychological reality.

28. Actually, even if Burge denies that he is privileging the expert's belief over the other beliefs, the fact is that so long as the expert's belief is one among the several beliefs that go into something like a "cluster" rewrite, the inconsistency—of the first horn—will still get attributed to the agent who says or thinks "I have arthritis in my thigh."

29. It should be clear from all this that I am not committed to the notion of sense in any standard conception of the term, not the Fregean conception, nor the cluster-theoretic conception.

30. It would be surprising if the motivations for something as minimal as (G.E.) were the same as the motivations for (O.E.). In spelling the motivations for my own specific version of externalism in Bilgrami (1992), I stick as closely as possible to the motivations that any one might have for something as minimal as (G.E.). These motivations are altogether different from those that have inspired (O.E.).

31. I try to answer these and other questions in Bilgrami (1992).

Bibliography

Almog, J.; Perry, J.; and Wettstein, H., eds. (1989). *Themes from Kaplan*. Oxford: Oxford University Press.

Aquila, R. (1977). *Intentionality: A Study of Mental Acts*. University Park: Pennsylvania State University Press.

Ayers, M. (1972). "Some Thoughts." *Proceedings of the Aristotelian Society* LXXIII: 69–96.

Bach, K. "*De Re* Belief and Methodological Solipsism." In Woodfield (1982).

———. (1988). "Burge's New Thought-Experiment: Back to the Drawing Room." *The Journal of Philosophy* 85: 88–97.

Bell, D., Cooper, N., eds. (forthcoming). *The Analytic Tradition*. New York: Blackwell.

Benacerraf, P. (1973). "Mathematical Truth." *The Journal of Philosophy* 70: 661–79.

Bilgrami, A. (1985). "Comments on Loar." In Grimm and Merrill, eds. (1988).

———. (1987). "An Externalist Account of Psychological Content." *Philosophical Topics* 15.

———. (1991). "Thought and Its Objects." E. Villanueva, ed. *Consciousness*. New Jersey: Rowman and Littlefield.

———. (1992). *Belief and Meaning*. Oxford: Blackwell Press.

Blackburn, S. (1984). *Spreading the Word*. Oxford: Clarendon Press.

Block, N., ed. (1981). *Readings in the Philosophy of Psychology*, 2 vols. London: Methuen.

———. (1987). "Functional Role and Truth Conditions." *Proceedings of the Aristotelian Society Supplementary Volume* 61: 157–81.

Bogdan, R., ed. (1986). *Belief*. Oxford: Oxford University Press.

Brueckner, A. (1986). "Brains in a Vat." *The Journal of Philosophy* LXXXIII, 3: 148–67.

Burge, T. (1977). "Belief *De Re*." *The Journal of Philosophy* 74: 338–62.

———. (1978). "Belief and Synonymy." *The Journal of Philosophy* 75: 119–38.

———. (1979a). "Individualism and the Mental." In French *et al.* (1979).

———. (1982). "Other Bodies." In Woodfield (1982).

———. (1982a). "Two Thought Experiments Reviewed." *Notre Dame Journal of Formal Logic* 23.

———. (1986). "Individualism and Psychology." *Philosophical Review* 95, 1: 3–45.

———. (1986a). "Cartesian Error and the Objectivity of Perception." In McDowell and Pettit (1986).

———. (1986b). "Intellectual Norms and the Foundations of Mind." *The Journal of Philosophy* 83: 697–720.

———. (1988). "Perceptual Individualism and Authoritative Self-Knowledge." In Grimm and Merrill (1988).

———. (1988a). "Individualism and Self-Knowledge." *The Journal of Philosophy* 85: 649–63.

———. (1989). "Individuation and Causation in Psychology." Manuscript, UCLA.

———. (1989a): "Wherein Is Language Social?" In George (1989).

———. (forthcoming). "Frege on Sense and Linguistic Meaning." In Bell and Cooper (forthcoming).

Butterfield, J. (1986a). "Content and Context." In Butterfield (1986b).

————. (1986b). *Language, Mind and Logic*. Cambridge: Cambridge University Press.

Carruthers, P. (1987). "Russellian Thoughts." *Mind* 96: 18–35.

Castaneda, H. N. (1966). " 'He': A Study in the Logic of Self-Consciousness." *Ratio* 8: 130–57.

————. (1967). "Indicators and Quasi-Indicators." *American Philosophical Quarterly* 4: 85–100.

————. (1968). "On the Logic of Attributions of Self-Knowledge to Others." *The Journal of Philosophy* 65: 439–56.

Chomsky, N. (1971). *Problems of Knowledge and Freedom*. New York.

Churchland, P. S., and Churchland P. M. (1983). "Stalking the Wild Epistemic Engine." *Nous* 17: 5–18.

Crane, T. (1990). "The Language of Thought: No Syntax Without Semantics." *Mind and Language* 5.

Crane, T., and Mellor, D. H. (1990). "There is No Question of Physicalism." *Mind* 99: 185–206.

Davidson, D. (1970). "Mental Events." Reprinted in *Essays on Actions and Events*. Oxford: Oxford University Press.

————. (1984). *Inquiries into Truth and Interpretation*. Oxford: Clarendon.

————. (1984a). "First Person Authority." *Dialectic* 38, 2–3:101–11.

————. (1987). "On Knowing One's Own Mind." *Proceedings and Addresses of the American Philosophical Association* 60: 441–58.

————. (1988). "Reply to Burge." *The Journal of Philosophy* 85: 664–65.

————. (1991). "What Is Present to the Mind." E. Villanueva, ed. *Consciousness*. New Jersey: Rowman and Littlefield.

Davies, M. (1986). "Externality, Psychological Explanation, and Narrow Content; Reply to Jerry Fodor's 'Individualism and Supervenience'." Paper delivered to the Joint Session of the Aristotelian Society and the Mind Association, July 1986.

Dennett, D. (1969). *Content and Consciousness*. London: Routledge & Kegan Paul.

————. (1978). *Brainstorms*. Cambridge: MIT Press.

————. (1982). "Beyond Belief." In Woodfield (1982), pp. 1–95.

————. (1984c). "Cognitive Wheels: The Frame Problem of AI." C. Hookway, ed. *Minds, Machines and Evolution*. Cambridge: Cambridge University Press.

————. (forthcoming). "Out of the Armchair and Into the Field." *Poetics Today* (Israel).

Devitt, M. (1974). "Singular Terms." *The Journal of Philosophy* 71: 183–205.

————. (1976). "Semantics and the Ambiguity of Proper Names." *Monist* 59: 404–23.

————. (1979). "Against Incommensurability." *Australasian Journal of Philosophy* 57: 29–50.

————. (1981). *Designation*. New York: Columbia University Press.

Devitt, M., and Sterelny, K. (1987). *Language and Reality*. Cambridge: Basil Blackwell.

Donnellan, K. (1966). "Reference and Definite Descriptions." *Philosophical Review* 75: 281–304.

————. (1970). "Proper Names and Identifying Descriptions." *Synthese* 21: 335–58.

————. (1974). "Speaking of Nothing." *Philosophical Review* 83: 3–31.

————. (1977). "The Contingent: A Priori and Rigid Designators." P. French *et al.*, eds. *Midwest Studies in Philosophy Vol. II*.

Dretske, F. (1981). *Knowledge and the Flow of Information*. Cambridge: MIT Press.

————. (1986). "Misrepresentation." In Bogdan (1986).

Dummett, M. (1973). *Frege: Philosophy of Language*. London: Duckworth.

————. (1974). "Postscript." *Synthese* 27: 523–34.

Dupre, John. (1981). "Natural Kinds and Biological Taxa." *Philosophical Review* 90: 66–90.

Enc, B. (1976). "The Reference of Theoretical Terms." *Nous* 10: 261–82.

Evans, G. (1977). "The Causal Theory of Names." In Schwartz (1977).

————. (1973). "The Causal Theory of Names." *Aristotelian Society Supplementary Volume* XLVII: 187–208.

————. (1980). "Understanding Demonstratives." H. Parret and J. Bouveresse, eds. *Meaning and Understanding*. New York, Berlin: Walter de Gruyter.

————. (1982). *The Varieties of Reference*. Oxford: Oxford University Press.

Feyerabend, P. (1962). "Explanation, Reduction, and Empiricism." H. Feigl and G. Maxwell, eds. *Minnesota Studies in the Philosophy of Science* 3: 28–97.

————. (1970). "Consolations for a Specialist." I. Lakatos and A. Musgrave, eds. *Criticism and the Growth of Knowledge*. Cambridge: Cambridge University Press, pp. 197–230.

Field, H. (1972). "Tarski's Theory of Truth." *The Journal of Philosophy* 69: 347–75.

————. (1973). "Theory Change and the Indeterminacy of Reference." *The Journal of Philosophy* 70: 462–81.

————. (1975). "Conventionalism and Instrumentalism in Semantics." *Nous* 9: 375–405.

————. (1978). "Mental Representation." Reprinted in Block (1981).

Fine, A. (1975). "How to Compare Theories: Reference and Change." *Nous*: 17–32.

Fodor, J. A. (1975). *The Language of Thought*. Harvester.

————. (1980). "Methodological Solipsism Considered as a Research Strategy in Cognitive Psychology." *The Behavioral and Brain Sciences* 3: 63–109. Reprinted in Fodor (1981).

————. (1981). *Representations*. Cambridge: MIT Press.

————. (1981a): "Methodological Solipsism as a Research Strategy in Cognitive Science." Reprinted in Fodor (1981).

————. (1982). "Cognitive Science and the Twin Earth Problem." *Notre Dame Journal of Formal Logic* 23.

————. (1986). "Individualism and Supervenience I." *Proceedings of the Aristotelian Society*, Supp. Vol. LX: 235–62.

————. (1987). *Psychosemantics*. Cambridge: MIT Press.

French, P.; Uehling, T.; and Wettstein, H., eds. (1979). *Midwest Studies in Philosophy Vol. IV*. Minneapolis: University of Minnesota Press.

Geach, P. T. (1969). *God and the Soul*. London: Macmillan.

George, A., ed. (1989). *Reflections on Chomsky*. Oxford: Blackwell.

Gibson, E. (1969). *Principles of Perceptual Learning and Development*. New York: Appleton-Century-Crofts.

Goodman, N. (1961). "About." *Mind* 71: 1–24.

————. (1978). *Ways of Worldmaking*. Indianapolis: Hackett.

Grimm, R., and Merrill, D., eds. (1988). *Contents of Thought (Proceedings of the 1985 Oberlin College Colloquium in Philosophy)*. Tucson: Arizona University Press.

Gunderson, K., ed. (1975). *Language, Mind and Knowledge*. Minnesota Studies in the Philosophy of Science, vol. VII. Minneapolis: University of Minnesota Press.

Haldane and Ross, eds. (1955). *The Philosophical Works of Descartes, vol. I*. New York: Dover.

Hampshire, S. (1975). *Freedom of the Individual*. Expanded edition. Princeton: Princeton University Press.

Harman, G. (1973). *Thought*. Princeton: Princeton University Press.

Haugeland, J. (1985). *Artificial Intelligence: The Very Idea*. Cambridge, MA, and London: MIT Press.

Heil, J., and Mele, A., eds. (1993). *Mental Causation*. Oxford: Clarendon Press.

Hintikka, J. (1962). *Knowledge and Belief*. Ithaca: Cornell University Press.

Hofstadter, D. (1979). *Gödel, Escher, Bach: An Eternal Golden Braid*. New York: Basic Books.

Hofstadter, D., and Dennett, D. (1981). *The Mind's I: Fantasies and Reflections on Mind and Soul*. New York: Basic Books.

Hornsby, J. (1986). "Physicalist Thinking and Behavior." In Pettit and McDowell (1986).

Jackson, F., and Pargetter, R. (forthcoming). "Causal Statements." *Philosophical Topics*.

Jackson, F., and Pettit, P. (1988). "Functionalism and Broad Content." *Mind* 97: 381–400.

James, W. (1890). *The Principles of Psychology*.

Kaplan, D. (1968). "Quantifying In." *Synthese* 19: 178–214.

———. (1978). "Dthat." P. Cole, ed. *Syntax and Semantics*. New York: Academic Press.

———. (1977). "Demonstratives." In Almog, Perry, and Wettstein (1989).

———. (1980). "Demonstratives." The John Locke Lectures, Oxford University.

Kitcher, P. (1978). "Theories, Theorists and Theoretical Change." *Philosophical Review* 87: 519–47.

Kripke, S. (1971). "Identity and Necessity." M. Munitz, ed. *Identity and Individuation*. New York: New York University Press, pp. 135–64.

———. (1972). "Naming and Necessity." In Davidson, D., and Harman, G., eds. *Semantics of Natural Languages*. New York: Humanities, pp. 253–355.

———. (1979). "A Puzzle About Belief." Avishai Margalit, ed. *Meaning and Use*. Dordrecht: Reidel, pp. 239–83.

———. (1980). *Naming and Necessity*. Oxford: Blackwell.

Kuhn, T. (1962). *The Structure of Scientific Revolutions*. Chicago: University of Chicago Press.

———. (1970). "Reflections on My Critics." Lakatos, I., and Musgrave, A., eds. *Criticism and the Growth of Knowledge*. Cambridge: Cambridge University Press, pp. 231–78.

Lewis, D. (1972b). "Psychophysical and Theoretical Identifications." *Australasian Journal of Philosophy* 50.

———. (1973). *Counterfactuals*. Oxford: Blackwell.

———. (1974). "Radical Interpretation." *Synthese* 27.

———. (1978). "Truth in Fiction." *American Philosophical Quarterly* 15: 37–46.

———. (1979). "Attitudes *De Dicto* and *De Se*." *Philosophical Review* 78: 513–43.

———. (1981). "What Puzzling Pierre Does Not Believe." *Australian Journal of Philosophy* 59: 283–89.

———. (1983). "New Work for a Theory of Universals." *Australasian Journal of Philosophy* 61: 343–77.

———. (1986). "Causal Explanation." Reprinted in *Philosophical Papers, vol. 2*. Oxford: Oxford University Press.

Loar, B. (1982). "Must Beliefs Be Sentences?" Asquith, P., and Nickles, T., eds. *PSA 1982: Proceedings of the 1982 Biennial Meeting of the Philosophy of Science Association*. East Lansing, Michigan: Philosophy of Science Association, pp. 627–42.

———. (1987). "Names in Thought." *Philosophical Studies* 51: 169–85.

———. (1988). "Social Content and Psychological Content." Grimm and Merrill, eds. *Contents of Thought*. Tucson: University of Arizona Press, pp. 99–110.

McCarthy, J., and Hayes, P. (1969). "Some Philosophical Problems from the Standpoint of

Artificial Intelligence." Meltzer, B., and Michie, D., eds. *Machine Intelligence*. Edinburgh: Edinburgh University Press.

McCulloch, G. (1986). "Scientism, Mind and Meaning." In Pettit and McDowell (1986).

———. (1989). *The Game of the Name*. Oxford: Clarendon Press.

McDowell, J. (1984). "*De Re* Senses." *The Philosophical Quarterly* 36: 283–94.

———. (1986). "Singular Thought and Inner Space." In Pettit and McDowell (1986).

———. (1991). "Intentionality and Interiority in Wittgenstein." In Puhl (1991), pp. 148–69.

McGinn, C. (1977). "Charity, Interpretation, and Belief." *The Journal of Philosophy*, LXXIV.

———. (1982). "The Structure of Content." In Woodfield (1982).

———. (1989). *Mental Content*. Oxford: Basil Blackwell.

McKinsey, M. (1978). "Names and Intentionality." *Philosophical Review* 87: 171–200.

———. (1986). "Mental Anaphora." *Synthese* 66: 159–75.

———. (1987). "Apriorism in the Philosophy of Language." *Philosophical Studies* 52: 1–32.

———. (1991). "The Internal Basis of Meaning." *Pacific Philosophical Quarterly* 72: 143–69.

Mellor, D. H. (1977). "Natural Kinds." *British Journal for the Philosophy of Science* 28: 299–312.

———. (1981). *Real Time*. Cambridge: Cambridge University Press.

———. (1989). "I and Now." *Proceedings of the Aristotelian Society* 89: 79–94.

Morton, A. (1975). "Because He Thought He Had Insulted Him." *The Journal of Philosophy* LXXII: 5–15.

Musgrave, A. (1976). "Why Did Oxygen Supplant Phlogiston?" Howson, C., ed. *Method and Appraisal in the Physical Sciences*. CUP.

Nagel, T. (1986). *The View from Nowhere*. Oxford: Oxford University Press.

Neisser, U. (1976). *Cognition and Reality*. San Francisco: Freeman.

Nelson, R. (1978). "Objects of Occasion Beliefs." *Synthese* 39: 105–40.

Noonan, H. (1984). "Fregean Thoughts." *The Philosophical Quarterly* 36: 205–24.

———. (1986). "Russellian Thoughts and Methodological Solipsism." In Butterfield (1986b).

Nozick, R. (1981). *Philosophical Explanations*. Cambridge: Harvard University Press.

Owens, J. (1987). "In Defense of a Different Doppelgänger." *Philosophical Review*: 521–54.

Papineau, D. (1979). *Theory and Meaning*. Oxford: Clarendon Press.

Parfit, D. (1984). *Reasons and Persons*. Oxford: Oxford University Press.

Pearce, G., and Maynard, P., eds. (1973). *Conceptual Change*. Dordrecht: D. Reidel.

Perry, J. (1977). "Frege on Demonstratives." *Philosophical Review* 86: 474–97.

———. (1979). "The Problem of the Essential Indexical." *Nous* 13: 3–21.

Pettit, P. (1986). "Broad-minded Explanation and Psychology." In Pettit and McDowell (1986).

Pettit, P., and McDowell, J., eds. (1986). *Subject, Thought, and Context*. Oxford: Oxford University Press.

Puhl, K., ed. (1991). *Meaning Skepticism*. Berlin and New York: De Gruyter.

Putnam H. (1967). "The 'Innateness' Hypothesis and Explanatory Models in Linguistics." *Synthese* 17: 12–22.

———. (1973). "Meaning and Reference." *The Journal of Philosophy* LXX, 19 (Nov. 8, 1973): 699–711.

———. (1974). "Comment on Wilfred Sellars." *Synthese* 27.

————. (1975). "The Meaning of 'Meaning'." Reprinted in Putnam (1975a).

————. (1975a). *Mind, Language, and Reality: Philosophical Papers, Volume 2*. New York: Cambridge University Press.

————. (1975b). "The Meaning of 'Meaning'." Gunderson, K., ed. *Language, Mind, and Knowledge*. Minneapolis: University of Minnesota Press.

————. (1975c). "Explanation and Reference." In Putnam (1975a).

————. (1975d). *Mathematics, Matter and Method: Philosophical Papers, Volume 1*. New York: Cambridge University Press.

————. (1975e). "Is Semantics Possible?" In Putnam (1975a).

————. (1978). *Meaning and the Moral Sciences*. Boston: Routledge & Kegan Paul.

————. (1981). *Reason, Truth and History*. Cambridge: Cambridge University Press.

————. (1988). *Representation and Reality*. Cambridge: MIT Press.

————. (1990). *Realism with a Human Face*. Cambridge: Harvard University Press.

Pylyshyn, Z. (1979). "Complexity and the Study of Artificial and Human Intelligence." Ringle, M., ed. *Philosophical Perspectives in Artificial Intelligence*. New Jersey: Humanities Press.

Quine, W.V.O. (1960). *Word and Object*. Cambridge: MIT Press.

Ramsey, F. (1928). "Universals of Law and of Fact." In *Philosophical Papers*. Cambridge: Cambridge University Press, 1990.

————. (1929). "General Propositions and Causality." In *Philosophical Papers*. Cambridge: Cambridge University Press, 1990.

Reichenbach, H. (1965). *The Theory of Relativity and A Priori Knowledge*. California.

Rosenberg, J., and Travis, C., eds. (1971). *Readings in the Philosophy of Language*. Englewood Cliffs, NJ: Prentice-Hall.

Schiffer, S. (1978). "The Basis of Reference." *Erkenntnis* 13: 171–206.

Schilpp, P., ed. (1951). *Albert Einstein Philosopher-Scientist*. New York.

Schlesinger, G. (1963). *Method in the Physical Sciences*. London: Routledge & Kegan Paul.

Schwartz, S., ed. (1977). *Naming, Necessity, and Natural Kinds*. Ithaca: Cornell University Press.

Searle, J. (1958). "Proper Names." *Mind* 67: 166–73.

————. (1979). *Expression and Meaning*. Cambridge: Cambridge University Press.

————. (1979a). "Referential and Attributive." *The Monist* 62: 190–308.

————. (1983). *Intentionality*. Cambridge: Cambridge University Press.

Segal, G. (1989a). "The Return of the Individual." *Mind* 98: 39–57.

————. (1989b). "Seeing What Is Not There." *The Philosophical Review* 97: 189–214.

Shoemaker, S. (1984). *Identity, Cause and Mind*. Cambridge: Cambridge University Press.

Smart, J. (1959). "Sensations and Brain Processes." *The Philosophical Review*: 141–56.

Stalnaker, R. (1984). *Inquiry*. Cambridge: MIT Press.

Sterelny, K. (1981). "Davidson on Truth and Reference." *Southern Journal of Philosophy* 19: 95–117.

Stich, S. (1978a). "Autonomous Psychology and the Belief-Desire Thesis." *The Monist* 61: 571–91.

————. (1983). *From Folk Psychology to Cognitive Science: The Case Against Belief*. Cambridge: MIT Press.

Ullman, S. (1979). *The Interpretation of Visual Motion*. Cambridge: MIT Press.

Van Gulick, R. (1989). "Metaphysical Arguments for Internalism and Why They Don't Work." S. Silvers, ed. *Rerepresentation*. Boston: Kluwer.

Wallas, Graham. *The Art of Thought*.

White, S. (1982). "Partial Character and the Language of Thought." *Pacific Philosophical Quarterly* 63: 347–65.

Winograd, T. (1972). *Understanding Natural Language*. New York: Academic Press.

Wittgenstein, L. (1953). *Philosophical Investigations*. Oxford: Blackwell.

Woodfield, A., ed. (1982). *Thought and Object: Essays on Intentionality*. Oxford: Clarendon Press.

Wright, C. (1989). "Wittgenstein's Later Philosophy of Mind: Sensation, Privacy and Intention." *The Journal of Philosophy* 86.

Zemach, E. (1976). "Putnam's Theory on the Reference of Substance Terms." *The Journal of Philosophy* 73: 116–27.

Ziff, P. (1972). *Understanding Understanding*. New York.

Index